Introduction to Sociology

A Text with Readings

Introduction to Sociology

A Text with Readings

Fourth Edition

Daniel E. Hebding

Leonard Glick

Community College of Philadelphia

McGraw-Hill, Inc.

New York St. Louis San Francisco Auckland Bogotá Caracas
Lisbon London Madrid Mexico Milan Montreal New Delhi
Paris San Juan Singapore Sydney Toyko Toronto

Introduction to Sociology: A Text with Readings

2 3 4 5 6 7 8 9 0 DOC DOC 9 0 9 8 7 6 5 4 3 2

ISBN 0-07-033750-0

This book was set in Palatino by Better Graphics, Inc.
The editors were Phillip A. Butcher, Marian Provenzano, and Curt Berkowitz;
the designer was Jack Ehn;
the production supervisor was Annette Mayeski.
The photo editor was Elyse Rieder.
R. R. Donnelley & Sons Company was printer and binder.

About the cover: At a naturalization ceremony held in the Orange Bowl arena in Miami, Florida, 10,000 people from countries around the world are sworn in as new citizens of the United States. The great cultural diversity found in American society is but one of many areas of interest to sociologists.

Photo Credits

Chapter 1 Opening Photo: Michael Dwyer/Stock, Boston; Page 13: John J. Krieger, Jr./The Picture Cube; Chapter 2 Opening Photo: Peter Menzel/Stock, Boston; Page 57: David M. Grossman/Photo Researchers; Chapter 3 Opening Photo: Elizabeth Crews/Stock, Boston; Page 81: Yan Lukas/Photo Researchers; Chapter 4 Opening Photo: Spencer Grant/Stock, Boston; Page 134: Elizabeth Crews/The Image Works; Chapter 5 Opening Photo: Laima Druskis/Photo Researchers; Page 192: Alan Carey/The Image Works; Chapter 6 Opening Photo: Fredrik Bodin/Stock, Boston; Page 225: Peter Menzel/Stock, Boston; Chapter 7 Opening Photo: Lionel Delevingne/Stock, Boston; Page 285: Eli Reed/Magnum; Chapter 8 Opening Photo: Michael Weisbrot/Stock, Boston; Page 306: Alan Carey/The Image Works; Chapter 9 Opening Photo: Peter Menzel/Stock, Boston; Page 357: Spencer Grant/The Picture Cube; Chapter 10 Opening Photo: Mark Antman/The Image Works; Page 387: Ellis Herwig/The Picture Cube; Chapter 11 Opening Photo: Sam C. Pierson, Jr./Photo Researchers; Page 443: Peter Menzel/Stock, Boston; Chapter 12 Opening Photo: East Midlands Pix/Sygma; Page 473: Mark Antman/The Image Works

Library of Congress Cataloging-in-Publication Data

Hebding, Daniel E.
Introduction to sociology: a text with readings / Daniel E. Hebding, Leonard Glick.—4th ed.
p. cm.
Includes bibliographical references and index.
ISBN 0-07-033750-0
1. Sociology. I. Glick. Leonard. II. Title.
HM51.H395 1992
301—dc20 91-20754

Contents

Preface

Over the years, our goal in writing an introductory text for sociology courses has been to present the field of sociology as clearly and explicitly as possible. We hope that by studying the new edition of *Introduction to Sociology* students will be better able to grasp the special contribution of sociology to the understanding of human social behavior and society. In this, our fourth edition of the text, student learning should be further enhanced through a unique combination of features that makes the basics of sociology more accessible to introductory students.

1. We have improved the organization of our text for this edition and expanded its contents.

Two new chapters on social institutions have been incorporated into this edition. New coverage includes materials on poverty, computer crime, the aging of the U.S. population, ecology and the environment, changing roles of women and men, and health and health care.

2. The book includes an expanded number of readings that are fully integrated into the text.

The book has matured into a comprehensive text-reader. Readings have been chosen not only for their illustrative value, but also for their readability and relevance to many of the major subject areas and issues explored in sociology.

For example, the article in Chapter 5 titled "Why We're Losing the War on Crime" provides a critical analysis of our current strategies for dealing with problems of crime and drugs in the United States. In Chapter 6, Stratification, the article "Address Unknown: Homelessness in Contemporary America" discusses the growing problem of homelessness in our society and various causes of this problem. Chapter 11, Population, Urbanization, and the Environment, contains the article "Protecting the Environment," which discusses new strategies for cleaning up our environment and keeping it clean. Subject areas addressed by other readings include women's roles (in "Trading Places: The Daughter Track") and family change (in "Step by Step").

Several classic sociology pieces have also been retained in the new edition, including "The Sociological Imagination" by C. Wright Mills, "Body Ritual Among the Nacirema" by Horace Miner, and "The Uses of Poverty: The Poor Pay All" by Herbert J. Gans. Through these readings, students are directly exposed to major thinkers at their most lucid and appealing. Each reading is preceded by a brief overview of its major points and an explanation of its significance to the issues discussed in the text. A numbered list of reading review questions follows each reading.

3. A comprehensive student Study Guide has been incorporated into each chapter of the text.

The study guide consists of **numbered chapter objectives, lists of key terms, a student self-test**—including **short answer, multiple-choice, true/false, fill-in-the-blank, matching,** and **essay questions**—and a separate section containing **applied interactive exercises.** This Study Guide is designed to help students organize their study of the textbook chapters, evaluate their understanding of the text material, and prepare for their examinations during the course of the semester.
sXX

4. The sociological I.Q. test has been retained in this edition.

This is designed to test the accuracy of common-sense assumptions about society. Students can gauge their own progress in the course by taking the test both at the beginning and the end of the course. (An "Answer Key" is provided at the end of the book, before the index.)

5. In addition to the built-in Study Guide, the book contains a wide range of pedagogical devices aimed at reinforcing fundamental textual material.

These learning aids include: **Chapter Pretests; margin notes** that create a chapter outline and emphasize **key terms; boldfaced key terms** in the text; **charts; graphs; tables; numbered chapter summaries;** and a **comprehensive glossary** and **index** at the end of the book. In this edition, we offer among the most thorough pedagogical packages available for introductory courses in sociology.

Acknowledgments

Our thanks go to the following reviewers for going over our manuscript and providing valuable suggestions for this revision: Ben Agger, State University of New York, Buffalo; Julie Brown, University of North Carolina, Greensboro; Rudolph Harris, Des Moines Area Community College; Margaret Haun, St. Louis Community College at Florissant Valley; Dick Marsh, Orange Coast College; James Satterlee, South Dakota State University; Steve Schada, Oakton Community College; and William Snizek, Virginia Polytechnic Institute. Our thanks also go to Dave Lewis of the U.S. Bureau of the Census, Philadelphia Regional Office, for his very competent and helpful assistance.

We would also like to express our deep appreciation to the highly competent people at McGraw-Hill for their help, dedication, and cooperation in the preparation of this fourth edition of our text. In particular, we would like to thank a group of outstanding editors including Phillip Butcher, Sylvia Shepard, and Marian Provenzano, and the following members of the production staff: Curt Berkowitz, editing supervisor; Annette Mayeski, production supervisor; Elyse Rieder, photo researcher; Jack Ehn, designer; and Alice Jaggard, copyeditor. Very special thanks must also be given to our wives and children, Nevie, Marie, Sonia, Gretchen, and Leonard, Jr., for their understanding and cooperation during the time spent on this book.

Daniel E. Hebding
Leonard Glick

Introduction to Sociology

A Text with Readings

Chapter 1

Sociology and the Scientific Approach

Chapter Pretest

Let's see how much you already know about topics in this chapter:

1. **Sociology originated in Europe during the twentieth century. True/False**
2. **The sociological approach to understanding human behavior is essentially the same as the literary or the philosophical approaches. True/False**
3. **Sociology is concerned primarily with the study of the individual and individual mental processes. True/False**
4. **The most common way sociologists gather data concerning human behavior is by observing people in their daily activities. True/False**
5. **In experiments, the control group receives the stimulus. True/False**
6. **Sociological explanations for human behavior involve the idea that social interactions cause or at least greatly influence people's behavior. True/False**
7. **For the most part, human behavior reveals very few patterns and regularities. True/False**
8. **Sociology, like other social sciences, makes predictions on the basis of probability. True/False**

The Nature of Sociology

Human beings are born into and spend their entire lives within groups. As such, they can be described as "social" animals who depend on others for the satisfaction of their needs. During infancy, humans must rely on close contact with and nurturing from others for their basic physical survival. Through childhood and into adulthood, groups give meaning and support to the individual. The stress in sociology is on human interaction, the groups that people form, and the relationships that occur within groups. Sociology is not concerned with the study of the human being as an isolated individual, but with the study of people in the group or social context. Therefore the major goal of sociological inquiry is to explain and understand human *social* behavior or interaction as well as the results of human interaction.

Sociology studies people in the group context

From the sociological perspective, much of human behavior is learned through interaction with others. It is through human interaction that the human biological animal *becomes* a human social animal. In other words, it is through relations with others that the individual derives values, attitudes, beliefs, and standards of behavior. Much behavior, including a person's ideas, actions, and so forth, can be explained only in terms of relationships with and learning from others. Thus sociological explanations for human behavior are tied to the idea that social interactions among individuals cause or at least greatly influence human behavior.

The human group is the central concept and subject matter of sociological study

Sociology may be defined as the scientific study of human interaction and the products of such interaction. Human interaction is a social or "group" concept because it necessarily involves two or more people relating to and influencing one another. Sociological study is focused therefore on the nature of human group life and the products of group living. In fact, one can say that the central concept and subject matter of sociological study is the "human group." As we shall see in later chapters, sociology provides answers to questions such as What is a group? How do groups come about, change, persist, and weaken? What functions or needs do groups serve for their members? What influence does group membership have on the person? What patterns of intergroup relations are found within society? What are the nature and characteristics of the most encompassing, or *total*, social group that sociologists term "society"?

Chief among the products of human interaction with others is the development of group customs, traditions, values, and standards of behavior. Much sociological analysis is given to elements such as these because they are present in every group, but more important, because they also constitute the *basis* on which human social life is organized and perpetuated. A society, for instance, as well as groups within it, is organized in certain ways. From the sociological viewpoint, much of this social organization (families, political and economic systems) reflects various group customs, traditions, values, and standards of behavior. Customs, traditions, and values warrant much sociological attention because they derive from group living and, in turn, have much influence on human social life.

The sociological "how" and "why" of human social life

Sociology is concerned with the ultimate questions of how and why human beings act the way they do. These questions have been central to every age, and today, as in the past, there are many ways at arriving at their answers. People may gain insight into these questions from many points of view—the supernatural or religious, the literary, the philosophical, or the biological. The sociological approach is distinct from these other approaches in two major respects: First, sociologists view human behavior as fundamentally *social* in nature; and second, sociologists use the scientific method to study human social behavior. The physical sciences, such as chemistry and physics, use the scientific method to answer questions concerning the nonhuman or material world. Sociology—a social science—assumes that there are uniformities in nature and, therefore, in human social nature and that these uniformities may be detected and understood.

Finally, it should be noted that sociology, like other sciences, often investigates traditional beliefs that people hold concerning the world about them.

Many of these beliefs have been handed down from generation to generation and have never been critically examined. Said to be matters of "common sense," the actual testing of such beliefs is often met with considerable resistance by the general public. Few people like to have their opinions and beliefs scientifically scrutinized. As a means of demonstrating the way in which sociological findings sometimes differ from common sense, you may wish to take Kezins' Sociological I.Q. Test, which appears on pages 6 and 7. Your performance on this test will give you a better idea of how knowledgeable you are about the society in which you live, as well as the contributions made by sociology to our understanding of this and other societies. See how well *you* score on various sociological facts concerning American society, which many believe to be simply matters of common sense.

Early Social Thought

Throughout the classical and medieval periods of human history, interpretations of human social and societal existence derived largely from an unwavering belief in an unchanging natural law and in the supremacy and sanctity of traditional and theological dogma. The philosophical systems of these periods were founded largely on rather simple speculative analogies to so-called *eternal truths,* emanating from the revered sources of tradition and divine will.

But the emergence of the Industrial Revolution signaled the beginnings of vast changes in this social world, in the patterns of relationships among people, and in social life. The Industrial Revolution radically changed and disrupted older patterns of human relationships and routines of everyday life. The revolution ultimately brought about an intellectual crisis throughout Europe. People began to question their beliefs about the nature of human existence and the nature of society. They increasingly came to the realization that they could no longer simply take society for granted and that new answers were needed to the questions of what society is, how it changes, and how it might be reorganized to meet the needs and challenges of the present. They also began to question their ideas about the sources of knowledge that they had previously relied on to answer such questions. It became evident that mere speculative philosophy and traditional authority could no longer provide suitable answers to questions concerning their present and future life circumstances.

The Industrial Revolution inspired intellectual revolution

It was in this historical context that sociology emerged in Europe during the nineteenth century as one facet of the European intellectual response to the Industrial Revolution. As we shall see, early sociologists such as Comte, Spencer, Durkheim, Marx, and Weber felt that society and social change could be studied and understood in a factual, objective, *scientific* way—a way quite distinct from the earlier forms of explanation incorporated within speculative social philosophies.

The 19th-century emergence of sociology

KEZINS' SOCIOLOGICAL I.Q. TEST*

Found below are a series of statements about American society. Read each statement carefully, and then indicate whether you believe it to be either *True* or *False*. You can measure the progress you have made in the course and your gains in understanding society by taking the I.Q. test again at the end of the course and comparing your scores. ("Answer Key" appears on pages 528 and 529.) After completing all statements, answer each of the background items found at the end of the test.

True False 1. Psychological disorders are more common among people in the lower class.

True False 2. Heart disease is far more likely to kill poor people than the affluent.

True False 3. Most suicides are committed by people in their 30s and 40s.

True False 4. Per-pupil expenditures by American school systems significantly affect student scores on achievement tests.

True False 5. More women are graduating from professional schools today than ever before.

True False 6. The vast majority of women today support sexual equality in the home.

True False 7. Most elderly persons ($\geq$ 65 years) depend on their children for at least some amount of financial assistance.

True False 8. Less than 1 percent of all welfare recipients are able-bodied employable males.

True False 9. Most welfare recipients are white.

True False 10. Approximately half the families on welfare have been on the rolls for five years or more.

True False 11. Whites have higher self-esteem than blacks.

True False 12. The suicide rate is higher among women than men.

True False 13. Suicide rates in the United States are higher among upper class people than among lower class people.

True False 14. Largely as a result of women's liberation, the frequency of marital coitus has declined noticeably over the last decade.

True False 15. Most married women work.

True False 16. Three out of four divorced women remarry within three years.

True False 17. It is more difficult for men to remarry than it is for women.

True False 18. In dating and mating, "absence makes the heart grow fonder."

True False 19. States with the death penalty have a lower murder rate than those without the death penalty.

True False 20. Crimes of violence and theft are far more likely to occur among teen-agers than among any other age group in our society.

---

*This test was prepared by William E. Snizek, Virginia Polytechnic Institute and State University at Blacksburg. Thanks go to Dave Demo, Ted Fuller, Mike Hughes, and Susan Mead for their assistance.

True False 21. The United States has one of the lowest rates of infant mortality in the world.

True False 22. The soaring birth rates in developing countries make it difficult, if not impossible, for those countries to feed their rapidly growing populations.

True False 23. Almost half the people currently in jail in this country have not been convicted of a crime.

True False 24. Northern schools are more integrated than schools in the South.

True False 25. Suicide is more prevalent in the South than in any other region of the United States.

True False 26. Rape is usually an impulsive uncontrollable act of sexual gratification.

True False 27. In dating and mate selection, "opposites attract."

True False 28. Women are more likely than men to abuse children.

True False 29. In most instances, marital happiness is likely to increase following the birth of children.

True False 30. By age 45, more than one-third of all males in this country have engaged in at least one homosexual act.

RESPONDENT BACKGROUND INFORMATION

SEX (Female = 1, Male = 2)

TERM STANDING (Freshman = 1, Sophomore = 2, Junior = 3, Senior = 4)

MAJOR (Liberal Arts = 1; Business = 2; Engineering = 3; Education = 4; Physical Sciences = 5; Other = 6)

AGE (18 or less = 1; 19 = 2; 20 = 3; 21 or more = 4)

The Beginnings of Sociology

Auguste Comte

Auguste Comte (1798–1857) developed the first complete approach to the *scientific* study of society. Before Comte, people had inquired into the nature of human behavior by various systems of social philosophy, some of which later evolved into specific social sciences. Comte, who is considered the founder of sociology, is best known for his six-volume *Positive Philosophy* (1855), in which he organized the social and scientific achievements of his time. In Comte's view, people might study society and human actions using methods similar to those in the physical sciences.

Comte's method of positivism

Comte felt that sociology should use the method of **positivism.** Positivism emphasizes the techniques of observation, comparison (particularly historical comparison), and experimentation in the development of knowledge concerning the nature of society and human action. Comte, in other words, was responsible for the development of a new philosophy or approach to the study of total, or whole, societies. His approach was quite different from earlier, more traditional, speculative systems of social philosophy.

Comte felt that sociology should be divided into two main areas, which he termed *social statics* and *social dynamics*. Social statics is concerned with the various parts of society, such as its political, economic, and family systems, and with how these parts interrelate. Social dynamics is concerned with the analysis of change within and among the various parts of society. The end product of each of these areas of study is the formulation of universal "natural laws" of social life and social change. The development of these universal laws, based on scientific knowledge, would, in turn, allow for the solution of problems within society, making "social progress" or social improvement possible.

Herbert Spencer

Herbert Spencer (1820–1903) was another major contributor to early sociology. He systematically defined the various areas of study within sociology—social control, politics, religion, the family, stratification, associations, communities, and the sociology of knowledge. Spencer had an "organismic" view of the nature of society in that he saw society as a living organism with specific parts (or organs), each performing specific functions.

Society—a living organism

In contrast to Comte, Spencer was an outstanding evolutionary theorist. Spencer's view of society was based on analogies to a biological model, with social change taking place like biological evolution within other living organisms. Spencer was heavily influenced by the evolutionary theories of Charles Darwin, and he emphasized the Darwinian notions of "natural selection" and "survival of the fittest" in his analysis of human societal evolution. Like Comte, Spencer stressed that sociology should not be limited to the study of society's parts, such as industry, family, and politics. He felt that sociology should be concerned with the total society, emphasizing the ways in which each part is related to other parts and how change in one part can affect change in another. For example, change in a society's system of industry can influence the quality of family life.

Spencer felt that social evolution would create a perfect society

But in contrast to Comte, Spencer's emphasis on social evolution led him to conclude that "natural" (in the sense of unplanned) change would inevitably bring about "progress" and, ultimately, perfection within society. Spencer therefore thought that the major focus of sociology should be social evolution rather than the suggestion and implementation of strategies for social improvement.

Emile Durkheim

Emile Durkheim (1858–1919) also occupies a central place in the development of sociology. Durkheim, along with Comte and Spencer, favored the development of specific areas or fields of inquiry within sociology, such as the sociology of religion, law, family, and politics. Durkheim recognized that sociology was the study of society, and he stressed the importance of studying societies as total units, or entities in themselves.

Durkheim viewed a society as an entity composed of various parts—the political system, the religious system, the family system, and so on. However,

Durkheim viewed society as a total entity, as something more than simply the sum of these parts. The nature of society as a unit is not observable in the parts viewed separately. By way of simple analogy, we know that when we combine hydrogen and oxygen in a certain proportion, the result is water. But water is a third new substance having qualities different from hydrogen or oxygen taken separately. Likewise, Durkheim viewed society as something that had a reality of its own. The combination of the parts produced a new substance, the nature of which could not be observed in the parts alone.

Society—an entity more than the sum of its parts

For Durkheim, the group or society rather than the individual was the central object for sociological study. Durkheim saw the individual as a rather passive being whose ways of behaving, thinking, and feeling were merely reflections of group expectations, laws, and customs. Durkheim also felt that the overall design or organization of each society has many consequences for people living within it. For instance, he noted that suicide is far less common in rural or agricultural societies than in modern urbanized societies. He theorized that this difference resulted from the fact that agricultural societies are organized in a much more uniform and unchanging manner and that because individuals feel a greater sense of meaning to their actions and relations with others, their lives are more stable (Durkheim, 1951).

Durkheim is considered one of the founders of a major sociological perspective known as **functionalism.** In this perspective, society is a system of interdependent units or parts, each of which plays an important role (fulfills a particular "need" or purpose) in helping maintain the total social system. With respect to our society's present-day institutional structure, for example, functionalists would be interested in analyzing how the family, education, and religion help maintain and perpetuate the society at large. Contemporary sociologists have also found the functionalist perspective useful in understanding a wide range of social phenomena, including poverty, inequality, health care, and social deviance. From the functionalist viewpoint, society and human interaction are characterized by harmony, cooperation, balance, and consensus.

According to Durkheim, sociology should focus on the study of a variety of phenomena, termed **social facts.** Social facts are ways of acting, thinking, and feeling that are characteristic of a group or society. Group customs and laws are common examples of social facts. Phenomena such as these exist outside and independent of individuals, yet they are capable of greatly influencing individual behavior. When we carry out family, religious, or occupational obligations, for example, we are responding to these phenomena. Because they are truly social in nature, they must be studied and explained on the basis of sociological rather than biological or psychological principles.

For Durkheim, social facts are the subject matter of sociology

Durkheim's ideas about social facts also may be applied to social phenomena such as crime, marriage, divorce, or births. Although an individual may commit a particular crime, a crime *rate* is a *social* fact—it is a social phenomenon that varies over time and among different groups and societies. Rates of crime, marriage, divorce, and birth are distinctively social phenomena that cannot be explained on the basis of individual psychology.

Durkheim was the first sociologist to engage in large-scale scientific research. His classic study *Suicide* (1897) marked the first attempt to systematically collect factual and statistical data for testing theories of *social* phenomena. We will discuss this study more thoroughly in Chapter 5.

Karl Marx

Karl Marx (1818–1883) made many important contributions to social philosophy, sociology, and other social sciences. He was one of the earliest and most important exponents of **conflict theory.** In many respects, conflict theory is quite different from the functionalist perspective. Whereas functionalists tend to view society as a mosaic of balance, cooperation, and harmony, conflict theorists see competition and social conflict as forming the basis of group or social life. Contrary to functionalists, conflict theorists feel that any "harmonious balance" present within society is simply an illusion. For them, dissension resulting from the competition among groups for advantage and power is the basic fact of social life. Rather than social harmony, there is a continuous struggle between those with advantages and privileges and those without them.

Marx saw conflict as the main source of social change

Like many other sociologists and social philosophers of his time, Marx had an evolutionary model of society. He believed that societies go through a fixed number of stages, such as ancient, feudal, and capitalist. For Marx, the history of civilization is the history of class struggles, and conflict is the main source of social change. Classes are always economically based and are defined by their relationship to the means of production. Regardless of the specific method of production, vested and opposed interests arise between those who own and control the means of production (and thus have advantage and power) and those who do not. Inevitably, through each period of history and societal evolution, the exploited, unpropertied class comes to recognize its exploitation and revolts against those in power. Finally, under the capitalist productive system, the proletarian (laboring) class joins in a revolution to overthrow the bourgeoisie (the owners of production). With the overthrow of the bourgeoisie, the dictatorship of the proletariat becomes a reality—signaling the onset of a utopian, classless society.

Today not all conflict theorists subscribe to all the elements of Marxist ideology. Nevertheless, Marx did provide many fresh insights into the nature of social change, social structure, and social classes. As we shall see in Chapters 6, 7, 8, and 12, contemporary sociologists have employed a conflict perspective for understanding a diversity of social arrangements and social phenomena, including prejudice and discrimination, social stratification, the family, social movements, and social change.

Max Weber

Few scholars have influenced sociology as much as Max Weber (1864–1920). Weber wrote extensively on such topics as social class, status, power, political organization, comparative religion, the division of labor, bureaucracy, economic systems, and the relationship of religious systems to economic systems.

Although Weber is known for his contributions to conflict theory, he is also widely recognized as one of the founders of a competing theoretical perspective known as **symbolic interactionism.** Whereas the functionalist and conflict perspectives focus on the study of society's institutions, organizations, class conflicts, and social structure, the interactionist perspective focuses on social life and human behavior from the standpoint of the individuals involved in day-to-day interaction. The interactionist perspective assumes that people bring into each social situation certain ideas about themselves, about the meaning of their behavior, about the nature of the situation, and about others. These ideas play a crucial role in determining how and why people act as they do. People learn ideas from others through the ongoing process of symbolic interaction. Through symbols—words, actions, and gestures—people communicate the meanings of events, situations, and behavior. Thus, from the interactionist perspective, to explain people's social behavior fully, one must go beyond a knowledge of their age, marital status, social class, and so forth. One must find out how they interpret the world and, specifically, what their behavior and their social situation symbolize to them.

The interactionist perspective

Contemporary sociologists find the interactionist perspective useful in attempting to understand and interpret the everyday interaction of people as they relate with others in the context of family, friendships, or any other social situation. As we shall see in Chapter 3, the interactionist perspective is also valuable in understanding the processes of socialization and the emergence of the "self" as explained in the theories of Charles H. Cooley and George H. Mead.

Weber felt that the principal task of sociology (and of all other social sciences) was to understand the nature and meaning of human social conduct. Weber was concerned specifically with those types of human behavior that have some sort of meaning or purpose to the actor. He called such meaningful behavior **social action.** Weber stated that social action occurs when a person intends to act in ways that others expect. Weber felt that sociology could achieve its primary objective, that of explaining social action, by a method that he termed ***verstehen*** ("understanding"). This method enables the sociologist to make subjective interpretations of the *actions* and *intentions* of other people (what the acts mean to the people themselves), because as a human being, the sociologist has developed a degree of understanding of behavior through personal experiences with others.

Social action—behavior intended to fulfill expectations

In many respects, Weber felt that social scientists could study society and human conduct with procedures used in the physical sciences, such as careful observation and precise gathering and analysis of data. To this end, he advocated that sociology employ a *comparative method* for data analysis. He developed a number of comparative systems (or typologies) by means of which he identified and described various categories of social action as well as various forms of religious, political, and economic systems.

Adaptation of scientific method to sociology

As a final note regarding the functionalist, conflict, and symbolic interactionist perspectives, it should be stressed that although a particular perspective may be well suited for explaining certain kinds of social phenomena, no one of these perspectives is clearly the "best" for understanding all facets of human social life. Each perspective provides us with a somewhat different, yet important, way of looking at and understanding the social world around us. A complete understanding of social phenomena requires that we give careful consideration to all views.

Sociology in America

The origins of sociology

As we have seen, sociology originated in Europe during the nineteenth century. But it matured in large part in America during the twentieth century. Following Comte's lead, many American sociologists of the late 1800s and early 1900s were interested in social reform and studying society's problems. At the time, America was experiencing massive industrialization, urbanization, and immigration. The scale and rapidity of this social change were problematic themselves yet brought a host of other problems, such as crime, urban ghettos, and group conflicts.

Early sociology studied many social problems

The first sociology department was organized at the University of Chicago in the early 1890s. During the early 1900s, a number of well-known sociologists at the university, such as Ernest Burgess and Robert E. Park, considered Chicago their laboratory for the study of social problems such as delinquency, drug addiction, crime, poverty, ghetto life, and prostitution. Meanwhile, scholars such as Charles H. Cooley and George H. Mead were studying the importance of social and group influences on human behavior, personality, and social identity. The work of these men provided the foundation for symbolic interactionism.

During the 1940s and 1950s, other schools, such as Harvard and Columbia, gained prominence as centers of sociological training and research. Sociology also began to change. It became less reformist and activist and more concerned with the development of comprehensive theories of society. For example, Talcott Parsons at Harvard University theorized about the nature and organization of total societies. His work became the basis for much of modern functionalism. Other sociologists also worked to refine research principles to make sociology more "scientific." These efforts resulted in improved research designs, data gathering, and statistical and computer data analysis.

Since the 1950s and 1960s, modern conflict theory, as evidenced in the writings of C. Wright Mills, Lewis Coser, and Ralf Dahrendorf, has gained influence in American sociology. The 1960s also marked a return to social activism that had characterized sociology early in this century. Today many sociologists feel that their science can play an important role in stimulating social change and social reform. Yet, as a whole, sociologists are keenly aware of the necessity of theory and research in their efforts to understand society and human social behavior.

Characteristics of the Scientific Approach

In science, factual information and verification are important

The scientific approach is based on factual observation and evidence that can be checked by others. In other words, scientists restrict their attention to things that can be seen, heard, or touched—things that can be experienced by or through the senses. In sociology, examples of such phenomena would be overt human acts such as group or interpersonal behavior, verbal statements, and written documents.

The scientific method demands exactness in all of its facets.

The scientific method also requires that the researcher be objective. **Objectivity** means making observations and drawing conclusions without personal bias, preconceptions, or personal feelings. For instance, although a researcher may believe that imprisonment is the best method for dealing with criminals, that belief must not interfere with his or her observations and conclusions on the subject. Objectivity is perhaps the most difficult quality for the sociologist to acquire. Not only does it demand that we see things as they really are rather than the way we would like or wish them to be, it also requires that we develop insight into our own feelings and biases that may interfere with our perception of the world as it actually exists.

Objectivity is basic to the scientific method

Closely related to objectivity is the idea that science must remain neutral with respect to human values. The study of various types of beliefs and values does not imply that scientists either accept or reject them. In other words, sociologists *as scientists* do not make personal value judgments as to the "rightness" or "wrongness" of beliefs and value systems under examination, because *as scientists* they cannot demonstrate that one value is more worthwhile than another. Sociologists may find, for instance, that most people in our society disapprove of divorce, but sociologists may not conclude that they are right or wrong in their opinions. But, as scientists, sociologists can identify values that people hold, study the ways in which certain values may conflict with others, and indicate the consequences of adopting one value rather than another.

Scientists do not permit personal value judgments to color their thinking

Finally, the scientific method demands exactness in all its facets, including observation, experimentation, the collection and analysis of data, and the drawing of conclusions. Accuracy in the development of sociological concepts and theory depends on such exactness.

The Research Process

The Selection of a Problem and the Construction of a Hypothesis

Scientific research begins with the formulation or selection of a research problem. As indicated in Figure 1.1, after the research problem or topic has been selected, the researcher will next want to restate the problem in very clear and precise terms. To this end, the scientist develops a **hypothesis**—a tentative statement capable of being tested by the scientific method. For example, many people believe that drug use is more prevalent among college students today than in previous years. A scientifically researchable hypothesis concerning this belief would be: "The use of illegal drugs among currently enrolled college students is significantly greater than among enrolled college students 10 years ago." Even here, certain terms would have to be carefully defined: The types of illegal drugs would have to be specified, the types of college students the researcher is interested in studying would have to be identified, and so forth. Hypotheses of this form are termed *descriptive* because they attempt to identify or describe one or more characteristics of a population.

Hypotheses may be descriptive or explanatory

In contrast, sociologists often develop a second type of hypothesis, an *explanatory* hypothesis. Suppose that one were to find that juvenile delinquency is greater in one-parent than two-parent homes. The question of why then might arise. A researcher might speculate that the degree of parental supervision differs greatly between one- and two-parent homes and that this factor would adequately explain the delinquency. The researcher therefore would try to answer the question with an explanatory hypothesis such as the following: "*If* homes are characterized by inadequate parental supervision, *then* they are more likely to foster delinquency regardless of whether one or two parents are present." The hypothesis would be confirmed if the researcher found that delinquency were more prevalent in inadequately than in adequately supervised homes.

The Research Design

After formulating a hypothesis to be tested, the scientist develops a research design that defines the types of data to be collected, the time needed and method to be used for gathering such data, and the methods by which the data will be classified and analyzed.

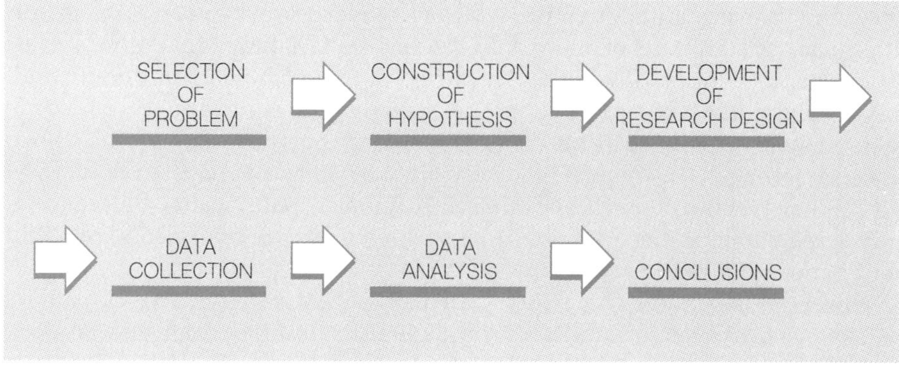

Figure 1.1 **Steps in the research process.**

Data Collection

The scientist next begins to collect data, gathering information in accordance with the methods specified in the research design. The three most common methods for data collection are observation, survey, and experimentation.

Observation. Sociologists use two basic types of observation: detached and participant. In **detached observation** (sometimes referred to as **nonparticipant observation**), the observer remains *outside* the group under study.

One of the best-known examples of detached observation is from a classic series of investigations, the Hawthorne of Western Electric studies, that were carried out over a period of several years. These studies analyzed the relationship of the productivity of workers to various human factors such as worker fatigue and morale. In one of these investigations, the "Bank Wiring Room" study, the observer used a controlled form of observation, remaining in the presence of the workers, but *not engaging in or modifying* group activities, over a period of several months (Roethlisberger and Dickson, 1939). During this time, the observer kept systematic and detailed records of the employees' behavior, conversations, and productivity, for the purpose of determining how the relations among the workers influenced their attitudes toward one another as well as their work.

A second type of observation often used by sociologists is **participant observation.** In this form of observation, the observer actually joins and participates in the group being studied. Participant observation provides an opportunity to experience and understand the world from the subjects' point of view.

Participant observation—insight through involvement

A classic example of participant observation is the study described in Elliot Liebow's well-known book, *Tally's Corner* (1967). For 18 months, Liebow studied a group of 24 poor black men who regularly met on a street corner in a ghetto area of Washington, D.C. Liebow examined the way of life of these men, their feelings toward themselves, their unstable work patterns, and their marginal and often nonexistent family relationships. Liebow's study focused on how the entire structure of this street-corner world rested largely on an ongoing network of "primary, face-to-face relationships" among its inhabitants.

In some instances, observation is carried out in a *laboratory* or under conditions like those in a laboratory. But many observational studies are conducted by observers who actually go out and study people in their real-life, natural, day-to-day social settings. This type of *field* work often relies on participant observation, as did Elliot Liebow's work. Sociologists have used participant observation to study small communities, the nature of various occupations, prison life, delinquent gangs, and many other topics.

Difficulties with observational studies

Observational studies have their problems—they are often time-consuming and expensive. Observers must try to generalize findings from one group to others. Particularly in participant observation, there is also the danger of losing objectivity or of interfering with the behavior of the subjects under study (Hunt, 1985). Nevertheless, observational methods provide the researcher with much information about people's behavior and a depth of insight into group life not often available through other data collection methods.

Survey. Without doubt, the most common method of data collection is the **survey.** Survey data are gotten through questionnaires and interviews.

Questionnaires often are mailed to a specific group of people whom the researcher considers representative of (that is, having certain characteristics or qualities in similar proportion to) a larger population. The subjects fill out the questionnaires and return them. Questionnaires are less expensive than other forms of data collection. They also give researchers a great deal of information from many people, in a short time, for little effort by researcher and respondent. But questionnaires pose two problems. First is the problem of nonresponse—many respondents fail to return a questionnaire. The partial return of data may, in turn, cause the researcher to draw distorted conclusions. The second problem is that some respondents may not understand or may misinterpret certain questions.

Interviews: time-consuming, expensive, but sometimes more accurate

Survey data also are obtained through *interviews.* An interview is a meeting between a subject and an interviewer. In an interview, a trained interviewer asks questions and records the answers. Interviews are almost always more time-consuming and expensive than questionnaires, but these disadvantages are often outweighed by the facts that interviews largely eliminate the problem of nonreturn, more intimate or personal questions may be asked, and the interviewer may reword or explain questions for respondents.

Surveys are used to gather information about a large category of people termed a **population.** This might be all middle-class housewives, all college students, all people 20 to 40 years of age, all lawyers, or all Democrats. The population is typically so large that the researcher cannot survey everyone. Thus the researcher must take a *representative* sample of the population. A representative sample has the same characteristics as the larger population being studied. For example, for a study of middle-class attitudes toward inflation and government spending, if 25 percent of all middle-class people are over 50 years of age, then the sample should contain an equal percentage of this age group.

There are several ways to increase the likelihood of obtaining a representative sample. One method is known as random sampling. In a **random sample,** people are selected at random from the entire population, with each individual having an equal chance of being picked. Another method is to design a *stratified* random sample. In this method, the entire population is first divided (or stratified) into different categories—by age, sex, income, or educational level, or any other characteristic germane to the study. A random sample of equal proportion to the population then is picked from each category or group.

Surveys have a number of important uses in sociological research (Baker, 1988). They can supply sociologists with a great deal of *factual data* concerning the opinions, attitudes, beliefs, and behaviors of large numbers of individuals. For example, surveys can tell us what people know and how they feel about many contemporary economic and social issues. Moreover, sociologists use surveys to discover *why* people behave the way they do. Large-scale survey research has shown, for example, that political opinions and people's rates of voting are related to factors such as education, occupation, age, and area of residence.

Surveys have many important uses

Experimentation. The most precise and rigorous method of data collection used by social scientists is the **controlled experiment,** in which all factors that are felt to influence the outcome of an experiment are held constant, with the exception of the factor hypothesized to account for some change in the objects under study. For instance, over the past several years, medical researchers have developed drugs to alleviate various mental disorders. In a controlled experiment of such a drug, a researcher would form two groups—an **experimental group** and a **control group.** The groups would be alike in age, social class, general personality characteristics, intelligence, diagnosed mental disorders, and so forth. The experimental group then would receive the drug. The control group would receive only water or some other harmless solution. Members of the groups would not know whether they were receiving the drug or an inert substance. (In a *double-blind* study, the researchers would not know at the time which subjects were in which groups.) Differences in the manifestation of illness later would be compared between the two groups.

The experimental group receives the stimulus

Similar experimental principles and procedures might be used in evaluating the effects of a counseling program on delinquent children. Two groups of children as similar to each other as possible—including, of course, their patterns of delinquent behavior and attitudes—would be selected. One group (the experimental group) then would receive treatment or counseling while the other (the control group) would not. A series of measurements of delinquency would be taken of both groups some time *after* treatment had ended. These measurements then would be compared with the children's delinquency as measured *before* the counseling. A reduction in delinquency in the experimental group compared with the control group would be considered a result of the experimental group's treatment. A visual model of the controlled experiment can be seen in Figure 1.2.

Control groups are important in experimental research. In our drug treatment example, if certain individuals in an institutional setting received the drug

Figure 1.2 **The controlled experiment.**

and their mental condition improved over several months of experimentation, we could not be sure that such improvement resulted from the drugs. The improvement might be due to factors unrelated to the experiment. Only a control group lets the researcher determine the effects of the drugs alone.

Control groups also guard against what has been termed the **Hawthorne effect,** or the effect of the experiment itself. In other words, there is a tendency for people to change their behavior when they know that they are *participating* in experiments. The classic investigations at the Western Electric Company's Hawthorne plant outside Chicago, actually began as a rather informal and unsophisticated series of experiments (distinct from the final "detached" observation phase previously discussed) to determine the influence of lighting on productivity. To the investigators' amazement, productivity of the subjects increased regardless of increases or decreases in lighting (Roethlisberger and

Dickson, 1939). Later the investigators realized that the increased productivity resulted from all the personal attention that the subjects got during the experiment.

Experiments allow researchers to test and validate cause-effect relationships. For example, they can find out how counseling affects delinquency. Experiments can be carried out in laboratory or laboratory-like settings, as the drug therapy and counseling experiments. In contrast, experiments conducted away from the laboratory in more natural social settings are termed **field experiments,** as illustrated by the beginning stages of the Western Electric experiments on lighting and productivity. Laboratory settings have the advantage of allowing the researchers to apply rigorous experimental controls. Yet because these settings are somewhat artificial, people do not always act as they would in real-life settings. In field experiments, which allow researchers to study behavior under more natural conditions, it is more difficult for them to control for other factors that could influence the outcome of the experiment. In either case, researchers must always be on guard against the Hawthorne effect. Although experiments may be viewed as the most rigorous data collection method, they may be extremely time-consuming and costly, particularly when large numbers of subjects are involved.

Experiments can be conducted inside or outside laboratory settings

Data Analysis and Conclusions

The two remaining phases in the research process consist of analyzing the data obtained and developing conclusions. In the initial stages of analysis, the researcher must assemble, classify, and tabulate the data, incorporating various statistical calculations and tests to obtain the research findings. Finally, the researcher draws conclusions from the findings and either confirms or rejects the original hypothesis.

The Development of Theory

One major goal of science is the development of **theory.** A theory is a set of general statements or principles that attempts to explain observations, experiences, or research findings. Theory also may shed light on other areas of inquiry and suggest new hypotheses to be tested. For example, according to a widely respected theory developed by Albert Cohen (1955), delinquency stems from the frustrations that working-class boys experience in their failure to achieve the American ideal of success. If the working-class boy fails to achieve this ideal, he reacts by *rejecting* middle-class values (which he previously aspired to and viewed as legitimate), and turns to a delinquent gang. The gang totally opposes middle-class values *because* they are beyond hope of attainment. For instance, the gang both accepts and expects physical aggression largely *because* aggression is unacceptable in the middle class. The gang also supports the boy in eliminating any guilt for his delinquent acts and for his choice to break with middle-class values.

The development of theory is a major goal of science

Theory and research go hand in hand

Cohen's theory deals primarily with working-class dimensions of delinquency, but it illustrates the interplay between theory and research. The theory stands as an attempt at the overall explanation and unification of much earlier sociological research into delinquency, but it raises many hypotheses for testing. For example, Upon failure, is *rejection* the *only* response left open to the working-class youth? Is it true that he suffers little or no guilt resulting from delinquent acts as a gang member? Researchers have tackled questions such as these. Their efforts illustrate the point that research and the development of theory go hand in hand.

Sociological Inquiry

Science is a method of study

Science includes a number of areas of inquiry: biology, chemistry, physics, psychology, sociology, and economics. All these disciplines are sciences because they share the method and principles of scientific inquiry. Thus we see **science** as a *method* of study. Science refers not to the *content* of subject matter, but to the *way* in which the subject matter of a given field is studied. Some people feel that any discipline that studies people cannot really be a science because people, unlike atoms, molecules, or stars, do not behave "scientifically." But atoms and molecules do *not* behave "scientifically." For example, blending hydrogen and oxygen in certain proportions produces water. In this process, hydrogen and oxygen are not behaving scientifically. But the person who sets up the conditions and proportions, and combines the substances is behaving scientifically.

It is sometimes argued that because the millions of people throughout the world are unique individuals whose behavior is so varied and complex, understanding of human behavior is not accessible by means of the scientific method. In contrast, sociologists assume that much human behavior does reveal patterns and regularities. Sociological descriptions and explanations of human behavior involve the notion of **social determinism**—the idea that social interactions cause or at least greatly influence people's behavior. Sociologists assume that patterns and regularities are predominant in human behavior—the existence of which should be self-evident even to casual observers of values, attitudes, speech, and dress. Perhaps most revealing of the existence of *order* within human behavior is the continuous existence of organized society itself. The sociologist, being more than a casual observer, is aided by the use of the scientific method in the discovery, understanding, and prediction of uniformities in human behavior.

Social determinism—social interactions influence behavior

Prediction in sociology and the other social sciences is much like prediction in the physical sciences. Yet there is one major difference that should be noted. *Prediction* in the physical sciences involves the notion of direct cause and effect. For example, if water is heated to a certain temperature, it changes to steam. In other words, you can predict that an increase in heat (seen as a *cause*) will have the *effect* of changing liquid water into steam. In contrast, sociology and other social sciences make predictions on the basis of **probability,** or the likelihood that certain things will be found to exist or occur given the presence of other things. For instance, a sociologist may predict (and also find) that families with

Sociological predictions are based on probability

higher incomes have fewer children or that suicide is more frequent in higher social classes than in lower social classes. In such instances, the sociologist is not saying that family income *in itself* causes or does not cause the presence of children or that social class *in itself* causes or does not cause suicide. Sociologists attempt to determine and estimate the association or relationship of certain things to one another, not causes and effects. Predictions made on this basis do not hold true in every single case. Statements of probability only assess the *likelihood* of things existing together under certain conditions.

Generally, sociologists and other social scientists have not engaged in prediction on as grand a scale as have physical scientists. Sociological predictions are less frequent and sometimes less accurate, largely because sociologists are not aware of and thus cannot control (at least mathematically) all the variables in human behavior. Even so, much human behavior does reveal pattern and regularity and therefore is susceptible to prediction. Future studies no doubt will increase our understanding of human behavior and allow for more extensive predictions in the social sciences

Many variables cause difficulties in prediction

Pure and Applied Science

Another important distinction is that between **pure** and **applied science.** Pure scientists are concerned with acquiring knowledge for the purpose of knowing and understanding more adequately the subject matter within their given field of inquiry. As such, they are not concerned with the ways in which knowledge might be used to solve practical problems. In contrast, applied scientists work under the assumption that their findings will benefit people in some practical way. From the standpoint of applied science, sociologists are involved in a vast number of applied scientific areas, ranging from studying the causes and consequences of family violence to analyzing the changing nature and growth of American suburbs, the consequences of recent trends toward longer prison terms for convicted criminals, and the effects of advertising on consumer behavior.

From a more general perspective, Otto Larsen has outlined in the American Sociological Association's publication *Footnotes* some of the major uses and activities of the social sciences, including sociology. These activities include:

1. producing information for business, government, organizations, and individuals on consumer behavior, changes in attitudes and values, crime victimization, cross-cultural comparisons, and other matters
2. creating technologies in survey research, demographic projections, political polling, and consumer research for use by business, industry, and the professions
3. supplying information and advice on policy matters to government and nongovernment bodies
4. pursuing the primary goal of science—that of adding to the overall growth of knowledge to enhance understanding of many facets of human behavior and social life

Some major uses and activities of sociology and other social sciences

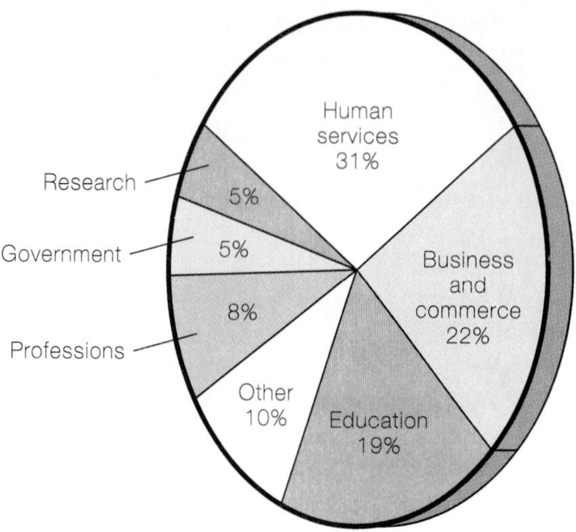

Figure 1.3 Areas of employment for those with bachelor degrees in sociology.
Source: R. A. Hedley and S. M. Adams. "The Job Market for Bachelor Degree Holders: A Cumulation." *The American Sociologist*, vol. 17, 1982, pp. 155–163.

Using sociology

Students who take undergraduate sociology courses find them useful in business and business administration, education, law, public service, government work, the allied health fields, and social work. Figure 1.3 shows some areas of employment for people with bachelor degrees in sociology. Graduate education is a basic requirement for those who want to pursue careers in sociology. Most professional sociologists are involved in undergraduate- and graduate-level teaching, research, consulting, and administrative work.

The Sociological Perspective

Using scientific principles and procedures

As we have seen, sociological inquiry is based on the use of scientific principles and procedures in the study of human social behavior. As such, objectivity and the gaining of precise, factual, and verifiable information all are important.

Developing generalizations and theories

As in other social sciences, a major goal of sociology is to develop a body of generalizations and theories about how and why human beings act the way they do. In their studies, sociologists will often examine specific groups and events, but the actual underlying purpose here is to discover patterns and regularities within social life. In turn, on the basis of this knowledge, sociologists are able to construct generalizations and develop theories that help them understand and predict human social behavior.

The sociological perspective involves two levels of analysis: the macro and the micro. **Macrosociology** is devoted to the study of the broad structure, organization, and features of society. Macrosociology is focused on large economic systems, class structure, patterns of ethnic relations, industrialization, urbanization, and other broad social processes. In contrast, **microsociology** is devoted to studying how people behave and interact in everyday social settings. It is focused particularly on how people's motives, goals, and perceptions of their social settings influence their behavior. At the macro level, for example, sociologists may be interested in studying the effects of long-term industrialization on a society's fertility rates and population growth. At the micro level, sociologists would focus on the various personal and interpersonal factors that influence couples' decisions about how many children to have, or they might focus on how patterns of family interaction differ in small and large families. The functionalist and conflict perspectives, which we discussed earlier in this chapter, offer macro-level analyses, whereas the interactionist perspective offers micro-level analyses.

Levels of sociological analysis

Finally, the sociological perspective involves the use of what C. Wright Mills (1959) called the **sociological imagination.** The sociological imagination lets people understand the relation between biography and history. It is an awareness of how events in personal life often are shaped by social forces. The following reading discusses the sociological imagination and how it broadens personal understanding.

Use of the sociological imagination

General Comments on Readings

As you read this text, you will see readings on a wide range of topics. Some readings are theoretical and stress generalizations concerning various aspects of human social behavior and social life. Others present facts about the dynamic relationship among human social behavior, social organization, and current social issues. The readings are intended to further your knowledge of your society, of social behavior, and of yourself as a member of society. The review questions following each reading relate to some of the important topics discussed within each reading selection.

THE SOCIOLOGICAL IMAGINATION

C. Wright Mills

The following selection is taken from C. Wright Mills's classic book, *The Sociological Imagination* (1959). For Mills, the sociological imagination is a quality of mind—a perspective that enables us to see ourselves and the society around us from a distinct

sociological point of view. It can help us gain a fuller awareness of the present structure of our society, where our society stands in history, the varieties of people who now live in our society, and the ways in which each of these elements is related to and influences one another. The sociological imagination helps us achieve a better understanding of ourselves and our own life experiences. Throughout our lifetimes, we all contribute in one way or other to shaping society, yet we are truly *products* of society and its history. "The sociological imagination enables us to grasp history and biography and the relations between the two within society" (C. W. Mills, 1959).

One important dimension of the sociological imagination is the benefit of seeing and understanding one's personal problems in relation to and partly as a *consequence* of the larger problems within society. Mills shows, for example, that although the problems of war, unemployment, and marital instability may be viewed from a personal and psychological level, the sociological imagination enables its possessor to understand the link between individual problems and their structural and institutional origins.

In these and in many other ways, the sociological imagination permits a broader and more adequate understanding of one's daily life experiences. Understanding one's own place in society is important for individual identity and self-awareness.

The sociological imagination enables its possessor to understand the larger historical scene in terms of its meaning for the inner life and the external career of a variety of individuals. It enables him to take into account how individuals, in the welter of their daily experience, often become falsely conscious of their social positions. Within that welter, the framework of modern society is sought, and within that framework the psychologies of a variety of men and women are formulated. By such means the personal uneasiness of individuals is focused upon explicit troubles and the indifference of publics is transformed into involvement with public issues.

The first fruit of this imagination—and the first lesson of the social science that embodies it—is the idea that the individual can understand his own experience and gauge his own fate only by locating himself within his period, that he can know his own chances in life only by becoming aware of those of all individuals in his circumstances. In many ways it is a terrible lesson; in many ways a magnificent one. We do not know the limits of man's capacities for supreme effort or willing degradation, for agony or glee, for pleasurable brutality or the sweetness of reason. But in our time we have come to know that the limits of "human nature" are frighteningly broad. We have come to know that every individual lives, from one generation to the next, in some society; that he lives out a biography, and that he lives it out within some historical sequence. By the fact of his living he contributes, however minutely, to the shaping of this society and to the course of its history, even as he is made by society and by its historical push and shove.

The sociological imagination enables us to grasp history and biography and the relations between the two within society. That is its task and its promise. To recognize this task and this promise is the mark of the classic social analyst. It is characteristic of Herbert Spencer—turgid, polysyllabic, comprehensive; of E. A. Ross—graceful, muckraking, upright; of Auguste Comte and Emile Durkheim; of the intricate and subtle Karl Mannheim. It is the quality of all that is intellectually excellent in Karl Marx; it is the clue to Thorstein Veblen's brilliant and ironic insight, to Joseph Schumpeter's many-sided constructions of reality; it is the basis of the psychological sweep of W. E. H. Lecky no less than of the profundity and clarity of Max Weber. And it is the signal of what is best in contemporary studies of man and society.

No social study that does not come back to the problems of biography, of history and of their intersections within a society has completed its intellectual journey. Whatever the specific problems of the classic social analysts, however limited or however broad the features of social reality they have examined, those who have been imaginatively aware of the promise of their work have consistently asked three sorts of questions:

1. What is the structure of this particular society as a whole? What are its essential components, and how are they related to one another? How does it differ from other varieties of social order? Within it, what is the meaning of any particular feature for its continuance and for its change?

2. Where does this society stand in human history? What are the mechanics by which it is changing? What is its place within and its meaning for the development of humanity as a whole? How does any particular feature we are examining affect, and how is it affected by, the historical period in which it moves? And this period—what are its essential features? How does it differ from other periods? What are its characteristic ways of history-making?

3. What varieties of men and women now prevail in this society and in this period? And what varieties are coming to prevail? In what ways are they selected and formed, liberated and repressed, made sensitive and blunted? What kinds of "human nature" are revealed in the conduct and character we observe in this society in this period? And what is the meaning for "human nature" of each and every feature of the society we are examining?

Whether the point of interest is a great power state or a minor literary mood, a family, a prison, a creed—these are the kinds of questions the best social analysts have asked. They are the intellectual pivots of classic studies of man in society—and they are the questions inevitably raised by any mind possessing the sociological imagination. For that imagination is the capacity to shift from one perspective to another—from the political to the psychological; from examination of a single family to comparative assessment of the national budgets of the world; from the theological school to the military establishment; from considerations of an oil industry to studies of contemporary poetry. It is the capacity to range from the most impersonal and remote transformations to the most intimate features of the human self—and to see the relations between the two. Back of its use there is always the urge to know the social and historical meaning of the individual in the society and in the period in which he has his quality and his being.

That, in brief, is why it is by means of the sociological imagination that men now hope to grasp what is going on in the world, and to understand what is happening in themselves as minute points of the intersections of biography and history within society. In large part, contemporary man's self-conscious view of himself as at least an outsider, if not a permanent stranger, rests upon an absorbed realization of social relativity and of the transformative power of history. The sociological imagination is the most fruitful form of this self-consciousness. By its use men whose mentalities have swept only a series of limited orbits often come to feel as if suddenly awakened in a house with which they had only supposed themselves to be familiar. Correctly or incorrectly, they often come to feel that they can now provide themselves with adequate summations, cohesive assessments, comprehensive orientations. Older decisions that once appeared sound now seem to them products of a mind unaccountably dense. Their capacity for astonishment is made lively again. They acquire a new way of thinking, they experience a transvaluation of values: in a word, by their reflection and by their sensibility, they realize the cultural meaning of the social sciences.

Perhaps the most fruitful distinction with which the sociological imagination works is between "the personal troubles of milieu" and "the public issues of social structure." This distinction is an essential tool of the sociological imagination and a feature of all classic work in social science.

Troubles occur within the character of the individual and within the range of his immediate relations with others; they have to do with his self and with those limited areas of social life of which he is directly and personally aware. Accordingly, the statement and the resolution of troubles properly lie within the individual as a biographical entity and within the scope of his immediate milieu—the social setting that is directly open to his personal experience and to some extent his willful activity. A trouble is a private matter: values cherished by an individual are felt by him to be threatened.

Issues have to do with matters that transcend these local environments of the individual and the range of his inner life. They have to do with the organization of many such milieux into the institutions of an historical society as a whole, with the ways in which various milieux overlap and interpenetrate to form the larger structure of social and historical life. An issue is a public matter: some value cherished by publics is felt to be threatened. Often there is a debate about what that value really is and about what it is that really threatens it. This debate is often without focus if only because it is the very nature of an issue, unlike even widespread trouble, that it cannot very well be defined in terms of the immediate and everyday environments of ordinary men. An issue, in fact, often involves a crisis in institutional arrangements, and often too it involves what Marxists call "contradictions" or "antagonisms."

In these terms, consider unemployment. When, in a city of 100,000, only one man is unemployed, that is his personal trouble, and for its relief we properly look to the character of the man, his skills, and his immediate opportunities. But when in a nation of 50 million employees, 15 million men are unemployed, that is an issue, and we may not hope to find its solution within the range of opportunities open to any one individual. The very structure of opportunities has collapsed. Both the correct statement of the problem and the range of possible solutions require us to consider the economic and political institutions of the society, and not merely the personal situation and character of a scatter of individuals.

Consider war. The personal problem of war, when it occurs, may be how to survive it or how to die in it with honor; how to make money out of it; how to climb into the higher safety of the military apparatus; or how to contribute to the war's termination. In short, according to one's values, to find a set of milieux and within it to survive the war or make one's death in it meaningful. But the structural issues of war have to do with its causes; with what types of men it throws up into command; with its effects upon economic and political, family and religious institutions, with the unorganized irresponsibility of a world of nation-states.

Consider marriage. Inside a marriage a man and a woman may experience personal troubles, but when the divorce rate during the first four years of marriage is 250 out of every 1,000 attempts, this is an indication of a structural issue having to do with the institutions of marriage and the family and other institutions that bear upon them.

Or consider the metropolis—the horrible, beautiful, ugly, magnificent sprawl of the great city. For many upper-class people, the personal solution to "the problem of the city" is to have an apartment with private garage under it in the heart of the city, and forty miles out, a house by Henry Hill, garden by Garrett Eckbo, on a hundred acres of private land. In these two controlled environments—with a small staff at each end and a private helicopter connection—most people could solve many of the problems of personal milieux caused by the facts of the city. But all this, however splendid, does not solve the public issues that the structural fact of the city poses. What should be done with this wonderful monstrosity? Break it all up into scattered units, combining residence and work? Refurbish it as it stands? Or, after evacuation, dynamite it and build new cities according to new plans in new places? What should those plans be? And who is to decide and to accomplish whatever choice is made? These are structural issues; to confront them and to solve them requires us to consider political and economic issues that affect innumerable milieux.

In so far as an economy is so arranged that slumps occur, the problem of unemployment becomes incapable of personal solution. In so far as war is inherent in the nation-state system and in the uneven industrialization of the world, the ordinary individual in his restricted milieu will be powerless—with or without psychiatric aid—to solve the troubles this system or lack of system imposes upon him. In so far as the family as an institution turns women into darling little slaves and men into their chief providers and unweaned dependents, the problem of a satisfactory marriage remains incapable of purely private solution. In so far as the overdeveloped megalopolis and the overdeveloped automobile are built-in features of the overdeveloped society, the issues of urban living will not be solved by personal ingenuity and private wealth.

What we experience in various and specific milieux, I have noted, is often caused by structural changes. Accordingly, to understand the changes of many personal milieux we are required to look beyond them. And the number and variety of such structural changes increase as the institutions within which we live become more embracing and more intricately connected with one another. To be aware of the idea of social structure and to use it with sensibility is to be capable of tracing such linkages among a great variety of milieux. To be able to do that is to possess the sociological imagination.

Review Questions

1. What is meant by "the sociological imagination"?
2. Contrast the difference between personal troubles and public issues. Give examples of each.
3. Give specific illustrations of the interdependence between self and the society.
4. State several ways in which the sociological imagination may be important for you.

Sociology and Other Social Sciences

Sociology is not the only social science that studies the behavior of people. Several other disciplines—anthropology, psychology, economics, and political science—also study human behavior. But each focuses on and emphasizes a different aspect of this behavior.

Physical anthropology: studies origins and evolution

Anthropology is usually divided into two main types: physical and cultural (or social) anthropology. Physical anthropology stresses the biological sciences and focuses on the origins and evolutionary aspects (that is, the changing physical characteristics) of human beings as well as their behavioral characteristics. Cultural anthropology is concerned with the study of total societies, that is, everything that goes into making up the society, including its systems of beliefs, customs, language, politics, family life, and so on. Cultural anthropology traditionally has emphasized the study of simple, nonliterate societies. Recently, however, cultural anthropologists have given some attention to the study of more contemporary, industrialized societies.

Cultural anthropology: studies cultural variations in time and space

Psychology: studies individual behavior

Rather than studying societies, psychologists study the person. Psychology focuses on individual behavior, examining the mind as well as the mental processes of the individual, including learning, perception, and motivation. Some psychologists concern themselves primarily with the human personality and its development. Often psychologists also systematically observe and study animal behavior. These psychologists feel that the study of animal behavior is an excellent aid in understanding many basic types of human behavior because of the many similarities between humans and the other members of the animal world.

Economics: focuses on production, distribution, and consumption of wealth

Economics is the study of the economic life of humans and is focused primarily on the various dimensions of wealth, such as its production, distribution, and consumption. Many economists stress a society's scarce resources (supply and demand) and their allocation within society.

Political science: studies governments and politics

Political science, like economics, concerns a specific aspect of human behavior. Political scientists study the political behavior of humans and focus on the various aspects of government, political institutions, political processes, and political parties.

To summarize, the social sciences are similar in that they all use the scientific method. Sociology's goal, like that of the other social sciences, is to understand human behavior. However, sociology focuses on and emphasizes different aspects and varieties of human behavior from these other scientific approaches. Whereas cultural anthropologists traditionally have emphasized the study of *total* societies, primarily the non-Western and nonliterate societies, sociologists have focused almost exclusively on the study of contemporary Western literate societies. They have stressed the study of social institutions and groups within societies, giving particular attention to patterns of internal organization of groups. Whereas psychologists study the individual, with some emphasis on the biological factors in human behavior, sociologists focus on human groups and the relationships within groups. Economics and political science are limited to certain aspects of human interaction, whereas sociology is concerned with all aspects of human social life.

Summary

1. Sociology is the scientific study of human interaction and the products of such interaction. Sociologists study the groups that people form and the relationships that occur within groups. Sociologists do not study people as isolated individuals. The products of human interaction include human beings as social animals, groups, societies, customs, traditions, values, and standards of behavior that organize and sustain human social life. In the process of scientifically investigating group behavior, sociology sometimes demonstrates commonly held beliefs to be potentially or completely false.

2. Sociology emerged during the nineteenth century as one facet of the European intellectual response to the Industrial Revolution. Early sociologists such as Comte, Spencer, Durkheim, Marx, and Weber made many significant contributions to the development of sociology. Each felt that human social life and social change could be studied in an objective, scientific manner, and that a new *science of society,* which Comte called *sociology,* was both possible and necessary.

3. Three major theoretical perspectives in sociology are functionalism, conflict theory, and symbolic interactionism. Functionalists view society as a system of interrelated parts, each fulfilling a particular purpose in helping maintain the total social system. Conflict theorists see competition and social conflict as the bases of group or social life. Symbolic interactionists seek to understand social life and human behavior from the standpoint of the interacting individuals themselves and emphasize the role of symbols (shared meanings) in influencing human actions.

4. Sociology began in Europe in the 1800s but largely matured in America in the 1900s. Sociologists have not agreed about whether sociology should actively stimulate social change and social reform. American sociology has made impressive strides in developing research methods and theories that have yielded a better understanding of human society and social behavior.

5. Sociologists use the scientific method to study human behavior. The scientific approach demands factual information, verification, objectivity, neutrality, and exactness on the part of the researcher. Scientists attempt to study only things that can be experienced through the senses so that others may verify their findings.

6. The research process involves several steps: (1) the formulation of a research problem, (2) the construction of a hypothesis, (3) the develop-

ment of a research design, (4) data collection, (5) data analysis, and (6) the development of conclusions based on findings.

7. Sociology is only one of many disciplines that use the methods and principles of scientific inquiry. "Science" refers to a method of study, not to the subject matter that is studied. Sociologists and other social scientists make predictions on the basis of probability, that is, the likelihood that certain things will be found to exist or occur given the presence of other things.
8. Pure science is based on the idea of acquiring knowledge for its own sake, whereas applied science is based on the idea of using scientific knowledge to solve practical problems. The social sciences, including sociology, have many uses and activities, including those of producing information, creating technologies, supplying information and advice on policy matters, and adding to the overall growth of knowledge with regard to human behavior and social life.
9. The sociological perspective incorporates (1) the use of scientific principles and procedures in the study of human social behavior, (2) the development of a body of generalizations and theories about how and why human beings act the way they do, (3) the study of both macro- and micro-level social phenomena, and (4) the exercise of the sociological imagination.
10. Sociology is one of the social sciences, which include physical and cultural anthropology, psychology, economics, and political science. All the social sciences are focused on human behavior, but each is focused on a different aspect of that behavior.

STUDY GUIDE

Chapter Objectives

After studying this chapter, you should be able to:

1. Give a clear and concise definition of sociology
2. Identify the major goal of sociological inquiry
3. Identify two differences between the sociological approach to understanding human behavior and religious, literary, and other approaches
4. Contrast Comte's and Spencer's views on the uses of scientific knowledge
5. Identify what Durkheim meant by "social facts"
6. Detail Marx's ideas about the nature of society and social change

7. Contrast the functionalist, conflict, and symbolic interactionist perspectives
8. Define "social action" and "*verstehen*"
9. Identify the scientific approach and give an example for each of its characteristics
10. List and briefly describe the various steps in the scientific research process
11. Identify and illustrate methods of data collection
12. List advantages and disadvantages of each method of data collection
13. Contrast by means of two examples the difference between cause-effect and probability relationships and predictions
14. Contrast by means of an example the difference between pure and applied science
15. Identify and briefly describe the major elements of the sociological perspective

Key Terms

Applied science (p. 21)
Conflict theory (p. 10)
Control group (p. 17)
Controlled experiment (p. 17)
Experimental group (p. 17)
Field experiments (p. 19)
Functionalism (p. 9)
Hawthorne effect (p. 18)
Hypothesis (p. 14)
Macrosociology (p. 22)
Microsociology (p. 23)
Objectivity (p. 13)
Observation (detached) (p. 15)
Observation (participant) (p. 15)
Population (survey research) (p. 16)
Positivism (p. 7)
Probability (p. 20)
Pure science (p. 21)
Random sample (p. 17)
Science (p. 20)
Social action (Weber) (p. 11)
Social determinism (p. 20)
Social facts (Durkheim) (p. 9)
Sociological imagination (p. 23)
Sociology (p. 4)
Survey (p. 16)
Symbolic interactionism (p. 10)
Theory (p. 19)
Verstehen (p. 11)

Self-Test

Short Answer

(p. 4) 1. "Sociology" can be defined as ______________________________
____
____

(p. 7) 2. Positivism emphasizes use of three techniques:
a. ______________________________
b. ______________________________
c. ______________________________

(p. 9) 3. Functionalism considers society to be ______________________________

(p. 10) 4. For conflict theorists, the basic fact of social life is ______________________________

(p. 11) 5. "Symbolic interactionism" can be defined as ______________________________

(p. 13) 6. "Objectivity" can be defined as ______________________________

(p. 15) 7. The six basic steps in the research process are:
a. ______________________________
b. ______________________________
c. ______________________________
d. ______________________________
e. ______________________________
f. ______________________________

(p. 19) 8. A theory is ______________________________

(p. 22) 9. Macrosociology studies (a), whereas microsociology studies (b):
a. ______________________________
b. ______________________________

(p. 21) 10. Four major uses and activities of the social sciences (including sociology) are:
a. ______________________________
b. ______________________________
c. ______________________________
d. ______________________________

Multiple Choice *(Answers are on page 37.)*

(p. 4) 1. The central concept and subject matter of sociology is:
a. values
b. the human group
c. human behavior
d. group beliefs

(p. 7) 2. The founder of sociology is:
a. Max Weber
b. Emile Durkheim
c. Auguste Comte
d. Herbert Spencer

(p. 8) 3. According to Spencer, sociology should focus upon the analysis of:
a. social facts
b. social statics
c. social action
d. social evolution

(p. 10) 4. For Marx, conflict:
a. is the main source of social change
b. occurs only in capitalist societies

c. has little influence upon social change
d. is always harmful to society

(p. 12) 5. Many American sociologists during the late 1800s and early 1900s were interested in:
a. studying social institutions
b. developing comprehensive theories of society
c. studying society's problems and effecting social reform
d. improving statistical methods in data analysis

(p. 14) 6. Statements that attempt to identify or describe one or more characteristics of a population are termed:
a. scientific theories
b. scientific laws
c. descriptive hypotheses
d. explanatory hypotheses

(p. 15) 7. Elliot Liebow's study of Tally's Corner is an illustration of:
a. survey research using questionnaires
b. participant observation
c. survey research using interviews
d. detached observation

(p. 16) 8. Survey data are obtained by means of:
a. questionnaires and interviews
b. questionnaires and field studies
c. interviews and field experiments
d. detached and participant observation

(p. 20) 9. Social determinism refers to the idea that:
a. social interactions cause or at least greatly influence people's behavior
b. everything depends on the individual
c. society remains unchanging
d. behavior is unpredictable

(p. 20) 10. Sociological predictions are based on:
a. cause and effect
b. common sense
c. subjective interpretations
d. probability

True/False *(Answers are on page 37.)*

T F 11. From the sociological perspective, much of human behavior is learned through interaction with others. (p. 4)

T F 12. Comte felt that sociology should be divided into the areas of social inquiry and social dynamics. (p. 8)

T F 13. Durkheim viewed the individual as a rather passive being. (p. 9)

T F 14. For Durkheim, sociology should focus upon the study of biological and psychological facts. (p. 9)

T F 15. Max Weber used the term "social action" to refer to meaningful social behavior. (p. 11)

T F 16. As a scientist, the sociologist makes value judgments about the "rightness" or "wrongness" of beliefs and value systems that he or she examines. (p. 13)

T F 17. Nonresponse is the major problem for interview surveys. (p. 16)

T F 18. The function of research is to test and evaluate theory; the function of theory is to explain one's research findings and stimulate additional research. (p. 19)

T F 19. Science is a method of study. (p. 20)

T F 20. Physical anthropology stresses the biological sciences and the origins and evolutionary aspects of human beings. (p. 28)

Fill In *(Answers are on page 37.)*

(p. 3) 21. Because humans spend their entire lives within groups, they can be described as ______ animals.

(p. 4) 22. Sociology is concerned with the ultimate questions of ______ and ______ humans act the way they do.

(p. 8) 23. Spencer's views on social evolution led him to conclude that natural change would bring about ______.

(p. 9) 24. Durkheim's classic study titled ______ tested various theories with respect to social phenomena.

(p. 12) 25. Since the 1950s and 1960s, modern ______ theory has gained influence as a major theoretical perspective in American sociology.

(p. 15) 26. The three most frequently used methods for data collection are ______, ______, and ______.

(p. 16) 27. A representative sample has the same characteristics as the larger ______ being studied.

(p. 17) 28. The experimental method uses two types of groups, which are termed the ______ group and the ______ group.

(p. 19) 29. According to Albert Cohen, delinquency stems from the frustrations that working-class boys experience in their failure to achieve ______.

(p. 21) 30. The ______ scientist seeks to obtain and use knowledge for some practical purpose.

Matching *(Answers are on page 37.)*

31. ______ Social facts
32. ______ Population
33. ______ Hawthorne effect
34. ______ Understanding
35. ______ Hypothesis
36. ______ Karl Marx
37. ______ Symbolic interactionism
38. ______ Probability

a. A tentative statement capable of being tested by the scientific method

b. Early important exponent of conflict theory

c. The likelihood that certain things will be found to exist or occur given the presence of certain other things

39. ______ Positivism

40. ______ Participant observation

d. Where the researcher joins the group under study

e. Comte's method

f. Ways of thinking, acting, and feeling characteristic of a group or society

g. The effect of the experimental situation itself on the subjects

h. English word for *verstehen*

i. Theoretical perspective that tries to understand human behavior from the standpoint of the individuals involved in day-to-day interaction

j. A large category of people

Essay Questions

1. What is sociology, and what is the main goal of sociological inquiry? What are the basic questions that sociology attempts to answer?
2. How does the sociological approach to understanding human behavior differ from religious, literary, and philosophical approaches?
3. What do sociologists mean by "social facts"? List five social facts. Why are they *social* rather than psychological or biological facts?
4. Which sociological orientation—functionalism, conflict theory, or symbolic interactionism—do you feel is most useful in explaining the workings of society? Why?
5. Contrast in an essay the functionalist and conflict orientations in sociology with the symbolic interactionist orientation.
6. How have American sociologists viewed the role and purpose of sociology during the twentieth century?
7. Write a brief essay on development of American sociology during the twentieth century.
8. Identify several ways in which sociology may be of benefit to you.
9. What are the major characteristics of the scientific approach?
10. What are the major steps in the scientific research process?
11. Which method(s) of data collection would you use when investigating a general hypothesis such as "American adult males use alcoholic beverages more frequently than American adult females" or "Viewing violence on television has little effect on the behavior of children"? What are the reasons for your choice?
12. What are the major advantages and disadvantages of surveys, observation, and experimentation as methods of data collection?

13. In what ways do cause-effect predictions differ from probability predictions? Give examples.
14. How does pure science differ from applied science? Can a person be both a pure and applied scientist simultaneously? Explain.
15. What are the major elements of the sociological perspective?
16. Compare and contrast how sociology differs from social sciences such as political science, psychology, anthropology, and economics. Write a brief essay.

Interactive Exercises

1. Having completed the first chapter in the text, you now have a fairly general idea of the nature of sociology, the scope of its subject matter, and the sociological perspective. In what ways do you feel that sociology can be of use to you in your present and/or future occupation? Do you feel that sociology can be beneficial to you in spheres of social life outside the context of work and career? How?

2. This chapter provides analysis of three major theoretical perspectives in sociology: functionalism, conflict theory, and symbolic interactionism. Which of these perspectives do you feel is most useful in describing and explaining the workings of our society and its institutions, and of social change? Which perspective do you feel can be best applied toward an understanding of various contemporary issues and social problems within our society? Is a certain perspective more useful for working with some social problems than with others? Discuss your ideas and conclusions with other students and with your instructor during class.
3. The following are examples of research questions. Of the various methods for data collection discussed in this chapter, choose the one that you feel would be most appropriate for the study of each research topic listed below. Why did you choose this particular method? This exercise is designed to reinforce your learning of much of the material presented in this chapter. The exercise should help you gain a better understanding of the research process in general as well as the advantages and disadvantages of various methods of data collection in particular.
   a. Do childless couples experience happier marriages than couples with children?
   b. Are children from one-parent homes more likely to become delinquent than children from two-parent homes?
   c. Does the overall size of a company influence employees' feelings of satisfaction and personal fulfillment with their jobs?
   d. Does a nonsmokers program "X" really work?
   e. What are the patterns of interaction and decision making found within a small group (for example, a delinquent gang, social club, small work group, and so on)?

4. At one time or other during their careers, many people are likely to become involved, either directly or indirectly, in some type of research endeavor related to their work. Many companies, for example, conduct

research aimed at determining the appeal of their products to the public. Other organizations may attempt to assess the efficiency of their employees and/or the quality of service provided by the company or organization. Within the particular occupational field that interests you, what kinds of specific information would be important for a company, agency, or organization to ascertain regarding the quality of its performance? Develop one or two hypotheses related to possible area(s) of study, and specify the method(s) of data collection most useful for obtaining information with regard to this research. Discussing your ideas with other students and your instructor should prove helpful.

Answers

Answers to Self-Test

1. b
2. c
3. d
4. a
5. c
6. c
7. b
8. a
9. a
10. d
11. T
12. F
13. T
14. F
15. T
16. F
17. F
18. T
19. T
20. T
21. social
22. how, why
23. progress
24. *Suicide*
25. conflict
26. observation, survey, experimentation
27. population
28. experimental, control
29. success
30. applied
31. f
32. j
33. g
34. h
35. a
36. b
37. i
38. c
39. e
40. d

Answers to Chapter Pretest

1. F
2. F
3. F
4. F
5. F
6. T
7. F
8. T

Chapter 2

Culture and Society

Chapter Pretest

Let's see how much you already know about topics in this chapter:

1. **People are always very much aware of the impact of culture on their everyday behavior. True/False**
2. **Sociologically, the term "culture" refers exclusively to things such as art, music, and ballet. True/False**
3. **Values cannot scientifically be proved true or false. True/False**
4. **The earliest societies in human history were hunting and gathering societies. True/False**
5. **Humans rely on various instincts for their physical and social survival. True/False**
6. **When sociologists use the term "role," they are talking about one's position relative to other positions in a group. True/False**
7. **Culture has very little influence over people's health and longevity. True/False**
8. **Cultural elements such as language, folklore, etiquette, and feasting are found in all known societies. True/False**

The Nature and Foundations of Culture

In Chapter 1, we stated that sociology is fundamentally concerned with the ultimate questions of how and why people act the way they do. We can begin to answer these questions by examining our inheritance from the past—ways of acting and thinking, values, ideas, customs, types of knowledge, and so forth. In other words, behavior may be explained by examining culture.

Culture has been defined in various ways over the years, but one classic definition developed by E. B. Tylor is frequently cited by sociologists. According to Tylor (1871), **culture** is "that complex whole which includes knowledge, beliefs, art, morals, law, custom, and any other capabilities and habits acquired by man as a member of society." Thus culture is not only art and music, as some may believe, but also consists of the values and rules we live by, our ideas of good and evil, our language, our religion, and so forth. Note the importance

Culture refers to all that is learned

of Tylor's idea of culture as that which is "acquired by man as a member of society." In other words, culture refers to *all* that is *learned* by humans in society. By examining that which people have learned, we can better understand their thoughts, actions, and feelings. For example, one's tastes regarding food (Chinese dislike milk; Americans view milk as nature's perfect food), the way one protects oneself from the elements (ice blocks in the Arctic, bricks and siding in the United States), and even one's type of marriage (one wife or one husband in the United States, multiple wives among the Baganda of Central Africa, multiple husbands among the Toda in South India) all are largely influenced by one's culture. Thus culture, like other concepts employed by sociologists, serves as a tool by which we can gain a better understanding of and more easily analyze human behavior.

Culture may be both explicit and implicit

It is important to note that many parts of culture are "explicit" while other parts are "implicit." **Explicit culture** consists of those rules, customs, and regularities in behavior that people are aware of and consciously recognize. Driving on the right side of the road or shaking hands when introduced to someone are examples of *explicit* American culture. In contrast, sociologists give considerable attention to the analysis of **implicit culture**—those aspects of culture that frequently are unrecognized by people but that give direction to behavior. Various types of values and beliefs may be *implicit* in the sense that they are so fundamental that people simply take them for granted and rarely, if ever, consciously think about them. For instance, in the reading "Mirror for Man" that appears later in this chapter, the author states:

> **Missionaries in various societies are often disturbed or puzzled because the natives do not regard "morals" and "sex code" as almost synonymous. The natives seem to feel that morals are concerned with sex just about as much as with eating—no less and no more (Kluckhohn, 1949).**

THE SILENT LANGUAGE

Edward T. Hall

Everyone is aware that people in different cultures often think, feel, and act in different ways. However, these differences may extend much further than we realize. The peoples of Latin America and North America, for example, often have considerable yet unsuspected differences in the ways in which they use and conceive of time and spatial distance. Likewise, there are often deep and subtle differences in the ways in which they regard the nature and purpose of friendship.

As we mentioned above, values and beliefs are often part of *implicit* culture. Yet, as American anthropologist Edward T. Hall's article "The Silent Language" points out,

Reprinted from *Américas,* Vol 14, 1962, a bimonthly magazine published by the General Secretariat of the Organization of American States in English and Spanish.

various other subtle aspects of culture tend to remain hidden but still have implications for human social life. Hall's article illustrates three such aspects—time, space, and friendship—and discusses the consequences of these silent languages for human interaction.

There is a great reservoir of mutual good will among the peoples of the Americas. Much of it is needlessly dissipated in the desert sands of misunderstanding because in today's troubled world good will alone is not enough. Between the people of the United States and their southern neighbors there are deep and subtle differences. What is needed is an understanding and an appreciation of each other's psychology that will help to bridge political and economic gaps when these exist. Surface differences can be seen and dealt with. What defeats all of us are the hidden elements in man's psychological make-up whose presence is all too often not even suspected.

I will use the Spanish word *ocultos*—"not seen"—in a new sense to stand for these hidden psychological patterns that stand between peoples. Like germs that can't be seen, there are many ocultos that cause psychological difficulty. All one sees are the symptoms, the outward manifestation of the oculto.

One can never hope to uncover all these unsuspected patterns that influence the communication between people. Even reviewing the principal elements at work here is virtually impossible, because each country in the Americas is unique and has a unique relationship with its fellow states.

DEFINING THE OCULTO

I will particularize about three specific topics to demonstrate a principle. These are Time, Space, and Friendship. Ocultos between the U.S. citizen and his neighbors differ in all three. One must keep in mind, however, that times are changing very fast: therefore, some of my examples no longer apply to regions where there has been a great influx of North Americans.

I first became aware of space as a patterned aspect of human behavior when I noted that people raised in other cultures handled it differently. In the Middle East I felt crowded and was often made to feel anxious. Fellow U.S. citizens, also, found it hard to adapt themselves to houses and offices arranged so differently, and often commented on how there was too little or too much space, and how much space was wasted. These spatial differences are not limited to offices and homes: towns, subway systems, and road networks usually follow patterns that appear curious to one not accustomed to the culture.

The "natural" way to describe space may be different in two cultures. For instance, I discovered in Japan that intersections of streets were named and the streets were not. Similarly, Europeans find it almost impossible to follow directions given by Arabs until a whole new system of visualizing space is learned. One reason for this is that the Arab takes so completely for granted the details of a familiar route that he thinks that if he identifies the desired destination as being near a well-known landmark, he has given adequate directions. He visualizes each area as a fixed unit, instead of focusing on the positional relationship between units.

These differing ideas of space—like the ideas of time and place—contain traps for the uninformed. A person raised in the United States is often likely to give an unintentional snub, without realizing it, to a Latin American because of the way he handles space relationships, particularly the physical distance between individuals during conversations. A Colombian or Mexican often feels that the *Norteamericano* he is talking to is cold and withdrawn.

A conversation I once observed between a Latin and a North American began at one end of a forty-foot hall. I watched the two conversationalists until they had finally reached the other end of the hall. This maneuver had been effected by a continual series of small backward steps on the part of the North American as he unconsciously retreated, searching for a comfortable talking distance. Each time, there was an accompanying closing of the gap, as his Latin friend attempted to reestablish his own accustomed conversation distance.

In formal business conversations in North America, the "proper" distance to stand when talking to another adult male who is simply a business acquaintance you don't know well, is usually about two feet. This distance diminishes, of course, at social functions like the cocktail party, but anything under eight to ten inches is likely to irritate. An easy way to test where the hidden line is, is to watch for the first point in closeness that causes the other person to back up, or move. To the Latin, with his own ocultos, a distance of two feet seems remote and cold, sometimes even unfriendly. One of the things that gives the South American or Central American the feeling that the North American is *simpático* is when he starts to use space in a sympathetic way and is no longer made uncomfortable by closeness or being touched.

North Americans, working in offices in Latin America, may keep their local acquaintances at a distance—not the Latin American distance—by remaining behind a desk or typewriter. Even North Americans who have lived in Latin America for years have been known to use the "barricade approach" to communication and to remain completely unaware of its cultural significance. They are aware only that *they* "feel comfortable" when not crowded, without realizing that the distance and the desk often create an oculto that distorts or gives a cold tone to virtually everything that takes place. The hold of the oculto is so strong, however, that the Latin is sometimes observed trying to "climb over" the intervening obstacles—leaning over the desk, for instance—in order to achieve a distance at which he can communicate comfortably. . . .

TIME—PATTERNS OF PUNCTUALITY

As with space, there are many time ocultos that characterize each people. The North American has developed a language of time that involves much more than being prompt. He can usually tell you when his own ocultos have been violated, but not how they work. His blood pressure rises and he loses his temper when he is kept waiting; this is because time and the ego have been linked. As a rule, the longer a North American is kept waiting *in his own setting,* the greater the discrepancy between the status of the two parties. Because of their high status, important people can keep less important people waiting. Also, very important business takes precedence over less important business. Five minutes brings a mild apology; thirty minutes a very long explanation; forty-five minutes is a slap in the face. In addition, the North American has developed a pattern for seeing one person at a time.

Individual appointments aren't usually scheduled by the Latin American to the exclusion of other appointments. The Latin often enjoys seeing several people at once even if he has to talk on different matters at the same time. In this setting, the North American may feel he is not being properly treated, that his dignity is under attack, even though this simply is not true. The Latin American clock on the wall may look the same, but it tells a different sort of time.

By the U.S. clock, a consistently tardy man is considered undependable. To judge a Latin American by the same time values is to risk a major error.

This cultural error may be compounded by a further miscalculation. Suppose the *Norteamericano* has waited forty-five minutes or an hour and finally gets to see the Latin American with whom he has an appointment, only to be told, with many apologies, that "there is only five minutes—maybe a meeting can be arranged for tomorrow or next week?" At this point, the North American's schedule has been "shot." If it is important, he will have to *make the time.* What he may not understand is an oculto common in Mexico, for example, and that is that one is very likely to take one's time before doing business, in order to provide time for "getting acquainted." First meetings leave the North American with the feeling he isn't getting anywhere. If not forewarned by a friendly advisor, or by experience, he keeps trying to get down to business and stop "wasting time." This, too, turns out to be a mistake. In the United States, *discussion* is used as a means to an end: the deal. One tries to make his point with neatness and dispatch—quickly and efficiently. The North American begins by taking up major issues, leaving details for later, perhaps for technicians to work out.

Discussion, however, is to the Latin American an important part of life. It serves a different function and operates according to rules of form; it has to be done right. For the Latin American, the emphasis is on courtesy, not speed. Close friends who see each other frequently shake hands when they meet and when they part. It is the invisible social distance that is maintained, not the physical distance. Forming a new friendship, or a business acquaintance, must be done properly. The Latin American wants to know the human values of a new acquaintance—his cultural interests, his philosophy of life—not his efficiency, before he can establish confidence. And this is all accompanied by elaborate and graceful formal verbal expressions, which people in the United States have long felt too busy to take time for. They tend to assume familiarity very quickly, to invite new acquaintances to their homes after one or two meetings. But the Latin American entertains only friends of very long standing in his home—and never for business reasons.

Of course, times are changing, and the North American can be fooled, too, because there is an increasing number of Latin businessmen who now demand punctuality even greater than in the North. However, there are still a great many times when the old patterns prevail and are not understood. The hidden differences seem to center around the fact that in the North, the ego of the man is more on the surface, whereas in the South preserving institutional forms is important.

THE LANGUAGE OF FRIENDSHIP

It has been observed that in the United States, friendships may not be longlasting. People are apt to take up friends quickly and drop them just as quickly. Friendships formed during school days persist when neither party moves away, but this is unusual. A feature influencing North American friendship patterns is that people move constantly (in the twelve-year period from 1946–1958, according to U.S. census data, two thirds of those owning homes had moved, while virtually all those renting property had moved). The North American, as a rule, looks for and finds his friends next door and among those with whom he works. There are for him few well-defined, hard and fast rules governing the obligations of friendship. At just what point our friendships give way to business opportunism or pressure from above is difficult to say. In this, the United States seems to differ from many other countries in the world.

In Latin America, on the other hand, while friendships are not formed as quickly or as easily as in the United States, they often go much deeper and last longer. They almost always involve real obligations. For example, it is important to stress that in Latin America your "friends" will not let you down. The fact that they, personally, are having difficulties is never an excuse for failing friends. You, in turn, are obligated to look out for their interests.

Thus friends and family around the world—and especially in Latin America—represent a kind of social insurance that is hard to find in the United States, where friends are often a means of getting ahead—or at least getting the job done. Frequently, friendship in the U.S. system involves a series of carefully, though silently, tabulated favors and obligations, doled out where they will do the most good. The least that North Americans expect in exchange for a favor is gratitude. . . .

SPEAKING ONE'S MIND

Europeans often comment on how candid the North American is. Being candid, he seeks this in others. What fools him is that the Latin American does not readily reciprocate. One has to be known and trusted—admitted into the circle of friendship—before this happens. Even then, what is not said may be just as important, and just as much noticed, as what is said. Much of the miscuing that takes place can be traced to the reciprocity oculto in the North American friendship pattern. North Americans tend to believe much too much of what they hear, and then are shocked when things turn out differently. The Latin American, in particular, will not speak his mind to someone involved in his own operation unless there is complete confidence.

UNCOVERING THE OCULTO CAN HELP

Latin Americans are tired of trying to find North Americans who will understand and who are *simpático.* Some have given up trying. They value the whole man, not just his skill or knowledge in one or two fields. They feel that North Americans are so engrossed in getting things done that they never take time to live. This observation is corroborated by the statistics that show how quickly U.S. men whose whole energy has been devoted to their jobs, to the exclusion of other interests and hobbies, die when forced to retire while still vigorous. These have much to learn from their southern neighbors. But there are today many people in the United States who, tired of the trapped feeling of being caught in their inflexible daily rounds, find these Latin American values deeply congenial.

Nevertheless, until we face up to the reality of the ocultos, and make them explicit, difficulties in communication are going to continue. Ocultos drain the great reservoir of good will that the people of the Americas feel in their hearts for each other.

The Latin American must help the North American to understand. And the North American must do everything in his power to reach his friends in Latin America. He must continue to inform himself about the tremendously rich heritage, and the vitality and subtlety, of Hispano-American culture.

Review Questions

1. What are the three aspects of ocultos identified by Hall as existing between the peoples of North America and Latin America?

2. List several ways in which the ocultos can hinder communication and cooperation between peoples of different cultures.
3. Describe various aspects of U.S. ocultos as they might be manifested between teachers and students, people being introduced to each other, and patients gathered in a doctor's waiting room.
4. List several methods by which the ocultos may be diminished between people of different cultural backgrounds.

The Components of Culture

Material Culture

Because culture is a rather complex concept, we will further examine it in terms of its major elements. First, we may discuss culture as material and nonmaterial. By **material culture,** we mean the material objects that people produce and use—from the simplest tools, utensils, furniture, and clothing to the most complex computer systems, architectural designs, automotive engines, and instruments used in space exploration. These and other material products are important for understanding the way in which people live. People employ knowledge and skills necessary to bring these material products into existence and also decide the ways in which they are used. For instance, a brass pot may be used exclusively for cooking in one culture, whereas it may be considered a decorative object in another culture. A sophisticated computer system might be viewed as an indispensable object in one culture, but in another culture, it might be seen as a totally worthless object. Thus our awareness of the kinds of objects created and how people use them brings about a greater understanding of the culture of a society.

Material culture means things people create and use

Nonmaterial Culture

In contrast, **nonmaterial culture** consists of elements termed norms, values, beliefs, and language.

Norms. The concept of *norm* frequently is defined in two different ways. In one sense, norms refer to behavior that is found to be "average," "typical," or "usual." Sociologists call such norms **statistical norms** because they represent what people actually do. Thus, when calculating a statistical norm, one would observe the actual behavior of people in a given situation and report the findings in some form of numerical average. For instance, if one wanted to calculate a statistical norm for smoking and nonsmoking on public buses in a certain city, one would have to ride the buses, count the number of people who smoked and did not smoke, and come up with some sort of mathematical figure summarizing

Norms can be ideal or statistical

one's findings—for example, that 19 out of every 20 people who use the city's buses do not smoke while traveling.

Sociology, however, is primarily concerned with analysis of what are termed *ideal* or *cultural* norms. **Ideal norms** are rules or standards of expected behavior in given situations. The ideal norm for smoking on buses might be "Smoking is not permitted." Thus a norm in the true sociological sense "is an idea in the minds of the members of a group, an idea that can be put in the form of a statement specifying what the members or other[s] should do, ought to do, are expected to do, under given circumstances" (Homans, 1950).

Ideal norms are important for explaining and understanding behavior

Although the sociologist is primarily concerned with analysis of ideal or cultural norms, the distinction beween these and statistical norms is important for various reasons. First, the sociologist is interested in *explaining* and *understanding* behavior and not simply counting behavior. Thus, if one observes a pattern of behavior of dress, speech, or smoking in certain places, the question arises as to why the pattern has arisen. In answering this question, one would almost inevitably have to consider normative standards relating to the behavior pattern. Likewise, one might note that various types of human behavior are almost never committed—such as murder. In contrast, certain types of behavior, such as male and female fashions of dress, may show great variation from place to place or time to time. Here again, one would resort to explanation of the intensity to which certain types of behavior are normatively forbidden, disapproved, tolerable, appropriate, or obligatory. Second, although statistical norms usually bear some resemblance to ideal or cultural norms, one's understanding and explanation of any pattern of social behavior would be largely meaningless if it failed to take into consideration the system of cultural and social expectations underlying it. (See Figure 2.1 for a graph showing both ideal and statistical norms.)

Norms influence the vast majority of human social behavior

In large part, culture is composed of vast and complex systems of ideal norms, many of which are implicit in that they are not consciously recognized by people. Hall's article illustrates well the concept of implicit norms of spatial and temporal relations. Likewise, norms also may be explicit in the sense that people are aware of them and consciously pattern their behavior (dress, speech, or whatever) in accordance with them. In either case, norms represent a vital element of culture. They influence the vast majority of human social behavior, such as how one eats, dresses, speaks, greets others, or behaves in a religious service or in a college classroom. In short, norms bring order into human behavior and thus can be found in all human societies.

There are several different types of norms in every society. Sociologists classify many of these norms as either *folkways* or *mores*. These terms originated with an important nineteenth-century sociologist, William Graham Sumner. **Folkways** are customary rules of conduct that are seen as appropriate for given situations but are not strongly insisted upon nor seen as vital to the welfare or survival of the group. Folkways apply to acts such as arranging a place setting at a dinner table or placing a postage stamp on the upper righthand corner of an envelope. Standards of polite behavior—such as making brief conversation when meeting acquaintances or neighbors—would also be categorized as folkways.

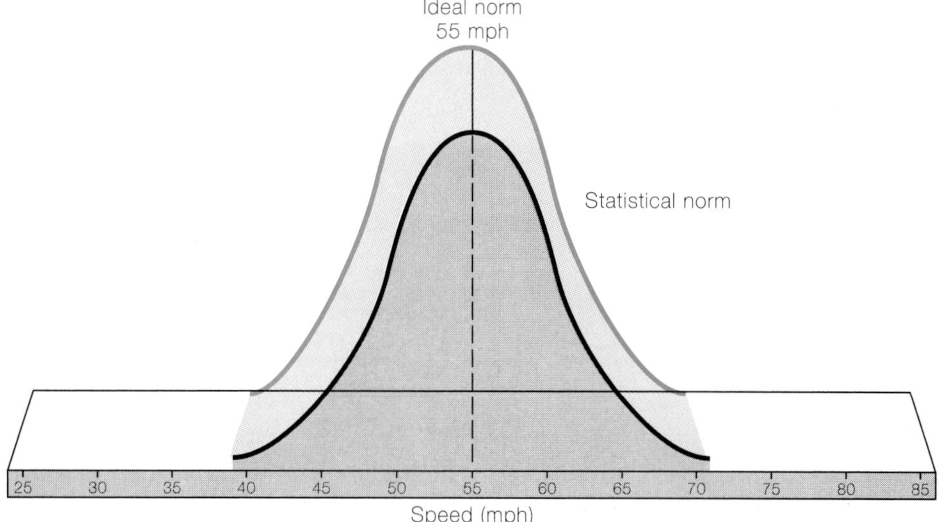

Figure 2.1 **Ideal and statistical norms for state turnpike driving. The ideal norm is stated in terms of the posted legal speed; the statistical norm generally tends to conform to the ideal expectation. However, the statistical norm indicates that some drivers deviate from the ideal to a significant degree, thereby creating hazardous conditions.**

In contrast, certain folkways are felt to have greater significance and more importance for the group. Sociologists term these folkways **mores.** Mores are standards of conduct that are highly respected and valued by the group, and their fulfillment is felt to be necessary and vital to group welfare. Examples of mores are rules prohibiting murder, treason, and cannibalism. Mores, therefore, represent a special type or variety of folkways. They are those folkways that represent obligatory behavior. Mores go beyond custom or etiquette, because they are viewed as highly important and necessary standards for group welfare and because their infraction results in far more severe punishment to the violator.

Folkways govern less significant actions than mores

In addition, both folkways and mores arise from the process of daily living and are viewed as ways by which people may deal with the problems of daily life. Daily living presents a series of challenges—such as how to relate compatibly to friends, acquaintances, and business associates; how to make a living; how to maintain a congenial and stable home and family life; and how to ensure safety and security for oneself as well as others. In short, human beings have various needs that require satisfaction, and over a period of time, certain methods are tried and developed that come to be regarded as proper and expedient ways of fulfilling such needs. Many ways of doing things become norms not by means of rational decision or planning, but simply through repetition and by eventual social acceptance of these patterns as legitimate, expected, and proper. Norms arise from people's daily attempts to satisfy needs and, once developed, are passed on from generation to generation as tradition.

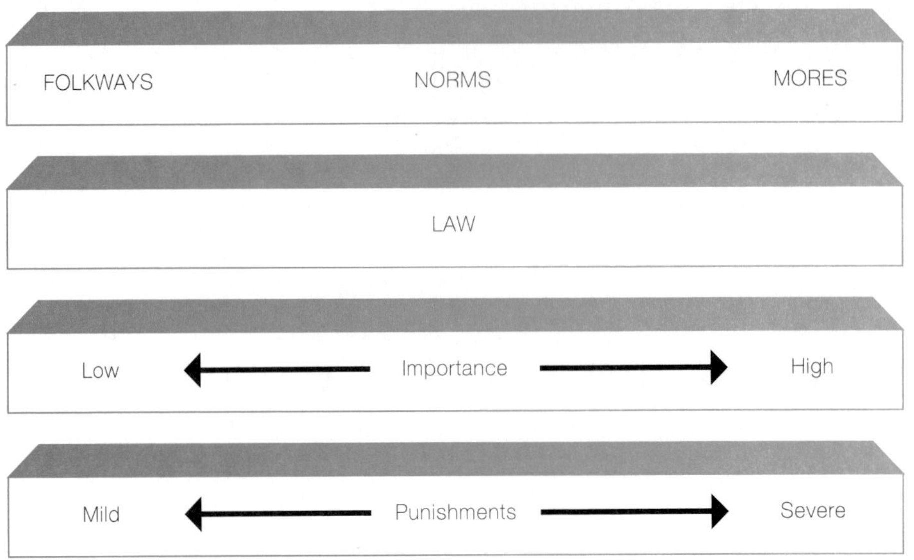

Figure 2.2 **Norms, including those codified in law, vary according to the degree of importance people assign to them and also to the degree of punishment (or sanction) that their violation elicits.**

Laws represent another type of norm with which sociologists deal, particularly in their analysis of complex modern societies. In the context of modern societies, sociologists frequently refer to laws as *formal norms* because they are formally written and typically enacted in a conscious and deliberate manner by federal, state, or local authority. Sociologists long have recognized the importance of law for modern societies, which continuously face extensive social change. Such societies typically cannot wait for custom to resolve conflicts and bring about smooth and orderly social exchange. Such societies face complex problems demanding speedy solutions, and therefore varieties of enacted laws are needed to meet changing circumstances (see Figure 2.2).

Interrelationships of laws, mores, and folkways

The relation of law to other norms (mores and folkways) is complex. Frequently, laws and other norms are consistent. We can see this in the case of prohibitions against murder as well as the requirement that one drive on the right side of the road. In this sense, laws derive from and codify mores and folkways. In a related manner, enacted laws ultimately may be responsible for the development of other types of norms. For instance, the president of the United States may decide that a certain day be declared a legal holiday in commemoration of a certain person or event. Over a period of years, it becomes customary to honor the person or event on that day. In other words, the day becomes not only a legal but also a traditional holiday.

But mores, folkways, and laws are not always in harmony, and therefore conflicts may arise among them. A familiar example of such conflict is the enactment of the prohibition amendment to the Constitution during the early 1900s, by which the sale of alcoholic beverages was forbidden. Although the amendment represented the mores of some people, it did not gain the support of many others. The amendment was repealed 15 years later. This case (and there are others) illustrates the point that when conflict occurs between laws and mores, mores have a tendency to win out. Sumner (1940) clearly recognized this principle and wrote:

To be strong, legislation must be consistent with mores

> **Acts of legislation come out of the mores. . . . Legislation . . . has to seek standing ground on the existing mores, and it soon becomes apparent that legislation, to be strong, must be consistent with the mores. . . . It is sometimes said that "public opinion" must ratify and approve police regulations, but this statement rests on an imperfect analysis. The regulations must conform to the mores, so that the public will not think them too lax or too strict.**

Values. **Values** refer to another major element of culture. Values refer to a person's ideas about worth and desirability. Values make up our judgments of moral and immoral, good and bad, right and wrong, beautiful and ugly, and so forth. Values are distinguished from norms in that values represent judgments of the worth of objects, events, courses of action, and conditions; norms are standards of behavior. Also, technically speaking, values may be held by one or any number of people, whereas norms are always shared, group standards for behavior. We are concerned here with *cultural* values rather than individual values. Shared values tend to serve as a foundation for societal unity. In American culture, for example, we value achievement, success, democracy, and equality. We do not value personal failure, totalitarianism, and social discrimination. Therefore norms as standards of behavior often reflect values, because the norms are tied to a group's conception of the desirable. For instance, in a culture that emphasizes the desirability of individual success, we would expect to find many norms encouraging personal effort and achievement and discouraging overreliance on others.

Values pertain to notions of desirability

Beliefs. **Beliefs** are defined by sociologists as ideas that people hold about the universe or any part of the total reality surrounding them. Defined in this way, the subject of human beliefs may be infinite and may include ideas concerning the individual, other people, and any and all aspects of the biological, physical, social, and supernatural world. Although both beliefs and values represent *ideas* held by people, beliefs may be distinguished from values in various ways. Beliefs concern convictions as to what "is" or "is not." In addition, some beliefs can be proved correct or incorrect. For example, at one time it was believed that the earth was the center of the universe. Evidence attesting to the falsity of this belief came into existence beginning with Copernicus. Other beliefs, however, cannot be proved true or false, such as beliefs about the existence of devils.

Beliefs: a person's conceptions of the surrounding world

In contrast to beliefs, values are concerned with standards of worthiness of what is "good" or "bad," what "should be" or what "should not be," and so forth. In contrast to many beliefs, values represent judgments that cannot be scientifically tested or proved true or false, because there is no way to demonstrate scientifically that a value in and of itself is right or wrong or more or less worthwhile than another. Beliefs give people ways to interpret and explain the

Values represent unprovable judgments

world. Various beliefs also help people cope with events over which they may have little, if any, control. Finally, similar to shared values, systems of shared beliefs contribute to social order and social integration, which are necessary for the continuation of society.

Language. Culture is found only within human societies because only humans can develop and use highly complex systems of symbols, and symbols are the foundation of culture. In simplest form, a **symbol** is something that stands for something else. The most frequent use of symbols is language. Put in another way, words are symbols because they stand for something else (objects, events, or whatever); **language** consists of a highly intricate set of symbols that is made by humans. However, language is far more than just a cluster of words that gives names to things around us. Language influences our ways of perceiving, behaving, and feeling and thus tends to define and shape the world around us. In other words, language affects our awareness, activities, and our ideas of right and wrong, moral and immoral, and good and bad. In turn, these ideas comprise important elements of culture.

Symbols: the foundation of culture

The relation of symbols to culture is so fundamental that sociologists sometimes define "culture" as the total of the symbols possessed by a human group or society. This definition is based on the idea that each fragment of knowledge, each belief, law, custom, and value (according to Tylor's definition) ultimately may be reduced to a set of symbols that is learned, shared, and passed on by means of language from generation to generation. Animals other than humans do communicate, interact, and learn, but virtually none of this behavior is symbolic communication, interaction, or learning. In addition, because other animals lack this symbolic capacity, their learning cannot be accumulated and passed on from generation to generation in the form of a "social heritage."

Characteristics of Culture

Human culture therefore is essentially symbolic. As such, culture is something that is made and developed by people. Traditions, values, beliefs, and standards of behavior are created human products and not simply instinctual givens that genetically program people to act or think in certain ways. That culture is created and developed by humans implies that it is *learned*. Each individual is born into a group that already possesses values, beliefs, and standards of behavior that are transmitted to the individual through interactions with others. Sociologists term this learning process *socialization;* it is the subject of the following chapter. For the present, it is sufficient to say that culture refers to learned behavior rather than to genetically inherited behavior. But not all human behavior is learned. Behaviors such as sneezing and breathing are not learned. But once one moves above the biological level and looks at human social life, there is very little, if any, behavior that does not involve learning. Sociology is concerned with the study of human cultural and social behavior, that is, behavior that is learned.

Culture is learned

In addition to being learned, culture also is *shared*. By this, we mean that culture is a quality of a group rather than of an individual. In this sense, no one person knows the entire culture, because it would be impossible for a single person to acquire the total experience and knowledge of the entire group or society. Culture is learned and shared by people as a result of belonging to various groups. In the reading that follows this section, Clyde Kluckhohn examines how this learning occurs in groups (which define appropriate ways of responding to nature's patterns) and also indicates that culture is shared.

Culture is shared

Finally, culture is *cumulative* and constantly *changing*. When we say that culture is cumulative, we mean that it has a tendency toward growth, expansion, or addition. Thus culture is handed down or communicated from one generation to another. Culture has been popularly termed human "social heritage," which emphasizes the idea of the historical nature or quality of culture. People therefore receive the experience of many previous generations, passed on in the form of social tradition. Change in culture is continuous. In other words, no culture is totally fixed or static. For example, American pioneer culture was quite different from mainstream nineteenth-century American culture, and, in turn, our contemporary technological culture is extremely different from the culture of the past century.

Culture constantly grows and changes

As we shall see in Chapter 12, there are several major sources of cultural change, including invention, discovery, and diffusion. Invention and discovery occur within cultures. Diffusion involves a borrowing or transfer from one culture to another. We, for example, have borrowed items such as corn, glass, umbrellas, and the game of lacrosse. Regardless of the source, the pace of cultural change can be very uneven, and adjustment to change at times may be a problem. But in broadest terms, cultural change generally results as people continuously face new problems that call on them to satisfy needs and goals in new ways. Thus culture must adapt to situations and forces within as well as outside of itself.

Cultures change from within and without

MIRROR FOR MAN

Clyde Kluckhohn

The following reading is from anthropologist Clyde Kluckhohn's book *Mirror for Man* (1949), which has contributed significantly to people's understanding of the world. In it, Kluckhohn examines the nature and significance of culture for human behavior and human social life. He views culture as a total way of life of a group of people; it is that part of our environment that is created, learned, and shared by people as members of

a given group or society. Kluckhohn stresses the influence of culture for understanding, explaining, and even predicting much of our behavior.

This reading is of special importance for a number of reasons. First, it is rich in cross-cultural comparisons, allowing the student insight into variations in the ways of living found within many societies past and present. Second, the reading emphasizes how culture influences much of our daily behavior and even "channels" some of our biological processes. As we shall examine in more detail later, recent evidence indicates that culture even influences how long people live. For years, researchers have noted that people in the Soviet Republic of Abkhasia often live to over 100 years of age. Factors such as diet and work habits (both of which are culturally patterned) have something to do with this. Yet other cultural factors that provide a high degree of integration, stability, and personal security in the lives of Abkhasians are also important (Benet, 1971). Finally, the reading examines the distinction between explicit and implicit culture. You will recall that explicit culture refers to those aspects of culture that people are consciously aware of, while implicit culture refers to those aspects of culture that are so taken for granted that people are not consciously aware of them. A fuller understanding of culture and its effects on our lives requires that we be keenly aware of both dimensions.

Why do the Chinese dislike milk and milk products? Why should the Japanese die willingly in a Banzai charge that seemed senseless to Americans? Why do some nations trace descent through the father, others through the mother, still others through both parents? Not because they were destined by God or Fate to different habits, not because the weather is different in China and Japan and the United States. Sometimes shrewd common sense has an answer that is close to that of the anthropologist: "because they were brought up that way." By "culture" anthropology means the total life way of a people, the social legacy the individual acquires from his group. Or culture can be regarded as that part of the environment that is the creation of man.

This technical term has a wider meaning than the "culture" of history and literature. A humble cooking pot is as much a cultural product as is a Beethoven sonata. In ordinary speech a man of culture is a man who can speak languages other than his own, who is familiar with history, literature, philosophy, or the fine arts. In some cliques that definition is still narrower. The cultured person is one who can talk about James Joyce, Scarlatti, and Picasso. To the anthropologist, however, to be human is to be cultured. There is culture in general, and then there are the specific cultures such as Russian, American, British, Hottentot, Inca. The general abstract notion serves to remind us that we cannot explain acts solely in terms of the biological properties of the people concerned, their individual past experience, and the immediate situation. The past experience of other men in the form of culture enters into almost every event. Each specific culture constitutes a kind of blueprint for all of life's activities.

One of the interesting things about human beings is that they try to understand themselves and their own behavior. While this has been particularly true of Europeans in recent times, there is no group which has not developed a scheme or schemes to explain man's actions. To the insistent human query "why?" the most exciting illumination anthropology has to offer is that of the concept of culture. Its explanatory importance is comparable to categories such as evolution in biology, gravity in physics, disease in medicine. A good deal of human behavior can be understood, and indeed predicted, if we know a people's design for living. Many acts are neither accidental nor due to personal peculiarities nor caused by supernatural forces nor simply mysterious. Even those of us who pride ourselves on our individualism follow most of the time a pattern not of our own making. We brush our teeth on arising. We put on pants—not a loincloth or a grass skirt. We eat three meals a day—not four or five or two. We sleep in a bed—not in a hammock or on a sheep pelt. I do not have to know the individual and his life history to be able to predict these and countless other regularities, including many in the thinking process, of all Americans who are not incarcerated in jails or hospitals for the insane. . . .

Some years ago I met in New York City a young man who did not speak a word of English and was obviously bewildered by American ways. By "blood" he was as American as you or I, for his parents had gone from Indiana to China as missionaries. Orphaned in infancy, he was reared by a Chinese family in a remote village. All who met him found him more Chinese than American. The facts of his blue eyes and light hair were less impressive than a Chinese style of gait, Chinese arm and hand movements, Chinese facial expression, and Chinese modes of thought. The biological heritage was American, but the cultural training had been Chinese. He returned to China.

Another example of another kind: I once knew a trader's wife in Arizona who took a somewhat devilish interest in producing a cultural reaction. Guests who came her way were often served delicious sandwiches filled with a meat that seemed to be neither chicken nor tuna fish yet was reminiscent of both. To queries she gave no reply until each had eaten his fill. She then explained that what they had eaten was not chicken, not tuna fish, but the rich, white flesh of freshly killed rattlesnakes. The response was instantaneous—vomiting, often violent vomiting. A biological process is caught in a cultural web. . . .

I have said "culture channels biological processes." It is more accurate to say "the biological functioning of individuals is modified if they have been trained in certain ways and not in others." Culture is not a disembodied force. It is created and transmitted by people. However, culture, like well-known concepts of the physical sciences, is a convenient abstraction. One never sees gravity. One sees bodies falling in regular ways. One never sees an electromagnetic field. Yet certain happenings that can be seen may be given a neat abstract formulation by assuming that the electromagnetic field exists. Similarly, one never sees culture as such. What is seen are regularities in the behavior or artifacts of a group that has adhered to a common tradition. The regularities in style and technique of ancient Inca tapestries or stone axes from Melanesian islands are due to the existence of mental blueprints for the group. . . .

A culture is learned by individuals as the result of belonging to some particular group, and it constitutes that part of learned behavior which is shared with others. It is our social legacy, as contrasted with our organic heredity. It is one of the important factors which permits us to live together in an organized society, giving us ready-made solutions to our problems, helping us to predict the behavior of others, and permitting others to know what to expect of us. . . .

Many aspects of a culture are explicit. The explicit culture consists in those regularities in word and deed that may be generalized straight from the evidence of the ear and the eye. The recognition of these is like the recognition of style in the art of a particular place and epoch. If we have examined twenty specimens of the wooden saints' images made in the Taos valley of New Mexico in the late eighteenth century, we can predict that any new images from the same locality and period will in most respects exhibit the same techniques of carving, about the same use of colors and choice of woods, a similar quality of artistic conception. Similarly, if, in a society of 2,000 members, we record 100 marriages at random and find that in 30 cases a man has married the sister of his brother's wife, we can anticipate that an additional sample of 100 marriages will show roughly the same number of cases of this pattern. . . .

Cultures do not manifest themselves solely in observable customs and artifacts. No amount of questioning of any save the most articulate in the most self-conscious cultures will bring out some of the basic attitudes common to the members of the group. This is because these basic assumptions are taken so for granted that they normally do not enter into consciousness. This part of the cultural map must be inferred by the observer on the basis of consistencies in thought and action. Missionaries in various societies are often disturbed or puzzled because the natives do not regard "morals" and "sex code" as almost synonymous. The natives seem to feel that morals are concerned with sex just about as much as with eating—no less and no more. No society fails to have some restrictions on sexual behavior, but sex activity outside of marriage need not necessarily be furtive or attended with guilt. The Christian tradition has tended to assume that sex is inherently nasty as well as dangerous. Other cultures assume that sex in itself is not only natural but one of the good things of life, even though sex acts with certain persons under certain circumstances are forbidden. This is implicit culture, for the natives do not announce their premises. The missionaries would get further if they said, in effect, "Look, our morality starts from different assumptions. Let's talk about those assumptions," rather than ranting about "immorality."

A factor implicit in a variety of diverse phenomena may be generalized as an underlying cultural principle. For example, the Navaho Indians always leave part of the design in a pot, a basket, or a blanket unfinished. When a medicine man instructs an apprentice he always leaves a little bit of the story untold. This "fear of closure" is a recurrent theme in Navaho culture. Its influence may be detected in many contexts that have no explicit connection. . . .

Every group's way of life, then, is a structure—not a haphazard collection of all the different physically possible and functionally effective patterns of belief and action. A culture is an interdependent system based upon linked premises and categories whose influence is greater, rather than less, because they are seldom put in words. Some degree of internal coherence which is felt rather than rationally constructed seems to be demanded by most of the participants in any culture. As Whitehead has remarked, "Human life is driven forward by its dim apprehension of notions too general for its existing language."

In sum, the distinctive way of life that is handed down as the social heritage of a people does more than supply a set of skills for making a living and a set of blueprints for human relations. Each different way of life makes its own assumptions about the ends and purposes of human existence, about what human beings have a right to expect from each other and the gods, about what constitutes fulfillment or frustration. Some of these assumptions are made explicit in the lore of the folk; others are tacit premises which the observer must infer by finding consistent trends in word and deed.

Review Questions

1. What does Kluckhohn mean by the statement "culture channels biological processes"?
2. List examples of how our biological processes are influenced by culture.
3. Distinguish between and give examples of explicit and implicit culture.
4. List examples of cultural relativity.

Society and Social Structure

Society

Sociologists traditionally have distinguished culture from society by indicating that culture consists of learned and shared ways of acting, thinking, and feeling (that is, a total way of life), whereas society refers to an actual group of people. Specifically, a **society** refers to a large number of people who form a relatively organized, self-sufficient, enduring body. We can see therefore that culture and society represent two sides of the same coin: "society" referring to *people* (who share a common culture) and "culture" referring to patterns or ways of group life.

Society refers to a group

During the course of human history, people have organized themselves into various types of societies depending upon their level of technology and the related methods of subsistence. The earliest societies were simple hunting and gathering societies where people hunted various animals and gathered basic vegetables and fruit. These were followed by pastoral societies, which used herded, domesticated animals for food. Next came horticultural societies in which people developed methods of planting and producing their own foods from the soil by using very small tools. These were followed by agricultural societies, after the invention of the plow—a device that enabled people vastly to increase the amount of available food. Industrial societies, with their more modern types of energy and machinery, developed only within the last couple of centuries. Although each of these social forms still exists, only a small number of hunting and gathering societies remain. Moreover, the postindustrial society, with its emphasis on high technology, mass computerization, and white-collar service occupations, is quickly becoming a reality.

The type of society depends on the level of technology and related methods of subsistence

Sociologists distinguish culture from society for many reasons but perhaps primarily because there exist various forms of societies that do not possess culture. Various animal species other than humans (ants, bees, and chimpanzees, for example) engage in *social* or group life, can distinguish or recognize themselves from other species, and possess a relatively complex division of labor

Only human societies have culture

to meet their basic needs for survival. Human societies, however, can be distinguished from nonhuman societies because only human societies have *culture.*

Human societal life is based on culture

Human beings rely on culture as the basis for their social life and organization because the human animal does not possess instincts. By **instinct,** we mean any complex behavior pattern that is genetically inherited and that is universal for every member of a species. Examples of instinctual behavior are the migration and nest building of various species of birds and the division of labor as reflected in the highly specialized functions of queen bees as well as worker ants.

Of course, according to some popular notions, humans do possess at least some instincts. It is not uncommon, for instance, to hear some people speak of "self-preservation," "species preservation," and "the maternal instinct." However, no scientific evidence exists to support such beliefs. If an instinct for self-preservation did exist, the act of suicide would not and could not even be contemplated, let alone performed. Likewise, the presence of maternal instinct or species preservation would make such acts as child abandonment, homicide, and war impossible. In short, when we say that humans possess no instincts, we mean that there are no complex human social behavior patterns that are and always have been the same or identical for every member of the human species. In contrast to other animals, our social behavior is the product of learning, and when sociologists speak of culture they refer to behavior that is *learned.*

Social Structure

Societies not only possess culture, but they also have an organization or social structure. **Social structure** refers to patterns of interactions and networks of relationships found within a society. The idea of social structure calls attention to the fact that the patterns and regularities seen in our behavior and the behavior of others in the context of family, work, recreation, and so forth, are not simply the result of accident or chance. Rather, people's behavior is very much influenced by social forces and the social network systems within which they participate. We can gain a clearer understanding of social structure by briefly examining some of its key elements, which would include role, status, groups, and institutions. Each of these brings order to social life and to our interactions with others.

Role and Status. When sociologists speak of **role,** they mean a pattern of behavior that is expected of an individual who occupies a particular status in society. By **status,** they mean a position relative to other positions. When an individual is occupying the status of father in the social structure, for example, he is expected to play the father role with all its rights and obligations. Roles help people structure their behavior in accordance with socially expected guidelines. In general, roles help ensure a relatively predictable course of social interaction. When an individual is occupying the status of doctor, for instance, he or she is expected to perform in ways that are appropriate to the status of doctor. The role, in other words, defines the pattern of behavior expected of the doctor to patients, colleagues, and others.

Roles and statuses help people pattern and structure their behavior

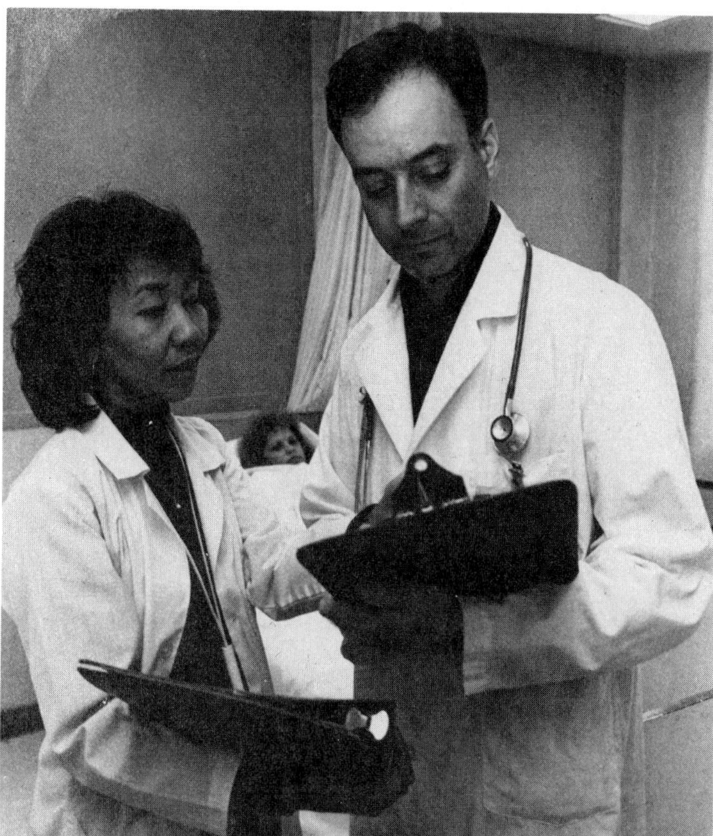

Roles are an important element in structuring social behavior.

Each individual occupies many statuses and plays the different roles associated with them. We occupy such statuses as sister, brother, mother, father, Catholic, Jew, student, and teacher. Each status has an accompanying socially appropriate role. We use the term **role expectancy** to define the way an individual is expected to act in a particular status. In contrast, **role performance** consists of the individual's actual response to this expectancy. For example, one expects managers to behave differently from workers and Catholics to behave differently from Moslems. Each status has its appropriate role, which consists of norms or rules that *pre*scribe socially appropriate behavior and *pro*scribe behavior considered inappropriate within a particular culture or subculture. In other words, the behavior that one exhibits and the norms that one follows depend to a great extent upon the status one happens to be occupying at a particular time and place. A foreman in an industrial plant is guided by norms that have been basically established by management for that position, and we usually find that he acts in ways that are appropriate to his status of foreman. At home, this same individual sheds the foreman role and plays the role of father to his children and husband to his wife. Occasionally, an individual finds it difficult to shed a

Each status has its appropriate role

One individual may have several roles

particular role even though it may be socially appropriate to do so—such as the army sergeant who makes his children march in step to church.

It should be noted that roles sometimes conflict with one another. A working mother, for example, may have to decide between working overtime at her job and preparing dinner for her children. When two or more roles conflict in this manner, the individual experiences **role conflict.** When an individual has too many role obligations and has difficulty fulfilling them all, the condition is called **role strain.**

To summarize, a social role is a part performed by an individual as he or she occupies a particular status, and it may be analyzed independently of the way in which it is performed by the individual.

Individuals come to occupy their statuses in two ways: by ascription and by achievement. **Ascribed statuses** are assigned to the individual at birth and are based on factors beyond the individual's control. Examples of ascribed statuses are sex, age, race, and social class at birth. Our culture, like all others, defines certain behaviors as appropriate or inappropriate to each particular sex, race, and age group. An **achieved status,** in contrast, must be earned. It is through the individual's own efforts and skill that she or he occupies an achieved status. One is not ascribed the status of pianist or doctor. Only through many years of education, study, and practice do individuals acquire such achieved statuses as these.

Groups. Social groups also form the basis of organized social life. As we shall see in Chapter 4, groups are of many sizes and are organized for a variety of human needs.

When sociologists employ the concept **social group,** they mean a unit "composed of two or more persons who come into contact for a purpose and who consider the contact meaningful" (T.M. Mills, 1967). The concept also has been defined as a "number of persons linked together in a network of social relationships" (Chinoy, 1963). The members of a social group:

Social groups defined

1. interact in more or less standardized ways according to the norms of the group
2. base their relationships mainly upon a set of interrelated roles and statuses
3. are united to a lesser or greater degree by similar interests or a sense of common identity, enabling them to differentiate members from nonmembers

Several people waiting for a subway or a bus and hardly aware of one another are not a sociological group, but an **aggregate** of people. Their superficial, fleeting interaction does not qualify them as a group. But if an aggregate of people begin to interact frequently over an extended period of time—such as a collection of people stuck in an elevator—their interactions are likely to become patterned. They also are likely to develop expectations about one another's behavior and come to identify one another as members of the same entity. Thus aggregates as well as other collectivities of people may become social groups.

A group is also to be distinguished from a **category,** which is a collection of people with similar characteristics but with no common identity, understanding of membership, and no involvement in patterned social interaction. All single mothers, all army privates, and all little people are social categories. But the Veterans of Foreign Wars, the family, and a college fraternity are social groups. Social categories, such as all voters or all football fans, are not groups because not all voters or all football fans interact with one another. The absence of interaction means that there is no group. Within groups, there must be frequent, patterned interaction and the carrying on of a variety of activities. In contrast to a social category, a social group consists of two or more individuals who share a common pattern of social interaction.

Categories lack group characteristics

Institutions. Finally, with respect to structural patterns, sociologists give considerable attention to the concept of institutions. As they have with the concept of culture, sociologists have defined "institution" in various ways. One of the most common contemporary definitions of **institution** is a pattern of norms (folkways and mores) centered around a major goal, value, or need for society. Every society has the continuous need to supply itself with new members. As such, in every society, some sort of family system evolves with the major goals of procreation and the care and early training of the young. The norms surrounding these needs specify the ways in which the needs are to be satisfied. In addition, networks of norms, statuses, and roles provide stability, order, or structure to family life, thus ensuring that needs will be met. Thus a family in the ideal normative sense is composed of a number of individuals, each of whom has a role and status, functions and responsibilities, toward the fulfillment of various institutional and societal ends.

An institution is a pattern of norms centered around a basic societal need

In addition to procreation and early childhood care, each society must meet a host of other basic needs. It must manufacture and distribute goods and services and deal with supply and demand, which give rise to the society's *economic* institution. The need for maintaining social control and the problems related to the regulation of the *power* of some individuals or groups over others necessitate the development of *political* institutions. The *educational* institution is connected with the continuing goal of socialization of the young. Finally, the *religious* institution is found in all societies. This institution serves a basic human need of bringing ethical principles and morality to people's lives and providing answers to the questions of their existence, meaning, and future.

Cultural Variation

We mentioned above that every society possesses certain institutions for fulfilling basic survival needs. In addition to these institutions, a host of common cultural elements can be found within every society. A well-known anthropologist, George Murdock (1945), listed some 88 common elements, including incest taboos, mourning, language, cooking, folklore, etiquette, feasting, and puberty rites. Sociologists term these common cultural elements found within all known societies **cultural universals.**

Murdock has given us general forms of cultural behavior, but the specific *content* of behavior composing each of these general categories varies remarkably from society to society. Thus, for example, though political institutions are found within every society, whether these institutions incorporate parliamentary, totalitarian, divine right, or democratic principles varies with the surrounding culture. An incest taboo prohibiting sexual intercourse by close relatives is found in every society. But whether this cultural prohibition applies to simply brothers and sisters, cousins (of some degree), or members of one's entire clan also varies from society to society. Likewise, all societies make cultural distinctions between age and sex categories, which, in turn, have implications for prestige, temperament, identity, and various other social and psychological characteristics. Here again, however, the specific *content* of these distinctions is different in each society. The elderly of one society may receive very little prestige and respect and may be looked upon (and come to view themselves) as a social problem. In another society, the elderly are highly valued and respected, because age culturally signifies wisdom, authority, and knowledge.

Different cultures mean different ways of living

With respect to cultural variations between the sexes, the well-known and classic work of Margaret Mead (1935) among three primitive societies on the island of New Guinea serves as an excellent example. Among the Arapesh, Mead notes that both sexes are cooperative and responsive to each other and behave in a way that Americans would describe as feminine or maternal. There is very little difference between male and female activities and personality. Much of the concern and many of the daily activities among the Arapesh center around family life and child rearing. In contrast, the Mundugumors of both sexes tend to be violent and aggressive, and both behave in ways that Americans would tend to feel are masculine. Family life and child care among the Mundugumors are not highly valued. The Tchambuli make the sharpest distinction between the sexes, but the sex roles and personality differences are somewhat different from those of American society: The women occupy the aggressive and dominant roles, and the men are more submissive, passive, and dependent.

Culture has implications for identity and personality organization

Variations in culture have implications for more than identity and personality. Some evidence suggests that differences in people's ways of life also may be related to how long they live. As we mentioned previously, many people in the Soviet Republic of Abkhasia live to be 80, 90, and 100 years old. Why? Throughout their lives, Abkhasians eat fresh fruits, many kinds of fresh and pickled vegetables, cheeses, cornmeal, and buttermilk. They do not eat much meat, and they consider overeating hazardous to health. Abkhasians also work throughout most of their lives. Work is highly valued and is paced according to capabilities and age. Other cultural factors also seem to be important for Abkhasian longevity. Abkhasians tend to value and manifest a high degree of stability and continuity in many activities—eating, working, recreation, and so forth. They have a strong, highly organized kinship structure that also adds a high degree of integration and personal security in their lives. Thus, as a whole, Abkhasian culture provides and promotes consistent, stable, and meaningful life patterns quite different from those characteristic of American society (Benet, 1971).

Culture and longevity

In recent years, there has been a growing awareness on the part of medical personnel and social scientists of the role that social and cultural factors play in promoting health and longevity. David Mechanic, for example, makes the point that health is influenced by the "personal decisions of individuals" and equally, if not more so, by the "routine organization of everyday settings and activities." His analysis stresses a number of factors conducive to promoting health, such as (1) the level of social integration within groups, (2) the degree of social and cultural constraints over people's behavior, and (3) the stability of social settings and daily life activities and routines—particularly in the context of family life and other forms of social and community participation. As Mechanic notes, "Health outcomes depend heavily on patterns of family life and social participation and how everyday activities and behavior are structured" (Mechanic, 1990).

The extent of cultural diversity cannot be overestimated. We have seen that there is a wide diversity even among many common elements found throughout cultures. Of course, cultures can be strikingly dissimilar in an almost infinite number of ways. For instance, the existence of books or the use of electricity are common to the point of being taken for granted in our own society, but material culture of this sort may be totally unknown in another society. Likewise, war may be recognized within some societies, and military defense and offense may take priority over many other social needs. In other societies, however, warfare may never occur, and, in fact, certain peoples may even find it impossible to conceive of war.

Cultural diversity cannot be overestimated

Intracultural Variation

When sociologists speak of **cultural variation,** they speak not only of diversity *between* cultures but also *within* cultures. Sociologists frequently note that in most societies, there are groups of people who maintain most of the values, customs, and beliefs characteristic of the dominant culture yet also maintain distinct values, customs, and beliefs of their own. In other words, particularly in large societies, one can observe certain groups or categories who share in the general culture but who maintain distinctive ways of thinking, acting, and feeling. Sociologists call this distinctive pattern of thinking, acting, and feeling a **subculture.** Sociologists have noted that many subcultural groups tend to be found within complex societies. In the United States, for instance, there is an abundance of religious, racial, ethnic, and occupational subcultures. Protestants, Catholics, Jews, and Amish exemplify religious subcultures. Blacks, Polish-Americans, and Italian-Americans are examples of racial and ethnic subcultures. Medical doctors, bricklayers, and teachers are examples of occupational subcultures. In addition, subcultures may be based on location (the subcultures of the West and South), on age (the adolescent subculture), or on social class (lower-, middle-, and upper-class subcultures).

Usually, the patterns of thinking, acting, and feeling of most subcultures do not conflict with those of the dominant culture. However, some subcultures have values and norms that sharply contradict the dominant values and norms of the larger society. These subcultures are called **countercultures** (Yinger 1960, 1977). Many delinquent gangs and extremist revolutionary and political groups exemplify countercultural systems. The 1960s youth movement and the contemporary "punk" movement are also countercultures. The members of counter-

Countercultures: special types of subcultures

cultures not only share distinctive ways of thinking and acting but also hold norms and values that are contradictory and hostile to the dominant norms of the larger society.

Ethnocentrism and Cultural Relativism

Each person is born into a particular society that has its own particular culture. At an early age, children begin to learn many aspects of this culture, such as language, standards of behavior, and beliefs. They also begin to learn many of the group's values concerning judgments of good and bad, proper and improper, and right and wrong. This learning continues into and throughout adulthood as people internalize, accept, and identify with their group's way of living. As a consequence of this limited experience within one particular society, most people feel that their particular way of life is superior, right, and natural and that all other cultures are inferior and often wrong and unnatural. This feeling is called **ethnocentrism.** It is basically an inclination to judge other cultures in terms of the values and norms of one's own culture. Thus the more dissimilar another culture is to one's own, the stranger, more absurd, and inferior the other culture appears to be. In this sense, ethnocentrism involves mistaking the familiar, customary, or merely conventional ways of one's own culture for what is "natural," "right," and "superior."

Ethnocentrism: my way of life is the best

The concept of **cultural relativism** is opposite to that of ethnocentrism. Basically, cultural relativism refers to the notion that each culture should be evaluated from the standpoint of *its own setting* rather than from the standpoint of a different culture. In other words, norms, values, and beliefs are *relative* to the particular culture in which they exist and should be judged only from the viewpoint of that culture. The ethnocentric American would consider the practice of polygamy (one person marrying two or more people of the opposite sex) in another society to be "uncivilized" and "immoral." In contrast, cultural relativists would judge the meaning, purpose, and worthwhileness of this practice in the context of the specific culture in which it is found, because they adopt the position that the goodness or badness of values, practices, or beliefs are relative to their cultural setting.

Cultural relativism: things must be judged in their own setting

Sociologists have noted that to some degree all societies (as well as subgroups within societies) are ethnocentric. In certain ways, ethnocentrism may have some disadvantages, particularly where the solution of various problems or the achievement of certain goals requires mutual recognition, respect, and cooperation among various peoples. But ethnocentrism also makes for loyalty and solidarity within groups. Ethnocentrism also tends to bring about stability and resistance to change within groups. Of course, resistance to change in itself can have a variety of consequences. In some instances, change may be a necessity, even to the point of continued group survival, but in other cases, change may disrupt group unity.

BODY RITUAL AMONG THE NACIREMA

Horace Miner

Even though ethnocentrism is present in all societies, people almost never recognize it in themselves. In the following reading, the people of the Nacirema society are so immersed within their culture that they consider women's baking their heads in small ovens and men's scraping and lacerating their faces desirable. Written by Horace Miner, this classic article examines Nacirema culture and its belief that the human body is "ugly and that its natural tendency is to debility and disease."

The anthropologist has become so familiar with the diversity of ways in which different peoples behave in similar situations that he is not apt to be surprised by even the most exotic customs. In fact, if all of the logically possible combinations of behavior have not been found somewhere in the world, he is apt to suspect that they must be present in some yet undescribed tribe. This point has, in fact, been expressed with respect to clan organization by Murdock.[1] In this light, the magical beliefs and practices of the Nacirema present such unusual aspects that it seems desirable to describe them as an example of the extremes to which human behavior can go.

Professor Linton first brought the ritual of the Nacirema to the attention of anthropologists twenty years ago,[2] but the culture of this people is still very poorly understood. They are a North American group living in the territory between the Canadian Cree, the Yaqui and Tarahumare of Mexico, and the Carib and Arawak of the Antilles. Little is known of their origin, although tradition states that they came from the east. According to Nacirema mythology, their nation was originated by a culture hero, Notgnihsaw, who is otherwise known for two great feats of strength—the throwing of a piece of wampum across the river Pa-To-Mac and the chopping down of a cherry tree in which the Spirit of Truth resided.

Nacirema culture is characterized by a highly developed market economy which has evolved in a rich natural habitat. While much of the people's time is devoted to economic pursuits, a large part of the fruits of these labors and a considerable portion of the day are spent in ritual activity. The focus of this activity is the human body, the appearance and health of which loom as a dominant concern in the ethos of the people. While such a concern is certainly not unusual, its ceremonial aspects and associated philosophy are unique.

The fundamental belief underlying the whole system appears to be that the human body is ugly and that its natural tendency is to debility and disease. Incarcerated in such a body, man's only hope is to avert these characteristics through the use of the powerful influences of ritual and ceremony. Every household has one or more shrines devoted

---

[1] G.P. Murdock, *Social Structure* (New York: Macmillan, 1949).

[2] R. Linton, *The Study of Man* (New York: Appleton-Century, 1936).

to this purpose. The more powerful individuals in the society have several shrines in their houses and, in fact, the opulence of a house is often referred to in terms of the number of such ritual centers it possesses. Most houses are of wattle and daub* construction, but the shrine rooms of the more wealthy are walled with stone. Poorer families imitate the rich by applying pottery plaques to their shrine walls.

While each family has at least one such shrine, the rituals associated with it are not family ceremonies but are private and secret. The rites are normally only discussed with children, and then only during the period when they are being initiated into these mysteries. I was able, however, to establish sufficient rapport with the natives to examine these shrines and to have the rituals described to me.

The focal point of the shrine is a box or chest which is built into the wall. In this chest are kept the many charms and magical potions without which no native believes he could live. These preparations are secured from a variety of specialized practitioners. The most powerful of these are the medicine men, whose assistance must be rewarded with substantial gifts. However, the medicine men do not provide the curative potions for their clients, but decide what the ingredients should be and then write them down in an ancient and secret language. This writing is understood only by the medicine men and by the herbalists who, for another gift, provide the required charm.

The charm is not disposed of after it has served its purpose, but is placed in the charm-box of the household shrine. As these magical materials are specific for certain ills, and the real or imagined maladies of the people are many, the charm-box is usually full to overflowing. The magical packets are so numerous that people forget what their purposes were and fear to use them again. While the natives are very vague on this point, we can only assume that the idea in retaining all the old magical materials is that their presence in the charm-box, before which the body rituals are conducted, will in some way protect the worshipper.

Beneath the charm-box is a small font. Each day every member of the family, in succession, enters the shrine room, bows his head before the charm-box, mingles different sorts of holy water in the font, and proceeds with a brief rite of ablution. The holy waters are secured from the Water Temple of the community, where the priests conduct elaborate ceremonies to make the liquid ritually pure.

In the hierarchy of magical practitioners, and below the medicine men in prestige, are specialists whose designation is best translated "holy-mouth-men." The Nacirema have an almost pathological horror of and fascination with the mouth, the condition of which is believed to have a supernatural influence on all social relationships. Were it not for the rituals of the mouth, they believe that their teeth would fall out, their gums bleed, their jaws shrink, their friends desert them, and their lovers reject them. They also believe that a strong relationship exists between oral and moral characteristics. For example, there is a ritual ablution of the mouth for children which is supposed to improve their moral fiber.

The daily body ritual performed by everyone includes a mouth-rite. Despite the fact that these people are so punctilious about care of the mouth, this rite involves a practice which strikes the uninitiated stranger as revolting. It was reported to me that the

---

* Wood and plaster—Ed.

ritual consists of inserting a small bundle of hog hairs into the mouth, along with certain magical powders, and then moving the bundle in a highly formalized series of gestures.

In addition to the private mouth-rite, the people seek out a holy-mouth-man once or twice a year. These practitioners have an impressive set of paraphernalia, consisting of a variety of augers, awls, probes, and prods. The use of these objects in the exorcism of the evils of the mouth involves almost unbelievable ritual torture of the client. The holy-mouth-man opens the client's mouth and, using the above mentioned tools, enlarges any holes which decay may have created in the teeth. Magical materials are put into these holes. If there are no naturally occurring holes in the teeth, large sections of one or more teeth are gouged out so that the supernatural substance can be applied. In the client's view, the purpose of these ministrations is to arrest decay and to draw friends. The extremely sacred and traditional character of the rite is evident in the fact that the natives return to the holy-mouth-men year after year, despite the fact that their teeth continue to decay.

It is to be hoped that, when a thorough study of the Nacirema is made, there will be careful inquiry into the personality structure of these people. One has but to watch the gleam in the eye of a holy-mouth-man, as he jabs an awl into an exposed nerve, to suspect that a certain amount of sadism is involved. If this can be established, a very interesting pattern emerges, for most of the population shows definite masochistic tendencies. It was to these that Professor Linton referred in discussing a distinctive part of the daily body ritual which is performed only by men. This part of the rite involves scraping and lacerating the surface of the face with a sharp instrument. Special women's rites are performed only four times during each lunar month, but what they lack in frequency is made up in barbarity. As part of this ceremony, women bake their heads in small ovens for about an hour. The theoretically interesting point is that what seems to be a preponderantly masochistic people have developed sadistic specialists.

The medicine men have an imposing temple, or *latipso*, in every community of any size. The more elaborate ceremonies required to treat very sick patients can only be performed at this temple. These ceremonies involve not only the thaumaturge* but a permanent group of vestal maidens who move sedately about the temple chambers in distinctive costume and headdress.

The *latipso* ceremonies are so harsh that it is phenomenal that a fair proportion of the really sick natives who enter the temple ever recover. Small children whose indoctrination is still incomplete have been known to resist attempts to take them to the temple because "that is where you go to die." Despite this fact, sick adults are not only willing but eager to undergo the protracted ritual purification, if they can afford to do so. No matter how ill the supplicant or how grave the emergency, the guardians of many temples will not admit a client if he cannot give a rich gift to the custodian. Even after one has gained admission and survived the ceremonies, the guardians will not permit the neophyte to leave until he makes still another gift.

The supplicant entering the temple is first stripped of all his or her clothes. In everyday life the Nacirema avoids exposure of his body and its natural functions. Bathing and excretory acts are performed only in the secrecy of the household shrine, where they are ritualized as part of the body-rites. Psycholog-

---

* Miracle worker—Ed.

ical shock results from the fact that body secrecy is suddenly lost upon entry into the *latipso.* A man, whose own wife has never seen him in an excretory act, suddenly finds himself naked and assisted by a vestal maiden while he performs his natural functions into a sacred vessel. This sort of ceremonial treatment is necessitated by the fact that the excreta are used by a diviner to ascertain the course and nature of the client's sickness. Female clients, on the other hand, find their naked bodies are subjected to the scrutiny, manipulation, and prodding of the medicine men.

Few supplicants in the temple are well enough to do anything but lie on their hard beds. The daily ceremonies, like the rites of the holy-mouth-men, involve discomfort and torture. With ritual precision, the vestals awaken their miserable charges each dawn and roll them about on their beds of pain while performing ablutions, in the formal movements of which the maidens are highly trained. At other times they insert magic wands in the supplicant's mouth or force him to eat substances which are supposed to be healing. From time to time the medicine men come to their clients and jab magically treated needles into their flesh. The fact that these temple ceremonies may not cure, and may even kill the neophyte, in no way decreases the people's faith in the medicine men.

There remains one other kind of practitioner, known as a "listener." This witch doctor has the power to exorcise the devils that lodge in the heads of people who have been bewitched. The Nacirema believe that parents bewitch their own children. Mothers are particularly suspected of putting a curse on children while teaching them the secret body rituals. The counter-magic of the witch doctor is unusual in its lack of ritual. The patient simply tells the "listener" all his troubles and fears, beginning with the earliest difficulties he can remember. The memory displayed by the Nacirema in these exorcism sessions is truly remarkable. It is not uncommon for the patient to bemoan the rejection he felt upon being weaned as a babe, and a few individuals even see their troubles going back to the traumatic effects of their own birth.

In conclusion, mention must be made of certain practices which have their base in native esthetics but which depend upon the pervasive aversion to the natural body and its functions. There are ritual fasts to make fat people thin and ceremonial feasts to make thin people fat. Still other rites are used to make women's breasts larger if they are small, and smaller if they are large. General dissatisfaction with breast shape is symbolized in the fact that the ideal form is virtually outside the range of human variation. A few women afflicted with almost inhuman hypermammary development are so idolized that they make a handsome living by simply going from village to village and permitting the natives to stare at them for a fee.

Reference has already been made to the fact that excretory functions are ritualized, routinized, and relegated to secrecy. Natural reproductive functions are similarly distorted. Intercourse is taboo as a topic and scheduled as an act. Efforts are made to avoid pregnancy by the use of magical materials or by limiting intercourse to certain phases of the moon. Conception is actually very infrequent. When pregnant, women dress so as to hide their condition. Parturition takes place in secret, without friends or relatives to assist, and the majority of women do not nurse their infants.

Our review of the ritual life of the Nacirema has certainly shown them to be a magic-ridden people. It is hard to understand how they have managed to exist so long under the burdens which they have imposed upon themselves. But even such exotic customs as these take on real meaning when they are viewed with the insight provided by Malinowski when he wrote[3]:

> Looking from far and above, from our high places of safety in the developed civilization, it is easy to see all the crudity and irrelevance of magic. But without its power and guidance early man could not have mastered his practical difficulties as he has done, nor could man have advanced to the higher stages of civilization.

[3] B. Malinowski, *Magic, Science, and Religion* (Glencoe, Ill.: The Free Press, 1948).

Review Questions

1. Identify the dominant belief of Nacirema culture.
2. List some of the masochistic practices for care of the body found in Nacirema society.
3. Identify some of the places within Nacirema society reserved for body ritual.
4. Describe the Nacirema's hierarchy of "magical practitioners" of body ritual.

Some of you probably found the Nacirema's way of life strange, irrational, perhaps even barbaric by American standards. Sometimes we are so immersed in our culture that it is difficult to recognize many aspects of our own way of life when described from another "outside" perspective. The fact is, however, that Horace Miner's article was written for an American audience. Nacirema, of course, is "American" spelled backwards.

The Functions of Culture

Culture's importance cannot be overemphasized. As we have noted, humans do not possess instincts. Thus we must rely on culture to ensure our safety, survival, and cooperation with others. In some cases, for example, a harsh, hazardous physical environment may bring about the destruction of many animal species. By means of culture, however, humans can adapt to the demands of most physical environments and in some cases even change the environment to suit their own interests and desires. Compared with many other animal species, we humans possess many physical limitations—our eyesight is nothing exceptional, we do not possess a great deal of physical strength, and we are obviously not built for flying. Yet through the technological knowledge stored in our culture, we have more than compensated for these limitations. Finally, humans live as social or group animals, and the satisfaction of many of

Culture aids people in survival

The human being is a social animal, not an isolated individual

our social and physical needs often requires collective or group action. Group life, however, necessitates that people develop ways to live in harmony and cooperation with others in the pursuit of personal and collective goals. Culture is also important in this regard because it serves to regulate our collective existence by providing us with relatively common systems of beliefs, values, goals, and behavioral standards by which we can judge and regulate the intentions and actions of ourselves as well as others.

The above examples have made clear the importance of culture for people's physical and social survival. One might now ask: "Of what practical value is the concept of culture?"

First, the concept can help each of us understand better our own as well as other people's behavior. The concept not only allows us to be more astute in our observations of behavior, but it also provides us with a framework of explanation for the behavior we observe. Second, the concept of culture is a tremendous aid for the prediction of human behavior. Thus, knowing the values, beliefs, and normative systems of a particular society is helpful in predicting how people within that society will react under a wide variety of circumstances. Finally, understanding how culture affects human behavior and personality permits us to take into account patterns of human thought and behavior similar to as well as different from our own. Thus the concept provides us with a key to greater self-awareness as well as heightened appreciation and respect for ways of living that are quite different from our own.

Summary

1. Culture consists of learned and shared patterns of acting, thinking, and feeling—that is, a total way of life. Culture may be both explicit and implicit.
2. Material culture consists of the material objects that people produce and use. In contrast, nonmaterial culture consists of norms, values, beliefs, and language. Only human societies possess culture, because only humans can develop and use highly complex systems of symbols. Symbols form the foundation of culture. Culture is learned, shared, and cumulative, as well as constantly changing.
3. Society refers to the actual group of people who share a common culture. In addition to culture, societies also possess a social structure—the key elements of which include role, status, groups, and institutions. Each of these elements brings order to social life and to our interactions with others.
4. Cultural patterns may vary considerably among and within societies, especially complex societies like our own. The concepts of subculture and counterculture help us account for the existence of cultural variation within specific societies. Ethnocentrism is the tendency to feel that one's own culture is superior, right, and natural compared with other cultures.

Cultural relativism refers to the notion that each culture should be evaluated from the standpoint of its own setting.

5. Culture serves many important functions. Culture can be seen as a form of survival mechanism for human beings. As such, culture helps people adapt to the demands of the surrounding physical environment, helps compensate for many human physical limitations, and provides ways and means to regulate human collective existence. The concept of culture is important because it allows for increased understanding, prediction, and appreciation of the varieties of human behavior found within societies both past and present.

STUDY GUIDE

Chapter Objectives

After studying this chapter, you should be able to:

1. Define the nature and significance of culture
2. Analyze and illustrate the importance of learning to social behavior
3. Identify and define the major components of culture
4. Contrast by means of examples the difference between ideal and statistical norms
5. Analyze the differences among folkways, mores, and laws
6. Describe how norms originate and develop
7. Contrast the differences between values and beliefs
8. Identify reasons why the concepts of symbols and language are important to an understanding of culture
9. Identify the major characteristics of culture
10. Describe and contrast the differences between culture and society
11. Identify and define the major elements of social structure
12. Give four original examples of elements that constitute cultural universals
13. Describe differences between countercultures and subcultures, with specific examples of each
14. List three examples of ethnocentrism in American society
15. List the major functions of culture

Key Terms

Achieved status (p. 58)
Aggregate (p. 58)
Ascribed status (p. 58)
Beliefs (p. 49)
Category (p. 59)
Counterculture (p. 61)
Cultural relativism (p. 62)
Cultural universals (p. 59)
Cultural variation (p. 61)
Culture (p. 39)
Culture (explicit) (p. 40)
Culture (implicit) (p. 40)
Ethnocentrism (p. 62)
Folkways (p. 46)
Instinct (p. 56)
Institution (p. 59)
Language (p. 50)
Laws (p. 48)
Material culture (p. 45)
Mores (p. 47)
Nonmaterial culture (p. 45)
Norm (ideal) (p. 46)
Norm (statistical) (p. 45)
Role (p. 56)
Role conflict (p. 58)
Role expectancy (p. 57)
Role performance (p. 57)
Role strain (p. 58)
Social group (p. 58)
Social structure (p. 56)
Society (p. 55)
Status (p. 56)
Subculture (p. 61)
Symbol (p. 50)
Values (p. 49)

Self-Test

Short Answer

(p. 39) 1. Culture is ______________________________
____
____

(p. 41) 2. The dimensions of implicit culture discussed by Hall are ____
____

(p. 45) 3. The five major components of culture are:
a. ______________ d. ______________
b. ______________ e. ______________
c. ______________

(p. 52) 4. The three reasons why the Kluckhohn reading is of special importance are:
a. ______________________________
b. ______________________________
c. ______________________________

(p. 55) 5. The six major types of societies are:
a. ______________ d. ______________
b. ______________ e. ______________
c. ______________ f. ______________

(p. 56) 6. The four key elements of social structure are:
a. ______________ c. ______________
b. ______________ d. ______________

(p. 58) 7. A social group is ______________________________
____
____

(p. 61) 8. Subcultures are ______________________________

(p. 61) 9. Countercultures are defined as ______________________________

(p. 63) 10. According to Horace Miner, a basic belief of the Nacirema is that ______________________________

Multiple Choice *(Answers are on page 75.)*

(p. 39) 1. Culture would include which of the following elements?
a. art
b. beliefs
c. knowledge
d. all the above

(p. 41) 2. Hall's article, "The Silent Language," illustrates the existence of various aspects of implicit culture with respect to:
a. time patterns
b. spatial distance
c. friendship patterns
d. all the above

(p. 45) 3. Material culture would not include:
a. houses
b. tools
c. values
d. automobiles

(p. 47) 4. Mores are:
a. unchanging
b. found in most, but not all, cultures
c. appropriate rules of conduct that are not regarded as vital to group welfare
d. rules of conduct whose fulfillment is regarded as vital to group welfare

(p. 55) 5. The earliest societies were:
a. pastoral societies
b. hunting and gathering societies
c. agricultural societies
d. horticultural societies

(p. 56) 6. Humans possess the following instincts:
a. self-preservation
b. species preservation
c. maternal
d. none of the above

(p. 59) 7. Which of the following is not a group?
a. a board of directors
b. the family
c. all football fans
d. a college fraternity

(p. 59) 8. Sociologists define "institutions" as:
a. patterns of norms centered on some major societal goal, value, or need
b. unchanging aspects of culture
c. patterns of behavior found within all societies, human and nonhuman
d. belief systems shared by all members of the society

(p. 62) 9. Ethnocentrism refers to:
a. inborn behavior patterns
b. the idea that cultures should be judged in relation to their own setting
c. the idea that other cultures are superior to one's own culture
d. the idea that one's own culture is superior to other cultures

(p. 62) 10. The term opposite to that of ethnocentrism is
a. cultural relativism
b. counterculture
c. subculture
d. cultural universal

True/False *(Answers are on page 75.)*

T F 11. According to Tylor, culture refers to all that which is not learned by humans. (p. 40)
T F 12. In general, there tends to be a resemblance between statistical norms and ideal, or cultural, norms. (p. 46)
T F 13. Norms always arise as a result of rational decision or planning. (p. 47)
T F 14. Sociologists term laws "formal norms." (p. 48)
T F 15. The terms "society" and "culture" are interchangeable and therefore synonomous. (p. 55)
T F 16. A collection of people waiting for a train is called a group. (p. 58)
T F 17. An aggregate can change into a group. (p. 58)
T F 18. The specific content of cultural universals varies from society to society. (p. 60)
T F 19. Many subcultural groups tend to be found within complex societies. (p. 61)
T F 20. According to cultural relativism, each culture should be evaluated from the standpoint of its own setting rather than that of other cultures. (p. 62)

Fill In *(Answers are on page 75.)*

(p. 45) 21. What people most typically do is termed a ______ norm.
(p. 51) 22. Culture is ______ in that it has a tendency toward growth, expansion, or addition.
(p. 53) 23. According to Kluckhohn, many aspects of culture are ______ as well as ______.
(p. 55) 24. ______ refers to a large number of people who form a relatively organized, self-sufficient, enduring body.
(p. 56) 25. A ______ is a pattern of expected behavior.
(p. 56) 26. A ______ is a position relative to other positions.
(p. 58) 27. An ______ status must be earned.
(p. 59) 28. The need for maintaining social control, and the problems related to the regulation of the power of some individuals and groups over others, necessitates the development of the ______ institution.

(p. 60) 29. A classic study of inhabitants on the island of New Guinea showing the influence of cultural variation upon personality and behavior was conducted by ______.

(p. 64) 30. Many of the Nacirema's body rituals take place in household shrines that we would commonly call ______.

Matching *(Answers are on page 75.)*

31. ______ Folkways
32. ______ George Murdock
33. ______ Statistical norm
34. ______ Language
35. ______ William Graham Sumner
36. ______ Symbol
37. ______ Implicit culture
38. ______ Diffusion
39. ______ Category
40. ______ Values

a. Aspects of culture that tend to be unrecognized by people but give direction to behavior
b. Something that stands for something else
c. Source of cultural change
d. Originator of mores and folkways concepts
e. Listed some 88 common cultural elements (cultural universals)
f. Their violation carries mild punishments
g. All blond-haired people
h. Most drivers stop their cars at red lights
i. The desirability of achievement, success, and democracy
j. A complex symbolic system

Essay Questions

1. What is culture? Why is culture indispensable to human social life?
2. What is the difference between implicit and explicit culture? What are some examples of each?
3. Identify the major components of culture. Give an example of each.
4. Why do symbols constitute the foundation of culture?
5. How does culture differ from society? What are the major types of societies that have developed during the course of human history?
6. What is meant by social structure? What are its key elements? Why is social structure important to human social life?
7. What is meant by the concepts of role and status? Give two or three examples of each.
8. What is a social group?
9. Contrast by way of examples the differences among a group, a category, and an aggregate of people.

10. Identify the two most important concepts that help sociologists understand and explain cultural variation.
11. Why is ethnocentrism important for groups? Are you ethnocentric? In what ways?
12. In your opinion, of what use or practical value is the concept of culture?

Interactive Exercises

1. Having been born and raised within one particular culture, most people have a tendency to assume that their own culture's most basic values, norms, and beliefs are pretty much the same everywhere else. For the purpose of learning more about the actual extent of cultural variation, interview or informally talk with three or four students from other cultural backgrounds, asking them to describe some of the most basic values, norms, and beliefs specific to their own culture's way of living. It would be a good idea to keep a written list or record of their responses, perhaps in table form, regarding the cultural diversity that you will discover.

2. During the course of our lifetimes, we occupy many statuses and play many roles. Select two or three statuses that you occupy. For each status (student, worker, husband, girlfriend, and so on):
   a. examine the roles you play
   b. describe some examples of role conflict and role strain
   c. explain how some of these conflicts and strains can be resolved

3. People are usually too ethnocentric to recognize many aspects of their own culture when presented from a more objective viewpoint of an outsider. Ask some of your friends, fellow students, or relatives to read Horace Miner's article, "Body Ritual Among the Nacirema," with the exception of the paragraph on page 67 where your authors reveal the true identity of these "strange" people. Ask your readers to tell what they think of the Nacirema, to comment on the Nacirema's rituals, and to identify who they think the Nacirema are. Most people's responses should help give you a clearer understanding of ethnocentrism and how common ethnocentrism really is.

4. A college campus typically is composed of students representing a broad range of subcultural groups from the standpoint of religion, ethnic background, geographical region, political affiliation, and so forth. In an effort to learn more about the diversity of subcultures on campus and in our society in general, ask students representing various groups to identify a few of the specific subcultural values, beliefs, language differences, and customs that provide them with a somewhat distinctive way of life and identity.

5. It is important to stress that an understanding of culture and other concepts presented in this chapter can be very useful to people working in many business, science, government, and professional fields. In what specific ways can an understanding of culture and related concepts such as subculture, cultural variation, ethnocentrism, norms, and so forth be

useful in your present and/or future occupation? It would be helpful if students would compose separate lists of uses for these concepts and get together afterward for discussion.

Answers

Answers to Self-Test

1.	d	11.	F	21.	statistical	31.	f
2.	d	12.	T	22.	cumulative	32.	e
3.	c	13.	F	23.	implicit, explicit	33.	h
4.	d	14.	T	24.	society	34.	j
5.	b	15.	F	25.	role	35.	d
6.	d	16.	F	26.	status	36.	b
7.	c	17.	T	27.	achieved	37.	a
8.	a	18.	T	28.	political	38.	c
9.	d	19.	T	29.	Margaret Mead	39.	g
10.	a	20.	T	30.	bathrooms	40.	i

Answers to Chapter Pretest

1. F
2. F
3. T
4. T
5. F
6. F
7. F
8. T

Chapter 3

Socialization

Chapter Pretest

Let's see how much you already know about topics in this chapter:

1. **Infants can survive physically with little or no support from adults. True/False**
2. **Personality and one's sense of self are very much determined by one's genetic background. True/False**
3. **Socialization is a process that basically occurs only during the developmental years. True/False**
4. **Men's and women's roles are essentially biologically determined. True/False**
5. **Males are more sensitive to light. True/False**
6. **Men are more creative than women in art and music. True/False**
7. **Television has little impact upon the way children learn about their gender/sex roles in society. True/False**
8. **One's peer group, especially during adolescence, is not as important as the family in the socialization process. True/False**

The Importance of Socialization

Humans, like other mammals, are helpless at birth. The newborn infant is highly dependent upon others for mere physical survival. If left alone, the infant would soon die of thirst, hunger, heat, or cold. To put it simply, the human infant lacks those instincts, or unlearned forms of behavior, that in other species serve to enable the survival of the young. Unlike newly hatched fish or ducks, which are capable of providing for their own needs in their new environments, the human infant is highly dependent upon others for satisfaction of basic human needs. Human young, born with an incomplete nervous system and having a long maturation period, will not survive unless adults feed them, protect them from the environment, and provide constant care.

Children are totally dependent beings

Human contact is necessary not only for the infant's physical well-being, but for healthy social and psychological development as well. As infants grow,

The personality of the child is formed by social contact

their inborn predispositions and social experiences combine to influence the development of their individual personalities. Without the social experiences provided by human contact within human groups, the individual's personality development is impaired to the extent that functioning within human society is not possible.

The necessity of human contact is shown in studies of social isolates. Children with little or no social experience cannot communicate verbally or by means of gestures with others. Secluded from human contact, many are unable to perform such basic functions as walking, feeding, or cleaning themselves. However, when these children are placed in environments where they are provided with human contact and training, they are able to achieve a more normal development and learn to behave in ways more appropriate for their age and status.

Cases of extreme isolation

Two such classic cases of extreme isolation have been documented by Kingsley Davis (Davis, 1940, 1947). In one case, a 6-year-old girl named Anna was discovered in a Pennsylvania farmhouse attic where she had been hidden by her family because she was illegitimate. Fed almost nothing but milk, Anna had received little physical care or emotional attention. When found by a social worker, she could not walk, talk, or take care of her own basic needs. She also showed no signs of intelligence, was withdrawn, apathetic, and totally indifferent to others. Having missed six years of socialization from her family, Anna never smiled or laughed.

After many months of care and training in a special school, Anna learned to wash herself, walk, talk, and play with other children. When she died at age 10, she was socially and mentally functioning at about a 2-year-old's level.

In a second case, a 6-year-old Ohio girl named Isabelle was discovered living with her deaf mother in a dark room. Unlike Anna, Isabelle had had the advantage of her mother's interaction. Because her mother was deaf, Isabelle did not learn conventional language nor develop speech. But she did communicate with gestures. When found, Isabelle was thought to be deaf because she did not seem to hear words. She also reacted wildly to the presence of others, especially men. After a slow start in an intensive training program, Isabelle began rapidly to learn to speak and to put sentences together. One and one-half years later, she had developed an extensive vocabulary and could ask complicated questions. Later she achieved an apparently normal level of development and attended school with other children. Isabelle's developmental success probably was greater than Anna's because during isolation, Isabelle had interacted with and received warmth and affection from her mother.

Human interaction is a prerequisite of a social self

The cases of Anna and Isabelle illustrate the effects of inadequate social interaction on human development. Without care, training, and love from adults, without the social experiences of group life, children are unable to develop a human personality. In other words, human interaction is a prerequisite for the development of a social self and personality in human beings. It is through socialization that people acquire their personalities and social capabilities.

In this chapter, we shall concentrate on the socialization process. **Socialization** is the way in which culture becomes a part of the individual. It is the process by which individuals internalize many of the socially approved values, attitudes, beliefs, and behavior patterns of their culture. Through socialization, the individual acquires a **social self**—an awareness of personal or social identity. Through socialization, the individual also acquires **personality**—an organization of attitudes, beliefs, habits, and behavior. As a newborn infant is socialized by others, he or she is transformed from a biological organism concerned with eating, sleeping, and crying into a social being with a complex network of attitudes, beliefs, values, and norms. The human personality and self, in other words, are developed as the individual grows, interacts, and learns from others.

Acquiring self through socialization

In addition to its importance in the development of a social self and personality, socialization is significant because it is the process by which human culture is transmitted from one generation to the next. It is the process by which the young are fitted into an organized society. It involves the learning of a variety of social roles, which are to be played on a social stage, and the learning of the skills that are necessary to ensure survival and the satisfaction of needs. An individual cannot adapt to the demands of the physical or social environment unless the knowledge, skills, roles, values, and attitudes that constitute the culture are passed along through such agents of socialization as the family, the school, and other social institutions.

But the human personality and self are products not just of the social environment. When explaining human personality and behavior, one must also take into account inherited traits. Human personality and self are products of a complex interaction between heredity and environment. Neither learning nor heredity alone determines human development.

In this chapter, we emphasize the emergence of the self and personality through the socialization process, the structure of the self, and an understanding of the importance of learning society's social roles. Before examining the actual process by which the social self and the human personality emerge through socialization, we must first examine the learning of social roles.

Learning Social Roles

As you read in the previous chapter, a **role** is a pattern of behavior that is expected of an individual who occupies a particular status in society. A **status** is a position relative to other positions. For example, when a person is occupying the status of mother in our society, she is expected to play the mother role with all its rights and obligations. Roles also help us structure our behavior in accordance with socially expected guidelines.

Status and role again defined

An essential part of the socialization process is the learning of social roles. Individuals learn social roles as they acquire the culture of their society through interaction with others. Roles are taught in direct, deliberately planned ways or in more subtle ways. A teacher may directly inform students of the behavior that is expected in the classroom, or these expectations may be transmitted less directly by means of a stare or tone of voice. In fact, gestures, expressions, and cues can at times convey much more than conscious, deliberate instructions.

Gender and Sex Role Socialization

Gender and sex defined

Gender refers to the differences that sex makes in a culture, and influences how we think of ourselves, how we interact with people, and how we fit into our society. It refers to human traits that are linked by culture to each sex. **Sex** refers to the division of human beings into biological categories of female and male. In America, females are socialized to be feminine and males are socialized to be masculine. In point of fact, American society demands the socialization of women and men into fixed social roles. This is done at great cost to the individual needs of both sexes. Although many traditional male-female role distinctions are not as absolute as they once were, sex roles still appear to be basic in American society—and in all other societies—because sex is such a basically differentiating characteristic.

The ascription and division of statuses according to sex appear in all cultures. All societies define certain behaviors and attitudes as appropriate to each sex; men and women are expected to think and act differently. Linton (1936) believes that most societies try to rationalize these prescriptions in terms of the physical differences between the sexes or their different roles in reproduction. Linton states, however, that a

> **comparative study of the statuses ascribed to women and men in different cultures seems to show that while such factors (physical and reproductive differences) may have served as a starting point for the development of a division, the actual ascriptions are almost entirely determined by culture (Linton, 1936).**

A self-fulfilling prophecy

The thoroughness of sex role socialization in a society is furthered by the fact that the social belief and expectation that boys and girls are very different tends to be a self-fulfilling prophecy. Wrongly believing a condition to be true can create the very condition that was not originally present. As long as the belief that boys and girls differ in abilities is perpetuated by the way our children are socialized, male and female children will grow up to be different in culturally expected ways.

Sex role socialization begins at birth

Sex role socialization begins at birth, when the infant is first dressed in blue or pink clothing. The socialization is very effective; the majority of children in our culture eventually grow and develop according to social expectations. Through parents, schools, friends, and the mass media, boys and girls are socialized into the "appropriate" sex role values, attitudes, beliefs, and behavior patterns.

By and large, parents base their child rearing on the idea that girls are naturally timid and dependent and boys are naturally brave, resourceful, and independent. Boys are therefore given their independence at an earlier age. They are permitted to play away from the house, walk to school by themselves, and pick their own activities earlier than their sisters. The boy's emancipation from the family is speeded up; the girl's is slowed down.

In many of our nation's nursery and elementary schools, teachers continue to maintain environments where children learn that girls are supposed to be

Young children learn sex role behavior early in life.

passive and submissive and boys are supposed to be aggressive and to solve problems. Teachers act and react differently to boys and girls. This then restricts the children's freedom to develop psychologically and intellectually. Many teachers of young children are less likely to react to a girl's appropriate or inappropriate behavior than to a boy's. Teachers reward girls for being cooperative, flexible, and willing to take direction, but not for being assertive. Boys are rewarded for being assertive, inquisitive, and independent. Teachers disapprove of boys when they are shy, passive, and fearful.

The importance of teachers

The importance of the peer group

A child's peer group is another important agent of socialization. The **peer group** consists of all the groups of children in which the child participates. It, as well as the family and the school, socializes boys and girls into sex appropriate attitudes and behavior; and it presents peer-approved concepts of femininity and masculinity.

The mass media

The mass media—television, movies, radio, newspapers, and books—is another important agent of sex role socialization. Television, for example, conveys to children the idea that boys are more capable than girls. School books, in spite of many changes, still reinforce the notion that males are more interesting and important than females and that such characteristics as passivity, dependence, fearfulness, and incompetence prevail among girls. Children's sections in libraries contain dozens of books that portray little girls as continually crying, baking, washing dishes, and cleaning house—and deriving much pleasure from these behaviors.

The transmission of a variety of cultural values, attitudes, and beliefs through the socialization process trains girls and boys in their respective sex roles. Because the learning of sex roles begins so early in life, the individual is very resistant to change. Early socialization of females is very important in the maintenance of sexual inequality and sexism in our society. All of us are socialized into sets of personality traits that are labeled either "feminine" or "masculine." Who we are, our emotions, and our reactions are very much defined by our sex roles.

GUNS AND DOLLS

Laura Shapiro

In the following reading, "Guns and Dolls," Laura Shapiro addresses the differences between boys and girls. The article contends that the main differences between boys and girls are caused by environmental factors that encourage gender stereotypes. Even though the author stresses that men have been very much responsible for many of the biases, one cannot deny that women have also contributed to the environment within which both boys and girls live.

Meet Rebecca. She's 3 years old, and both her parents have full-time jobs. Every evening Rebecca's father makes dinner for the family—Rebecca's mother rarely cooks. But when it's dinner time in Rebecca's dollhouse, she invariably chooses the Mommy doll and puts her to work in the kitchen.

Now meet George. He's 4, and his parents are still loyal to the values of the '60s. He was never taught the word "gun," much less given a war toy of any sort. On his own, however, he picked up the word "shoot." Thereafter he would grab a stick from the park, brandish it about and call it his "shooter."

Are boys and girls *born* different? Does every infant really come into the world programmed for caretaking or war making? Or does culture get to work on our children earlier and more inexorably than even parents are aware? Today these questions have new urgency for a generation that once made sexual equality its cause and now finds itself shopping for Barbie clothes and G.I. Joe paraphernalia. Parents may wonder if gender roles are immutable after all, give or take a Supreme Court justice. But burgeoning research indicates otherwise. No matter how stubborn the stereotype, individuals can challenge it; and they will if they're encouraged to try. Fathers and mothers should be relieved to hear that they do make a difference.

Biologists, psychologists, anthropologists and sociologists have been seeking the origin of gender differences for more than a century, debating the possibilities with increasing rancor ever since researchers were forced to question their favorite theory back in 1902. At that time many scientists believed that intelligence was a function of brain size and that males uniformly had larger brains than women—a fact that would nicely explain men's pre-eminence in art, science and letters. This treasured hypothesis began to disintegrate when a woman graduate student compared the cranial capacities of a group of male scientists with those of female college students; several women came out ahead of the men, and one of the smallest skulls belonged to a famous male anthropologist.

Gender research has become a lot more sophisticated in the ensuing decades, and a lot more controversial. The touchiest question concerns sex hormones, especially testosterone, which circulates in both sexes but is more abundant in males and is a likely, though unproven, source of aggression. To postulate a biological determinant for behavior in an ostensibly egalitarian society like ours requires a thick skin. "For a while I didn't dare talk about hormones, because women would get up and leave the room," says Beatrice Whiting, professor emeritus of education and anthropology at Harvard. "Now they seem to have more self-confidence. But they're skeptical. The data's not in yet."

Some feminist social scientists are staying away from gender research entirely—"They're saying the results will be used against women," says Jean Berko Gleason, a professor of psychology at Boston University who works on gender differences in the acquisition of language. Others see no reason to shy away from the subject. "Let's say it were proven that there were biological foundations for the division of labor," says Cynthia Fuchs Epstein, professor of sociology at the City University of New York, who doesn't, in fact, believe in such a likelihood. "It doesn't mean we couldn't do anything about it. People can make from scientific findings whatever they want." But a glance at the way society treats those gender differences already on record is not very encouraging. Boys learn to read more slowly than girls, for instance, and suffer more reading disabilities such as dyslexia, while girls fall behind in math when they get to high school. "Society can amplify differences like these or cover them up," says Gleason. "We rush in reading teachers to do remedial reading, and their classes are almost all boys. We don't talk about it, we just scurry around getting them to catch up to the girls. But where are the remedial math teachers? Girls are *supposed* to be less good at math, so that difference is incorporated into the way we live."

No matter where they stand on the question of biology versus culture, social scientists agree that the sexes are much more alike than they are different, and that variations within each sex are far greater than variations between the sexes. Even differences long taken for granted have begun to disappear. Janet Shibley Hyde, a professor of psychology at the University of Wisconsin, analyzed hundreds of studies on verbal and math ability and found boys and girls alike in verbal ability. In math, boys have a moderate edge; but only among highly precocious math students is the disparity large. Most important, Hyde found that verbal and math studies dating from the '60s and '70s showed greater differences than more recent research. "Parents may be making more efforts to tone down the stereotypes," she says. There's also what academics call "the file-drawer effect." "If you do a study that shows no differences, you assume it won't be published," says Claire Etaugh, professor of psychology at Bradley University in Peoria, Ill. "And until recently, you'd be right. So you just file it away."

The most famous gender differences in academics show up in the annual SAT results, which do continue to favor boys. Traditionally they have excelled on the math portion, and since 1972 they have slightly outperformed girls on the verbal side as well. Possible explanations range from bias to biology, but the socioeconomic profile of those taking the test may also play a role. "The SAT gets a lot of publicity every year, but nobody points out that there are more women taking it than men, and the women come from less advantaged backgrounds," says Hyde. "The men are a more highly selected sample: they're better off in terms of parental income, father's education and attendance at private school."

Another longstanding assumption does hold true: boys tend to be somewhat more active, according to a recent study, and the difference may even start prenatally. But the most vivid distinctions between the sexes don't surface until well into the preschool years. "If I showed you a hundred kids aged 2, and you couldn't tell the sex by the haircuts, you couldn't tell if they were boys or girls," says Harvard professor of psychology Jerome Kagan. Staff members at the Children's Museum in Boston say that the boys and girls racing through the exhibits are similarly active, similarly rambunctious and similarly interested in model cars and model kitchens, until they reach first grade or so. And at New York's Bank Street preschool, most of the 3-year-olds clustered around the cooking table to make banana bread one recent morning were boys. (It was a girl who gathered up three briefcases from the costume box and announced, "Let's go to work.")

By the age of 4 or 5, however, children start to embrace gender stereotypes with a determination that makes liberal-minded parents groan in despair. No matter how careful they may have been to correct the disparities in "Pat the Bunny" ("Paul isn't the *only* one who can play peekaboo, *Judy* can play peekaboo"), their children will delight in the traditional male/female distinctions preserved everywhere else: on television, in books, at day care and preschool, in the park and with friends. "One of the things that is very helpful to children is to learn what their identity is," says Kyle Pruett, a psychiatrist at the Yale Child Study Center. "There are rules about being feminine and there are rules about being masculine. You can argue until the cows come home about whether those are good or bad societal influences, but when you look at the children, they love to know the differences. It solidifies who they are."

WATER PISTOLS

So girls play dolls, boys play Ghostbusters. Girls take turns at hopscotch, boys compete at football. Girls help Mommy, boys aim their water pistols at guests and shout, "You're dead!" For boys, notes Pruett, guns are an inevitable part of this developmental process, at least in a television-driven culture like our own. "It can be a cardboard paper towelholder, it doesn't have to be a miniature Uzi, but it serves as the focus for fantasies about the way he is going to make himself powerful in the world," he says. "Little girls have their aggressive side, too, but by the time they're socialized it takes a different form. The kinds of things boys work out with guns, girls work out in terms of relationships—with put-downs and social cruelty." As if to underscore his point, a 4-year-old at a recent Manhattan party turned to her young hostess as a small stranger toddled up to them. "Tell her we don't want to play with her," she commanded. "Tell her we don't like her."

Once the girls know they're female and the boys know they're male, the powerful stereotypes that guided them don't just disappear. Whether they're bred into our chromosomes or ingested with our cornflakes, images of the aggressive male and the nurturant female are with us for the rest of our lives. "When we see a man with a child, we say, 'They're playing'," says Epstein. "We never say, 'He's nurturant.'."

The case for biologically based gender differences is building up slowly, amid a great deal of academic dispute. The theory is that male and female brains, as well as bodies, develop differently according to the amount of testosterone circulating around the time of birth. Much of the evidence rests on animal studies showing, for instance, that brain cells from newborn mice change their shape when treated with testosterone. The male sex hormone may also account for the different reactions of male and female rhesus monkeys, raised in isolation, when an infant monkey is placed in the cage. The males are more likely to strike at the infant, the females to nurture it. Scientists disagree—vehemently—on whether animal behavior has human parallels. The most convincing human evidence comes from anthropology, where cross-cultural studies consistently find that while societies differ in their predilection toward violence, the males in any given society will act more aggressively than the females. "But it's very important to emphasize that by aggression we mean only physical violence," says Melvin Konner, a physician and anthropologist at Emory University in Atlanta. "With competitive, verbal or any other form of aggression, the evidence for gender differences doesn't hold." Empirical findings (i.e., look around you) indicate that women in positions of corporate, academic or political power can learn to wield it as aggressively as any man.

Apart from the fact that women everywhere give birth and care for children, there is surprisingly little evidence to support the notion that their biology makes women kinder, gentler people or even equips them specifically for motherhood. Philosophers—and mothers, too—have taken for granted the existence of a maternal "instinct" that research in female hormones has not conclusively proven. At most there may be a temporary hormonal response associated with childbirth that prompts females to nurture their young, but that doesn't explain women's near monopoly on changing diapers. Nor is it likely that a similar hormonal surge is responsible for women's tendency to organize the family's social life or take up the traditionally underpaid "helping" professions—nursing, teaching, social work.

Studies have shown that female newborns cry more readily than males in response to the cry of another infant, and that small girls try more often than boys to comfort or help their mothers when they appear distressed. But in general the results of most research into such traits as empathy and altruism do not consistently favor one sex or the other. There is one major exception: females of all ages seem better able to "read" people, to discern their emotions, without the help of verbal cues. (Typically researchers will display a picture of someone expressing a strong reaction and ask test-takers to identify the emotion.) Perhaps this skill—which in evolutionary terms would have helped females survive and protect their young—is the sole biological foundation for our unshakable faith in female selflessness.

INFANT TIES

Those who explore the unconscious have had more success than other researchers in trying to account for male aggression and female nurturance, perhaps because their theories cannot be tested in a laboratory but are deemed "true" if they suit our intuitions. According to Nancy J. Chodorow, professor of sociology at Berkeley and the author of the influential book "The Reproduction of Mothering," the fact that both boys and girls are primarily raised by women has crucial effects on gender roles. Girls, who start out as infants identifying with their mothers and continue to do so, grow up defining themselves in relation to other people. Maintaining human connections remains vital to them. Boys eventually turn to their fathers for self-definition, but in order to do so must repress those powerful infant ties to mother and womanhood. Human connections thus become more problematic for them than for women. Chodorow's book, published in 1978, received national attention despite a dense, academic prose style; clearly, her perspective rang true to many.

Harvard's Kagan, who has been studying young children for 35 years, sees a different constellation of influences at work. He speculates that women's propensity for caretaking can be traced back to an early awareness of their role in nature. "Every girl knows, somewhere between the ages of 5 and 10, that she is different from boys and that she will have a child—something that everyone, including children, understands as quintessentially natural," he says. "If, in our society, nature stands for the giving of life, nurturance, help, affection, then the girl will conclude unconsciously that those are the qualities she should strive to attain. And the boy won't. And that's exactly what happens."

Kagan calls such gender differences "inevitable but not genetic," and he emphasizes—as does Chodorow—that they need have no implications for women's status, legally or occupationally. In the real world, of course, they have enormous implications. Even feminists who see gender differences as cultural artifacts agree that, if not inevitable, they're hard to shake. "The most emancipated families, who really feel they want to engage in gender-free behavior toward their kids, will still encourage boys to be boys and girls to be girls," says Epstein of CUNY. "Cultural constraints are acting on you all the time. If I go to buy a toy for a friend's little girl, I think to myself, why don't I buy her a truck? Well, I'm afraid the parents wouldn't like it. A makeup set would really go against my ideology, but maybe I'll buy some blocks. It's very hard. You have to be on the alert every second."

In fact, emancipated parents have to be on the alert from the moment their child is born. Beginning with the pink and blue name tags for newborns in the hospital nursery—I'M A GIRL/I'M A BOY—the gender-role juggernaut is overwhelming. Carol Z. Malatesta, associate professor of psychology at Long Island University in New York, notes that baby girls' eyebrows are higher above their eyes and that girls raise their eyebrows more than boys do, giving the girls "a more appealing, socially responsive look." Malatesta and her colleagues, who videotaped and coded the facial expressions on mothers and infants as they played, found that mothers displayed a wider range of emotional responses to girls than to boys. When the baby girls displayed anger, however, they met what seemed to be greater disapproval from their mothers than the boys did. These patterns, Malatesta suggests, may be among the reasons why baby girls grow up to smile more, to seem more sociable than males, and to possess the skill noted earlier in "reading" emotions.

The way parents discipline their toddlers also has an effect on social behavior later on. Judith G. Smetana, associate professor of education, psychology and pediatrics at the University of Rochester, found that mothers were more likely to deal differently with similar kinds of misbehavior depending on the sex of the child. If a little girl bit her friend and snatched a toy, for instance, the mother would explain why biting and snatching were unacceptable. If a boy did the same thing, his mother would be more likely to stop him, punish him and leave it at that. Misbehavior such as hitting in both sexes peaks around the age of 2; after that, little boys go on to misbehave more than girls.

Psychologists have known for years that boys are punished more than girls. Some have conjectured that boys simply drive their parents to distraction more quickly; but as Carolyn Zahn-Waxler, a psychologist at the National Institute of Mental Health, points out, the difference in parental treatment starts even before the difference in behavior shows up. "Girls receive very different messages than boys," she says. "Girls are encouraged to care about the problems of others, beginning very early. By elementary school, they're showing more caregiver behavior, and they have a wider social network."

Children also pick up gender cues in the process of learning to talk. We compared fathers and mothers reading books to children," says Boston University's Gleason. "Both parents used more inner-state words, words about feelings and emotions, to girls than to boys. And by the age of 2, girls are using more emotion words than boys." According to Gleason, fathers tend to use more directives ("Bring that over here") and more threatening language with their sons than their daughters, while mothers' directives take more polite forms ("Could you bring that to me, please?"). The 4-year-old boys and girls in one study were duly imitating their fathers and mothers in that very conversational pattern. Studies of slightly older children found that boys talking among themselves use more threatening, commanding, dominating language than girls, while girls emphasize agreement and mutuality. Polite or not, however, girls get interrupted by their parents more often than boys, according to language studies—and women get interrupted more often than men.

Despite the ever-increasing complexity and detail of research on gender differences, the not-so-secret agenda governing the discussion hasn't changed in a century: how to understand women. Whether the question is brain size, activity levels or modes of punishing children, the traditional implication is that the standard of life is male, while the entity that needs explaining is female. (Or as an editor put it, suggesting possible titles for this article: "Why Girls Are Different.") Perhaps the time has finally come for a new agenda. Women, after all, are not a big problem. Our society does not suffer from burdensome amounts of empathy and altruism, or a plague of nurturance. The problem is men—or more accurately, maleness.

"There's one set of sex differences that's ineluctable, and that's the death statistics," says Gleason. "Men are killing themselves doing all the things that our society wants them to do. At every age they're dying in accidents, they're being shot, they drive cars badly, they ride the tops of elevators, they're two-fisted hard drinkers. And violence against women in incredibly pervasive. Maybe it's men's raging hormones, but I think it's because they're trying to be a *man.* If I were the mother of a boy, I would be very concerned about societal pressures that idolize behaviors like that."

Studies of other cultures show that male behavior, while characteristically aggressive, need not be characteristically deadly. Harvard's Whiting, who has been analyzing children cross-culturally for half a century, found that in societies where boys as well as girls take care of younger siblings, boys as well as girls show nurturant, sociable behavior. "I'm convinced that infants elicit positive behavior from people," says Whiting. "If you have to take care of somebody who can't talk, you have to learn empathy. Of course there can be all kinds of experiences that make you extinguish that eliciting power, so that you no longer respond positively. But on the basis of our data, boys make very good baby tenders."

In our own society, evidence is emerging that fathers who actively participate in raising their children will be steering both sons and daughters toward healthier gender roles. For the last eight years Yale's Pruett has been conducting a ground-breaking longitudinal study of 16 families, representing a range of socioeconomic circumstances, in which the fathers take primary responsibility for child care while the mothers work full time. The children are now between 8 and 10 years old, and Pruett has watched subtle but important differences develop between them and their peers. "It's not that they have conflicts about their gender identity—the boys are masculine and the girls are feminine, they're all interested in the same things their friends are," he says. "But when they were 4 or 5, for instance, the stage at preschool when the boys leave the doll corner and the girls leave the block corner, these children didn't give up one or the other. The boys spent time playing with the girls in the doll corner, and the girls were building things with blocks, taking pride in their accomplishments."

LITTLE FOOTBALLS

Traditionally, Pruett notes, fathers have enforced sex stereotypes more strongly than mothers, engaging the boys in active play and complimenting the girls on their pretty dresses. "Not these fathers," says Pruett. "That went by the boards. They weren't interested in bringing home little footballs for their sons or little tutus for the girls. They dealt with the kids according to the individual. I even saw a couple of the mothers begin to take over those issues—one of them brought home a Dallas Cowboys sleeper for her 18-month-old. Her husband said, 'Honey, I thought we weren't going to do this, remember?" She said, 'Do what?' So that may be more a function of being in the second tier of parenting rather than the first."

As a result of this loosening up of stereotypes, the children are more relaxed about gender roles. "I saw the boys really enjoy their nurturing skills," says Pruett. "They knew what to do with a baby, they didn't see that as a girl's job, they saw it as a human job. I saw the girls have very active images of the outside world and what their mothers were doing in the workplace—things that become interesting to most girls when they're 8 or 10, but these girls were interested when they were 4 or 5."

Pruett doesn't argue that fathers are better at mothering than mothers, simply that two involved parents are better than "one and a lump." And it's hardly necessary for fathers to quit their jobs in order to become more involved. A 1965-66 study showed that working mothers spent 50 minutes a day engaged primarily with their children, while the fathers spent 12 minutes. Later studies have found fathers in two-career households spending only about a third as much time with their children as mothers. What's more, Pruett predicts that fathers would benefit as much as children from the increased responsibility. "The more involved father tends to feel differently about his own life," he says. "A lot of men, if they're on the fast track, know a lot about competitive relationships, but they don't know much about intimate relationships. Children are experts in intimacy. After a while the wives in my study would say, 'He's just a nicer guy'."

Pruett's study is too small in scope to support major claims for personality development; he emphasizes that his findings are chiefly theoretical until more research can be undertaken. But right now he's watching a motif that fascinates him. "Every single one of these kids is growing something," he says. "They don't just plant a watermelon seed and let it die. They're really propagating things, they're doing salad-bowl starts in the backyard, they're breeding guinea pigs. That says worlds about what they think matters. Generativity is valued a great deal, when both your mother and your father say it's OK." Scientists may never agree on what divides the sexes; but someday, perhaps, our children will learn to relish what unites them.

Review Questions

1. Are you in agreement with the statement that social scientists agree that the sexes are (a) much more alike than they are different, and that (b) variations within each sex are far greater than variations between the sexes?
2. Comment on the statement that "the case for biologically based gender differences is building up slowly . . ."
3. Discuss the findings of Pruett's longitudinal study of sixteen families.

The Development of Self and Personality Through Socialization

Society consists of the many roles and statuses that are surrounded and determined by the normative aspects of culture. The norms of the particular culture define the nature of these roles and statuses, but it is *people* who are guided by the norms and who play the roles.

To a large extent, individuals play the roles expected of them because of a system of general rewards and punishments that is built into social roles and statuses. Individuals who properly play the roles prescribed by society receive such rewards as recognition, economic security, and social privileges. Conversely, individuals who do not play their roles properly receive negative sanctions. Yet although systems of rewards and punishments do much to ensure

Culture develops needed personality attributes

that a society functions, they are inadequate in and of themselves to elicit desirable behavior. The primary way by which society brings forth "appropriate" behavior is by encouraging the development of personality types who want to play society's roles and play them properly. In other words, every culture attempts to develop those kinds of personalities among its members that are best suited to its needs—personalities that consist of the "proper" attitudes, beliefs, values, emotions, and repressions. Let us now examine more closely the development of personality and the social self as they emerge through socialization. We will begin our examination of the emerging self with an analysis of the "looking glass self," a concept developed by the sociologist Charles H. Cooley in his studies on childhood socialization.

Charles Horton Cooley: The "Looking Glass Self"

The looking glass self

Charles Horton Cooley (1864–1929), a founder of the symbolic interactionist school of sociology, believed that individuals and their personalities are the products of social interaction and social forces. According to Cooley (1922), our attitudes, behaviors, and self-concepts develop from our interactions with others; we develop a feeling about ourselves by imagining what others think about the way we look and act. To show how others influence the image we have of ourselves, Cooley developed the concept of the **looking glass self.** The "self," which is essentially an individual's awareness of his or her social or personal identity, was for Cooley a social development. Three major elements compose Cooley's concept of the looking glass self: our imagination of how others see us, our imagination of how others judge our appearance, and the feeling of self that results from our imagination of the thoughts others have of us.

We see ourselves as we think others see us

One important aspect of the genesis of the looking glass self is that how we see ourselves is influenced by how we think others perceive us. In everyday life, we continually interact with others and judge their behavior. We also try to imagine what judgments others have made of us. Just as we look into a mirror (or looking glass) to establish an idea of what we are like, we use other people's responses to our appearance and behavior to establish a self-concept. In this way, our perception of self is based upon our imagination of what we believe to be the judgments others have made of us. This is what Cooley means by the "looking glass self."

George Herbert Mead: The Social Self

Another important contributor to the concept of self was George H. Mead (1863–1931). Mead (1934) developed a detailed analysis of the self as it emerges through the process of socialization. He, like Cooley, believed that the self is not present at birth, but is a social product that develops through social experience and interaction with others. We will begin our analysis of Mead with an examination of the importance of social interaction, preverbal communication, and language.

For Mead, the development of language and self must be preceded by social interaction. Nonverbal communication (gestures) between individuals also must precede and is a prerequisite to communication through language. For example, children cannot understand the meaning of the word "angry" until they understand an angry gesture; the word has no meaning to them until they have interacted with an individual or group of individuals who communicates through gestures the meaning of "angry."

Interaction, preverbal communication, and language

Language makes possible the replacement of behavior and gestures with ideas. When a child learns what a word means, the child then has the *idea* of that word. By sharing language (ideas) with another person, the child can respond to what the other person says as well as to what the other person does. The other individual's language or ideas and not merely the other individual's gestures communicate. With language, the word "anger" can have meaning to the child even when the angry person is absent or not angry. Thus language makes possible the replacement of behavior with ideas because the child is able to share conceptions or ideas with others. As children acquire language, they acquire *mind,* or the ability to symbolize and to relate symbols to one another. Children thus become *self*-conscious by reflecting about themselves, their behavior, and the behavior of others.

Language permits communication of ideas

As children mature, they learn the names of objects in the environment. They learn, for instance, that a "dog" is a furry four-legged animal that wags its tail. While learning the names of objects, they also learn the attitude that "significant others"—people whose attitudes affect one's self-esteem, such as parents, siblings, and playmates—have toward the objects. A child learning about fire, for instance, learns to associate it with caution, danger, and fear. In the process of learning to take those attitudes expressed by others toward objects in the environment, children also learn to take an attitude toward themselves. Young children become self-conscious and begin to acquire a *social self* when they begin to use the attitudes of others to think about themselves and their behavior. Through interaction, children become aware of themselves as objects relative to others. It is through the attitudes and definitions of others that a self is formed. The specific mechanism that enables an individual to view him- or herself as an object is that of role taking.

Acquiring a social self

others' eyes. They gain a view of their own selves and behavior. Role taking also provides people with a basis for anticipating the responses of others and for understanding the meaning of their own actions.

George Mead: Self Development Stages. According to Mead, there are three stages in the development of the self: the preparatory, the play, and the game stage. During the preparatory stage, children imitate the behavior of others in the environment. During the play stage, they assume or play several roles, one after another. They learn the meanings associated with particular roles in relation to other roles and learn to "take the role of the other." During the game stage, children assume several roles simultaneously and finally are able to take the role or attitude of what Mead called the "generalized other," the attitude of the entire community or organized social group. In the game stage,

Preparatory, play, and game stages

the child begins to understand his or her position in terms of the organized community or society as a whole. The "generalized other," in addition to providing a guideline for behavior in a variety of social settings, provides the individual with a frame of reference for developing his or her self-concept.

Mead's "I" and "me"

George Mead: "I" and "Me." Mead's theory of the relationship between the individual self and society is based on his analysis of the self as divided into what he called the "I" and the "me." There is, for Mead, an unsocialized and impulsive, yet creative, aspect to the self, called the "I." The "I" represents the unorganized, undirected tendencies of the self. It creatively, as well as actively, influences cultures where individuals are much less controlled by the internalized attitudes of others. The socialized or conventional self—the "me"—consists of the internalized social attitudes of others. The "me" emerges when the child starts to act toward himself or herself from the perspective of the community. It represents the internalization of an organized set of attitudes, expectations, and meanings that are common to the group or community. An individual finds it very satisfying when the demands of the "me," or conventional self, enable the "I," or creative self, to find expression. The interaction between the two provides the basis for an understanding of the relationship between society and individual.

Erving Goffman: The Dramaturgical Approach

Social life as a stage

Cooley and Mead examine the development of our conceptions of self through social interaction with others. They also examine how we act toward others based upon the feedback about ourselves gained from others. In his classic work *The Presentation of Self In Everyday Life,* Erving Goffman (1959) stresses that it is only by influencing other's ideas of us that we can hope to predict or even control what happens to us. Goffman views social life as a stage where people interact with one another. All people are viewed both as members of the audience and as actors. The parts that are played are the roles people play in the course of their respective daily routines. Goffman, in other words, analyzes everyday interaction using the **dramaturgical approach.**

Every encounter is an "event"

In the dramaturgical approach, Goffman views performances staged in the theater as an analogy and tool for depicting and understanding social life. This perspective, or approach, examines those dimensions of the lives of everyday people that are similar to the behavior of stage performers. Every encounter between two or more people is an "event." As in any stage performance, this event calls for each "actor" to present one or more of his or her social roles to the other(s). In order to have impact on the common definition of the situation, people are motivated to present selected information about themselves to others. Goffman terms this process "impression management." For example, we all have a stake in presenting ourselves to others in ways that will lead others to view us favorably. Therefore, when one goes for a college admissions or job interview, one engages in "impression management" in choosing what clothing to wear, how to style the hair, and how to speak.

Goffman further illustrates his perspective by using the behavior of waiters as they move to and from their kitchens to the dining rooms. When their audience changes, from co-workers in the kitchen to customers in the dining areas, their behavior changes. From situation to situation, they alter their self-expression from one of servility to one of perhaps ridiculing the servility they perform front stage. Our daily routines involve many such shifts to and from the front and backstages as we shift from playing one role to playing another. At home, we are on the backstage. At our jobs, we are front stage and our demeanor shifts as we become more aware of our actions. As social actors, we present different aspects of ourselves to different people in various situations. From this perspective, a person does not have a "real self," but many "real selves."

We are all actors

For Goffman then, much social interaction is "on stage" and is socially structured with a script, a responding audience, and the "stage" itself. Within the confines of the social situation and the cultural norms and values the audience will tolerate, people seek to take dramatic license to confirm their self-conceptions. Options, however, can or may be limited. At times, individuals have little or no choice over scripts, stages, and audience. Goffman stresses that individuals attempt to sustain their self-conceptions, but must do so in a "theatrical world" not always of their own making.

Sigmund Freud: The Psychoanalytic Viewpoint

Another important contributor to the theories of the development of self and personality was Sigmund Freud (1856–1939), the founder of psychoanalysis. Freud (1949), like Cooley and Mead, believed that the self is largely the product of social experience. However, unlike Cooley and Mead, he portrayed the self as frustrated and repressive rather than creative and somewhat harmonious. He divided the self into three parts—the *id*, the *ego*, and the *superego*—and emphasized their conflict. Freud believed that at birth, we are dominated by the **id.** The id has no sense of time, order, or morality. It constantly seeks pleasure and consists of impulses and primitive drives. Throughout life, the id remains unconscious and highly charged with energy.

Id, ego, and superego

The **ego** is that segment of the self that is conscious and rational. It develops as the child begins to realize that he or she is separate from other individuals and objects in the environment. The ego acts as a mediator between the unconscious impulses of the id and the restrictions and morality of the superego.

The **superego**—or conscience—is the last part of the self to emerge. As children interact with others, they are subject to external parental authority. While growing, they begin to identify with the parental image (the son with the father, the daughter with the mother) and thus incorporate it into their own personalities.

Freud believed that the major work of society is carried on by the superego in that it molds the individual's personality according to society's dictates. It is the superego that permits the expression of those impulses that society considers appropriate and that represses those that are considered asocial. The superego is in continual conflict with the impulses of the id. Serving as a conscience, it enables us to observe our actions and to judge them.

Although there appears to be some similarity between Freud's superego and Mead's "me" in that both represent social consciousness, the resemblance is more apparent than real.

Freud: Psychosexual Stages. Freud viewed personality development as a progression in the satisfaction of basic human needs. He stressed the significance of basic biological drives, child-parent relationships, and unconscious thoughts and drives. His theory involves five steps: the oral, anal, phallic (Oedipal), latency, and genital stages. Freud called these stages **psychosexual stages** because he believed that they were sexual in nature and that they progressed from impulses of the id to a successively more mature self, or ego. Each psychosexual stage represents a need for a different kind of bodily gratification. Freud believed that a person must pass through each of these stages to develop into a whole, well-functioning individual.

1. *The oral stage.* During the first year of life, the infant seeks satisfaction through stimulation to the mouth, by sucking, biting, and chewing. If the need for oral gratification is not met, the individual, by adulthood, would have developed an oral fixation, characterized by a smoking habit, talkativeness, dependence, and a general need for oral gratification.

2. *The anal stage.* Between ages 1 and 3, the period of toilet training, the infant achieves satisfaction from the withholding or expelling of feces. Much of the child's activity is anal-centered during this period. Satisfaction of basic impulses from the id is achieved by the child when he or she has learned to control bowel movements with pride. Freud believed that if anal satisfaction is unfulfilled at this stage, the individual may develop an anal fixation, characterized by excessive neatness, excessive punctuality, stinginess, and possessiveness.

Psychosexual stages of development

3. *The phallic stage.* By age 4 or 5, the child seeks satisfaction through exploration of the genitals. According to Freud, a male child is attracted to, and seeks satisfaction from, his mother. A female child seeks affection from her father. In the case of the male, this is termed the "Oedipal" stage; in the case of the female, it is termed the "Electra" stage. The male child resolves his Oedipus complex by sublimating his sexual desire for his mother and identifying with his father; the female child identifies with her mother. By identifying with parental figures, children internalize the standards of their culture, and their superego emerges. Failure to resolve the Oedipus or Electra complex may lead to later personality problems, such as the inability to function in an adult sexual role.

4. *The latency stage.* Between age 5 and the beginning of adolescence, the attention of the individual is focused on the surrounding world, where the person is dominated by his or her intellectual as well as social de-

velopment. Sexual urgings become dormant, and no dynamic conflicts or basic personality changes occur.

5. *The genital stage.* Occurring at puberty, this stage marks the beginning of adult sexual desires and behavior. The genital stage is dominated by the emotional patterns that have been developed in infancy and childhood. From this point on, the individual must integrate the variety of demands within him- or herself. True maturity requires the taming of aggressive and sexual urges, allowing their release in only a socially acceptable manner. The self must be adequately mature before it can surrender itself to another and achieve true intimacy.

Most personality theorists reject the Freudian idea that the sexual urge is our only drive. Nevertheless, Freud's treatment of the socialization of early impulses has influenced many recent theorists.

For Freud, Mead, and Cooley, our social selves and personalities are the product of the socialization process. For Freud, the individual and society are in conflict with each other, and socialization is a conflict between the individual's needs and society's demands. Mead believed that the self is a social structure that develops and forms through social experience. The development of self, however, must be preceded by social interaction and language. With language, the child acquires mind and becomes "self"-conscious. Children acquire a social self when they begin to use the attitudes of others to think about themselves and their behavior and become aware of themselves as objects. For Mead, individuals can be objects of their own actions, and he regarded the ability of people to act toward themselves as the "central mechanism with which the human being fares and deals with the world." For Cooley, also, the self is not present at birth, but is a social development. The individual and the individual's society are one—and in Cooley's theories, the unity, interrelation, and indivisibility of individual and society are emphasized.

Personality is the product of social processes and experiences

Erik H. Erikson: Psychosocial Stages of Development

Erik H. Erikson's theory of the psychosocial stages of personality development is an alternative to and outgrowth of Freud's theory of psychosexual stages. Freud assumed that all important socialization takes place during the early years of life, but Erikson (1963) believes that personality development occurs throughout the lifespan of the individual, beginning at birth and continuing into old age.

Erikson's theory of eight **psychosocial stages** of ego development integrates the psychological, physical, and social aspects of the socialization process. As individuals progress through these stages, they establish a series of orientations to themselves as individuals and to their social environment. Erikson notes that just as various parts of the body develop in interrelated ways when we are in the mother's womb, so does the personality develop as the ego progresses through these eight interrelated stages. In each stage of psychosocial development, the growing individual deals with a crisis. The crisis is brought about by physical changes that take place within the individual as well as by changes that take place in the social environment to which the individual must respond and adapt. It should be noted that Erikson's stages, unlike Freud's, are not rigid. What this means is that if a person does not solve a particular psychosocial conflict when it initially arises, the conflict may be solved later on in life.

First stage: basic trust vs. mistrust

Erikson's first stage of development involves *basic trust versus mistrust.* The infant is highly dependent on the mother or mother-substitute for care. This adult is responsible for the nurturance of the infant, and social interactions such as talking, singing, playing, and cuddling between the adult and infant determine the infant's later attitudes. Infants learn to trust the environment if their affectional needs have been adequately met. But they learn to fear and mistrust both themselves and others if treatment has been inadequate or inconsistent.

Second stage: autonomy vs. shame and doubt

The second stage, *autonomy versus shame and doubt,* occurs at age 2 or 3 when children are learning to walk, talk, explore, and act independently. If during these important years, the parents encourage independence, indicate approval when the children act on their own initiative, and are consistent in their discipline, the children will feel sure of themselves and their behavior and thus be better able to cope with situations that require control, choice, and autonomy. But if the parents are overprotective, tend to discourage or disapprove of the children's own initiatives, and discipline inconsistently, the children will be doubtful, uncertain, and ashamed of their behavior and themselves.

Third stage: initiative vs. guilt

The third stage, *initiative versus guilt,* occurs between ages 4 and 5. During this stage, children broaden their social environment to include school friends, relatives, and neighbors. If parents, teachers, and other significant adults give children the freedom to experiment and explore, and if they take time to answer the children's questions, they encourage tendencies toward initiative. But if they restrict children's activity and cause the children to believe that their questions and activities are annoying and pointless, the children develop feelings of guilt about doing things on their own.

Fourth stage: industry vs. inferiority

The fourth stage, *industry versus inferiority,* occurs between ages 6 and 11. The behavior of children in this stage is dominated by intellectual curiosity and performance. If parents and teachers encourage the children to do and make things, allow them to complete tasks, and praise them for trying, industry results. But if parents and teachers are annoyed with children's attempts to do things, and if their efforts are treated as bothersome, the children develop a sense of inferiority and may not be inclined to complete tasks.

Fifth stage: identity vs. role confusion

The fifth stage, *identity versus role confusion,* occurs during adolescence. Adolescents face a crisis in finding their place in society. As they are achieving physical maturity and becoming independent from their parents, adolescents become concerned about their futures. Adolescents must integrate all their past experiences to find their own sense of identity. They ask themselves, Who am I? What do I believe in? What do I want from life? The sense of identity develops if the adolescent succeeds (as reflected by the reactions of others) in integrating his or her roles in various situations so as to experience a sense of continuity in his or her self-perceptions. If adolescents cannot integrate earlier experiences, they cannot form an ego identity. The inability to establish a sense of stability in various aspects of one's life—a clear sense of self—leads to role confusion. For Erikson, identity versus role confusion is the most significant conflict that a person must face.

Sixth stage: intimacy vs. isolation

The sixth stage, *intimacy versus isolation,* occurs in young adulthood. Once identity has been established, individuals are able to form close contacts and relationships with others and to share themselves with others. A person who has not established an identity may develop a feeling of isolation. Some young people cannot enter into an intimate relationship with another person because they have not adequately established their identity and cannot risk losing it through intimate giving.

Seventh stage: generativity vs. self-absorption

The seventh stage, *generativity versus self-absorption and stagnation,* occurs in middle age. Generativity is the concern for establishing and guiding the next generation. It involves the ability to look beyond oneself and to be concerned about others. Those individuals who are unable to become engaged in this process of guiding others become victims of self-absorption and stagnation.

Eighth stage: integrity vs. despair

The final stage, *integrity versus despair,* occurs in old age. Old age is a time of reflection. The aged see most of their life's work as complete and begin to recognize their mortality. Integrity is the acceptance of one's life cycle as "something that had to be and that, by necessity, permitted no substitutions" (Erikson, 1963). Remembering life with pleasure, the aged are able to establish a sense of unity in themselves and with others. Despair, according to Erikson, "expresses the feeling that the time is now short, too short for the attempt to start another life and to try out alternative roads to integrity" (1963). When an aged person sees his or her life as a series of failures and disappointments and realizes that a new life cannot be lived, the person feels despair.

Erikson and Freud

To summarize, Erikson, like Freud, assumed that there are specific stages of human development. The two differ, however, in their areas of concern. Freud was concerned with sexuality and emotion, and Erikson was concerned with the individual in his or her environment. Freud viewed the psychosexual stages of development as biologically determined, and Erikson viewed the psychosocial stages as determined by the individual's interactions with others. Although Erikson considers factors within the individual as important, he places a greater importance than Freud on social and cultural factors in socialization.

Jean Piaget: Stages of Cognitive Development

Another theory of specific stages of human development was formulated by an important Swiss psychologist, Jean Piaget. Unlike Erikson, who sees the stages as being determined by the individual's interaction with others, Piaget (1970) sees the stages as being biologically determined. Piaget's primary focus is on the development of cognitive activity—the use of thinking and language. From his scientific observations of children, Piaget developed a theory that cognitive development occurs in stages. **Cognition** develops as the child masters particular nonverbal, unlearned, and universal mental operations that are characteristic of each stage. To a great extent, intellectual development is an inwardly programmed process. It is important for us to examine Piaget's stages because a child's interpretation and understanding of the social environment—the type of socialization that can occur—are limited to the child's particular stage of cognitive maturation. Let us look at the stages of cognitive development as formulated by Piaget.

Sensorimotor stage

The first stage, called the *sensorimotor stage,* lasts from birth to about 18 months of age. At this age, infants are primarily concerned with their own senses and motor activities. Very little of their behavior involves language or thinking. For example, because they do not have the concept of self, infants do not see objects or other people as being different from themselves; they are unable to differentiate between themselves and their parents or between their feet and a toy in the crib. Once infants begin to distinguish their own bodies from others and the environment, they develop *object permanence,* the realization that people or objects do exist even when they cannot be seen or grasped. During this stage, the infant is involved in a process of adapting basic reflexes to interact with objects and others in the environment.

At about 18 months of age, infants move their arms to make a plastic toy move or to bring a rattle to their mouths. Being aware of various objects and being able to identify some of them, infants are able to adapt a learned solution to a new problem or use the same solution for different situations. A characteristic test for operations performed at this stage is to have an 18-month-old pick up small blocks and place them in a cup. This demonstrates the infant's ability to direct the manipulation of objects.

Preoperational stage

The next stage, the *preoperational stage,* lasts from about 18 months to 7 years of age. By this time, children have total object permanence and are learning to use language and to communicate with others. Children now also imitate the actions of others but view the world from their own perspective because they cannot take the role of others. In other words, children in this stage are highly egocentric and do not make a distinction between their own thoughts and feelings and those of others. With respect to language development, words have a meaning that is unique to each child, thus limiting the child's ability to consider others' points of view.

Piaget calls this stage *preoperational* because children in this stage are unable to understand basic concepts such as weight, number, quantity, and speed, and are therefore incapable of performing simple intellectual operations. Children at this stage invariably assume that the larger of two objects must be the heavier, and they cannot understand that one dime is worth more than nine pennies.

Concrete operational stage

During the third stage, the *concrete operational stage,* which lasts from about 7 to 11 years of age, the thinking of children remains tied to the concrete world. Because children of this age have difficulty thinking and communicating in abstract concepts, they think and talk in terms of concrete images, events, and real situations. In this stage, children can perform a variety of operations that are related to weight, number, quantity, and speed. An example of this is exemplified in the principle of conservation, by which children can recognize that it is possible to change the shape of liquids as well as solids without changing their volume or mass. Children at this stage have no ability to generalize beyond their own actual experience. However, they are no longer highly egocentric. At this stage, they begin to realize the existence of other points of view, and they become able to take the role of others and effectively participate in organized games and social relationships.

Formal operational stage

The fourth and final stage, the *formal operational stage,* begins with the onset of adolescence at about age 11. At this stage, children begin to think abstractly—in terms of general principles, abstract concepts, and theories—and also are able

Table 3.1. **Perspectives on Socialization**

STAGE	MEAD	FREUD	ERIKSON	PIAGET
1	Preverbal period (birth–1 year)	Oral stage (birth–1 year)	Basic trust vs. mistrust (birth–2 years)	Sensorimotor stage (birth–18 months)
2	Verbal period and preparatory stage (1–3 years)	Anal stage (1–3 years)	Autonomy vs. shame and doubt (2–3 years)	Preoperational stage (18 months–7 years)
3	Play stage (3–7 years)	Phallic stage (4–5 years)	Initiative vs. guilt (4–5 years)	Concete operational stage (7–11 years)
4	Organized game stage (7–8 years)	Latency period (5 years—adolescence)	Industry vs. inferiority (6–11 years)	Formal operational stage (begins at about 11 years)
5		Genital stage (11–14 years)	Identify vs. role confusion (12–18 years)	
6			Intimacy vs. isolation (young adulthood)	
7			Generativity vs. self-absorption (middle age)	
8			Integrity vs. despair (old age)	

to think scientifically. They can approach a problem with several solutions and weigh these solutions by discussion and reasoning. Children at the formal operational stage can also put the solutions to practical tests until they find the correct solution. Not all people reach this stage of cognitive development. The development of some people ends at the concrete operational stage, and they have trouble dealing with abstract concepts and thought.

For Piaget, this process of cognitive development is universal. In every culture, people progress through these four stages. This development is both psychologically and socially prescribed. For an individual to be conscious of his or her own mind, social experience is a necessity. Without the relevant social experiences, the mind cannot develop beyond a particular stage. Table 3.1 presents an outline of the stages of development described above.

Agents of Socialization

The self and personality are largely the product of social processes and individual experiences. As noted in Chapter 2, a particular society can foster the development of a particular type of personality. Certain social structures and certain types of personalities also seem to correspond. For example, there appear to be similarities in the personalities of urban dwellers that contrast sharply with the personalities of rural dwellers. Individuals raised under similar social conditions tend to develop somewhat similar personalities. However, each individual is brought up subject to many different influences and is affected by many different agents of socialization. The personality of each individual is the product of a particular community, family, religion, and peer group. We turn now to the more important agents of socialization and note their importance in the socialization process.

Family: The Most Important Agent of Socialization

The family is the most important unit of socialization

Children first acquire their attitudes, beliefs, and values from those individuals who first provide for their needs. The family is the most important agent of socialization in that it is usually the first group to provide meaning and support to the individual. The family is a socially sanctioned, relatively permanent grouping of people who are united by blood, marriage, or adoption, who generally live together and cooperate economically. Sisters, brothers, and parents establish roots for the emergence of an infant with distinctive physical composition and potential for growth into a person with the capacity to participate in society. Within the family, young children learn the socially approved means of satisfying their needs and begin to develop an understanding of the many basic roles of society. The family is the child's first reference group, and its attitudes, norms, values, and practices are the source of the child's first interpretation of the world. Within the family, the child first learns society's most basic skills, language, and the "proper" attitudes. A child's family experiences are the most important series of contacts he or she ever has.

As children, we rely heavily upon close contact and nurturing from family members, particularly our mothers or mother-substitutes. The extent to which parents provide basic needs, such as food, shelter, and love, to a great extent determines how a child's personality develops, both mentally and emotionally. The parent-child relationship in the years from birth to age 3 is critical in human development.

The necessity of close parental contact

Human stimulation is a basic requirement for the development of healthy people. Various child development studies and cases of isolated children like Anna and Isabelle stress the critical importance of human contact. Research indicates that children who have been deprived of this contact, who have not been cuddled and carried, tend to become listless and withdrawn. Monkeys raised in isolation develop humanlike schizophrenia, behaving violently toward each other and themselves. Without close nurturing from adults, children become withdrawn from their environment and unable to learn the basic behavior patterns and skills that are necessary to function in society. Clearly, the family is essential in that it provides the child with the intimate, personal relationships that are necessary for physical, social, and psychological development.

A family may provide a child with abusive relationships and violent role models. In many American families, violence is an everyday occurrence and a fundamental part of family life. When children are socialized in a family that uses violence to solve problems, they learn parental and marital roles centered on violence. When these children themselves are parents, they reenact the behavior learned in childhood, especially in stressful situations. Many husbands who abuse their wives and parents who abuse their children usually had as role models abusive parents. Whether children learn violent behavior depends on whether their role models are violent or not.

Learning violence in the family

But violence and aggression are learned not only through social interaction with family members. They also are learned in other socializing experiences, such as peer groups and school, and from violent films and television programs. Even though the family is the most important agent of socialization and is usually the first group to provide positive meaning and support to the individual, it may provide negative meaning and socialize children into an unsupportive social setting.

Peer Group

Another important agent of socialization is the child's peer group. It consists of the many groups, made up of children, in which the child participates. A peer group may consist of neighbors' children, children who make up a neighborhood gang, those in the school, those at the playground, and so forth. Each peer group has its own system of rules and regulations and its own language and activities, which are supported by a child-oriented system of values and beliefs. Separated from the adult world, the peer subculture is governed by children's rituals, rules, interests, and logic. Elkin and Handel (1972) believe that a major function of the peer group is "to keep children from being completely immersed in the process of socialization." As they say:

> **Although it is probably true that the peer group retards socialization in the sense of keeping the child from being totally concerned by the rules, values, and norms of the adult world, there are other ways in which it contributes to socialization.**
>
> **First, the peer group gives the child experience in egalitarian types of relationships. In this group he engages in a process of give and take not ordinarily possible in his relationships with adults. . . . In the peer group he gains his first substantial experience of equality. The child entering a peer group is interested in the companionship, attention, and good will of the group, . . . and the group is in a position to satisfy this interest. . . . As with other socializing agencies, the child comes to view himself as an object from the point of view of the group and in some measure to internalize its standards. While he is a member, these standards are reinforced by the feelings of solidarity and support that he obtains from others. . . . The peer group provides the setting within which the child develops close relationships of his own choosing. . . .**
>
> **Through this distinctive peer culture of childhood and through the new kinds of relationships that children establish in the peer group, they become more independent of parents and other adult authorities. In the peer group, the child develops new emotional ties and identifies with new models. He seeks the attention, acceptance, and good will of peer group members and views himself according to the group's standards. . . . When he (the child) reaches adulthood**

The peer group provides the first inkling of equality

> and sees his children and their peer culture, he becomes aware that his own childhood was passed in a particular time and under historically limited circumstances that make him a member of a particular generation (Elkin and Handel, 1972).*

Primary Group

Small primary groups strongly influence personality

The family and peer group, which are characterized by intimate face-to-face association and cooperation by their members and are considered what Cooley calls a **primary group,** will be discussed in detail in the following chapter. However, it should be noted that the primary group is one of the major agents of socialization. Primary groups, being small, intimate, and face-to-face, go far in determining the personality of the individual. They strongly influence personality and character development. They make us human in that we are able to sympathize, love, resent, and so on. These sentiments, impulses, and human feelings are developed within us as we are molded by primary groups. Cooley believes that human beings may be molded in a variety of ways by the social environment. Cooley (1956) describes the functions of primary groups as follows:

> By primary groups I mean those characterized by intimate face-to-face association and cooperation. They are primary in several senses but chiefly in that they are fundamental in forming the social nature and ideas of the individual. The result of intimate association, psychologically, is a certain fusion of individualities in a common whole, so that one's very self, for many purposes at least, is the common life and purpose of the group. Perhaps the simplest way of describing this wholeness is by saying that it is a "we"; it involves the sort of sympathy and mutual identification for which "we" is the natural expression. One lives in the feeling of the whole and finds the chief aims of his will in that feeling. . . .
>
> The most important spheres of this intimate association and cooperation—though by no means the only ones—are the family, the playgroup of children, and the neighborhood or community of elders. These are practically universal, belonging to all times and all stages of development; and are accordingly a chief basis of what is universal in human nature and human ideals (Cooley, 1956).

School and Mass Media

Schools weaken dependence on family

The school is another major agent of socialization. For most children in our culture, the school provides an environment that is somewhat less personal than the family and the neighborhood playgroup. As children are socialized by teachers, administrators, and classmates, their dependence upon the family is lessened, emotional ties to the family are to some extent loosened, and they begin to develop loyalties and ties to a wider social environment. The values and norms the community considers important are taught to children so that they may fit into the roles of the community.

---

* From *The Child and Society: The Process of Socialization,* by Frederick Elkin and Gerald Handel.

The mass media—newspapers, radio, movies, television, books—are also important in communicating to individuals a society's beliefs, values, mores, and traditions. Children and adults in our culture spend many hours each week listening to the radio and watching television. Old as well as young people are continually socialized by what is expressed in the mass media. The power of the mass media to socialize is enormous, and it is by no means always beneficial. Many social scientists believe that there is a link between violence in society and the violent programs viewed by people who watch television. A six-year study of over 1500 teenage boys by William Belson at the Survey Research Centre of the London School of Economics examined the relationship between television and delinquent behavior. He noted that the "evidence was strongly supportive of the hypothesis that long term exposure to violence increases the degree to which boys engage in violence of a serious kind" (Munson, 1978).

Socialization, then, occurs primarily within the family, in peer and primary groups, in schools, and through the mass media. However, socialization does not come to a halt the day a student graduates from school or leaves home. Many social groups and organizations—the social club, the military, the church, and work groups—socialize and resocialize individuals throughout their lives. For example, in the military, young adults unlearn many of the civilian attitudes and beliefs and are resocialized into those more appropriate to a military role.

Adult Roles: The Changing Roles of Women and Men

American society maintains many traditional views about women and men, and the roles they play in American culture. Many women's roles, however, are stereotypes that characterize women in negative terms. In this section, we will examine some of the traditional views of women in terms of their behavior, temperament, intelligence, and creativity.

Women's Behavior and Temperament

A major traditional view of women in American society is based on the idea that the female temperament—and therefore behavior—is innately different from that of the male. Experiments on animals suggest that sex hormones can account for variations in behavior and temperament. But are these experiments applicable to humans? Even though it is quite obvious that men and women differ physically, we are not certain how these biological differences affect behavior and temperament, if at all. Cultural dimensions must also be considered before determining which behaviors are acquired and which are biologically inherited.

Behaviors: acquired or inherited

All societies make cultural distinctions between sex and age categories. These cultural distinctions have various implications for identity, prestige, social and psychological characteristics, temperament, and behavior. Of course, the specific content of these distinctions varies from one society to another. For example, old women receive little respect and prestige in American society. In many other societies, however, they are highly valued and respected, because age may signify authority, knowledge, and wisdom.

Temperament, biology, and conditioning

The effect of biological differences upon the temperament and behavior of women must be questioned after examining the classic studies of the famous cultural anthropologist Margaret Mead (M. Mead, 1935). As briefly noted in Chapter 2, her analysis of three primitive societies of New Guinea introduced an awareness of the cultural variations that exist between the sexes. Responsive and cooperative, both sexes among the Arapesh people behave in ways that would be defined by the majority of Americans as feminine or maternal. The personalities and activities of males and females are very similar and center on family life and child rearing. Among the Mundugumors, females and males are aggressive and violent, and both sexes devalue family life and child rearing. Americans would label the behavior of female Mundugumors as masculine. Among the Tchambuli, sex roles, temperament, and behaviors are basically the opposite of ours. Tchambuli men are submissive, passive, and dependent. Tchambuli women are aggressive and dominant; they play what most Americans would consider "bread-winning" roles.

For Margaret Mead, the link between sex, behavior, and temperament must be critically questioned. She states that personality traits that we have termed masculine or feminine are "as lightly linked to sex as the clothing [and] the manners . . . that a society at a given period assigns to either sex. . . . the differences between individuals who are members of different cultures, like the differences between individuals within a culture, are almost entirely to be laid to differences in conditioning, especially during early childhood, and the form of conditioning is culturally determined" (M. Mead, 1935).

Women's Intelligence

Sex and intelligence

Another traditional view about women in American culture concerns the relationship between sex and intelligence. It was once believed that brain size indicated intelligence. Because it was also believed that female brains were smaller than male brains, women were considered to be less intelligent. There is still a tendency among many Americans to believe that women cannot deal with abstract thought or that they cannot think as clearly as men. Some people have even believed that women had a different type of intelligence, one linked to their emotions (S. Feldman, 1974).

Differences can be explained in terms of cultural conditioning and socialization

John Stuart Mill, many years ago, noted no differences in basic intelligence between the sexes; what differences did exist were due to environmental factors, such as education. The famous anthropologist Ashley Montagu noted that scientific research refutes the theory linking intelligence and brain size. In fact, in relation to the size of the body, the female brain is at least as large as, and, in general, larger than, that of the male (A. Montagu, 1968). In the 1990s, it is widely believed that the commonly observed differences in the intellectual capabilities of women and men are determined not by biology, but by social conditioning. There appears to be virtually no concrete evidence of a biological explanation for any differences in intellectual capabilities. Sociologists explain that the very attempt to uncover basic intelligence differences between men and women reflects cultural biases that make the research invalid. Today the great majority of scientists believe that our intellectual capabilities are distributed by nature without regard to sex. The differences that do exist can probably be explained in terms of socialization and cultural conditioning. According to Feldman (S. Feldman, 1974), women are taught to emphasize their emotions and are often discouraged from developing their minds. What, if any, intellectual differences exist between men and women are difficult to detect because of our prejudices and unwillingness to treat men and women as equals.

Women's Creativity

In American society, women have been traditionally viewed as less creative than men. For example, there have been few women artists, playwrights, inventors, and composers; however, women have also had much less opportunity to realize their creative potential. Women have faced discrimination whenever they have attempted to enter fields dominated by men. The traditional idea of women's "proper" role in society was that of wife and mother. Only the female can bear children and naturally feed them: The child-care role is primarily an extension of a female's biological function beyond pregnancy, and a woman was considered to be naturally fulfilled and content in these roles.

Women's "proper" role in society

The perspective that rejects the traditional view of woman as wife and mother rejects the idea that child rearing is a full-time job. Proponents of this perspective believe that restricting women to the roles of wife and mother tends to diminish human beings and harm our society. No longer considered justifiable, these traditional roles can create unhappy, dissatisfied women who resent their husbands and children and who, as a result, often hinder them from achieving their potential. Viewing women in the traditional way contributes to the growth of a dehumanized society, for which, "unless sexual roles disappear and sexual equality is realized, there is no hope for more humane relationships between people for a more humane world" (S. Feldman, 1974).

MEN VS. WOMEN

Merrill McLoughlin with Tracy L. Shryer, Erica E. Goode, and Kathleen McAuliffe

In the following reading, "Men vs. Women," the authors examine some of the research on how men and women do, in fact, differ. They view their physiology, their psychology, and the interplay between them. They also examine how society influences men's and women's physical and psychological differences. The reading stresses the point that women are at least as well equipped as men for life in today's world—and that in some ways they are, in fact, the stronger sex.

There was a time, not so long ago, when all the answers seemed clear. Everyone *knew* which was the weaker sex: Analyzed in terms of political power and bodily brawn, wasn't it obvious? Turn-of-the-century scientists produced learned tracts solemnly warning against an excess of exercise or education for girls: Too much activity—or thinking—would divert needed blood from their reproductive systems. Pseudoscientists meticulously measured human brains and found women's wanting (along with those of blacks and Irishmen). And when the new science of intelligence testing turned up repeated and systematic superiority among girls, researchers kept tinkering with the tests until they produced the "right" results.

We've come a long way since those bad old days. We have also moved beyond a backlash of 1970s feminist scholarship, which insisted with equal ideological fervor that apart from the obvious dimorphism of human beings, there were *no* real differences between the sexes—that seeming disparities in mental abilities, emotional makeup, attitudes and even many physical skills were merely the product of centuries of male domination and male-dominated interpretation.

Lately, in bits and pieces that are still the subject of lively debate, science has been learning more about the fine points of how men and women differ—more about their physiology, their psychology, the interplay between the two and the subtle ways society influences both. Among the questions these studies may help answer:

- Are more women doomed to die of heart attacks as they rise to positions of power in the work world? Or are they peculiarly protected from the stresses that beleaguer modern men?
- Is there something to be learned from female longevity that might help improve and prolong the lives of men?
- Are boys always going to be better at math than girls? And why is it that there have been relatively few women of acknowledged artistic genius?
- Are men, by nature, better suited than women to lead and manage other people? Or is it possible that society would be better off with women's ways in the board rooms, female fingers near the nuclear buttons?

The old answers, once so sure, just won't do any more. In *The Myth of Two Minds,* her provocative 1987 book analyzing findings on sex differences, Beryl Lieff Benderly put the argument succinctly: "Who had the stronger shoulders, who might unpredictably become pregnant, clearly meant a great deal when work and warfare ran on muscle power and conception lay as far beyond human control as the weather. But now, when every American fingertip commands horsepower by the thousands, when the neighborhood drugstore and clinic offer freedom from fertility, those two great physical differences weigh very lightly indeed in the social balance."

While scientists still have a long way to go, research in a dozen disciplines—from neurology, endocrinology and sports medicine to psychology, anthropology and sociology—is beginning to point in the same direction: There are differences between the sexes beyond their reproductive functions, the pitch of their voices, the curves of elbows and knees, the fecundity of hair follicles. Many of these differences suggest that women are at least as well equipped as men for life in the modern world—and that in some ways they are, in fact, the stronger sex.

BODY

The distinctions are more than just skin-deep

If God created man first, He or She apparently took advantage of hindsight when it came to women. Except for the moment of conception (when 13 to 15 males are conceived for every 10 females), the distaff side simply has a better chance at survival. Spontaneous abortions of boys outnumber those of girls. More males than females die during infancy, youth and adulthood. In every country in the world where childbirth itself no longer poses mortal danger to women, the life expectancy of females exceeds that of males. And in the United States, the gap is growing. A baby girl born today can look forward to nearly 79 years—seven more than a baby boy.

Why? Some of the answers seem to lie deep in the genes. Others doubtless float in the hormones that carry messages from organ to organ, even, some researchers believe, "imprinting" each human brain with patterns that can affect the ways it responds to injury and disease. The research suggests that females start out with some distinct biological advantages. Among them:

■ *The Genetic Code.* Genesis was wrong: Women came first—embryologically speaking, at least. Genetically, the female is the basic pattern of the species; maleness is superimposed on that. And this peculiarity of nature has the side effect of making males more vulnerable to a number of inherited disorders.

The reason lies in the way our genes determine who's a male and who's a female. A normal embryo inherits 23 chromosomes from the mother and 23 from the father. One of these chromosome pairs, the 23rd, determines what sex the baby will be. From the mother, the embryo always receives an X chromosome. From the father, it receives either an X, creating a female, or a Y, creating a male.

The Y chromosome carries little more than the genetic signal that, in the sixth week of development, first defeminizes the embryo, then starts the masculinization process. In a female, the X chromosome supplied by the father duplicates much of the genetic information supplied by the mother. Thus, if there are potentially deadly genetic anomalies on one of the female's X chromosomes, the other may cancel their effects. But the male embryo has no such protection: What's written on his sole X chromosome rules the day. Among the X-linked troubles he is more likely to inherit: Colorblindness, hemophilia, leukemia and dyslexia.

■ *The Estrogen Factor.* The main task of the female sex hormones, or estrogens, is to keep the female body prepared to carry and care for offspring. But as it turns out, what's good for female reproduction is also good for the arteries. One effect of estrogens, for example, is to keep blood vessels pliable in order to accommodate extra blood volume during pregnancy. That also reduces the risk of atherosclerosis. And because a developing fetus needs lots of carbohydrates but is unable to use much fat, the mother's body must be able to break down the extra fat left behind after the fetus's demands are met. Estrogen makes this happen by stimulating the liver to produce high-density lipoproteins (HDL), which allow the body to make more efficient use of fat—and help to keep arteries cleared of cholesterol.

The male hormone testosterone, by contrast, causes men to have a far higher concentration of *low*-density lipoprotein. "LDL forms and fixes in large amounts to the lining of the blood vessels," explains endocrinologist Estelle Ramey. "They become narrower and more fragile." That didn't matter 2 million years ago, when men were far more physically active: Exercise lowers the LDL count.

Long after menopause, when estrogen production drops dramatically, women maintain the cardiovascular advantages built up during their childbearing years. The Framingham study, a 24-year examination of the health of almost 6,000 men and women between the ages of 30 and 59, found approximately twice the incidence of coronary heart disease in men as in women, even in the upper age range. And in an analysis of the health patterns of 122,000 U.S. nurses, Graham Colditz, assistant professor at Harvard Medical School, has found that women who use estrogen supplements after menopause cut their risk of heart attacks by a third.

So—would men live longer if they took doses of estrogens? So far, the answer is a resounding no. In experiments where men received estrogen supplements, "they dropped like flies," says Elaine Eaker, an epidemiologist at the National Institutes of Health—from heart attacks. Eaker speculates that men don't have the proper receptor sites for estrogen.

But there may be hope for greater longevity in highly experimental work on macrophages, cells that form part of the immune system. Macrophages, Ramey explains, "gobble up" unmetabolized glucose that randomly affixes itself to DNA—and would eventually cause damage. As people age, the macrophage system slows, and the damage gets worse. "Macrophage activity in females, because of estrogen, is much higher," says Ramey. It's the hope of researchers that they can find a way to increase and prolong that activity in both sexes.

■ *The Stress Syndrome.* "Women," Ramey declares flatly, "respond better to stress." Although the evidence on how stress hurts the human body is still equivocal, there are two main hypotheses. The first is mechanical: Elevation of heart rate and blood pressure due to stress promotes damage to the inner lining of the artery wall, laying the groundwork for heart disease. The second is chemical: Increased production of stress hormones promotes arterial damage.

Ramey is one scientist who is convinced that stress does damage. And she puts the blame squarely on testosterone—and the fact that while the world has changed substantially, men's bodies have not. In the world where primitive man evolved, "testosterone is the perfect hormone." In effect, it orders neuroreceptors in the brain to drop everything else and react as quickly as possible to a release of stress hormones. This greater reaction to stress may be damaging in the long run, but the short-term benefits were much more important in an age when "the life expectancy was about 23," says Ramey. Today, when the average man is less likely to be threatened by a saber-toothed tiger than by a corporate barracuda, his stress reaction is exactly the same—and just as damaging to long-term health.

Perhaps because testosterone isn't egging them on, women seem to respond to stressful situations more slowly, and with less of a surge of blood pressure and stress hormones. Some researchers suspect that psychosocial factors also play a big role. Dr. Kathleen Light, a specialist in behavioral medicine at the University of North Carolina, thinks women may have a different perception of just what situations are threatening. Women show much less stress than men, for instance, when asked to solve an arithmetic problem. But Light's preliminary data in a study of public speaking show that women experience about the same surge in blood pressure as men. "Women may respond more selectively than men," she suggests. "We think this reflects learned experience."

But Karen Matthews is not so sure. Postmenopausal women, she observes, show higher heart rates and produce more stress hormones than women who are still menstruating. This leads her back to the reproductive hormones. One possible conclusion: Estrogens may be better adapted than testosterone for the flight-or-fight situations of modern life.

■ *The Brain Plan.* Men's and women's brains really are different. Over the last decade, researchers have discovered that in women, functions such as language ability appear to be more evenly divided between the left and right halves of the brain; in men, they are much more localized in the left half. After strokes or injuries to the left hemisphere, women are three times less likely than men to suffer language deficits.

What accounts for these differences in brain organization? One clue: The central section of the corpus callosum, a nerve cable connecting the left and right halves of the brain, seems to be thicker in women than in men, perhaps allowing more right-brain-left-brain communication.

Many researchers think that sex hormones produced early in fetal development—as well as after birth—literally "sex" the brain. In young animals, says neuroendocrinologist Bruce McEwen of New York's Rockefeller University, "the brain cells respond to testosterone by becoming larger and developing different kinds of connections."

These changes add up to big behavioral differences. Inject a female rat pup with testicular hormones, for instance, and it will mount other females just like a male. And it's not just a matter of mating. Male rat pups deprived of testicular hormones perform more poorly on maze tests than normal males; young females injected with testicular hormones do better. Many researchers are convinced that hormones have similar effects on human brains. Males produce testosterone from the third to the sixth month of gestation. Another burst is released just after birth, and then one final spurt at the onset of puberty—roughly coinciding with the time boys begin to surpass girls in math. What's more, males with an abnormality that makes their cells insensitive to testosterone's effects have cognitive profiles identical to girls: Their verbal IQ is higher than in normal males and their "performance" IQ (correlated with mechanical ability) is inferior to that of normal males.

Such findings are highly controversial. Feminist scholars, in particular, fear that they will give new life to the notion that biology is destiny—and that females just aren't the equal of men at certain tasks. But biodeterminists tend to ignore a critical difference between humans and other animals: The hugely complex human brain is not simply the sum of its synapses. There are other factors at play.

MIND

Different ways of thinking, from math to morals

Declare that women are more sensitive to the color red, and you get a few raised eyebrows. Argue that females are—by nature—not as good as males at mathematics, and you'll get outrage. Not surprisingly, intellectual ability is the arena in which sex differences are most hotly disputed. The stakes are high: Research findings can influence funding and policy decisions in everything from education to employment.

Most of the controversy over sex differences has focused on the longstanding male edge on tests of math aptitude. And it was further fueled in 1980, when Johns Hopkins University researchers Camilla Benbow and Julian Stanley reported on a study of 10,200 gifted junior-high students who took the Scholastic Aptitude Test between 1972 and 1979. Their conclusion: Boy were far more likely than girls to be mathematically talented. The researchers went on to speculate that there may be 13 male math geniuses for every female with such talent—and that the sex differences in math are the result of biological factors, perhaps exposure to the male sex hormone testosterone.

The Johns Hopkins studies were savagely attacked from the moment they were released. For one thing, the SAT's regularly have shown wider differences in male-female scores than other math tests. And the population that Benbow and Stanley studied is by definition exceptional: Its performance does not necessarily mean anything about boys and girls in general.

But many other tests have consistently turned up a male superiority in math as well. And the explanation of the results offered by critics—that boys traditionally have been *expected* to do better at math, so they got more encouragement from parents and teachers—doesn't quite wash, either. Girls get better average *grades* in math at every level.

Lately, some researchers have found hints that testosterone plays a role in enhancing math aptitude: Girls who have received abnormal doses of it in the womb seem to do better than average on the tests.

Whatever the explanation, however, the gap is narrowing. According to psychologist Janet Hyde of the University of Wisconsin, a preliminary analysis of dozens of studies of sex differences suggests that the gap has been cut in half in the past seven years.

But on another cognitive front—visual-spatial ability—males still hold an undisputed edge. The male advantage begins to show up around the age of 8, and it persists into old age.

Some simple explanations are tempting: A few researchers have even suggested that a single, sex-linked gene is responsible for the male edge in analyzing and mentally manipulating three-dimensional objects. Like hemophilia, such a sex-linked trait could be carried by both men and women but would become active in a woman only rarely—when both of her X chromosomes carried the gene. Men, who have only one X chromosome, would by contrast need only a single copy of the gene to acquire the ability.

But there are no rigorous data to support the idea: No gene has been identified, nor has anyone been able to trace the inheritance of an enhanced spatial ability from mothers to sons—as has been done extensively in the case of hemophilia. Moreover, most researchers are skeptical that such a complex ability as spatial reasoning could possibly rest in a single gene.

Many researchers are thus beginning to suspect that the male superiority is the product of a combination of factors—genetic, hormonal and cultural—with roots deep in humanity's hunting-gathering past.

Nature vs. nurture

Separating out those various factors is a daunting task. One promising approach is to study sex differences as they develop, rather than merely focusing on aptitude-test scores. Among the recent findings:

■ Females are more attracted to people and males to objects.

Numerous studies show that girl infants between 5 and 6 months detect differences in photographs of human faces, while males of the same age do not. In addition, writes psychologist Diane McGuinness, studies on very young infants show that "females smile and vocalize only to faces, whereas males are just as likely to smile and vocalize to inanimate objects and blinking lights." McGuinness concludes that there probably is a biological predisposition in females to caretaking behavior that is later reinforced by observing adults.

■ Boys have a shorter attention span.

McGuinness has conducted a series of studies of sex differences in preschool children. Her results are intriguing: In a given 20-minute interval, boys did an average of 4.5 different activities, while girls concentrated on 2.5. Girls started and finished more projects than the boys. Boys were more distractible, interrupting their play to look at something else almost four times as often as girls—and they also spent more time in general watching other kids. Why the difference? "Maybe boys are just more visually oriented, and they learn by watching," McGuinness suggests.

■ Boys and girls differ in their approach to moral problems.

The pioneering work in the study of moral development was carried out 20 years ago by Harvard psychologist Lawrence Kohlberg. But as one of his former students, Carol Gilligan, notes, Kohlberg's research seemed to assume that "females simply do not exist": He studied 44 boys over 20 years, but no girls.

Gilligan has retraced some of Kohlberg's steps, including girls this time, and found some highly interesting differences between the sexes. One example: Gilligan posed one of the "moral dilemmas" Kohlberg used in his studies to a boy and a girl, both 11 years old. The dilemma involves the case of "Heinz," who faces the choice of stealing a drug his wife needs to stay alive but which he cannot afford, or obeying the law and letting her die. Jake, the boy, thought Heinz should steal the drug because a life is worth more than property. Amy, the girl, argued that the problem was more complicated: "I think there might be other ways besides stealing it, like if he could borrow the money or make a loan or something. If he stole the drug, he might save his wife then, but if he did, he might have to go to jail, and then his wife might get sicker again and he couldn't get more of the drug."

In Gilligan's analysis, Amy sees the moral problem in terms of "a narrative of relationships that extend over time." Jake, by contrast, sees a "math problem."

Even a few years ago, research on sex differences still met enormous resistance from feminists and others who believed that merely posing the question was unscientific at best, politically inspired at worst. Diane McGuinness recalls the rejection she received once from a scientific journal when she submitted a paper on cognitive processes in males and females. One of the scientific referees who reviewed the paper wrote: "The author *purports* to find sex differences. Who cares!"

That attitude is beginning to change. "As time passes, people are less frightened and less rigid," says Grace Baruch, associate director of the Center for Research on Women at Wellesley College. Scholars are finding that a focus on "female" psychology and behavior can add much to a body of knowledge built almost exclusively upon studies of males. And new statistical techniques have also made the investigation of sex differences more reliable.

The new wave of results has even made converts of researchers who were skeptical that sex differences existed. "I've had to revise my view considerably," confesses Purdue University social psychologist Alice Eagly. Still, she adds, "the public needs to be warned that knowing a person's sex doesn't allow you to predict much of anything about him or her." The overlap between men and women is still much greater than their average differences. There are males who are every bit as adept at verbal skills as even the best females—and women who are better at math than most men.

ATTITUDE

In politics and management, the "gender gap" is real

There is one difference between the sexes on which virtually every expert and study agree: Men are more aggressive than women. It shows up in 2-year-olds. It continues through school days and persists into adulthood. It is even constant across cultures. And there is little doubt that it is rooted in biology—in the male sex hormone testosterone.

If there's a feminine trait that's the counterpart of male aggressiveness, it's what social scientists awkwardly refer to as "nurturance." Feminists have argued that the nurturing nature of women is not biological in origin, but rather has been drummed into women by a society that wanted to keep them in the home. But the signs that it is at least partly inborn are too numerous to ignore. Just as tiny infant girls respond more readily to human faces, female toddlers learn much faster than males how to pick up nonverbal cues from others. And grown women are far more adept than men at interpreting facial expressions: A recent study by University of Pennsylvania brain researcher Ruben Gur showed that they easily read emotions such as anger, sadness and fear. The only such emotion men could pick up was disgust.

What difference do such differences make in the real world? Among other things, women appear to be somewhat less competitive—or at least competitive in different ways—than men. At the Harvard Law School, for instance, female students enter with credentials just as outstanding as those of their male peers. But they don't qualify for the prestigious *Law Review* in proportionate numbers, a fact some school officials attribute to women's discomfort in the incredibly competitive atmosphere.

Students of management styles have found fewer differences than they expected between men and women who reach leadership positions, perhaps because many successful women deliberately imitate masculine ways. But an analysis by Purdue social psychologist Alice Eagly of 166 studies of leadership style did find one consistent difference: Men tend to be more "autocratic"—making decisions on their own—while women tend to consult colleagues and subordinates more often.

Studies of behavior in small groups turn up even more differences. Men will typically dominate the discussion, says University of Toronto psychologist Kenneth Dion, spending more time talking and less time listening.

Political fallout

The aggression-nurturance gulf even shows up in politics. The "gender gap" in polling is real and enduring: Men are far more prone to support a strong defense and tough law-and-order measures such as capital punishment, for instance, while women are more likely to approve of higher spending to solve domestic social problems such as poverty and inequality. Interestingly, there is virtually no gender gap on "women's issues," such as abortion and day care; in fact, men support them slightly *more* than women. . . .

Applied to the female of the species, the word "different" has, for centuries, been read to mean "inferior." At last, that is beginning to change. And in the end, of course, it's not a question of better or worse. The obvious point—long lost in a miasma of ideology—is that each sex brings strengths and weaknesses that may check and balance the other; each is half of the human whole.

Review Questions

1. List and briefly examine several ways women and men differ in terms of their physiology and psychology.
2. How does American society influence men's and women's psychological and physical differences?
3. Critique the following statement: "Women are, in fact, the stronger sex."

Adult Roles: The Aged

Socialization is a lifelong process. It does not end in our early years, but continues through the middle years and into our aged years. Even when we join the ranks of the aged, we are socialized into playing a particular role in society. Just as our society prescribes particular roles for women solely on the basis of sex, it also prescribes particular roles for people solely on the basis of age. The roles associated with becoming old are negatively valued in America, and there are very few, if any, rewards for obtaining the position of "old person." Let us briefly examine some of the role changes that accompany later life.

The "aged role" is negatively valued

One new role the aged experience is dependence. Many of America's aged fear becoming physically or financially dependent on others after having been self-sufficient for many years. In the family, advancing age can bring role reversals between parent and child. With the parent now having to depend on the child, anger, frustration, and guilt may develop on the part of both. Millions of aged Americans experience financial dependence. Income is a major problem of the elderly in America. It has been estimated that several million of the elderly population live below the poverty level. At retirement, income can drop 40 to 50 percent. As the elderly become even older, income continues to decline. Very few of the aged have significant income from earnings or assets such as rents, interest, and dividends from investments. In fact, Social Security is the major source of income for the great majority of aged Americans. The payments for those elderly who have no other source of income do little more than keep them at subsistence level.

The dependence role

One of the most important role changes accompanying old age is the shift from the role of worker to the role of retiree. Many aspects of a person's life are affected by mandatory retirement. For example, retirement brings a loss of the occupational identity that for many provided the social substance by which other identities were maintained and various social roles coordinated. Each year, thousands of Americans retire from the labor force. For many, the retirement period they have been anticipating becomes a serious problem.

The retiree role

Unlike many other societies, America does not provide institutionalized roles for the aged. For those who can afford it, there are leisure communities with golf courses and swimming pools. But joining a leisure retirement community in Florida or California is not an alternative for those who cannot afford the costs or for those who cannot or will not move from their old neighborhoods.

With advancing years, health becomes a very important influence on the individual's participation in the community, in family life, and on the job. When we are not in good health, it is difficult to perform our various social roles and have a satisfying life. As people grow older, health expenditures increase, and chronic conditions such as heart disease, high blood pressure, arthritis, and diabetes increasingly appear. Health then is a major determinant of the situation of the elderly and the role changes they experience.

In all these ways, the aged are socialized into playing a lesser role in society. American society socializes its members to devalue the capabilities of the aged, and this devaluation is reflected in the operation of our social institutions. An example of this is the restrictions placed on the opportunities available to the aged, such as the necessity to retire at a certain age or the inability to obtain a mortgage. Political, legal, and economic barriers have had the result of underutilizing the skills, talents, and capabilities of the aged in America.

THE CHANGING MEANINGS OF AGE

Bernice L. Neugarten and Dail A. Neugarten

In the following reading, "The Changing Meanings of Age," the authors report that age is a major dimension of social organization. It also plays an important part in how we all relate to one another, how we organize our lives, and how we view and interpret our lives.

Childhood, adulthood, and old age—the life periods—were much more closely associated with chronological age in past decades. Today the distinctions between life periods and the social roles that accompany them are becoming increasingly blurred. Today we are less sure where to place the punctuation marks in the "life line." We are not even sure what the punctuation marks should be. Is the line between adolescence and adulthood becoming increasingly obscured? Is the line between childhood and adulthood fading? Is there, as noted in the previous section of this chapter, an aged role in American society?

In our society, as in most others, age is a major dimension of social organization. Our school system, to name one example, is carefully arranged around the students' ages, and the behavior of all students is clearly differentiated from the behavior of adult teachers. Similarly, to a greater or lesser extent, families, corporations, even whole communities are organized by age.

Age also plays an important part in how people relate to one another across the whole range of everyday experience. When a young man sits down in an airplane and glances at the person in the next seat, the first thing to cross his mind is likely to be "That's an old man," or "That's a young man like me," and he automatically adjusts his behavior accordingly—his language, manners and conversation.

Age is also a major touchstone by which individuals organize and interpret their own lives. Both children and adults continually ask of themselves, "How well am I doing for my age?"

From all three perspectives, our changing society has brought with it changes in the social meanings of age: blurred boundaries between the periods of life, new definitions of age groups, new patterns in the timing of major life events and new inconsistencies in what is considered age-appropriate behavior.

In all societies, lifetime is divided into socially relevant periods, age distinctions become systematized and rights and respon-

---

sibilities are distributed according to social age. Even the simplest societies define at least three periods: childhood, adulthood and old age. In more complex societies, a greater number of life periods are differentiated, and transition points are differently timed in different areas of life. In modern America people are considered adults in the political system when they reach 18 and are given the right to vote; but they are not adults in the family system until they marry and take on the responsibilities of parenthood. Or people may be adult in the family system, but if they are still in school they are not yet adult in the economic system.

Historians have described how life periods became demarcated in Western societies over the past few centuries. Only with industrialization and the appearance of a middle class and formally organized schools did childhood become a clearly definable period of life. Adolescence took on its present meaning in the late 19th century and became widespread in the 20th, as the period of formal education lengthened and the transition to adulthood was increasingly delayed. A stage called youth took on its modern meaning only a few decades ago, as growing numbers of young people, after leaving high school and before marrying or making occupational choices, opted for a period of time to explore various life roles.

It was only a few decades ago, too, that middle age became identified, largely a reflection of the historically changing rhythm of events in the family cycle. With fewer children per family, and with births spaced closer together, middle age became defined as the time when children grow up and leave the parents' home. In turn, as the concept of retirement took hold, old age came to be regarded as the time following retirement from the labor force. It was usually perceived as a distinct period marked by the right to lead a life of leisure, declining physical and intellectual vigor, social disengagement and, often, isolation and desolation.

Life periods were closely associated with chronological age, even though age lines were seldom sharply drawn.

But the distinctions between life periods are blurring in today's society. The most dramatic evidence, perhaps, is the appearance of the so-called "young-old." It is a recent historical phenomenon that a very large group of retirees and their spouses are healthy and vigorous, relatively well-off financially, well-integrated into the lives of their families and communities and politically active. The term "young-old" is becoming part of everyday parlance, and it refers not to a particular age but to health and social characteristics. A young-old person may be 55 or 85. The term represents the social reality that the line between middle age and old age is no longer clear. What was once considered old age now characterizes only that minority of older persons who have been called the "old-old," that particularly vulnerable group who often are in need of special support and special care.

When, then, does old age now begin? The usual view has been that it starts at 65, when most people retire. But in the United States today the majority begin to take their Social Security retirement benefits at 62 or 63; and at ages 55 to 64 fewer than three of every four men are in the labor force. At the same time, with continued good health, some people are staying at work, full-time or part-time, into their 80s. So age 65 and retirement are no longer clear dividers between middle age and old age.

Alternatively, old age is often said to begin when poor health creates a major limitation on the activities of everyday life. Yet in a 1981 survey, half of all people 75 to 84 reported no such health limitations. Even in the very oldest group, those older than 85, more than a third reported no limitations due to health, and another one-third reported minor limitations; only one in three said they were unable to carry out any of their everyday activities. So health status is also becoming a poor age marker.

It is not only in the second half of life that the blurring of life periods can be seen. Adults of all ages are experiencing changes in the traditional rhythm and timing of events of the life cycle. More men and women marry, divorce, remarry and divorce again up through their 70s. More stay single. More women have their first child before they are 15, and more do so after 35. The result is that people are becoming grandparents for the first time at ages ranging from 35 to 75. More women, but also increasing numbers of men, raise children in two-parent, then one-parent, then two-parent households. More women, but also increasing numbers of men, exit and reenter school, enter and reenter the work force and undertake second and third careers up through their 70s. It therefore becomes difficult to distinguish the young, the middle-aged and the young-old—either in terms of major life events or the ages at which those events occur.

The line between adolescence and adulthood is also being obscured. The traditional transitions into adulthood and the social competencies they implied—full-time jobs, marriage and parenthood—are disappearing as markers of social age. For some men and women, the entry into a job or profession is being delayed to age 30 as education is prolonged. For others, entry into the work force occurs at 16 or 17. Not only are there more teenage pregnancies but also more teenage women who are mothering their children. All this adds up to what has been aptly called "the fluid life cycle."

This is not to deny that our society still recognizes differences between adolescents, young people and old people, and that people still relate to each other accordingly. Yet we are less sure today where to place the punctuation marks in the life line and just what those punctuation marks should be. All across adulthood, age has become a poor predictor of the timing of life events, just as it is a poor predictor of health, work status, family status, interests, preoccupations and needs. We have conflicting images rather than stereotypes of age: the 70-year-old in a wheelchair, but also the 70-year-old on the tennis court; the 18-year-old who is married and supporting a family, but also the 18-year-old college student who brings his laundry home to his mother each week.

Differences among individuals, multiple images of age groups and inconsistencies in age norms were surely present in earlier periods of our history, but as our society has become more complex, the irregularities have become increasingly a part of the social reality.

These trends are reflected in public perceptions, too. Although systematic research is sparse, there are a few studies that show a diminishing public consensus about the periods of life and their markers. In the early 1960s, for instance, a group of middle-class, middle-aged people were asked about the "best" ages for life transitions (such as completing school, marrying, retiring) and the ages they associated with such phrases as "a young man," "an old woman" and "when a man (or woman) has the most responsibilities." When the same questions were asked of a similar group of people two decades later, the earlier consensus on every item of the questionnaire had disappeared. In the first study, nearly 90 percent had replied that the best age for a woman to marry was between 19 and 24; in the repeat study, only 40 percent gave this answer. In the first study, "a young man" was said to be a man between 18 and 22; in the repeat study, "a young man" was anywhere from 18 to 40. These findings are based on a very small study, but they illustrate how public views are changing.

In some respects, the line between childhood and adulthood is also fading. It is a frequent comment that childhood as we once knew it is disappearing. Increasingly children and adults have the same preferences in styles of dress, forms of language, games and television shows. Children know more about once-taboo topics such as sex, drugs, alcoholism, suicide and nuclear war. There is more adult-like sexual behavior among children, and more adult-like crime. At the same time, with the pressures for achievement rising, we have witnessed the advent of "the hurried child" and the "harried child."

We have also become accustomed to the descriptions of today's adults as narcissistic, self-interested and self-indulgent. Yuppies are described in the mass media as the pacesetters. While they work hard to get ahead, they are portrayed as more materialistic even than the "me" generation that preceded them, interested primarily in making money and in buying the "right" cars, the "best" housing and the most expensive gourmet foods. Overall, today's adults have fewer lasting marriages, fewer lasting commitments to work or community roles, more uncontrolled expressions of emotion, a greater sense of powerlessness—in short, more childlike behavior.

This picture may be somewhat overdrawn. Both children and adults are continually exhorted to "act your age," and they seldom misunderstand what that means. Yet the expectations of appropriate behavior for children and adults are certainly less differentiated than they once were. We are less sure of what intellectual and social competencies to expect of children—not only because some children are teaching their teachers how to use computers, but also because so many children are streetwise by age 8 and so many others, in the wake of divorce, are the confidantes of their parents by age 12.

Some observers attribute the blurring of childhood and adulthood primarily to the effects of television, which illuminates the total culture and reveals the secrets that adults have traditionally withheld from children. But it is not only television. A report in *The New York Times* underlines the fact that children are being socialized in new ways today by parents, schools, churches and peer groups as well. The Girl Scouts of the U.S.A., according to the *Times* article, had decided finally to admit 5-year-olds. The national executive director was quoted as saying, "The decision to admit five-year-olds reflects the change in the American labor market. Women are working for part or all of their adult lives now. The possibilities are limitless but you need to prepare. So we think six is not too early to learn about career opportunities, and we also think that girls need to learn about making decisions. When you're five, you're not too young."

The blurring of traditional life periods does not mean that age norms are disappearing altogether. We still have our regulations about the ages at which children enter and exit from school, when people can marry without the consent of parents, when they are eligible for Social Security benefits. And less formal norms are still operating. Someone who moves to the Sun Belt to lead a life of leisure is socially approved if he is 70, but not if he is 30. An unmarried mother meets with greater disapproval if she is 15 than if she is 35. A couple in their 40s who decide to have another child are criticized for embarrassing their adolescent children. At the door of a discotheque a young person who cannot give proof of being "old enough" may be refused admission, while inside a gray-haired man who dances like those he calls youngsters meets the raised eyebrows and mocking remarks of the other dancers. As in these examples, expectations regarding age-appropriate behavior still form an elaborate and pervasive system of norms, expectations that are woven into the cultural fabric.

Both legal and cultural age norms are mirrored in the ways people behave and the ways they think about their own lives. Today, as in the past, most people by the time they are adolescents develop a set of anticipations of the normal, expectable life cycle: expectations of what the major life events and turning points will be and when they should occur. People internalize a social clock that tells them if they are on time or not.

Although the actual timing of life events for both women and men has always been influenced by various life contingencies, the norms and the actual occurrences have been closely connected. It may be less true today, but most people still try to marry or have a child or make a job change when they think they have reached the "right" age. They can still easily report whether they were early, late or on time with regard to one life event after another. "I married early," we hear, or "I had a late start because I served in Vietnam."

The life events that occur on time do not usually precipitate life crises, for they have been anticipated and rehearsed. The so-called "empty nest," for instance, is not itself stressful for most middle-aged parents. Instead, it is when children do not leave home at the appropriate time that stress occurs in both the parent and the child. For most older men, if it does not occur earlier than planned, retirement is taken in stride as a normal, expectable event. Widowhood is less often a crisis if it occurs at 65 rather than at 40.

It is the events that upset the expected sequence and rhythm of the life cycle that cause problems—as when the death of a parent comes during one's adolescence rather than in middle age; when marriage is delayed too long; when the birth of a child comes too early; when occupational achievement is slowed; when the empty nest, grandparenthood, retirement, major illness or widowhood occurs "out of sync." Traditional timetables still operate.

For the many reasons suggested earlier, the traditional time schedules do not in today's society produce the regularities anticipated by adolescents or young adults. For many men and women, to be out of sync may have lost some of its importance, but for others, the social clocks have not stopped ticking. The incongruities between the traditional norms and the fluid life cycle represent new freedoms for many people; for other people, new uncertainties and strains.

There is still another reality to be reckoned with. Some timetables are losing their significance, but others are more compelling than ever. A young man may feel he is a failure if he has not "made it" in his corporation by the time he is 35. A young woman may delay marriage because of her career, but then hurry to catch up with parenthood. The same young woman may feel under pressure to marry, bear a child and establish herself in a career all within a five-year period—even though she knows she is likely to live to 85.

Sometimes both traditional and nontraditional views are in conflict in the mind of the same person. The young woman who deliberately delays marriage may be the same woman who worries that she has lost status because she is not married by 25. A middle-aged man starts a second family, but feels compelled to justify himself by explaining that he expects to live to see his new children reach adulthood. Or an old person reports that because he did not expect to live so long, he is now unprepared to take on the "new ways" of some of his peers. Some people live in new ways, but continue to think in old ways.

Given such complications, shall we say

that individuals are paying less or more attention to age as a prod or a brake upon their behavior? That age consciousness is decreasing or increasing? Whether or not historical change is occurring, it is fair to say that one's own age remains crucial to every individual, all the way from early childhood through advanced old age. A person uses age as a guide in accommodating to others, in giving meaning to the life course, and in contemplating the time that is past and the time that remains.

In sum, there are multiple levels of social and psychological reality based on social age, and in modern societies, on calendar age as the marker of social age. The complexities are no fewer for the individual than for society at large.

Review Questions

1. Age is a major dimension of social organization. Specifically, give examples of how age plays an important role in (a) how you relate to others and (b) how you view as well as organize your life.
2. Are the distinctions between "life periods" and the social roles that accompany them becoming increasingly blurred in American society? Support your position with examples.
3. Is there no longer an "aged role" in American society? Explain your answer.

In sum, humans do not possess any automatic forms of behavior to ensure their safety, survival, or cooperation with others, so we are dependent upon culture to secure these ends. Socialization is important because it is the process by which the individual learns and internalizes culturally approved ways of thinking and behaving. It is the process by which the individual learns basic behaviors and skills and thus becomes a part of the community. It develops knowledge and motivation within the individual and serves the function of teaching the individual particular roles, thus forming an identity or self-image. In addition, socialization ensures the survival and perpetuation of the social system. It is the process by which human culture is transmitted from one generation to the next.

As a concept, socialization functions as a tool for analyzing and understanding human behavior. It helps us understand how a new member of society becomes a social being and how the human personality is formed. Finally, socialization helps us understand the social processes by which new members are integrated into a culture.

Summary

1. Socialization is the process by which individuals internalize many of the socially approved values, attitudes, beliefs, and behavior patterns of their culture.

2. Socialization is important because it is the process by which human culture is transmitted from one generation to the next. It is also the process by which the young become part of organized society. Through socialization, the individual acquires a social self and personality.

3. Human personality and self are products of a complex interaction between heredity and environment. Neither learning nor heredity alone determines human development.

4. Role is a pattern of behavior that is expected of an individual who occupies a particular status in society. Status is a position relative to other positions. Roles help people structure their behavior in accordance with socially expected guidelines.

5. An essential part of the socialization process is the learning of social roles, including sex/gender roles. Individuals learn social and gender roles as they acquire the culture of their society through interaction with others.

6. The ascription and division of statuses according to sex/gender appear in all societies. The family, peer group, schools, and mass media are all important agents of sex/gender role socialization. Many differences between boys and girls are caused by environmental factors that encourage gender stereotypes.

7. An important dimension of socialization is the development of a self-concept and personality. Several theorists explain how the social self and personality develop. Cooley developed the "looking glass self" theory. Mead developed a detailed analysis of the self as it emerges through socialization. Goffman developed the dramaturgical approach. Freud's theory of psychosexual stages presented a psychoanalytic viewpoint. Erikson stressed the interaction between the personality and the social environment. Piaget viewed the stages of cognitive development as a social as well as psychological unfolding.

8. The most important agents of socialization are the family, the peer and primary groups, the schools, and the mass media. Children acquire their initial attitudes, values, and beliefs from their families and peer group.

9. Socialization into the various roles we play is not only a childhood process but also one that continues throughout one's life. Throughout the life cycle, many of the traditional roles and views about men and women have been changing. Researchers also have been finding some significant differences between the sexes.

10. Even when we join the ranks of the aged, we are socialized into playing a particular role. However, whether we are young, old, or in-between, "acting your age" can mean many more things today than it did in previous decades.

STUDY GUIDE

Chapter Objectives

After studying this chapter, you should be able to:

1. Examine the nature and importance of socialization
2. Discuss the process of gender and sex role socialization
3. Discuss the differences between boys and girls in American society
4. Describe Cooley's and Mead's ideas on the origin and development of the self
5. Discuss Goffman's dramaturgical approach
6. List and examine Freud's psychosexual stages of personality development
7. List and examine Erikson's psychosocial stages of development
8. List and examine Piaget's stages of cognitive development
9. Understand the importance of the family, peer group, primary group, school, and mass media as agents of socialization
10. Examine the changing roles of women and men in American society
11. Examine several of the significant differences between men and women
12. Describe two role changes that occur during old age
13. Examine how "acting your age" can mean many more things today in American society than it did in past decades

Key Terms

Cognition (p. 97)
Dramaturgical approach (p. 92)
Ego (p. 93)
Gender (p. 80)
Gender roles (p. 80)
Id (p. 93)
Looking glass self (p. 90)
Peer group (p. 101)
Personality (p. 79)
Primary group (p. 102)

Psychosexual stages (p. 94)
Psychosocial stages (p. 95)
Role (p. 79)
Self (p. 79)
Sex (p. 80)
Sex role (p. 80)
Social self (p. 79)
Social role (p. 79)
Socialization (p. 78)
Status (p. 79)
Superego (p. 93)

Self-Test

Short Answer

(p. 78) 1. Socialization is ____________________

(p. 78) 2. Human contact is important and necessary for the child because ____________________

(p. 80) 3. Gender and sex role socialization deals with the ____________________

(p. 79) 4. The social self is ____________________

(p. 90) 5. Cooley's "looking glass self" is ____________________

(p. 91) 6. For G. H. Mead, the three stages in the development of the self are:
a. ____________________
b. ____________________
c. ____________________

(p. 92) 7. Goffman's approach to the self stresses the ____________________

(p. 94) 8. Freud's five psychosexual stages of personality development are:
a. ____________________
b. ____________________
c. ____________________
d. ____________________
e. ____________________

(p. 94) 9. E. H. Erikson's eight psychosocial stages of personality development are:
a. ____________________
b. ____________________
c. ____________________
d. ____________________
e. ____________________
f. ____________________
g. ____________________
h. ____________________

(p. 98) 10. J. Piaget's four stages of cognitive development are:
a. ______
b. ______
c. ______
d. ______

(p. 100) 11. Five important agents of socialization are:
a. ______
b. ______
c. ______
d. ______
e. ______

(p. 103) 12. Some of the traditional views of women stressed that they differ from men in terms of their:
a. ______
b. ______
c. ______
d. ______

(p. 105) 13. Men differ from women in:
a. ______
b. ______
c. ______

(p. 113) 14. Two roles changes that come with old age are:
a. ______
b. ______

(p. 114) 15. How has the meaning of "age" changed in American society?
a. ______
b. ______
c. ______

Multiple Choice *(Answers are on page 127.)*

(p. 78) 1. When infants are deprived of human social contact, they are unable to:
a. speak a language
b. learn their culture
c. organize their experiences
d. all the above

(p. 90) 2. Which of the following is *not* a component of the "looking glass self" concept?
a. what others think of us
b. how we think our behavior appears to others
c. how we think others judge our behavior
d. how we feel about others' judgments of us

(p. 79) 3. Socialization is:
a. lifelong and important in the development of the social self
b. not always smooth and uniform

c. intense in the early primary groups
d. all the above

(p. 94) 4. The earliest of the psychosexual stages of development cited by Freud is:
a. genital c. oral
b. anal d. phallic

(p. 92) 5. Concepts important in G. H. Mead's perspective on the development of the social self include:
a. superego and id
b. role taking and generalized other
c. ego and latency
d. none of the above

(p. 95) 6. Erik Erikson suggested that as people develop, they pass through eight stages, each one marked by:
a. guilt c. conflict
b. sexual problems d. harmony

(p. 80) 7. A child's sex role is reinforced by:
a. parents
b. parents and counselors
c. the books he or she reads
d. all the above

(p. 78) 8. Isabelle and Anna are examples of:
a. the conflict between the "me" and the "I"
b. the effects of social isolation
c. the "looking glass self"
d. none of the above

(p. 98) 9. Which one of Piaget's stages occurs between approximately 2 and 7 years of age?
a. concrete operations c. sensorimotor
b. formal operations d. preoperational

(p. 100) 10. Which of the following is *not* a major agency of socialization?
a. the family c. the school
b. the peer group d. none of the above

True/False *(Answers are on page 127.)*

T F 11. The human infant is born at a more developed stage than other animals. (p. 77)

T F 12. Socialization is the process by which the social self develops. (p. 78)

T F 13. Gender refers to the division of human beings into the biological categories of female and male. (p. 80)

T F 14. According to Freud, we see ourselves as we think others see us. (p. 90)

T F 15. Goffman views social life as a stage where people interact with one another. (p. 92)

T F 16. For Erikson, the oral stage is the first stage in psychosexual development. (p. 94)

T F 17. The family is no longer the most important agent of socialization. (p. 100)

T F 18. Women are, in point of fact, less creative than men. (p. 105)

T F 19. Women are more aggressive than men. (p. 103)

T F 20. In all societies, lifetime is divided into socially relevant periods, age distinctions become systematized, and rights and responsibilities are distributed according to social age. (p. 114)

Fill In *(Answers are on page 127.)*

(p. 79) 21. _______ is important because it is the process by which human culture is transmitted from one generation to the next.

(p. 79) 22. A _______ is a position relative to other positions.

(p. 79) 23. Through socialization, the individual acquires a _______ and personality.

(p. 80) 24. _______ refers to the differences that sex makes in a culture, and influences how we think of ourselves, how we interact with others, and how we fit into society.

(p. 91) 25. For Mead, _______ permits communication of ideas.

(p. 97) 26. _______ was concerned with emotion and sexuality.

(p. 100) 27. The _______ is the most important agency of socialization.

(p. 95) 28. For _______, in each psychosocial stage, the growing individual deals with a crisis.

(p. 79) 29. A _______ is a pattern of expected behavior.

(p. 90) 30. The _______ is an important concept of C. H. Cooley.

Matching *(Answers are on page 127.)*

31. _______ K. Davis
32. _______ Psychoanalytic theory
33. _______ Erikson's theory
34. _______ Socialization
35. _______ C. Cooley
36. _______ G. Mead
37. _______ E. Goffman
38. _______ Family
39. _______ J. Piaget
40. _______ M. Mead

a. The process of learning the beliefs, values, norms, and roles of one's society
b. "Looking glass self"
c. Superego
d. Isabelle and Anna
e. The "I" and the "me"
f. Trust or mistrust
g. The stage
h. Mundugumors
i. The most important agent of socialization
j. Concrete operational stage

Essay Questions

1. What does "socialization" mean? What is its importance to the individual and society?
2. Why are the concepts of role and status important in socialization?
3. How are boys socialized differently from girls?
4. In what ways are boys different from girls according to Laura Shapiro?
5. What are the basic ideas of Cooley, Mead, Goffman, Freud, Erikson, and Piaget on the development of the self and of personality?
6. What have traditionally been some of the major views of women and the roles they have played in American society?
7. According to McLoughlin et al., what are some of the significant differences between the sexes?
8. What are some of the role changes that accompany latter life?
9. According to the Neugartens, what are some of the changing meanings of age in American society?

Interactive Exercises

1. As we discussed in the text, in many of our country's schools, many teachers and parents have maintained environments where children have learned that girls are supposed to be passive and submissive and boys are supposed to be aggressive and to solve problems. Examine some of the experiences you (and your friends) have had in terms of how your teachers and parents raised you (and your friends).

2. The family, the peer group, and the media are important agents of socialization. How much have you and your friends been influenced by your families, your peer groups, radio, television, and films? Have your families or peer groups had a negative or positive influence upon you and your behavior?

3. According to various theorists, our social selves and personalities develop as we progress through a series of stages. Using the theories and models examined in the chapter:
   a. examine your own development in terms of the various stages (and also your situations and relationships with significant others)
   b. explain whether any particular stages have had an especially important meaning to you
   c. explain how the way you have been socialized affects (or might possibly affect) your current (or future) performance in various roles you (will) play (for example, son, daughter, mother, father, employer, employee, and so on).

Answers

Answers to Self-Test

1.	d	11.	F	21.	socialization	31.	d
2.	a	12.	T	22.	status	32.	c
3.	d	13.	F	23.	social self	33.	f
4.	c	14.	F	24.	gender	34.	a
5.	b	15.	T	25.	language	35.	b
6.	c	16.	F	26.	Freud	36.	e
7.	d	17.	F	27.	family	37.	g
8.	b	18.	F	28.	Erikson	38.	i
9.	d	19.	F	29.	role	39.	j
10.	d	20.	T	30.	"looking glass self"	40.	h

Answers to Chapter Pretest

1. F
2. F
3. F
4. F
5. T
6. F
7. F
8. F

Chapter 4

Social Groups, Formal Organization, Bureaucracy, and Work

Chapter Pretest

Let's see how much you already know about topics in this chapter:

1. **Several people waiting for a bus on a street corner could be called a group of people. True/False**
2. **Conflict occurs when individuals or groups struggle to reach the same goals. True/False**
3. **In America, a police officer-citizen relationship can be considered a primary relationship. True/False**
4. **Large bureaucratic formal organizations are not considered to be new twentieth-century phenomena. True/False**
5. **In bureaucracies, employees tend to rise to their level of incompetence. True/False**
6. **Since the mid-1980s, hundreds of thousands of jobs have been cut from the managerial and professional ranks of America's corporations. True/False**
7. **During the past decade, a significant number of women have been dropping out of the corporate world. True/False**
8. **The feud of the 1990s will be "mothers against mothers." True/False**

In this chapter, we examine the actual forms of social relationships. We look at how people within society are organized into many different types of relationships, groups, and organizations. Interpersonal relationships and social groupings must be examined for a better understanding of people as social animals.

The Nature and Types of Social Groups

The understanding of social groups is of primary importance to the understanding of human behavior. People do not live as isolated creatures; they live in groups, and through their activities within groups, social life is sustained. We are all born into and spend our entire lives within groups. We can be described

Humans are social animals. They rely on close contact and nurturing

therefore as social animals who depend on others for the satisfaction of our needs. You will recall from our discussion of socialization that humans rely on close contact and nurturing from others within groups for their basic physical and psychological survival. Groups give meaning and support to the individual from childhood into adulthood.

Human traditions, customs, standards of behavior, and values are found within social groups, are the products of human interaction within groups, and also form the basis of organized social life. Groups are organized to reflect society's values, customs, and standards of behavior, which are then reflected in the behavior of individuals. Groups are of many sizes and are organized for a variety of human needs. Before we begin to examine social groups in depth, we should first determine how the sociologist defines "social group."

Social groups defined

When sociologists use the concept of **social group,** we mean a unit consisting of two or more people who come into meaningful contact for a purpose. It is also defined as people connected in a network of social relationships. As examined in Chapter 2, a social group is different from an **aggregate**—a number of persons in the same place at the same time with no sense of belonging and no patterned social interaction. A group is also different from a **category**—a collection of people with similar characteristics but no common identity, no understanding of membership, and no involvement in patterned interaction.

Aggregate

Category

Human Interaction

Cooperation

There are three important processes of human interaction: cooperation, competition, and conflict. **Cooperation** is the interaction among individuals or groups of people to achieve shared goals or promote common interests. A Pennsylvania Amish farm family, for example, would have trouble building a barn by itself. However, when several families join together in a cooperative effort, they can achieve an otherwise unobtainable goal. In many respects, communities and societies are based on cooperation. People cooperate with each other to provide mutual protection from external threats and to meet group as well as individual needs efficiently.

Competition

Some social scientists believe that competition rather than cooperation is the most basic social process. **Competition** occurs when individuals or groups struggle to reach the same goals. In general, if a particular value or goal is plentiful in a society, cooperation between groups is likely to occur. But if the value or goal is scarce, competitive behavior is likely to predominate. Whatever the goal may be—money, power, or prestige, for example—each group's aim is simply to obtain the goal, not to harm or destroy its competitors. Like cooperation, competition occurs in all societies. Unlike cooperation, in competition, the primary concern of the individuals or groups is directed toward goal achievement, not toward each other. The competing groups or individuals seek the goal separately and in rivalry with one another.

Conflict

Unlike competition, which is a kind of cooperative conflict, **conflict** is a social process whereby two or more groups consciously seek either to block one another in achieving a desired goal or to defeat, harm, or annihilate one another. In "pure" conflict, the goal is to immobilize, destroy, or harm an opponent.

Groups then may be cooperative, competitive, or in conflict with one another. But why and how do groups form in the first place? In the following section, we examine the formation of social groups.

The Formation of Groups

All groups begin at particular points in time and are formed under particular sets of social conditions. One may ask: Why do social groups form? How does a particular collection of people come to constitute a group? What are the different conditions under which groups form?

At first, it may appear that the reasons for the formation of a family, a committee, an ethnic group, and a business association have little in common. When one or more people decide that a collection of individuals can accomplish some purpose not otherwise possible, they have established the basic condition for the deliberate creation of a group. We can identify three general sets of circumstances under which groups come into existence. According to Cartwright and Zander (1968), a group may be created deliberately by one or more people to accomplish a particular objective. A group may be formed spontaneously by people who participate in it. Also, a collection of individuals may become a group because they are treated in a homogeneous way by others.

Why groups form

Groups form to meet different kinds of purposes. Thus a work group might form to perform a particular task efficiently through the pooling and coordination of the behavior and resources of a collection of individuals. For example, a small business to manufacture a new product or an expedition to examine hunger in a distant country might form. In contrast, problem-solving groups form to solve particular problems. Task forces, commissions, research teams, and committees work to solve problems. They may use social action, legislation, and mediation to accomplish their purpose.

Groups may be formed spontaneously

In addition to being created deliberately, a group may be formed spontaneously by the people who come to participate in it. Social groups, in other words, can also develop because people expect to derive satisfaction and have personal needs met by associating with others in groups. Social clubs and friendship cliques, informal clusterings in formal organizations, and juvenile gangs usually have this type of spontaneous origin.

Finally, some groups in our society form because certain people are treated alike by others. Under certain conditions, personal traits such as age, sex, race, skin color, income, place of birth, and language become socially relevant, and individuals possessing them are clustered into perceptual categories such as teenagers, older people, the poor, migrants, and so forth. Because of this external designation, groups form. The experience of a common fate may lead to the emergence of such group properties as cohesiveness, norms, standards, and goals.

Thus many groups form because of a desire to achieve an objective or to meet the needs of members, and because certain people are treated alike by others.

Group Boundaries

Human interaction by definition is a group concept in that it necessarily involves two or more people relating to and influencing one another. As people influence and relate to one another within groups, there develops a consciousness of belonging together—a feeling of common membership. People in groups create boundaries to maintain a distinction between the "we" of the group and the "they" outside the group. To describe the "we" and "they" feelings that develop through group membership, William Sumner, an early American sociologist, developed the concepts of in-group and out-group.

In-groups

In-groups are those to which a person belongs. They consist of people in whose presence the person feels comfortable and with whom he or she shares common experiences. Examples are friendship groups, families, and religious groups.

Group boundaries may be either formal and clearly defined or informal and unclear. When the boundaries are formal, group membership is determined by predetermined criteria, such as being accepted into a college fraternity or a particular religion. Formal group boundaries may be maintained and group members identified by such things as a particular mode of dress, an unusual handshake, or a union card. When boundaries are informal, group membership is determined by nonspecific criteria, as in a college peer group. Member and nonmember boundaries are informal when a group develops around a temporary activity, such as playing street football during a lunch break or soliciting funds for a local public television station.

Out-groups

Out-groups are groups to which a person does not belong. If you are a union member, those who are not members are the out-group. If you are not a union member, those who belong to the union are the out-group. In other words, out-groups are "they-groups" and in-groups are "we-groups." The out-group includes those people who are excluded when we use the word "we."

Members of groups tend to believe that their group is something special, and they seek to maintain its boundaries. Conflict between in-groups and out-groups is an effective method of creating as well as maintaining group boundaries. A common enemy often unites group members. A sense of solidarity and cohesion develops from confrontation and conflict with out-groups. However, conflict with out-groups alone cannot keep a group together. A group must carry on activities that its membership needs and values, and it must have a basis for consensus and cohesion to stand up to and grow more cohesive from external pressure.

Other Characteristics of Groups

Some groups exist for extended periods of time; others die out quickly. Groups depend on their members for their existence. If a group's members lose their reasons for belonging to the group and no longer feel bound to it, the group ceases to exist.

Conversely, groups persist and may even develop a "consciousness of kind"—a strong sense of group unity—when a sharing of valued and needed activities is present.

Various groups and social categories in society provide social standards against which people analyze and evaluate themselves and their behavior. These groups are called reference groups. A **reference group** is any group that an individual takes into account when evaluating his or her own behavior and self-concept. It is a group that has a strong influence on a person's identity and values. A person may or may not actually belong to his or her reference groups, but a reference group is always a group that an individual accepts as a model for his or her judgments and actions.

Reference groups

In our society, each individual belongs to many social groups, such as school, work, religious, friendship, and family groups. A person may belong to special interest groups, athletic groups, and professional groups. The list of groups, especially in a complex society such as ours, is unending. Sociologists therefore deal with many characteristics of groups, such as size, interaction patterns, group goals, formality of the group, degrees of permanence, and organization. Many sociologists focus particularly on two broad types of groups—primary groups and secondary groups.

Primary Groups and Relationships

The concept of **primary group** was formulated by sociologist Charles H. Cooley (1956). Cooley believed that primary groups are an extremely important unit of social organization—a necessary part of social life. Essential elements of primary groups are intimacy, intrinsically valued relationships, and shared attitudes and values emanating from experiences within the primary groups themselves. Within primary groups, people get to know and understand one another intimately as individual personalities. The need for intimate, personal, and spontaneous relationships exists within all societies that are characterized by high degrees of formality and rationality.

Importance of primary groups

Within the primary group, an individual may express emotions of all kinds, such as love, anger, and happiness. There is a freedom and spontaneity of response between members of primary groups that is not found in more formally organized groups. Primary groups are always small and are characterized by intimate, face-to-face relationships. Ties between primary group members are personal and warm. They are founded on sentiments. Relationships are total as well as personal in that they involve many aspects of an individual's life experiences.

Characteristics of primary groups

Members of primary groups have common goals and standards and a common spirit of cooperation and sympathy. Primary groups do not exist solely to achieve certain goals. The members consider one another as ends in themselves and not as means to other ends. In other words, relationships within primary groups are desired for their own sake and are unconditional. Within the family, for example, a mother caring for her sick child is not concerned about getting anything out of the situation. The relationship is a **primary relationship,** which means it is never instrumental. A primary relationship is characterized by love, affection, and emotional involvement; the relationship is personal and valued as an end in itself. There is a high degree of durability and frequency in a primary relationship. Erratic, occasional interaction is not conducive to an inti-

The family is a primary group where relationships characterized by love, affection, and emotional involvement exist.

Primary groups fulfill the basic human need for intimacy

mate relationship. One only gets to know the whole person through frequent contact over an extended period. Primary relationships meet the need for intimate human contact and companionship, a need that all humans have. Relaxed and informal, primary relationships occur most frequently within peer groups, families, and small communities whose members are in continuous close contact over extended periods of time. The basic qualities of primary groups then are:

Basic qualities of primary groups

1. small size
2. face-to-face relationships
3. relatively frequent contact
4. a sharing of mutual concern—that is, a sharing of a variety of interests and activities in sympathetic, intimate atmosphere

As we noted in Chapter 3, one of the most important functions of primary groups is the training and socialization of the individual. Such primary groups as the family and peer group play a significant role in effectively developing and controlling individual behavior.

Cooley has stated that primary groups are "fundamental in forming the social nature and ideals of the individual." Arising from the intimate association occurring in primary groups is a:

certain fusion of individualities into the common whole, so that one's very self, for many purposes at least, is the common life and purpose of the group . . . it is a "we," it involves the sort of sympathy and mutual identification for which "we" is the natural expression (Cooley, 1922).

The primary group functions as a place where the individual can be a whole person—a total personality. Within the primary group, a person can give release to all kinds of emotions. The group functions as a place where people can communicate their deepest feelings to others. Primary groups provide a feeling of security for the individual, a feeling of protection from the complexity and conflict in society. In other words, primary groups provide a very important supporting and sustaining function to the individual.

Because fo these functions, primary groups are considered by sociologists to be of great significance. They are considered to be the basic units of social cohesion and control. The very strength of a society is dependent upon the strength of its primary groups.

Secondary Groups and Relationships

Within a contemporary urban industrial society such as the United States, there are many social groupings other than the small primary group. Such groupings are categorized as **secondary groups.** A secondary group is usually large and is created for a clearly defined, limited purpose. The principal purpose of the secondary group is to meet a specific need or fulfill a particular function. The functions of the group, established to achieve group goals, dictate the types of relationships expected among its members.

The importance of secondary groups

Secondary groups are characterized by **secondary relationships.** A secondary relationship is nonemotional, formal, and specialized; it does not involve the entire personality of the individual participants. It tends to be segmented, utilitarian, and impersonal. People in secondary groups interact for limited and specific purposes. A secondary relationship is specialized and involves only a segment of the personality, excluding a wider variety of interests and roles.

Secondary groups are characterized by secondary relationships

The relationship between a bus driver and a passenger is secondary. Each has a specific role to play, and under ordinary circumstances, no other interests or roles enter into the relationship. A police officer-citizen relationship is secondary in that the citizen is not interested in whether the police officer loves his children or takes a shower, and conversely, the police officer is not interested in the citizen's eating or sleeping habits. The police officer and the citizen, in other words, view each other within a specific working role that does not involve the whole personality.

Within the secondary relationship, communication is restricted and specific. It does not include the free communication of personal attitudes and feelings that reflect one's total personality. Communication is limited to the specifics of the relationship. For example, a shopper interested in buying a pair of shoes need communicate only his or her needs with respect to shoe style, size, and color.

Limited communication

Table 4.1. **Primary and Secondary Relationships**

	PRIMARY	SECONDARY
Physical Conditions	Spatial proximity Small number Long duration	Spatial distance Large number Short duration
Social Characteristics	Identification of ends Intrinsic valuation of the relation Intrinsic valuation of other person Inclusive knowledge of other person Feeling of freedom and spontaneity Operation of informal controls	Disparity of ends Extrinsic valuation of the relation Extrinsic valuation of other person Specialized and limited knowledge of other person Feeling of external constraint Operation of formal controls
Sample Relationships	Friend-friend Husband-wife Parent-child Teacher-pupil	Clerk-customer Announcer-listener Performer-spectator Officer-subordinate Author-reader
Sample Groups	Play group Family Village or neighborhood Work team	Nation Clerical hierarchy Professional association Corporation

Reprinted by permission of Kingsley Davis, author and copyright holder, from *Human Society* (New York: Macmillan, 1949), p. 306.

The secondary relationship is contractual and limited to those specific, well-understood obligations that each interacting individual has to the others. In other words, relationships among members of a secondary group are clearly defined, restricted to a particular purpose, and oriented toward a specific goal. Individual goals are subordinated to group goals. While participating in the secondary group, individuals subordinate themselves to the requirements and functions of the group. With little flexibility in their relationships with others, secondary group members disregard individual characteristics and perform their specified functions within the group. In secondary groups, an individual's importance lies not in his or her personal qualities, but in the ability to perform a specific role. The secondary relationship is transferable in that participants are interchangeable. If one bank teller annoys a customer, the customer may transfer to another individual playing the bank teller role. As can be seen in Table 4.1, participants in a secondary relationship or members of a secondary group are not concerned with one another as people, as in primary relationships or groups; they are concerned with one another as means to other ends and their capacity as functionaries playing particular roles.

Within secondary groups, such as a local business club or the Federal Trade Commission, interpersonal relationships are often formalized and established by written regulations enforced through hierarchical channels. Secondary groups are judged by their efficiency in meeting a particular need. They are goal-oriented, in contrast to primary groups, which are judged by the emotional and psychological satisfaction they supply to their members. Personal and private relationships are excluded or controlled according to the formalized requirements of the group. Personal emotions have little place among a secondary work group along an assembly line in an industrial plant.

Secondary groups are judged by their efficiency

In the United States, as in most other urban industrial societies, secondary groups and formal organizations have gained in importance and have tended to dominate one sphere of life after another. In fact, one can analyze much of what is happening in American society in terms of a shift from primary groups and relationships to secondary groups and relationships.

Before going on to the next section of this chapter, one must remember that the importance of human interaction within groups is great. It is through interaction within groups that people learn much of their behavior. Many of our ideas, values, and actions can be accounted for only in terms of how others relate to us and how we have learned from others within social groups. Sociological explanations for human behavior are based on the belief that social interactions within groups greatly influence the individual's behavior. An individual's attitudes, orientation toward life, and conceptions of self are influenced and developed through social interaction within groups.

Formal Organizations and Bureaucracy

For many decades, a primary mode of relationships and group life existed in the United States. With urbanization and industrialization came a shift from the primary mode to a secondary, or associational, type of social organization. Today we are much more dependent on secondary relationships and groups to meet our needs. Primary groups and relationships no longer dominate our culture as they did in the past.

In modern urban society, individuals tend to spend much of their lives within groups formed to accomplish special purposes. Sociologists term these groups organizations. According to Talcott Parsons (1960), **organizations** are human groupings or social units deliberately constructed and reconstructed to meet specific goals. They include such groupings as hospitals, prisons, churches, schools, and corporations. They are characterized by a deliberately planned division of labor, by power, by communication responsibilities, and by the presence of goal-oriented and controlling power centers.

Organizations defined

Life in the urban community is dominated by organizations. In fact, large-scale formal organizations are the most distinctive feature of industrial societies. It should be noted, however, that organizations are not a new phenomenon. They existed in the early civilizations of Egypt, Rome, and China. Through the centuries, people have used organizations to accomplish a multitude of functions: to find food, to make war, and to build cities and churches.

Today organizations fill a broader variety of social and personal needs than they did in the past. In the Egyptian and Oriental empires of pharaohs and emperors, organizations did not permeate and affect large segments of people's lives, but were utilized for such needs as the construction of pyramids and the building of irrigation systems.

The organization is a powerful social tool that coordinates many human actions to achieve its goal. For example, the organization of an industrial plant combines raw materials with people and intertwines workers, machines, and specialists so that a product needed by the members of a society can be efficiently produced. Because urban societies stress rationality and scientific efficiency, there is an extension of organizations into every aspect of our lives. Every urbanized society has its business corporations, government organizations, schools, churches, and hospitals.

Organizations permeate every aspect of urban life

Many large organizations command enormous social power. American organizations such as General Motors and Exxon employ hundreds of thousands of individuals and have billions of dollars in assets. Large organizations also command a significant share of an urban society's social resources. In the United States today, the majority of the population is not self-employed, as it was at the turn of the century. Today the bulk of the work force consists of "organization" women and men. Centralized, large organizations occupy an increasingly significant and strategic position in American society.

There also exist today organizations that function to coordinate and mediate other organizations. These large, complex organizations are utilized at an unprecedented level in human history. Our contemporary American society places great value upon efficiency, effectiveness, and rationality. We are, as noted by the organizational sociologist Amitai Etzioni (1964), dependent on organizations as "the most rational and efficient form of social groupings known."

There are social as well as human costs involved in the growth of organizations in American society. Alienation and frustration exist among many who work for organizations. Much of what enhances rationality within organizations reduces human happiness. However, Etzioni (1964) notes:

> **Not all that enhances rationality reduces happiness, and not all that increases happiness reduces efficiency. Human resources are among the major means used by the organization to achieve its goals. Generally the less the organization alienates its personnel, the more efficient it is. Satisfied workers usually work harder and better than frustrated ones. Within limits, happiness heightens efficiency in organizations and, conversely, without efficiency in organizations much of our happiness is unthinkable. Without well run organizations our standard of living, our level of culture, and our democratic life could not be maintained. Thus, to a degree, organizational rationality and human happiness go hand in hand. But a point is reached in every organization where happiness and efficiency cease to support each other. Not all work can be well paid or gratifying, and not all regulations and orders can be made acceptable. Here we face a true dilemma.**

According to Etzioni then, the problem of modern organizations is how to develop highly rational groups while producing a minimum of unwanted side effects and a maximum of satisfaction.

Our society is the associational society

Our lives are increasingly spent in the rational, formalistic, emotionally neutral world of organizations. As noted by William Dobriner (1969), our society is the associational society—"a world of bureaucracy in which millions of persons each day are caught up in social structures so vast and complex that no one individual, not even the corporation president, the general . . . or the President has full understanding or, indeed, 'control' over what is happening." American society is a "mass" society—a world of mass production, mass communication, and mass consumption.

In most organizations, especially large ones, there is a division of labor so that organizational goals may be achieved more efficiently. Goals are clearly understood in an organization. Within organizations, people know one another in specialized roles. Primary relationships may exist, but they are not essential to the operation of the organization.

Power in an organization is usually concentrated in the hands of a few individuals who control and lead the organization's activities toward the fulfillment of organizational goals. Membership in organizations is not fixed; it changes on a routine basis. Individuals retire and resign, are fired and hired.

Organizations may be either formal or informal. The distinction is made in terms of the types of social relationships in the organization. Rules and regulations specifically define the types of relationships that occur in a formal organization. As we shall examine later, within informal organizations, the relationships are more informal. They form spontaneously out of the needs and interests of members. In a formal organization, tasks are divided among the membership. Each member's relationship to others within the organization is specified and clearly defined. Expected patterns of communication, decision making, and authority are established as people coordinate to meet organizational goals.

When the activities of several people have to be coordinated in terms of explicit impersonal goals, bureaucracies tend to arise. It is in the interests of achieving greater efficiency that organizations undergo bureaucratization, or the adoption of bureaucratic principles and procedures.

To understand contemporary urban society, it is necessary to understand the nature of a bureaucracy, its functions, and its effects on people. In advanced urban societies, the bureaucracy is the most common type of organizational structure in such areas as government, the military, the economy, and education. The increasing size of the American population has caused Americans to utilize the bureaucratic form of group structure to meet growing needs. Perhaps the most important reason for the trend toward bureaucratization is the increasing technological complexity of our society. There is no other form of social organization currently available that can deal with the complex administrative tasks that the increase in population and technological complexity has created.

Bureaucracy is the only known mode of government that can deal with our present complex state

Bureaucracy and Max Weber

A **bureaucracy** is a form of organizational structure. It is a "formal, rationally organized, social structure with clearly defined patterns of activity in which, ideally, every series of actions is functionally related to the purposes of the organization" (Merton, 1957). Max Weber, a scholar of the social sciences, wrote a classic analysis of bureaucracy that is extremely useful in the study of organizations. According to Weber (1964), when the culture of a particular society places great value on the effectiveness and efficiency of administration, a rational model of organization such as a bureaucracy develops. Weber believed that there has been a growth of bureaucratic organizations because they are technically superior to any other form of organization. A bureaucracy compares with "other organizations exactly as does the machine with nonmechanical modes of production. Precision, speed, unambiguity, knowledge of the files, continuity, discretion, unity, strict subordination, reduction of friction and of material and personal costs—these are raised to the optimum point in the strictly bureaucratic organization." The effort to efficiently coordinate the activities of many individuals toward a particular goal leads to the formation of a bureaucracy.

Bureaucratic organizations are technically superior to other forms of organization

Weber identified six basic characteristics of an ideal bureaucracy: office, rules, impersonality, hierarchy, specialization and technical competence, and career.

Office. In a bureaucratically structured organization, each individual occupies an **office**, or specific position. The duties and tasks of each official are explicitly defined, as is the relationship of one office to all other offices. Activities of individuals within a bureaucracy are limited by the office occupied; the office does not belong to any individual. Office claimants are those individuals who possess explicit qualifications based on duties and functions. No individual can claim an office by virtue of special rank, privilege, or inherited position. No one individual is indispensable within a bureaucracy.

Activities of individuals within bureaucracy are limited by the individual's office

The office exists as an explicit definition of functions and duties. It is separate from the individual holding the office. This interchangeability of people means that the organization can continue to function even when its officeholders resign, retire, or die. It continues to function effectively by filling vacant positions with appropriately qualified individuals. The first component of a bureaucracy then is the division of people and work into units called offices or bureaus.

Rules. In a bureaucracy, norms are usually spelled out in written sets of regulations and **rules**. Written, not oral, agreements and documents guide the officeholders of an organization. The officeholder's behavior is dictated by the organization's formal regulations and rules, which are specific and apply to definite situations and circumstances. Rules and regulations, in addition to being specific, are also general in that they formally apply in an impersonal manner to all within the scope of the rule. When problems arise, rules rather than personal judgments dictate the behavior of officeholders. Personal judgments and biases are minimized by the following of rules and regulations. Even though the following of rules and regulations renders social relations impersonal, it provides for continuous and uniform treatment of clients and members of the organization in addition to enabling workers to do their jobs in spite of personality differences.

Regulations provide continuity and uniformity and limit power

The second characteristic of a bureaucracy then is that the amount of responsibility and authority and the exact duties of an office are governed by specified rules and regulations. These rules limit the amount of authority certain employees have over others.

Impersonality. Relationships in a bureaucracy are not among people but among offices. The formally prescribed relationships between offices are impersonal. This **impersonality** helps render objective and rational judgments and ensures cooperation among people who must interact in order that their assigned duties may be carried out efficiently and with detachment. The spirit of impersonality is uninfluenced by likes and dislikes of particular persons; it is one of detachment and distance. The third component of bureaucracy then is impersonality.

Hierarchy. A bureaucracy is characterized by a **hierarchy** of offices ("a clearly established system of super- and subordination") with a chain of command "in which there is a supervision of the lower offices by the higher ones" (Weber, 1968). Bureaucracies are similar to pyramids in shape, with many offices at the bottom and very few at the top. They are also characterized by a centralization of authority and decision making within an administration or a management. A bureaucracy makes explicit the location of authority and limits each office's exercise of authority. Within the bureaucracy, officeholders are responsible for the actions of those under their authority and are also responsible to those above them. The hierarchy, in other words, locates responsibility within particular positions and permits an exact determination of policy.

The hierarchy locates responsibility

Employees of a bureaucracy then are hierarchically organized. The responsibility and authority at each level are clearly established, with each individual being responsible to the individual above him or her. These established lines of responsibility and authority help coordinate organizational activities into one policy.

Specialization and Technical Competence. Bureaucracy develops a high degree of **specialization** of function within an organization. Only personnel who are professionally and technically qualified for the bureaucratic offices are selected to fill these positions. This selection of individuals for offices in terms of their professional and technical competence makes it necessary to develop instruments and tests to measure individual abilities.

Within a bureaucracy, each position demands specific skills and technical or professional qualifications. Whether or not an individual is employed within a bureaucracy depends on his or her ability to meet these demands.

Career. Employment within the bureaucracy of an organization provides a **career** for officials. To ensure loyal, unbiased performance, employees are given security of tenure. Promotions are based on merit, seniority, or demonstrated ability.

Within the bureaucratic structure, the individual participant is provided with a career and a system of rewards consisting of tenure and seniority. These chief characteristics of a bureaucracy are summarized in Table 4.2.

The structural and functional characteristics of a bureaucracy as set forth by Weber help us understand how bureaucracies operate. As an ideal type—a mental construct that in reality does not exist—a bureaucracy also functions to

Table 4.2. Weber's Basic Characteristics of a Bureaucracy

Office	A clear-cut division of labor among the individual officials
Rules	A formal system of rules and regulations governing decisions and actions
Impersonality	An impersonal orientation by the officials toward their clients, who are treated as "cases"
Hierarchy	A hierarchical authority structure, with the scope of each individual's responsibility clearly defined
Specialization	A specialized administrative staff that maintains the organization and its internal communication system
Career	A promotion system based on merit, seniority, or both, so that officials typically anticipate a lifelong career in the organization

Source: Based on Weber's chief characteristics of a bureaucracy, as listed in the *Encyclopedia of Sociology* (Guilford, Conn.: Dushkin Publishing, 1974).

specify and define several important variables that can be used as a basis by which to compare and contrast different types of bureaucracies. As noted earlier, Weber believed that the bureaucratic form of organization has grown because the rationality of its form makes it more efficient than alternative methods of administration and forms of organization.

Weber saw bureaucracy as a social structure within which people would be treated impartially and fairly. He believed that prejudice and personal capriciousness in business and governmental decisions would be eliminated by bureaucracy. Bureaucracy would also control favoritism and replace spontaneous, traditional, informal ways of doing things with calculated rules and logical procedures.

Bureaucratic Problems

"Ideal" bureaucracies do not exist

Formal organizations do not conform exactly to Weber's ideal type of bureaucracy. In fact, Weber himself was aware that one aspect of bureaucratic organization (or government)—the efficient control over people's lives—could have adverse consequences. Even when bureaucracies approach his ideal type, sociologists have questioned whether they are actually the most rational and efficient structure by which to organize human resources for achieving desired ends.

Bureaucratic inefficiency

Inflexibility leads to inefficiency

Robert Merton criticizes Weber's ideas on bureaucratic organizations in his classic essay, "Bureaucratic Structure and Personality" (Merton, 1957). Merton notes that when bureaucratic officials stress the following of rules—and rules are the means established to achieve organizational goals—the rules tend to become ends in themselves, resulting in inefficiency. This inflexibility of following the rules actually can inhibit the achievement of organizational goals that the bureaucracy is supposed to achieve efficiently. When unanticipated situations or unusual problems arise, organizational rules and regulations cause inefficiency, because the bureaucrat, unable to find a rule or precedent covering the situation, has a tendency to do nothing. That is, personnel within a bureaucracy who continually follow rules are unable to act when conditions not covered by the rules arise. The bureaucratic employee may not be able to act in a manner constructive to the organization because the rules and regulations do not provide for exceptions.

Bureaucratic rule following strangulates the ability to act on an unfamiliar situation

The following of rules and regulations within the segmented roles of the bureaucratic hierarchy can discourage initiative, imagination, and the acceptance of responsibility. The inability to use one's own rational judgments and imagination can result in feelings of alienation.

Initiative discouraged

An additional inefficiency of bureaucratic structures has been noted by Laurence Peter (1969). According to his Peter Principle, within any bureaucracy, "every employee tends to rise in the hierarchy to his own level of incompetence." That is, an individual who is doing a good job in the bureaucracy is usually promoted out of it until he or she reaches a job beyond his or her capacity, where the person tends to remain. The well-known Parkinson's Law describes another aspect of bureaucratic inefficiency: "Work expands to fill the amount of time available for its completion."

Peter M. Blau also questions the efficiency of Weber's ideal type of bureaucracy with regard to reserve detachment or impersonality, the exercise of authority, and the insistence on conformity. Blau states: "If reserved detachment characterizes the attitudes of the members of the organization toward one another, it is unlikely that high 'esprit de corps' will develop among them. The strict exercise of authority in the interest of discipline induces subordinates, anxious to be highly thought of by their superiors, to conceal defects in operations from superiors, and this obstruction of the flow of information upward in the hierarchy impedes effective management. Insistence on conformity also tends to engender rigidities in official conduct and to inhibit the rational exercise of judgment needed for efficient performance of tasks" (Blau, 1956). In other words, impersonality can prohibit the growth of "spirit" among organizational members, the strict exercise of authority can lead to problems of concealment and communication, and strict conformity can lead to rigidity in the performance of tasks. In the following section, we examine an additional dimension of social organization.

Blau on bureaucracy

Informal Groups and Organization

Organization should not be thought of solely in terms of formal organization. There is a continuum from extremely formalized and persisting structures to transitory, informal structures. One misses many important aspects of social organization if only the formal structures are examined. Therefore we will more closely examine informal organization and the importance of informal groups.

Informal groups are those within which an individual's social as well as personal relationships are not prescribed nor defined by the formal organization. They develop wherever and whenever people come together with some

Informal groups defined

frequency. They appear in such diverse organizations as industrial plants, the military, and prisons.

Informal groups have their own structures of interrelated roles, statuses, shared beliefs, and values. They can appear without formal organization of any kind, such as in play or friendship groups. They also develop as a reaction to formal organizations with their bureaucracies and formalized structures. They operate to counter many of the impersonal effects of secondary groups.

Importance of informal groups

It is important to have an understanding of informal groups and relationships in order to have a better and more complete understanding of social organization in such places as factories, offices, and prisons. For example, in order to have a complete picture of social organization in an industrial plant, it is necessary to understand the informal network of relationships among workers, the informal groups of which they are members, and the more formal organization, with its technological systems, bureaucracy, and formal structure. We can begin to appreciate the importance of informal relationships and groups by examining their functions, their effects on members, and their activities within the setting of an industrial organization.

In industrial organizations, as in many other work organizations, for many years, workers were viewed as individuals. It was not until the now classic Mayo studies at the Hawthorne plant of Western Electric (Roethlisberger and Dickson, 1939) that the view of workers as group members emerged.

The worker as a group member

Workers maintain work group values as well as personal values, and they respond to both personal and group interests. In many organizations, informal groups and relationships form spontaneously out of workers' psychological and social needs. In organizations with technologically advanced systems of production, work is routinized, specialized, diversified, and simplified in accordance with the needs of efficiency and rationalization. In industrial organizations, many jobs are boring and monotonous. Informal groups function to reduce this boredom and monotony.

Speed and amount of work produced are socially regulated

Within an industrial organization, as in other types of work organizations, new workers are quickly socialized into a variety of norms defined by the informal organization of workers. Two such norms are the amount-of-work standard and the speed standard, both of which are rigidly enforced by the informal organization of the workers. Basically, these norms require that a person should not work too hard nor too fast. When workers restrict their work and production, their motive may be to increase their security on the job.

An additional norm held by informal work groups is that a worker should not inform a supervisor of any behavior that would prove detrimental to a fellow worker. Ostracism, harassment, and at times, physical force can be used by informal groups to enforce the above values at work. By enforcing these values, work groups maintain their informal organization and protect it from unwanted outside interference.

Causes and significance of informal groups

Informal groups are not to be seen as being accidental or tangential. Formal organizations must contain a parallel, spontaneous network of interpersonal relations (informal groups) if they are to function effectively. A formal organization's rules and regulations do not cover unforeseen problems. Informal groups and norms can help the organization as a whole survive unforeseen difficulties.

The informal group is an integral part of the organizational structure. In the following section, we examine the effects of bureaucracy on the worker.

Bureaucracy, Work, and the Individual

In the United States, workers are increasingly employed by large bureaucratic organizations. More than 90 percent of all employed people are wage and salary workers. With most Americans working in bureaucratic organizations, it is important to understand their effects on workers.

Work defined

First, we have to define "work." **Work** is defined as an activity that produces something of value for others. Defining work in this manner, rather than equating it with paid employment, keeps us from ignoring its social and personal aspects. For example, a housewife or househusband doing housework is certainly working, even though it is not paid employment.

Functions of work

Work has many important functions. It is the means by which society's desired and needed goods and services are provided. Through the economic rewards of work, people obtain many of the material things they need and want. Work also serves social purposes. At work, people meet and form friendships. Work also confers a particular social status on the worker and his or her family. In point of fact, one's work is a major determinant of a family's social class, including where a family lives and attends school, and the people with whom a family associates.

Self-esteem and work

Work also contributes to a person's self-esteem. It does this by enabling a worker to acquire a sense of mastery over him- or herself and his or her environment. Work also enables a person to provide a service or product that is valued by others. That is, work "tells" the worker that he or she has something of value to offer others. For a person not to have a job is not to have something that is valued by others. Conversely, to work is to have evidence that one is needed by others.

A person's sense of identity is very much shaped by work. Most working people describe themselves in terms of the work groups or organizations to which they belong. When asked who they are, people respond with, "I work for General Motors," or, "I'm an Aetna agent," or "I'm a nurse." In other words, people become what they do.

For the majority of people in our society, working conditions have improved along with standards of living—such as higher real income and life expectancy. However, even though they are better off materially than past generations, many workers still express dissatisfaction with work.

Maslow's order of needs

Some social scientists have explained dissatisfaction in terms of workers' changing values, needs, and aspirations. In a now classic study, Abraham Maslow (1964) has suggested that people's needs are hierarchical. When needs are met at one level, the next level becomes important to the person. Maslow's order of needs is as follows: physiological requirements such as food and water; safety and security; companionship and affection; self-esteem and the esteem of others; self-actualization, or being able to realize one's potential to the fullest.

Some social scientists believe that industry's and organized labor's success in meeting the basic needs of workers has unintentionally created demands for fulfilling jobs. In point of fact, much sociological research has indicated that what workers want most is to control their immediate environments and to feel that both their work and they themselves are important—the twin ingredients of self-esteem (Report on Work, 1980).

Workers' social, psychological, and personality needs may be adversely affected at work because they conflict with the nature of bureaucracy. As we have seen, bureaucracy is characterized by impersonality, specialization, rules and regulations, chain of command, and close supervision. These characteristics deny the worker control over job activities. They also inhibit the expression of a worker's creative abilities and make a worker passive and dependent.

Work satisfaction

In general, for the past 15 years, there has been a continuing decrease in the work satisfaction among both white- and blue-collar workers, men and women, and all occupational groups (National Opinion Research Center, 1985). But people in the professions and higher-level jobs are more satisfied with their work than are people in lower-level, unskilled jobs. In general, one finds less self-regulation and autonomy in lower-level jobs. Dissatisfaction, however, is a problem not only among blue-collar workers. In offices, white-collar workers complain of being slaves to their office machines where work is highly specialized, monotonous, and noisy. Computer operators and typists share much with factory workers. Even managers have shown discontent with the intrinsic factors of work, such as its lack of achievement, accomplishment, responsibility, and challenge.

THE DISAPPEARING COMPANY MAN

Mitchell Lee Marks

In the following reading, "The Disappearing Company Man," Mitchell Marks examines the discontent that men are having in the bureaucratic corporate world. He notes how many managers, shaken by mergers and cutbacks, are fending for themselves, placing their trust not in corporations, but in their own capabilities.

In today's lean and mean companies, a new breed of workers, professionals and executives has shed the traditional gray flannel suits and put on their personal running shoes. They are not company men or women but entrepreneurs whose business is themselves.

A recent survey by the Employment Management Association found that 79 percent of the 259 companies studied had reduced their staff for economic reasons within the last five years. Managerial and professional ranks have been hardest hit, with more than a half million positions cut in some 300 companies since 1984. The slashes have affected some of the largest and seemingly most stable corporations, including Apple Computers, IBM, General Motors, Du Pont, CBS, Eastman Kodak, Control Data and Dow Chemical.

These shake-ups reflect a major change in what organizational psychologists call the "psychological contract" between employer and employee. As Denise Rousseau of Northwestern University's Kellogg Graduate School of Management points out, long-term employees had come to believe that there was "more to their job than just the money they make, just as a spouse might think there is more to a marriage than the obligation of financial support." This psychological contract committed both sides to maintaining the relationship, with the employees supplying loyalty and the company steady employment.

In my work as a consultant and researcher on corporate mergers and reorganizations, I regularly come across people with 20, 25 and even 30 years of service to one firm. In playing by company rules, many missed watching their children grow up, moved themselves and their families across the country and back again and took job assignments that fitted the company needs rather than their own. Their rewards were security and self-esteem as well as the pay and perks of higher management positions. The rules of the corporate game have changed, however, changing the psychological contract with them.

One reason is that the business environment has altered dramatically in the past few years. To stay competitive in the face of increased global competition, rapid technological change and government deregulation, firms have reorganized to cut costs, streamline corporate hierarchies and improve product lines. With corporate missions redefined, some firms have shed subsidiaries and narrowed their focus to core businesses; others have gone the other way, gobbling up businesses in their haste to diversify.

But there is more behind the lean, mean corporate culture than fierce competition and new technology First, there are corporate raiders, people like Carl Icahn, Frank Lorenzo and T. Boone Pickens, who buy up shares of what they consider undervalued companies. To maximize short-term gains for themselves and other stockholders, they often break up companies and sell off their assets piece by piece. Such tactics ignore long-term employee loyalty and consistent management direction.

And now the giants have picked up the habit. Huge mergers of large organizations, such as GE with RCA, Chevron with Gulf Oil and Philip Morris with General Foods, have made entire levels of management redundant. Wall Street investment bankers, inspired by the handsome fees and profits generated by financial restructurings, tell anxious executives to "eat or be eaten." Third, the urge to merge has created a backlash of defensive layoffs to head off unwanted suitors by reducing overhead and pumping up stock prices. Finally, it has simply become fashionable to cut back. Even the most financially successful companies have jumped on the job-cutting bandwagon.

A new generation of chief executives, often cash-flow experts with little savvy in production or marketing, seems ready to abandon many employee morale and community service programs. One result: a growing wall of distrust between employer and employee. Greg Borax, who works at the Boston headquarters of the Gillette Company, is a case in point. "I had done an internship with Gillette while in college," he told me, "liked what I saw and looked forward to rejoining them after I graduated, which I did. Then, one day in November, I walked into work and it was nothing but rumors about the company being taken over. Then our stock price began to go up—someone was buying it but no one knew who. I let it slide over me, but lots of people were really affected by it. They lost weight, became increasingly nervous and had trouble sleeping."

Gillette eventually averted an unfriendly takeover bid by paying greenmail—buying back investor stock at a premium. "We didn't hear anything from the company until January," Borax recalls, "when they announced a 'restructuring,' just a fancy term for layoffs to pay the debt of buying back their shares. Most of the people let go on our floor were middle- and upper-level managers. We looked around and thought, 'There is no security in staying here.'

"In May they announced a second 'restructuring' and then another in November. There was no warning or explanation for the cutbacks, but each time they assured us that this was the last round. I learned more from the gossip going around than from anything the company told us. My feelings about the company have changed: I don't feel the company is being up-front with us. Everyone in my department is ready to jump to another company."

These feelings of distrust and helplessness have found expression in a bitter riddle that's made the company rounds in recent years: "Why is an executive in a merged corporation like a mushroom?" "Because he's kept in the dark, fed manure and prepared for canning."

Despite assurances that cutbacks are strictly for business reasons and have nothing to do with job performance, many people who are laid off blame themselves and feel they've lost control of their lives. "Everything I counted on before," one man told me, "turned topsy-turvey. The things I thought would make me successful—hard work and commitment—didn't pay off. Now I wonder, 'What was the use of it all?'"

Social psychologists Dorothea and Ben Braginsky anticipated these problems when they studied laid-off middle managers back in the 1970s. They found that unemployment produced drastic changes in how the executives viewed themselves and the world around them. Most regained their self-esteem soon after they found jobs, but their alienation remained, a lasting suspicion of the organization that broke its psychological contract with them.

Even people who survive cuts suffer from them. Executives in firms that have been merged or reorganized often tell me that their employees are "paralyzed" and that work comes to a standstill as people wonder whether they'll survive with their jobs and careers intact.

Terry Elledge has seen reorganization from both sides of the fence. Six years ago the Pacific Financial Company cut its work force by about one-third—quite a shock for a firm that hadn't laid off anybody in more than 100 years. Elledge helped orchestrate this shake-up, but when Pacific Financial later cut back further, he decided to leave. Now a management consultant in southern California, Elledge sees the current psychological work contract this way:

"It used to be, 'You have something I need and I have something you need.' Now both employers and employees have become more protective, distant and skeptical. And to validate these feelings, both sides have come to believe that 'people are taking advantage of me.' Individuals these days are more likely to walk out for something better, while companies are more inclined to fire people."

The changing psychological contract clearly places more responsibility on individuals to assess and design their own careers. William Ellermeyer, president of the Ellermeyer Company, a California-based outplacement firm, says that "people need to take control of their situation. The belief that 'I'm going to hang my hat here and bet that the company will give me a gold watch after 40 years' just isn't valid any more. Companies have game plans and goals and individuals must do the same. Those who don't are lambs waiting to be shorn."

The first step in taking control of your career is to assess your skills against your firm's needs now and in the future. Watch carefully to see how the psychological contract is changing at your company and use the information to establish realistic expectations. Does your company reward more effort and accomplishment with more pay and more perks? Public-opinion analyst Daniel Yankelovich believes that too many companies, enamored of a lean and mean corporate policy, shortsightedly ignore the potential of what he calls "discretionary effort"—the large, usually untapped area between the minimum amount of work employees have to do to slide by and the full effort they're eager to give, if they see that it pays off.

Before joining a new company, check its history as well as you can. How have previous reorganizations and cutbacks been handled? Were employees given adequate warning, proper explanations, fair severance agreements and outplacement counseling? Were terminations voluntary, involuntary or some combination of the two?

Keep your résumé updated and have a battle plan for whom you would call and what firms you would contact if you have to reenter the job market. This helps minimize the crisis orientation that follows a rumor or announcement of cutbacks. Read the newest edition of *What Color is Your Parachute?* by Richard Bolles. Be alert to trends and changes within your company—cuts in one department can portend cutbacks in others—and in your field as a whole. Cutbacks by one firm often create a "keep down with the Joneses" mentality in other similar companies.

Stay alert to these signs, but don't panic and move on just because you see changes in other departments or companies. Rather, use these changes as a cue to start asking questions of yourself, your boss and associates you trust. When change does hit close to home, avoid the temptation to hide your feelings of insecurity and put on a phony "everything is great" facade. Talk with coworkers, a counselor or family members about what may happen and how it can be handled. Give and get support.

Most important, always keep your options open. Crisis brings opportunity as well as danger. Being pushed out of the corporate nest is just the goad many people need to take on their dreams of opening their own business or getting in on the exciting start-up of a new enterprise. The changing psychological contract is driving the business world toward an individualistic work force—men and women who place their trust not in giant corporations but in their own capabilities, self-entrepreneurs who run their careers like privately held corporations.

Review Questions

1. How have the "rules of the corporate game" changed the psychological contract between companies and their employees? Explain your answer.
2. Examine some of the author's suggestions for "taking control of your career" in today's corporate world.

Women and Work

Women work hard in American society, as wives, as mothers, and as members of the paid work force. Many Americans still do not view housekeeping and child rearing as work. Husbands and children can still be heard saying, "My wife (mother) doesn't work; she just stays home." At times, even a woman herself will tell a person, "I don't work; I'm just a housewife." Housewives do not draw salaries, and the value of their work is not figured into the gross national product of the United States. Yet economists have determined that the average full-time housewife works a total of almost 100 hours a week, or an average of more than 14 hours a day, 7 days a week. The different jobs a woman performs as homemaker include maid, housekeeper, cook, dishwasher, laundress, seamstress, nurse, and tutor. If women were paid for this work, they would receive salaries of several hundred dollars a week. Housewives receive only the money (unless thay also are in the paid work force) their husbands give them, however, and their work is excluded from Social Security. They are underpaid and overworked, with little, if any, financial security.

100 hours a week

American women also work in the paid labor force, and almost all who do are homemakers as well. Today over 90 percent of all American women do paid work during some part of their lives. Between the 1950s and today, the number of working women greatly increased. In the 1950s, few working-age women were employed outside the home. Today over half of working-age women are employed outside the home.

Why women work

Why do women work in our society today? Some people still believe they work for a few extra dollars or for pleasure. The fact is that women work out of necessity. Millions of women work in the paid labor force because high rates of inflation over most of the past two decades have considerably eroded disposable earnings and have forced many families to rely on two incomes in order to maintain their standard of living. Because of divorce, widowhood, and other reasons, many women work because they are the sole support of their families.

Some social scientists have explained the increase of women in the paid work force in terms of industries' growing demands. This is especially true in the service industries (a major job market for women) because service jobs have expanded at such a high rate in our economy. The increase can also be explained in terms of smaller families, which free mothers at an earlier age from caring for their children. Technological advances, which have simplified work at home, have also somewhat freed women's time for paid work in the labor market.

STRATEGIES OF CORPORATE WOMEN

Barbara Ehrenreich

In the following reading, "Strategies of Corporate Women," Barbara Ehrenreich examines women in the bureaucratic, corporate work world. She examines what women have learned at the office, and notes how a small, but significant, segment of women workers are deciding not to "have it all" and are leaving the corporate world for home.

Some of us are old enough to recall when the stereotype of a "liberated woman" was a disheveled radical, notoriously braless, and usually hoarse from denouncing the twin evils of capitalism and patriarchy. Today the stereotype is more likely to be a tidy executive who carries an attaché case and is skilled in discussing market shares and leveraged buy-outs. In fact, thanks in no small part to the anger of the earlier, radical feminists, women have gained a real toehold in the corporate world: about 30 percent of managerial employees are women, as are 40 percent of the current MBA graduates. We have come a long way, as the expression goes, though clearly not in the same direction we set out on.

The influx of women into the corporate world has generated its own small industry of advice and inspiration. Magazines like *Savvy* and *Working Woman* offer tips on everything from sex to software, plus the occasional instructive tale about a woman who rises effortlessly from managing a boutique to being the CEO of a multinational corporation. Scores of books published since the mid-1970s have told the aspiring managerial woman what to wear, how to flatter superiors, and when necessary, fire subordinates. Even old-fashioned radicals like myself, for whom "CD" still means civil disobedience rather than an eight percent interest rate, can expect to receive a volume of second-class mail inviting them to join their corporate sisters at a "networking brunch" or to share the privileges available to the female frequent flier.

But for all the attention lavished on them, all the six-figure promotion possibilities and tiny perks once known only to the men in gray flannel, there is a malaise in the world of the corporate woman. The continuing boom in the advice industry is in itself an indication of some kind of trouble. To take an example from a related field, there would not be a book published almost weekly on how to run a corporation along newly discovered oriental principles if American business knew how to hold its own against the international competition. Similarly, if women were confident about their role in the corporate world, I do not think they would pay to be told how to comport themselves in such minute detail. ("Enter the bar with a briefcase or some files. . . . Hold your head high, with a pleasant expression on your face. . . . After you have ordered your drink, shuffle through a paper or two, to further establish yourself [as a businesswoman]," advises *Letitia Baldridge's Complete Guide*.)

The New Republic, Jan. 27, 1986, pp. 28–31.

Nor, if women were not still nervous newcomers, would there be a market for so much overtly conflicting advice: how to be more impersonal and masculine (*The Right Moves*) or more nurturing and intuitive (*Feminine Leadership*); how to assemble the standard skirted suited uniform (de rigueur until approximately 1982) or move beyond it for the softness and individuality of a dress; how to conquer stress or how to transform it into drive; how to repress the least hint of sexuality, or alternatively, how to "focus the increase in energy that derives from sexual excitement so that you are more productive on the job" (*Corporate Romance*). When we find so much contradictory advice, we must assume that much of it is not working.

There is a more direct sign of trouble. A small but significant number of women are deciding not to have it all after all, and are dropping out of the corporate world to apply their management skills to kitchen decor and baby care. Not surprisingly, these retro women have been providing a feast for a certain "I told you so" style of journalism; hardly a month goes by without a story about another couple that decided to make do on his $75,000 a year while she joins the other mommies in the playground. But the trend is real. The editors of the big business-oriented women's magazines are worried about it. So is Liz Roman Gallese, the former *Wall St. Journal* reporter who interviewed the alumnae of Harvard Business School, class of '75, to write *Women Like Us*.

The women Gallese interviewed are not, for the most part, actual dropouts, but they are not doing as well as might have been expected for the first cohort of women to wield the talismanic Harvard MBA. Certainly they are not doing as well as their male contemporaries, and the gap widens with every year since graduation. Nor do they seem to be a very happy or likable group. Suzanne, the most successful of them, is contemptuous of women who have family obligations. Phoebe, who is perhaps the brightest, has an almost pathological impulse to dominate others. Maureen does not seem to like her infant daughter. Of the 82 women surveyed, 35 had been in therapy since graduation; four had been married to violently abusive men; three had suffered from anorexia or bulimia; and two had become Christian fundamentalists. Perhaps not surprisingly, given the high incidence of personal misery, two-fifths of the group were "ambivalent or frankly not ambitious for their careers."

What is happening to our corporate women? The obvious anti-feminist answer, that biology is incompatible with business success, is not borne out by Gallese's study. Women with children were no less likely to be ambitious and do well than more mobile, single women (although in 1982, when the interviews were carried out, very few of the women had husbands or children). But the obvious feminist answer—that women are being discouraged or driven out by sexism—does gain considerable suport from *Women Like Us*. Many of the women from the class of '75 report having been snubbed, insulted, or passed over for promotions by their male coworkers. Under these circumstances, even the most determined feminist would begin to suffer from what Dr. Herbert J. Freudenberger and Gail North call "business burnout." For non-feminists—or, more precisely, post-feminists—like Gallese and her informants, sexism must be all the more wounding for being so invisible and nameless. What you cannot name, except as apparently random incidents of "discrimination," you cannot hope to do much about.

Gallese suggests another problem, potentially far harder to eradicate than any form of discrimination. There may be a poor fit between the impersonal, bureaucratic culture of the corporation and what is, whether as a result of hormones or history, the female personality. The exception that seems to prove the rule is Suzanne, who is the most successful of the alumnae and who is also a monster of detachment from her fellow human beings. In contrast, Gallese observes that men who rise to the top are often thoroughly dull and "ordinary"—as men go—but perhaps ideally suited to a work world in which interpersonal attachments are shallow and all attention must focus on the famed bottom line.

To judge from the advice books, however, the corporate culture is not as impersonal, in a stern Weberian sense, as we have been led to believe. For example, *The Right Moves,* which is a good representative of the "how to be more like the boys" genre of books for corporate women, tells us to "eliminate the notion that the people with whom you work are your friends"—sound advice for anyone who aspires to the bureaucratic personality. But it also insists that it is necessary to cultivate the "illusion of friendship," lest co-workers find you "aloof and arrogant." You must, in other words, dissemble in order to effect the kind of personality—artificially warm but never actually friendly—that suits the corporate culture.

Now, in a task-oriented, meritocratic organization—or, let us just say, a thoroughly capitalist organization dedicated to the maximization of profit—it should not be necessary to cultivate "illusions" of any kind. It should be enough just to get the job done. But as *The Right Moves* explains, and the stories in *Women Like Us* illustrate, it is never enough just to get the job done; if it were, far more women would no doubt be at the top. You have to impress people, win them over, and in general project an aura of success far more potent than any actual accomplishment. The problem may not be that women lack the capacity for businesslike detachment, but that, as women, they can never entirely fit into the boyish, glad-handed corporate culture so well described three decades ago in *The Lonely Crowd.*

There may also be a deeper, more existential, reason for the corporate woman's malaise. It is impossible to sample the advice literature without beginning to wonder what, after all, is the point of all this striving. Why not be content to stop at $40,000 or $50,000 a year, some stock options, and an IRA? Perhaps the most striking thing about the literature for and about the corporate woman is how little it has to say about the purposes, other than personal advancement, of the corporate "game." Not one among the Harvard graduates or the anonymous women quoted in the advice books ever voices a transcendent commitment to, say, producing a better widget. And if that is too much to expect from postindustrial corporate America, we might at least hope for some lofty organizational goals—to make X Corp. the biggest damn conglomerate in the Western world, or some such. But no one seems to have a fast and guiding vision of the corporate life, much less a Gilderesque belief in the moral purposefulness of capitalism itself. Instead, we find successful corporate women asking, "Why am I doing what I'm doing? What's the point here?" or confiding bleakly that "something's missing."

In fact, from the occasional glimpses we get, the actual content of an executive's daily labors can be shockingly trivial. Consider Phoebe's moment of glory at Harvard Business School. The class had been confronted with a real-life corporate problem to solve. Recognizing the difficulty of getting catsup out of a bottle, should Smucker and Co. start selling catsup out of a wide-mouthed container suitable for inserting a spoon into? No, said Phoebe, taking the floor for a lengthy disquisition, because people like the challenge of pounding catsup out of the bottle; a more accessible catsup would never sell.

Now, I am not surprised that this was the right answer, but I am surprised that it was greeted with such apparent awe and amazement by a professor and a roomful of smart young students. Maybe for a corporate man the catsup problem is a daunting intellectual challenge. But a woman must ask herself: Is *this* what we left the kitchen for?

Many years ago, when America was more innocent but everything else was pretty much the same, Paul Goodman wrote, "There is nearly 'full employment' . . . but there get to be fewer jobs that are necessary or unquestionably useful; that require energy and draw on some of one's best capacities; and that can be done keeping one's honor and dignity." Goodman, a utopian socialist, had unusually strict criteria for what counted as useful enough to be a "man's work," but he spoke for a generation of men who were beginning to question, in less radical ways, the corporate work world described by William H. Whyte, David Riesman, Alan Harrington, and others. Most of the alienated white-collar men of the 1950s withdrew into drink or early coronaries, but a few turned to Zen or jazz, and thousands of their sons and daughters eventually joined with Goodman to help create the anticorporate and, indeed, anti-careerist counterculture of the 1960s. It was the counterculture, as much as anything else, that nourished the feminist movement of the late 1960s and early 1970s, which is where our story began.

In the early years, feminism was torn between radical and assimilationist tendencies. In fact, our first sense of division was between the "bourgeois" feminists who wanted to scale the occupational hierarchy created by men, and the radical feminists who wanted to level it. Assimilation won out, as it probably must among any economically disadvantaged group. Networks replaced consciousness-raising groups; Michael Korda became a more valuable guide to action than Shulamith Firestone. The old radical, anarchistic vision was replaced by the vague hope (well articulated in *Feminine Leadership*) that, in the process of assimilating, women would somehow "humanize" the cold and ruthless world of men. Today, of course, there are still radical feminists, but the only capitalist institution they seem bent on destroying is the local adult bookstore.

As feminism loses its critical edge, it becomes, ironically, less capable of interpreting the experience of its pioneer assimilationists, the new corporate women. Contemporary mainstream feminism can understand their malaise insofar as it is caused by sexist obstacles, but has no way of addressing the sad emptiness of "success" itself. Even the well-worn term "alienation," as applied to human labor, rings no bells among the corporate feminists I have talked to recently, although most thought it an arresting notion. So we are in more or less the same epistemological situation Betty Friedan found herself in describing the misery—and, yes, alienation—of middle-class housewives in the early 1960s; better words would be forthcoming, but she had to refer to "the problem without a name."

Men are just as likely as women to grasp the ultimate pointlessness of the corporate game and the foolishness of many of the players, but only women have a socially acceptable way out. They can go back to the split-level homes and well-appointed nurseries where Friedan first found them. (That is assuming, of course, they can find a well-heeled husband, and they haven't used up all their child-bearing years in the pursuit of a more masculine model of success.) In fact, this may well be a more personally satisfying option than a work life spent contemplating, say, the fluid dynamics of catsup. As Paul Goodman explained, with as much insight as insensitivity, girls didn't have to worry about "growing up absurd" because they had intrinsically meaningful work cut out for them—motherhood and homemaking.

There is no doubt, from the interviews in *Women Like Us* as well as my own anecdotal sources, that some successful women are indeed using babies as a polite excuse for abandoning the rat race. This is too bad from many perspectives, and certainly for the children who will become the sole focus of their mothers' displaced ambitions. The dropouts themselves would do well to take a look at *The Corporate Couple,* which advises executive wives on the classic problems such as: how to adjust to the annual relocation, how to overcome one's jealousy of a husband's svelte and single female co-workers, and how to help a husband survive his own inevitable existential crisis.

Someday . . . a brilliantly successful corporate woman will suddenly look down at her desk littered with spread sheets and interoffice memos and exclaim, "Is this really worth my time?" At the very same moment a housewife, casting her eyes around a kitchen befouled by toddlers, will ask herself the identical question. As the corporate woman flees out through the corporate atrium, she will run headlong into a housewife, fleeing into it. The two will talk. And in no time at all they will reunite those two distinctly American strands of radicalism—the utopianism of Goodman and the feminism of Friedan. They may also, if they talk long enough, invent some sweet new notion like equal pay for . . . meaningful work.

Review Questions

1. Write a brief critique on the following statement: "Women have gained a real foothold in the corporate world."
2. Comment on the position that a small but significant number of women are deciding "not to have it all" after all, and are dropping out of the corporate world to apply their management skills to kitchen decor and baby care.

MOMMY VS. MOMMY

Nina Darnton

In the 1990s, there is a conflict occurring between many of the mothers who work at home and those who work in the paid work force (and at home—in that there are very few, if any, working mothers who are working solely in the paid work force). In the following reading, "Mommy vs. Mommy," Nina Darnton addresses an important

---

decision that more and more mothers must make in their lives—whether or not to become part of the work force. As you read the article, however, keep in mind that the great majority of employed wives carry a double work load in that they are wage earners and hold almost exclusive responsibility for housework. Calling this the "second shift," Arlie Hochschild reported that husbands do about a third of household chores, but working wives do most of the daily routine chores, such as cooking and cleaning (Hochschild, 1989).

These are the Mommy Wars:

Elaine Cohen, an executive with a New York television company, moved to suburban Westchester County when her son was 3 years old. Although she had a full-time babysitter while she worked, she wanted to find a play group for him. It should have been easy, but it wasn't. "I called everywhere," she says. But the mothers she spoke with made it very clear that children with babysitters weren't welcome. "As soon as I said that I was a working mother, it was as if I had a disease."

Seven hundred miles away, near Chicago, Joanne Brundage ran into very different problems. Brundage quit her job as a letter carrier to take care of her two children. After a few weeks, a friend telephoned and, busy with the baby, Brundage didn't pick up the phone until the fourth ring. "Oh . . . sorry," drawled her friend. "Did I interrupt a crucial moment in your soap opera?"

Every so often a feud erupts that helps to define an era. In the '60s, it was hippies vs. rednecks. In the '70s, the decade of the women's movement, it was women against men. By the mid-'80s, and now into the '90s, it's mothers against mothers—more precisely, mothers who stay at home against mothers who work. This conflict is played out against a backdrop of frustration, insecurity, jealousy and guilt. And because the enemies should be allies, the clash is poignant.

The tension has been building for some time, as women have chosen divergent paths—either devoting themselves to traditional homemaking roles or entering the work force and turning over the daily care of their kids to someone else. The breach was brought into sharp relief recently when Wellesley College students objected to inviting Barbara Bush to speak at the commencement, because they believed that as a stay-at-home wife and mother, who gained recognition through her husband's achievements, she was not a proper role model. And the skirmishes continue. Here are actual bulletins from the front:

"How *nice* that you can walk little Bobby to school every morning," gushes a stay-at-home mother to a harried working mom as she arrives at her son's school. "Otherwise, you'd never *see* him." (Opening salvo.)

"Listen, Sophie *really needs* some fake fur for her princess costume," wheedles a working mom talking to her next-door neighbor. "Since you're home with *so much time,* would you mind picking some up at the store for me?" (Direct hit.)

"Oh, you're a lawyer. How *exciting.* It must be *so much fun* to get dressed up and go to an office all day. And I'm sure that Joey does *just fine* at the day-care center." (Heavy artillery.)

"It's just *great* that you can stay home with your kids all day. You know, you really have to be a *special kind* of person to be able to *do* that. *I* would go *crazy* just talking to kids all day." (Bombs away!)

How did things get so bad? In her recent

book, "Women Together, Women Alone," women's issues writer Anita Shreve comments on confrontations she observed between working and stay-at-home moms. "It was impossible not to draw the conclusion that there exists in America today a deep and sharp division among women," Shreve writes. "And no small cause of that split is that one group feels exploited and/or dismissed by the other."

Picture the working mother. Like most mothers of her generation, she probably grew up in a family with an at-home mom, so she's vulnerable to criticism that she's not spending enough time with her children. She worries about how her kids will turn out. She reads psychological studies about "bonding," and fears she can't do it on a six-week maternity leave, which she's lucky if she gets and which usually comes without pay. She hears media reports—and follows them with self-punishing intensity—about day-care horror stories: sexual abuse, neglect, indifference.

She is anxious that her children are growing up without her, that she's missing the important landmarks in their lives, that someone else will record their first words and first steps. She is rent with conflicts. She wonders if she should exchange career advancement for flexible hours and resign herself to the famous "mommy track." But she chafes at being penalized for motherhood when fathers don't have to make such choices. She's angry because she hasn't many options: her family simply can't get by on one salary. Or, she believes she has a right to a career. Yet she can't help feeling guilty. Moreover, she feels surrounded by moms who are home with their kids. Sure, 56 percent of mothers with kids under 6 are working. But that still means 44 percent are at home.

Mutual attack: No wonder the working mom is jealous of her stay-at-home neighbors. A Boston doctor describes a birthday party her 4-year-old was invited to. "The mother made a pirate party, complete with maps *with burnt edges* stuck in little bottles she buried for a treasure hunt," she says. "I thought, 'I could do that if I had nothing else to do all day too'." She's even jealous of her babysitter. "Sometimes, when I come home, the baby smiles at me, and then puts his arms out to *her*," says a Minneapolis saleswoman. "I *want* him to love her. I just want him to love me more."

The at-home mothers don't make it any easier. A New York secretary leaves her 3-year-old son with another mother during working hours. "She complained that my son didn't like the sandwich I brought him," the secretary says. "I told her that he loves that sandwich. She asked me how I would know since I'm not with him all day. She made me feel like an outsider, like I wasn't part of his life."

The working mother doesn't need this. She is under so much stress trying to be both a good employee and a good mother that even just getting to work in the morning is a major accomplishment. Never mind remembering that she needs to bring 24 valentines for the other kids in the class, or find six yogurt containers for an art project; she also has to make sure her kid brushes her teeth and hair and eats something before the school bus comes.

In the middle of this maelstrom, it's hard for the working mom to feel empathy for her at-home neighbors, especially when she knows they are critical of her. Most working mothers have their particular neighborhood nemesis—the most disapproving at-home mom whom the working mother goes out of her way to avoid. June Lyndsay Hagman, a Minneapolis video producer, describes hers: "She even counted the number of times I went to my son's soccer practice," Hagman says. "She made sure she let me know that she couldn't *imagine* not being there when her child came home from school, as if that proves I love my kids less than she does."

Angry and defensive, the working mom strikes back. She complains that at-home mothers spend so much time doing volunteer work and taking aerobics classes that they don't see their kids much more than the working mother does. She argues that stay-at-home mothers are less interesting than working mothers, even spoiled. When a vice president of a Los Angeles film company—the mother of two young daughters—heard of a "stress workshop" given for the at-home wives of male executives, she laughed. "What stress?" she asks. "Like where to get their nails manicured?"

Now cross the battle lines for a look at the working-at-home mother.

She's usually there because she believes that's best for her children. Either she's lucky and her husband can support them easily, or they've agreed to sacrifice and economize so that they can live on one salary. Once ensconced, however, she is often isolated. She imagined that staying home would be like it was for her mother, with busy neighbors and friends. But she feels surrounded by moms who leave home every day, making her the only at-home mother on her street—her house the one at which the UPS man drops everyone's packages, her phone number the one working friends give to the schools for emergencies. She feels underappreciated by her husband, harried by the housework and the demands of her children.

She reads about "the empty-nest syndrome" and worries about what will happen to her when her kids grow up. She is afraid she will never be able to get back on track with her career. She wishes she could talk to more adults, wishes her husband would come home earlier and, sometimes, is afraid her brain is turning into mashed potatoes. But she disapproves of most of what she sees working mothers do. She thinks they don't spend enough time with their kids, bribe them with expensive presents and keep them up too late at night. She can't help thinking that most of them are selfish: Yuppies who never believe they have enough money. Yet she may still think of herself as a feminist, and she is concerned that by not working she is perpetuating the idea that women belong in the home. She worries that her children won't respect her when they grow up.

Women's movement: No wonder she envies the working mothers she sees getting on trains and buses every morning. They are dressed in clothes she can't afford and doesn't have any place to wear anyway. They look well groomed. She can't remember when she last had time to put makeup on during the day or didn't get something spilled on her blouse. She feels the working mom's children are getting neglected at home, and she is the one expected to pick up the slack. "I used to run the Brownie troop," says Judy Higby, a Connecticut mother. "Pickup time was 4:30, but there was this working mother who never arrived until at least 5. You kind of get fed up."

It's the stay-at-home moms who keep the schools going, the at-home mom grouses. They drive to soccer practice, chaperone class trips, act as class mothers. The children of working moms benefit from these services, but the working moms don't respect the mothers who perform them. "For the latchkey kids who are all over this neighborhood, where do they come when they're lonely, or scared?" asks Gae Bomier, a Burke, Va., mother. "To us."

Nowhere is the resentment more striking than at professional dinners where employees and their spouses "get to know" one another. Psychologist Jay Belsky says his wife, who stayed home to take care of their child, found faculty dinners a nightmare. "The professional women treated the at-home mothers as if they came from another planet," says Belsky. "They were treated like second-class citizens."

It's hard to believe it came to this. In 1960, three years before Betty Friedan published "The Feminine Mystique," only 19 percent of women with children under the age of 6 were in the labor force. By the 1970s, when women first started surging into the workplace, they felt the solidarity of fighting a common oppressor and were exhilarated by their new freedom and independence. They were setting new goals, proving that sex didn't dictate destiny, and they tended to downplay—even denigrate—the traditional roles of wives and mothers. "Families were seen as the problem, not the solution," says Sylvia Hewlett, author of the 1986 controversial book "A Lesser Life: The Myth of Women's Liberation in America." The solution, for some, was not to have families.

But by the late '70s, many women began to find that strategy unfulfilling. Like every generation of women before them, they wanted kids. A few, like Deborah Fallows in The Washington Monthly, gave voice to a rationale for choosing motherhood without guilt. "The boardroom or the corner office, where men have traditionally gone to search for challenge and reward . . . are not the only places to find these rewards . . .," Fallows wrote in her book "A Mother's Work." "There is an honor and legitimacy about . . . raising children."

An economic necessity: But it wasn't as easy as that. Strong economic forces have been at work through the '80s, and as things have gotten tougher, for many families two salaries are not a luxury but a necessity. And many of the women who found fulfillment at work found they also wanted the satisfaction of having children. Why not? They began to speak of having it all. By 1988, 73 percent of mothers of school-age children were working outside the home, as were about half the mothers with infants a year old or younger. But they found the physical and emotional price higher than they expected. Some mothers had limited options: no nationally guaranteed maternity leave (in spite of years of attempts to pass a parental-leave bill, the United States remains the only industrialized nation besides South Africa to have none), few quality day-care centers and almost no part-time professional jobs. With full-time schedules, inflexible hours and only minimal help from their husbands, the exhilaration of having it all turned to exhaustion, and then to anger, a kind of postfeminist backlash among some of the women themselves.

A few dropped out and decided to stay home with their children. Feeling isolated, some joined support groups to encourage their members to feel good about themselves and their choice. One of them, Mothers-At-Home, publishes a monthly newsletter called Welcome Home, which has 13,000 subscribers. It doesn't shy away from gooey maternal aphorisms, such as "My favorite part of the day is . . . seeing my girl's smiling face first thing in the morning," or "If I ever wrote a book about being a mother at home, I would call it . . . 'How to Make Sure You Live a Valuable Life'."

Different solutions: Nostalgia for the days when men were men and women were at home is still strong among some men, perhaps not surprisingly. Esquire, in a June issue dedicated to the American wife, published a collection of articles glorifying life before liberation. Treating women as if they were creatures from a catalog, the magazine offers a section called "Your Wife: An Owner's Manual" (a phrase that would have been unprintable just five years ago). It contains helpful hints about those little female mysteries that bewilder the macho man—everything from the contents of a woman's pocketbook to "her plumbing." In a feature article in praise of a stay-at-home mom, which the magazine incorrectly calls "an endangered species," a male reporter describes her day: "She reaches for the laundry," he writes. "There is a smile on her face, and soon she begins to whistle."

There's a lot more than whistling, however, going on in the trenches of the Mommy Wars. There is an increased sense of purpose, and a growing policy struggle. Both sides have explicit political agendas. Working moms are fighting for all-day kingergarten, guaranteed leave for new parents, improved day care and better tax breaks to deflect the cost. At-home mothers argue against using their tax money for full-day kindergartens they don't need. They want tax breaks to help them stay home and raise their own kids. Some are even against federal aid for better day care, because they say it would encourage mothers to abandon their children for work. Mothers-At-Home published a position paper, "Mothers Speak Out on Child Care," arguing for other solutions for women who need to work and can work out temporary child care from family members: part-time work, flex time and home-based businesses.

In spite of all the tensions, however, there are signs of reconciliation. Recently, in Chicago, 30 mothers got together to discuss themselves and their children. About half of them were members of Women Employed, a working woman's advocacy group. The other half belonged to FEMALE (Formerly Employed Mothers At Loose Ends), an at-home mom's support group. It didn't take long for the mothers to discover their common ground. Most of the at-home moms said they would work if they could find decent part-time jobs, flexible schedules and acceptable child care. All the working moms said they would be home at least part time if they could afford it. Both groups agreed that they needed more options. "Let's face it, being a mother is hard no matter what you do," says June Lindsay Hagman. "We all want what's best for our children."

The problem is we don't all know what the best is. After years of research, most child-development experts agree that different families need to work out different child-care solutions. "I think the notion that one way is right is wrong," says psychologist Sandra Scarr, of the University of Virginia. The most widely accepted research finding also makes the most common sense: depressed mothers on either side tend to have unhappy children. Women who feel happy or satisfied with their role—whatever it is—usually have the healthiest, most self-confident children.

Making peace: Those women also have the most tolerance for the other side. Most mothers remember the special bond they felt with other pregnant women when they carried their own children. They are pained by the current hostilities. Many feel that feminism's first wave didn't give them the alternatives they need. Because of that, some gave up on feminism. But others are determined that the second wave will respond to their needs as workers and as mothers. "This time we're trying to figure it out again," says at-home suburban Chicago mother Michele Miller. "We need to get it right for those women who come after us." But perhaps the mothers can't "get it right" all on their own. It seems likely that a truce won't be possible until Congress passes legislation to give families more choices, without sacrificing either the children's welfare or the mother's individual needs. After all, isn't choice what feminism was supposed to be all about?

Review Questions

1. Examine the various dimensions/factors that differentiate the position of mothers who work in the paid work force from the position of mothers who do not work in the paid work force.
2. Assuming you are, or will become, a mother, do you, or will you, work in the paid work force? Why? If you are, or will become, a father, do you, or will you, want your child's mother to be in the paid work force? Why or why not?

Summary

1. People are organized into a variety of relationships, groups, and organizations. The understanding of social groups and interpersonal relationships is of primary importance to an understanding of human behavior.
2. People's traditions, values, customs, and standards of behavior are found within social groups, are the products of people's interaction within groups, and also form the basis of organized social life.
3. A social group is a unit composed of two or more people who come into contact for a purpose and who consider the contact meaningful. Through group interaction, people learn much about their behavior.
4. Three important processes of human interaction are cooperation, competition, and conflict.
5. Social groups may be deliberately created, spontaneously formed, or externally designated.
6. Primary groups are an important unit of social organization. Within them, people get to know and understand one another intimately and are free to express emotions. Members have common goals and standards and a common spirit of cooperation and sympathy.
7. Primary groups have the following characteristics: small size, face-to-face relationships, relatively frequent contact, and mutual concern. Primary groups have many important functions, such as socializing the individual and offering people a place to be total personalities.
8. Secondary groups have become increasingly important in the United States. They are large and are created for a clearly defined purpose.
9. Secondary relationships characterize secondary groups. A secondary relationship is nonemotional, specialized, and formal; it does not involve the whole personality of the participants. In the United States, secondary groups have tended to dominate one sphere of life after another.

10. Formal organizations are human groupings or social units deliberately constructed or reconstructed to meet specific goals. Filling a broader variety of social and personal needs than they did in the past, organizations command enormous, pervasive social power. Our lives are increasingly lived in the rational, formalistic, emotionally neutral world of organizations.

11. A bureaucracy is a form of organizational structure. It is a formal and rationally organized structure with clearly defined patterns of activity in which, ideally, every series of actions is functionally related to the purposes of the organization.

12. Some sociologists have questioned whether a bureaucracy is actually the most efficient and rational means by which to organize resources to achieve desired ends. Means tend to become ends, and inflexibility and impersonality may cause inefficiency within bureaucratic structures.

13. Informal groups are an outgrowth of and a reaction to bureaucracy. They have their own structures of interrelated roles, statuses, shared beliefs, and values. They operate to counter many of the impersonal effects of bureaucracies.

14. Work is an activity that produces something of value for others. It is also the means by which society's desired and needed goods and services are provided.

15. Work affects one's style of living, life chances, and sense of identity.

STUDY GUIDE

Chapter Objectives

After studying this chapter, you should be able to:

1. List three reasons for studying social groups
2. Give a good sociological definition of "social group"
3. Define the three processes of human interaction
4. Briefly describe how groups come into existence
5. List the major characteristics and functions of primary and secondary groups
6. Define "organizations" and explain their importance in the American society
7. Identify and briefly explain the major components of bureaucracy according to Max Weber

8. Briefly explain the concept of "informal group"
9. Define "work" and its functions
10. Explain what is happening to both men and women in today's work world

Key Terms

Aggregate (p. 130)
Bureaucracy (p. 139)
Career (p. 141)
Category (p. 130)
Competition (p. 130)
Conflict (p. 130)
Cooperation (p. 130)
Formal organization (p. 137)
Hierarchy (p. 141)
Impersonality (p. 141)
Informal group (p. 143)
Office (p. 140)
Organization (p. 137)
Primary relationship (p. 133)
Primary group (p. 133)
Reference group (p. 133)
Rules (p. 140)
Secondary group (p. 135)
Secondary relationship (p. 135)
Social category (p. 130)
Social group (p. 130)
Social organization (p. 137)
Specialization (p. 141)
Work (p. 145)

Self-Test

Short Answer

(p. 137) 1. Social organization refers to ______________________________

(p. 130) 2. A social group is ______________________________

(p. 130) 3. The members of a social group come into meaningful contact for a ______________________________

(p. 130) 4. An aggregate is ______________________________

(p. 130) 5. Three important processes of human interaction are:
a. ______________ c. ______________
b. ______________

(p. 131) 6. Three different kinds of circumstances during which groups come into existence are:
a. ______________________________
b. ______________________________
c. ______________________________

(p. 132) 7. In-groups are ______________________________

(p. 132) 8. Out-groups are ______________________________

(p. 133) 9. According to Cooley, the essential elements of primary groups are ______________________________

(p. 135) 10. A secondary group is ______________________________

(p. 137) 11. According to Parsons, organizations are ______________________________

(p. 137) 12. List three characteristics of organizations:
a. ____________ c. ____________
b. ____________

(p. 139) 13. According to Merton, a bureaucracy is ____________
____

(p. 140) 14. List Weber's six basic characteristics of a bureaucracy:
a. ____________ d. ____________
b. ____________ e. ____________
c. ____________ f. ____________

(p. 142) 15. A criticism of Weber's bureaucratic model is ____________
____

(p. 142) 16. An additional criticism of Weber's model is ____________
____

(p. 143) 17. Informal groups are ____________
____

(p. 144) 18. Prime concerns of informal groups are ____________
____

(p. 144) 19. Informal groups are important because ____________
____
____

(p. 145) 20. Work affects ____________, ____________, and ____________

Multiple Choice *(Answers are on page 169.)*

(p. 130) 1. Groups:
a. are collections of people with similar characteristics and a common identity or understanding of membership
b. give meaning and support to the individual from childhood into adulthood
c. are important in explaining the behavior of people
d. all the above

(p. 130) 2. Which of the following is *not* a group?
a. the V.F.W.
b. the family
c. people waiting for a bus
d. a college fraternity

(p. 130) 3. Which of the following is *not* a social category?
a. all voters
b. all football fans
c. all single mothers
d. none of the above

(p. 130) 4. Which of the following is *not* a major process of human interaction?
a. conflict
b. competition
c. aggression
d. cooperation

(p. 131) 5. Groups are:
a. deliberately created
b. spontaneously formed
c. externally designated
d. all the above

(p. 132) 6. Out-groups:
   a. are groups to which we belong
   b. consist of people in whose presence we feel comfortable
   c. are groups to which we do not belong
   d. none of the above

(p. 135) 7. Secondary groups are:
   a. small
   b. face-to-face
   c. large
   d. none of the above

(p. 133) 8. Primary groups are:
   a. small
   b. formal
   c. specialized
   d. none of the above

(p. 136) 9. A sample primary relationship is:
   a. friend-friend
   b. clerk-customer
   c. author-reader
   d. performer-spectator

(p. 136) 10. A sample secondary physical condition is:
   a. short duration
   b. small number
   c. long duration
   d. spatial proximity

(p. 137) 11. Organizations:
   a. permeate every aspect of urban life
   b. command much social power
   c. are powerful social tools that coordinate many human actions in order to achieve their goals
   d. all the above

(p. 139) 12. Bureaucracy:
   a. is a form of organizational structure
   b. is a social structure with undefined patterns of acting
   c. is technically inferior to other more formal forms of organization
   d. none of the above

(p. 140) 13. Which of the following is *not* one of Weber's basic characteristics of an ideal bureaucracy?
   a. office
   b. rules
   c. personality
   d. hierarchy

(p. 143) 14. In bureaucracies:
   a. rules can become ends in themselves
   b. inflexibility can lead to inefficiency
   c. initiative, imagination, and acceptance of responsibility can be discouraged
   d. all the above

(p. 144) 15. Informal groups:
   a. are no longer an important dimension in formal organizations
   b. form spontaneously as a result of the psychological as well as social needs of the workers
   c. are prescribed or defined by the formal organization
   d. rarely appear in the military or in prisons

(p. 144) 16. Informal groups:
   a. are accidental and tangential
   b. can help the organization as a whole survive unforeseen difficulties
   c. rarely reduce the boredom, monotony, and fatigue of many jobs
   d. none of the above

(p. 145) 17. Today workers in the United States:
   a. are increasingly being employed by large-scale organizations
   b. are mainly self-employed
   c. rarely work in bureaucracies
   d. none of the above

(p. 145) 18. Work:
   a. is the means by which society's desired and needed goods and services are provided
   b. is simply "paid employment"
   c. has few important functions
   d. none of the above

(p. 145) 19. Which of the following is *not* one of Maslow's "order of needs"?
   a. safety
   b. trust
   c. self-esteem
   d. self-actualization

(p. 150) 20. Most women work in American society:
   a. for the fun of it
   b. out of economic necessity
   c. for self-expression
   d. none of the above

True/False *(Answers are on page 169.)*

T F 21. Primary groups are always large. (p. 133)
T F 22. A collection of people waiting for a train is called a group. (p. 130)
T F 23. An aggregate is the same as a group. (p. 130)
T F 24. Primary groups are always small. (p. 133)
T F 25. Face-to-face contact is a characteristic of secondary groups. (p. 135)
T F 26. At times, a social group may consist of only one person. (p. 130)
T F 27. Competition occurs in all societies. (p. 130)
T F 28. Secondary groups are characterized by frequent intimate interaction. (p. 135)
T F 29. In-groups are those to which one belongs. (p. 132)
T F 30. Within the secondary relationship, communication is restricted and specific. (p. 135)
T F 31. Bureaucracies are twentieth-century phenomena. (p. 137)
T F 32. For Weber, a characteristic of bureaucracy is "office." (p. 140)
T F 33. Informal groups are the same as bureaucracies. (p. 143)
T F 34. Bureaucracy is an example of a secondary group. (p. 139)

T F 35. Organizations conform exactly to Weber's ideal type of bureaucracy. (p. 142)

T F 36. Bureaucrats basically function in terms of rules and regulations that are established to meet standard situations. (p. 140)

T F 37. Work is the means by which society's desired and needed goods and services are provided. (p. 145)

T F 38. A person's sense of identity is no longer shaped by work. (p. 145)

T F 39. For Maslow, when people's needs are met at one level, the next level becomes important. (p. 145)

T F 40. In America, most women work out of economic necessity. (p. 150)

Fill In *(Answers are on page 169.)*

(p. 130) 41. _______ give meaning and support to the individual from childhood into adulthood.

(p. 130) 42. _______ is the interaction among individuals or groups of people to achieve shared goals or promote common interests.

(p. 132) 43. _______ are groups to which we belong.

(p. 132) 44. _______ are characterized by frequent intimate interaction.

(p. 135) 45. Within the _______ relationship, communication is restricted and specific.

(p. 130) 46. A _______ is a collection of people with similar characteristics but no common identity or understanding of membership and no involvement in patterned social interaction.

(p. 133) 47. A _______ is any group that an individual takes into account when evaluating his or her behavior and self-concept.

(p. 131) 48. _______ may be deliberately created, spontaneously formed, or externally designated.

(p. 135) 49. _______ relationships characterize secondary groups.

(p. 135) 50. In the United States, _______ relationships have tended to dominate one sphere of life after another.

(p. 137) 51. _______ are characterized by a deliberately planned division of labor, power, and communication responsibilities and the presence of goal-oriented and controlling power centers.

(p. 143) 52. Organizations can be formal or _______ .

(p. 137) 53. _______ organizations are technically superior to other forms of organization.

(p. 141) 54. For Weber, the hierarchy locates _______ .

(p. 143) 55. _______ expands to fill the amount of time available for its completion.

(p. 145) 56. A person's sense of _______ is very much shaped by work.

(p. 145) 57. For Maslow, _______ is the ability to realize one's potential to the fullest.

(p. 144) 58. _______ groups can appear without formal organization of any kind.

(p. 144) 59. The Hawthorne study indicated that workers are to be viewed as ______ members.

(p. 145) 60. ______ is an activity that produces something of value for others.

Matching (Answers are on page 169.)

61. ______ Group
62. ______ Cooperation
63. ______ Secondary relationship
64. ______ Out-groups
65. ______ Bureaucracy
66. ______ Rules and career
67. ______ Peter Principle
68. ______ Work
69. ______ Bureaucratic inefficiency
70. ______ Maslow

a. Groups to which we do not belong
b. A family or the V.F.W.
c. Clerk-customer
d. Social process
e. Hierarchical needs
f. Robert Merton
g. Weber's characteristics of bureaucracy
h. Rise to your level of incompetence
i. "Pyramid"
j. An activity that produces something of value for others

Essay Questions

1. What is a social group?
2. Explain why social groups are important.
3. Identify and compare the three processes of human interaction.
4. What are the three different kinds of circumstances under which groups come into existence?
5. What is the difference between an in-group and an out-group?
6. What are the major characteristics and functions of primary groups?
7. What are the major characteristics and functions of secondary groups?
8. What is a bureaucracy?
9. What are the basic characteristics of a bureaucracy according to Max Weber?
10. Why are bureaucracies important, and what are some of their problems?
11. What are informal groups, and why are they important?
12. What is work, and why is it important?

Interactive Exercises

1. In this chapter, we have examined how members of primary groups such as peer groups and families are bound together by primary, emotional relationships. Which primary relationships—your family or peer relationships—have had the greatest impact upon your life? Why have they had this impact?

2. Secondary relationships and groups have gained in importance and have tended to dominate one sphere of life after another. Briefly analyze the future of America in terms of a continuing shift from primary groups and relationships to secondary groups and relationships. What kind of impact do you believe this shift will have upon your personal life? Give examples.

3. Virtually all of us have been members of, or have had contact with, some large bureaucratic organizations. How has bureaucracy had an impact upon you in your role of student (the college bureaucracy), and citizen (the town, city, state, or federal bureaucracy)? Was this a positive or negative experience?

4. Today many Americans are employed in large bureaucratic organizations. Most bureaucratic organizations are structured so as to clash with the expectations and needs of workers. This may result in worker dissatisfaction and poor health. How do people in your current or future career or profession deal with the issues and problems that arise in their bureaucratic organizations (or those with which they come in contact)?

Answers

Answers to Self-Test

1. d
2. c
3. d
4. c
5. d
6. c
7. c
8. a
9. a
10. a
11. d
12. a
13. c
14. d
15. b
16. b
17. a
18. a
19. b
20. b
21. F
22. F
23. F
24. T
25. F
26. F
27. T
28. F
29. T
30. T
31. F
32. T
33. F
34. T
35. F
36. T
37. T
38. F
39. T
40. T
41. groups
42. cooperation
43. in-groups
44. primary groups
45. secondary
46. category
47. reference group
48. social groups
49. secondary
50. secondary
51. organizations
52. informal
53. bureaucratic
54. responsibility
55. work
56. identity
57. self-actualization
58. informal
59. group
60. work
61. b
62. d
63. c
64. a
65. i
66. g
67. h
68. j
69. f
70. e

Answers to Chapter Pretest

1. F
2. F
3. F
4. T
5. T
6. T
7. T
8. T

Chapter 5

Deviant Behavior and Social Control

Chapter Pretest

Let's see how much you already know about topics in this chapter:

1. **Deviant behavior is found only within complex industrial societies. True/False**
2. **Deviant behavior may help strengthen group norms and values. True/False**
3. **Lying is a fairly uncommon form of behavior in our society. True/False**
4. **All forms of drug use and crime decline sharply as offenders grow older. True/False**
5. **At present, there are approximately 8 million alcoholics and alcohol abusers in the United States. True/False**
6. **In our society, about one out of every four homes has been affected by some type of alcohol-related family problem. True/False**
7. **About one-third of Americans experience some type of mental disorder during their lifetime. True/False**
8. **In the United States, suicide occurs more frequently among females than among males. True/False**

The Nature of Deviant Behavior

When sociologists speak of deviant behavior, they are referring to behavior that does not conform to norms—behavior that in some way does not meet with the expectations of a group or of society as a whole. Although this definition represents an adequate starting point for our analysis, we will present a more specific definition of deviant behavior in the pages to come. First, however, we will develop a few general points about the nature of social control and deviant behavior.

It should be evident from the preceding chapters that many mechanisms that have the sole purpose of bringing about conformity are built into social life. Chief among these, as we have seen in Chapter 3, is the socialization process itself. Shortly after birth, the child begins to have experiences with others. Through these experiences, the child is taught what he or she should and should not do, what is good or bad, and what is right or wrong. Early socialization consists largely of the development of habits that conform to the customs and traditions of the groups into which the child is born. Children also learn a system of values that provides justification and motivation for wanting to do certain types of things that are approved by parents and peers and, likewise, for wanting to refrain from behavior that is disapproved. Ultimately, as we have seen, socialization results in the development of a system of internal or self-controls—a self-regulating conscience, a *superego* or *me*—that incorporates the internalized values and norms of parents and peers. Thus, to a large degree, conformity results from a system of internal controls or restraints developed *within* the individual during the process of socialization.

Early socialization: the development of internal social control

In addition to internal controls, conformity is induced through external mechanisms. Thus each day the person experiences pressures to meet the expectations of others. Often we think of these expectations as obligations that we owe to others in return for things they have done for us. From a sociological point of view, many of these expectations are of this reciprocal nature and become standardized over time as a result of being linked to the roles we play within groups and society. Thus each role carries with it a set of rights as well as duties to be carried out in our relationships with others. A failure to meet these expectations usually results in the application of sanctions that might involve snubbing, ridicule, or ostracism within small informal primary groups. Within large formal groups, such as corporations, unions, professional associations, and churches, sanctions are often more formal—loss of pay, suspension, or permanent expulsion.

External control may be formal and/or informal

The form and severity of sanctions vary, depending on the type of group and also on the degree of importance assigned to the fulfillment of certain expectations. The ultimate external mechanism used to maintain conformity and order within society is the state. The state represents the final authority within society and possesses a monopoly over the use of coercion for the purpose of maintaining order. Thus the state has legitimate authority to apply a variety of penalties for behavior that violates society's laws. These penalties range from fines, to imprisonment, to the ultimate penalty, death. Reliance on formal authority for the maintenance of order and social control tends to increase as societies become larger, more industrialized, and urbanized. The development of formal law and the increased use of the state's law enforcement and judicial machinery is usually a result of the deterioration of more informal social control mechanisms characteristic of smaller and less complex societies.

Despite the presence of various mechanisms for the maintenance of social control and conformity, deviance can be found throughout human history and in every society. Indeed, deviance and the accompanying social reactions may have both negative as well as positive consequences.

Deviance is a universal phenomenon

On the negative side, large-scale deviance may harm group stability, and it may induce distrust and ill will. Combating deviance may drain a society of important human and economic resources that otherwise might be used for worthwhile purposes. Finally, if deviance were to become the norm, it might weaken people's faith in and conformity to social norms and values.

The positive and negative consequences of deviance

Deviance also has a number of positive consequences. For one, each time a group defines a particular act as deviant, it teaches people what is acceptable social behavior. For this reason, all groups, even the most highly disciplined and regimented, have (and in a sense *need*) social deviants. Second, rather than producing social havoc, deviance may strengthen group norms and values. In opposing the deviant, group members actually reinforce their commitment to the group and its standards. Finally, deviance may be both sign and source of needed social change. The history of a number of social movements in our society clearly shows that commitment to change may begin in deviance from existing norms.

The Relativity of Deviance

Although, simply described, deviant behavior is that behavior that does not conform to social norms, adequate sociological analysis of just what constitutes specific types of deviant behavior faces many problems and ambiguities. These difficulties, in large part, arise from the fact that deviant behavior is *relative* to many complex factors and conditions, all of which must be taken into consideration.

Time

The specification of the types of behavior viewed as deviant and the degree to which these behaviors are considered deviant changes over time.

The meaning of deviance changes through the years

Homosexuality, for example, although no doubt still considered deviant by many Americans, does not often produce the severe ridicule and contempt that it did a generation or so past. Smoking by teen-agers and women (at least in public) was at one time branded as a sign of demoralization and corruption, and laws were enacted during the early part of this century forbidding young people to smoke. The sale of patent medicines containing opium derivatives was legal prior to the passage of the Pure Food and Drug Act in 1906. Thereafter such practices became crimes. Likewise, the late 1950s and early 1960s witnessed an increased concern over the rise of drug use, particularly that of marijuana and LSD. This concern eventually led to the passage of more restrictive drug-control legislation and enforcement practices. As a result, the number of arrests for the possession, use, and sale of various drugs increased dramatically in the 1960s compared with the previous decade, with the majority of arrests involving people 21 years of age or younger.

Place

Behaviors considered deviant also vary according to geographic area. Homosexuality, for instance, meets with general public disapproval in the majority of western European countries; but in most of these societies, a homosexual act is not a criminal offense, at least when performed in private. In the United States, many but not all states currently define only publicly committed homosexual acts as criminal. Prostitution and some forms of gambling are legal in some states and not in others. The sale of alcoholic beverages is legally prohibited in thousands of counties throughout the United States. Legal penalties for the use of marijuana range from 5 to 10 years imprisonment in some states to a small fine in others.

Subcultures

A conforming act within a subculture may be considered deviant by the larger society

As we mentioned previously, complex modern societies are usually composed of a multitude of subcultures based on class, occupation, race, and nationality. Each of these subcultures shares in the larger culture in the sense that it is aware of and conforms to many of the norms and values of the general culture. But subcultures maintain distinctive values and norms that tend to distinguish their members from the larger society. In certain respects, the existence of subcultures complicates the understanding of deviant behavior. Because different subcultures hold at least some different norms, behavior considered deviant also varies from subculture to subculture. Likewise, and perhaps more important, what is seen as conformity to the norms of the subculture may be viewed as deviant from the norms of the society. Thus a delinquent gang member who carries a gun or knife, who gets involved in an occasional gang war, and who displays aggression with a minimum of provocation could be defined as a conformist to the norms of the gang subculture and at the same time as deviant and perhaps even criminal in terms of the norms of the general society (Yablonsky, 1961).

Deviant Behavior as Disapproved Behavior

Although deviance may occur in both approved and disapproved modes, we are generally concerned with disapproved behavior

Reactions of others to deviance range from social approval to severe disapproval. Thus, for instance, from the standpoint of general norms of society, certain types of behavior—such as exceptionally high academic performance, great thrift, ambition, or dedication to the needs of others—may constitute approved deviation. These qualities or achievements far exceed the standards and expectations of others.

In almost all cases, however, when sociologists speak of deviant behavior, they are concerned with behavior that deviates from norms and expectations of others in a disapproved direction. Behaviors such as crime, delinquency, and drug addiction constitute *disapproved* forms of deviation. For the most part, society is far more aware of and concerned about these forms of deviation than with behaviors that constitute overconformity to its norms.

Deviant Behavior and Social Tolerance

Reactions to deviance also vary by *intensity*. Violations of some norms of etiquette, for instance, may meet with only mild disapproval and sanctions, whereas violations of other norms, such as those prohibiting murder, rape, or robbery, may meet with strong disapproval and severe sanctions. Each particular norm has a **tolerance limit,** the degree to which norm violations are tolerated or suppressed by a group. As one would expect, the severity of the sanctions serves as an index of the group's willingness to tolerate violations of the norms. Because some norms are seen as more important or vital than others, more stringent tolerance limits and more severe sanctions are applied to violations of them.

The degree of tolerance of deviance also is relative to *who* is engaging in the behavior. For example, petty theft or minor acts of vandalism that might be thought of as mischief or practical jokes when acted out by upper- or middle-class teenagers might be defined as criminal when performed by lower-class teenagers. One's position within a group or society thus influences how others react to and judge one's behavior.

Tolerance toward deviance depends greatly on who is engaging in the behavior

The preceding analysis has illustrated an important idea; namely, that deviant behavior refers to those human acts that are *socially* defined by the group or society as deviant. Thus deviance is relative to the norms of the group. We have emphasized that norms defining behavior as deviant show tremendous variation. What is deviant in one culture may not be deviant in another culture. What is deviant at one time, in one geographic area of a society, or in one subculture may not be deviant in another time, area, or subculture. Finally, social reactions to deviance vary from approval to disapproval. Ultimately, therefore, *"social groups create deviance by making the rules whose infraction constitutes deviance"* (Becker, 1963). From the sociological point of view, what is considered deviant behavior is entirely relative to and dependent on group or social definitions. In this sense, no human act is inherently evil or immoral. Even the act of killing someone is not necessarily defined as criminal when it is acted out in self-defense, by a police officer in the line of duty, or by a soldier against the enemy in war. Acts *become* deviant only when groups define them as such, and this social definition is relative to various situations, circumstances, and conditions. Likewise, the general conception that "deviant" people are in some respects really different (in the sense of abnormal or pathological) from the rest of us "normal" people warrants criticism (Becker, 1963). Because, as we have said, norms are *relative*, the carrying of a knife by a member of a juvenile gang may very well constitute conformity to the norms of the subculture to which he or she has been socialized. In fact, it is generally true that all people at one time or another are deviant because they have violated at least some norms—sometimes "important" norms. Thus people are not generally or totally deviant. They are deviant from some norms some of the time but probably not from most norms most of the time.

Deviance is relative to group norms

Everyone commits deviant acts at one time or another

We now define **deviant behavior** as referring to "only those deviations in which behavior is in a disapproved direction and of sufficient degree to exceed the tolerance limit of the community" (Clinard, 1968). In the rest of this chapter, we describe some of the most strongly disapproved forms of deviant behavior in American society and some of the sociological explanations for these types of deviant behavior.

Deviance is a matter of social definition

GROUND RULES FOR TELLING LIES

As we have noted, deviance is a matter of group or social definition. Over time, groups develop norms about which acts, under what conditions, are to be judged as deviant. The following reading discusses a form of behavior with which we all are familiar—lying. Lying has become widespread in society, yet as the reading points out, there are few norms for judging when and under what conditions it should be considered deviant. In her book *Lying* (1978), Sissela Bok argues that only certain kinds of lies—those that are approved in advance by the public—should be permitted. The reading illustrates the difficulties and deliberations that groups face in trying to determine the conditions under which behaviors should be defined as deviant.

When is it permissible to tell a lie? Never, according to Augustine and Kant. Machiavelli approved lying for princes, Nietzsche for the exceptional hero—the Superman. Most other philosophers and ordinary folk are less certain, allowing some lies, but not others. After some 2,500 years of moral speculation, says Philosopher Sissela Bok, mankind is still trying to work out ground rules for acceptable lying.

In her new book, *Lying,* Bok—the wife of Harvard president Derek Bok and daughter of Swedish sociologist Gunnar Myrdal—traces the history of convoluted arguments on the subject. For instance, Grotius said that speaking falsely to an intruder is not a lie. This, Bok suggests, would be something like knocking a man to the ground, then explaining that you did not hit him because he had no right to be there. Kant insisted that all lies were immoral—even those told to a murderer to protect an innocent life. Erasmus disagreed, but Cardinal Newman sympathized with Kant. His solution: instead of lying to the murderer, knock him down and call the cops. Casuists invented the "mental reservation." Example: "Mr. Smith is not in today"—a lie that is magically transformed into a truth by adding the unspoken thought "to you." The Talmud allows lies for "bed" (inquiries into one's sex life) and "hospitality" (if a host was generous, one could lie about it so that the host would not be inundated by unwelcome guests).

Most norms on lying, Bok writes, grow out of elaborate moral systems of thought that "are often elegant in operation, noble in design. But when we have to make difficult concrete moral choices, they give us little help." In the absence of clear social guidelines, she says, casual lying has become entrenched in America. Indeed, Social Psychologist Jerald Jellison estimates that the average American outstrips Pinocchio by telling a whopping 200 lies a day, including white lies and false excuses ("Sorry I'm late. I was tied up at the office").

Bok thinks that the problem is a practical one, because lying by the government has begun to corrupt our politics: 69% of the public, according to Cambridge Survey Research, believe that the country's leaders have consistently lied to them over the past ten years. Bok also argues that lying is now an accepted part of many professions, including law and the behavioral sciences. In a typical experiment in social psychology, for example, a subject is misled about the aims of the study to see how he reacts under pressure.

In medicine, prescribing placebos and lying to patients are commonplace. Says Bok, who teaches medical ethics at the Harvard Medical School: "The requirement to be honest with patients has been left out altogether from medical oaths and codes of ethics, and is often ignored, if not actually disparaged, in the teaching of medicine." Bok sees problems in journalism too. Reporters Bernstein and Woodward, she says, seemed untroubled by "the whole fabric of deception" they used to uncover the Watergate scandal. Those lies, she maintains, were not clearly necessary and may encourage other reporters to use such tactics routinely.

What kinds of lies should be permitted? Bok's answer: only those approved in advance by the general public. The use of unmarked police cars is one example of socially approved deception. By this standard, she argues, political lies are rarely justifiable. "If government duplicity is to be allowed in exceptional cases," Bok concludes, "the criteria for these exceptions should themselves be openly debated and publicly chosen. Otherwise government leaders will have free rein to manipulate and distort the facts."

Bok feels that doctors should stop virtually all lying to patients, universities should root out fraudulent and deceptive research, and government officials should be expected to stick to the truth. Her point: the public is now so cynical about being lied to that only extraordinary efforts to avoid lying will restore a feeling of trust. Or, as Mark Twain once observed, "Always do right. This will gratify some people, and astonish the rest."

Review Questions

1. Discuss the positions of various philosophers and religious scholars about lying.
2. List several examples of lying and deceptive practices found within our institutional systems (government, education, medicine, law, and science).
3. Formulate your own ground rules for lying, and give reasons for them.

Major Varieties of Deviant Behavior

This section briefly examines some highly disapproved varieties of deviant behavior in American society. There is a wide variety of such behavior, and we can choose only a few examples for analysis: crime, drug abuse, alcoholism, mental disorders, and suicide.

Crime

A **crime** is a violation of any one of the specific types of norms that we call laws. Conviction for violation of a law results in application of certain sanctions or

Crime violates a legislated norm

punishments to the offender, which can range from fines, to imprisonment, to death. More serious offenses, such as criminal homicide, rape, aggravated assault, and robbery, are legally termed **felonies** and receive penalties of a minimum of one year of imprisonment in a state or federal penitentiary, a very heavy fine, or both. Less serious offenses, such as petty theft, disorderly conduct, and vagrancy, are legally termed **misdemeanors,** the punishment for which involves confinement in a local or county jail for a period of less than one year, a limited fine, or both.

Major Crime. Since 1930, the Federal Bureau of Investigation (FBI), through the U.S. Department of Justice, has published a bulletin entitled *Uniform Crime Reports.** This publication contains data with respect to the FBI's list of Crime Index offenses consisting of murder and nonnegligent manslaughter, forcible rape, robbery, aggravated assault, burglary, larceny, auto theft, and arson. These data indicate that in 1989, 14.3 million offenses were reported throughout the United States. During the period from 1985 to 1989, *Uniform Crime Reports* indicated an increase of 15 percent in the number of reported Crime Index offenses throughout the United States. The number of violent crimes (murder and nonnegligent manslaughter, forcible rape, robbery, and aggravated assault) increased 23.9 percent, and the number of property crimes (burglary, larceny, and auto theft) increased 13.5 percent within this five-year period. Figure 5.1 shows the total change over the same period. Over the 10-year period from 1980 to 1989, the number of reported Crime Index offenses increased by 6.3 percent, with violent crimes increasing 22.4 percent and property crimes 4.5 percent.

The actual meaning of these statistics is difficult to determine, because such increases may reflect, in part, improvements in data reporting by the public and recording by law enforcement agencies. Statistics such as these, of course, do not tell the whole story, for there are, no doubt, many crimes that go unreported. In addition, various offenses are difficult to detect and are not usually included in official crime statistics. Such offenses include organized crime and various white-collar crimes.

Sutherland's definition of white-collar crime

White-Collar Crime. Criminologist Edwin H. Sutherland has defined **white-collar crime** as "crimes committed by persons of respectability and high social status in the course of their occupations." In his classic study, *White Collar Crime* (1949), Sutherland examined various forms of white-collar crime, including violations of patent infringement, restraint of trade, false advertising, and unfair labor practices. Today the concept of white-collar crime has been expanded to include a number of "occupational" crimes, including fraud, embezzlement, false advertising, political bribery, fee splitting, antitrust violations, and employee theft. We do not know the exact economic cost to society of white-collar crime, but it is surely greater than that of property index crime (those crimes against property that have been included in the Crime Index total).

One dimension of white-collar crime that has increased dramatically in

* In the following sections, all statistical data on reported crime and arrests as they concern adult crime, delinquency, drug abuse, and use of alcoholic beverages come from the *Uniform Crime Reports,* August 1990, as well as other specifically selected years.

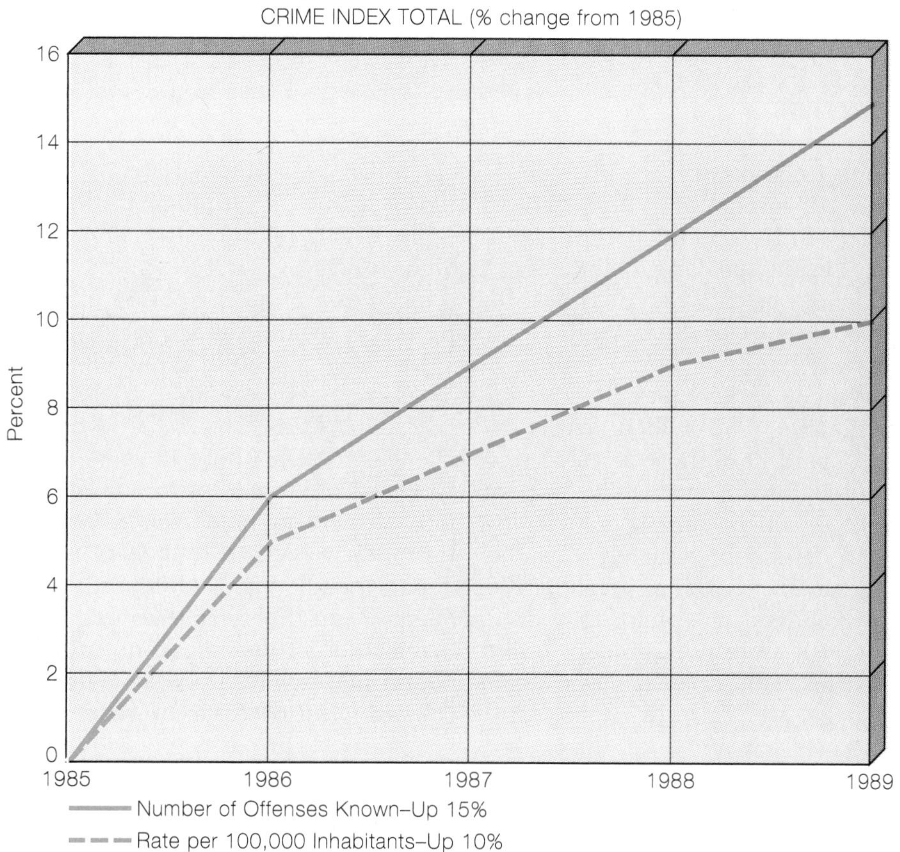

Figure 5.1 **Crime and population, 1985–1989.**
Source: *Uniform Crime Reports, 1989,* p. 45.

recent years is that of computer crime—also referred to as computer-related crime or computer abuse. The increased availability and use of computers in recent decades has brought with it greater opportunities to use this new technology for both legal as well as illegal purposes. Although computer crimes often take the form of embezzlement or employee theft, it appears that the variety of computer-related crimes is expanding. C. R. Swanson and Leonard Territo (1980), for example, have outlined a number of categories within which computer crimes often fall. This list would include, in part, (1) theft of services, where an individual who is authorized makes use of a computer for a purpose which is unauthorized or where an individual who is unauthorized gains access to the computer system; (2) information crimes, where individuals use data found within a computer for personal advantage and profit; (3) financial crimes, where computers used in financial processing are employed to obtain assets in fraudulent ways; and (4) property crimes, in which a computer is used to illegally acquire property which, in turn, is either sold or used for personal

There is a wide diversity of computer crime

benefit. Annual losses from computer crimes have been estimated to be as much as $5 billion (Barlow, 1990). Still, this is relatively small compared with the cost of white-collar crime in general, which has been estimated at $44 billion annually (Velocci, 1978).

Juvenile Delinquency. Juvenile delinquency is an additional area of crime not fully incorporated within general crime statistics. **Delinquency** refers to violations of laws on the part of young people, usually 16 to 18 years of age and under. Legally speaking, delinquency pertains to all acts that if committed by an adult would be considered crimes. It also includes a number of other offenses that pertain specifically to youth, including acts of truancy, incorrigibility, running away, and violation of curfew laws. Just as in the adult population, the involvement of juveniles in criminal acts is high. For example, there were approximately 14.3 million arrests made throughout the United States during 1989; 15 percent of those arrested were juveniles. People under 18 years of age accounted for approximately 39 percent of all the arrests for vandalism, 29 percent of all the arrests for larceny-theft, 32 percent of all the arrests for burglary, and approximately 42 percent for motor vehicle theft and arson.

Juveniles contribute far more than their share to certain crimes

Generally speaking, juvenile offenders are handled quite differently from adult offenders. The philosophy of juvenile law and the juvenile court system accentuates protection, guidance, and rehabilitation of juveniles—not punishment. This philosophy is based on the notion that juveniles, because of their young age, are not really capable of the *criminal intent* necessary to harm other people maliciously.

The philosophy of juvenile law and juvenile court has tended to stress "rehabilitation"

According to juvenile law, the offender is admitted into custody and receives a hearing. Upon the decision of the juvenile court, the offender is committed into a school or home for juvenile offenders. Thus the offender is not actually tried, convicted, or sentenced as in the adult criminal justice system.

In recent years, increasing numbers of people have begun to question the philosophy of the juvenile justice system. Because of the substantial growth in juvenile crime—particularly violent crime—and the criticism that the system for handling youths neither punishes nor reforms, a number of reforms soon may be instituted within the juvenile justice system. Such reforms would ensure a more lenient approach to the handling of the nonviolent status offender—the curfew violator, truant, or runaway child. The aim would be to decriminalize some of these offenses and find help for the juvenile in the broader community. But the new reforms would mean a much tougher approach to the handling of juveniles who commit violent crimes. In these cases, definite and longer-term punishment would be emphasized. The juvenile courts would be guided by the principle of letting the punishment fit the crime.

As in the case of juvenile crime, more and more of the public (and many experts) are also of the opinion that punishment and retribution rather than rehabilitation and reform should be the new philosophy in dealing with the adult offender—particularly the serious offender. Today a number of changes aimed at correcting certain inadequacies and imbalances within our criminal justice system are being considered and acted upon. There has been a growing trend toward replacing indeterminate prison sentences with mandatory and fixed sentences.

WHY WE'RE LOSING THE WAR ON CRIME

Michael Gottfredson and Travis Hirschi

As we have seen, crime is a serious social problem in the United States. In recent years, a "get-tough" approach to fighting crime has been the dominant strategy. Mandatory prison sentences have become more and more common, and the prison population across the country has increased greatly. The following article questions the idea that more law enforcement personnel, more prosecutors, and more prisons will act to bring down the crime rate. The authors argue that current crime policy fails to consider the diversity of crimes that individuals commit and ignores the importance of focusing crime prevention efforts on children.

President Bush's long-awaited national strategy to combat the drug problem puts great faith in the potential of conventional law-enforcement strategies and governmental intervention. The Democrats' response differs chiefly in degree, not in kind, with the high ground seeming to belong to those who would spend more.

But the hard-line programs proposed by the president—more prisons, more prosecutors, more hardware for the border patrol, more law enforcement officials, more drug testers—taken together, will have little impact on the crime rate or the drug problem.

The $8 billion earmarked by President Bush for the New War on Drugs would go atop the $44 billion already spent each year at all levels of government for police and prisons—along with tens of billions more for customs agents, judges, probation and parole officers.

Since the early '70s and the backlash against Great Society programs, everyone seems to agree that the key to crime and drug abuse is to be found in the criminal justice system—in the workings of the police, courts and prisons—and not in economic or social conditions. This consensus has powered the immense growth in law-enforcement organizations, anti-crime programs (e.g., drug testing, "career-criminal" units, mandatory sentencing), and the number of people in jails and prisons.

According to the federal Bureau of Justice Statistics, expenditures for criminal justice in the last few years have increased four times as rapidly as for education, and twice as rapidly as for health and hospitals. Since 1980, the number of adults behind bars has doubled. As of January, 627,000 adults were incarcerated in federal and state prisons. The latest figures show that 1 adult in 55 is under some form of correctional supervision.

But all the effort and money have not bought relief from crime. According to FBI figures, the crime rate peaked about 1980, declined for a few years, and then increased for the past four years. (The mild downturn of the early '80s resulted from the aging of baby-boomers. The peak age of incarceration comes a few years after the peak age of crime. This fact, coupled with tougher sentencing policies, accounts for the increase in the numbers incarcerated.)

No one can substantiate the slightest reduction in drug use or the rate of crime as a

---

From *The Washington Post Magazine*, September 10, 1989, p. C3.

consequence of increases in expenditures in the '80s, and there is no reason to think these failed government programs will now work simply because even more money is thrown their way. In fact, there are good reasons to believe otherwise. The latest scientific research on crime and drug use does not accord with the law-enforcement image of criminals and drug dealers as sophisticated, cunning, persistent and highly organized. Nor does it support the view that strengthening the crime-control apparatus is our only hope.

In fact, the research paints quite a different picture. Studies of the most common criminal events show that they are generally acts of force, fraud or mood enhancement in the pursuit of immediate self-interest. The typical burglary or robbery takes little effort, little time and little skill.

The typical burglar takes advantage of opportunities of the moment; he lives in the neighborhood and victimizes easy targets—such as houses with unlocked doors—carrying away whatever seems of value. The typical car thief finds a car with the keys in the ignition and drives until the gas tank is empty. The typical drug user is satisfied with whatever drug is available at a suitable price. Consequently, most lavish police operations involving costly high-tech hardware are irrelevant to reducing the number of typical crimes. Solid research studies show that most ordinary crimes can be prevented by the presence of even the most minor obstacles: locks on doors, keys taken out of ignitions, reduced late-night hours for convenience stores, and the like.

Nor do the crime data indicate that putting more cops on the street will decrease the frequency of offenses. Daily life presents practically limitless opportunities for crime or drug use. As a result, prevention by policing is nearly impossible. In fact, a growing body of research documents the negligible impact of police patrols in lowering the crime rate.

Moreover, it is becoming clear that criminals and drug abusers are also less complex and less driven than current policies suggest. Indeed, two facts about offenders are directly at odds with the assumptions found in law-enforcement policies. Unless these misconceptions are corrected, there is little hope for efficient and realistic crime policy.

RANDOM PATTERNS

The first fact is this: Offenders are extraordinarily versatile in their choice of criminal and deviant acts. That is, the same people who use drugs also steal cars, commit burglaries, assault and rob others and drive recklessly. Indeed, they are so versatile that knowing their prior offenses does not permit us to predict what crimes they will commit in the future. Despite decades of study, criminologists have failed to discover meaningful numbers of criminal specialists—people who commit particular crimes to the exclusion of others.

For example, when researchers at the University of Pennsylvania followed to age 30 nearly 10,000 boys born in 1945, they discovered virtually no pattern or specialization in each individual's offenses recorded in police files.

The versatility of offenders goes beyond conventional crime categories to include alcohol abuse, spouse and child abuse, accidents, truancy from school and work, and sexual promiscuity. Research repeatedly shows that these behaviors are consistently found together in the same people. A celebrated study by Lee Robins at Washington University tracked over 500 children referred to a guidance clinic over the course of 30 years, comparing them with a control group. As adults, the clinic children were more likely to be arrested for a wide variety of offenses, more likely to be divorced, to be unemployed, to be on welfare, to use alcohol excessively and to be hospitalized for psychiatric problems.

What explains this amazingly dependable correlation among such diverse acts? We believe it is a common element: All of them produce immediate pleasure without regard to potential long-term consequences. This general tendency to engage in such acts we call "low self-control."

Indeed, recent research into offender motivation casts doubt on the standard explanations of drug use and criminal behavior, and on the supposed connection between them. It suggests instead that when adolescents use drugs they are merely seeking an immediate good feeling—and that no deeper social, psychological or economic motives are involved.

Thus, in committing auto theft, the offender is not pursuing upward mobility, doing what his culture requires him to do or pondering the possibility that a third felony on his record will make him eligible for career criminal sentencing. Instead, he is merely seeking easy transportation in a good looking car. If auto theft and drug use go together, it is not because one is the cause of the other, but because both produce immediate benefits for an offender who pays little attention to long-term costs. This directly contradicts two basic assumptions of contemporary law enforcement: that fear of lengthy prison terms deters offenders from their acts; and that a war on drugs can be separated from a war on crime in general.

A TIME FOR EVERY PURPOSE

The second problematic fact about criminal behavior is that all forms of drug use and crime decline sharply as offenders grow older. This phenomenon has proven astonishingly stable through time. Early in this century, the British criminologist Charles Goring reported that age statistics of conviction "obey natural laws of frequency."

Current research reaffirms Goring's findings: The age-distribution curve of crime in the United States today is virtually identical to the one produced by English convicts over three-quarters of a century ago. That is, the propensity to commit crime increases very rapidly throughout adolescence, peaks in the late teens, then declines quickly and steadily throughout adulthood.

The implications for current drug and crime policy are profound. The decline in crime and drug use with age is so steep that it overwhelms most crime-control strategies that focus on the offender, such as incarceration and rehabilitation. After all, if the vast majority of offenders are teenagers, and if they rapidly quit using drugs and committing crimes of their own accord, what is the point of incarcerating them well into adulthood, or, for that matter, treating them after the problem is over? The present fascination with ever-longer sentences and abolition of parole implies enormous expenditures for almost no payoff in terms of crime reduction.

The age effect is so strong and so obvious to correctional officials that it tends to undermine the resolve to hold prisoners "for the rest of their natural lives." After 30 years in prison, what danger does the 50-year-old "career robber" pose to society? The rate of robbery in that age group is one-fiftieth the rate for 17-year-olds. More to the point of the proposed drug sentencing policies (and arguments about large financial benefit from imprisonment), what can be the advantage of adding 10 years to sentences that already exceed the active life of the typical offender? Why lock up drug offenders well beyond the age of active substance abuse? Taxpayers may be fooled into thinking they are safer with longer sentences, but when these sentences keep offenders behind bars into middle age (at an average cost, per year, of $25,000 per offender), they should keep their hands more firmly on their wallets.

BRINGING THE WAR HOME

Any potentially successful plan to combat crime must acknowledge that individual differences in the tendency to commit crimes and use drugs remain reasonably stable over the life course. People who do these things when they are very young tend to do them as adolescents, and to have higher rates than others as adults. People who abstain as adolescents, on the other hand, tend to abstain throughout life. Even when the "crime years" are essentially over, those active as adolescents will be found to have relatively high rates of noncriminal deviant behavior—such as excessive drinking, marital problems and employment instability. For example, psychologists studying aggression have discovered that differences in the rate of pushing, shoving, and disobedience at age 8 are reasonably good predictors of criminal convictions at age 30.

The president's drug plan conspicuously ignores the notion of prevention. Yet the stability of differences from early childhood suggests that any worthwhile crime or drug policy must focus on the early years of life; that wars on crime and drugs, if they are to be successful, must target children.

Research clearly demonstrates that children who are taught early to respect the property of others, to delay gratifications of the moment if they conflict with long-term goals and to understand the negative consequences of drug and alcohol abuse are unlikely to abuse drugs or commit criminal acts, no matter what the criminal justice system looks like. The same research shows that children not taught these things are likely to run into trouble with the law.

Parents, not police, are the key to the drug crisis. Today, drug and crime policies focus on the wrong institution of social control (the government), treat an inappropriate age category (adults), falsely assume specialization of offenders, falsely assume a causal connection between drug use and criminal acts, and misperceive the motives of offenders. As long as this continues, no amount of taxpayer's money will win the war on crime.

Review Questions

1. Discuss the strategy of current government programs aimed at reducing crime.
2. Identify some of the basic findings of scientific research on crime and criminals.
3. Identify two basic facts concerning offenders that are at odds with the assumptions of current law enforcement policies.

Drug Abuse

Arrests for drug abuse have increased

The use of narcotics, and drug abuse in general, has shown significant increases in recent years throughout American society. The magnitude of the problem is indicated to some degree in terms of arrest data. For example, in 1953, only 1.3 percent of the total arrests were for narcotics offenses; by 1970, this figure had increased to 5 percent. In 1989, 9.5 percent of total arrests were for drug-abuse (including heroin and cocaine) violations. During the period from 1985 to 1989, arrests for drug-abuse violations increased 55.4 percent. Statistics also support the notion that drug abuse is heavily concentrated among young people. In 1989, 43 percent of those arrested for drug abuse were under 25 years of age.

American society as a whole is highly involved in the consumption of drugs. Millions of people use alcohol, barbiturates, amphetamines, milder tranquilizers, nicotine, caffeine, and nonprescription drugs, and many abuse these drugs. The prevalence of addiction to narcotics remains unknown, but estimates from the National Institute on Drug Abuse indicate that there are approximately 500,000 heroin addicts in the United States (*U.S. News & World Report,* 1985).

Contemporary narcotics use and addiction represent key examples of how social reactions determine which behaviors are deviant and what should be done about them. Lindesmith and Gagnon (1964), for instance, show that the overwhelming social reaction to narcotics use and addiction throughout the twentieth century has been punitive and legally suppressive. They point out that by and large, the population of drug users within the United States has radically changed in this century. In the early 1900s, the drug-using and addict population was concentrated among middle-class, middle-aged women living in rural as well as urban areas. Today the population of narcotics users and addicts is composed heavily of males, young people, blacks and whites, within the lower social classes. Lindesmith and Gagnon feel that the growth of suppressive legal measures and law enforcement tactics has largely been responsible for the changes in the population of narcotics users and addicts. Heightened public concern about drug abuse has led to increased criminal legislation and strict law enforcement that tends to define and stereotype the addict or user primarily as *criminal,* thus bringing about "punitive" reactions on the part of the public. Law enforcement measures also, paradoxically, have led to the development of a criminal underworld and increased involvement and dependence of the addict upon such avenues of supply.

Drug laws may have created the current drug problem

The use of cocaine has also increased—particularly during the 1970s and 1980s in our society. Crack, a potent, relatively cheap, crystalline form of cocaine, has become widespread since the mid-1980s. As distinct from narcotics that are depressants, cocaine is a potent stimulant. The cocaine user initially experiences an elevation in mood, a sense of well-being, and feelings of exhilaration. However, as the drug's effects subside, the user typically experiences feelings of depression, edginess, and tenseness. Cocaine and crack constrict the blood vessels of the heart, and their use has been linked with heart attacks even among people less than 30 years of age. These substances can also cause brain seizures. In terms of psychological effects, paranoid, violent, erratic, and hallucinatory behavior can accompany the use of these drugs. Frequent daily cocaine or crack usage can induce significant personality changes, depression, confusion, and anxiety. The more these substances are consumed, the greater the possibility that the user will develop psychosis (National Institute on Drug Abuse, 1989). With respect to the extent of usage, a large-scale National Institute on Drug Abuse survey has estimated that approximately 21 million Americans have used cocaine or crack at least once during their lifetime. Of these, 8.2 million people reported using the drug within one year prior to the survey and of these, in turn, approximately 3 million people were current users—having used the drug in the month prior to the survey (National Institute on Drug Abuse, 1989).

Many Americans have used cocaine or crack at least once during their lifetime.

Some evidence also indicates a tendency for cocaine users to increase the frequency of their cocaine use over time (Goode, 1990).

During recent times, social reaction to drug abuse and addiction has been diverse and conflicting. Some people have advocated the increased utilization of treatment and rehabilitation approaches for the addict. In this view, the addict is seen as a patient with a disease. Others have advocated educational programs aimed at the prevention of addiction among potential future users—particularly children. In contrast, however, many people define the user and addict as both a deviant and a criminal.

CYCLES OF CRAVING

Dan Hurley

As we have discussed above, both drug use as well as drug abuse are common in our society. The following article points out, however, that drug abuse is not random or haphazard—rather, it occurs in cycles and reveals certain patterns. The article discusses a number of these patterns in terms of regional trends, social class distinctions, and the tendency of certain drugs to "travel together." The article identifies a number of factors that shape drug-abuse patterns and looks at the prospects of drug abuse in the future.

Society's drugs of choice appear to come in waves: LSD and marijuana, cocaine, now crack. But cutting across the gradual shifts in drug-use patterns and the severe crisis in many of our cities is a growing disenchantment with it all. Lenard Hebert is an expert of sorts on America's patterns of drug abuse over the past 25 years. He hasn't studied them; he's lived them.

"I did each drug of the decade," says Hebert, a 40-year-old man now glad to be recovering in New York City's Phoenix House, one of the largest residential drug treatment centers in the world. Sitting in a lounge at the center, dressed neatly in white shirt and tie, he recalls his time as a Marine in Vietnam in 1967: "We'd wear peace signs on our helmets and love beads around our necks. Drugs were another way to get in touch with home. And LSD was definitely the most popular drug at the time."

When he returned home in the early '70s, Hebert became a black militant, bought a beret and, as he says, "did strictly reefer. A good militant did natural, herbal things. Then I went disco. I snorted cocaine for 10 years. It was chic because it was so expensive."

Along came crack, the smokable, highly addictive form of cocaine with its five-minute high. Hebert stopped dealing cocaine and turned his middle-class high-rise apartment into a crack den. Before he made it to Phoenix

---

House, he was sleeping in abandoned cars and shelters for the homeless.

SPOTTING NATIONAL TRENDS

The cycles of drug abuse that nearly ruined Hebert's life represent fairly well the way that different drugs sweep across our country in waves. "It's as if we've been conducting a huge social experiment since the early 1960s," said the late Norman E. Zinberg, a psychiatrist at Harvard who, since 1963, had been studying national drug-abuse patterns. (He died in April.) In his view, the nation has gone through four major waves of drug use, beginning with LSD in the early 1960s, marijuana in the mid- to late-'60s, heroin from 1969 to 1971 (Hebert escaped this heroin wave somehow) and cocaine in the late '70s and '80s.

Zinberg believed shifting patterns in drug abuse are signs of the times, reflections of the country's shifting zeitgeist. "Cocaine became the drug of the '80s because it's a stimulant," he said. "People were looking for action. It fit the mood, just like psychedelics fit the mood of the early '60s."

For years, experts have been trying to spot large trends in drug abuse with the hope that they might better prepare and adapt treatment, prevention and law enforcement efforts, according to David E. Smith, a specialist in addiction medicine who opened the Haight Ashbury Free Clinic in 1967 and has been monitoring drug-use patterns ever since. Although we have become increasingly sophisticated in identifying patterns, several factors muddy tidy calendars of drug usage such as Zinberg's. Most notably, researchers have found that: 1. Drug use varies tremendously from region to region, even city to city; 2. Drugs of choice move with some predictability through the social class structure; and 3. Rather than a simple succession of drugs in use, one drug often will piggyback on another, complicating efforts at prevention.

THE EAST-WEST TRANSFER

In 1976 the National Institute on Drug Abuse (NIDA) took the first step toward monitoring regional trends when it formed the Community Epidemiology Work Group, an assembly of drug-abuse experts from 20 cities around the country who meet biannually to exchange data. "Drug-abuse problems sometimes develop very quickly at the local level," says Nicholas J. Kozel, chief of NIDA's statistical and epidemiologic analysis branch and chairman of the group.

"Up until about a year and a half ago, there wasn't much of a crack problem in Washington, DC," Kozel explains. "Then all of a sudden we had more violence and murder than we'd ever seen, most of it associated with drugs, especially crack. Drug abuse is different from Boston to Buffalo to Washington. It pops up this month and recedes the next. That's why we need local surveillance. It keeps you on the edge of your seat, trying to stay alert to these changes and their impact on the health of our nation."

CLASS DISTINCTIONS

Compounding these regional variations is the movement of particular drugs through social classes. In a fairly predictable pattern, drug epidemics seem to begin among a small, elite group, then filter down into the broad middle class and finally permeate the ghetto. In 1983, half of the callers to 1-800-COCAINE, the national cocaine-abuse hot line, were college-educated, 52% had family incomes of at least $25,000 and only 16% were unemployed. By 1987, only 16% of the callers were college-educated, a mere 20% had incomes of $25,000 and fully 54% were among the unemployed.

"Cocaine use is going down among the people who work and can't afford not to show up for their jobs," says psychiatrist David F. Musto, a Yale medical historian and author of *The American Disease: Origins of Narcotic Control.* "The first people to go on a drug are the avant-garde and the wealthy, and they're the first to go off it, too. But in the inner city, drugs become a source of status and money, at least for the dealers."

Demand for illegal drugs has been dropping in the middle class for 10 years, according to two national surveys sponsored by NIDA. The most recent National Household Survey on Drug Abuse showed that drug use among 18- to 25-year-olds leveled off between 1979 and 1985. The first substantial decline in cocaine consumption among American high-school seniors, college students and young adults showed up in a 1987 survey conducted by the University of Michigan's Institute for Social Research. The most recent available poll shows that the decline continued in 1988.

DRUGS THAT TRAVEL TOGETHER

Despite regional variations, there do appear to be predictable patterns of abuse once a drug arrives on the scene. For instance, heavy abusers of cocaine or speed often use heroin simultaneously, usually at the end of a binge to ease themselves down. It shouldn't be surprising, then, that in 27 cities across the country the number of deaths associated with both heroin and cocaine leapt between 1984 and 1988. From 1987 to 1988 alone, domestic heroin seizures by the Drug Enforcement Agency more than doubled, jumping from 382.4 kilograms to 793.9 kilograms.

"It's predictable that we've had an increase in heroin abuse," says Smith. "Anytime you see a stimulant up-swing, you see an opiate upswing. The stimulant epidemic was the door for the opiate epidemic."

And Smith is now worried by a disturbing new trend—a simultaneous increase in the use of *both* speed and cocaine. "Normally the trends go in different directions," he says. "The speed curve went up and the cocaine curve went down. But since the advent of crack, it's the first time I've ever seen both the speed curve and the cocaine curve go up. The current stimulant epidemic is without a doubt the worst I've seen since 1967—and in fact it's worse than 1967."

WHAT SHAPES THE PATTERNS?

Experts have found the patterns of drug abuse are formed not only by vague national moods and fashions but also by the ordinary stuff of any business: packaging, marketing, distribution, research and development. "Crack has grown because of new marketing techniques," says Jim Hall, executive director of Up Front, a national drug-information center based in Miami. "When the yuppies were buying cocaine, they bought it in somebody's apartment, usually at prices of at least $50. The crack user buys it on the street or at a crack den in a vial that costs $10. This less-expensive alternative is what has brought cocaine to a whole new user group in the poverty pockets." It's not unlike the single-serving marketing strategy that has been successfully adopted by the food industry.

Arguably the strongest regulator of drug use is the public's perception of a drug's safety. America's first epidemic of cocaine abuse a century ago began when doctors had only good things to say about it. In 1884, Sigmund Freud wrote in *Uber Coca* that "The psychic effect of cocaine consists of exhilaration and lasting euphoria which does not differ from normal euphoria of a healthy person. . . . Absolutely no craving for further use of cocaine appears after the first or repeated taking of the drug." Thirty years later, the U.S. Congress passed the Harrison Act, designed to restrict severely traffic in opiates and cocaine, which by then had come to be considered serious public health hazards.

Cocaine's perceived risks have followed much the same trajectory in its second epidemic. As recently as 1985, psychiatrist Lester Grinspoon and lawyer James B. Bakalar wrote in a chapter of *The Comprehensive*

Textbook of Psychiatry that "High price still restricts consumption for all but the very rich, and those involved in trafficking. . . . If used moderately and occasionally, cocaine creates no serious problems." In that same year, the University of Michigan's annual survey of high-school students and young adults found that only 34% believed that trying cocaine once or twice was a "great risk." By 1987, amidst thundering anti-drug news in the national media, that proportion had jumped to 47.9%, and by 1988 more than half of those polled thought that even experimenting with cocaine was very risky. "The perceived risks have shifted enough that they could fully account for the shifts in use," says Jerald G. Bachman, one of the survey researchers.

DRUGS FOR THE '90s

Even now, as the uproar of negative publicity about crack's debilitating effects has checked its spread among middle-class users, another stimulant—a smokable, fast-acting form of methamphetamine—has entered the drug scene in the West and, according to some experts, has begun moving eastward. Police officers in various areas have been seizing unprecedented numbers of clandestine methamphetamine laboratories, and there has been a sharp rise in both hospital emergency-room reports and deaths related to use of the stimulant.

In contrast to crack, which gained its foothold in the East and then began moving westward, methamphetamine seems to be a West Coast phenomenon. It also differs from crack in that "methamphetamine use tends to be highest among white, blue-collar types," says Smith. "The clandestine labs tend to be controlled by the white biker gangs, while crack tends to be controlled more by inner-city blacks."

The growth of methamphetamine seems to stem from the ease with which it is manufactured in secret labs. A drug that can be made here at home avoids the problem of smuggling across our increasingly patrolled borders. In addition, its effects are advertised as similar to those of cocaine, without the reputation for deadliness. Hall, of Up Front, says that the spread of methamphetamine "looms as a potential national drug crisis of the 1990s."

THE EMPATHY DRUG

A case study in the progression of a new drug trend can be seen in the recent emergence of MDMA, better known as Ecstasy. First produced in 1914 but forgotten for years, the drug attracted the attention of psychotherapists in the '70s because, besides its stimulant and mildly psychedelic qualities, it could also increase patients' insight and empathy. "There's very little question in my mind that it can facilitate insight-oriented psychotherapy," says psychiatrist Lester Grinspoon.

By 1985, however, Ecstasy had become a recreational drug associated with a distinct type of music and dancing called "acid house" that originated on the Spanish island of Ibiza where wealthy people vacation. It served as a sort of new, improved brand of cocaine: It was exclusive, it provided the energy for dancing until dawn, it was allegedly "harmless," and—perhaps most attractive—it made people not only want to talk—as most stimulants do—but also to listen.

Researchers quickly found, however, that Ecstasy can damage brain cells in animals, even in low doses that correspond to the dosages people use for recreation, and the DEA outlawed it for most purposes in 1985. Recently made illegal in most of Europe, it drew the kind of sensational headlines there last summer that crack had garnered in America. Yet that publicity failed to cross the Atlantic, and Ecstasy continues to enjoy a safe and exclusive image here.

"It's a very white, very middle-class

drug," says Bill Brusca, general manager of The Tunnel, a popular Manhattan nightclub. "It's not the kind of drug you're going to hear a lot about, because it's not habit-forming."

But positive accounts such as these, says Nicholas Kozel of NIDA, "are similar to what was said about cocaine in the early '80s. They're looking for the safe drug, and we're realizing that there isn't any." Even so, Kozel isn't prepared to predict that Ecstasy abuse will reach epidemic proportions. "Forecasting is difficult," he says, "and MDMA is an especially difficult drug to track."

WHAT DOES THE FUTURE HOLD?

Despite the advances in trend analysis for drug abuse, nobody seems prepared to forecast the future. Some—including, most notably, psychiatrist Jerome Jaffe, the country's first "drug czar" under President Richard Nixon and the current head of federal addiction research efforts—are skeptical about our ability to make accurate predictions at all. Although he concedes that, without question, drug abuse follows a "trendy, fashionable popularity cycle," he doesn't believe we know enough about those cycles to predict what will happen next.

Historian Musto thinks that the most important trend is the decreased use of illegal drugs by the middle class that has cut through all of the various cycles since 1979. "We're 10 years into a phase of growing intolerance toward drugs," says Musto. "If history is a guide, it will take 20 to 30 more years for drug use to hit the nadir." History is indeed a guide to Musto, who investigated long-forgotten documents on America's first drug epidemic at the turn of the century for *The American Disease.* To him, the year-to-year shifts in drug use are all-but-imperceptible "blips" in our declining interest in illicit drugs.

According to Musto, "Crack seemed to be the ultimate drug problem, one so frightening that it crystallized our intolerance toward all drugs. It has created a consensus in society against drugs and ended the ambivalence that had been prevalent for decades."

Musto fears that America's turn against drugs could have serious social repercussions. "My concern is that as demand goes down in the middle class, instead of channelling efforts into long-term plans to help, people will get angrier and angrier at those in the inner city who still use drugs," he explains. "If we triple the amount of money we spend to battle the drug problem and if we pass a death-penalty measure expecting to solve the problem in a year, we'll only become frustrated by the results. The decline in drug use will be a long, gradual process. We're going down a road, and we've still got a long way to go."

A drug epidemic takes on a different character when it reaches the ghetto: There are more deaths—including the killing of innocent standers-by—and other tragedies such as addiction in newborns. Failure to recognize these people as victims, Musto says, and consequent failure to pursue aggressive public education and jobs programs, will only exacerbate an already difficult social problem.

BREAKING THE CYCLE

Once this, America's second drug epidemic, bottoms out, will we begin cycling inexorably into a third? Musto is willing to make one prediction: A society that forgets its history of abuse is doomed to repeat it. Unfortunately, says Musto, when America's first cocaine epidemic began fading in the '20s, "it became policy in the federal government to mention drugs as little as possible, and if they did mention them, to give descriptions so exaggerated and disgusting that no one would try them even once." Many adults are familiar with the 1936 propaganda film *Reefer Madness* that was circulated in the late 1950s and became a cult favorite in the '60s and '70s. When the young people who experimented with drugs in the '60s discovered that the exaggerations couldn't be trusted, they discarded all cautions to explore the reality of drugs in earnest.

Tragically, America's ahistorical attitude toward drug abuse continues to this day. "The Department of Education in California recently came up with a new syllabus of American history," Musto says. "There's no mention of the history of drug abuse. And in one place it lists drug abuse among the unacceptable topics for history electives. The largest education system in America gives no space on its syllabus for the important history of drug abuse in the United States."

In Musto's opinion, "The history of drugs and alcohol should be integrated into American history. If people had had a vivid knowledge of the first cocaine epidemic, the second epidemic might have taken a different route."

As we live with the fallout of America's second great drug-abuse epidemic in decline, a national commitment to remember the toll it has taken may be the only way to avoid a third.

Review Questions

1. Describe various patterns of drug abuse that have been identified by researchers in recent years.
2. Identify the factors that shape drug-abuse patterns in our society.
3. Discuss the prospects of drug abuse in the future.

Alcoholism

Types of drinking patterns

Although people have used alcoholic beverages throughout history, alcoholism is viewed as a distinct violation of group norms. As such, it represents another form of deviant behavior. Alcoholic beverages are consumed by the American public for various reasons and in various quantities. It is common for sociologists and others to speak of various categories or types of drinkers. *Social drinkers,* for instance, indulge only in light to moderate alcohol consumption. They may have a drink or two at a party or on a special occasion. Thus they tend to drink only when a particular situation calls for it. *Heavy drinkers* sometimes drink to the point of intoxication and generally drink much larger quantities of alcohol than social drinkers. Alcoholics fall into the category of *excessive drinkers.* They frequently drink in order to become intoxicated, and their drinking is of such degree as to interfere with normal family, occupational group, and community relations. Alcoholics are dependent on alcoholic beverages to the extent that they lose a substantial amount of personal control over their drinking. Frequently, they cannot refrain from the first drink and cannot stop drinking after they have started. The most serious alcoholics are termed **chronic alcoholics.** For the most part, these people have lost all control over their drinking. They literally live to drink and drink to live. Their relationships with their family, occupational groups, and friends show marked deterioration, often to the point

In our society, subcultural norms sometimes encourage drinking at a young age.

of extinction. Their continuous drinking leads to neurological and other forms of physical deterioration and sometimes culminates in death.

Estimates indicate that the number of alcoholics and alcohol abusers 18 years and over will increase

Alcoholism constitutes a large and growing problem in American society. It has been estimated that between 1985 and 1995, the number of alcoholics and alcohol abusers 18 years and over will increase from 17.6 million to 18.4 million. The numbers of alcoholics alone has been projected to increase from 10.5 million to 11.2 million people during this period (Williams et al., 1987). About one out of every four American homes has been affected by some type of alcohol-related family problem. Estimates indicate that alcoholism treatment expenditures cost $15 billion annually (*Facts on Alcoholism and Alcohol-Related Problems,* 1987).

The use of alcohol presents substantial law enforcement and judicial problems. In 1989, there were approximately 14.3 million arrests in the United States. Nearly 3.4 million were for offenses involving the use of alcohol, such as drunkenness, disorderly conduct, driving while intoxicated, and vagrancy. The use of alcohol also is frequently connected with other crimes, such as homicide, and aggravated and other assaults.

There exist, of course, medical definitions of excessive drinking. But excessive drinking is also defined as deviant behavior because it violates social norms that specify acceptable levels of and acceptable situations for drinking. Such norms vary from society to society and from group to group within society. What would be considered social drinking in one subculture might be viewed as heavy drinking in another. Nevertheless, when an individual consumes alcohol to such a degree that he or she cannot function in his or her social roles and maintain relatively stable relationships with others, alcoholism is present. It is at this *problematic* point that medical and social definitions of alcoholism tend to coincide.

Mental Disorders

Mental disorder is viewed by sociologists as another major form of deviant behavior. In previous times, it was considered reasonable to view mental disorder as representing some form of illness similar to a physical illness within the human organism. Although this view exists today, it has become increasingly common within social and psychological theory to see mental disorder as representing certain varieties of social deviance. In this view, mental disorder involves deviation from the expectations of others. Mental disorder as deviance from norms focuses attention on the social definitions with respect to violation of certain norms and the degree of social tolerance accorded to certain types of nonconforming behaviors. Thus behaviors felt to indicate mental disorder at one time or in one society may not indicate mental disorder in another time or society. According to Thomas Scheff (1966), mental disorders as deviance simply represent a form of **residual rule breaking.** Each society sets up certain rules and typically applies certain labels to people who violate certain social conventions. Thus we have the terms "drunkard," "thief," and "prostitute." The remaining (or residual) forms of deviance for which a group has no specific labels simply become packaged under the broad category of **mental disorder.** Types of nonconformity labeled mental disorder often include excessive aggressiveness, types of speech felt to be incoherent or nonrational, withdrawal from interpersonal relations, compulsive actions, delusions, phobias, states of depression, and often simply a general awkwardness in personal relations.

Mental disorder as deviance

Psychiatric terminology traditionally has divided mental disorders into two broad categories called neurosis and psychosis.* *Neurosis* usually refers to less serious forms of mental disorder. Neurosis is far more common than psychosis, and the neurotic usually functions more or less satisfactorily in relations with others. Categories of neuroses include phobias, psychosomatic disorders, obsessive compulsive behavior, hypochondria, and anxiety reactions.

Psychiatric categories of mental disorder

More serious forms of mental disorders are called *psychoses.* Psychotic individuals often have severe problems in relating to other people, and many psychotics cannot function adequately as members of society. Some psychoses involve impairment of brain functioning and may be caused by a wide variety of factors, including heredity, physical brain damage, and alcoholism. Major types of psychoses include schizophrenia, affective disorders, and paranoid disorders.

In recent years, the American Psychiatric Association has developed a new system for classifying mental disorders (*Diagnostic and Statistical Manual of Mental Disorders,* 1987). Rather than using the traditional, broadly descriptive terms of "neurosis" and "psychosis," the new system classifies mental disorders in terms

* Diagnosis of cases is not always precise. Each disorder category denotes only general descriptive characteristics and professional diagnosis of specific cases may reveal some inconsistency. Specific people may also manifest a variety of symptoms of more than one form of disorder.

of a large number of more specific and precise categories. Examples of such categories include organic mental disorders; psychoactive substance use disorders, including alcohol dependence, and abuse of various other drugs; schizophrenia; paranoid disorder; mood disorders, such as depression; anxiety disorders, such as panic disorders and phobias; and sexual disorders, such as fetishism and sexual sadism.

Many Americans experience some type of mental disorder during their lifetime

In prevalence as well as treatment, statistics substantiate the fact that mental disorder is a major form of deviant behavior and a major social problem today. A recent National Institute of Mental Health study has estimated that approximately 32 percent of Americans experience some type of mental disorder during their lifetime. The study estimates, for example, that among people 18 years of age and older, 14.6 percent have experienced anxiety disorders such as phobias and panic disorders, while 8.3 percent have experienced affective disorders such as major depression (Regier et al., 1988). Compared with other illnesses, mental disorder is the leading reason why people are admitted to hospitals. Many people need some form of treatment but do not receive it (*Facts About Mental Illness,* 1979).

Suicide

Suicide is the act of taking one's own life voluntarily and intentionally. Although suicide is considered a major form of deviance in contemporary American society, social reactions to it have shown wide variations from society to society and in different periods of human history. Various Oriental cultures have looked upon suicide with some ambivalence and have not disapproved of it in certain circumstances. Among the Chinese, suicide was permitted for reasons of revenge against an enemy. In Japan, it was *expected* that a soldier would commit a form of self-destruction known as hara-kiri rather than permit himself to be seized by the enemy. During World War II, Japanese suicide divers received military decorations in ceremonies before their suicide flights. Western European and American societies, in contrast, traditionally have been strongly opposed to suicide. The Jewish and Christian religions also have highly disapproved of suicide. In eleventh-century England, suicide was defined as a crime as well as a sin. Throughout the medieval period and into relatively recent times, suicide was punished as a felony. The suicide's body was denied burial in a Christian cemetery, and the suicide's possessions were confiscated by the Crown. Similar penalties were put into effect in the New England colonies and remained until the early 1800s in Massachusetts. Attempted suicide was a crime in North Dakota, South Dakota, and New Jersey until the 1950s and in England until 1961.

In some instances, suicide was expected and approved

Statistics indicate that the rate of suicide in the United States was 12.3 per 100,000 population in 1985. This rate has remained fairly stable over a number of years. The United States suicide rate was 11 per 100,000 population in 1970 and 12.3 per 100,000 population in 1978. Suicide rates have been comparatively high in various other countries in recent years. In the mid-1980s, suicide rates in Switzerland, West Germany, Czechoslovakia, Finland, Sweden, Austria, and Hungary exceeded 18 per 100,000 population. In other countries, including Italy,

Spain, Greece, and Ireland, suicide rates were less than 8 per 100,000 population during the early to mid-1980s (*United Nations Demographic Yearbook,* 1987).

Differentials in suicide

Suicide in the United States tends to occur more frequently among males than among females. The sex ratio for suicide is approximately three to one. More older people commit suicide than younger people. The relation of increasing age to rates of suicide is direct and highly consistent. The rate of suicide among married people is lower than the rate among the single, widowed, or divorced. In addition, the rate of suicide is lower among married couples with children than among childless couples. Whites commit suicide far more frequently than nonwhites, particularly blacks. Protestants tend to have a higher suicide rate than Catholics and Jews.

One of the most important studies of suicide was made by Emile Durkheim. According to Durkheim (1951), suicide could be explained in terms of a variety of social or group factors as they affected individuals. Durkheim felt that the likelihood of suicide was related to the degree of integration or involvement of individuals within groups or society. Specifically, suicide was more likely to occur in the extreme circumstances in which individuals lacked adequate integration within groups or society or in instances where individuals were too highly integrated into society.

Social and group factors in suicide

Durkheim classified three major types of suicide: egoistic, anomic, and altruistic. Egoistic and anomic suicide characterized a weak attachment of individuals to groups or society. For Durkheim, **egoistic suicide** was a form of self-centered suicide. The individual lacked full participation within groups, together with the emotional involvement that participation entails. Durkheim felt that this fact could explain the higher rates of suicide among Protestants than Catholics and the unmarried than the married. Protestantism advocates free inquiry into the Bible and religious matters and the doctrine of individual salvation. Catholicism stresses theological interpretation of the Bible and salvation through the church. Durkheim thus reasoned that Protestants would experience more isolation and detachment and less integration into a church as a form of group or association. The higher rates of suicide that Durkheim found among Protestants thus reflect basic weaknesses in social constraints over behavior (including the act of suicide) characteristic of Protestant religious groups. Likewise, unmarried people were not subject to the group ties and the social constraints of marriage and family life. Durkheim felt that the lack of attachments to others and greater emotional isolation among the unmarried was a prime factor in explaining their higher rates of suicide compared with the rates of married persons.

On the other hand, **anomic suicide** is not the result of a lack of close interpersonal or group relations, but instead, occurs as a result of a breakdown of the values and norms of the group or society *itself.* Thus higher suicide rates are often found during times of political crisis or economic depression.

Altruistic suicide occurs as a result of extreme integration into a group or society to the point where group norms and goals are the only things that matter. The individual identifies with and becomes so highly involved with and committed to the group that he or she would willingly commit suicide if the values and norms of the group so required. The practice of hara-kiri among the

Japanese and the self-destruction in India of a widow at her husband's funeral illustrate this form of suicide.

Explanations for Deviant Behavior

Biological Theories

Biological explanations for deviance

During the past century, a wide variety of explanations have been developed to account for deviant behavior. Early explanations tended to relate biological characteristics and biological inheritance to deviant and criminal behavior. Cesare Lombroso (1836–1909) attempted to demonstrate on the basis of various physiological and cranial measurements that criminals constituted a special class of primitive or atavistic throwbacks on the human scale of evolution. In more recent times, researchers such as Ernest Kretschmer and William Sheldon have tried to link various aspects of personality and tendencies toward deviant behavior to different physiques or body types. Sheldon, for instance, classified physiques in terms of three major types: **endomorphs** (predominantly soft, round, heavyset individuals), **ectomorphs** (tall, lean, flat-chested people), and **mesomorphs** (heavy chested, muscular, athletic people). Sheldon contended that mesomorphic individuals were most prone to crime and delinquency.

Modern biological theory and research has stressed the influence of biochemical factors (such as dietary factors and hormonal imbalances), neurophysiological factors (such as brain dysfunctions and brain wave abnormalities), and genetic influences (such as chromosome abnormalities), as possible explanations for some forms of deviant behavior—particularly violent crime (Siegel, 1989). While biological theory may provide some degree of explanatory insight into certain forms of crime, the biological perspective has been open to a number of criticisms. For example, it is highly likely that many, if not most, individuals who have engaged in violent, antisocial, or even criminal behavior, do not have some sort of biological abnormality. Biological theories also give major attention to violent crime, while giving little, if any, consideration to other numerous forms of criminal activity, such as fraud, embezzlement, drug-abuse violations, larceny-theft, and so forth. Finally, as many have pointed out, biological theory tends to ignore or at least minimize the influence of social environmental factors in crime causation (Siegel, 1989).

Psychological and Psychiatric Theories

In contrast to biological theories, psychological and psychiatric explanations tend to stress the relationship of personality factors to deviant behavior. From this perspective, personality is derived largely from one's interpersonal experiences, primarily those occurring in early childhood. As such, abnormal personalities are developed through experience *after* birth and thus characterize individuals who have been improperly or inadequately socialized to the values, needs, or demands of society. Psychological and psychiatric theories then attempt to utilize varieties of mental and psychological abnormalities as the basis of explanations for most other types of behavior defined as deviant.

Psychological and psychiatric theories tend to stress the relationship of personality factors to deviant behavior

In the area of crime and delinquency, psychological and psychiatric theories have tended to focus on the areas of mental capabilities (such as low intelligence), personality structures (personality traits associated with crime and delinquency), and personality development (the failure to achieve higher levels of maturity), as explanations of these forms of deviance (Mannle and Hirschel, 1988). Psychological and psychiatric theories have also come under a variety of criticisms. For example, the accuracy and reliability of tests and techniques that psychologists use to identify and measure mental abilities and personality traits have been called into question. Psychologists, so far, have not been able to identify specific personality traits or stages of development characteristic of delinquents or of criminals in general. Finally, psychological and psychiatric theories give little attention to various large-scale social and economic factors involved in crime and delinquency causation (Mannle and Hirschel, 1988).

Sociological Theories

The sociological perspective incorporates the most diverse and inclusive variety of explanations for deviant behavior. The sociological approach to deviant behavior differs from biological and psychological approaches in a number of ways. From the sociological viewpoint, what is *deviant* or *normal* from the standpoint of personality and behavior is always *relative* to the norms of the group or society. Thus deviance is ultimately a product of group or *social* definitions. Individuals perceived to be in violation of group norms are typically labeled as deviants of one type or another—"nut," "drunk," or "dope fiend," or perhaps in more sophisticated terms as "neurotic," "disturbed," or "addicted." Sociologists recognize the many important consequences that such labeling has for individuals and their relations with others.

Basic assumptions of the sociological viewpoint

In addition, sociologists see many similarities between deviant and nondeviant behavior. First, they assume that both types of behavior are *learned* in the course of one's interaction with others. Thus they give special attention to the individual's group affiliations. Sociologists take into consideration the norms and values to which an individual has been socialized within the context of the family, peer groups, school, and occupational groups. Second, sociologists assume that the vast majority of individuals engaged in deviant behavior are not sick or abnormal. Often they are actually conforming to the deviant norms of some subculture to which they have been socialized. Their deviant behavior may also be a normal response to frustrations, tensions, and stresses generated by pressures and conflicts within the structure of society and social life itself.

There are many varieties of sociological explanation for deviant behavior. Therefore we can present in brief only what we consider to be some of the leading and most popular approaches to the understanding of deviance. Accordingly, we have selected for analysis the following major varieties of theoretical explanation: labeling theory, conflict theory, the theory of anomie, and learning theory.

Labeling Theory. **Labeling theory** was largely popularized by a well-known sociologist, Howard Becker. Starting with the basic idea that deviance is relative to social or group norms and not inherently characteristic of certain human acts or people, Becker states: "*Social groups create deviance by making the rules whose infraction constitutes deviance,* and by applying those rules to particular people and labeling them as outsiders." Thus, "deviance is *not* a quality of the act the person commits, but rather a consequence of the application by others of rules and sanctions to an 'offender.' The deviant is one to whom that label has successfully been applied; deviant behavior is behavior that people so label" (Becker, 1963, p. 9).

From this perspective, an individual might engage in deviant actions on an occasional or perhaps even on a regular basis. As long as the deviance is unknown to others, the individual would not be considered deviant or abnormal. But when the individual's deviance becomes known and others are not willing to accept excuses for it, the individual becomes labeled and identified as "deviant." He or she is thus assigned a deviant identity and role by the group. This situation in and of itself has serious consequences for the individual. It typically brings about a type of self-fulfilling prophecy. In effect, this deviant label or identity renders the individual an "outsider." As such, according to Becker, the deviant "tends to be cut off, after being identified as deviant, from participation in more conventional groups, even though the specific consequences of the particular deviant activity might never of themselves have caused the isolation had there not also been the public knowledge and reaction to it" (1963, p. 34). As an outsider, the individual has little or no choice other than to live with and accept the view others have toward him or her. As such, the individual is literally compelled to assume and conform to the role and social identity of "deviant."

Labeling as deviant renders the person an "outsider"

The fact of labeling results in additional deviant behavior, drastic and simultaneous changes in one's self-image as a deviant, and the severing of many relationships with others. The individual known or discovered to be a homosexual or drug addict may wind up losing a job and may be forced into unrespectable or illegitimate types of work or activity. According to Becker, the final stage in the establishment of a deviant identity and deviant career is the individual's movement into an organized deviant group. The deviant group provides the individual with needed emotional support, encouragement, and reinforcement for deviant activities. Membership in a deviant group confirms the self-image of deviant, allows the individual to engage in deviance with a minimum of trouble and outside interference, and provides ready-made rationales for continuing in deviant acts.

The consequences of labeling

Becker's theory represents a somewhat radical approach to the understanding of deviance. His theory emphasizes several points that we made earlier in this chapter. There are no human acts *inherently* evil and deviant in themselves. Acts *become* deviant only when groups define them as such. Likewise, deviance is not a quality characteristic of some people and not of others. In truth, we are probably all deviants because we all violate norms—sometimes regularly. The crucial questions are:

1. whether a person becomes identified and labeled as deviant
2. whether sanctions are applied to that person by others
3. whether he or she is cast into a deviant role by others

Labeling as deviant is crucial

When these conditions come to pass, a person is isolated from more conventional roles, strengthened in his or her self-image as deviant, and increasingly assimilated into deviant activities and groups.

Becker's theory has been criticized on several counts. First, it must not be assumed that a person once labeled as deviant continues to commit deviant acts and progresses toward a deviant career. Second, Becker's theory deals almost entirely with reactions to acts labeled as deviant. This does not really explain *why* some people commit deviant acts to begin with, while others refrain from such behaviors. In spite of these and other criticisms, Becker's theory allows significant insight both into the nature of social reaction and social response to behavior and, in a sense, into the implications of such factors for the actual creation of deviance.

Conflict Theory. **Conflict theory** directs attention away from labeling and its consequences for generating deviant identities and deviant careers. It focuses on issues such as who makes rules and laws, who decides who is deviant, and which groups benefit from or suffer by these decisions.

Central to the conflict perspective are the ideas of dominance and power. The dominant groups in society have the power to decide which norms and laws govern the society and to ensure that these norms favor their own values, interests, and standards of morality. Other groups having conflicting interests and norms therefore are judged deviant and are subject to punishment by authorities who represent and enforce the views and norms of the dominant groups. Erich Goode sums up his analysis of conflict theory's central concern:

Central ideas of the conflict perspective

> **Conflict theory . . . abandons the question of why some people break the rules. Instead, it deals with the issue of *making* the rules, especially the criminal law. Why is certain behavior outlawed? And why is other, often even more damaging behavior, *not* outlawed? Conflict theorists answer these questions by arguing that laws are passed and rules are approved because they support the customs or the interests of the most powerful members of a society. In a large, complex society, no rule or law is accepted or believed as right by the whole society—only certain segments of it. Likewise, no rule or law protects everybody's rights or interests—again, only those of certain social groups or categories. It is the powerful groups that are able to impose their will on the rest of the society and make sure that laws and rules favorable to themselves, and possibly detrimental to other, less powerful groups, are instituted. That, in a nutshell, is the central concern of conflict theory (Goode, 1984, pp. 31, 32).**

Conflict theorists feel that laws support the powerful

A number of conflict theorists adopt a Marxist position to the analysis of deviance. From this perspective, crime and other forms of deviance are rooted in class and economic conflicts in the capitalist system. Crime and deviance are not only outcomes of the exploitation of the proletariat by capitalists but result when the wealthy capitalists define as deviant acts that threaten their economic interests. Marxists question, for example, why acts such as drunkenness, robbery, theft, and drug use are defined as crimes, while many questionable business practices are not defined as crimes. Moreover, some Marxist theorists feel that the only true solution to crime lies in the creation of a society based on socialist rather than capitalist principles (Quinney, 1974, 1975).

Marxian conflict theorists

Not all conflict theorists agree in total with the Marxist perspective. Non-Marxist conflict theorists feel, for example, that not all conflicts in social life are based on class or economic factors and that crime and deviance will continue to persist regardless of whether a system is capitalist or socialist. In addition, many deviance theorists object to the Marxists' notion that capitalism is responsible for all forms of crime (Goode, 1984). Conflict theory thus has its critics both from within and without. Other criticisms include, for example, that the theory does not adequately explain the specific processes by which a person becomes a criminal or deviant, that the law does not always operate for the exclusive benefit of the elite and powerful while ignoring the needs and interests of others, and that to date, conflict theory has not been supported by a sufficient body of empirical evidence (Clinard and Meier, 1979).

Criticisms of conflict theory

Conflict theory provides a view of crime and deviance quite different from that provided by other theoretical perspectives. Conflict theory challenges the widespread view that a consensus regarding values, morality, and ideas of deviance exists within society and that the law is simply the embodiment of this consensus. Conflict theorists also reject the notion that laws serve to benefit and protect everyone in society (Goode, 1984). Even so, many people feel that the conflict approach adds a valuable dimension to an understanding of crime and deviance in that it stresses the importance of power and political processes in both defining and controlling deviant behavior.

The Theory of Anomie. A third major theoretical explanation for deviant behavior is called the theory of **anomie.** In the section on suicide, we spoke of Durkheim's concept of anomic suicide, which resulted from a breakdown of societal norms. Sociologist Robert Merton (1957) has modified Durkheim's concept of anomie for explaining deviant behavior. For Merton, anomie involves a disjunction or lack of integration between cultural goals and the legitimate means for attaining them. Thus American society places great emphasis on the attainment of goals such as economic success and material possessions and prescribes certain approved means (higher education, well-paying jobs) for goal attainment. However, there are certain groups (the lower class and certain racial and ethnic groups) who because of their structural position within society are severely limited or denied adequate access to legitimate means for goal attainment. The pressures and frustrations experienced by people in this situation are often of such severity as to lead or induce them into deviant behavior. For Merton, "social structures exert a definite pressure upon certain persons in the society to engage in nonconforming rather than conforming conduct." Individuals located within these structural positions of society that limit or deny access to culturally approved goals tend to become anomic, or alienated from society.

Structural factors in deviance

Table 5.1. **A Typology of Individual Adaptation**

MODES OF ADAPTATION	CULTURE GOALS	INSTITUTIONALIZED MEANS
Conformity	+	+
Innovation	+	−
Ritualism	−	+
Retreatism	−	−
Rebellion	±	±

Source: Data from R. K. Merton, *Social Theory and Social Structure.* New York: Free Press, 1957, p. 140

Such individuals or groups thus have a greater tendency to deviate from conventional societal goals and norms.

Merton suggests five methods of adaptation to the use of means and goal attainment. With the exception of conformity (which results when the individual accepts both legitimate means and goals and is in a social position that allows access to both), the remaining methods of adaptation constitute deviant or anomic types of responses. These occur when legitimate means to goal attainment are blocked. According to Merton, the four types of deviant adaptations are innovation, ritualism, retreatism, and rebellion. Table 5.1 has been adapted from Merton's writings. In this table, a plus sign (+) signifies "acceptance," a minus sign (−) signifies "rejection," and a plus-minus sign (±) signifies "rejection of prevailing values and substitution of new values."

Innovation occurs when the individual accepts the cultural goals but his or her position within society prevents adequate access to legitimate means for goal attainment. The innovator winds up rejecting legitimate means and uses illegitimate means to achieve culturally approved goals such as economic success, material possessions, and social status. A prime example of innovation is crime—particularly organized crime, crimes against property (theft or burglary), robbery, drug pushing, and prostitution.

Types of deviant adaptations

Ritualism occurs when, in failing to achieve the goals, the person inwardly gives up or abandons "true" efforts to achieve them. Nevertheless, the person outwardly conforms in strict fashion to the use of legitimate means that are socially defined as necessary for goal attainment. Thus the ritualist finds solution to failure and frustration by actually reducing or ignoring the importance of the goals. Outwardly, however, ritualists manifest a compulsive conformity to legitimate means. They exaggerate the importance of the means to the point at which the means become ends in themselves. The ritualist's appearance to others would suggest anything other than deviance. In reality, however, ritualists are deviant because they have inwardly withdrawn from the struggle for goal attainment. The overzealous bureaucrat or the hardworking shop owner who, in fact, realizes that he or she is not "going anywhere" exemplifies ritualism.

Retreatism occurs when the individual blocked in goal attainment gives up on both goals and means to goals. In rejecting conventional goals and means, the retreatist frequently turns to other illegitimate ones. The suicide, drug addict, chronic alcoholic, and, at times, the severely mentally disturbed exemplify contemporary forms of retreatist escape and withdrawal.

Rebellion occurs when individuals not only reject and withdraw from legitimate goals or societal means but also attempt to introduce new goals and means to replace the conventional ones. Various radicals and revolutionaries exemplify this form of deviant adaptation.

Merton's theory, in large part, is directly opposed to the view that deviation is a manifestation of personal sickness or abnormality. Merton's theory assumes that anomic forms of deviation represent normal responses to frustrations, tensions, and stresses generated by conflicts within the structure of society itself. Thus the causes for deviation lie not in individuals, but in the contradictions between the emphasis placed on cultural goals and the lack of opportunities for some people to use legitimate means to reach these goals.

Learning Theory. As we have mentioned, sociology stresses the notion that deviant (as well as nondeviant) behavior is *learned* in the course of one's interactions with others. Thus, in attempting to explain various forms of deviant behavior, such as white-collar crime and certain kinds of drug abuse, **learning theory** is concerned with an individual's group affiliations and contacts with others.

Deviant behavior is socially learned behavior

Some sociologists emphasize that deviant behavior is learned as a result of participation in deviant subcultures. Individuals nearly always function as members of subcultures within complex societies. Thus, to a certain degree, individuals orient their thinking, acting, and feeling to the norms, values, and beliefs characteristic of these subcultures.

The subcultural approach bases its explanations for deviance on the fact that a multitude of subcultures exist in complex societies, some of which contain systems of norms and values different from or in opposition to those of society at large. No doubt, many advocates of the subcultural approach would not deny the significance of structural conditions (in terms of Merton's analysis) for generating tendencies toward deviance. In opposition to Merton, however, they would emphasize that deviant behavior is simply a product of *learning* through one's participation in and gradual absorption into deviant subcultures. In broadest terms, they would argue that much deviance is a product of deviant subcultures. Thus the major and perhaps only important factor ultimately deciding whether a person *becomes* deviant is the degree of his or her differential exposure to people in the deviant subculture. Socialization into a deviant subculture is like socialization into any other group. It involves the acquisition of a variety of skills, techniques, attitudes, values, and motives that rationalize and justify engaging in deviant behavior. All these are acquired gradually as a person participates in group life and comes to be accepted by other deviant group members.

The learning process: deviant subcultures

Sociologists generally assume that deviant subcultures develop among people who face similar types of problems. These problems tend to arise in situations in which there is a conflict between a culture that encourages high aspirations and a social structure that limits or denies fulfillment of such aspirations. Thus subcultures exist in one form or another because they provide solutions to such problems. Such solutions may offer escape or withdrawal (the alcoholic or drug subcultures); rebellion, violence, or conflict (violent gangs, revolutionary groups); or goal attainment by illegitimate means (criminal and delinquent subcultures engaging in theft, robbery, extortion, prostitution, organized and professional crime).*

Cohen's subcultural analysis of delinquency

One of the classic studies with regard to subcultural analysis of deviant behavior is Albert Cohen's work on juvenile delinquency (1955). According to Cohen, much delinquency can be accounted for in terms of a **delinquent subculture,** the existence of which is most clearly manifested in the delinquent gang. For Cohen, the delinquent subculture exists primarily because it provides some sort of solution to the status problems of working-class boys. These status problems arise as a result of the clash between middle-class values and goals to which working-class youth have been socialized to some degree and various structural barriers to mobility. This situation ultimately results in frustration of their aspirations.

Cohen sees the working-class boy as one who aspires to middle-class goals and lifestyles. Nevertheless, his background does not prepare him for entrance into the middle class. Socialization for middle-class boys incorporates suppression of aggression, postponement of immediate gratification, academic achievement, ambition, rationality, and self-reliance. By comparison, socialization for the working-class boy, although emphasizing goal attainment, nevertheless falls short in emphasizing these middle-class standards necessary for goal attainment. Thus the working-class boy develops aspirations similar to those of the middle-class youth but is deficient in the development of personal qualities deemed necessary for success. With increased contact with the middle-class world, particularly through his participation in school and other activities outside the immediate family and neighborhood, he increasingly comes to realize that his background has left him ill-equipped for success in school and in the other avenues necessary for upward mobility.

Alternatives for the working-class youth

At this point, there are several possibilities available to the working-class boy. First, despite his handicaps, he may reject much of his working-class values and background, sever relationships with his peers, and strive to conform to middle-class standards. He pulls himself up by his bootstraps and goes to college. Second, he may not reject his working-class background, associates, or circumstances and may decide to make the best of his situation as it is, simply taking life as it comes. Third, he may develop a delinquent response. In this case, he reacts by rejecting middle-class values and norms (which to some degree he has internalized). He turns to the delinquent subculture of the gang, which provides a solution to the status problems that he faces. Thus, in turning to the delinquent subculture, the youth discovers another form of status through membership in the gang.

---

* Cloward and Ohlin (1960) speak of similar varieties of subcultures that are termed retreatist, conflict, and criminal subcultures. Their use of these concepts is limited, however, specifically to delinquent or gang subcultures.

Gang norms and values

Cohen sees the delinquent subculture as malicious, nonutilitarian, and negativistic. Its members engage in vandalism and theft for kicks and display hostility and resentment toward anything suggestive of middle-class values, conventions, and lifestyles. The gang represents an entity having a need to be totally opposed to the middle class. For instance, it both accepts and expects physical aggression because outward aggression is forbidden in the unachievable middle class. The gang also gives the boy support in eliminating any guilt he might experience resulting from delinquent acts through mechanisms Sykes and Matza (1957) term "techniques of neutralization." Such techniques actually comprise sets of rationalizations and justifications that come to be developed and shared within the subculture. Thus, in rationalizing deviant acts, the delinquents may claim that they only "borrowed" and did not steal a car, assert that the victim of an attack really deserved it, or brand those who disapprove of their delinquent acts as hypocrites.

Richard Cloward and Lloyd Ohlin (1960) have modified and extended Cohen's analysis by classifying three basic types of delinquent subcultures. The **criminal subculture** comprises delinquent youth who typically engage in robbery, fraud, and theft; the **conflict subculture** characterizes delinquents who achieve status through acts of violence or force; and the **retreatist subculture,** for the most part, is involved in the consumption of drugs. The particular type of delinquent subculture that is formed and the fate of delinquents when they mature depend on several factors, including the area in which they live. In adulthood, some or perhaps most of the delinquents adopt noncriminal lives. Those who have been exposed to adult criminal models may progress under their guidance into adult criminal careers. The remainder will probably become involved in various retreatist activities.

Summary

1. When sociologists speak of deviant behavior, they are referring to behavior that does not conform to social norms.

2. Deviance has a number of positive and negative consequences. It is always relative to the norms of a particular group. Group norms, however, show tremendous variation; what is deviant in one group or society may not be deviant in another group or society. Deviance also varies over time, in different geographical areas, and in different subcultures. In this chapter, we presented a general discussion of the nature and extent of several highly disapproved forms of deviant behavior found within American society, including crime, delinquency, drug abuse, alcoholism, mental disorders, and suicide.

3. During the past century, many explanations have been developed to account for deviant behavior. Biological explanations have stressed the role of biological characteristics and biological inheritance. Psychological theo-

ries tend to stress the relation of personality factors to deviant behavior. Sociology stresses the influence of social and group factors in explaining deviance. Four major sociological theories concerning deviant behavior are labeling theory, conflict theory, the theory of anomie, and learning theory.

4. Labeling theory is concerned with the analysis of social reactions to deviance and the implications of this labeling for individuals labeled as deviant.

5. Conflict theory focuses upon issues such as who makes rules and laws, who decides who is deviant, and which groups benefit or suffer by these decisions. In general, conflict theory stresses the importance of power and political processes in both defining and controlling deviant behavior. In Marxist conflict theories, crime and other forms of deviance are rooted in class and economic conflicts of capitalism.

6. The theory of anomie traces the origin of major forms of deviant behaviors to conditions of social or structural disorganization. Anomie involves a disjunction between cultural goals and the availability of legitimate means for attaining these goals.

7. Learning theory emphasizes the idea that deviant behavior is learned through interactions with others. The subcultural approach illustrates many of the principles of learning theory, emphasizing the notion that deviant behavior is a product of learning through participation in deviant subcultures. Cohen's analysis of the delinquent subculture provides an excellent illustration of the subcultural approach to explaining deviance.

STUDY GUIDE

Chapter Objectives

After studying this chapter, you should be able to:

1. Contrast internal and external social control
2. List the positive and negative consequences of deviance
3. Define "social tolerance" and "deviant behavior"
4. Define "crime" and list several examples of computer crime
5. Contrast the legal distinction between juvenile delinquency and crime in general

6. Compare and contrast the various types of drug use and drinking
7. Distinguish, by way of example, the difference between mental disorder as illness and as deviation
8. Define "egoistic," "anomic," and "altruistic suicide" and give examples of each
9. Contrast biological, psychological, and sociological explanations for deviant behavior
10. Evaluate the contributions of labeling theory and conflict theory to understanding of deviant behavior
11. Define "anomie" and give examples of the four basic forms of deviant adaptations to anomie, according to Merton
12. Describe Cohen's theory of the delinquent subculture

Key Terms

Altruistic suicide (p. 195)
Anomic suicide (p. 195)
Anomie (p. 200)
Chronic alcoholic (p. 191)
Conflict subculture (p. 204)
Conflict theory (of deviance) (p. 199)
Crime (p. 177)
Criminal subculture (p. 204)
Delinquency (p. 180)
Delinquent subculture (p. 203)
Deviant behavior (p. 175)
Ectomorphs (p. 196)
Egoistic suicide (p. 195)
Endomorphs (p. 196)
Felonies (p. 178)
Innovation (p. 201)
Labeling theory (p. 198)
Learning theory (p. 202)
Mental disorder (p. 193)
Mesomorphs (p. 196)
Misdemeanors (p. 178)
Rebellion (p. 202)
Residual rule breaking (p. 193)
Retreatism (p. 202)
Retreatist subculture (p. 204)
Ritualism (p. 201)
Suicide (p. 194)
Tolerance limit (p. 174)
White-collar crime (p. 178)

Self-Test

Short Answer

(p. 171) 1. Deviant behavior is ______

(p. 172) 2. The positive consequences of deviance are:
a. ______
b. ______
c. ______

(p. 172) 3. The negative consequences of deviance are:
a. ______
b. ______
c. ______

(p. 176) 4. The *Time* Magazine article, "Ground Rules for Telling Lies," illustrates: ______________________________

(p. 177) 5. Crime is ______________________________

(p. 195) 6. Durkheim's three types of suicide, (a) egoistic, (b) anomic, and (c) altruistic, can be defined as follows:
a. ______________________________
b. ______________________________
c. ______________________________

(p. 198) 7. According to Becker, social groups create deviance by ______________________________

(p. 199) 8. The conflict theory of deviance focuses upon issues such as ______________________________

(p. 201) 9. Merton's four types of deviant responses or adaptations include:
a. ______________ c. ______________
b. ______________ d. ______________

(p. 202) 10. Learning theory stresses the notion that ______________________________

Multiple Choice *(Answers are on page 212.)*

(p. 172) 1. With respect to deviance, sociologists note that:
- a. it can be found in every society
- b. it really does not exist
- c. it refers only to mental abnormality
- d. it is not relative to factors such as time and place

(p. 172) 2. In terms of negative consequences, large-scale deviance:
- a. can help ascertain what is acceptable social behavior
- b. may harm group stability
- c. can strengthen group norms and values
- d. can be a sign and source of needed social change

(p. 175) 3. From the sociological point of view:
- a. deviance is absolute, not relative
- b. certain acts are inherently evil
- c. deviance is relative to and dependent on social definitions
- d. deviant people are quite different from nondeviant people

(p. 178) 4. White-collar crime would include:
a. political bribery
b. embezzlement
c. antitrust violations
d. all the above

(p. 185) 5. According to Lindesmith and Gagnon, the overwhelming social reaction to narcotics use and addiction during the twentieth century has been:
a. punitive and legally suppressive
b. therapeutic
c. permissive
d. liberal

(p. 185) 6. The National Institute on Drug Abuse estimates the number of Americans who have used cocaine or crack at least once during their lifetime at:
a. 8 million
b. 21 million
c. 32 million
d. 12 million

(p. 196) 7. With respect to deviance, psychological and psychiatric explanations stress:
a. The role of chromosomes
b. inherited characteristics
c. anomie
d. personality and early life experiences

(p. 199) 8. Central to the conflict perspective of deviance are the ideas of:
a. labeling and the development of deviant identities
b. anomie and structural disorganization
c. dominance and power
d. learning and deviant subcultures

(p. 201) 9. According to Robert Merton, an innovator is one who:
a. rejects legitimate means and turns to illegitimate ones in order to acquire approved goals
b. rejects only the approved goals
c. rejects both approved goals and legitimate means
d. rebels against the entire order

(p. 204) 10. According to Sykes and Matza, techniques of neutralization are:
a. stereotypes
b. rationalizations for delinquency shared within the subculture
c. a variety of actions that the middle-class boy can adopt in solving his status problems
d. delinquent acts

True/False *(Answers are on page 212.)*

T F 11. Deviance is found only within complex societies. (p. 172)
T F 12. Deviance always elicits social disapproval. (p. 174)
T F 13. People tend to be either totally deviant or totally nondeviant. (p. 175)

T F 14. Generally speaking, the juvenile law and court system emphasizes protection, guidance, and rehabilitation of juveniles, not punishment. (p. 180)

T F 15. According to Michael Gottfredson and Travis Hirschi, increased government expenditures during the 1980s had a significant impact in reducing drug use and the rate of crime during this period. (p. 181)

T F 16. The article "Cycles of Craving" indicates that the demand for illegal drugs has been decreasing in the middle class for 10 years. (p. 188)

T F 17. According to Durkheim, suicide is related to the degree of integration or involvement of individuals within groups or society. (p. 195)

T F 18. According to Becker, labeling an individual as "deviant" and "outsider" can often result in additional deviant behavior. (p. 198)

T F 19. Merton feels that the anomic type of person does not have a tendency to deviate from conventional societal goals and norms. (p. 200)

T F 20. According to Cohen, a delinquent response involves an acceptance of middle-class values and conformity to middle-class norms. (p. 203)

Fill-In *(Answers are on page 212.)*

(p. 172) 21. Social control operates on the basis of both ______ and ______ mechanisms.

(p. 173) 22. Deviance is ______ to many factors such as time, place, and subculture.

(p. 175) 23. ______ create deviance by making rules whose infraction constitutes deviance.

(p. 177) 24. ______ is a violation of any one of the specific types of norms that we call laws.

(p. 193) 25. According to psychiatric terminology, the word ______ usually refers to less serious forms of mental disorder.

(p. 196) 26. William Sheldon felt that ______ were most prone to crime and delinquency.

(p. 197) 27. Sociology assumes that both deviant and nondeviant behaviors are ______ in the course of one's interactions with others.

(p. 199) 28. From the Marxist conflict perspective, crime and other forms of deviance are rooted in ______ and ______ conflicts in the capitalist system.

(p. 202) 29. ______ occurs when individuals not only reject and withdraw from legitimate goals or societal means but attempt to introduce new goals and means for the society.

(p. 202) 30. Some sociologists emphasize that deviant behavior is learned as a result of participation in ______ subcultures.

Matching (Answers are on page 212.)

31. _______ Social control
32. _______ Edwin H. Sutherland
33. _______ Retreatism
34. _______ Tolerance limit
35. _______ Computer crime
36. _______ Felonies
37. _______ Howard Becker
38. _______ Conflict subculture
39. _______ Brain dysfunction
40. _______ Anomic suicide

a. Degree to which norm violations are tolerated or suppressed by a group or community
b. Composed of delinquents who achieve status through acts of violence or force
c. Popularized labeling theory
d. Total withdrawal from goals as well as means to goals
e. Author of classic study *White Collar Crime*
f. Serious crimes such as criminal homicide, rape, and robbery
g. Results from a breakdown of the values and norms of the group or society itself
h. Methods whereby a group or society attempts to bring about conformity of its members to group norms and expectations
i. Biological explanation for some forms of deviant behavior
j. Theft of services

Essay Questions

1. What is meant by internal and external social control? Which do you think is more influential in bringing about conformity to social norms? Why?
2. What are some of the positive and negative consequences of deviance for groups and society?
3. In what ways is deviance relative to time, place, and subcultural factors? What are some examples?
4. Sociologically speaking, can deviance exist without norms? Why?
5. What are six examples of behaviors that you feel are deviant? Why do you feel they are deviant?
6. Do groups actually need social deviants? Why or why not?
7. What are the major forms of deviant behavior discussed in this chapter? Describe each briefly.

8. How do biological and psychological theories explain deviant behavior?
9. What are the four major sociological explanations for deviant behavior presented in this chapter? List and briefly discuss these theories.

Interactive Exercises

1. This chapter has emphasized the idea that deviance is a matter of social definition and is always relative to group norms. However, in some cases, there is an absence of agreed-upon norms for judging and regulating certain forms of behavior. In our society, this is surely the case with regard to the widespread use of lying, which is discussed in the article "Ground Rules for Telling Lies." Ask some other students at your school to read this brief article. Are they aware that lying is as commonplace in our society as the article indicates? In general, do they view lying to be deviant or nondeviant behavior? Do they agree with philosopher Sissela Bok that certain lies should be permitted? What kind of ground rules do they suggest be established for telling lies? This exercise should aid in your understanding of the role of social definitions in producing deviance and the difficulties people face in evaluating and regulating their behavior in the absence of clear normative guidelines.

2. This chapter has discussed in some detail four major sociological explanations for deviant behavior: labeling theory, conflict theory, the theory of anomie, and learning theory. Select a certain form of deviant behavior, perhaps a particular type of crime or specific type or types of drug abuse, and prepare a brief written analysis of how each of these theories would explain such deviance. Compare your analysis with those of other students in your class. This form of applied exercise should aid in your understanding of the theoretical perspectives as well as the strengths and weaknesses of each.

3. Take at least one of the major forms of deviant behavior discussed in this chapter, and attempt to locate and familiarize yourself with two or three major published sources of descriptive and/or statistical information with regard to the form(s) of deviance you have selected. For example, if you choose the area of crime, an important source of information that you should thoroughly examine would be the Federal Bureau of Investigation annual publication *Uniform Crime Reports.* If you choose the area of mental disorders, be sure to examine the third edition of the American Psychiatric Association's *Diagnostic and Statistical Manual of Mental Disorders.* Your instructor and reference librarian should be helpful in suggesting additional standard sources of information in these and other areas. This exercise has informative value for everyone and should be particularly useful to those intending to pursue careers in the social sciences, law, criminal justice, law enforcement, social and human services, and mental health.

Answers

Answers to Self-Test

1. a
2. b
3. c
4. d
5. a
6. b
7. d
8. c
9. a
10. b
11. F
12. F
13. F
14. T
15. F
16. T
17. T
18. T
19. F
20. F
21. internal, external
22. relative
23. social groups
24. crime
25. neurosis
26. mesomorphs
27. learned
28. class, economic
29. rebellion
30. deviant
31. h
32. e
33. d
34. a
35. j
36. f
37. c
38. b
39. i
40. g

Answers to Chapter Pretest

1. F
2. T
3. F
4. T
5. F
6. T
7. T
8. F

Chapter 6

Stratification

Chapter Pretest

Let's see how much you already know about topics in this chapter:

1. **One's social class position has very little, if any, influence upon one's life expectancy. True/False**
2. **In 1988, there were 32 million people below the poverty level in the United States. True/False**
3. **One's occupation is a key indicator of one's social class position. True/False**
4. **In many respects, social classes represent subcultures. True/False**
5. **Poverty is harmful to our society as a whole. True/False**
6. **In recent years, one-fifth of the American population has received about one-half of the national income. True/False**
7. **Today, in general, the income difference between full-time year-round female and male workers is virtually nil. True/False**
8. **The vast majority of homeless people in our society are alcohol abusers. True/False**

The Nature and Importance of Stratification

There is a commonly held notion that all people are created equal. Equality represents an ideal of many peoples past and present and is a major American cultural value, but the existence of social stratification contrasts sharply with this ideal.

When sociologists speak of **stratification,** they are referring to a system whereby people rank and evaluate each other as superior or inferior and, on the basis of such evaluations, unequally reward one another with wealth, authority, power, and prestige. One result of such differentiation is the creation of a number of levels within society. Stratification always involves social inequality and social ranking and thus stresses the *differences* among people. Some of these differences—for example, birth into a particular level of society, occupation, education, age, sex, and race—serve as criteria according to which people and groups are ranked. In theory, any number of differences among people, such as personality characteristics, intelligence, height, hair color, or others, may be used as a basis for ranking. In practice, however, out of an almost infinite number of differences among people, very few are criteria for ranking. Because stratification also involves unequal distribution of rewards, if occupation, education, or race serve as criteria for ranking, individuals in certain occupational, educational, and racial categories will receive different income, wealth, status, prestige, and power (Williams, 1970).

Though people may be "created equal," they are not treated equally

Sociologists have long been interested in the study of stratification for a number of reasons, of which the following two seem paramount. First, some form of stratification system has been found within every human society. It is possible, at least in a theoretical sense, that all people might be taken simply as they are and evaluated equally, but this never happens. Second, the existence of a social stratification system has many consequences for individuals and groups. For example, within one form of stratification system, the social class system, practically every aspect of an individual's behavior, such as religious preference, voting behavior, vocabulary, recreational activities, early socialization, marital status, size of family, and even sex life, is related to social class.

Social class also influences what Max Weber termed one's **life chances.** By way of a few contemporary examples, as class position increases, individual life expectancy also increases, the rate of infant mortality decreases, the rate of physical sickness decreases, the level of education increases, the chance of arrest and commitment for a criminal act decreases, and the likelihood of serious mental disorder decreases. Thus the study of social stratification is of prime interest to sociologists because stratification appears universally and because it so deeply affects virtually every aspect of people's chances to obtain those things considered important and desirable.

Higher social class position generally improves all "life chances"

Although the existence of stratification is universal, the question of why stratification exists in every society has been a subject of debate among sociologists for many years. From the functionalist perspective, stratification renders an important service to a society. It rewards occupations vital to group welfare and requiring special abilities and arduous training—such as medical and legal occupations—with a greater share of wealth, income, prestige, and power than less vital and less difficult occupations. This system of rewards helps motivate competent people to make the necessary sacrifices and commitments to prepare for and carry out difficult occupational roles. Thus, although stratification involves inequality, it benefits society at large by helping guarantee that the more difficult and critically important kinds of work will be accomplished.*

Functionalist position: stratification benefits society in general

In contrast to the functionalist, the conflict perspective views stratification as neither important nor advantageous to the welfare of most members of society. Conflict theorists view stratification as an unjust system inflicted on

* This analysis generally follows the line of functionalist reasoning developed by Kingsley Davis and Wilbert Moore (1945). For additional analysis of functional and conflict theories see also Beth E. Vanfossen, *The Structure of Social Inequality* (Boston: Little, Brown, 1979), pp. 21–51, and Leonard Beeghley, *Social Stratification in America: A Critical Analysis of Theory and Research* (Santa Monica, Calif.: Goodyear Publishing, 1978), pp. 1–91.

society by people with a monopoly of power and wealth to safeguard their own interests, advantages, and power. Stratification thus is seen to exploit the many while rewarding the few.

Conflict perspective: stratification benefits the wealthy and powerful

Over the years, functionalist and conflict theories of stratification have been the subject of criticism and debate by sociologists. In addition, sociologists such as Gerhard Lenski (1966) and Robin Williams (1966) have attempted a synthesis of the two theoretical perspectives. While neither conflict nor functionalist theories can explain to everyone's satisfaction the reasons why stratification exists, each provides valuable insights into the nature, causes, and consequences of stratification for human societies.

Types of Stratification Systems

Sociologists distinguish among three major ideal types of stratification systems: the caste system, the estates system, and the open class system.

The **caste system** represents a *closed* system of stratification in the sense that an individual's rank or position within the society is fixed for life on the basis of some ascribed or inherited characteristic. Within this system, the individual is simply born into a particular level, called a **caste**, and remains in that caste for life. Thus, in a true caste system, mobility from one caste to another is impossible.

There are no pure caste systems in the world today. One historical example of a nearly pure caste system was that of India. The Indian system was divided into four major castes: the Brahmins, who were priests and scholars; the Kshatriya, who were warriors; the Vaisya, who were merchants and farmers; and the Sudra, who were laborers and peasants. In addition to these, there were many smaller castes and subcastes, a number of *untouchables* who did not have any caste, as well as *outcastes,* who at one time or another had been expelled from their caste for violation of caste taboos. In the Indian caste system, marriage was endogamous in that one was required to select a marriage partner from within one's own caste, and contact with members of other castes was not allowed. These and other caste regulations were enforced on religious, philosophical, and traditional grounds. Today many of India's castelike qualities have disappeared as a result of modernization, industrialization, and legislation forbidding many practices associated with caste.

The caste system was comprised of many castes

A second major type of stratification system is called the **estates system.** This system was characteristic of Europe during medieval times. It was similar to the caste system in that it was relatively closed and rigid. Nevertheless, mobility was possible, even though it was the exception. There were three major feudal estates: the nobility, the clergy, and the peasantry. The nobility comprised the kings, the nobles, and the military aristocracy (who in most cases were nobles); the clergy ranged from high-ranking religious leaders to lower-ranking officials of the church. The peasantry was composed of farmers, laborers, as well as serfs. The European estates system was characteristic of an agrarian (agri-

The estates system was characteristic of Europe during medieval times

cultural) economy and was based on ownership of property (particularly land) and inheritance. The estates system, essentially ascriptive in nature, remained in existence in Europe for several hundred years. Unlike the Indian caste system, which was sustained primarily by religion, the estates system was sustained primarily by tradition and law.

In an open class system, rewards are based on achievement

The third major ideal type of stratification system is called the **open class system.** In this system, an individual's class position within the society is determined by his or her personal effort and ability rather than by factors relating to birth. Thus there is a great deal of social mobility, with people moving up and down the class scale and everyone having an equal chance to attain social and economic rewards. An open class society encourages competition among individuals, and rewards are based upon achievement rather than ascription.

Pure open class systems, like pure caste systems, do not actually exist. Those societies that most resemble true open class systems tend to be the modern, technological, industrialized societies in which opportunities for mobility are usually high. The United States, for instance, with its emphasis on competition and personal achievement, tends to approach the open class model, yet even here there are barriers and limitations to mobility for some individuals that derive from castelike ascriptive factors, such as inheritance of wealth, race, religion, sex, and age.

Stratification and Social Class

Karl Marx

For Marx, one's class position was a function of one's position in the economic system of the society

One of the earliest and most important contributors to the analysis of the nature of social class was Karl Marx. As we discussed in Chapter 1, Karl Marx was a leading exponent of conflict theory, and his analysis of stratification and social class illustrates his conflict perspective. For Marx, human history was the history of class struggle. He believed that a class system results from and reflects the relations of production within a particular society. Each society has a particular mode of production and people fulfill particular economic or productive roles, the combination of which constitutes the "relations of production." In agricultural societies, there are the people who own land and the tenants; in industrial societies, there are the employers (the owners of productive property) and the workers (the nonowners, or people who work for wages). For Marx, one's class position was a function of one's position in the economic (productive) system of the society.

Marx was an *economic determinist,* which means that he believed that the entire structure of a society derived from its economic organization and that the individual's position in the productive system determined virtually every aspect of his or her life chances, beliefs, behavior, and consciousness. Therefore he believed that people in similar productive positions (classes) tend to hold and share similar life chances, consciousness, wealth, power, and prestige. Thus, for Marx, one's social existence determined one's consciousness and virtually every other aspect of one's life.

According to Marx, classes arise out of the productive system of a society. The relationships between the ruling classes (masters, overlords) and the ruled classes (slaves, serfs) would be marked by struggle and conflict over the unequal distribution of wealth and power within the society. With the dissolution of feudalism and the development of industrialization, new classes would emerge with diametrically opposed interests. On one side were capitalists, or **bourgeoisie**—those who owned productive property such as land, factories, and machinery. The aim of the bourgeoisie was to increase and maximize profit gained through the labor of others. Marx regarded the bourgeoisie as parasites because they gained wealth, power, and profit through the labor of others rather than through their own labor. Much of this profit would be used by the bourgeoisie for their own self-interest in terms of reinvestment in additional markets or machinery. On the other side were the **proletariat,** or workers, who constituted the exploited laboring class. This class did not own anything except their own labor power. They sold this labor to the bourgeoisie in return for a mere subsistence wage, even though by means of their labor, they created much "surplus value" (profit after operating costs and payment of wages) for the bourgeoisie. Workers might be angered by this exploitative situation, but they could not do much about it, because the powerful bourgeoisie used political power to sustain and reinforce their domination.

The continuation of the capitalist system, however, would eventually bring about additional change. With time, the gulf between the positions of the bourgeoisie and the proletariat would become wider and wider, with the bourgeoisie becoming more wealthy and powerful and the proletariat becoming more and more exploited. However, because consciousness is determined by activity, the increasingly exploited and subservient productive role of the proletariat would bring about new forms of class consciousness on the part of the workers. The proletariat would begin to realize that through *collective* action, the bourgeoisie could be overthrown. At this point, Marx felt that the class struggle would become open, deliberate, and conscious. In the end, the proletariat would join together and, with the help of various alienated intellectuals within society, would revolt against the bourgeoisie. With the overthrow of capitalism, the "dictatorship of the proletariat" would become a reality—signaling the onset of the communist, classless society.

The rich get richer while the poor get poorer

In spite of Marx's highly respected and enlightening analysis of the relevance of economic and class factors to human behavior and social organization, his predictions for the revolution of the proletariat have not come true. Particularly in the case of western, industrialized societies, he did not anticipate, among other things, the development of giant national and international labor unions, modern corporate stock companies, and the vast growth of the middle classes. It would appear that each of these factors has tended to lessen class consciousness as well as class conflict, which Marx felt were absolutely necessary for revolution.

Marx foresaw complete revolution—not labor unions and the resulting middle class

Max Weber

Another major contributor to the analysis of stratification was Max Weber. Although Weber's theory of stratification differed from Marx's in several respects, his analysis of stratification systems was based on a conflict perspective. Moreover, he agreed with Marx that the economic aspect of stratification (that is, the ownership and control over property) was of great importance. For Weber, stratification was comprised of three dimensions: wealth, prestige, and power. In his writings, he referred to these three dimensions more specifically as class, status, and party (that is, political power). For Weber, all three serve as sources of conflict and competition among groups within society.

Weber's dimensions of stratification: class, status, and political party

In stressing the economic (wealth) factor, Weber believed that people compose a **class** when they have similar economic interests, occupations, (particularly as these reflect ownership or nonownership of property), and incomes. For Weber, in contrast to Marx, classes did not have to share an explicit form of consciousness. A class simply consisted of a number of individuals who possessed similar economic standing within society. The economic position of some gives them the opportunity to live similarly and, more important, to share common types of life chances. In this sense, certain classes, by virtue of their ownership of property, occupations, and incomes, possess specific types of life advantages compared with those who have nothing to give or sell in the marketplace but their labor. Thus, according to Weber, a class exists when:

Class is determined by wealth

> (1) a number of people have in common a specific causal component in their life chances, in so far as (2) this component is represented exclusively by economic interests in the possession of goods and opportunities for income, and (3) is represented under the conditions of the commodity or labor markets.

Weber indicates that:

> It is the most elemental economic fact that the way in which the disposition over material property is distributed among a plurality of people . . . in itself creates specific life chances. . . . this mode of distribution excludes the non-owners from competing for highly valued goods; it favors the owners and, in fact, gives to them a monopoly to acquire such goods. . . . "Property" and "lack of property" are, therefore, the basic categories of all class situations (Weber, 1946).

Weber termed the second major dimension of stratification **status.** In contrast to classes, which derive from the property relations of the marketplace, Weber believed that "status groups" tended to form "communities" in the sense that the members of each status group often have frequent contact with one another out of friendship, similar values, attitudes, and ways of living.

For Weber, status groups exist because each is ranked and accorded various degrees of prestige within society. Weber recognized that differences in property (class) could and often did make for differences in status, but he believed that this was not always the case. Even relatively nonpropertied classes could and sometimes did share membership in the same status group. The distinctive quality of status is that it makes for differences in lifestyles. Common status symbols, behaviors, tastes, vocabularies, and manners are shared and expected within each status group. Expectations also limit associations and define appropriate friendship cliques. In addition, status groups take on virtually castelike aspects—for instance, with choice of marriage partners limited to the same

Status is castelike and based on similar lifestyles

status group. Status groups therefore take on qualities of highly exclusive, castelike subcultures.

Weber termed the third dimension of stratification **power.** He defined power as the chance of people "to realize their own will . . . even against the resistance of others." Weber's analysis of power tends to emphasize the role of political parties. A party's "action is oriented toward the acquisition of social 'power,' that is to say, toward influencing a communal action no matter what its content may be." Thus, whereas classes are organized on an economic basis, and status groups involve levels of prestige or "honor," parties are based on power. They exist to gain and use power to attain particular goals. These goals may be particular social causes as well as personal and party goals. Some parties are composed of specific class or status groups and thus represent specific economic interests. Parties may attain power through methods ranging from "naked violence of any sort to canvassing for votes with coarse or subtle means: money, social influence, the force of speech, suggestion, clumsy hoax, and so on."

Party is the banding together to attain power

C. Wright Mills

Although Weber stressed the nature of party in his analysis of power, contemporary American sociologists have tended to view power as emanating from a variety of different sources. C. Wright Mills, for instance, sees power as the most important element influencing and determining individual and group relations within a society. Mills advanced a concept of the power structure based on his view that there exists within American society a **power elite.** The elite is composed of those individuals who hold positions at the highest corporate, military, and political levels. By virtue of their commanding positions within the major bureaucratic organizations of the society, Mills felt that this small elite (which numbered fewer than 300 people) made decisions that had major consequences for national and world affairs. According to Mills (1956): "They rule the big corporations. They run the machinery of the state and claim its prerogatives. They direct the military establishment. They occupy the strategic command posts of the social structure." Moreover, these individuals tend to have common interests, concerns, and perspectives; thus the bureaucratic and institutional spheres that they control do not represent a balance of power. Next under the elite are those who have some (but actually very little) power, such as the Congress, which does not really represent the interests of the masses anyway. Finally, there are the masses, who are politically powerless and, for the most part, apathetic.

The power elite; those with little power; the powerless and apathetic masses

Some social scientists do not share Mills's views. Economist John Kenneth Galbraith (1956), for instance, speaks of "countervailing power"—the notion that power centers are not in harmony, do not cooperate, and do not act in the interests of other power centers, but rather are engaged in conflict and competition for power. The power of one sphere tends to balance and offset the power of others. David Riesman (Riesman, Glazer, and Denny, 1950) argues for an "amorphous power structure" that in the long run tends toward a balance of power among veto groups, each having the ability to reject the decisions of others that go against its own interests. Finally, Talcott Parsons (in Bendix and

Galbraith: countervailing power

Riesman: balance of power

Parsons: power circulates

Lipset, 1957) believes that the power in American society is neither limited nor fixed, but actually circulates from one area to another.

Social Class in the United States

What Are Social Classes?

When sociologists speak of a **social class,** they usually refer to a group of people who have relatively equal status (in the sense of position or rank) within a hierarchy of class statuses or positions. As we mentioned above, one's position in the social hierarchy is closely related to one's income, occupation, and education—the combination of factors that sociologists generally include in *socioeconomic status.* In addition, as we have seen, other factors, such as the possession of wealth and power, family background, lifestyle, and associations with and acceptance by others, also play a significant role in determining one's social class. In this sense, economic factors are important but are not the only determinants of class position. Thus college professors are likely to have higher class positions than skilled blue-collar workers by virtue of their occupational and educational prestige, even when the professors' incomes are lower than the blue-collar workers'. Factors such as socialization into class-typed ways of living and acceptance into certain circles of associates and friends are also important determinants of social class.

Classes represent subcultures

Thus classes are more than simply economic categories. Classes also represent subcultures with class-typed ways of thinking, acting, and feeling. Sociologist Harold Hodges (1968) astutely points this out in his description of social class. He states that social class is "a distinct reality which embraces the fact that people live, eat, play, mate, dress, work, and think at contrasting and dissimilar levels. These levels—social classes—are the blended product of shared . . . occupational orientations, educational backgrounds, economic wherewithal, and life experiences." People at different levels, "because of their approximately uniform backgrounds and experiences . . . will share comparable values, attitudes, and lifestyles. Each of these likenesses will be reinforced in turn by clique, work, and friendship ties which are limited, in the main, to persons occupying the same class level" (Hodges, 1968, p. 13). Classes develop a "consciousness of kind" and certain "class conditioned components of personality."

How many social classes are there?

Sociologists do not agree on the number of social classes in the United States. Some sociologists do not speak of class in terms of specific and distinct categories of people. They see social class as representing a continuum of status with no major, clear-cut class divisions or lines. Although this view of stratification for American society is in some measure probably correct, most sociologists (and, in fact, most Americans) tend to think and speak of class in terms of different levels or class categories, such as white-collar and blue-collar or upper, middle, and lower class, and so on. Such conceptualizations allow sociologists to make comparisons among large numbers of people found at relatively distinct positions along the status continuum.

During the past several decades, various sociological studies of social class have identified and described different numbers of classes. In one very early but classic study of Middletown, Robert and Helen Lynd (1929) identified two social classes—the working class and the business class. On a reexamination of Middletown some ten years later, the Lynds (1937) realized that this classification was too simple because some families in the community could not be readily classified as members of the working class or the business class.

Although in more recent times, some sociologists have used the threefold classification system of upper, middle, and lower class, most tend to use a five- or sixfold classification system such as upper upper, lower upper, upper middle, lower middle, upper lower, and lower lower. This approach was characteristic of Warner's study of "Yankee City" during the 1930s (Warner and Lunt, 1941).

Similarly, Harold Hodges's early 1960s description of the class structure of metropolitan San Francisco (the inhabitants of which he termed "Peninsula" people) used five class profiles, ranging from a small upper-class elite to a larger lower-lower class, comprising a poverty-stricken one-sixth of the peninsula population (Hodges, 1961).

Coleman & Neugarten's study of social classes

Aside from investigations of the class structure at the community level, there have been a number of attempts to describe the American class structure nationwide. Coleman and Neugarten (1971), for example, speak of a national class structure composed of five social classes. These include a small upper class (about 1 percent of the total population) centering around a professional and executive corporate elite; an upper middle professional and managerial class (10 percent); a lower middle class comprised of nonmanagerial white-collar workers, blue-collar technicians, and some service workers (32 percent); a working class consisting largely of unionized blue-collar workers (39 percent); and finally, a lower class largely made up of unskilled workers living in poverty (18 percent).

Rossides's Profile of the American Class System

Rossides identifies five social classes in the U.S.

Daniel Rossides (1990) has provided a profile of the American class system that is consistent with much current research. As Rossides indicates, contemporary research has identified five relatively distinct social classes in the United States. Following Rossides, we will now outline many of the characteristics of each of these classes. We should keep in mind, however, as Rossides points out, that class boundaries are not always clear-cut. Moreover, the following profiles are based on many generalizations. Thus not every member of a particular class can be expected to think or behave exactly like others.

The upper class in the United States is composed of a small number of families (approximately 1 to 3 percent). These families occupy a highly stable position in the American stratification structure. They enjoy high personal income, inherited wealth, and economic power. The upper class has high family stability, and it emphasizes the importance of family lineage, education, "breeding," and lifestyle. The upper class maintains a high degree of participation in

Upper class: small, wealthy, tradition-conscious, "leisure class"

both primary and secondary groups—most of which are open only to the "right" people. They also have a high degree of participation in political processes and receive many legislative and government benefits. The upper class is tradition-conscious, civic-minded, and supportive of many cultural and charitable organizations and causes. It is truly a "leisure class," in Rossides's words (although the males do work), highly involved in the consumption of material and symbolic culture. The upper class exercises considerable control over corporations and government. The power of this class stems from its great wealth, enabling it to control much capital investment, and also from its capacity to "set the terms of membership for new wealth"—its control over elite prestige groups and elite private schools is significant in this regard.

Upper middle class: professional, educated, high income, politically active

The upper middle class comprises about 10 to 15 percent of the total population. This class is composed of professionals, business executives, and high-ranking military and civil officials. Upper-middle-class families are characterized by high incomes, high occupational prestige, high education, and a pattern of stable family life. It is expected that children of both sexes receive at least a college education. The economic status and power of this class is frequently a function of its members' professional roles, business ownership, and educational achievement. Rossides points out that members of the upper middle class do not possess certain prestige assets characteristic of the upper class, and its members do not possess great wealth. Nevertheless, its members have high incomes and lead comfortable, affluent lives. The upper middle class tends toward high participation in many voluntary organizations and in political life. It receives many legislative and government benefits. It tends to be economically conservative yet liberal on matters of civil rights and foreign policy.

Lower middle class: modest incomes, high school graduates, "civic-minded," the lower-ranking professionals and white-collar workers

The lower middle class comprises an additional 30 to 35 percent of the national population. This class is diverse. It consists, for example, of small businesspeople and small farmers, lower-ranking professionals and semiprofessionals (teachers, nurses, clergy, local political officials, social workers), and clerical and sales workers. People within this class have modest incomes, some savings, and a certain amount of prestige derived from their occupations. They are high school graduates, and many have attended college at least for a while. In some cases, the incomes of members of the lower middle class are similar to those of the working class. Nevertheless, their overall class standing is higher than that of the working class for a number of reasons. Compared with the working class, lower-middle-class people manifest a higher level of social existence, a higher level of occupational prestige, and more family stability. In addition, their children are more likely to receive a college education. Members of the lower middle class are civic-minded and tend to be more politically aware and active than members of the working and lower classes.

The working class is the largest social class of all, comprising approximately 40 to 45 percent of the total population. This class also is characterized by great occupational and economic diversity. It is composed of skilled, semiskilled, and unskilled workers. Although some working-class members may earn incomes comparable to some middle-class people, the working class as a whole (in spite of unions) is not economically well off. Rossides points out that because working-class people often earn low incomes, they can afford to live only plain, simple lives and they have little or no savings. Despite the relatively high hourly

Some blue-collar workers may earn fairly high incomes, yet their occupational prestige is relatively low.

pay of some skilled workers, their yearly incomes can often be low, due in part to seasonal employment and underemployment. Members of the working class are grade school graduates who may have received some high school or technical training. The education of their children often is restricted to vocational and technical programs. Compared with the upper and middle classes, the working class has less social and occupational prestige, less marital and family stability, and is less active and interested in the political sphere and community activities. Rossides notes that the working class is usually politically liberal when it comes to economic-welfare issues. However, its nonminority members tend to be politically conservative on questions of civil rights.

Working class: not well off economically, little formal education, blue collar, not much interest in political and community activities

The lower class comprises approximately 20 to 25 percent of the population. This class consists of the poor—the continually unemployed and underemployed, the severely underpaid, the elderly poor, and the physically and mentally sick and incapacitated. This class has no economic worth in the labor market. This problem not only perpetuates its poverty but also results in little prestige, social recognition, or power. As Rossides points out:

Lower class: poor, no economic worth in labor market, socially isolated, poor health

> **The worthlessness of the lower class comes from the normal operation of capitalist institutions. The problems of the lower class result from the solutions that the upper classes have found for their own problems. The upper classes fight inflation with unemployment and bankruptcy. They favor technology over labor, oppose trade unions, and support immigration. Secure in their own identities and families, they stress individualism, thus making marriages and family life for**

> **those below them difficult. They oppose taxes for public services, helping to drive people into the labor market, creating yet another way to maintain labor surpluses. And they jealously guard their absolute right to control investment, including the right to use cheap labor overseas (Rossides, 1990).**

Rossides states that, as a whole, the lower class has many other disabilities: Its physical and psychological health is poor, its life expectancy is lower than that of other classes, and it is socially isolated from participation in the broader sphere of social life.

Poverty in America

It is evident from the above analysis that poverty constitutes a major social problem in American society. Unfortunately, many people are not aware of the scope of the poverty problem in our society. They also often fail to recognize that poverty is particularly serious in that it is often intertwined with a host of other problems that affect our society in general and the poor in particular. The poor, for example, must often face the situation of homelessness or the necessity of living in substandard housing. They are less healthy, both physically and mentally, than are nonpoor and affluent groups, and their chances of staying in school and getting a good education are far less than those who are not poor. The poor are more at risk of being victims of violent crime, yet they have a greater chance of being arrested and imprisoned for various types of crimes compared with nonpoor and affluent people.

Poverty is often intertwined with many other problems

Who Are the Poor? In 1988, there were 31.9 million people, a rate of approximately 13.1 percent of the entire United States population, who fell below the federal government's official poverty level. These figures are substantially higher compared with the 1970s, when the number of people in poverty ranged from 23 million to 25.9 million. Every year, the government establishes a poverty line (in terms of money income), which changes in relation to a number of factors, such as family size and composition and the Consumer Price Index. In 1988, the poverty level or "threshold" for a family of four was set at $12,091 (Census Bureau, 1989, P-60, #166).

The number of people in poverty has increased

Examination of poverty data for 1988 reveals a number of important facts that conflict with some popular misconceptions regarding the poor. Approximately one out of every five children (19.7 percent) in the United States under 18 years of age lives in poverty, while 12 percent of all Americans 65 years of age and over are poor. Since 1975, children have had the highest poverty rate of any age group. Children and the elderly constitute one-half of the entire poverty population in our society. In 1988, 65.1 percent of all people living in poverty were white, 29.6 percent were black, and 5.3 percent were of other races. Still, the poverty rate is much higher for blacks compared with whites: 31.6 percent of black people are poor compared with 10.1 percent of white people. Approximately 44 percent of black children under 18 years of age are poor. The poverty rate was higher in nonmetropolitan areas than in metropolitan areas, 33.5 percent of all female householder families (no husband present) ranked below the poverty level, and nearly half (48.3 percent) of poor family householders

Poverty varies by age, race, area of residence, and type of household

Table 6.1. **Poverty Rates Among Various Categories: 1988**

CATEGORY	PERCENTAGE OF POOR WITHIN EACH CATEGORY
Total population of United States	13.1
Under 18 years of age	19.7
Persons 65 years and over	12.0
Whites	10.1
Blacks	31.6
Living in the South	16.2
Living in the Northeast	10.2
Living in the Midwest	11.5
Living in the West	12.7
Female householder families (no spouse present)	33.5
Male householder families (no spouse present)	11.8
Householders completing one or more years of college	3.5
Householders who are high school graduates (no college)	8.9
Householders not completing high school	20.8

Source: U.S. Bureau of the Census, Current Population Reports, Series P–60, No. 166, *Money Income and Poverty Status in the United States: 1988 (Advance Data from the March 1989 Current Population Survey)* (Washington, D.C.: U.S. Government Printing Office, 1989), pp. 6, 8.

worked during the year (Census Bureau, 1989, P-60, #166). Table 6.1 presents further information about poverty and the poor.

Explanations for Poverty. Poverty has been explained in many ways. No one theory or perspective can adequately deal with it, however, because it has different origins and takes on a variety of forms.

One major theory that has attempted to explain the existence and persistence of poverty was popularized by a well-known social scientist, Oscar Lewis, and is termed the **culture of poverty** theory.* According to this theory, the various social strata manifest distinct cultures and the values of the poor are substantially different from the values of people in the mainstream of society (Fave, 1974). There are, according to Lewis, a large number of traits that characterize the "culture of poverty." Examples are feelings of powerlessness, a sense of helplessness, unemployment, an inability to defer gratification, the lack of privacy, and a predisposition to authoritarianism. Many traits of this "culture" inhibit the poor from the adjustment to a success-oriented middle-class society and from upward mobility in that society. In fact, the culture of poverty viewpoint stresses that the poor do not even value upward mobility. This is indicated by a "general lack of commitment to any endeavor requiring sustained effort, self-discipline, and renunciation of present for future gratification" (Fave, 1974). According to Lewis, the culture of poverty is, for the poor, a series of reactions and adaptations to their marginal position in American society. He believes America's poor could not continue to carry on without this culture of poverty

Characteristics of the "culture of poverty" inhibit upward mobility

* For a discussion of this and other theories of poverty, see Beth E. Vanfossen, *The Structure of Social Inequality* (Boston: Little, Brown, 1979), pp. 355–372, and Leonard Beeghley, *Social Stratification in America: A Critical Analysis of Theory and Research* (Santa Monica, Calif.: Goodyear Publishing, 1978), pp. 141–144.

and its structure, rationale, and defense mechanisms. It is a stable and persistent way of life, transmitted from generation to generation in the family (Lewis, 1964).

The culture of poverty is often seen by theorists as having a dual role. On the one hand, it helps the poor cope with their feelings of hopelessness and the harshness of their environment. Yet, at the same time, it incorporates a set of values and behaviors that tends to perpetuate their poverty.

A number of theorists have been critical of the culture of poverty approach. They argue that poverty is basically *situational* rather than "culturally" passed on from generation to generation. From this point of view, the poor do not have a unique set of values; rather they have learned, and in fact subscribe to, middle-class values. In turn, differences in lifestyles and behavior patterns among the poor are not the result of basic value differences, but should be seen as methods of adaptation and adjustment to living in poverty.

Traits are situational conditions of poverty

Charles Valentine, an advocate of the situational approach, believes that unemployment, unskilled work, poor wages, poor housing, and poor education are not ingrained patterns of social response, but are "conditions of poverty." Other sociologists' research supports Valentine by suggesting that the majority of traits that lent support to Lewis's perspective might be "better classified as situational conditions of poverty rather than a bonafide 'culture' of poverty" (Coward, Feagin, and Williams, 1974). Low expectations and low levels of aspiration are, according to Valentine, consistent with the poor's situation; however they should not be viewed as ingrained subcultural values, but as "inevitable emotional responses to the actual conditions of poverty." He also believes that government programs criticize the poor for their cultural inadequacies, such as low achievement motivation, instead of dealing with the problems of income distribution, which are the basis of our nation's poverty (Valentine, 1968).

Social, economic, and political structures exploit the poor

In contrast to the above perspectives, the conflict approach to poverty stresses that the social, economic, and political structures of America deprive the poor from a decent living standard. Some conflict theorists, most notably Marx, view the problem as a product of capitalism. In a market economy, those in poverty are exploited by the few who continually amass privileges and power. Class being the significant fact of social life, the poor become merely a tool for those in power. The social problem of poverty develops out of the dynamics of class struggle and is the product of capitalistic power relations and economic structure.

Sociologist Herbert Gans feels that people in power profit from the poor. He sees poverty as being "deeply connected to the structure of society" (Rossides, 1990). Although Gans maintains a basic conflict perspective, he has attempted to explain poverty from the standpoint of its uses and positive functions. In the following reading, Gans discusses some of these positive functions and suggests a number of functional alternatives to poverty.

THE USES OF POVERTY: THE POOR PAY ALL

Herbert J. Gans

In the following reading, Herbert Gans examines poverty from the standpoint of its "uses" and positive functions. Many people conceive of poverty as harmful to society as a whole. Gans points out that poverty is harmful to some but beneficial economically, socially, and politically to others. For example, poverty helps guarantee that society's dirty work gets done, and it also creates jobs for professions that provide service to the poor. Gans also examines a number of functional alternatives to poverty. For example, if poverty were eliminated, automation still could handle society's dirty work and new roles could be found for those professionals who now prosper by poverty. Gans does not endorse poverty. He points out that poverty does, in fact, exist because it often benefits groups in our society.

Some twenty years ago Robert K. Merton applied the notion of functional analysis* to explain the continuing though maligned existence of the urban political machine: if it continued to exist, perhaps it fulfilled latent—unintended or unrecognized—positive functions. Clearly it did. Merton pointed out how the political machine provided central authority to get things done when a decentralized local government could not act, humanized the services of the impersonal bureaucracy for fearful citizens, offered concrete help (rather than abstract law or justice) to the poor, and otherwise performed services needed or demanded by many people but considered unconventional or even illegal by formal public agencies.

Today poverty is more maligned than the political machine ever was; yet it, too, is a persistent social phenomenon. Consequently, there may be some merit in applying functional analysis to poverty, in asking whether it also has positive functions that explain its persistence.

Merton defined functions as "those observed consequences [of a phenomenon] which make for the adaptation or adjustment of a given [social] system." I shall use a slightly different definition; instead of identifying functions for an entire social system, I shall identify them for the interest groups, socioeconomic classes, and other population aggregates with shared values that "inhabit" a social system. I suspect that in a modern heterogeneous society, few phenomena are functional or dysfunctional for the society as a whole, and that most result in benefits to some groups and costs to others. Nor are any phenomena indispensable; in most instances, one can suggest what Merton calls "functional alternatives" or equivalents for them, i.e., other social patterns or policies that

From *Social Policy*, July/August 1971, SOCIAL POLICY published by Social Policy Corporation, New York, New York 10036.

* "Manifest and Latent Functions," in *Social Theory and Social Structure* (Glencoe, Ill: The Free Press, 1949), p. 71.

achieve the same positive functions but avoid the dysfunctions.†

Associating poverty with positive functions seems at first glance to be unimaginable. Of course, the slumlord and the loan shark are commonly known to profit from the existence of poverty, but they are viewed as evil men, so their activities are classified among the dysfunctions of poverty. However, what is less often recognized, at least by the conventional wisdom, is that poverty also makes possible the existence or expansion of respectable professions and occupations, for example, penology, criminology, social work, and public health. More recently, the poor have provided jobs for professional and paraprofessional "poverty warriors," and for journalists and social scientists, this author included, who have supplied the information demanded by the revival of public interest in poverty.

Clearly, then, poverty and the poor may well satisfy a number of positive functions for many nonpoor groups in American society. I shall describe thirteen such functions—economic, social, and political—that seem to me most significant.

THE FUNCTIONS OF POVERTY

First, the existence of poverty ensures that society's "dirty work" will be done. Every society has such work: physically dirty or dangerous, temporary, deadend and underpaid, undignified and menial jobs. Society can fill these jobs by paying higher wages than for "clean" work, or it can force people who have no other choice to do the dirty work—and at low wages. In America, poverty functions to provide a low-wage labor pool that is willing—or, rather, unable to be *un*willing—to perform dirty work at low cost. Indeed, this function of the poor is so important that in some Southern states, welfare payments have been cut off during the summer months when the poor are needed to work in the fields. Moreover, much of the debate about the Negative Income Tax and the Family Assistance Plan has concerned their impact on the work incentive, by which is actually meant the incentive of the poor to do the needed dirty work if the wages therefrom are no larger than the income grant. Many economic activities that involve dirty work depend on the poor for their existence: restaurants, hospitals, parts of the garment industry, and "truck farming," among others, could not persist in their present form without the poor.

Second, because the poor are required to work at low wages, they subsidize a variety of economic activities that benefit the affluent. For example, domestics subsidize the upper middle and upper classes, making life easier for their employers and freeing affluent women for a variety of professional, cultural, civic, and partying activities. Similarly, because the poor pay a higher proportion of their income in property and sales taxes, among others, they subsidize many state and local governmental services that benefit more affluent groups. In addition, the poor support innovation in medical practice as patients in teaching and research hospitals and as guinea pigs in medical experiments.

Third, poverty creates jobs for a number of occupations and professions that serve or "service" the poor, or protect the rest of society from them. As already noted, penology would be minuscule without the poor, as would the police. Other activities and groups that flourish because of the existence of poverty are the numbers game, the

† I shall henceforth abbreviate positive functions as functions and negative functions as dysfunctions. I shall also describe functions and dysfunctions, in the planner's terminology, as benefits and costs.

sale of heroin and cheap wines and liquors, pentecostal ministers, faith healers, prostitutes, pawn shops, and the peacetime army, which recruits its enlisted men mainly from among the poor.

Fourth, the poor buy goods others do not want and thus prolong the economic usefulness of such goods—day-old bread, fruit and vegetables that would otherwise have to be thrown out, secondhand clothes, and deteriorating automobiles and buildings. They also provide incomes for doctors, lawyers, teachers, and others who are too old, poorly trained, or incompetent to attract more affluent clients.

In addition to economic functions, the poor perform a number of social functions.

Fifth, the poor can be identified and punished as alleged or real deviants in order to uphold the legitimacy of conventional norms. To justify the desirability of hard work, thrift, honesty, and monogamy, for example, the defenders of these norms must be able to find people who can be accused of being lazy, spendthrift, dishonest, and promiscuous. Although there is some evidence that the poor are about as moral and law-abiding as anyone else, they are more likely than middle-class transgressors to be caught and punished when they participate in deviant acts. Moreover, they lack the political and cultural power to correct the stereotypes that other people hold of them and thus continue to be thought of as lazy, spendthrift, etc., by those who need living proof that moral deviance does not pay.

Sixth, and conversely, the poor offer vicarious participation to the rest of the population in the uninhibited sexual, alcoholic, and narcotic behavior in which they are alleged to participate and which, being freed from the constraints of affluence, they are often thought to enjoy more than the middle classes. Thus many people, some social scientists included, believe that the poor not only are more given to uninhibited behavior (which may be true, although it is often motivated by despair more than by lack of inhibition) but derive more pleasure from it than affluent people (which research by Lee Rainwater, Walter Miller, and others shows to be patently untrue). However, whether the poor actually have more sex and enjoy it more is irrelevant; so long as middle-class people believe this to be true, they can participate in it vicariously when instances are reported in factual or fictional form.

Seventh, the poor also serve a direct cultural function when culture created by or for them is adopted by the more affluent. The rich often collect artifacts from extinct folk cultures of poor people; and almost all Americans listen to the blues, Negro spirituals, and country music, which originated among the Southern poor. Recently they have enjoyed the rock styles that were born, like the Beatles, in the slums; and in the last year, poetry written by ghetto children has become popular in literary circles. The poor also serve as culture heroes, particularly, of course, to the left; but the hobo, the cowboy, the hipster, and the mythical prostitute with a heart of gold have performed this function for a variety of groups.

Eighth, poverty helps to guarantee the status of those who are not poor. In every hierarchical society someone has to be at the bottom; but in American society, in which social mobility is an important goal for many and people need to know where they stand, the poor function as a reliable and relatively permanent measuring rod for status comparisons. This is particularly true for the working class, whose politics is influenced by the need to maintain status distinctions between themselves and the poor, much as the aristocracy must find ways of distinguishing itself from the *nouveaux riches.*

Ninth, the poor also aid the upward mobility of groups just above them in the class hierarchy. Thus a goodly number of Americans have entered the middle class through the profits earned from the provision of goods and services in the slums, including illegal or nonrespectable ones that upper-class and upper-middle-class businessmen shun because of their low prestige. As a result, members of almost every immigrant group have financed their upward mobility by providing slum housing, entertainment, gambling, narcotics, etc., to later arrivals—most recently to Blacks and Puerto Ricans.

Tenth, the poor help to keep the aristocracy busy, thus justifying its continued existence. "Society" uses the poor as clients of settlement houses and beneficiaries of charity affairs; indeed, the aristocracy must have the poor to demonstrate its superiority over other elites who devote themselves to earning money.

Eleventh, the poor, being powerless, can be made to absorb the costs of change and growth in American society. During the nineteenth century, they did the backbreaking work that built the cities; today, they are pushed out of their neighborhoods to make room for "progress." Urban renewal projects to hold middle-class taxpayers in the city and expressways to enable suburbanites to commute downtown have typically been located in poor neighborhoods, since no other group will allow itself to be displaced. For the same reason, universities, hospitals, and civic centers also expand into land occupied by the poor. The major costs of the industrialization of agriculture have been borne by the poor, who are pushed off the land without recompense; and they have paid a large share of the human cost of the growth of American power overseas, for they have provided many of the foot soldiers for Vietnam and other wars.

Twelfth, the poor facilitate and stabilize the American political process. Because they vote and participate in politics less than other groups, the political system is often free to ignore them. Moreover, since they can rarely support Republicans, they often provide the Democrats with a captive constituency that has no other place to go. As a result, the Democrats can count on their votes, and be more responsive to voters—for example, the white working class—who might otherwise switch to the Republicans.

Thirteenth, the role of the poor in upholding conventional norms (see the *fifth* point, above) also has a significant political function. An economy based on the ideology of laissez faire requires a deprived population that is allegedly unwilling to work or that can be considered inferior because it must accept charity or welfare in order to survive. Not only does the alleged moral deviance of the poor reduce the moral pressure on the present political economy to eliminate poverty but socialist alternatives can be made to look quite unattractive if those who will benefit most from them can be described as lazy, spendthrift, dishonest, and promiscuous.

THE ALTERNATIVES

I have described thirteen of the more important functions poverty and the poor satisfy in American society, enough to support the functionalist thesis that poverty, like any other social phenomenon, survives in part because it is useful to society or some of its parts. This analysis is not intended to suggest that because it is often functional, poverty *should* exist, or that it *must* exist. For one thing, poverty has many more dysfunctions than functions; for another, it is possible to suggest functional alternatives.

For example, society's dirty work could be done without poverty, either by automation or by paying "dirty workers" decent wages. Nor is it necessary for the poor to subsidize the many activities they support through their low-wage jobs. This would, however, drive up the costs of these activities, which would result in higher prices to their customers and clients. Similarly, many of the professionals who flourish because of the poor could be given other roles. Social workers could provide counseling to the affluent, as they prefer to do anyway; and the police could devote themselves to traffic and organized crime. Other roles would have to be found for badly trained or incompetent professionals now relegated to serving the poor, and someone else would have to pay their salaries. Few penologists would be employable, however. And pentecostal religion could probably not survive without the poor—nor would parts of the second- and third-hand-goods market. And in many cities, "used" housing that no one else wants would then have to be torn down at public expense.

Alternatives for the cultural functions of the poor could be found more easily and cheaply. Indeed, entertainers, hippies, and adolescents are already serving as the deviants needed to uphold traditional morality and as devotees of orgies to "staff" the fantasies of vicarious participation.

The status functions of the poor are another matter. In a hierarchical society, some people must be defined as inferior to everyone else with respect to a variety of attributes, but they need not be poor in the absolute sense. One could conceive of a society in which the "lower class," though last in the pecking order, received 75 percent of the median income, rather than 15-40 percent, as is now the case. Needless to say, this would require considerable income redistribution.

The contribution the poor make to the upward mobility of the groups that provide them with goods and services could also be maintained without the poor's having such low incomes. However, it is true that if the poor were more affluent, they would have access to enough capital to take over the provider role, thus competing with, and perhaps rejecting, the "outsiders." (Indeed, owing in part to antipoverty programs, this is already happening in a number of ghettos, where white storeowners are being replaced by Blacks.) Similarly, if the poor were more affluent, they would make less willing clients for upper-class philanthropy, although some would still use settlement houses to achieve upward mobility, as they do now. Thus "Society" could continue to run its philanthropic activities.

The political functions of the poor would be more difficult to replace. With increased affluence the poor would probably obtain more political power and be more active politically. With higher incomes and more political power, the poor would be likely to resist paying the costs of growth and change. Of course, it is possible to imagine urban renewal and highway projects that properly reimbursed the displaced people, but such projects would then become considerably more expensive, and many might never be built. This, in turn, would reduce the comfort and convenience of those who now benefit from urban renewal and expressways. Finally, hippies could serve also as more deviants to justify the existing political economy—as they already do. Presumably, however, if poverty were eliminated, there would be fewer attacks on that economy.

In sum, then, many of the functions served by the poor could be replaced if poverty were eliminated, but almost always at higher costs to others, particularly more affluent others. Consequently, a functional analysis must conclude that poverty persists not only because it fulfills a number of positive functions but also because many of the functional alternatives to poverty would be quite dysfunctional for the affluent members of society. A functional analysis thus ultimately arrives at much the same conclusion as radical sociology, except that radical thinkers treat as manifest what I describe as latent: that social phenomena that are functional for affluent or powerful groups and dysfunctional for poor or powerless ones persist; that when the elimination of such phenomena through functional alternatives would generate dysfunctions for the affluent or powerful, they will continue to persist; and that phenomena like poverty can be eliminated only when they become dysfunctional for the affluent or powerful, or when the powerless can obtain enough power to change society.

Review Questions

1. List several of the positive functions that, according to Gans, poverty serves for the nonpoor.
2. Identify, in contrast to Gans's analysis, some of the negative aspects of poverty for the poor as well as for society as a whole.
3. List some of the functional alternatives to poverty together with their costs to other members of society.

Mobility in the United States: Caste and Class

In general terms, social mobility can be discussed with reference to the *type* of stratification system characteristic of particular societies. As we mentioned earlier, at one extreme, there is the caste system in which a person's rank or position is determined and fixed on the basis of birth. Societies based upon the caste system are termed "closed" societies in the sense that there is no opportunity for individuals to move up or down. In contrast to the closed society is the "open" society, in which mobility is not only possible but frequent and based on individual achievement.

Sociologists traditionally distinguish between two types of mobility. One of these is **vertical mobility,** the movement upward or downward from one class level to another. The office worker who eventually becomes a personnel director for a company exemplifies vertical mobility. In contrast, **horizontal mobility** refers to a change of position that does not involve any real alteration of class rank. Thus the architect who becomes a lawyer is horizontally mobile. We are primarily concerned in this section with an analysis of *vertical* mobility in the United States.

Whether one is upwardly mobile in American society is related to many factors. Place of residence is important—mobility is usually higher in urban areas than in rural areas. People who marry late, have only one or two children, and get a college education (sometimes at Ivy League universities) tend to be upwardly mobile. In general, there is a strong and positive relationship between the amount of education one acquires and one's estimated lifetime income. Probably the most important indicator of an individual's mobility (either upward or downward) is occupation, and this, in turn, is related to the person's ability and chance to acquire education that provides the knowledge, skills, and technical training necessary to qualify anyone for particular work. When sociologists study mobility in the United States, they tend to focus on people's occupational changes. However, they also look at differences in class standing between parents and children. This is referred to as **intergenerational mobility,** and it is typically indexed by comparing occupational differences between generations.

From these studies, sociologists have gained a great deal of information with regard to mobility patterns in American society. The following represent only a few of the most basic observations they have made with respect to mobility in the contemporary United States. First, mobility (both career and intergenerational) appears to be widespread. Second, however, when sociologists look at general occupational categories such as white-collar and blue-collar (that is, nonmanual as opposed to manual categories), they find that mobility is more common within these categories than between them. For instance, a truck driver working for a large company has a better chance of becoming a foreman or dispatcher for the company than of becoming a white-collar administrator. Mobility usually occurs in small stages over time. Thus, although mobility tends to be common in American society, many people do not have a very high degree of mobility during their working careers.

Some basic observations regarding mobility

Third, sociologists generally agree that the rate of upward mobility (from manual to nonmanual) exceeds the rate of downward mobility, but the difference is not very great. In fact, there is some evidence that the rate of upward intergenerational mobility is roughly similar to the rate of downward intergenerational mobility (Miller, 1969). Comparing fathers' and sons' occupations in data from the Department of Commerce (1977) shows that in most cases, sons of white-collar workers end up in white-collar occupations, and sons of blue-collar workers end in up in blue-collar occupations. Moreover, only about 20 percent of the sons whose fathers were employed in lower-level manual positions had themselves attained upper-level, white-collar positions. But only 16 percent of the sons whose fathers were employed in white-collar occupations were engaged in lower-level, manual occupations.

Analysis of mobility patterns from 1982 also shows that, in general, sons of nonmanual workers often end up in some form of nonmanual occupation, and sons of manual workers tend to end up in manual occupations (Tausky, 1984). Upward occupational mobility was more common than downward occupational mobility. One-third of sons moved into a specific higher occupational level than their fathers', but one-quarter moved into a specific lower occupational level than their fathers'. Women were more likely to move up from their fathers' occupational group than were men. But even so, about two-thirds of these moves on the part of women were into lower-level, nonmanual clerical and sales jobs.

Mobility in the U.S.: the present situation

Fourth, although factors such as individual effort and motivation are important for mobility, changes in the occupational structure itself also affect mobility. Changes in occupational structure are, in turn, related to the degree of economic growth, industrial expansion, and technological change in society. For example,

Changes in occupational structure are important for mobility

during the first half of this century, industrialization and technological change in American society caused a decrease in the number of farm and unskilled manual occupations. Over the long run, children of manually employed parents had to acquire the training for more skilled and perhaps nonmanual occupations rather than face downward mobility. Industrial and bureaucratic expansion after World War II also made for large changes in the occupational structure—creating vast opportunities for mobility in white-collar and new technical fields. Such expansion was significantly responsible for the growth of white-collar middle classes during the 1950s and 1960s. Finally, current economic and technological change, associated with the beginning of the postindustrial era, has created additional changes in the occupational structure. Jobs in high-technology areas and a vast and rapidly expanding service sector have become the main avenues for social mobility for many Americans.

The economy's rapidly expanding service sector

Thus economic, industrial, and technological change have been the sources of much mobility in American society. But evidence indicates that American mobility has not been exceptionally high compared with many other industrial nations. France, Great Britain, Sweden, and Japan, for example, have rates of mobility similar to that of the United States.

Mobility and Class of Origin

As we mentioned previously, American stratification is characterized not only by class aspects of ranking but also by castelike qualities. In many respects, the system is castelike in the sense that some ascribed qualities (those acquired at birth) play a role in determining an individual's present class position as well as her or his opportunities for mobility. A person's class position at birth (sometimes referred to as class of origin), for example, is highly important in this regard.

The poor often stay poor; the rich, rich

People born into the highest social levels (the upper class) have simply "made it." They cannot go higher, and the possibility of losing their vast wealth, power, and prestige is remote. People born into the bottom levels find upward mobility very difficult to achieve because they have relatively little opportunity to acquire the skills and advanced education necessary for occupational improvement. Generally speaking, the life circumstances and life chances for these people have changed very little over the years. For example, Table 6.2 indicates that in 1987, the lowest fifth of the American population according to income received only 5 percent of the national income, whereas the highest fifth received about one-half of the national income. Moreover, this pattern has remained virtually the same over the last 30 years. In 1968, 25.4 million people were living in poverty. As of 1988, despite all the government programs and billions of tax dollars spent to improve this situation, the number of poor actually increased to 31.9 million (Census Bureau, 1989, P-60, #166).

Not everyone living in poverty remains there. Some poverty results perhaps from short-term illness, disability, displacement, or layoff. However, for millions of other low-income people, this is not the case. Many of these people remain in or near poverty over many years (perhaps generations) because of discrimination or economic or technological change that renders them unem-

Table 6.2. Percentage of National Income Received by Each Fifth of the U.S. Population (Families)

	1953	1987
Highest fifth	40.9	43.7
Second highest fifth	23.9	24.1
Middle fifth	18.0	16.9
Second lowest fifth	12.5	10.8
Lowest fifth	4.7	4.6

Source: U.S. Bureau of Census, Current Population Reports, Series P-60, No. 162, *Money Income of Households, Families, and Persons in the United States: 1987* (Washington, D.C.: U.S. Government Printing Office, 1989), p. 42. See also U.S. Bureau of the Census, *Statistical Abstract of the U.S.: 1990* (Washington, D.C.: U.S. Government Printing Office, 1990), p. 451.

ployable or because they are trapped in a cycle of poverty. Of course, as we have seen in the reading "The Uses of Poverty: The Poor Pay All," the persistence of poverty also may be partly explained in terms of the positive functions it serves for the nonpoor. Regardless of the reasons for poverty, the poor in American society stand a slim chance for mobility. Thus stratification in the United States tends to manifest certain castelike qualities, particularly at the extreme top and bottom levels. Although mobility does occur at these levels, for the most part, it is horizontal rather than vertical.

In contrast to the lower class, the middle class has traditionally encountered relatively few barriers to mobility. Statistics indicate that historically, most mobility has occurred at or near the middle of the American stratification system. By and large, the middle class has believed in the American dream of success, and for many, it has become a reality. However, whether many middle-class people will continue to experience upward mobility remains to be seen. A combination of inflation and increased taxation during the 1970s, plus a major recession during the early 1980s, eroded the standards of living of many people, particularly those in the middle class. The 1980s also witnessed a number of changes in the occupational structure, which tended to dampen mobility prospects for many. In particular, there was a large increase in the numbers of lower-status, lower-paying service-sector jobs together with the loss of large numbers of higher-paying jobs, especially in the manufacturing area.

The numbers of lower-status, lower-paying service-sector jobs grew during the 1980s

Perhaps more problematic is the possibility that in the future, the economy may not be able to generate enough occupational opportunities necessary to maintain lifestyles and ensure upward mobility for many people within the middle- or near-middle-class levels. Jobs in various computer and other high-technology areas will continue to increase. Nevertheless, we can expect continuing growth in the massive service sector of the economy, and in many instances, among those service jobs (such as office clerks, sales clerks, secretaries, waiters, and cashiers) that require little higher education and do not pay very well. Government projections indicate that between 1988 and the year 2000, there will be approximately twice as many new jobs for janitors as for computer programmers (U.S. Bureau of the Census, *Statistical Abstract of the U.S.: 1990*).

Some scholars argue that trends in household income and recent changes in the occupational structure reveal that the middle class is in a state of decline and/or possibly shrinking. While this is a matter of some debate, there is nevertheless a distinct possibility that upward mobility for those in the middle and near middle classes will become more difficult. Thus, in the future, many people will be forced to adjust their expectations and behavior in line with less affluent lifestyles.

Mobility and Women

In addition to class of origin, sex is another ascribed quality that is important in determining one's class position and one's opportunities for mobility. Studies dealing with the relative mobility of women and men have yielded inconsistent evidence. Some studies show that the mobility of women in our society is far less than that of men. Others show that the social mobility of women is roughly similar to that of men. For women, mobility is usually a function of two factors: marriage and, increasingly, occupational achievement. Marriage may influence a woman's mobility in various ways. Obviously, marriage that produces a large family is not often very conducive to mobility. On the other hand, some mobility by women results from the fact that they have "married well" (sometimes in addition to pursuing careers before or after marriage).

Factors that influence the mobility of women

Increasingly, however, as more women have entered the labor force, their mobility has become more closely related to their own occupational status and achievements. When we compare male and female mobility patterns on these bases, significant differences become apparent. Occupationally, although there has been a growth in the number of women engineers, scientists, physicians, lawyers, and managers, women continue to be found primarily in certain kinds of jobs—clerical, secretarial, elementary school teaching, and selling—and the types of service jobs that do not carry much prestige and in general pay badly. Moreover, even when women work in positions deemed comparable to those of men, they usually are paid less than men are. As a whole, income differences between the sexes are substantial. In 1987, the median income of all full-time year-round female workers was only 66 percent of the median income of all full-time year-round male workers. Perhaps more distressing is the fact that this difference has shown little change since the early 1960s (Census Bureau, 1989, P-60, #162).

Comparable work does not often mean comparable pay

We must conclude that these occupational and income differentials are in some measure the direct result of overt discrimination against women. In addition, these differentials also result from traditional (but no less discriminatory) restrictions within the occupational system itself. As Beth Vanfossen notes:

> **. . . women workers are channeled into a very few occupations. The occupational system is, of course, highly differentiated by sex; some jobs are performed mostly by women and other jobs mostly by men. . . . Because women are offered employment in such a narrow range of jobs, the effect is to limit the opportunity for women for advancement and self-development and to reduce competition with men so that men's mobility chances are not materially threatened (Vanfossen, 1979, p. 196).**

There are significant differences in the mobility patterns and opportunities of males and females. In general, men are more mobile than women.

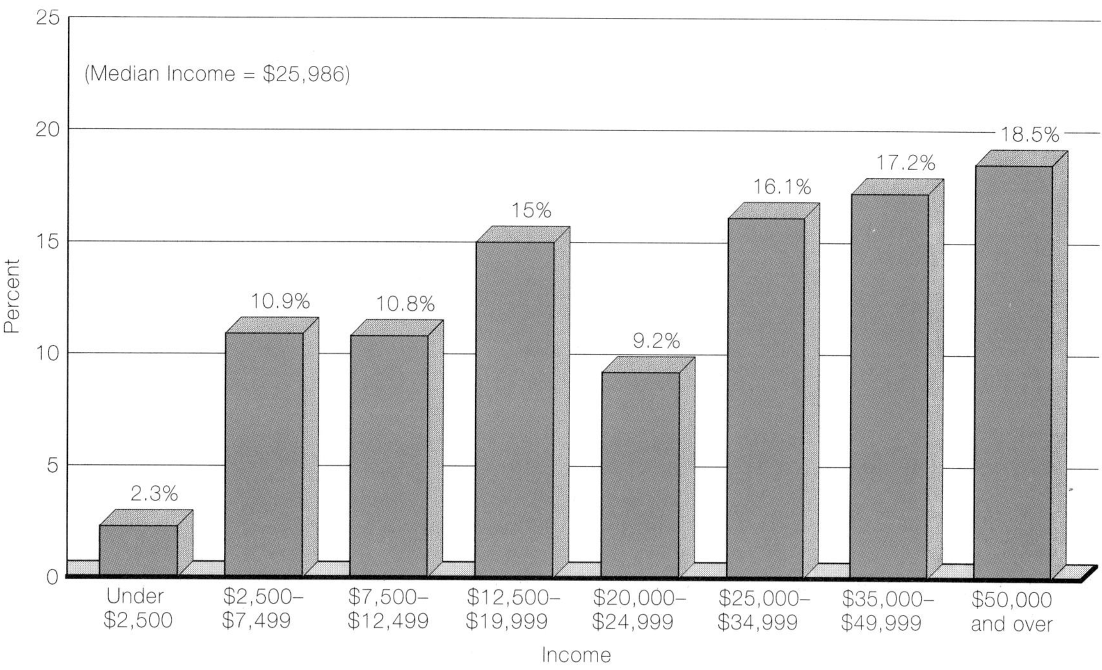

Figure 6.1 **Stratification of United States households by income for 1987.**
Source: U.S. Bureau of the Census, Current Population Reports, Series P-60, No. 162, *Money Income of Households, Families, and Persons in the United States: 1987* (Washington, D.C.: U.S. Government Printing Office, 1989), p. 10.

Mobility and Blacks

Finally, castelike aspects are also evident in the social positions of blacks and whites. Racial identity still serves as an element by which people are ranked, evaluated, and rewarded. But several sociological studies indicate that certain racial aspects of caste in the United States have weakened. There is also evidence of a growing black middle class. Mobility for blacks from the standpoint of income, occupation, and education has become more common than ever before.

Mobility for blacks is more common, but substantial inequalities still remain

Yet, although racial aspects of caste are perhaps less salient today than they once were, a disproportionate number of blacks remain in lower income and occupational levels, and patterns of segregation still exist in housing and in education (particularly at the elementary and high school levels). In terms of income, for example, as Figures 6.1 and 6.2 show, the 1987 median income of all households in the United States was $25,986. But the median household income of blacks was only 56.4 percent that of whites. In 1988, the poverty rate for blacks was 31.6 percent (Census Bureau, 1989, P-60, #166). Factors of income, occupation, and education tap only the socioeconomic dimension of social class. When it comes to other dimensions (as described by Weber), such as prestige and power, black gains have been modest at best. In general, mobility for blacks has

The poverty rate for blacks is high

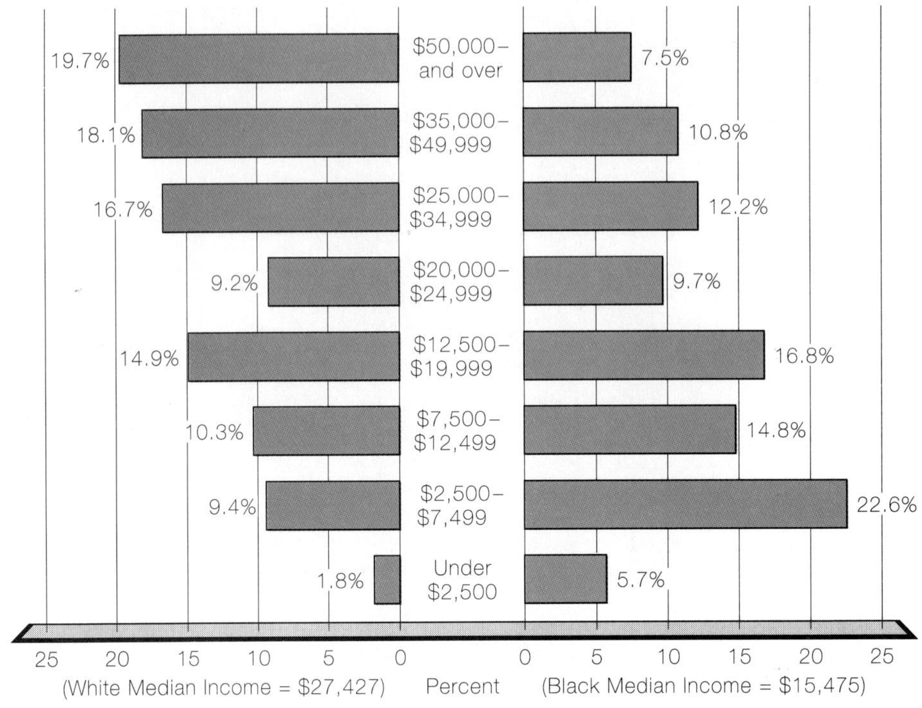

Figure 6.2 Stratification of black and white households by income for 1987.
Source: U.S. Bureau of the Census, Current Population Reports, Series P-60, No. 162, *Money Income of Households, Families, and Persons in the United States: 1987* (Washington, D.C.: U.S. Government Printing Office, 1989), pp. 10–11.

increased, but substantial differences in class position and mobility patterns between blacks and whites remain.

Conclusions on mobility

A number of general conclusions can be drawn from this analysis of mobility. First, the popular assumption that mobility is common in American society seems to be correct, particularly where intergenerational mobility is concerned. However, mobility is a two-way street, and downward mobility occurs more frequently than most people suspect. Second, individual effort and motivation are important for mobility, but many barriers to mobility derive from class as well as from castelike features in the American stratification system. Economic, industrial, and occupational structures themselves also play a vital role in determining upward and downward mobility. Third, despite some popular notions to the contrary, mobility—particularly upward—is not easy. We may hear of an occasional "overnight success," but in reality, such happenings are rare indeed. Upward social mobility for most people tends to be slow, and it occurs in small stages—if it occurs at all.

ADDRESS UNKNOWN: HOMELESSNESS IN CONTEMPORARY AMERICA

James D. Wright

In the following reading, James D. Wright discusses the phenomenon of homelessness in contemporary American society. Evidence indicates that there has been a significant growth of this problem during the 1980s. Wright points out that contrary to commonly held stereotypes, the homeless comprise a diverse, heterogeneous population. The reading links the causes of homelessness to poverty and poverty-related factors.

The past decade has witnessed the growth of a disturbing and largely unexpected new problem in American cities: the rise of what has been called the "new homeless." Homeless derelicts, broken-down alcoholics, and skid row bums have existed in most times and places throughout our history. But the seemingly sudden appearance of homeless young men, women, children, and whole families on the streets and in the shelters was, in retrospect, a clear signal that something had gone very seriously wrong.

The sudden intensity and new visibility of the homelessness problem took most observers by surprise. Ten or fifteen years ago, a walk along the twenty-odd blocks from Madison Square Gardens to Greenwich Village would have been largely uneventful, a pleasant outing in an interesting part of New York City. The same walk today brings one across an assortment of derelict and indigent people—old women rummaging in the trash for bottles and cans, young kids swilling cheap wine from paper bags, seedy men ranting meaninglessly at all who venture near. Who are these people? Where did they come from? What, if anything, can or should be done to help?

Many stereotypes about the homeless have sprung up in the last decade. One of the most popular is that they are all crazy people who have been let loose from mental hospitals. A variation is that they are all broken-down old drunks. One writer has described them as the "drunk, the addicted, and the just plain shiftless"; the implication is that most of the homeless could do better for themselves if they really wanted to. Still another view is that they are welfare leeches, living off the dole. A particularly popular view that sprang up during the Reagan years was that most of the homeless are, as Reagan put it, "well, we might say, homeless by choice," people who have chosen to give up on the rat race of modern society and to live unfettered by bills, taxes, mortgage payments, and related worries. In truth, all these stereotypes are true of some homeless people, and none of them are true of all homeless people. As with any other large group in the American population, the homeless are a diverse, heterogeneous lot. No single catch phrase or easy myth can possibly describe them all.

As in times past, most homeless people in America today are men, but a sizable fraction are women and a smaller but still signifi-

Society, vol. 26, no. 6, September/October 1989, pp. 45–53.

cant fraction are the children of homeless adults. All told, the women and children add up to between one-third and two-fifths of the homeless population. Indifference to the plight of homeless adult men comes easily in an illiberal era, but indifference to the plight of homeless women and children, groups society has traditionally obligated itself to protect, comes easily only to the coldhearted.

Likewise, alcohol abuse and homelessness are tightly linked in the popular stereotype, but recent studies confirm that less than 40 percent of the homeless population abuses alcohol to excess; the majority, the remaining 60 percent, do not. Focusing just on the adult men, the studies show that alcohol abuse still runs only to about 50 percent: about half the men are chronic alcoholics, but then, the other half are not.

In like fashion, mental illness is certainly a significant problem within the homeless population, but severe chronic psychiatric disorder characterizes only about a third; the remaining two-thirds are not mentally ill, at least not according to any meaningful clinical standard.

Being among the poorest of the poor, it is also true that many homeless people receive governmental assistance in the form of general assistance (welfare), food stamps, disability pensions, and the like. Yet, nationwide, the studies show that only about half the homeless receive any form of social welfare assistance; the remaining half survive on their own devices, without government aid of any sort.

And so: Some of the homeless *are* broken-down alcoholics, but most are not. Some *are* mentally imparied, but most are not. Some *are* living off the benefit programs made available through the social welfare system, but most are not. Clearly, the popular mythologies do not provide an adequate portrait of the homeless in America today.

ON DEFINITIONS AND NUMBERS

Defining homelessness for either research or operational purposes has proven to be a rather sticky business. It is easy to agree on the extremes of a definition: an old man who sleeps under a bridge down by the river and has nowhere else to go would obviously be considered homeless in any conceivable definition of the term. But there are also many ambiguous cases. What of persons who live in rooming houses or flophouses? Even if they have lived in the same room for years, we might still want to consider them homeless in at least some senses of the term. What of persons who live in abandoned buildings? In tents or shacks made from scrap materials? In cars and vans? What of a divorced woman with children who can no longer afford rent on the apartment and who has an offer from her family "to live with us for as long as you need"? What of people who would be homeless except that they have temporarily secured shelter in the homes of their families or friends? Or those that would be homeless except that they are temporarily "housed" in jails, prisons, hospitals, or other institutions? What of the person on a fixed income who rents a cheap hotel room three weeks a month and lives on the streets or in the shelters for the fourth week because the pension is adequate to cover only three-quarters of the monthly room rent?

Clearly, to be homeless is to lack regular and customary access to a conventional dwelling unit. The ambiguities arise in trying to define "regular and customary access" and "conventional dwelling unit."

These examples demonstrate that *homelessness is not and cannot be a precisely defined condition.* A family who sleeps in its pickup truck and has nowhere else to go would be considered homeless by almost everyone. A long-distance trucker who sleeps regularly—perhaps three or four nights a week—in the cab of his $100,000 rig, who earns $30,000 or $40,000 a year, and who has a nice home where he sleeps when he is not on the road, would not be considered "homeless" by anyone. Our long-distance trucker has options; our homeless family living in its pickup does not.

Thus, choice is implied in any definition of homelessness. In general, people who choose to live the way they do are not to be considered homeless, however inadequate their housing may appear to be, while those who live in objectively inadequate housing—in makeshift quarters or cheap flophouses or in the shelters and missions—because they do not have the resources to do otherwise *would* be considered homeless in most definitions, clearly in mine.

"The resources to do otherwise" implies yet another aspect of my definition of homelessness: that true homelessness results from extreme poverty. One hears from time to time of "street people" who are found to have a locker in the bus station stuffed with cash, or of vagabonds who, in a former life, traded stock on Wall Street but cashed in for the unfettered romance of life on the road. In some sense, these people are "homeless," but they are homeless by choice. Ronald Reagan notwithstanding, they comprise no important part of the homeless problem in this nation and I shall say nothing further about them.

Poor people living in objectively inadequate housing because they lack the means to do otherwise number in the tens of millions. Indeed, if we adopt a sufficiently inclusive definition of "objectively inadequate housing," we would capture virtually the entire poverty population of the country, some 35 million people, within the homeless category. And yet, surely, being homeless is more than just being poor, although, just as surely, being poor has a lot to do with it.

My colleagues and I have therefore found it useful to distinguish between the *literally homeless* and the *marginally housed.* By "literally homeless" I mean those who, on a given night, have nowhere to go—no rented room, no friend's apartment, no flophouse—people who sleep out on the streets or who *would* sleep out on the streets except that they avail themselves of beds in shelters, missions, and other facilities set up to provide space for otherwise homeless people. And by "marginally housed" I mean those who have a more or less reasonable claim to more or less stable housing of more or less minimal adequacy, being closer to the "less" than the "more" on one or all criteria. This distinction certainly does not solve the definitional problem, but it does specify more clearly the subgroups of interest.

This discussion should be adequate to confirm that there is no single, best, correct, easily agreed upon definition of "homelessness," and thus, no single correct answer to the question: "How many homeless people are there?" There is, rather, a continuum of housing adequacy or housing stability, with actual cases to be found everywhere along the continuum. Just where in the continuum one draws the line, defining those above as adequately if marginally housed and those below as homeless, is of necessity a somewhat arbitrary and therefore disputable decision.

Nonetheless, despite the unavoidable arbitrariness, the discussion calls attention to three pertinent groups: (1) the poverty population as a whole, (2) the subset of the poverty population that is marginally housed, and (3) the subset of the poverty population that is literally homeless. . . .

I have reviewed the results from a number of studies done in single cities, discarding those that I felt were obviously deficient and giving the greatest weight to those that I felt had been the most scientifically respectable. Based on these studies and the usual simplifying assumptions, my conclusion is that the total literally homeless population of the nation on any given night numbers in the hundreds of thousands, although probably not in the millions. As a rule of thumb, we can speak of a half million homeless people in America at any one time. And if the ratio of one-night to annual homelessness estimated for the city of Chicago (about 3 to 1) is generally true, then the *annual* homeless population of the nation is on the order of one-and-a-half millions. . . .

WORTHY AND UNWORTHY HOMELESS

What have we learned in the research of the past decade about these half-million or so Americans who are homeless on any given night? We have learned, first of all, that they are a very diverse group of unfortunates: men and women, adults and children, young and old, black and white. We have also learned that relatively few of them are chronically homeless. Indeed, only a quarter to a third would be considered chronically or permanently homeless. The majority are *episodically* homeless; that is, they become homeless now and again, with the episodes of literal homelessness punctuated by periods of more or less stable housing situations. And of course, many homeless people on any given night are recently homeless for the first time, so that no pattern is yet established. . . .

Homelessness . . . is not a new problem in the larger historical sweep of things, but the current rash of homelessness certainly exceeds anything witnessed in this country in the last half-century. More to the point, the last major outbreak occurred as a consequence of the worst economic crisis in American history; the current situation exists in the midst of national prosperity literally unparalleled in the entire history of the world.

Not only did homelessness make a "comeback" in the early 1980s, but the character of homelessness also changed; this is another sense in which today's problem could be described as "new." In 1985, my colleagues and I had occasion to review medical records of men seen in a health clinic at the New York City Men's Shelter, in the very heart of the Bowery, for the period 1969–1984. Among the men seen in the early years of this period (1969–1972), almost half (49 percent) were white, 49 percent were documented alcohol or drug abusers, and the average age was forty-four. Among men seen at the end of the period (1981–1984), only 15 percent were white, only 28 percent were documented alcohol or drug abusers, and the average age was thirty-six. Thus, during the 1970s and early 1980s, the homeless population changed from largely white, older, and alcohol-abusive, into a population dominated by younger, non-substance-abusive, nonwhite men. Between the Great Depression and the 1980s, the road to homelessness was paved with alcohol abuse; today, quite clearly, many alternative routes have been opened.

In *Without Shelter* Peter Rossi presents a detailed comparison of results from studies of the homeless done in the 1950s and early 1960s with those undertaken in the 1980s, thus contrasting the "old" homeless and the "new." The first point of contrast is that the homeless of today suffer a more severe form of housing deprivation than did the homeless of twenty or thirty years past. Bogue's 1958 study in Chicago found only about a hundred homeless men sleeping, literally, out on the streets, out of a total homeless population estimated at twelve thousand. Rossi's 1986 survey found nearly fourteen hundred homeless persons sleeping out of doors in a total population estimated at about three thousand. Nearly all of the old homeless somehow found nightly shelter indoors (usually in flophouses and cubicle hotels, most of which have disappeared), unlike the new homeless, sizable fractions of whom sleep in the streets.

A second major difference is the presence of sizable numbers of women among today's homeless. Bogue's estimate in 1958 was that women comprised no more than 3 percent of the city's skid row population; in the middle 1980s, one homeless person in four is a woman. A third important contrast concerns the age distribution, the elderly having disappeared almost entirely from the ranks of the new homeless. Studies of the 1950s and 1960s routinely reported the average age of homeless persons to be somewhere in the middle fifties. Today, it is in the middle thirties.

Rossi points out two further differences: the substantially more straitened economic circumstances and the changing racial and ethnic composition of the new homeless. In 1958, Bogue estimated the average annual income of Chicago's homeless to be $1,058; Rossi's estimate for 1986 is $1,198. Converted to constant dollars, the average income of today's homeless is barely a third of the income of the homeless in 1958. Thus, the new homeless suffer a much more profound degree of economic destitution, often surviving on 40 percent or less of a poverty-level income.

Finally, the old homeless were mostly white—70 percent in Bahr and Caplow's well-known study of the Bowery, 82 percent in Bogue's study of Chicago. Among the new homeless, racial and ethnic minorities are heavily overrepresented.

We speak, then, of the "new face of homelessness" and of the "new homeless" to signify the very dramatic transformation of the nature of the homeless population that has occurred in the past decade.

IS HOMELESSNESS A GROWING PROBLEM?

Granted that the character of homelessness has changed, what evidence is there that the magnitude of the problem has in fact been increasing? Certainly, the amount of attention being devoted to the topic has grown, but what of the problem itself?

Since, as I have already stressed, we do not know very precisely just how many homeless people there are in America today, it is very difficult to say whether that number is higher, lower, or the same as the number of homeless five or ten or twenty years ago. The case that homelessness is in fact a growing problem is therefore largely inferential. The pertinent evidence has been reviewed in some detail by the U.S. General Accounting Office (GAO). Rather than cover the same ground here, let me simply quote GAO's conclusions:

> In summary, no one knows how many homeless people there are in America because of the many difficulties [in] locating and counting them. As a result, there is considerable disagreement over the size of the homeless population. However, there is agreement in the studies we reviewed and among shelter providers, researchers, and agency officials we interviewed that the homeless population is growing. Current estimates of annual increases in the growth of homelessness vary between 10 and 38 percent.

The most recent evidence on the upward trend in homelessness in the 1980s has been reviewed by economists Richard Freeman and Brian Hall. Between 1983 and 1985, they report, the shelter population of New York City increased by 28 percent, and that of Boston by 20 percent. Early in 1986, the U.S. Conference of Mayors released a study of twenty-five major U.S. cities, concluding that in twenty-two of the twenty-five, homelessness had indeed increased. There has also been a parallel increase in the numbers seeking food from soup kitchens, food banks, and the like. Thus, while all indicators are indirect and inferential, none suggest that the size of the homeless population is stable or declining; to the contrary, all suggest that the problem is growing rapidly.

HOW DID IT COME TO BE?

To ask how it came to be is to ask of the causes of homelessness, a topic about which everyone seems to have some opinion. *My* opinion is that many of the most commonly cited and much-discussed "causes" of contemporary homelessness are, in fact, not very important after all.

Chief among these not-very-important factors is the ongoing movement to deinstitutionalize the mentally ill. I do not mean to make light of the very serious mental health problems faced by many homeless people, but it is simply wrong to suggest that most, or even many, people are homeless because they have recently been released from a mental hospital.

What is sometimes overlooked in discussions of homelessness and deinstitutionalization is that we began deinstitutionalizing the mentally ill in the 1950s. The movement accelerated in the 1960s, owing largely to some favorable court orders concerning less-restrictive treatments. By the late 1970s, most of the people destined ever to be "deinstitutionalized" already had been. So as a direct contributing factor to the rise of homelessness in the 1980s, deinstitutionalization cannot be that important.

Many also seem to think that the rise of homelessness in the 1980s was the direct responsibility of Ronald Reagan particularly the result of the many cutbacks that Reagan engineered in human-services spending. This, like the deinstitutionalization theme, is at best a half truth. Certainly, the Reagan years were not kind or gentle to the nation's poor, destitute, and homeless. A particular problem has been the federal government's absolute bail-out from its commitment to the subsidized construction of low-income housing units, a point that I will return to shortly. But at the same time, many of the factors that have worked to increase or exacerbate the problem of homelessness in the 1980s are rooted in the larger workings of the political economy, not in specific political decisions made by the Reagan administration.

What, then, *has* been the cause of this growing problem? Like most other social problems, homelessness has many complex causes that are sometimes difficult to disentangle. We can begin to get a handle on the complexity, however, by stating an obvious although often overlooked point: homeless people are people without housing, and thus, the *ultimate* cause of the problem is an insufficient supply of housing suitable to the needs of homeless people. Although this means, principally, an inadequate supply of low-income housing suitable to single individuals, the housing problem cuts even more deeply.

In twelve large U.S. cities, between the late 1970s and the early 1980s, the number of low-income housing units dropped from 1.6 million units to 1.1 million units, a decline of about 30 percent. Many of these "lost" units have been taken from the single room occupancy hotels or flophouse hotels and rooming houses, those that have always served as the "housing of last resort" for the socially and economically marginal segments of the urban poverty population. Many likewise have been lost through arson or abandonment. And many have disappeared as low-income housing only to reappear as housing for the affluent upper-middle class, in a process that has come to be known as gentrification.

Saying that the homeless lack housing, however, is like saying that the poor lack money: the point is a correct one, even a valuable one, but it is by no means the whole story. A second critical factor has been the recent increase in the poverty rate and the growing size of the "population at risk" for homelessness, the urban poor. In the same twelve cities mentioned above, over the same time frame, the poverty population increased from about 2.5 million poor people to 3.4 million, an increase of 36 percent. Dividing poor people into low-income units, these twelve cities averaged 1.6 poor people per unit in the late 1970s, and 3.1 poor people per unit in the early 1980s. In a five-year span, in short, the low-income housing "squeeze" tightened by a factor of two. Less low-income housing for more low-income persons necessarily predestines a rise in the numbers without housing, as indeed we have dramatically witnessed in the early years of the decade.

My argument is that these large scale housing and economic trends have conspired to create a housing "game" that increasingly large numbers are destined to lose. Who, specifically, will in fact lose at the housing game is a separate question, and on this point, attention turns to various personal characteristics of the homeless population that cause them to compete poorly in this game. Their extreme poverty, social disaffiliation, and high levels of personal disability are, of course, the principal problems. Thus, it is not entirely *wrong* to say that people are homeless because they are alcoholic or mentally ill or socially estranged—just as it is not entirely wrong to blame "bad luck" for losing at cards. Given a game that some are destined to lose, it is appropriate to ask who the losers turn out to be. But it is wrong, I think, to mistake an analysis of the losers for an analysis of the game itself.

Another important factor that is often overlooked in discussions of the homeless is the seemingly endless deterioration of the purchasing power of welfare and related benefits. Converted to constant dollars, the value of welfare, aid to families with dependent children (AFDC), and most other social benefit payments today is about half that of twenty years ago. Twenty years ago, or so it would seem, these payments were at least adequate to maintain persons and families in stable housing situations, even in the face of the loss of other income. Today, clearly, they are not. To cite one recent example, the state of Massachusetts has one of the more generaous AFDC programs of any state in the country, and yet the state has been ordered by the courts twice in the past few years to increase AFDC payments. Why? The court compared the average AFDC payment in the state to the average cost of rental housing in the Boston area and concluded that the payment levels, although already generous by national standards, could only be contributing to the homelessness problem among AFDC recipients.

What we witness in the rise of the new homeless is a new form of class conflict—a conflict over housing in the urban areas between that class in the population whose income is adequate to cover its housing costs, and that class whose income is not. In the past, this conflict was held largely in check by the aversion of the middle class to downtown living and by the federal government's commitment to subsidized housing for the poor. As the cities are made more attractive to the middle class, as revitalization and gentrification lure the urban tax base back to the central cities, and as the federal commitment to subsidized housing fades, the intensity of this conflict grows—and with it, the roster of casualties, the urban homeless.

No problem that is ultimately rooted in the large-scale workings of the political economy can be solved easily or cheaply, and this problem is no exception. Based on my analysis, the solution has two essential steps: the federal government must massively intervene in the private housing market, to halt the loss of additional low-income units and to underwrite the construction of many more; and the benefits paid to the welfare-dependent population—AFDC, general assistance, Veterans Administration income benefits, Social Security, and so on—must approximately double.

Either of the above will easily add a few tens of billions to the annual federal expenditure, and thus, neither is the least bit likely to happen in the current political environment, where lowering the federal deficit and reducing federal spending are seen as a Doxology of Political Faith, widely subscribed to by politicians of all ideological persuasions. Thus, in the short run, which is probably to say for the rest of this century, the focus will be on amelioration, not on solutions. We will do what we can to improve the lives of homeless people—more and better temporary shelters, more adequate nutrition, better and more accessible health care, and so on. In the process, we will make the lives of many homeless people more comfortable, perhaps, but we will not rid ourselves of this national disgrace.

Review Questions

1. Identify some of the commonly held stereotypes that have developed in recent years about the homeless.
2. Describe the major differences between the "new" homeless population of the 1980s and the "old" homeless population of the 1950s.
3. List the factors that Wright identifies as causes of the growing problem of homelessness in our society.

WHY ISN'T THERE MORE EQUALITY?

Nathan Glazer

In the following reading, Nathan Glazer poses the basic question, Why isn't there more equality? As the reading points out, our concept of social justice involves the notion of equality. Yet our idea of justice also involves a number of competing values that make it impossible for government to strive for more equality (specifically, equality in income) "as a general and overriding goal." In general, Americans support efforts aimed at "relieving distress" and not the goal of redistributing income across the board.

Whatever justice, unqualified, may mean, it now seems established that social justice means equality. And one would think we must know much more about equality today than we did a dozen years ago, before the publication of John Rawls' *A Theory of Justice*. That is, we must know more if the measure of knowledge is the number of books and articles that have been devoted in the past dozen years to justice as equality. Much of the discussion has been sparked by Rawls' book, which seems to have become the text and the starting point for any discussion of justice. I will also use it as such, but only as a prelude to what will be basically an empirical discussion. The question I would like to consider is: Why is it, when so many philosophers agree that the measure of social justice is equality, that we do not have more of it?

There are many anomalies mixed up in this simple question. Consider that apace with this huge outpouring of discussion of justice as equality—and for the most part, of strong advocacy of justice as equality (who, after all, is for inequality?)—there seems to have been no increase in equality in this country, as measured by the distribution of income. It has remained remarkably stable for some 30 years or more. This is surprising, not because of the near universal commitment by American social philosophers to justice as equality (for, after all, philosophers do not rule the world), but because we have had in the past 20 years an amazing outpouring of measures to increase social justice—social justice *defined* as equality.

If one looks at the domestic part of the national budget, which has grown enormously in the past two decades, much more than has the military part of the budget, one finds that almost all of the growth has been occasioned by measures of social justice instituted, if not to create equality, to achieve more equality. These great measures include expansion of Social Security, the institution of Medicaid, Medicare, food stamps, grants and loans to college students, assistance to communities for education of poor children, an expansion of rent subsidies, of welfare, and of various kinds of assistance to expand the rights (and presumably the income) of minorities, of women, of the handicapped, and of the aged. In the face of this enormous outpouring of activity, which has greatly increased the properties of personal income taken by the Federal government for purposes of expanding equality, the distribution of income remains stable—and unequal.

Now, clearly, I am using only one kind of measure to judge the effectiveness of the expansion of social policies to increase equality, the measure of the distribution of income. But that happens to be the favored measure of most proponents of more equality. By other measures, all would have to acknowledge there has been substantial movement toward more equality. By the measure of political representation, blacks are much more equal than they were 20 years ago. By the measure of participation in key professions, in government, and in business, blacks, Hispanic Americans, and women are far more equal than they were two decades ago. If representation in schools of medicine, law, and business foreshadows an increase of income, then women and blacks will become more equal, so long as they follow, to the same degree as white males, the more lucrative fields of practice.

It is not only through growth of the gross Federal budget that we can mark these enormous efforts to achieve equality. If we consider other equally important interventions, those summed up by the expansion of regulation, we find that they too have been motivated both by a concern for social justice and a concern for more equality. So we have created major government agencies such as the Equal Employment Opportunity Commission and the Office of Federal Contract Compliance Programs, mobilizing thousands of professionals to achieve more income equality for minorities and women, and created or expanded other major regulatory agencies designed to increase the power of consumers and ordinary people as against that of manufacturers of cars, drugs, and other products, and manufacturers who pollute the air, water, and soil. But by the measure of gross income equality, despite all this thrashing and pulling, we are an unequal society—somewhat more unequal than Japan and Australia, perhaps a touch more equal (until recently) than France, somewhat more unequal than other major developed countries of Europe.

THREE EXPLANATIONS

We do have a dilemma here. So our question: If thought, argument, and policy have been directed toward more equality, why isn't there more?

I will present three explanations for why we do not have more equality. The first is that, surprisingly, perhaps, we don't want more. And by we, I do not mean the rich and powerful (that would be understandable), but most of us, including the poor who on a simple reading would be helped by more equality.

The second is an explanation of this first fact. Despite the enormous role the discussion of equality has taken in social philosophy, most people seem to hold equally strongly a number of other values, which seem to them an equal part of justice, and these compete with equality as an overriding part of justice.

The third is that because of these conflicting and competing values it is literally not possible for government, at any rate democratic government, to move to more equality in income as a *general* and overriding goal. It must move toward more equality in more piecemeal and concrete ways—for the aged, the sick, the handicapped, women, the young, students, the low-income renter, farmers, the unemployed, and on and on. It turns out, not for any reason that I can find written in the heavens, that the battle for more *different* kinds of equality, whatever satisfaction it may give one group or another, does not lead, or has not led, to any *overall* movement toward equality.

It is the first point that is perhaps the most surprising and that receives the least attention. Yet it directly ties up with the Rawls-influenced analysis of justice as equality. Rawls argued that if we were to conduct an opinion poll under very strictly limited circumstances—under a "veil of ignorance," in which each person did not know whether he was black or white, a man or a woman, young or old, sick or ablebodied, slow-witted or quick-witted, dexterous or not—that we would then all vote (I leave aside some complexities) for strict equality. Obviously, the poll cannot be conducted. But interestingly enough, social science techniques potentially permit something like it. We *could,* in theory, conduct a public opinion survey on how much equality people wanted, and hold everything that might bias the results constant. Through statistical techniques, we could eliminate all the factors that Rawls wants us to be ignorant of, such as intelligence, skill, heredity. Nothing like this has actually been done.

Yet there is an even simpler approach to the problem. We can ask the poor what they want in the way of equality. Or, we might ask all those below the median income. This has been done, and—as we would all recognize if we ponder that this *is* a democratic society and the will of the people *does* in some rough measure prevail—*most people don't want much more equality than we have.*

Jennifer Hochschild has examined this anomaly—if anomaly it is—in an interesting book, *What's Fair?* It seems to be a fact, she writes, that:

> the American poor apparently do not support the downward redistribution of wealth. The United States does not have, and seldom ever has had, a political movement among the poor seeking greater economic equality. The fact that such a movement could succeed constitutionally makes its absence even more startling. Since most of the population have less than the average amount of wealth . . . more people would benefit than would lose from downward distribution.[1]

Indeed, Hochschild points out:

> Redistribution has been so far from the national consciousness than even voracious pollsters and doctoral students have, for the most part, ignored it. As a result, we know very little about how most citizens actually feel about distributive changes. In the past forty years, only eight questions on national surveys have investigated some aspect of redistribution of income. Only three of the eight mention wealth. . . .

These surveys do show, which is not surprising, that the poor, unemployed, and blue-collar workers do support redistribution more than do others. But even among the poor, only 55% (at most) strongly support redistribution. And the more radical the question, the less support. If we translate Rawlsian equality into its crudest form (it has to be crude to get into a national survey), almost no one is for it. Thus, in 1969 the question was put: "Every family in this country should receive the same income, about $10,000 or so." (To take account of inflation, if the question were asked today that figure would have to be raised to about $25,000.) The figure selected, by the way, was not unduly low—it was about 15% above the median income of households in 1970. It was therefore *above* what the median family was then getting, and the majority of Americans would have been able to get a raise of at least 15% in family income by just saying "yes." They weren't even warned about any possible unwanted consequences of the redistribution. The responses, one must say, are startling, and should appear as a footnote in all further philosophical discussions of equality.

The respondents were divided into four income levels. Only 14% of the lowest quarter answered "yes" to the redistribution question, 17% of the next, 16% of the third quarter, and 7% of those in the top quarter of income. Support for a radical measure of income equality in the United States, one must say, is an eccentric minority position, not particularly affected by income earned (after all, we have millionaire socialists), and perhaps reaching significant proportions—if one may judge by the debates in philosophical journals—only among philosophers.

What is the basis for this denial of equality? Professor Hochschild has gone beyond the bare facts of public opinion survey answers—which never tell us "why"—to discuss their views of justice and equality with a few dozen citizens, rich and poor. What she discovers, I would argue, is that other conceptions of justice are at work which undermine commitment to justice as equality. Take the views of the poor—they are more interesting for us than the views of the rich, for the defense of self-interest is nothing that has to be explained, but the defense of a value that opposes crude self-interest does seem to require explanation.

So consider one of Professor Hochschild's respondents, Maria Pulaski, who cleans other people's homes. She feels her wealthy employers should pay her more—her work is worth it. But concerning their

---

[1] Jennifer L. Hochschild, *What's Fair?—American Beliefs About Distributive Justice* (Harvard University Press, 1981).

income—their $60,000 a year, as against her $7,000 (from both her efforts and her husband's; it is the 1974 recession, and he is unemployed), she says: "They worked for it, why not? You work for it, it's fair. If I got a good education and I'm doing a different job and a harder job, I deserve more. . . . I don't believe in this equal, all equal . . ." Even those who did not work for it, who "got it through their parents," deserve to keep their wealth. "Sure, if I had money, and if I gave it to my children, that's good. Good luck to them."

Or consider Sally White, now unemployed after various clerical jobs which give her an average income of $6,000. She thinks she can make a lot of money someday—and doesn't want to give up the chance for a uniform equality. She even rejects equal pay within occupations: "Not all secretaries are the same." She even can see some point, not that she likes it, to her boss's son starting a job that is better than he deserves and running a show he didn't start: "Somebody worked to get there in this family, and if they want to give it to him, really, it's their business." And when company presidents take it easy, she doesn't see why they still shouldn't enjoy their high salaries: "I know if I got my business going and I decided to be lazy and have someone [run it], I would still expect my full share of the profits. I'm the one that got the whole thing started."

ANOTHER KIND OF JUSTICE

What we have is a strong idea of another kind of justice competing with the idea of justice as equality. It is the idea that what is legitimately acquired, and even more, legitimately handed down to one's children, is legitimately owned. People are entitled to keep what they can fairly get, and pass it on after they are gone.[2] Professor Hochschild's respondents make no sophisticated argument about inequality being necessary for economic growth or suchlike. They simply believe things worked for, owned, are properly to be kept. A second belief which comes out very strongly is that one has the right to benefit one's children, regardless of their efforts. These beliefs quite overwhelm any commitment to strict equality.

But this does not mean that Professor Hochschild's respondents are rampant individualists who would let the devil take the hindmost, à la Herbert Spencer. They believe in guaranteed jobs, in minimum decency, and are quite willing to pay taxes for it. What emerges—in contrast to the philosophical discussion of social justice—is a kind of rough and ready pragmatism, combined with sympathy for those who suffer hardship, and even a willingness to provide for those who suffer hardship because of their own failures. There is also a preference for giving more, on easier terms, to those who suffer because of no fault of their own—the workingman out of a job because his plant has closed—than to those who suffer because of drink, or drugs, or unwillingness to learn and work. The notion of making any distinction between the "deserving" and the "undeserving" poor may be considered old-fashioned and reactionary—it is not to be seen much anymore in schools of social work, or among the majority of those who think about social problems—but it lives a hardy and determined life among ordinary people. . . .

[2] This is just about the position argued in Robert Nozick's *Anarchy, State and Utopia* (Basic, 1974). The fact that an awful lot of people—and an awful lot of poor people—agree, is no argument among philosophers. Yet, though Nozick has made his argument not on the basis of what ordinary people believe, but on the basis of the kind of reasoning that passes muster among philosophers, there is a surprising similarity between his position and the popular one.

I would insist these are sensible views we see expressed, solidly based in deeply held values, which are in no simple sense selfish values (as we have seen, the poor hold them almost as much as the rich). They are moral rather than pragmatic positions.

Some sophisticated defenders of inequality claim we need inequality of income in order to motivate people to work and to encourage investment by those who earn more than their consumption needs, but they have argued that these objectives would not be hampered by confiscatory inheritance taxes. Indeed, they have asserted this would help implement the equality of opportunity that all favor, and would have no harmful effects on the economy. The New Havenites disagree, reports Hochschild: "Respondents see taxes on inheritance or wealth as unfair, because they tax property more than once and they apparently preclude saving for the future of one's children." Or as one of the more prosperous respondents asserts: "Why should I work all my life and run the risk that three idiots who got jobs out of patronage are going to decide whether my daughter is going to get my money? No way. Before I'll do that, I'll stop working." Cutting inheritance taxes, I would guess, is one of the more popular things the Reagan administration has done. It caters to a basic and widely held sense of fairness.

Of course one question comes up about this widespread acquiescence in and indeed favoring of economic inequality, or more specifically the freedoms that lead to it and perpetuate it. Perhaps people are brainwashed—or perhaps they think that taking the egalitarian position will subject them to ridicule. In these long—very long—interviews, in which at least one respondent even felt free enough to say he was contemplating a robbery, there was simply no hint of this. This is not an issue of "false consciousness," as Marxists will have it. In any case, "false consciousness," as Guenter Lewy has pointed out in a book analyzing this peculiar idea, is a very flawed concept. It simply makes it possible for the ascriber of false consciousness to insist, quite independently of those whose interests he claims to be advancing, that anyone who disagrees with him about how to advance his own interests has been bamboozled. There is no hint of bamboozling here—there is strong enough evidence that people are using their eyes and their experience, and, yes, their values. They would like to restrict the role of government to limiting distress rather than redistributing income.

RELIEVING DISTRESS AND ENSURING EQUALITY

Let us leave Jennifer Hochschild's respondents and suggest a third reason why we do not have more equality. The programs that most Americans favor under the rubric of relieving distress, and that others may favor because they advance equality, have specific and discrete aims—and *in toto* they seem to indeed relieve distress, but not to basically adjust the distribution of income. This is to me something of a mystery. How is it possible that the huge redistribution of income to the aged, once one of the poorest groups in the society, does not redistribute income away from the rich, to the poor? This is our largest social program, and it is well known that it takes considerably less from the low-paid worker than it pays back in benefits, and probably, as the social security tax goes up, it takes more from the well-to-do than it returns to them in benefits.

We could make the same analysis for programs which have become quite large and didn't exist years ago, such as food stamps—or programs which did exist but have grown substantially, such as welfare. It is true that some of our major new social programs could be analyzed as not particularly assisting redistribution. For example, Medicaid and Medicare go to doctors, hospitals, and drug companies, and may well serve to redistribute more to the rich (though they have also permitted hospitals, for example, to increase the wages of low-paid hospital workers). Similarly, student grants and loans may not serve redistribution, since so much goes to the middle classes and to colleges and universities. And yet I remain mystified at the stability of the American distribution of income after all these efforts. The only explanations I have seen that make sense are two. First, as Edgar Browning and Morton Paglin have argued, if we properly value some of the elements in the redistribution that are not distributed as money (e.g., rent subsidies), we will find that as a matter of fact there has been considerable redistribution to the poor. I think more and more people now agree with this. There is a second explanation: that is the change in the composition of the bottom fifth or quarter of income earners. The bottom rung may still be getting a very modest share of income, but it is now composed of fewer families headed by working males, more families headed by nonworking females, and more people living alone.

Now this change in composition has considerable bearing on the question of why we do not have more equality after having instituted so many social programs. For the change in composition is itself in large measure the result of the expansion of social programs. This is not to say that people in the bottom fifth are not truly poor, but it is to say that the social programs have had a dynamic impact, which creates new classes of poor that take up the bottom position as those assisted by social programs have risen out of poverty. Two such dynamic interactions are familiar. Social Security permits more old people to live alone rather than with their children. Thus it encourages independence, while also reducing the incomes of households created. Thus a program giving assistance to elderly people permits them to move out of a household and set up their own. The two new households have more income than the one old household (they also have more expenses). The old couple or individual may now qualify as poor, but only because Social Security enabled them to become a poor *separate* household.

We now have much more in the way of support to young single individuals—young people who cannot work because of alcoholism or drug addiction, or the mentally ill and retarded released from institutions by the powerful movement for deinstitutionalization. This increases the number of single-person households and of poor households. Social policy has aimed at it—it is not a perverse effect—but it also thereby creates a new class of single-member households which will now join the bottom fifth, when formerly they might have lived in institutions and not been so classified. Perhaps the most important change in the composition of the bottom fifth is the increase in female-headed families—and it is clearly unnecessary to rehearse the argument that the increase in the number of such households is a result of the increase in and wider availability of welfare benefits.

Thus various social policies designed to create equality have certain effects which indeed do foster equality (the nonworking aged are now more equal to the working people; the mother on welfare is better off monetarily than she would have been before the expansion of welfare benefits), but they also *increase* certain categories which replace the groups formerly numbered in the lowest income stratum. It would clearly be wrong to say simply that efforts to increase equality are counterproductive, because what has happened to the aged who now live alone, or the mentally ill and retarded released from institutions, is exactly what social policy has aimed at. But in some cases, and the argument could be made for welfare, we do hit one target—the poverty of mothers without working males—but in hitting it expand the category substantially.

The point, in a word, is that there is no final answer to social problems—including the condition of poverty. It was perhaps the great illusion of the long period of prosperity of the 1950s and 1960s that there was, or could be. We now know that that long period of prosperity and of rising social expenditures to accommodate every major need—in some societies, such as Sweden and the Netherlands, just about every need for which public provision could be made—was based on exceptional circumstances. Perhaps it was because the rising tide of social expenditures was not yet producing massive deficits, and major inflation—as was the case in the 1970s, and is increasingly the case in the 1980s. But whatever the explanation for that good period, a bad period has followed it, and poverty reemerges as a problem even in societies that have gone further than we have in creating a net of services. . . .

Review Questions

1. Identify and discuss Glazer's three reasons for why we do not have more equality in American society.
2. Identify various American values that compete with that of equality.
3. According to Glazer, how is it that government programs relieve the distress of some yet produce "new classes of poor"?

Summary

1. Stratification refers to a system whereby people are unequally ranked and rewarded on the basis of wealth, authority, power, and prestige. Stratification exists in every society and has many consequences for individuals and groups. Functionalists feel that although stratification involves inequality, it nevertheless benefits society at large because it helps guarantee that the more difficult and critically important kinds of work will be accomplished. In contrast, conflict theorists view stratification as an unfair system inflicted on society by people holding a monopoly of power and wealth to safeguard their own interests, advantages, and power.
2. There are three ideal types of stratification systems: the caste system, the estates system, and the open class system. The caste system is a closed form of stratification system based exclusively on birth; a person is born into a particular caste and remains in it for life. The estates system repre-

sents a relatively closed and rigid stratification system. Mobility from one level (or estate) to another is possible but very uncommon. The open class system is based on individual effort and achievement rather than birth. There is much upward and downward mobility within this system. Modern industrialized societies resemble most closely the open class system.

3. Karl Marx and Max Weber have made major contributions to the analysis of stratification systems. As an economic determinist, Marx believed that classes arise out of the productive system of a society. For Marx, industrial societies were composed of two major social classes: bourgeoisie and proletariat. Max Weber believed that stratification systems were based on three elements: wealth, status (or prestige), and power.

4. Daniel Rossides's general descriptive profile of the American class system identifies five relatively distinct social classes, ranging from a small, wealthy upper class (1 to 3 percent of the population) to an impoverished lower class (20 to 25 percent of the population).

5. Poverty constitutes a major social problem in the United States. Children and the elderly make up one-half of the entire poverty population in our society. Three major theoretical explanations for poverty include the culture of poverty theory, the situational approach, and the conflict approach.

6. Social mobility (both upward and downward) is fairly common in American society. Upward mobility is, in part, a function of individual motivation and achievement, but there are also many class and castelike barriers to mobility, and occupational and industrial changes tend to play an important role in long-term mobility trends. Mobility for most people occurs slowly.

STUDY GUIDE

Chapter Objectives

After studying this chapter, you should be able to:

1. Define "social stratification"
2. Identify two reasons why the study of stratification is important in sociology
3. List several examples of life chances
4. Compare and contrast the functionalist and conflict perspectives on why stratification exists in every society

5. Identify and briefly describe the three major ideal types of stratification systems
6. Identify and compare, by way of example, the bourgeoisie and proletariat in Marxist theory
7. Identify and define Max Weber's three major dimensions of stratification
8. Define "power elite"
9. Define "social class"
10. List and briefly describe the five major social classes in the United States as identified by Daniel Rossides
11. Describe and contrast the culture of poverty, situational, and conflict explanations for poverty
12. Define and illustrate, by way of example, "vertical" and "horizontal mobility"
13. Identify major factors in upward mobility
14. Describe how changes in occupational structure are related to mobility
15. Illustrate, by way of example, castelike qualities in the American stratification system

Key Terms

Bourgeoisie (p. 219)
Caste (p. 217)
Caste system (p. 217)
Class (p. 220)
Culture of poverty (p. 227)
Estates system (p. 217)
Horizontal mobility (p. 234)
Intergenerational mobility (p. 235)
Life chances (p. 216)
Open class system (p. 218)
Power (p. 221)
Power elite (p. 221)
Proletariat (p. 219)
Social class (p. 222)
Status (p. 220)
Stratification (p. 215)
Vertical mobility (p. 234)

Self-Test

Short Answer

(p. 215) 1. Stratification is ______________________________

(p. 218) 2. In an open class system, one's class position is determined by ______________________________

(p. 218) 3. As an economic determinist, Marx believed that ______________________________

(p. 220) 4. Weber's three dimensions of stratification, class (a), status (b), and power (c), can be defined as:
a. ______________________________
____
b. ______________________________
____
c. ______________________________
____

(p. 222) 5. A social class is ______________________________
____
____

(p. 221) 6. According to Mills, the power elite is composed of ______
____
____

(p. 223) 7. Rossides's profile of the American class system identified five social classes, including:
a. ______________________________
b. ______________________________
c. ______________________________
d. ______________________________
e. ______________________________

(p. 229) 8. Herbert Gans points out that poverty does, in fact, continue to exist because ______________________________
____

(p. 234) 9. Vertical mobility is ______________________________
____

(p. 234) 10. Horizontal mobility is ______________________________
____

Multiple Choice *(Answers are on page 263.)*

(p. 215) 1. Stratification always involves:
a. equality
b. social similarities
c. equality and social ranking
d. social inequality and social ranking

(p. 216) 2. The conflict perspective sees stratification as:
a. a system that fulfills important needs for the society as a whole
b. a system that safeguards the interests and advantages of the rich and powerful
c. a system that ensures the accomplishment of important kinds of work
d. an essentially fair and just system

(p. 218) 3. In an open class stratification system, one's class position would be determined by one's:
a. class of origin
b. age
c. sex and/or race
d. personal effort and ability

(p. 220) 4. Weber felt that:
   a. classes are always the same as status groups
   b. power is the principal determinant of one's social class
   c. people constitute a class when they have similar economic interests, occupations, and incomes
   d. one's status determines one's power in the society

(p. 222) 5. Sociologists are in agreement that the United States is composed of:
   a. three social classes
   b. four social classes
   c. six social classes
   d. none of the above

(p. 225) 6. According to Rossides's profile of the American class system, the lower class:
   a. is composed of average-income Americans
   b. has growing economic worth in the labor market
   c. is socially isolated, but has a stable family life
   d. none of the above

(p. 226) 7. Since the mid-1970s, the age group with the highest poverty rate in the United States has been:
   a. children
   b. the elderly
   c. young adults
   d. middle-aged adults

(p. 234) 8. The office worker who eventually becomes the personnel director of a company exemplifies:
   a. intergenerational mobility
   b. horizontal mobility
   c. vertical mobility
   d. nonmobility

(p. 235) 9. Regarding mobility in the United States, which of the following statements would be correct?
   a. mobility is uncommon
   b. mobility is more common within white-collar and blue-collar categories than between them
   c. many people are highly mobile during their working careers
   d. caste aspects for mobility are virtually nonexistent

(p. 239) 10. According to your text, statistics show that the 1988 poverty rate for blacks stood at approximately:
   a. 32 percent
   b. 8 percent
   c. 14 percent
   d. 43 percent

True/False *(Answers are on page 263.)*

T F 11. As social class position increases, one's life expectancy decreases. (p. 216)

T F 12. From the functionalist perspective, stratification helps guarantee that society's more difficult and important kinds of work will be accomplished. (p. 216)

T F 13. In the Indian caste system, marriage was endogamous within each caste. (p. 217)

T F 14. According to Daniel Rossides, the lower middle class comprises 30 to 35 percent of the national population. (p. 224)

T F 15. Changes in the occupational structure have very little effect on mobility and mobility trends. (p. 235)

T F 16. Mobility in the United States is much higher than in many other industrial nations, such as France, Great Britain, and Japan. (p. 263)

T F 17. Historically, most mobility has occurred at or near the middle of the American stratification system. (p. 237)

T F 18. When women work in positions comparable to those of men, women usually receive pay equivalent to that of their male counterparts. (p. 238)

T F 19. According to James D. Wright, a major factor in the rise of contemporary homelessness has been the deinstitutionalization of the mentally ill. (p. 246)

T F 20. According to Nathan Glazer, most Americans desire to restrict government's role to that of relieving distress rather than redistributing income. (p. 253)

Fill In *(Answers are on page 263.)*

(p. 217) 21. In the estates system, the ______ comprises kings, nobles, and the military aristocracy.

(p. 219) 22. Marx felt that the ______ are parasites because they gain wealth and power, and profit through the labor of others.

(p. 221) 23. John Kenneth Galbraith speaks of ______, the idea that there is competition and conflict for power among various power centers.

(p. 221) 24. ______ sees power as something that circulates from one area to another.

(p. 222) 25. Classes represent ______ with specific class-typed ways of thinking, acting, and feeling.

(p. 234) 26. The architect who becomes a lawyer exemplifies ______ mobility.

(p. 235) 27. ______ mobility is typically indexed by comparing occupational differences between generations.

(p. 236) 28. The American system of stratification is characterized by both ______ and ______ aspects of ranking.

(p. 243) 29. James D. Wright uses the term "______ homeless" to refer to those who, on a given night, have nowhere to go.

(p. 249) 30. Glazer's article, "Why Isn't There More Equality?," speaks specifically about equality in ______.

Matching *(Answers are on page 263.)*

31. ______ Caste system
32. ______ C. Wright Mills

a. Views stratification as being comprised of three dimensions

33. ______ Functionalist perspective
34. ______ Karl Marx
35. ______ Estates system
36. ______ Occupation
37. ______ Max Weber
38. ______ Conflict perspective
39. ______ Intergenerational mobility
40. ______ Situational approach

b. Stratification system characteristic of Europe during medieval times
c. Estimated by comparing occupational differences between generations
d. An economic determinist
e. A closed system of stratification
f. Theoretical perspective that attempts to explain poverty
g. Used the concept of the power elite
h. Sees stratification as benefiting the wealthy and powerful in a society
i. Probably the most important indicator of an individual's mobility
j. Sees stratification as beneficial to the society at large

Essay Questions

1. What do sociologists mean by "social stratification"? Why is this an important area for sociological study?
2. How do functionalist theory and conflict theory account for the existence of stratification?
3. What are the three ideal types of stratification systems? Which do you think best describes the United States? Explain.
4. Compare Marx's and Weber's theories of stratification, and explain which you feel best describes the American stratification system.
5. Do you think a power elite actually exists in American society? If so, in your opinion, who makes up this elite?
6. What do sociologists mean by "social class"? What do you feel are the most important elements in determining a person's social class?
7. To what social class do you belong? Explain.
8. How does Daniel Rossides describe the social class system in our society?
9. Who are the poor? How have sociologists explained the existence and persistence of poverty in our society?
10. How do a person's sex, race, and class position at birth influence his or her chances for mobility? How do patterns of mobility differ among different sexes, races, and classes in American society?

Interactive Exercises

1. As discussed in this chapter, the question as to why stratification exists in every society constitutes one of the central concerns and debates among sociologists. Two answers to this question have come in the form of the functionalist and the conflict perspectives on stratification. Select a small number of students (perhaps five or ten), explain the functionalist and conflict perspectives on stratification as discussed in this chapter, and ask them why they think stratification exists in our society. Do they adopt a functionalist position or a conflict position, or do they have another viewpoint altogether? This exercise will reinforce your learning of these basic concepts and perspectives and also will increase your understanding of the various ways in which people perceive stratification and the reasons for its existence.

2. One of the most important social issues discussed in this chapter is poverty in the United States. Comparing the 1970s with the late 1980s, there has been a substantial increase in the number of people living in poverty. On the other hand, a recent study by the Joint Economic Committee of Congress found that between 1963 and 1983, the concentration of wealth among the rich in the United States actually increased: in effect, the rich got richer. Interview or informally talk with some other students, relatives, and friends for the purpose of learning more about how others perceive poverty and the extent of inequality in our society. Are they aware of the magnitude of economic inequality in the United States? Do they realize that poverty is a growing problem in our society? How do your respondents explain the existence of poverty? Do they blame poverty on the poor themselves? What suggestions do they have for alleviating poverty? It would be interesting to make note of the age, occupation, and so forth of your respondents in order to see how various background factors influence their views with respect to poverty and inequality in our society.

3. Stratification constitutes one of the most important areas of sociological study. For example, in our society, people in different social classes manifest different lifestyles, values, attitudes, behaviors, and also experience different life chances and opportunities. A number of these differences were illustrated in the Rossides profile of the American class system. In this exercise, you are to identify and list at least 10 occupational fields in which you feel a knowledge of social class and people's social class position would be useful and important. How would such knowledge be of use to you in your present and/or future job? As a footnote to this exercise, you may wish to contact the American Sociological Association at 1722 N Street, Washington, D.C. 20036. The Association has published various articles and pamphlets describing a number of occupations and careers for which sociological training and degrees on the undergraduate and graduate levels can be useful.

Answers

Answers to Self-Test

1.	d	11.	F	21.	nobility	31.	e
2.	b	12.	T	22.	bourgeoisie	32.	g
3.	d	13.	T	23.	countervailing power	33.	j
4.	c	14.	T	24.	Parsons	34.	d
5.	d	15.	F	25.	subcultures	35.	b
6.	d	16.	F	26.	horizontal	36.	i
7.	a	17.	T	27.	intergenerational	37.	a
8.	c	18.	F	28.	class, caste	38.	h
9.	b	19.	F	29.	literally	39.	c
10.	a	20.	T	30.	income	40.	f

Answers to Chapter Pretest

1. F
2. T
3. T
4. T
5. F
6. T
7. F
8. F

Chapter 7

Inequalities: Gender, Race, Age, and Ethnicity

Chapter Pretest

Let's see how much you already know about topics in this chapter:

1. **Some people are born prejudiced. True/False**
2. **Women account for less than one-half of the work force. True/False**
3. **Discrimination is basically the same as prejudice. True/False**
4. **In the United States, there are over 10 million Native Americans. True/False**
5. **After coming to America, the majority of immigrants vote. True/False**
6. **In the area of education, there has been progress for young blacks. True/False**
7. **Prejudice is learned. True/False**
8. **Hispanic Americans are expected to be America's largest minority group by the year 2000. True/False**
9. **There is less prejudice and discrimination in the United States today compared with 20 years ago. True/False**
10. **Five million legal immigrants are allowed to come to the United States each year. True/False**

In the United States, as in all other societies, some people are set apart for a variety of reasons, such as physical features or behavior patterns. On the basis of skin color, religion, sex, physical handicap, or cultural characteristics, people are prevented from participating equally and fully in many aspects of social life. Women, racial groups, the aged, and other minorities experience a limited range of life choices and encounter more prejudice, restrictions, and discrimination than do the dominant groups in society. These groups are all minorities.

Minority groups are prevented from participating fully in society

Our primary focus in this chapter is on the prejudice and discrimination that minorities experience in American society. We first define "minority group" and examine varieties of minority situations. We then examine prejudice, discrimination, and some of America's largest minority groups. We conclude with explanations of prejudice and minority responses to it.

"Minority Group" Defined

A **minority group** is any culturally or physically distinctive, self-conscious social aggregate that is subject to political, economic, or social discrimination by a dominant segment of a surrounding political society. In other words:

1. A minority is a social grouping that experiences a variety of disabilities in the form of prejudice, discrimination, segregation, or persecution (or any combination of these) at the hands of another group.

Minority groups are discriminated against and held in low esteem

2. The disabilities (prejudice, discrimination, and so forth) experienced by minorities are related to special characteristics that its members share, either physical or cultural or both, which the dominant group holds in low esteem.

In his classic analysis of minority groups, Louis Wirth (1945) defines a minority as:

> **a group of people who, because of their physical or cultural characteristics, are singled out from the others in the society in which they live for differential and unequal treatment, and who therefore regard themselves as objects of collective discrimination. The existence of a minority in a society implies the existence of a corresponding dominant group with higher social status and greater privileges (Wirth, 1945).**

Minority status excludes people from full participation in the life of society.

The dominant group in a dominant-minority situation does not necessarily have to be, numerically speaking, the larger group. For example, many counties in Mississippi have many more blacks than whites. Blacks also constitute a higher proportion of the population in South Africa. A majority-minority situation is a pattern of relationships and distribution of power, not necessarily a relationship of numbers.

Varieties of Minority Situations

There are many different ways of classifying minorities or minority situations. One highly regarded classification system, developed by Louis Wirth (1945), is based on the ultimate objectives of the minorities. In this classification system, there are four types of minorities:

1. pluralistic
2. assimilationist
3. secessionist
4. militant

A **pluralistic minority** is one that wants peaceful existence with the dominant group and other minority groups. It wants tolerance for its differences, whether they be religious, cultural, or racial. Pluralism varies from one setting to another. In some societies, it means toleration but little active cooperation. It may mean economic and political unity but little common participation and exchange in other matters. An example of a culturally pluralistic nation is Switzerland, where the Swiss have learned to live harmoniously despite their differences in language, dialect, costume, and patterns of life.

Unlike the pluralistic minority, which strives to maintain its group integrity, the **assimilationist minority** wants to be absorbed into the dominant group. Assimilation is a two-way process, in which a new people and culture emerge through a fusion of cultural traditions and racial stocks. The various European immigrant groups within the United States are examples of assimilationist minorities.

A **secessionist minority** wants full political self- determination and independence. It does not want to be absorbed into a dominant group and is not satisfied with mere toleration. A secessionist minority seeks cultural independence. The black Garveyite movement of the 1920s and the Jewish Zionist movement are examples of secessionist movements. These movements occur most frequently among minorities who once had political independence.

The ultimate objective of a **militant minority** is totally to reverse its status. It wants and demands domination over others, not equality with them. It is convinced of its own superiority and is highly ethnocentric.

There are many different policies toward minority groups

One may also develop an understanding of majority-minority situations by examining the aims of the dominant group. Dominant groups have developed six major types of policies toward minority groups:

1. assimilation
2. pluralism
3. legal protection of minorities
4. population transfer
5. continued subjugation
6. extermination

The dominant group's policy toward *assimilation* often differs from the minority policy in that it can be a forced assimilation. Dominant groups may adopt an extreme ethnocentrism and refuse minorities the right to practice their own religion and customs or to speak their own language. Dominant groups may force minorities to assimilate, or they may permit minorities to absorb dominant patterns at their own speed and in their own ways.

Policies range from assimilation to extermination

Similar to the *pluralistic* aims of some minorities, some dominant groups wish to permit cultural variability within a range consonant with national unity and security. Other dominant groups have a policy of *protecting* minority groups by legal, constitutional, or diplomatic means.

In an attempt to solve minority problems, some dominant groups have adopted a policy of *population transfer* and physical separation. Even though those who advocate population transfer may have good intentions, it usually expresses only hostility and discrimination as a policy of the majority. The transfer may be either of two types: direct or indirect. In a direct transfer, a minority is required and forced to leave. For example, many nations and cities drove out Jews in the late medieval period; the United States drove Native Americans out of area after area. An indirect transfer involves making life so unbearable for minority members that they "choose" to migrate.

At times, the dominant group wants neither to incorporate the minority nor to drive it out, but wants to keep it around in a servile, *exploitable state.* Some powerful interests in the southwestern part of the United States, for example, want to keep Mexican illegal aliens as an exploitable minority.

The final policy of dominant groups toward minority groups is that of *extermination*. Conflict between dominant and minority groups may develop to the point where elimination of the minority group becomes a goal of the dominant group. The Nazis exterminated the Jews, and the Americans exterminated the Native Americans.

The six policies of dominant groups may occur simultaneously—they are not mutually exclusive. Some of these policies are conscious, long-run plans; some are ad hoc adjustments to specific situations; some are the by-products (perhaps unintended) of other policies. In some instances, they are the official actions of majority group leaders. In other instances, they are the everyday responses of individual members of the dominant group.

Prejudice and Discrimination

Blacks, the handicapped, Jews, Indians, Mexican-Americans, Puerto Ricans, Asian-Americans, women, and other minorities suffer greatly from prejudice, discrimination, and segregation.

Prejudice defined

Prejudice is a state of mind and a system of negative conceptions, attitudes, feelings, and actions toward members of a particular group. It is an emotional, rigid attitude or belief, or a predisposition to respond to a particular stimulus, in a particular way, toward a group of people.

Prejudice is not the same as discrimination. Discrimination, as we shall see later, involves action whereby members of a particular group are accorded negative treatment on the basis of racial, ethnic, or religious background. Prejudice is a prejudgment of an individual or group of people before, or independent of, an examination of evidence or facts in the matter. One is not born prejudiced. Prejudices are learned, and they are learned by the individual primarily through interaction with people who are prejudiced rather than through contact with the group toward whom prejudice is felt.

Prejudice is a negative attitude or belief, and any negative attitude has the tendency somehow, somewhere, to express itself in action. In his classic study *The Nature of Prejudice* (1954), Gordon Allport notes that few people are able to keep their dislikes to themselves. If an individual has an intensely negative attitude, there is a likelihood of its resulting in hostile action. Allport distinguishes five degrees of negative action, which range from negative talk to extermination.

1. *Antilocution.* Most people who have prejudices talk about them. With like-minded friends or occasionally with strangers, they may express their antagonism freely. Many people never go beyond this mild degree of antipathetic action.

There exists a wide range of negative actions

2. *Avoidance.* If the prejudice is more intense, it leads the individual to avoid members of the disliked group, perhaps even at the cost of considerable inconvenience. In this case, bearers of prejudice do not directly inflict harm on the group they dislike, but take the burden of accommodation and withdrawal entirely upon themselves.
3. *Discrimination.* Prejudiced people who discriminate make detrimental distinctions of an active sort. They undertake to exclude all members of the group in question from certain types of employment, housing, political rights, educational or recreational opportunities, hospitals, churches, or other social rights. Segregation is an institutionalized form of discrimination, enforced legally or by custom.
4. *Physical attack.* Under conditions of heightened emotion, prejudice may lead to acts of violence or semiviolence. An unwanted black family may be forcibly ejected from a neighborhood or so severely threatened that it leaves in fear. Gravestones in Jewish cemeteries may be desecrated. The northside's Italian gang may lie in wait for the southside's Irish gang.
5. *Extermination.* Lynchings, pogroms, massacres, and Hitler's program of genocide mark the ultimate degree of violent expressions of prejudice.

These five degrees of negative action call our attention to the wide range of activities that may be caused by prejudice. When there is activity at one level, it is much easier to move up to the next level.

It was Hitler's antilocution that led Germans to avoid their Jewish neighbors and erstwhile friends. This preparation made it easier to enact the Nurnberg laws of discrimination which, in turn, made the subsequent burnings of synagogues and street attacks upon Jews seem natural. The final step in the macabre progression was the oven at Auschwitz (Allport, 1954, pp. 14–15).

Discrimination involves action and therefore is different from prejudice. Discrimination is the differential treatment of a person or persons considered to belong to a particular social group. Discrimination is not just an attitude, belief, or a predisposition to act, as is prejudice. Discrimination is not a state of mind, but entails overt action by which members of a group are accorded unfavorable treatment on the basis of their religious, ethnic, or racial membership.

Discrimination defined

Discrimination may be part of the behavior of people who have strong prejudices. It may be the result of social or cultural expectations, customs, or laws. For example, a white hairdresser may not have any personal animosity or prejudice against blacks but still may refuse their trade because he or she believes their presence may hurt business. Here we have an example of an individual who is not prejudiced yet who discriminates against a minority. But there are also individuals who are prejudiced and who fail to translate their prejudice into overt action. Many employers are prejudiced against minority groups but do not discriminate in their hiring procedures. Institutional policies, common custom, or laws may prohibit such discriminatory action. Most of the time prejudice and discrimination are mutually reinforcing. Many people who are prejudiced also discriminate. In fact, there exists a correlation between discrimination and prejudice in that those who are more prejudiced are more likely to discriminate.

Consequences of Prejudice and Discrimination

All groups suffer from prejudice and discrimination

Prejudice has many consequences for minority groups in the United States. But the costs of prejudice and discrimination to the dominant segments of society are also high. For example, discrimination in employment creates an inefficient and less productive use of the labor force. These effects, in turn, mean less purchasing power, less consumer demand, less production, and a lower living standard for dominant as well as minority groups. All American groups are affected by prejudice and discrimination to the extent that they affect our relationships with other nations of different races and religions. Many other nations regard the people of the United States as hypocrites when they speak of human rights because of the way minority groups are treated in American society.

Most minority groups suffer greatly from prejudice and discrimination. Three groups—women, blacks, and the aged—are America's largest minorities. Many of the problems they encounter parallel the inequities encountered by other minority groups. In the following sections, we focus on these three minority groups and on Hispanic and Native Americans.

Women: America's Largest Minority Group

Numerically speaking, there are more women than men in society. However, they are a minority group because, as we have noted above, a minority-dominant group situation is a pattern of relationships or a distribution of power. Women in America experience discrimination and prejudice in many areas, such as income, work, and education.

Women experience much prejudice and discrimination

Women contributed two-thirds of the total growth of the U.S. labor force between the mid-1970s and the late 1980s, as their numbers rose from 37 million to well over 50 million. Today over half of all women 16 years of age and over are working or looking for work. By 1995, the total U.S. employment will be reaching the 140 million level, and women will account for half of those workers (*Burlington County Times*, 1990).

American women work out of necessity

Most women in our society work out of necessity, not because they need a few extra dollars or because they seek pleasure. Millions of women work in the paid labor force because past high rates of inflation have considerably eroded disposable earnings and have forced many American families to rely on two incomes to maintain their standard of living. Many women also work because they are the sole support of their families as a result of divorce, widowhood, or other reasons.

In the United States, women earn two-thirds as much as men. This gap is wider than it was 30 years ago. Some people believe that women have less education and training than men and should therefore receive lower wages, because people are paid what they are worth. The fact is that women have basically the same education as men (an average of 12 years plus). Although there has been, in many areas, a slight narrowing of the earnings differential during the past decade, women workers still did not approach earnings parity with men, even when they worked in similar occupations. Back in 1975, the median earnings of women who worked at full-time jobs throughout the year were 59 percent of the amount that similarly employed men earned. Today women, as noted above, earn two-thirds of what men earn. The traditional pattern of concentration of women in lower-paying jobs persists even though women workers have completed about the same number of years of school as men. During the late 1970s and throughout the 1980s, a significant change for women has been increased representation among executive, administrative, and managerial occupations. Women constituted 22 percent of this group back in 1975. Today they constitute well over a third. Women still, however, were underrepresented in comparison with their overall participation in the labor force (*Burlington County Times*, 1990).

The earning gap between women and men remains in the 1990s

A woman of 25 who works year-round, full-time and who has four or more years of college earns *less* than a man with a high school diploma. This relationship has remained essentially unchanged over time. Some explanations traditionally offered are that women enter and leave the work force more frequently than men, resulting in less work experience; that women's education and skills are not equal to men's; and that women and men are concentrated in different occupations that pay differently. The first two explanations are false: Women are a stable part of the work force, and their educational attainment is equal to that of men. The major reason for the income gap is the difference in the types of jobs that the two sexes hold. These facts explain the income gap but do not excuse it. Women have low-paying jobs because these are the jobs considered "fitting" for women; this is the only rank to which woman are welcomed. Recent research shows that after all measurable variables are included in an equation on earnings differences for men and women, the variance that cannot be explained is attributed to unmeasured factors such as personal attitudes, quality of education, and discrimination (*U.N. Decade for Women*, 1985).

Some things have not changed

A survey by the Office of Technology Assessment (1985) found that American women are discouraged from seeking science and engineering jobs because of discrimination in the work force and sex-stereotyped career expectations. Female scientists and engineers generally receive lower salaries and have a smaller chance of promotion than men. The survey further noted that women's salaries are significantly lower than men's in almost all fields of science, in every employment sector, and at comparable levels of experience. In academia, men are far more likely than women to hold tenure track positions, to be given tenure, and to achieve full professorships. The differential treatment of women in the work force directly violates the principle of equality of opportunity.

Women are still discouraged from seeking many jobs

Younger working women have made greater gains

With regard to gender gaps then, relatively speaking, working U.S. women have been faring better than working U.S. men, even though on average they still earn only two-thirds as much. Gains have been promising for younger working U.S. women. Working women ages 20 to 24 years of age earn 86 percent as much as their male counterparts. One reason for this smaller gap may be that women are choosing longer working careers with fewer interruptions. In addition, many younger working women are entering higher-paying fields that traditionally have been dominated by males. An economist at the RAND Corporation, James P. Smith, predicts that as more women attend colleges and universities and gain work experience, the gap between women and men will narrow to where women as a group earn 80 percent or more of what men earn by the year 2000 (*Burlington County Times*, 1990).

WHAT KEEPS WOMEN "IN THEIR PLACE"?

Anthony Layng

In the following reading, "What Keeps Women 'in Their Place'?" the author, Anthony Layng, examines how sexual equality in the United States will not be acheived until Americans confront and deal with the fact that inequality is a product of our own attitudes and behavior.

During the decade of the 1970's, women in numerous nations called for the elimination of sexual discrimination. In the U.S., this latest feminist resurgence ambitiously attempted to end all inequalities between the sexes—including those involving employment, political participation, property rights, recreation, language, and education—and some reforms were achieved. An increasing number of women began to act like they were socially equal to men; there has been much talk about teaching girls to be more assertive; and there is now considerable confusion about what constitutes appropriate sex roles. Yet, judging by the fact that the Equal Rights Amendment did not pass and that it presently shows little promise of being resuscitated in the near future, many seem to have concluded that most American women are, by and large, content to remain where they are in relation to men. Further, since women in other industrialized nations have remained essentially "in their place," it appears that there are other formidable obstacles to overcome if we are to bring about such fundamental social change.

Why do sexual inequalities persist in the face of concerted feminist challenges? Is there any realistic basis for us to hope that sexual discrimination ever will be eliminated? What must be done to bring about full emancipation of women? What is it that keeps women "in their place"?

To understand fully how women have been kept "in their place," we first must learn how they came to be there. This requires consideration of the course of human evolution. Prior to 4,000,000 years ago, there was probably little social differentiation based on gender, because the two sexes were not economically interdependent; one could survive quite well without assistance from the other. It is likely that economic interdependence developed only after the evolving human brain reached a size that necessitated earlier birth, before the cranium of an infant was too large to pass through the birth canal. Giving birth earlier meant that the babies were less mature and would be more dependent on their mothers for a longer period of time. Prolonged helplessness of infants eventually created a need for mothers to depend on others for food and protection.

At the same time, more evolved brains enabled us to invent and use tools that resulted in our becoming effective hunters, in addition to being scavengers. Females with helpless infants still could gather and scavenge a variety of foods, but they were likely to be relatively handicapped hunters and so came to depend on males to provide them with a more reliable source of meat.

Increasing brain size and improved hunting skills also meant that some of our ancestors could begin to occupy northern regions where successful hunting was necessary for survival, since those foods that could be gathered were insufficient during some seasons. In such an environment, females with infants would not live long without food provided by others. Under these circumstances, a sexual division of labor made very good sense.

Although biological factors created the especially long dependency of human infants, the solution to this problem may have been entirely cultural. There is little evidence to suggest that any instinct developed at this time which led females to restrict their economic activities to gathering roots and fruits and men to go off in search of game, but doing so was sound strategy. Such specialization—encouraging females to learn and concentrate on gathering, and teaching only males to be hunters—was an efficient and realistic adaptation requiring only a change in our ancestors' learned behavior and attitudes.

So, a sexual division of labor emerged, but what about sexual inequality? The subordination of females was not brought about by this economic change alone, for, although economic specialization by sex made women dependent on men, it also made men dependent on women. Where human populations subsist entirely by what can be hunted or gathered, most of the food consumed is provided by the gatherers—women. Meat acquired by hunters may be given a higher social value than nuts and berries and the like; but, if the technology employed in hunting is very primitive, meat is difficult to acquire and frequently absent from the menu. Thus, when men began to concentrate on hunting, an interdependence between the sexes emerged, each relying on the other to provide food that made survival possible.

BELIEFS AND CUSTOMS

The development of a sexual division of labor may have preceded and even facilitated social inequality, but it did not create male dominance. Although male dominance would be very difficult to achieve in the absence of a sexual division of labor, it takes firm beliefs and customs as well to retain a higher status for men. The following examples illustrate how societies in various parts of the world have directed the socialization of their children to assure that women will be kept "in their place."

■ Mythology which justifies maintaining female subordination. Mythology and folklore are used in tribal societies to explain and justify the social *status quo*. The story of Adam and Eve illustrates how sexist myths can be, but some are even less subtle than Genesis in rationalizing male preeminence. Frequently found tales of Amazons or an era when our ancestors lived in matriarchal communities may be functionally equivalent to the Adam and Eve account; although they serve as inspiring models for some women, they may be far more instrumental in reminding men why they must be ever-vigilant in protecting their favored status. So, such tales become an important part of the conservative social learning of children.

■ Seclusion based on the concept of pollution. In many horticultural societies, women must retire to a special hut during menstruation, since it is believed that their condition magically would jeopardize the well-being of the community. Their economic inactivity during these and other periods of seclusion serves to indicate symbolically that their economic contributions are of secondary importance. This subconsciously may suggest to children in the community that the labor of men is too important to be so restricted by taboos.

■ Segregation of male domains. Many tribal societies have a men's house in the center of each village in which nearly all important political and ritual plans are made. Women are not allowed to enter this house, under the threat of severe punitive sanctions such as gang rape. Since this form of segregation effectively precludes the participation of women in the political arena, they are not likely to develop any political aspirations while growing up.

■ Exclusion from sacred public rituals. Tribal societies customarily devote much energy to elaborate religious events, believing that the health of the community depends on these. With very few exceptions, men direct these rituals and play all the key roles; commonly, women merely are observers or participate only in a support capacity. A primary function of these public rituals is to reinforce social values. Since they even attract the full attention of young children, tribal members learn early that men are far more important than women, for they are the ones charged with magically protecting the people.

■ Exclusion from military combat. As in the case of religious ritual in tribal societies, war is considered necessary to insure the survival of the community and almost always is conducted exclusively by men. Success as a warrior brings conspicuous prestige and admiration from women and children alike. Here again, the socialization process, instilling norms and attitudes of correct conduct, leads easily and inevitably to the conclusion that everyone's welfare depends on the performance of the men, and that the women should be suitably grateful.

■ Exclusion from high-status economic roles. Women in most tribal societies are important producers and consumers, but their economic role is restricted largely to domestic concerns, producing food and goods for kinsmen. When it comes to regulating the exchange of goods between kin groups or with outsiders, men usually dominate such activities. This division of economic roles is fully consistent with the assumption that men are more important socially and more skillful politically. Given such an assumption, the economic differences between the behavior of men and women are likely to seem both proper and inevitable.

■ Veneration of female virginity. If the religious, political, and economic activities of women are of secondary importance, then what, besides producing children, is their real value? One might be tempted to speculate that, because children in primitive societies are taught to venerate female virginity, this indicates that the status of women is not so lowly as might otherwise be assumed. However, it seems far more likely that this concern with virginity is an extension of the double standard and a reflection of the belief that the major value of women is their sexuality and fertility, their unexalted role as wife and mother.

■ Preference for male children. When parents usually prefer that their next child will be a boy, this attitude may be considered as both a consequence of and contributor to the higher status of men. Before young children are mature enough to appreciate that one sex socially outranks the other, they can understand that their parents hope to have a boy next time. Impending childbirth in a home is given much attention and takes on real importance; this often may be the earliest opportunity for children to learn that males are more valued than females.

■ Sexist humor and ridicule are used as important socialization methods in all societies and lend themselves quite effectively to maintaining a sexual hierarchy. Girls who behave like boys, and boys who behave like girls, almost inevitably inspire ridicule. Sexist jokes, particularly when they are considered to be good-natured, are especially effective in this regard. Women who take offense or fail to find such jokes amusing are accused of having no sense of humor, thus largely neutralizing their defense against this social control mechanism.

■ Sexual stereotyping. Stereotypes of any sort are likely to be of little use in teaching social attitudes to children unless they are accepted by the children as true images of nature. To believe that women and men behave differently because it is the way they were created helps to prevent misgivings from arising about the social inequality of men and women. To the extent that such status differences are believed to be imposed by human nature, the cultural supports of such inequality are not likely to be recognized and, therefore, will not be questioned.

DO WOMEN ACCEPT SUBJUGATION?

A society which effectively keeps women "in their place" need not employ all of the above techniques to do so; just a few will suffice, so long as there is general agreement throughout the population that the *status quo* of sexual inequality is both appropriate and natural. It is just as necessary that women accept this view as it is for men. Although some reformist writers argue that the subjugation of women was instigated by a male chauvinist plot forced upon unwilling victims, it seems amply evident that these social control mechanisms could not work effectively without the willing cooperation of women. They, too, must believe that they were designed by their creator to be subordinate; religious, political, and economic leadership are less suitable for them; and they have their own domains and should not be so immodest as to attempt to interfere where they do not belong. They, too, must consider military exploits as unsuitable for themselves.

Is this asking too much? Do not women value their virginity and that of their daughters as much as men do? Do they not condemn promiscuous women and at the same time tolerate promiscuous men? Is it not common for women to hope to have male children, in preference to daughters? Most women accept sexual stereotypes as an accurate reflection of nature to some degree, and they continue to encourage sexist humor by their laughter.

It seems clear that the "lowly" status of women was not brought about by a conspiracy, nor is it perpetuated only by men. There is no reason to view the above social controls as sinister or perverse where women willingly, even enthusiastically, teach their sons to be "real" men and their daughters to admire such men without wanting to be like them. In other words, in tribal societies, it is not male suppression which makes women subordinate.

It is only when we assume a missionary mentality, viewing such societies in light of our own society's values, that we think these women long for emancipation. Such an ethnocentric view fails to recognize that inequality, where it is accepted by all concerned as inevitable and proper, can be advantageous to lower-status individuals as well as to those who outrank them. Dominance hierarchies, like pecking orders, establish and maintain social order, a condition which tribal societies understandably prefer to disorder and uncertainty. Women in traditional societies do not contribute to their own subordination because they do not know any better or because they are forced to comply with the wishes of the men; they do so because they are socialized appropriately in any orderly society which is culturally well-adapted to its environment.

In tribal societies, sexual inequality is relatively high and protest against such inequality is relatively low. However, an increasing number of women in other societies are protesting sexual discrimination and their subordinate position. Most of this dissent comes from stratified and heterogeneous populations, where gossip, ridicule, and taboos are relatively ineffectual social control techniques. Social order in these more complex societies tends to be enforced by laws and specialized agencies, rather than depending upon voluntary compliance. Even in such complex societies, women need not necessarily feel unjustly deprived, for here, too, as in tribal societies, most may be wholly supportive of the social *status quo*, in spite of their own lowly status. Nevertheless, most of the discontent about sexual inequality comes from these populations.

In spite of such feminist discontent, sexual hierarchies still survive in even highly modernized societies like our own. American women have gained important rights in recent years, but many Americans continue to find Biblical justification for sexual discrimination. Many still think that our nation's economy appropriately remains under the domination of men, and, although the number of exclusively male domains (athletic teams, lodges, clubs, etc.) have been reduced greatly in recent years, a large number still find general endorsement and remain very much intact. Sexual stereotypes continue to enjoy robust health, the double standard is far from moribund, and sexist humor and ridicule seem to have recovered from their recent bout with militant feminism in the 1970's.

Today, in spite of a recent Gallup poll indicating that more than half the women in the U.S. consider themselves to be feminists, the most ambitious goals of the feminist movement have not been realized. However, it has grown increasingly difficult to convince American women that it is proper for them to be socially inferior to men, or that they should behave submissively. It seems that those customs and beliefs which deny opportunity to women in America are going to continue to be questioned by some who are very persuasive. Since a sexual division of labor has become largely anachronistic for our technologically advanced society, we may anticipate that efforts to preserve exclusive privileges for either sex will encounter increasing resistance.

Although tribal societies need to depend on a system of ascriptive statuses to maintain an orderly social structure, we do not. Tribal populations are not at risk in assigning economic roles strictly by sex, because not basing such assignments on individual aptitude and inclination is of little importance where the economy requires only a narrow range of tasks. In modern industrial society, however, where much highly skilled specialization is essential, selecting candidates for such positions from a limited talent pool, from only half of the adult population, places such a society at an unnecessary disadvantage, one which shows up very clearly if that society must compete with other nations which do not handicap themselves in this fashion. Also, traditional American values which exalt equality, opportunity, and achievement (matters of relatively little concern in tribal societies) are bound to give us increasing difficulty if we continue to deny equality to women and so restrict their ability to achieve the success that they desire and that our economy requires.

Since men have been politically dominant in all human societies, it is not surprising that many scholars have concluded that it is our nature, not our nurture, that has necessitated this inequality. Still, if sexual inequality is inevitable, given our nature, why must tribal populations resort to so many cultural methods to keep women subordinate and submissive?

Knowing how women have been kept "in their place" so long is essential if attempts to combat sexual inequality are to have some success. Just as the most effective medical cure is based on accurate causal diagnosis of an illness, so much social reform efforts take into account the nature of that which we would alter. If we recognize the various ways that our society uses cultural means to perpetuate differential socialization for boys and girls, we are prepared better to redesign that process to foster equality between the sexes. Similarly, if we are aware of the customary practices which encourage women to be submissive, we are more able to challenge and change such customs effectively. To fully understand how and to what extent women are kept "in their place" in the U.S., it is important that we understand how various societies effectively accomplish stable inequality.

Before all of this can enable us to eradicate male dominance, it may be that we first must learn why our society continues to deny equality of opportunity to women, for it is unlikely that we do so only as a result of cultural inertia. It may be that inequality is socially functional in ways that we do not understand fully.

Nevertheless, if women are to achieve total equality, if such a fundamental change can be brought about, it will require far more than passing the Equal Rights Amendment or changing discriminatory laws piecemeal. Since longstanding customs which encourage inequality thoroughly are ingrained in our culture, sexual equality will not be achieved until we face up to the fact that inequality is a product of our own behavior and attitudes. Only then might we discard this vestige of our tribal heritage.

Review Questions

1. Briefly comment on the statement ". . . Sexual equality will not be achieved until we face up to the fact that inequality is a product of our own behavior and attitudes."
2. Briefly examine four examples of how American society has directed the socialization of its children to assure that women will be kept "in their place."

The Black Minority

The effect of prejudice and discrimination on blacks has been great. Although blacks have advanced in certain areas, such as education, health, and election to public office, problems remain in income, employment, housing, and many other areas.

Many problems for blacks remain

Black Americans must contend with deteriorating conditions in sharp contrast to many other minority groups. The black poverty rate is triple that of whites and double that of many other minorities. Black unemployment is double that of whites. In urban ghettos, the black youth unemployment rate often exceeds 40 percent. It is not uncommon for young men to leave school at age 16 and reach their mid-20s without ever having held a steady job. Black infant mortality is not only double that of whites, but it also may be rising for the first time in a decade. We are already at a point where more than half of black children are born out of wedlock, most to teenage parents. Black girls between the ages of 15 and 19 constitute the most fertile population of that age group in the industrialized world. Their birth rate is twice as high as any other group in the western world.

Improvement has occurred in employment and education

Research indicates that for blacks in America, jobs and the education to get them are the major factors in the achievement of a better life. Of all the forces of discrimination affecting them, blacks themselves consider these to be the most important. As recent census data indicate, some improvement in the employment situation has occurred. There has also been progress in the area of education for young blacks. This area is critical, because no area of discrimination is as damaging as this starting point. A decade ago, well over half of black women had not finished high school. By the mid-1980s, two-fifths had not completed high school.

With respect to income, black families earn about two-thirds as much as white families (Census Bureau, 1990). The gap between family incomes of blacks and whites is no longer as great as it was in 1947, when black families earned 51 percent of what white families earned. However, the general income disparity that exists between the races is still very great. The income disparity may be accounted for in terms of the types of jobs that each group holds. Basically, the same explanations for the differences between men's and women's earnings apply to differences between whites' and blacks' earnings. Many blacks are in low-paying occupations because of the myths that blacks have no desire for better jobs, that they are happier in jobs in which they are welcome, and that they are not able to perform certain jobs as well as whites.

There have been changes in black employment patterns during the past two decades. Whites are still overrepresented in the more advantaged occupational categories, but blacks have experienced an occupational upgrading in the past 20 years. In fact, between 1960 and 1990, more occupational upgrading occurred among blacks and other races than among whites. Between 1970 and 1990, black women increased their proportions in many technical and professional jobs, working as nurses, therapists, dieticians, and engineering and science professionals. In point of fact, in 1985, the median income for black women passed and is now higher than that for white women. There is a gap between the earnings of black and white men, but it has narrowed considerably. In 1940, the earnings of black men as a percentage of white men's earnings was 40 percent. Today it is in the low 70 percent range (*Burlington County Times*, 1990).

Positive change in black incomes

Education has been a significant major force in narrowing the income gap between black and white workers. Finis Welch of the University of California and Kevin Murphy of the University of Chicago reported that during the past decade, blacks earned a higher return than whites by investing in their own education. In addition, both the black middle class and the black economic elite have been growing rapidly. Their achievements will be even more apparent in future generations. Today many blacks are very much financially able to secure the American dream for their children (*Burlington County Times*, 1990).

Housing segregation remains in many communities

One area of minority relations that has changed very little over the years is housing and neighborhood segregation. There is no shortage of law with respect to housing segregation. Federal fair housing statutes have existed for over 20 years. There are also many local and state antidiscrimination laws. However, there never has been strong enforcement of these laws. In some urban communities, there has been compliance, and middle-class blacks also have made some inroads into some formerly all-white suburbs.

In spite of certain improvements in such areas as income, employment, and education, blacks still occupy a distinct position in the American stratification system. Their color differentiates them from dominant groups in America, and they are prevented from being equal participants in many of the phases of social life.

The Aged

The aged in America also have been viewed as a minority group by sociologists. There is a strong relation between the basic cultural values of our society and the various patterns of structured social inequality based on age. Prejudice against old age is used as criterion for discrimination.

Prejudice against old age is the result of the unjust stereotypes that many people hold. Like women and blacks, the aged are subject to stereotyping and discrimination. For example, the attitudes that old people are rigid in their ways, sexless, constantly sick, and devoid of useful skills are typical stereotypes. Noting that in this culture, men are considered more socially valuable than women, and the young are considered more valuable than the old, Payne and Whittington (1976) state that elderly women are viewed as socially unimportant and are the recipients of more negative stereotypes than any other age or sex group. Older women are viewed as:

Many stereotypes about old age remain

> **weak, ineffective, inactive, asexual old maids or widows. . . . Older people and women . . . are groups which have traditionally fared quite badly in this country's social and economic market place and which continue to suffer discrimination motivated, at least in part, by such negative stereotypical images (Payne and Whittington, 1976, pp. 488–504).**

Research indicates that aged women are not significantly more sick or weak than men of the same age. The elderly woman is not asexual, widowhood is not necessarily a social or emotional grave, and leisure time is not always spent inactively or alone. These stereotypes affect what the aged think of themselves as well as what others think about them.

Sex, Race, and Age: A Comparison Compared with racial and sexual inequality, inequality based on age is a relatively new topic of sociological investigation. Although age discrimination is a common feature of society and both young and old share stereotypes about the aged, older people typically do not report a great deal of discrimination. Also when problems were reported in the past, they were seldom attributed to age by the elderly respondents. Unlike blacks, women, or other minority groups, the aged are probably far less likely to see and report conditions as being discriminatory:

> **Factors including the individual's ambiguous personal response to his [or her] own aging, the ambiguous legal definition of the older American's civil rights, and the relatively low public visibility of the nature and magnitude of age discrimination all militate against the older person's developing a definition of any particular situation as discriminatory and, therefore, unjust and intolerable (Kasschau, 1977, pp. 728–742).**

Because of these factors, discrimination on the basis of age appears to be more subtle and elusive than discrimination on the basis of race or sex. Therefore, it may be more difficult to control or eliminate. Age discrimination depends on a person's aged appearance. Elderly who do not look their age escape the consequences of age discrimination.

Hispanic Americans

Hispanic Americans constitute one of America's largest minority groups

Hispanic Americans are expected to be America's largest ethnic minority before the year 2000. When unofficial calculations are included, it is estimated that there are currently over 20 million Hispanics in the United States. Hispanics include ethnic groups from Cuba, Puerto Rico, and Mexico. Although many diversities exist among the Hispanic population, most are Roman Catholic and have a rich Spanish heritage.

Hispanic Americans are also victims of discrimination and prejudice in income, education, and employment. Hispanics' income is significantly lower than that of whites. In fact, virtually one-third of all Hispanics live below the poverty line. With the exception of Cubans, the Hispanic median educational level is two to three years less than that of the total American population. Hispanic women lag behind other women in the years of school completed, although younger Hispanic women are narrowing this gap. In general, Hispanic men and women have one of the highest unemployment rates in America. Hispanic workers are primarily concentrated in less skilled, lower-paid jobs.

Native Americans

In the United States, there are over 1.5 million Native Americans. The ancestors of Native Americans were the original occupants of America. Many were captured, killed, or displaced by whites.

Because many can no longer support themselves on their depleted reservations, more than half of all Native Americans live in urban communities where they continue to experience much prejudice and discrimination. Less than half of Native Americans are high school graduates. The median number of years of education for the total Native American population remains at less than 10. As with other minorities, Native Americans work at lower-level jobs. Two-thirds of the men are concentrated in blue-collar jobs. In addition, two-thirds of employed Native American women are concentrated in clerical, operative, and service jobs.

Native Americans are subject to much prejudice and discrimination

Explanations for Prejudice and Discrimination

Prejudice and discrimination may be explained in many ways, but no one theory can adequately explain all prejudice or all discrimination. Prejudice and discrimination have many different origins and are of many types. Although we cannot examine all of these, we will present some major theories.

Sociocultural Explanation

The sociocultural explanation of prejudice and discrimination is based on the belief that human attitudes and behavior are, to a great extent, patterned by culture. Social norms are a part of culture and are learned by people as they are socialized. These norms also inform people of socially appropriate behavior and guide them in intergroup relations. Cultural norms inform dominant and minority group members alike how they are expected to think, act, and feel toward one another. A rigid example of this exists in South Africa, where the culture specifies through its normative structure—its laws, customs, and traditions—how whites and blacks are expected to act toward each other.

Social norms are important

In the sociocultural explanation then, prejudices and discriminatory patterns are considered to be part of the folkways and mores of the society. They are among the learned responses acquired as part of the standard cultural equipment through socialization. Children grow up prejudiced to the extent that they are exposed to prejudiced traditions and beliefs by their reference groups.

The sociocultural explanation provides answers to the question of why prejudice against a particular minority remains, even though the causes of the prejudice are no longer present. For example, prejudice still exists against Japanese-Americans in the west. The prejudice exists because it remains a part of the cultural value system in that area, even though the cause of the prejudice—job competition from Japanese-Americans—is no longer present.

Frustration-Aggression: The Scapegoat Theory

In contrast to the sociocultural explanation for prejudice, the scapegoat theory stresses the importance of the individual personality. Individuals have many needs and goals. At times, however, needs are not met, and goals are blocked. Having one's goals and desires blocked may create frustration and anger in the individual, and this, in turn, can cause a person to vent hostility. Aggression, in other words, is the product of frustration.

Frustration may produce prejudice

In some cases, this aggression is directed at the source of the frustration, but at times, this may not be possible because the source—such as an employer or the government—may be unknown or too powerful to attack. Therefore minority groups become the target—the **scapegoat**—for this hostility. A displacement from the source of frustration to the scapegoat occurs. A scapegoat can be a group or someone or something that is forced to bear the blame or misfortune for others. Jews became the scapegoat for Hitler and Germany before and during World War II. They were blamed for the great bulk of the social and economic problems of the period. In many cases, white southerners after the Civil War were unable to vent their frustrations on the north and therefore directed their hostility against southern blacks. In his classic analysis of prejudice, Gordon Allport (1948) believes that suitable scapegoats have several characteristics. They are "easily recognizable; either physically or through some behavior or trait of dress; already unpopular; and a symbol of something hated."

The scapegoat theory helps explain some, but not all, prejudice. First, it does not explain why one minority group and not another is a scapegoat. Why are some minorities and not others selected for displacement? Second, frustration does not always result in aggression. Individuals can react to frustration by becoming apathetic, by seeking a substitute goal, or by increasing or decreasing their efforts to achieve their goals. Even so, the theory gives some insight into the sources of prejudice.

Economic Explanations for Prejudice

Economics also plays an important role in explaining prejudice. Many theorists consider economics, vested interests, and power as important variables in explaining prejudice, discrimination, and minority relations. Prejudice exists partly because some people, politically, socially, or economically, gain by prejudice. Marxists believe that the basic cause of prejudice and discrimination is class conflict.

In another classic study, Oliver Cox (1948) notes that racial prejudice and exploitation "developed among Europeans with the rise of capitalism and nationalism" and that "all racial antagonisms can be traced to the policies and attitudes of the leading capitalistic people, the white people of Europe and North America." He also believes that, in the United States, racial prejudice is the "socio-attitudinal matrix supporting a calculated and determined effort of a white ruling class to keep some people or peoples of color and their resources exploitable."

Economic exploitation theories emphasize prejudice's functional nature in maintaining an exploited minority group for its resources or labor. Persecution of a minority is justified in the interests of those in power. Dominant groups throughout the world have vested interests in the maintenance of a minority group's subordination. Economic and social advantages and privileges are preserved through the instrument of prejudice.

Herbert Blumer (1961) feels that dominant groups believe that they are entitled to rights and privileges with respect to occupations, property, social position, and so forth. Prejudice develops because dominant groups fear that the minority group or groups threaten or will challenge their dominant position. Prejudice, he states, is a "defensive reaction," a "protective device." It functions to protect and "to preserve the position of the dominant group."

Prejudice may be a defensive device

Groups that compete for scarce goods often develop prejudices toward and begin to discriminate against one another. For example, in times of sharp competition for jobs, housing, and other goods and services, antagonisms between competing groups intensify. Other studies also support the idea that prejudice is "most likely at the point of greatest sensed threat from social and economic competition." Basically, "Groups that have an economic, political or social advantage over other groups employ prejudice and discrimination as a means of protecting their advantageous position. Groups that compete with one another for particular scarce values tend to develop prejudice" (Vander Zanden, 1982, 1990).

Just as there are limitations to the sociocultural and personality theories, there are limitations to the economic theories of prejudice. For example, the economic competition theory may be able to account for the appearance of a particular dominant-minority pattern, but not for its continuation when the economic factor—such as job competition—has ended.

Each of the theories above emphasizes different factors in an attempt to account for prejudice and discrimination. There are, of course, many other theories. Some emphasize a historical approach and regard the Reconstruction period and slavery as variables in an explanation for black-white relations. Some theories, as we have seen, emphasize an economic approach. As Daniels and Kitano (1970) have stated, a case may be made for "urbanization, for industrialization, for the effects of materialism, depersonalization, and the mass culture; another point of view . . . emphasizes mobility in our society. . . . Broader theories . . . find the roots of prejudice in the unsavory nature of man himself. . . . Others emphasize inadequate socialization."

There is no simple one-factor explanation

All the above theories can be supported with a reliable and respectable body of research. In America, prejudice is a deep-rooted part of culture, a part of the adjustment systems of most people, a weapon in economic and political conflict, and a part of a tradition that brings the influences of the past into the present and puts them to use in conflicts.

Minority Group Reactions to Prejudice and Discrimination

There are several different ways in which minority groups react to their subordinate position in American society. Responses vary with the degree to which minority groups have been made the targets of prejudice and discrimination and to the extent that the minority group customs and norms are similar to those of the dominant society.

In a now-classic analysis of prejudice and discrimination, Peter I. Rose (1974) suggests that an understanding of minority group reactions can be obtained by asking two questions: "Does the minority group member accept or reject the image of subordinate status imposed by the majority?" and "Is the minority group member willing to play the humble role expected by those in positions of power?"

There exist many reactions to prejudice and discrimination

The answers to these questions reveal a minimum of four reactions: submission, withdrawal, separation, or integration. A particular person may manifest one or more of these reaction patterns at different times or in different circumstances.

Submission basically means the acceptance of a subordinate status. Many minority group members believe that their submission to a dominant group of society is necessary for survival. For many others, it is simply conformity to cultural traditions, a "conditioned reaction in a prejudiced society."

Withdrawal occurs when individuals deny their identity and accept the image that the majority has of their group. Because of self-hatred or expediency, the individual withdraws from the group. Many minority group members who accept this negative image try to pass into the dominant group. Passing is available to people who possess no identifying racial or ethnic characteristics or who can mask them. It is the only method of assimilation available to those who want to enter an environment that would reject them if their true identity were known.

With **separation**, the minority group does not accept the dominant group's negative image and avoids contact with the dominant group.

With **integration**, the minority rejects the idea that it is inferior. However, minority group members do not avoid contact with members of the dominant group; they attempt to integrate with and take their places alongside those in the dominant group.

Vander Zanden (1982, 1990), in his analysis of several studies, suggests that four models of minority group responses should be considered: acceptance, aggression, avoidance, and assimilation.

1. **Acceptance**. Minority group members may come to acquiesce to—to accommodate themselves to—their disadvantaged and subordinate status.

2. **Aggression**. Minority group members may respond to dominance by striking out against—engaging in hostile acts against—a status that is subordinate and disadvantaged.

3. **Avoidance**. Minority group members may attempt to shun—to escape from—situations in which they are likely to experience prejudice and discrimination.

4. **Assimilation**. Minority group members may attempt to become socially and culturally fused with the dominant group.

Minority group members may respond to dominance by striking out against a status that is subordinate and disadvantaged.

A combination of response patterns may exist

Avoidance and assimilation, and acceptance and aggression are viewed by Vander Zanden and others as opposites. These opposites reflect the choices that a minority group member must make in an intergroup situation. The minority group member allows intergroup contact or avoids the contact. If minority group members make contact with dominant group members, they must accept and acquiesce or be aggressive and strike out against their subordinate status.

A single, exclusive response pattern is never followed by a minority. Group relations are too complex for any one pattern to be used at all times. Usually, a combination predominates (Vander Zanden, 1968, 1982, 1990).

Lewis M. Killian (1970) gives an excellent illustration of the acceptance-aggression continuum in his analysis of black militance in the south:

> **The most obvious change in the social order of the south resulted directly from a shift of black southerners from a posture of accommodation to one of aggressive action. From the moment that Martin Luther King, Jr., led thousands of protestors into the streets of Montgomery, it became evident that black southerners would no longer depend either on the good will of white southerners or on intervention from outside for changes in their status. In cities all over the south, protest leaders arose to precipitate confrontations with their white fellow citizens. The old style black leaders who had enjoyed a cordial but subservient relationship with white influentials lost both their power in the black community and the confidence of their white sponsors. While indignant white southerners publicly ascribed the unrest in their communities to "outside agitators" and "newcomers," they knew**

> **in their hearts that there was a new spirit of rebellion even among "their colored folks." Although the outside aid of civil rights workers, white and black, was an essential force sustaining the civil rights movement in the south, it should never be forgotten that black southerners themselves participated in large numbers, as both leaders and followers, in challenging segregation and disenfranchisement. Enough participated to tear down the legal structure of segregation and to cause white southerners to view all black southerners through new eyes (Killian, 1970).**

Efforts to classify minority group reactions to dominance have not been entirely satisfactory. Rose's and Vander Zanden's models do attempt to overcome this difficulty with examinations of the most common reaction patterns to dominance. But they are obviously not the only responses of minority group members to dominance. Reactions are of many kinds and degrees. Together, though, they provide a great deal of insight into the wide range of behaviors that emanate from subordinate statuses.

BLACK BOY

Richard Wright

Learning that we are black or white is part of the process by which we acquire self-identity. As we learn other social roles, we learn our racial role. As children acquire the symbols and expectations of their racial roles, they learn who they are. In America during the 1930s and 1940s, learning one's racial role was both direct and subtle. The following reading, a selection from *Black Boy* by Richard Wright, relates an experience from his youth, as he applied for a job in a white woman's home.

The next day at school I inquired among the students about jobs and was given the name of a white family who wanted a boy to do chores. That afternoon, as soon as school had let out, I went to the address. A tall, dour white woman talked to me. Yes, she needed a boy, an honest boy. Two dollars a week. Mornings, evenings, and all day Saturdays. Washing dishes. Chopping wood. Scrubbing floors. Cleaning the yard. I would get my breakfast and dinner. As I asked timid questions, my eyes darted about. What kind of food would I get? Was the place as shabby as the kitchen indicated?

"Do you want this job?" the woman asked.

"Yes, ma'am," I said, afraid to trust my own judgment.

"Now, boy, I want to ask you one question and I want you to tell me the truth," she said.

"Yes, ma'am," I said, all attention.

"Do you steal?" she asked me seriously.

I burst into a laugh, then checked myself.

"What's so damn funny about that?" she asked.

"Lady, if I was a thief, I'd never tell anybody."

"What do you mean?" she blazed with a red face.

I had made a mistake during my first five minutes in the white world. I hung my head.

"No ma'am," I mumbled, "I don't steal."

She stared at me, trying to make up her mind.

"Now, look, we don't want a sassy nigger around here," she said.

"No, ma'am," I assured her. "I'm not sassy."

Promising to report the next morning at six o'clock, I walked home and pondered on what could possibly have been in the woman's mind to have made her ask me point-blank if I stole. Then I recalled hearing that white people looked upon Negroes as a variety of children, and it was only in the light of that that her question made any sense. If I had been planning to murder her, I certainly would not have told her and, rationally, she no doubt realized it. Yet habit had overcome her rationality and had made her ask me: "Boy, do you steal?" Only an idiot would have answered: "Yes, ma'am, I steal."

What would happen now that I would be among white people for hours at a stretch? Would they hit me? Curse me? If they did, I would leave at once. In all my wishing for a job I had not thought of how I would be treated, and now it loomed important, decisive, sweeping down beneath every other consideration. I would be polite, humble, saying yes sir and no sir, yes ma'am and no ma'am, but I would draw a line over which they must not step. Oh, maybe I'm just thinking up trouble, I told myself. They might like me . . .

The next morning I chopped wood for the cook stove, lugged in scuttles of coal for the grates, washed the front porch and swept the back porch, swept the kitchen, helped wait on the table, and washed the dishes. I was sweating. I swept the front walk and ran to the store to shop. When I returned the woman said:

"Your breakfast is in the kitchen."

"Thank you, ma'am."

I saw a plate of thick, black molasses and a hunk of white bread on the table. Would I get no more than this? They had had eggs, bacon, coffee . . . I picked up the bread and tried to break it; it was stale and hard. Well, I would drink the molasses. I lifted the plate and brought it to my lips and saw floating on the surface of the black liquid green and white bits of mold. Goddamn . . . I can't eat this, I told myself. The food was not even clean. The woman came into the kitchen as I was putting on my coat.

"You didn't eat," she said.

"No, ma'am," I said. "I'm not hungry."

"You'll eat at home?" she asked hopefully.

"Well, I just wasn't hungry this morning, ma'am," I lied.

"You don't like molasses and bread," she said dramatically.

"Oh, yes, ma'am, I do," I defended myself quickly, not wanting her to think that I dared to criticize what she had given me.

"I don't know what's happening to you niggers nowadays," she sighed, wagging her head. She looked closely at the molasses. "It's a sin to throw out molasses like that. I'll put it up for you this evening."

"Yes, ma'am," I said heartily.

Neatly she covered the plate of molasses with another plate, then felt the bread and dumped it into the garbage. She turned to me, her face lit with an idea.

"What grade are you in school?"

"Seventh, ma'am."

"Then why are you going to school?" she asked in surprise.

"Well, I want to be a writer," I mumbled,

unsure of myself; I had not planned to tell her that, but she had made me feel so utterly wrong and of no account that I needed to bolster myself.

"A what?" she demanded.

"A writer," I mumbled.

"For what?"

"To write stories," I mumbled defensively.

"You'll never be a writer," she said. "Who on earth put such ideas into your nigger head?"

"Nobody," I said.

"I didn't think anybody ever would," she declared indignantly.

As I walked around her house to the street, I knew that I would not go back. The woman had assaulted my ego; she had assumed that she knew my place in life, what I felt, what I ought to be, and I resented it with all my heart. Perhaps she was right; perhaps I would never be a writer; but I did not want her to say so.

Had I kept the job I would have learned quickly just how white people acted toward Negroes, but I was too naive to think that there were many white people like that. I told myself that there were good white people, people with money and sensitive feelings. As a whole, I felt that they were bad, but I would be lucky enough to find the exceptions.

Fearing that my family might think I was finicky, I lied to them, telling them that the white woman had already hired a boy. At school I continued to ask about jobs and was directed to another address. As soon as school was out I made for the house. Yes, the woman said that she wanted a boy who could milk a cow, feed chickens, gather vegetables, help serve breakfast and dinner.

"But I can't milk a cow, ma'am," I said.

"Where are you from?" she asked incredulously.

"Here in Jackson," I said.

"You mean to stand there, nigger, and tell me that you live in Jackson and don't know how to milk a cow?" she demanded in surprise.

I said nothing, but I was quickly learning the reality—a Negro's reality—of the white world. One woman had assumed that I would tell her if I stole, and now this woman was amazed that I could not milk a cow, I, a nigger who dared live in Jackson . . . They were all turning out to be alike, differing only in detail. I faced a wall in the woman's mind, a wall that she did not know was there.

"I just never learned," I said finally.

"I'll show you how to milk," she said, as though glad to be charitable enough to repair a nigger's knowledge on that score. "It's easy."

Review Question

1. Write a brief essay on the behavior expected of Richard Wright because he was black.

BEYOND THE MELTING POT

William A. Henry III

In the following reading, "Beyond the Melting Pot," the author, William A. Henry III, reports that in the next century, ethnic and racial groups in the United States will outnumber whites. As he states, "The 'browning of America' will alter everything in society, from politics and education to industry, values and culture."

Someday soon, surely much sooner than most people who filled out their Census forms last week realize, white Americans will become a minority group. Long before that day arrives, the presumption that the "typical" U.S. citizen is someone who traces his or her descent in a direct line to Europe will be part of the past. By the time these elementary students at Brentwood Science Magnet School in Brentwood, Calif., reach midlife, their diverse ethnic experience in the classroom will be echoed in neighborhoods and workplaces throughout the U.S.

Already 1 American in 4 defines himself or herself as Hispanic or nonwhite. If current trends in immigration and birth rates persist, the Hispanic population will have further increased an estimated 21%, the Asian presence about 22%, blacks almost 12% and whites a little more than 2% when the 20th century ends. By 2020, a date no further into the future than John F. Kennedy's election is in the past, the number of U.S. residents who are Hispanic or nonwhite will have more than doubled, to nearly 115 million, while the white population will not be increasing at all. By 2056, when someone born today will be 66 years old, the "average" U.S. resident, as defined by Census statistics, will trace his or her descent to Africa, Asia, the Hispanic world, the Pacific Islands, Arabia—almost anywhere but white Europe.

While there may remain towns or outposts where even a black family will be something of an oddity, where English and Irish and German surnames will predominate, where a traditional (some will wistfully say "real") America will still be seen on almost every street corner, they will be only the vestiges of an earlier nation. The former majority will learn, as a normal part of everyday life, the meaning of the Latin slogan engraved on U.S. coins—E PLURIBUS UNUM, one formed from many.

Among the younger populations that go to school and provide new entrants to the work force, the change will happen sooner. In some places in America beyond the melting pot has already arrived. In New York State some 40% of elementary- and secondary-school children belong to an ethnic minority. Within a decade, the proportion is expected to approach 50%. In California white pupils are already a minority. Hispanics (who, regardless of their complexion, generally distinguish themselves from both blacks and whites) account for 31.4% of public school enrollment, blacks add 8.9%, and Asians and other amount to 11%—for a nonwhite total of 51.3%. This finding is not only a reflection of white flight from desegregated public schools. Whites of all ages account for just 58% of California's population. In San Jose bearers of the Vietnamese surname

Nguyen outnumber the Joneses in the telephone directory 14 columns to eight.

Nor is the change confined to the coasts. Some 12,000 Hmong refugees from Laos have settled in St. Paul. At some Atlanta low-rent apartment complexes that used to be virtually all black, social workers today need to speak Spanish. At the Sesame Hut restaurant in Houston, a Korean immigrant owner trains Hispanic immigrant workers to prepare Chinese-style food for a largely black clientele. The Detroit area has 200,000 people of Middle Eastern descent; some 1,500 small grocery and convenience stores in the vicinity are owned by a whole subculture of Chaldean Christians with roots in Iraq. "Once America was a microcosm of European nationalities," says Molefi Asante, chairman of the department of African-American studies at Temple University in Philadelphia. "Today America is a microcosm of the world."

History suggests that sustaining a truly multiracial society is difficult, or at least unusual. Only a handful of great powers of the distant past—Pharaonic Egypt and Imperial Rome, most notably—managed to maintain a distinct national identity while embracing, and being ruled by, an ethnic mélange. The most ethnically diverse contemporary power, the Soviet Union, is beset with secessionist demands and near tribal conflicts. But such comparisons are flawed, because those empires were launched by conquest and maintained through an aggressive military presence. The U.S. was created, and continues to be redefined, primarily by voluntary immigration. This process has been one of the country's great strengths, infusing it with talent and energy. The "browning of America" offers tremendous opportunity for capitalizing anew on the merits of many peoples from many lands. Yet this fundamental change in the ethnic makeup of the U.S. also poses risks. The American character is resilient and thrives on change. But past periods of rapid evolution have also, alas, brought out deeper, more fearful aspects of the national soul.

POLITICS: NEW AND SHIFTING ALLIANCES

A truly multiracial society will undoubtedly prove much harder to govern. Even seemingly race-free conflicts will be increasingly complicated by an overlay of ethnic tension. For example, the expected showdown in the early 21st century between the rising number of retirees and the dwindling number of workers who must be taxed to pay for the elders' Social Security benefits will probably be compounded by the fact that a large majority of recipients will be white, whereas a majority of workers paying for them will be nonwhite.

While prior generations of immigrants believed they had to learn English quickly to survive, many Hispanics now maintain that the Spanish language is inseparable from their ethnic and cultural identity, and seek to remain bilingual, if not primarily Spanish-speaking, for life. They see legislative drives to make English the sole official language, which have prevailed in some fashion in at least 16 states, as a political backlash. Says Arturo Vargas of the Mexican American Legal Defense and Educational Fund: "That's what English-only has been all about—a reaction to the growing population and influence of Hispanics. It's human nature to be uncomfortable with change. That's what the Census is all about, documenting changes and making sure the country keeps up."

Racial and ethnic conflict remains an ugly fact of American life everywhere, from working-class ghettos to college campuses, and those who do not raise their fists often raise their voices over affirmative action and other power sharing. When Florida Atlantic University, a state-funded institution under pressure to increase its low black enrollment, offered last month to give free tuition to every qualified black freshman who enrolled, the school was flooded with calls of complaint, some protesting that nothing was being done for "real" Americans. As the numbers of minorities increase, their demands for a share of the national bounty are bound to intensify, while whites are certain to feel ever more embattled. Businesses often feel whipsawed between immigration laws that punish them for hiring illegal aliens and antidiscrimination laws that penalize them for demanding excessive documentation from foreign-seeming job applicants. Even companies that consistently seek to do the right thing may be overwhelmed by the problems of diversifying a primarily white managerial corps fast enough to direct a work force that will be increasingly nonwhite and, potentially, resentful.

Nor will tensions be limited to the polar simplicity of white vs. nonwhite. For all Jesse Jackson's rallying cries about shared goals, minority groups often feel keenly competitive. Chicago's Hispanic leaders have leapfrogged between white and black factions, offering support wherever there seemed to be the most to gain for their own community. Says Dan Solis of the Hispanic-oriented United Neighborhood Organization: "If you're thinking power, you don't put your eggs in one basket."

Blacks, who feel they waited longest and endured most in the fight for equal opportunity, are uneasy about being supplanted by Hispanics or, in some areas, by Asians as the numerically largest and most influential minority—and even more, about being outstripped in wealth and status by these newer groups. Because Hispanics are so numerous and Asians such a fast-growing group, they have become the "hot" minorities, and blacks feel their needs are getting lower priority. As affirmative action has broadened to include other groups—and to benefit white women perhaps most of all—blacks perceive it as having waned in value for them.

THE CLASSROOM: WHOSE HISTORY COUNTS?

Political pressure has already brought about sweeping change in public school textbooks over the past couple of decades and has begun to affect the core humanities curriculum at such elite universities as Stanford. At stake at the college level is whether the traditional "canon" of Greek, Latin and West European humanities study should be expanded to reflect the cultures of Africa, Asia and other parts of the world. Many books treasured as classics by prior generations are now seen as tools of cultural imperialism. In the extreme form, this thinking rises to a value-deprived neutralism that views all cultures, regardless of the grandeur or paucity of their attainments, as essentially equal.

Even more troubling is a revisionist approach to history in which groups that have gained power in the present turn to remaking the past in the image of their desires. If 18th, 19th and earlier 20th century society should not have been so dominated by white Christian men of West European ancestry, they reason, then that past society should be reinvented as pluralist and democratic. Alternatively, the racism and sexism of the past are treated as inextricable from—and therefore irremediably tainting—traditional learning and values.

While debates over college curriculum get the most attention, professors generally can resist or subvert the most wrongheaded changes and students generally have mature enough judgment to sort out the arguments. Elementary- and secondary-school curriculums reach a far broader segment at a far more impressionable age, and political expediency more often wins over intellectual honesty. Exchanges have been vituperative in New York, where a state task force concluded that "African-Americans, Asian-Americans, Puerto Ricans and Native Americans have all been victims of an intellectual and educational oppression . . . Negative characterizations, or the absence of positive references, have had a terribly damaging effect on the psyche of young people." In urging a revised syllabus, the task force argued, "Children from European culture will have a less arrogant perspective of being part of a group that has 'done it all.'" Many intellectuals are outraged. Political scientist Andrew Hacker of Queens College lambastes a task-force suggestion that children be taught how "Native Americans were here to welcome new settlers from Holland, Senegal, England, Indonesia, France, the Congo. Italy, China, Iberia." Asks Hacker: "Did the Indians really welcome all those groups? Were they at Ellis Island when the Italians started to arrive? This is not history but a myth intended to bolster the self-esteem of certain children and, just possibly, a platform for advocates of various ethnic interests."

VALUES: SOMETHING IN COMMON

Economic and political issues, however much emotion they arouse, are fundamentally open to practical solution. The deeper significance of America's becoming a majority nonwhite society is what it means to the national psyche, to individuals' sense of themselves and their nation—their idea of what it is to be American. People of color have often felt that whites treated equality as a benevolence granted to minorities rather than as an inherent natural right. Surely that condescension will wither.

Rather than accepting U.S. history and its meaning as settled, citizens will feel ever more free to debate where the nation's successes sprang from and what its unalterable beliefs are. They will clash over which myths and icons to invoke in education, in popular culture, in ceremonial speechmaking from political campaigns to the State of the Union address. Which is the more admirable heroism: the courageous holdout by a few conquest-minded whites over Hispanics at the Alamo, or the anonymous expression of hope by millions who filed through Ellis Island? Was the subduing of the West a daring feat of bravery and ingenuity, or a wretched example of white imperialism? Symbols deeply meaningful to one group can be a matter of indifference to another. Says University of Wisconsin chancellor Donna Shalala: "My grandparents came from Lebanon. I don't identify with the Pilgrims on a personal level." Christopher Jencks, professor of sociology at Northwestern, asks, "Is anything more basic about turkeys and Pilgrims than about Martin Luther King and Selma? To me, it's six of one and half a dozen of the other, if children understand what it's like to be a dissident minority. Because the civil rights struggle is closer chronologically, it's likelier to be taught by someone who really cares."

Traditionalists increasingly distinguish between a "multiracial" society, which they say would be fine, and a "multicultural" society, which they deplore. They argue that every society needs a universally accepted set of values and that new arrivals should therefore be pressured to conform to the mentality on which U.S. prosperity and freedom were built. Says Allan Bloom, author of the best-selling *The Closing of the American Mind:* "Obviously, the future of America can't be sustained if people keep only to their own ways and remain perpetual outsiders. The society has got to turn them into Americans. There are natural fears that today's immigrants may be too much of a cultural stretch for a nation based on Western values."

The counterargument, made by such

scholars as historian Thomas Bender of New York University, is that if the center cannot hold, then one must redefine the center. It should be, he says, "the ever changing outcome of a continuing contest among social groups and ideas for the power to define public culture." Besides, he adds, many immigrants arrive committed to U.S. values; that is part of what attracted them. Says Julian Simon, professor of business administration at the University of Maryland: "The life and institutions here shape immigrants and not vice versa. This business about immigrants changing our institutions and our basic ways of life is hogwash. It's nativist scare talk."

CITIZENSHIP: FORGING A NEW IDENTITY

Historians note that Americans have felt before that their historical culture was being overwhelmed by immigrants, but conflicts between earlier-arriving English, Germans and Irish and later-arriving Italians and Jews did not have the obvious and enduring element of racial skin color. And there was never a time when the nonmainstream elements could claim, through sheer numbers, the potential to unite and exert political dominance. Says Bender: "The real question is whether or not our notion of diversity can successfully negotiate the color line."

For whites, especially those who trace their ancestry back to the early years of the Republic, the American heritage is a source of pride. For people of color, it is more likely to evoke anger and sometimes shame. The place where hope is shared is in the future. Demographer Ben Wattenberg, formerly perceived as a resister to social change, says, "There's a nice chance that the American myth in the 1990s and beyond is going to ratchet another step toward this idea that we are the universal nation. That rings the bell of manifest destiny. We're a people with a mission and a sense of purpose, and we believe we have something to offer the world."

Not every erstwhile alarmist can bring himself to such optimism. Says Norman Podhoretz, editor of *Commentary*: "A lot of people are trying to undermine the foundations of the American experience and are pushing toward a more Balkanized society. I think that would be a disaster, not only because it would destroy a precious social inheritance but also because it would lead to enormous unrest, even violence."

While know-nothingism is generally confined to the more dismal corners of the American psyche, it seems all too predictable that during the next decades many more mainstream white Americans will begin to speak openly about the nation they feel they are losing. There are not, after all, many nonwhite faces depicted in Norman Rockwell's paintings. White Americans are accustomed to thinking of themselves as the very picture of their nation. Inspiring as it may be to the rest of the world, significant as it may be to the U.S. role in global politics, world trade and the pursuit of peace, becoming a conspicuously multiracial society is bound to be a somewhat bumpy experience for many ordinary citizens. For older Americans, raised in a world where the numbers of whites were greater and the visibility of nonwhites was carefully restrained, the new world will seem ever stranger. But as the children at Brentwood Science Magnet School, and their counterparts in classrooms across the nation, are coming to realize, the new world is here. It is now. And it is irreversibly the America to come.

Review Questions

1. Briefly comment on the following statement: The "browning of America" will alter everything in society, from politics and education to industry, values, and culture.
2. How will your ethnic, social, or religious group fit into America in the 21st century? Explain your answer.

In conclusion, relations between minority and dominant groups in the United States are quite complex and, at times, contradictory. We have made an attempt in this chapter to provide a basic foundation upon which to develop an understanding of minority group relations in the United States. Minority group membership is a major factor that inhibits full realization of the American ideal of equal opportunity. An important dimension of placement in the status hierarchy of society is that of group membership.

Many complex forces within American society create, perpetuate, and, at times, ameliorate intergroup tensions. The causes and consequences of intergroup conflict are many. Insights into the dynamics of intergroup relations, prejudice, and discrimination have been made possible through a growing wealth of social scientific knowledge and theory. Because many problems and tensions exist between America's many ethnic groups, there remains a need to continually examine minority group relations within a social scientific perspective.

Summary

1. A minority group is any culturally or physically distinctive, self-conscious social aggregate that is subject to political, economic, or social discrimination by a dominant segment of a surrounding political society.
2. Prejudice is basically a negative attitude or belief. Discrimination involves action. Prejudice is learned and tends to express itself in action. People discriminate because of their prejudices. People also develop prejudices because they discriminate. Prejudice and discrimination may exist together or independently.
3. The consequences of prejudice and discrimination are great. Blacks, women, the aged, Hispanics, Native Americans, and other Americans feel prejudice and discrimination in income, jobs, and housing.
4. Prejudice and discrimination have many explanations. The sociocultural explanation stresses the idea that prejudices are part of the folkways of a

culture and are learned. Other theories stress frustration-aggression, economics, vested interests, power, and competition.

5. Four major reactions by minority groups to their subordinate status are acceptance, aggression, avoidance, and assimilation.

STUDY GUIDE

Chapter Objectives

After studying this chapter, you should be able to:

1. Define "minority group" and describe the four types of minorities, according to Louis Wirth
2. Compare and contrast the six major policies dominant groups have developed toward minority groups
3. Define "prejudice" and "discrimination"
4. Briefly describe the relation between prejudice and discrimination
5. Briefly describe the consequences of prejudice and discrimination to women, blacks, and the aged
6. Identify the major explanations for prejudice and discrimination and their limitations
7. List and compare minority group reactions, according to Rose and Vander Zanden

Key Terms

Acceptance (p. 284)
Aggression (p. 284)
Antilocution (p. 269)
Assimilation (p. 284)
Assimilationist minority (p. 267)
Avoidance (p. 284)
Continued subjugation (p. 267)
Discrimination (p. 269)
Extermination (p. 268)
Integration (p. 284)
Legal protection (p. 267)
Militant minority (p. 267)
Minority group (p. 266)
Pluralism (p. 267)
Pluralistic minority (p. 267)
Prejudice (p. 268)
Scapegoat (p. 282)
Secessionist minority (p. 267)
Separation (p. 284)
Submission (p. 284)
Withdrawal (p. 284)

Self-Test

Short Answer

(p. 266) 1. List and define four variations of minority situations.

(p. 267) 2. List the six major types of dominant group policies toward minority groups.

(p. 269) 3. List Allport's five degrees of negative action.

(p. 268) 4. Briefly describe the relationship between prejudice and discrimination.

(p. 270) 5. Briefly describe the impact that prejudice and discrimination have had on the black minority or on women.

(p. 281) 6. Briefly describe the sociocultural explanation of prejudice.

(p. 281) 7. Briefly explain the scapegoat theory of prejudice.

(p. 282) 8. Briefly describe the economic explanation of prejudice.

(p. 284) 9. List and define Rose's reactions to prejudice and discrimination.

(p. 284) 10. List and define Vander Zanden's four models of minority group responses.

Multiple Choice (*Answers are on page 299.*)

(p. 268) 1. Prejudice is:
a. an attitude
b. behavior
c. both
d. none of the above

(p. 269) 2. Overt actions that categorically exclude all members of a group from certain privileges or rights are called:
a. prejudice
b. discrimination
c. stereotypes
d. violence

(p. 268) 3. The most extreme forms of racism include:
a. absorption
b. genocide
c. assimilation
d. none of the above

(p. 281) 4. Leading theories of prejudice include:
a. sociological
b. economic
c. psychological
d. all the above

(p. 284) 5. Which of the following is *not* one of Vander Zanden's "responses"?
a. separation
b. avoidance
c. assimilation
d. aggression

(p. 268) 6. Prejudice is:
a. the same as discrimination
b. aggression
c. a defensive device
d. all the above

(p. 286) 7. Richard Wright is:
a. an important economic theorist
b. the author "Beyond the Melting Pot"
c. the author of *Black Boy*
d. none of the above

(p. 266) 8. Which of the following is *not* one of Wirth's four types of minorities?
a. pluralistic minority
b. assimilationist minority
c. secessionist minority
d. subjected minority

(p. 269) 9. Which of the following is *not* one of Allport's degrees of negative action?
a. antilocution
b. avoidance
c. assimilation
d. extermination

(p. 270) 10. Women:
a. constitute the larger group in society
b. are a minority group
c. experience discrimination and prejudice in many areas of their lives
d. all the above

True/False (*Answers are on page 299.*)

T F 11. Prejudice is learned. (p. 268)
T F 12. Prejudice is the same as discrimination. (p. 268)
T F 13. All minority groups are essentially the same. (p. 266)
T F 14. You can be prejudiced without being discriminatory. (p. 270)

T F 15. Prejudice is genetically determined. (p. 268)

T F 16. Segregation continues to exist in the United States. (p. 279)

T F 17. The economic theories of prejudice stress the importance of learning. (p. 282)

T F 18. Today's women's movement is as strong as it was in the 1970s. (p. 270)

T F 19. For Allport, extermination is the final degree of negative action. (p. 269)

T F 20. Women experience much less discrimination today than they did in the past. (p. 270)

Fill In *(Answers are on page 299.)*

(p. 266) 21. A ______ is any culturally or physically distinctive, self-conscious social aggregate that is subject to political, economic, or social discrimination by a dominant segment of a surrounding political society.

(p. 268) 22. ______ is an emotional, rigid attitude or belief toward a group.

(p. 269) 23. ______ involves action and is the differential treatment of individuals considered part of a particular group.

(p. 269) 24. ______ is an institutionalized form of discrimination, enforced legally or by common custom.

(p. 269) 25. For Allport, ______ refers to prejudiced statements.

(p. 268) 26. ______ is learned.

(p. 270) 27. ______ are America's largest minority group.

(p. 284) 28. For Rose, ______ basically means the acceptance of a subordinate status.

(p. 284) 29. For Vander Zanden, with ______, minority group members may come to acquiesce to their disadvantaged and subordinate status.

(p. 284) 30. For Vander Zanden, with ______, minority group members may respond to dominance by striking out against a status that is subordinate and disadvantaged.

Matching *(Answers are on page 299.)*

31. ______ Prejudice		a. A type of minority group
32. ______ Discrimination		b. Forced to bear others' blame
33. ______ Degrees of negative action		c. Prejudice is learned
34. ______ Scapegoat		d. An institutionalized form of discrimination
35. ______ Avoidance		e. An attitude or belief
36. ______ Cultural explanation of prejudice		f. Antilocutions
37. ______ Women		g. Largest minority group
38. ______ Segregation		h. Involves action

39. _______ Stereotype
40. _______ Assimilationist

i. Response to prejudice and discrimination
j. Image of minority group member that is not based on fact

Essay Questions

1. What is a minority group?
2. What are the different types of minority groups?
3. What different policies have dominant groups developed toward minorities?
4. What is the nature of prejudice and discrimination?
5. What are some of the problems experienced by minorities?
6. What are the major explanations for prejudice and discrimination?
7. What are the major response patterns of minority group members to their subordinate status in the United States?

Interactive Exercises

1. Examine the advantages and disadvantages of being a male or female (black or white, or other ethnic group member) in American society today.

2. Compare your own (or a close friend's) family's ethnic history (its adjustments, difficulties, benefits, and so on) with those of (other) recent immigrant groups in America. Do today's immigrant groups have it "easier"?

Answers

Answers to Self-Test

1. a
2. b
3. b
4. d
5. a
6. c
7. c
8. d
9. c
10. d
11. T
12. F
13. F
14. T
15. F
16. T
17. F
18. F
19. T
20. F
21. minority
22. prejudice
23. discrimination
24. segregation
25. antilocution
26. prejudice
27. women
28. submission
29. acceptance
30. aggression
31. e
32. h
33. f
34. b
35. i
36. c
37. g
38. d
39. j
40. a

Answers to Chapter Pretest

1. F
2. F
3. F
4. F
5. F
6. T
7. T
8. T
9. F
10. F

Chapter 8

Social Institutions: Family and Marriage

Chapter Pretest

Let's see how much you already know about topics in this chapter:

1. **The family is a dying social institution. True/False**
2. **One out of every two marriages ends in divorce. True/False**
3. **There are fewer single-parent families today than there were 10 years ago. True/False**
4. **More men than women desert their families. True/False**
5. **The typical American family consists of husband, wife, and two children. True/False**
6. **The divorce rate is higher among people who have remarried. True/False**
7. **There is more child abuse today than there was a century ago. True/False**
8. **Husband abuse is one of the nation's most unreported crimes. True/False**
9. **Polygamy no longer exists in the United States. True/False**
10. **The future of the American family is bleak. True/False**

Introduction: Social Institutions

Social institutions exist in all societies to meet a variety of important social needs and goals. These needs and goals must be met if societies are to survive. The family, for example, is a basic, major social institution that meets society's vital need of supplying itself with new members. If the society does not replace its members from one generation to the next, it will quickly become extinct.

Many people commonly use the term "institution" to mean a prison, a hospital, or some other concrete structure. In the social sciences, however, an **institution** is defined as a pattern of norms centered around a major social goal, value, or need.

Institution defined

As one of the most important concepts in the field of sociology, institution refers to an organized procedure, a definite, patterned way of doing something. It refers to specific areas of social life that have become organized into discernible patterns. It is also the principle organized means by which the essential tasks of a society are organized, directed, and carried out.

Major social institutions—including the family and political, educational, religious, and economic systems—are found in every society. They provide for the socialization of new members, the maintenance of social order, the preparation for social and occupational roles, the establishment of ethical and moral principles, and the production and distribution of goods and services. These institutions are sets of norms that cohere around a relatively distinct and socially important complex of values and organize human behavior into stable patterns of activity.

Major social institutions are highly organized and structured around expected sets of values and norms. For example, schools, the social organizations of the educational institution, are basically large, highly structured bureaucracies run by educational specialists. These specialists socialize people into society through a formalized, standardized procedure that emphasizes learning, accumulating knowledge, cooperation, and conformity. In addition, social institutions consist of many social groups and have a number of procedures that define how the activities of the institution are to be carried out. In large, complex societies, social institutions are highly specialized and differentiated. People therefore separate their activities into such areas as work, school, and worship. In small, less complex societies, institutions are not so sharply differentiated and everyday activities are not necessarily defined into many separate and distinct areas. In nonurban, less complex societies, family activities, work, and play are much more likely accomplished together.

In this chapter, we examine the institutions of family and marriage. In the following two chapters, we will examine the political, economic, religious, educational, and health-care institutions, in addition to their functions in society. Many functions of social institutions are interrelated, and changes that occur in one social institution may cause changes in others. For example, changes in the American political institution may have great influence on American economic stability, the quality of American education, and the stability of the American family.

Many functions of social institutions are interrelated

Family: Definition, Functions, and Changes in Family Functions

The family is the most fundamental, universal social institution. Social scientists have been studying the family for many decades. But there is still no agreement about exactly what constitutes a family. Definitions of family abound in sociology and anthropology. After surveying family forms in 250 cultures, George Murdock (1949) in his now-classic research attempted to develop an encompassing definition. He defined a family as "a social group characterized by common residence, economic cooperation and reproduction. It includes adults of both sexes, at least two of whom maintain a socially approved sexual relationship, and one or more children, owned or adopted, of the sexually cohabitant adults." Murdock distinguishes family from marriage, which he called a "complex of customs centering upon the relationship between a sexually associating pair of adults within the family."

Murdock's definition of family has been criticized because it does not apply to all cultures. For example, among the Nayar of Southern India, families do not contain adults who live or work together. They also do not contain sexually cohabiting adults.

According to Burgess (1963), the following characteristics are common to the institution of the family in all places and at all times. These characteristics also differentiate the family from other social groups:

1. The family is composed of people united by ties of marriage, blood, or adoption.
2. The members of a family typically live together under one roof and constitute a single household, or if they live apart, they consider the household their home.
3. The family is composed of people who interact and communicate with each other in their social roles, such as husband and wife, mother and father, son and daughter, brother and sister.
4. The family maintains a common culture. It is derived mainly from the general culture, but each family has some distinctive features.

Keeping in mind the fact that definitions of the family vary and that the issue of how a family should be defined remains unresolved, we will use the following for a general definition of **family:** a socially sanctioned, relatively permanent grouping of people who are united by blood, marriage, or adoption and who generally live together and cooperate economically.

Family defined

The family has many important functions. They vary over time and from one society to another. As we will examine in more detail later, many sociologists believe that a number of traditional American family functions have been taken over by other social institutions. The following are among the functions of the family found throughout time and in all societies.

The first universal function of the family is reproduction and the regulation of sexual behavior. Reproduction is a prerequisite for the survival of a society. The family provides institutionalized means by which society's members are replaced from one generation to the next. The family also allows and regulates the sexual drive. All societies regulate their members' sexual activity. Some societies do not accept nonmarital sex; others are more liberal and accept nonmarital sex. But even in cultures that permit nonmarital sex, it may be implicitly accepted that those couples engaging in such behavior eventually marry. Furthermore, such societies usually are concerned with delaying children until after marriage.

Basic universal functions of the family

Another basic function of the family is the care, training, and protection of the young. Young children's needs, especially through their long period of dependency, must be met by their families. In addition, the family often functions as a protector for its members, especially the young, against dangers from others both inside and outside the clan, tribe, or society.

One of the most important universal functions of the family is socialization. The family is virtually the only social institution responsible for the early development of personality in the individual. It is the first group to provide meaning and support to the young. The family is also the first group to instill in a child attitudes, norms, values, and practices in evaluating his or her own behavior. An individual's first interpretation of the physical and social world and first establishment of likes and dislikes are derived from the network of family relationships.

An additional major function of the family is to provide the means by which an individual's social status is initially fixed. It serves, in other words, as the basis for the assignment of status to family members. For example, through the family, individual members are assigned their ethnic or racial status, their initial religious status, and their class status. Changes in status do occur during a family member's lifetime. However, much of the initial status individuals acquire from their families is retained throughout their lives.

In addition to the above functions, the family also provides the affection, love, and emotional support vital to human happiness. As infants, children, and adults, we need the warmth and affection that the family can provide. Emotional support and love are not easily obtained outside the context of the family.

Other functions of the family include providing recreation, providing a basis for the transmittal of private property, and providing an economic base for producing family goods and services.

Changing family functions

When the United States was an agricultural society, the family performed many functions with little help from other social institutions. With industrialization and urbanization, however, fathers who had previously farmed at their homes began to work away from home in urban factories and mills. Many mothers also began working in factories. Items that previously had been made in the home began to be mass-produced in factories. People then began to consume more and more products and services. With these changes, functions that were previously the family's responsibility began to be taken over by other institutions. For example, schools and churches largely took over education and religious training; the police largely became the protectors; the hospital largely became the health-care provider. Recreational functions also shifted away from the family.

Because of such changes as the mass movement of people to cities, the growth of schools for young children, and the shift in manufacturing from home to factory, some social scientists of that time believed that the institution of the American family had outlived its usefulness and was in a state of decline. Later generations of social scientists agreed that the family had lost the functions of providing economic support, education, and health care. But these social scientists were critical of their predecessors and stressed that some family functions—such as the nurturing and rearing of children and the offering of refuge to adults from an impersonal and competitive society—were now more important than before. Today certain family functions have been taken over by specialized institutions such as government agencies and churches, schools and factories. But the family still performs many important functions that no other institution can.

Family Structures and Variations

In addition to having a variety of functions, the family has various structures. Two major types of family structures are the nuclear family and the extended family. The **nuclear family** consists of a wife, a husband, and their children. This type of family structure is found in every human society, past or present. Most American families are of the nuclear type.

Nuclear family defined

George Murdock (1974) believes that the nuclear family "is a universal human social grouping. Either as the sole prevailing form of the family or as the basic unit from which more complex familiar forms are compounded, it exists as a distinct and strongly functional group in every known society." Other anthropologists doubt the validity of Murdock's statement, pointing to cultures like the Nayar of India, which lacks the nuclear family.

The other major type of family structure is the **extended family,** which consists of all those people defined as kin. **Kin** are people who are related by birth or marriage, such as brothers and sisters, husbands and wives, uncles and aunts, nephews and nieces. An extended family consists of several generations of blood relations that live together. For example, when a young couple marry, they may move in with the parents of the bride or groom. The household containing these two generations is an extended family. The household consists of three generations when children are born to the young couple.

Extended family: all those people defined as kin

The family into which a person is born or adopted is termed by sociologists that person's *family of orientation*. The family that a person establishes through marriage is termed the *family of procreation*. As children, we belong to the family of orientation. As parents, we belong to the family of procreation. A newly married couple who moves in with, or near, the husband's parents has **patrilocal residence;** a couple who moves in with, or near, the wife's parents has **matrilocal residence.** In the United States, a young married couple usually is expected to set up housekeeping in its own apartment or house. This pattern is called **neolocal residence.** When a relative other than a parent, such as an aunt, uncle, or grandparent, moves into a household of a nuclear family, the nuclear family becomes what is termed a **modified extended family.** Thus the nuclear family is a part of the extended family, which consists of "two or more nuclear families affiliated through an extension of the parent-child relationship . . . i.e., by joining the nuclear family of a married adult to that of his parents" (Murdock, 1974).

Murdock, in his survey of 250 representative human societies, discovered a third distinct major type of family organization. This type, termed the **polygamous family,** is formed by the marriage of one woman to two or more men or the marriage of one man to two or more women. But it should be noted that

Polygamous family defined

An extended family consists of all those people defined as kin.

Murdock still viewed nuclear families as separate units in these complex forms of family organizations. Other social scientists disagree that "these larger family organizations could be viewed as being made up of nuclear families; rather, it seemed, the nuclear families were submerged by them" (A. Skolnick, 1978).

Patterns of Marriage, Authority, and Inheritance

In addition to variations in family structures, many variations in family and marriage patterns exist in various cultures throughout the world. Even within our own society, we find many variations in forms of marriage, the selection of marriage partners, authority patterns, and descent and inheritance patterns.

First let us define marriage. According to Eshleman (1981, 1985), there appears to be a consensus that marriage involves several criteria. These criteria are found to exist across cultures and throughout time. They include:

1. a heterosexual union, including at least one male and one female
2. the legitimizing or granting of approval to the sexual relationship and the bearing of children without any loss of standing in the community or society
3. a public affair rather than a private, personal matter

4. a highly institutionalized and patterned mating arrangement
5. an assuming of mutual and reciprocal rights and obligations between spouses
6. a binding relationship that assumes some permanence

We will define **marriage** as a socially accepted union of two people in wife and husband roles, with the important function of ligitimation of parenthood.

Marriage defined

Forms of Marriage

There are two major forms of marriage relationships: *monogamy* and *polygamy*. **Monogamy** is the marriage of one male and one female; it is the most common type of marriage relationship. It is, in fact, the only form permitted in the United States. **Polygamy,** as noted above, means many wives or husbands. It consists of one person of one sex and a minimum of two persons of the other sex. The marriage of one woman to two or more men is called **polyandry.** The marriage of one man to two or more women is called **polygyny.** Even though many societies permit or even encourage polygamous marriages, it does not follow that in such societies all or even most married individuals have more than one spouse. In fact, in most polygamous societies, monogamy is statistically the prevailing form. The reason for this is explained by cultural anthropologists Beals and Hoijer:

Monogamy: marriage of one male and one female

Polygamy: many wives or husbands

> **The proportion of male to female births in any human society is roughly the same, and if this proportion is maintained among the sexually mature, a preponderance of plural marriages means that a considerable number of either men or women must remain unmarried. No society can maintain itself under such conditions; the emotional stresses would be too great to be survived (Beals and Hoijer, 1971).**

According to Beals and Hoijer, polygyny had been found on a wide scale among the Baganda living in Uganda, East Africa, because of the following factors:

> **The wide dispersal of polygyny among the Baganda is made possible by the high mortality rate among Baganda males. In chiefly families, male children are often killed at birth; the princes of the royal house, once the successor to the throne has been chosen, are put to death; the king arbitrarily kills off male retainers and servants who displease him; males, never females, must be sacrificed in great numbers to the gods at appropriate ceremonies; and great numbers of men are killed in the annual wars the Baganda conduct with their neighbors. As a result of these factors, plus the fact that large numbers of women are taken as booty in war expeditions, the women outnumber the men by three to one. It is this disparity in the relative numbers of men and women that makes polygyny on so wide a scale possible (Beals and Hoijer, 1971).**

There is an additional marriage form found in the world, but it is very rare. This form is called **group marriage** and is a combination of polyandry and polygyny, in which sets of women and men enjoy more or less equal conjugal

Group marriages are rare

rights with each other. The Marquesans, a fishing and agricultural people of Polynesia, have practiced such marriages.

Mate Selection and Patterns of Authority and Descent

Endogamy: marriage within

Exogamy: marriage outside

Different cultures accept different methods for selecting marriage partners. Customs or laws within each society prescribe whom a person may marry. **Endogamy** is a marriage within a specific group—whether religious, racial, class, or another type. **Exogamy,** in contrast, is marriage outside a specific group. For example, in the Navaho culture, marriage is exogamous—individuals are forbidden to marry within their clan of birth. A Navaho clan may consist of hundreds of individuals. In many cultures throughout the world, incest prohibitions keep individuals from marrying close blood relatives or people within their clan.

Authority patterns also vary from culture to culture. When the authority of the family is vested primarily in the husband, a **patriarchy** exists. A **matriarchy** exists when the authority is vested primarily in the wife. When the authority is more equally balanced between husband and wife, an **equalitarian (or egalitarian) family** exists.

Matrilineal, patrilineal, and bilineal systems defined

There are three basic systems of descent and inheritance: the *matrilineal, patrilineal,* and *bilineal* systems. Descent and inheritance pass through the female side of the family in the **matrilineal system.** The father's relatives are not considered kin. Property passes only through the female line. Descent and inheritance pass through the male side of the family in the **patrilineal system.** Males, not females, inherit property rights. The mother's relatives under this system are not considered kin. Descent and inheritance are traced through both sides of the family under the **bilineal system.** Familiar to us in the United States, but alien in most cultures of the world, the bilineal system considers as kin both the mother's and father's relatives and property passes to both females and males.

Marriage and Family in the United States

In this section of the chapter, we will examine the "typical" American family in terms of the family and marriage patterns presented above. However, it is important to remember that there are many variations of these patterns and that this typical picture of the U.S. family has not always been the same, and is in the process of changing in many ways, as we will examine in the following section.

The U.S. family system is nuclear

In the United States, the family system is nuclear. Despite our high divorce rate and informal living arrangements during the past 25 years, the great majority of Americans are still members of nuclear families. This pattern represents a shift from large, extended kin groups living in preindustrial agricultural

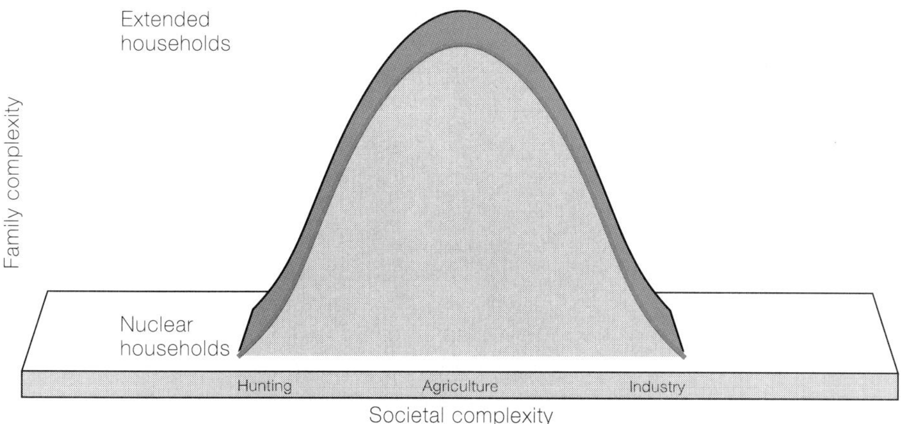

Figure 8.1 Societal complexity and family form.

communities to the nuclear family of modern industrial societies. However, the classical farm family of Western nostalgia is a myth. The nuclear family form predominated in America well before the era of industrialization. In other words, the nuclear family appears in advanced modern cultures; yet it appears in the most technologically simple (such as hunting) societies. The extended family then is dominant in agricultural societies. The nuclear family reappears in modern industrial societies and remains in postindustrial societies. As stated by A. Skolnick, "If all known societies were listed in the order of their complexity along the horizontal part of a graph and family type plotted on the vertical part of the scale, the relationship between societal development or complexity and family form would be curvilinear" (A. Skolnick, 1978). Figure 8.1 illustrates this curvilinear relationship and shows that the percentage of extended households is highest in agricultural societies.

The American family is monogamous

In addition to being nuclear, the American family is monogamous. That is, an individual is permitted to marry only one person at a time. A well-known exception to this monogamous pattern occurred during the late nineteenth century when the Mormons of Utah practiced polygyny. Some of the communal families of the 1970s also practiced marriage relationships other than monogamy. For most Americans, however, monogamy remains the preferred arrangement.

With the high American divorce rate and with most divorced people remarrying shortly after their divorces, we are experiencing what has been termed serial monogamy. **Serial monogamy** is the practice of marrying one person at a time but marrying more than one time.

American families are endogamous and homogamous

The average American in today's family is also endogamous. Most Americans marry *within* their social class and religious, ethnic, racial, and age groups. Most American families are also *homogamous*. The term **homogamy** is used to describe mate selection among people who share similar characteristics. It means that people marry others like themselves.

Both endogamy and homogamy are critical factors in the continuity of the American family system and other basic social institutions. Homogamy functions to conserve traditional values and maintain the status quo. These functions can also be dysfunctional by reducing and perhaps even eliminating contacts with others outside one's own group and by restricting the free choice of a mate.

Most marriages in the United States are between people within the same social class. There is a tendency among both men and women to marry within their own class. Sociologists also have noted that those in a second large segment of our population marry not within their own social class but into a neighboring social class. When marriage occurs outside of one's social class, **hypergamy** (the marriage of a female into a higher position) appears to be more prevalent in our society than **hypogamy** (the marriage of a female into a lower social class). When one considers the fact that most Americans associate mainly with people of their own class and share class-related interests and tastes, it is not surprising to find this persistence of endogamy and homogamy.

Marriage and social class

Marriage and religion

People tend to marry partners who are of the same religion. But, in the past few decades, religious homogamy has been declining in the United States.

Interracial marriages, although legally permitted in the United States, are low in frequency. People tend to marry others of the same race. Most studies have indicated an upward trend in interracial marriages over the past 25 years. Although there is no agreement as to which variable is most important for understanding the change, explanations for the increase in interracial marriage include cultural, value, psychological, and demographic factors, as well as factors of spatial and social propinquity (nearness).

Individuals are also likely to marry within their own ethnic group, although this pattern has declined markedly during the past two decades.

Marriage and age

People also tend to marry partners who are within two to three years of their own age; husbands usually are older than their wives.

The incest taboo

Even though endogamy and homogamy are important norms regarding marriage, they are not the only norms. An exogamous norm—the **incest taboo** (the prohibition of sexual relations between members of a family)—is the most widespread of all norms regarding marriage. Exogamy rules that members of a society marry outside their kin group. In fact, all marriages are exogamous to the extent that they are forbidden between members of the same nuclear family.

The American family is patriarchal

In addition to being nuclear, monogamous, and endogamous, the typical American family is patriarchal. There are, however, many signs that it has become increasingly egalitarian under the influence of various changes in authority patterns, family life, and roles. The average American family is also neolocal in that it establishes a household separate from its families of orientation.

The average family in America is also bilineal. That is, no differentiation between the father's and mother's kin is made, and property passes both to daughters and sons. Rules of descent are closely associated with the rules of inheritance. In the United States, most families make no distinction by sex or age in the distribution of wealth to their children.

In America, there are many variations on the typical pattern. The American family has significantly changed during the past two decades. In the following section, we examine many of these changes.

Changing Family and Marriage Patterns

The importance of a good family life

For almost 90 percent of Americans, good family life ranks first in importance. This is up from 82 percent reported in a poll from the early 1980s. Americans, in other words, value a good family life above self-respect (85 percent), good health (84 percent), a sense of accomplishment (69 percent), an exciting life (58 percent), and having a good time (41 percent) (Gallup, 1989).

Although the family and a good family life are considered important by Americans, it cannot be denied that this important institution has changed, and continues to change throughout the 1990s. According to P. C. Glick, the family today is not the same as a generation ago because social conditions have changed and family life has adapted to these changes. Only a few decades ago, a third of the American population lived on farms. Today only 2 percent of the United States population lives on farms. As P. C. Glick states: "One could venture a guess that half of the grandparents or great-grandparents of adults in 1990 grew up on a farm or heard about farm life from their parents. In those earlier days, farm life was close to nature, families were large, and the thought of growing up with several brothers and sisters tends to produce some nostalgia" (P. C. Glick, 1990).

In America today, studies indicate that almost two-thirds of young married couples will have only one or two children. In point of fact, the marriages of couples who have sons are more likely to remain intact than marriages of couples who have daughters and no sons (Spanier and P. C. Glick, 1981; Morgan, Lye, and Contran, 1988; P. C. Glick, 1990).

In 1960, 75 percent of American households contained a married couple, and more than half of those couples had one or more dependent children. In 1970, 40 percent of all households consisted of husband, wife, and children. Today that figure is 25 percent. In fact, the nuclear family of mother, father, and two children accounts for less than a tenth of all American households. America's average household size also continues to decline, from approximately three and one-half people in 1970 to two and one-half people in 1990 (Census Bureau, 1990; P. C. Glick, 1990).

The fastest growing type of family

America's fastest-growing type of family is the single-parent family. A quarter of all American families with children are single-parent families. In fact, the majority of America's children will spend at least several years in a single-parent family. In the following section, we examine single-parent families.

Single-Parent Families

Living with one parent

More than half of the children born in the 1990s will spend part of their childhood living with only one parent. Today one-quarter of U.S. families with children under 18 are maintained by a single parent. **Single-parent families** are families maintained by a parent who has never been married, who is in between marriages, or who never remarried. Half of the single-parent families are below the poverty line—a majority headed by a divorced or separated parent. A quarter are maintained by a parent who never married (P. C. Glick, 1990).

Whether single-parent families are viewed as a consequence of moral decay, as integral units of our society, or as legitimate redefinitions of the family, the fact is that their members have to contend with many difficulties.

A drop in the standard of living

For the single parent, one of the many difficulties caused by divorce is a drop in the standard of living. This drop happens in the great majority of cases, and it usually is greater for the mother. Many single mothers have limited incomes and must take time away from their children to earn a living. Today, even though many divorced women are financially better off than in the past, many—and older women in particular—do not have the skills or training to obtain jobs that pay well. Women also are paid less than men for comparable skills. Those single mothers who do not work and remain at home to take care of their children may enter the ranks of those on permanent welfare. Single parenthood appears to be a major factor in the feminization of poverty. The economic demands of raising a family alone are creating a new class of poor women, who head 90 percent of America's one-parent households. Many single mothers count on child support and alimony payments to provide for their children. Unfortunately, a high percentage of families that are supposed to receive recurrent, court-ordered payments actually receive few or none.

Even though courts still tend to favor mothers as parents, households headed by fathers have more than doubled since 1970. More than 500,000 children in the United States live with their divorced or separated fathers.

Single parents can raise healthy children

The myth that single parents cannot raise healthy children increases parents' anxiety and guilt. These feelings then may affect their ability to rear children. Single parents—male and female—also must maintain discipline, educate their children, and promote healthy emotional development. Children of divorce experience many difficulties, although in some cases, the problems are not as severe as living in a tense household filled with hatred and fighting. Many parents fail to explain to their children why they are separating and what it will mean to the children's future. But most children adapt to their new circumstances within a year of the divorce.

Higher educational levels

According to P. C. Glick and Lin, a favorable development with regard to single parenting is the fact that today's single parents have a much higher educational level than their counterparts several years ago (P. C. Glick and Lin, 1987; P. C. Glick, 1990). They note that about 40 percent of the increase in single-parent families between the early 1970s and late 1980s occurred among those with at least some college education. They state that "This situation reflects not only a general increase in college attainment among young adults but also an increasing tendency for lone mothers with little education to marry and to do so more quickly than lone mothers with more education" (P. C. Glick and Lin, 1987, P. C. Glick, 1990).

Blended Families

One out of every two marriages ends in divorce

Approximately one out of every two American marriages ends in divorce. Young divorced adults are much more likely to marry again than persons of the same age are likely to marry for the first time (P. C. Glick, 1990). A recent study indicated that almost three-quarters of recently divorced women will eventually remarry (Bumpass, Sweet, and Castro, 1988). Men are more likely than women to remarry. However, their remarriage rate has dropped off sharply in recent years. In any event, almost half of recent marriages involve a second (or subsequent) marriage for the bride, groom, or both (P. C. Glick, 1990). Because most Americans who divorce remarry, family relationships may become very complex. During the past decade, there has been a dramatic increase in the number of stepfamilies, or what we now call **blended families**.

America's 36 million blended families

There are well over 36 million blended families in America. In fact, most of the time, children in single-parent families are moved into remarried families where they become stepchildren (P. C. Glick, 1990). About 10 million children under 18 years of age are in stepfamilies. As P. C. Glick indicates, 7 million of these children are stepchildren because they were born before the remarriage. The other 3 million are siblings of the stepchildren because they were born after the remarriage (P. C. Glick, 1988). The above 7 million children constitute one out of every seven children under 18 years of age who are living in a two-parent home. In point of fact, a third of the children under the age of 18 "have already experienced being a stepchild in a two-parent family or will do so before they reach the age of eighteen" (P. C. Glick, 1988, 1990). In terms of the future, over half of today's American youth may be identified as stepdaughters or stepsons by the turn of the century (P. C. Glick, 1989, 1990).

Many stepdaughters and stepsons

Sociologists have been studying blended families and stepchildren and have identified factors that affect family stability. Pasley and Tallman (1985) note that the presence of stepchildren does not appear to be the most important factor affecting the blended family's stability. They believe that the most important factor is a couple's perception of how frequently they agree upon family issues. When there is frequent agreement, there is also stability.

In blended families, the sheer multitude of relationships can cause confusion among children. Stepparents may even resist relationships with their stepchildren:

> **Stepfathers tend not to claim their stepchildren as part of their family when they're asked to list family members. And stepmothers whose husbands do not have custody of their children, but who have a common child living with them, tend not to accept the stepkids (Pasley and Tallman, 1985, pp. 33–34).**

Other research indicates that conflicts over loyalty often result when a stepparent tries to assume a parental role prematurely. The sooner a stepparent tries to be a parent, the sooner problems may develop in the blended family (Clingempeel, 1985). Because there are few institutional role models for stepmothers, and because the role carries negative cultural stereotypes—as in the tale of Cinderella and other stories—many stepmothers try hard to assume the maternal role, but this trying to fill a mother's role "leads to problems because youngsters in stepfamilies resist anyone trying to take a biological parent's place. Stepdaughters have more problems with stepmothers than stepsons do, possibly because of the daughters' closer ties to their biological mothers. A daughter may also consider the stepmother a threat to her relationship with her father" (Jarmulowski, 1985).

But Wallerstein (1985) believes that for children, stepmothers are less important figures than stepfathers. Children in a blended family are more likely to live with their stepfathers full-time because women get custody of the children in most divorces.

A blended family may have its problems, but it also has its positive dimensions. It can offer people a larger number of relationships and support systems than those available in nuclear families (Clingempeel, 1985). Good relationships between stepparents and stepchildren are especially gratifying because they are not a given (Visher, 1985).

STEP BY STEP

Barbara Kantrowitz and Pat Wingert

In the following reading, "Step by Step," Barbara Kantrowitz and Pat Wingert examine many of the issues and dynamics of American step-, or blended, families.

The original plot goes like this: first comes love. Then comes marriage. Then comes Mary with a baby carriage. But now there's a sequel: John and Mary break up. John moves in with Sally and her two boys. Mary takes the baby Paul. A year later Mary meets Jack, who is divorced with three children. They get married. Paul, barely 2 years old, now has a mother, a father, a stepmother, a stepfather and five stepbrothers and stepsisters—as well as four sets of grandparents (biological and step) and countless aunts and uncles. And guess what? Mary's pregnant again.

This may sound like an unusually complicated family tree. It's not. Some demographers predict that as many as a third of all children born in the 1980s may live with a stepparent before they are 18. According to the latest available Census figures, there were close to 7 million children living in stepfamilies in 1985, an increase of 11.6 percent in just five years. As startling as these statistics are, some experts think the figures underestimate the number of children involved. For example, there's no way to accurately count youngsters in unofficial stepfamilies: homes where a child's biological parent is living with, but not married to, a new partner. Another group excluded by the Census is children who have stepsiblings or half siblings in another household. These relationships have brought stepfamily ties to millions more homes. "Most people have a personal connection with a stepfamily," says University of Pennsylvania sociologist Frank Furstenberg. "If it's not their parents, it's their child or their grandparents or their husband's parents."

As their numbers grow in the next few decades, stepfamilies will become even more prominent. Demographers expect that half of all people entering first marriages in the 1970s and 1980s will eventually divorce. The majority of them will probably remarry. "We will all have to work toward changing our internal maps of what a family should be," says Mala Burt, a Baltimore family therapist and president of the Stepfamily Association of America, a 10-year-old group with 60 chapters in 17 states. All kinds of institutions, from schools to hospitals to the courts, will have to adapt to the special needs of stepfamilies. The way things are set up now, stepfamilies have to contend with small—and large—indignities. Most school activities, for example, are structured around intact families. Parents are often allowed only two tickets for special events, like graduation. Although they may be full-time parents to their spouses' kids, stepparents, in many cases, have no legal rights. If, for example, a child needs emergency surgery, hospitals almost always require the consent of a biological parent or legal guardian. "That's a big issue in the law right now," says Furstenberg. "You bring up a child for 14 years, and yet you have no legal standing, while someone who has never lived with the child does have legal standing. Does that make any sense?"

Even more important than the legal issues are stepfamilies' unique history. "Every stepfamily is a family born of loss," says John Visher, a California psychiatrist, who, with his wife, Emily, a psychologist, has written books on stepfamilies. Each family member has experienced the tragedy of divorce or death or separation from a parent or spouse; the aftershock can linger for years. When these survivors form a new family, the reactions can be volatile. "The myth is that once you are remarried, you ride off into the sunset and everybody lives happily ever after," says Emily Visher. "It's not that way at all."

Research has shown that some children in stepfamilies have more than their share of difficulties adjusting to their new households. Psychologists say that as a group, stepchildren have more developmental, emotional and behavioral problems than children in intact families. Stepchildren are more likely to be victims of child abuse, especially sexual abuse, than other youngsters. Nicholas Zill, a Washington, D.C., researcher who has studied remarried families, says that from a psychological perspective, stepchildren most resemble kids in single-parent families—even though they may be living in two-parent households. "One of the consistent findings in research is that stepparenthood does not re-create the nuclear family," says Furstenberg. "It does not put the family back together again, in Humpty Dumpty fashion."

At least half of children living in stepfamilies are likely to face an additional trauma—the birth of a half sibling to their parent and the new spouse. This new addition, often intended by the parents as a way to bring the new family together, can have the opposite effect. The older kids often "feel they've been cast in an outsider role," says Zill. What's even more disturbing is that the new family may not last. Sixty percent of all second marriages are expected to end in divorce, sending everybody—parents and children—into a new emotional maelstrom.

Of course, not all stepchildren are troubled. Some studies have indicated that youngsters who come from families with higher incomes and educational levels do better. The child's age at the time of the parent's remarriage may also be a factor. The University of Virginia's E. Mavis Hetherington has found that younger kids and older teenagers are most likely to accept a stepparent. Youngsters in early adolescence, roughly ages 9 to 15, do the poorest.

The attitude of the outside world makes a difference as well. Just a few years ago, people in stepfamilies used to complain that they were the deliberately hidden pages in the American family album. If they were noticed, it was almost always in a negative connotation. Fairy tales hundreds of years old featuring wicked stepmothers set the tone. When Patricia (who didn't want her real name used), a New York artist, was growing up in the 1950s, her biggest secret was that her "mother" was not really her mother (who died when she was 3), but her stepmother. She remembers that her stepmother would always wink conspiratorially at her when someone would comment on how much mother and daughter resembled each other.

With Patricia's son Michael, the situation was completely different. In the years between Patricia's childhood and her son's, the divorce rate doubled. Multiple marriages are no longer unusual. Patricia was divorced from Michael's father when the boy was only 2. Michael is now 18 and hasn't seen his father since he was 12. Thirteen years ago Patricia married her current husband, Jack. Despite some very rough times, Patricia says Michael never suffered the same stigma that she did. "He knows so many other families with various configurations," she says. "He doesn't feel odd."

Until the 1970s, most of the people who studied families looked at the problems of nuclear families, not single-parent families or stepfamilies. Even the best informed stepparents did not understand the special nature of their families. When John and Emily Visher were married in 1959, they each brought along four children from their previous marriages. "We thought that in a few weeks, things would settle down," John recalls. It took a lot longer than that. Because there was so little information available, says Emily, "we just kind of muddled through."

Today, the Vishers' children are married with families of their own. And psychologists know much more about how stepfamilies work. Researchers such as the Vishers have shown that stepfamilies evolve in patterns that are very different from nuclear families. Situations that new stepmothers or stepfathers might perceive as insurmountable hurdles—such as feelings of guilt and anger between the new spouse and the children—are actually an inevitable part of the adjustment process. "One of the things that I think we've contributed," says John Visher, "is a sense that what they're going through is normal and even predictable."

When they first get together, stepfamilies often have unreasonably high expectations. Patricia Papernow, a Cambridge, Mass., psychologist who has studied the phases of stepfamily development, calls this the "fantasy" stage. If both spouses have been through a divorce, they may dream of fixing past wrongs and making everyone whole through the new marriage. A spouse who has never had children may be determined to be "supermom" or "superdad" to the new stepkids and may dream of rescuing the children from their misery. Or the new spouse may underestimate the amount of time the husband or wife will spend with the children and think that there will be plenty of time for a honeymoon phase in the marriage. That probably won't happen, even if the children aren't living with the new couple.

Terry and Diane Barter of Sterling, Mass., knew from the start that their family life would be complicated. Terry had three daughters from his previous marriage and Diane hoped they would have children of their own someday. But after seven years of marriage and the birth of three sons, Diane, 32, concedes that she was naive about her role in the girls' lives. "I lived in Fantasyland," she says. "I thought I could be the mother their mother wasn't to them." Everybody got along well when Diane and Terry, 41, were dating. But when the couple told the girls they were getting married, one of Terry's daughters reacted with anger and bitterness. She told Diane and Terry: "I don't know why I can't have a *real* mother and father."

After the fantasy phase, says psychologist Papernow, comes the reality phase, and it can be a shock. The original dreams of unified family life are destroyed and there's no easy substitute. All the members feel they have lost something. The children often mourn the death of their dearest dream—

that somehow their biological parents will get back together. The new spouse makes that reunion impossible. The newly married couple see that the transition is much harder than they ever imagined.

When Susan Borkin married Jerry Hurwitz almost nine years ago, she became an "instant mother" to Jerry's three children, Dan, Noah and Ramee. Susan had never planned on having a family; her career as a psychotherapist always came first, she says. Jerry's ex-wife, who lived in Oregon, had custody so Susan and Jerry expected the kids to visit them in San Francisco only on holidays and vacations. But as the children became teenagers, the living arrangements changed. Both Noah and Ramee spent long and sometimes difficult periods with Susan and Jerry; the family sought outside therapy several times. Now, with the older boys in college and Ramee, 16, finishing high school, Susan and Jerry believe they have overcome most of the hurdles—although they haven't forgotten them. "You have to have a commitment that you're going to stay married," says Jerry. "That has to be your bottom line."

In this reality phase, children who have spent many years in a single-parent family often feel especially threatened by the new spouse. The new partner is often viewed as an interloper. Esther Sullivan, a Chicago high-school senior, lived alone with her father, Michael, for 10 years after her parents' divorce. In May, Michael Sullivan, an anthropologist, married Lorel Pfaff, a social worker. Esther is glad her father has found someone, but she sometimes feels uncomfortable in her own house. "It's like having a permanent guest," she says. "My father is always reminding me to watch how I behave. Home has definitely changed." Esther thinks her father is trying hard to bring his wife and daughter together. "She's used to living by herself and I'm used to doing things by myself," says Esther. "He made us say hello to each other every morning. I don't want to talk to anyone in the morning and I don't think she does, either." The new spouse also has to adjust. "When you marry, you always marry the family, but they usually don't live in the house with you," says Lorel.

For couples who each bring children to the marriage, child-rearing styles are often a problem. Terry and Leanne Hochstein of Norfolk, Neb., each had two children when they got married five years ago. Terry had custody of his two daughters, Niki, now 14, and Angie, 13. Leanne and her two sons, Phillip, now 11, and Joey, 9, moved into Terry's house. Each was critical of the other's methods of discipline. Says Terry: "I was more strict and would punish more. I felt that Leanne would just talk to them and they would keep it up." At first they tried just disciplining their own kids, but now, as the situation has settled down, they have been acting more as a couple. Their rule is to try to present a unified front; otherwise, they say, the kids play one parent off against the other.

In this phase of stepfamily life, many couples just decide to give up. "Remarriages are very fragile," says Johns Hopkins University sociologist Andrew Cherlin. "There's a high rate of divorce for the first several years, almost as though these couples have gone through one bad marriage and they're determined not to go through another. Their antennae are up and they're prepared to leave if necessary."

Happy endings mean hard work from everybody. The commitment begins with the couple. Family therapists Jerry and Helen Devine of The Woodlands, Texas, had been longtime friends and colleagues when they married 3½ years ago. They moved into a house big enough for their five children, now ages 6 to 23. In any stepfamily situation, "there's a whole lot of pain," Helen says. "There's no getting away from it." But she says their combined family has succeeded so far because she and Jerry work hard at being a couple first. Even though the children may initially fight against the marriage, as the new union becomes more solid, "it is their security blanket," Helen says.

For newly remarried families, Burt of the Stepfamily Association thinks education is the first step. "It's enormously helpful for people to get as much information as possible," she says, "so they know what the pitfalls are and can deal with them when they come up." Some people seek private or group counseling; others turn to self-help support groups, like the Stepfamily Association.

Even people who aren't in remarried families will have to begin thinking about some of these issues as stepfamilies become more and more prominent. Nontraditional family forms may force us to change our expectations of the role of the family. "The complexity of families has reached astounding proportions," says Furstenberg. "It has become difficult to reckon who is kin, in many respects." In a recent national survey of stepchildren, he found that nearly a quarter did not include their stepsiblings as part of their family even though they were living with them.

One of the big questions for the 21st century, says Furstenberg, is "whether the people we count as kin can be counted on." Will, for example, stepchildren care for stepparents when they get old? Many experts think that the current generation of stepchildren will rewrite the rules of family life as they grow up. And they'll be looking for role models in families who have made it. Patricia, the New York artist, says that it took a long time, but now she feels that Michael considers Jack a real parent. In fact, she had proof when she looked at the quotations next to her son's picture in his high-school yearbook when he graduated this spring. "There it was," she recalls, "in between the quotes from Emerson and Led Zeppelin: 'Thanks Mom and Jack. Thanks for everything'."

Review Questions

1. Briefly examine three important issues that tend to develop in stepfamilies.
2. Select a stepfamily that you know, and describe two or three of the major problems with which they have to deal.

TRADING PLACES

Melinda Beck with Barbara Kantrowitz, Lucille Beachy, Mary Hager, Jeanne Gordon, Elizabeth Roberts, and Roxie Hammill

Many American women are becoming increasingly unhappy in their marriages and families. A major factor in the increase of unhappiness is the stress resulting from the many responsibilities, pressures, and conflicting roles married women play in family life. The following reading, "Trading Places," by Melinda Beck et al. addresses the emotional and economic stress that many American women encounter as they are "sandwiched between child care and elder care."

Like many daughters of aging parents, Sandy Berman didn't recognize at first how far her mother and father had slipped. "You are so used to your parents being mentally competent that you don't realize what you're dealing with for a long time," says the Northridge, Calif., schoolteacher, 47. Her parents had been living with trash piling up in their home for almost a year when Berman finally convinced them to move closer. But the move only hastened their decline. Berman's father, 83, became forgetful and overdosed on his insulin. Her mother, 74, couldn't find her way from the bedroom to the bathroom. For months, Berman called every morning before going to work, and stopped by every afternoon. "I was going to make everything right, and better and perfect," she says. "But everything I did turned into mush."

While her mother was sweet and cooperative, Berman says, age turned her father mean. He called at all hours of the night and thought his daughter was stealing his money. He hired a detective and changed the locks on the door. Berman was haunted by anxiety attacks. Her job teaching third grade was her only refuge. "When the bell rang at the end of the day, my stomach started to clench," she says. She worried that she was neglecting her husband and son, and longed to be mothered herself again. She lost 30 pounds and had fantasies of running away: "*San Fernando Valley schoolteacher disappears. No one knows why she didn't come home for dinner . . .*"

In February 1989, Berman snapped. "I was nurturing at home, at school and at my parents', and getting nothing back," she says. She quit work and stopped seeing her parents for two months, all the while making decisions for them with the help of a geriatric counselor and a lawyer. Diagnosed with Alzheimer's disease and paranoia, her father went from one nursing facility to another, and died in May 1989. Berman found a board-and-care home for her mother and enrolled her in an adult day-care center to keep her mind stimulated. These days, Berman visits her twice a month, and calls once a week, though her mother doesn't seem to know if she has called or not. Berman has returned to work, but she still wonders—and always will—"Did I do the right thing?"

Anguish, frustration, devotion and love.

A fierce tangle of emotions comes with parenting one's aged parents, and there isn't time to sort out the feelings, let alone make dinner, fold the laundry and get to work. More than 6 million elderly Americans need help with such basics as getting out of bed and going to the bathroom; millions more can't manage meals, money or transportation. Most are cared for by family members, at home, for free—and most families wouldn't have it any other way. There are myriad variations: "children" in their 60s looking after parents in their 80s; spouses spending their golden years tending ailing mates; empty-nesters who had paid the last tuition check only to have an aged relative move in. Increasingly, men are shouldering such responsibilities. Still, three fourths of those caring for the elderly are women, as it has always been. Until the last couple of decades, women were home," explains Diane Piktialis of Work/Family Directions, a Boston consulting firm. "Caregiving was their job."

But today they have other jobs as well. More than half the women who care for elderly relatives also work outside the home; nearly 40 percent are still raising children of their own. In fact, just when many women on the "Mommy Track" thought they could get back to their careers, some are finding themselves on an even longer "Daughter Track," with their parents, or their husband's parents, growing frail. The average American woman will spend 17 years raising children and 18 years helping aged parents, according to a 1988 U.S. House of Representatives report. As the population ages and chronic, disabling conditions become more common, many more families will care for aged relatives. And because they delayed childbirth, more couples will find themselves "sandwiched" between child care and elder care. The oldest baby boomers are now in their mid-40s; their parents are mostly in their late 60s and early 70s, when disabilities tend to begin. In the next few years, predicts Dana Friedman of the Families and Work Institute, there will be a "groundswell of baby boomers experiencing these problems."

The strains on women, long evident in their personal lives, are now showing up in the workplace. In recent years, about 14 percent of caregivers to the elderly have switched from full- to part-time jobs and 12 percent have left the work force, according to the American Association of Retired Persons. Another 28 percent have considered quitting their jobs, other studies have found. That's just what's aboveboard. Many employees are afraid to let on that they spent that "sick day" taking Mom to the doctor, visiting nursing homes or applying for Medicare. Many women shop, cook and clean for their parents before work, after work and on lunch hours, stealing time to confer on the phone during the day. "Caring for a dependent adult has become, for many, a second full-time job," says Bernard M. Kilbourn, a former regional director of the U.S. Health and Human Services Department, now with a consulting group, Caregivers Guidance Systems, Inc.

To date, only about 3 percent of U.S. companies have policies that assist employees caring for the elderly. But Friedman predicts that such programs will become "the new, pioneering benefit of the 1990s." Businesses may have no choice. With the baby bust sharply reducing the number of young workers entering the job market, the U.S. Bureau of Labor Statistics warns that 60 percent of the growth in the labor force this decade will be women, virtually all aged 35 to 54. "This is the age group that's feeling the brunt of child-care responsibilities," says the BLS's Jesse Benjamin. "This is also the age group where elder care hits. It's a double whammy."

Congress is encouraging more family-friendly work policies—at least, it has tried.

After five years of debate, lawmakers recently passed the Family and Medical Leave Act, requiring companies with more than 50 employees to grant them up to 12 weeks' unpaid leave to care for newborn or adopted children or relatives who are seriously ill. But President George Bush vetoed the bill, on the ground that government should not dictate corporate benefits.

American society is just waking up to the needs of an aging population. Even the words "elder care" and "caregiver" are new to the lexicon. Now, "there's a name and a description, and people are beginning to say, 'I fit into that'," says Louise Fradkin, cofounder of the support group Children of Aging Parents (CAPS), which has more than 100 chapters nationwide. For years, Fradkin says, caring for aged relatives was a hidden responsibility, one that most women assumed in silence. Even the major feminist groups have been slow to make it a cause. The National Organization for Women, for example, has been more concerned with abortion rights and advancement for women in the workplace than with family roles. "The problem today's midlife woman faces is that the rhetoric of the '70s and the realities of the '90s are somewhat discordant," says Michael Creedon of the National Council on the Aging.

Only the Older Women's League (OWL), a Washington advocacy group, has made elder care a pressing issue. "No matter what else we talk about, our members always come back to caregiving—it has a big impact on all their other roles," says OWL executive director Joan Kuriansky. "We get letters from women who are taking care of their children, and their parents and possibly *their* parents. They are running from place to place. How do we expect them to do that and stay employed?"

That is the dilemma of the Daughter Track. While women have become a major force in the American workplace, their roles as caregivers remain entrenched in the expectations of society and individual families. "Often it's the woman's own sense of what's required of her," says Kuriansky. "Some of it is emotional. Some of it is economic—she may feel that she cannot contribute financially as much as a man does." And just as with child care, says CAPS's Fradkin, "women feel they have to be superwomen and do it all themselves."

Those who do ask for help at home are often frustrated. Many husbands are unable—or unwilling—to confront the emotional demands of elder care, even when the aged parents are their own. Two years ago, Pamela Resnick of Coral Springs, Fla., quit her job and moved her ailing father-in-law in. While he was in and out of hospitals, she says, "he always wanted to see me—not even my husband. My husband doesn't deal very well with that type of scene." Joan Segal, 49, who quit her job to care for her mother, threatened to leave her husband unless he helped her mother more. Since then, Segal says, "He's so protective you'd think she was his own mother."

Grandchildren may also be swept into the changing family dynamics, and that adds to the guilt many women feel. Kristeen Davis, 43, a divorced accounting supervisor, has cut down her work hours since her 63-year-old mother, an Alzheimer's victim, came to live with her in Kansas City. Still, Davis's 13-year-old daughter must be home by 3:30 each day when her grandmother returns from an adult day-care center. "It's been hard on all of us," says Davis. Yet she says her mother "did for me when I was young. What's a couple of years out of my life?"

Time is often the most precious commodity for caregivers. "We were used to being George and Nancy with no kids at home," says Nancy Erbst, 38, of Minneapolis, whose mother-in-law, Hazel, lived with them for four years. "We used to take off on weekends and go camping. Our camping went down to one weekend in the summer." Nancy, an executive secretary, was also working to earn a bachelor's degree at the time. She would get up at 4 a.m. to study, then tend to Hazel before leaving for work at 7:45. Her husband's two grown daughters, who lived nearby, also helped watch over their grandmother until last spring, when her deteriorating health forced her into a nursing home. "It's what a family does for each other," Nancy says. "It's something you want to do."

Not all families rally so gracefully. Deciding who should do the caring, and where, can stir up old sibling rivalries—and create new bitterness. For several years, Linda Hunt, a 54-year-old Kansas widow, has been the primary caregiver for her mother, now in a nearby nursing home. Her brother has been mostly uninvolved. "Sometimes when he calls, he doesn't ask about her," she says. "It sets me hard against him."

Responsibility for an elderly relative usually falls to the woman who is nearest. And sometimes no one is close. Roughly one third of caregivers manage care for their aged parents long distance, assessing changing needs over the phone and with reports from neighbors. Even though her mother and father lived in a residential community that provided housekeeping and meals, Saretta Berlin, 60, flew from Philadelphia to Ft. Lauderdale, Fla., every 10 days during much of 1989, when her parents were failing. "I would tell myself that if I just made it to the plane, I would be OK," she says. "Then perfect strangers would ask me how I was doing, and the floodgates would open." Even now, with her father dead and her mother in a retirement home, Berlin calls daily and visits every three weeks or so.

As Berlin found, even when families put a parent in a nursing home, their responsibilities don't end. Many grown children rearrange their lives to visit as often as possible, and field lonely phone calls, night and day. Only about 10 percent of the disabled elderly are in such facilities—and the decision can haunt their families long afterward. Linda Hunt still feels guilty about putting her mother in a home three years ago—even though she was blind and Hunt was holding down two full-time jobs. "You think you should be able to do it all, but you can't," she says. "First you care for your children, then your mother. Pretty soon you just give your whole self to other people."

Unlike child care, the responsibilities of elder care often come suddenly. A stroke or broken hip can mean the difference between a parent living independently and needing round-the-clock care. And while a child's needs can be planned for, an older person's requirements are often difficult to assess. Can Dad still manage in his own home? Will he need care for a few months—or many years? What's more, says Kilbourn, "in dealing with your parents, you do not have total control. Any decision . . . can be met with resistance if not total refusal to cooperate."

Reversing roles is one of the hardest aspects of caring for an aged parent. Kristeen Davis says her mother was "a really sharp lady—and one of my best friends" before Alzheimer's set in. Now, Davis says, "sometimes she just sits there like a little lump that used to be a person." Elderly people find it even harder to relinquish their old parental roles. Many are desperately afraid of burdening their busy children, yet desperately afraid of being alone.

Dot von Gerbig's mother and father moved in to help her in 1969, when she was a widow raising small children. Today, they still share her Honey Brook, Pa., home, along with her second husband and their 15-year old son. Von Gerbig's father, 92, is confined to a wheelchair; her mother, 84, is mentally confused, and both are legally blind. Before leaving for work at 7 a.m., von Gerbig arranges every aspect of their lives, laying out clothes and organizing food in the refrigerator, so they can manage by themselves until she returns. "So far, we're making it," says von Gerbig, 52. But she lives in fear that something will go wrong and make her break her vow to keep them out of a nursing home. What troubles her even more, she says, is how terribly cruel the aging process is. "It makes me angry and it makes me fearful," she says. "It's an awful thing that a person does a good job all his life and this is his reward."

Most caregivers lament that they can't do more for their parents. Some of the toughest constraints are financial. Medicare does not cover the costs of long-term care, anywhere. Medicaid will pay for nursing homes, and home care in some states, but only after a patient has depleted his assets nearly to the poverty level. Thus, many elderly people exhaust their life savings paying for care, and families dig deep into their own pockets to help them.

Many married women, particularly those in low-paying jobs, find it cheaper to quit work and care for aging relatives themselves than to hire home health care. Professional women are less inclined to quit and more apt to hire help. Many are torn between the parents they cherish and the work they love. Just when many have gotten a long-awaited promotion, they find their parents in need of care.

Charlotte Darrow decided she had to abandon her career as a social psychologist at Yale and move to Ann Arbor, Mich., when her widowed mother fell ill in the late 1970s. She spent much of the next seven years cooking and chauffeuring for her. As a result, Darrow says, 'I really lost everything—it was much too late to go back and recapture my career." She devoted the next six years to studying how 15 other professional women combined work and caregiving. Her manuscript tells how they hired help and sacrificed weekends, lunches and vacations to spend time with their parents. Despite enormous stresses, all 15 continued their careers. "What these women showed is that people don't have to say, 'My God, this is it!'" says Darrow, 67. "It is possible to go on with your life."

What can employers do to make that easier? One of the most helpful things is to acknowledge the situation. "Corporate America needs to create an environment where employees can say, 'I have a problem with an elder who needs care'," says OWL president Lou Glasse. The Travelers Companies was one of the first to do so; after a 1985 survey found that 28 percent of its workers over 30 cared for an aged parent, on an average of 10 hours a week, Travelers started a series of support programs. Today's leader may be The Stride Rite Corp., which this year opened the nation's first on-site intergenerational day-care center.

Other forward-looking firms have devised a wide range of programs and benefits. One of the most common, and least costly, is simply to educate employees about social services available in their communities. Some firms hold lunchtime seminars or "Caregiver Fairs," where local agencies describe their programs. Some publish detailed handbooks for employees, covering everything from how to select a nursing home to how to locate and pay for respite care. Growing numbers of companies also contract with private consulting firms that can help employees manage care even for relatives in distant cities. Work/Family Directions has developed programs for 21 national firms, linking their clients' employees with 175 agencies across the country. It also provides an 800 number for support and advice. In a few cities, government agencies provide similar services. Employees "don't want a way out of their caregiving responsibilities—they just want some help in coping," says Barbara Lepis, director of Partnership for Eldercare, a New York City program working with American Express, Philip Morris and J.P. Morgan.

The same Employee Assistance Programs (EAPs) that assist workers with drug and alcohol problems can often help with strains on the home front. In fact, EAP counselors frequently find that caregiving duties are at the root of employees' financial, marital or job-performance difficulties. Teresa Freeman, EAP manager at Travelers, says one employee was referred to her office because she was crying at work; another had been put on warning because she was unable to learn new skills. Both, it turned out, were caring for elderly parents and were cracking under the strain. Freeman formed a support group of caregiving employees. But other firms have found that support groups don't work well in situations where bosses and their subordinates may be reluctant to share intimate problems. Lepis says the chemistry works better when such sessions are called "caregiver exchanges" that deal with a specific topic, such as filling out a medical form. "Then we are able to get a cross-strata of the work force to commiserate together about this stupid form," she says.

Some firms are training supervisors to be compassionate about the demands workers face at home. Managers must also be reminded that the Mommy Track, and the Daughter Track, should not be slower roads to advancement. Otherwise, warned OWL in its 1989 Mother's Day report, "only orphans with no children could be placed on the fast track to professional success."

Growing numbers of firms are granting unpaid leaves to employees with family needs. IBM is perhaps the most generous. Full-time employees can take up to three years off, with benefits, and find their jobs waiting: "If we give our employees help in managing their personal lives, it helps us attract and retain the workers we need," says IBM spokesman Jim Smith. That has proved true at Aetna Life and Casualty as well. When it extended its family leave from a few weeks to as long as a year in 1988, the turnover rate among its female caregivers dropped from 22 to 13 percent. About 15 percent of U.S. companies offer flexible work hours. Some 35 percent of U.S. Sprint's 16,000 employees are on an "alternative" schedule—flextime, part time or job sharing, though most do so for child care or other reasons. Since January, Travelers has also granted every employee three "family-care days" a year that do not count as absences.

Alas, some elder-care programs are underutilized. In 1987, Remington Products offered to pay half the cost of respite care for workers' dependents during nonwork hours. Two years later, it dropped the program when fewer than six employees had signed up. Michael Creedon, who conceived the idea through his work at the neighboring University of Bridgeport (Conn.), speculates that Remington's highly ethnic work force may not have been comfortable with the idea of strangers in their home. Indeed, says OWL's Glasse, "many caregivers want to be so supportive of elders that they are reluctant to ask for help" and try to do it all on their own. Out of embarrassment, or their own individual work ethic, many employees are also reluctant to burden their bosses with family problems.

In the end, there is only so much the business world can do to help America's caregivers. Many liberal lawmakers and more than 100 special-interest groups are pressing the federal government to do more. In March, the U.S. Bipartisan Commission on Comprehensive Health Care proposed a giant new long-term care program that would guarantee home health care and three free months in a nursing home to all severely disabled

Americans who need it, regardless of age or income. But the price tag—an estimated $42 billion a year—virtually assures that no legislative action will be taken any time soon.

Even without creating a massive new entitlement program, the federal government could do more to help the elderly and those who care for them. Federal funding for the network of social-service programs serving the elderly is a paltry $710 million a year; services are sparse and fragmented in many areas. Most offices are open only 9 to 5, forcing caregivers to deal with them during work hours. OWL is pressing the Social Security Administration to rewrite rules that penalize workers who take time out to care for children or aged dependents. Upon retirement, a worker's monthly benefit is determined by averaging his or her earnings over the past 35 years. A zero is entered for any year not worked, no matter what the reason. Caregiving, says OWL executive director Kuriansky, "is a wonderful dimension of woman as nurturer—and it's something we don't want to undermine. But in playing that role, we want to make sure she is rewarded, not penalized."

Most women on the Daughter Track do not want to give up their family responsibilities—no matter what personal or professional sacrifices it entails. Many see their efforts as a chance to repay the time and care their parents gave them—a chance to say, again, *I love you*, before it's too late. What they would like is more understanding at work, more support from the men in their lives, more community services to help them—and a little applause from a world that often turns too fast to take time out for love.

Review Questions

1. Briefly describe two or three problems that develop from daughters having to care for their aging parent(s).
2. Briefly describe how you or your spouse plan to (or currently) deal with an aging parent's needs.

Cohabitation and Singlehood

Because of the many problems and hassles that complicate remarriage, family sociologists have indicated that many divorced people are discouraged from remarrying and are opting for cohabitation or for living alone (P. C. Glick, 1990). Many Americans who have never been married have also opted for cohabitation. In 1960, under a half million heterosexual unmarried couples were living together. By the late 1980s, over five times as many—over 2.6 million unrelated couples—were living together. Almost a third of these couples have young children, three-quarters of whom are the woman's children (P. C. Glick, 1990).

Many Americans couples live together

P. C. Glick reports that some young adults have never had the experience with cohabitation, but will do so later on. Other young adults who have experienced living together have become married (P. C. Glick, 1990). Thorton reports that among unmarried adults age 18 to 35, one-third will eventually cohabit while being unmarried (Thorton, 1988).

Many Americans remain single

In the 1950s, only above 5 percent of American adults did not marry. Today that figure is over 10 percent. During the 1960s, approximately 11 percent of women (30 to 34 years of age) did not marry. Today two and a half times that many are not married (P. C. Glick, 1990).

Could it be that marriage and family life are becoming less popular in America? According to sociologists Glenn and Weaver in a study of attitudes toward marriage, there is a significant decline between the early 1970s and the late 1980s in the relationship between being married and reported happiness. They reported an increase of happy men who never married, and a decrease of happily married women (Glenn and Weaver, 1988).

Families of Divorce: Factors and Explanations

The American marital system involves two people who live together and who have individual values and needs. This can create a high potential for stress, conflict, violence, and marital and family breakdown. In the United States, marriage is a civil contract, and each state has specific conditions whereby the marriage may be dissolved. Divorces are obtained for reasons ranging from violation of marital obligation to mutual agreement.

Divorce: an unfortunate event

In most societies, divorce is viewed as an unfortunate event for the people involved. It can also be viewed as an index of failure for the family system or as an escape valve, a way out of the marriage itself. The United States has one of the highest divorce rates in the world. One out of every two marriages ends in divorce. Several million Americans have been divorced during the past decade. Many other American couples have also separated or deserted.

Marriage: an enduring social institution

This may suggest that marriage is no longer an enduring social institution. On the contrary, the data suggest that marriage remains a pervasive, enduring institution. The Skolnicks state that, "With 90 to 95 percent of the population marrying at least once, America is one of the world's most marrying nations. High divorce rates do not mean people are rejecting marriage, since most divorced people remarry within five years after their divorce (A. Skolnick and J. Skolnick, 1989). Despite high divorce rates then, most marriages are long-term, and few Americans marry more than twice.

Divorced people are not unhappy with family life

In addition, divorced people are not unhappy with family life. In fact, divorced Americans place a high premium on family life, as do married people. Americans who have chosen divorce do not believe that the family is unimportant. For example, three out of every four American women still think that the ideal way to live is to be married and to have children (Gallup, 1982, 1989). Why is it then that people divorce? In the following section, we examine some of the explanations.

Factors Affecting Divorce Rates

Many factors affect the divorce rate in the United States. First, divorce rates vary with social class. The divorce rate is higher for lower socioeconomic levels, although the difference is decreasing. This relationship holds true regardless of the index used for determining socioeconomic level (occupation, income, or education). High rates of divorce and marital instability at lower socioeconomic levels have been attributed to lower income levels and greater frustration in meeting expenses.

Three factors make it difficult, in terms of costs and desirability, for those in the upper class to obtain a divorce. First, the kin and friendship networks in the upper classes are larger and more tightly knit, making the social consequences of divorce greater. Second, exemption from family obligations in the upper classes is more difficult because of the complexities of long-range property investments and expenditures, such as annuities, houses, and insurance. Third, the wife's potential loss through divorce is greater at higher levels; therefore, she is less willing to give up the marriage (Goode, 1976; A. Skolnick and J. Skolnick, 1989).

Divorce and geography

Divorce rates in the United States also vary according to geographic and social factors. For example, with respect to geographic distribution, statistics indicate a general trend toward a higher divorce rate in the west than in the east. Divorce rates are up to four times higher in the west than in the northeast. Some sociologists attribute these geographical variations in part to the fact that different geographical areas contain different types of communities. They believe that "divorce rates will be lower in culturally homogeneous, rather than heterogenous, communities with primary face-to-face interactions in contrast to communities with anonymous and/or segmentalized relationships" (Eshleman, 1981, 1985).

Divorce and religion

With respect to religion, we find that, because of the Catholic church's stand against divorce, there tends to be a lower rate of divorce among Catholics than among Protestants. However, the rate of separation among Catholics is higher than among non-Catholics. The divorce rate tends to be the highest among couples who have no religious preference.

Divorce and social class

Desertion is a more common form of dissolving marriages among lower than higher social classes. **Desertion** occurs when a husband or wife leaves the family against the will of the other. Desertion by husbands, similar to divorce in many respects, places much economic strain on wives and children because the husbands generally fail to support their abandoned families. Although in the past, desertion was primarily a male phenomenon, today the ratio of male to female deserters is almost even.

Divorce and mobility

The high divorce and desertion rates in the United States are attributable to mobility, stresses on the nuclear family system, and changes in family functions. Some social scientists believe that geographical and social mobility have weakened many of the nuclear family's ties to kin. With the weakening of these ties, there is a loss of emotional support, financial advice, and various other forms of help that are important in maintaining family and marriage.

Spouses in the nuclear family must rely heavily on each other for the satisfaction of emotional needs. Some sociologists believe that this affectional function of the family is the only remaining justification for the family as a social institution. They believe that people turn more and more to the family as a source of affectional security as community contacts become increasingly formal and segmented. The competitiveness, isolation, and mobility of our society place strains on family members, whose increased anxiety levels lead them to other family members for emotional support. There is an insistent demand for affection from an institution that no longer has the traditional supporting structure. Many of the reasons given by couples for ending their marriages reflect the difficulty some families have in meeting the affectional function. Spouses have reported such complaints as mental cruelty, neglect, physical abuse, and problems in psychological and emotional interaction.

Divorce and family structure

High rates of divorce also have been explained in terms of the structure of the nuclear family. In the past, some social scientists have responded to the divorce problem by proclaiming that the nuclear family is either dying or dead. Others believe that the nuclear family is in a period of transition rather than decay. The instability of marriage is to be viewed as a misfortune and as a legitimate cause for complaint and remedy. However, these and other problems also may be viewed as incidental results of social changes to which neither society in general nor families in particular yet have been able to accommodate themselves.

The changing role of women has also been considered a factor in the breakup of some marriages. Many women have taken jobs outside the home for both economic and emotional reasons. Many women, in addition to supplementing their spouses' incomes, are emotionally and intellectually unfulfilled in the roles of child rearer, housekeeper, and supportive companion. Despite many barriers that continue to restrict women in their efforts toward economic and social equality, many wives have become economically independent from their husbands. This, in turn, has weakened the traditional role of husbands. For some wives, economic independence means that it is easier to divorce their husbands and establish lives outside of marriage.

Divorce and love expectations

Higher rates of divorce in America also have been explained in terms of higher expectations for romantic love in marriage. In contrast to earlier periods in history, romantic love rather than economic factors is now considered to be the important factor in choosing a marriage partner. Romantic love fades somewhat or is lost altogether when routines of marriage and family life begin. Job and household pressures, economic problems, and dirty dishes and diapers tend to push romantic feelings aside. Many couples interpret the loss of romantic love as indicative of a failed marriage. There are feelings of frustration and a loss of faith in the marriage itself. There are also many myths couples have about parenthood and the rearing of children (LeMasters, 1970). Parenthood is surrounded by folklore (widely held beliefs that are not supported by facts), and many men and women do not really know what being a parent means until they are parents themselves.

Dissimilar backgrounds and failure

In urban areas, there is also a greater probability of marrying someone who is socially, ethically, or religiously different. People with dissimilar backgrounds tend to have higher rates of marital failure than those whose backgrounds are similar. There also tend to be fewer social and economic proscriptions against divorce in urban than in rural environments.

There is much debate about the impact of urbanization, industrialization, and social change on the American family. In general, however, social scientists agree that the family has been weakened by the loss of its economic functions and that emotional functions have become increasingly important because the family is the best institution for fostering child care and adult intimacy. A. Skolnick and J. Skolnick (1989), in an analysis of domestic relations and social change, have examined these changes in functions. They state that the conditions of life in America today do undermine family ties and do create strong needs for nurturant, intimate, and enduring relationships. The primary changes that have created this dilemma are:

Emotional functions have become increasingly important

1. the loss of constraints and restrictions in work and marriage
2. a general emotional and task overload
3. contradictory social demands and values
4. demographic change

With respect to the loss of constraints and restrictions, in preindustrial societies, marriage and work were determined by tradition, hereditary status, and economic necessity, not by individual choice. Familial, community, and economic sanctions were imposed on families to ensure the continuity of marriages and their conformity to prescribed behavior. People have been liberated from such restrictions by modernization. The Skolnicks report that whenever a traditional pattern of work and family is replaced by a modern pattern, it is accompanied by an "ideology of liberation." They state: "Modernization promises freedom of opportunity to work that suits one's talents, freedom to marry for love and dissolve the marriage if it fails to provide happiness, and greater equality in the family between husband and wife, and between parents and children. The freedom of modern family life is bought at the price of fragility and instability of family ties" (A. Skolnick and J. Skolnick, 1989).

With regard to emotional and task overload, even sociologists who stress the vital societal functions played by the family acknowledge that societies can put strain on families. As Talcott Parsons stated in his now-classic studies: "When the family and the home no longer functioned as an economic unit, women, children, and old people were placed in an ambiguous position outside the occupational world. For children, the shift to industrial work, and the removal of the father from the home, also meant that the mother became more of a central figure. Little boys could no longer observe and participate in father's work. This created a strain on both child and mother" (Parsons, 1958). The family, through warmth, affection, and companionship, is supposed to somewhat compensate for the cold impersonal world. However, families have little on which to base their relationships after work, education, and other functions have been eliminated from the nuclear family.

Societies put strain on families

With respect to contradictory demands and values, the ideology concerning today's family emphasizes the qualities of personal freedom, individualism, and sexual equality. But the realities of everyday life of most Americans prevent them from achieving these values. For all members of the family, there is a contradiction between a morality of duty, responsibility, work, and self-denial (A. Skolnick and J. Skolnick, 1989).

Demographic factors are important

With regard to demographic change, it is difficult to comprehend how profoundly family life has been affected by changes such as longer life expectancy and the use of contraceptive devices. Marriage at an earlier age and extended lifespans have increased the possible length of a marriage from about 20 to more than 50 years. As the Skolnicks report, "The prospect of fifty years with the same person increases tensions in marriage and makes it more likely that dissatisfaction will lead to divorce. . . . In a rapidly changing society, the couple who seemed well suited to each other in their early twenties may find themselves growing in different ways and at different rates later on" (A. Skolnick and J. Skolnick, 1989).

Families of Violence

Families tend to be characterized by love and affection. They are, however, also characterized by violence. **Violence** in the family can take several forms: violence between spouses, violence between siblings, and violence against children by their parents, or **child abuse.** In this section of the chapter, we will examine spouse abuse, child abuse, and the explanations for violence in families.

Spouse Abuse

Estimates of spouse abuse vary

With respect to spouse abuse, estimates of the extent of violence between husbands and wives vary. A study in Chicago estimated that more police calls were made for conflict between family members than for all criminal incidents combined (L. Glick, 1990). In a national survey of several thousand representative families, about 2 million wives and an equal number of husbands commit one or more serious attacks on their spouses each year. Serious attacks range from kicks, punches, and bites to homicidal assaults with deadly weapons (L. Glick, 1990). In significant numbers of divorce applications, spouses mention overt violent behavior as a factor in their wanting a divorce. Many estimates of violence between spouses are low, however, because many incidents simply go unreported. And it is usually women who are on the receiving end of the worst violence at home. When there is a fight between a husband and a wife, the wife usually comes out the loser (L. Glick, 1990).

Husband beating: one of the most unreported crimes

Wives, however, are not the only victims of family violence. Husband beating is considered by some sociologists to be one of the most unreported crimes in America. It has been estimated that each year at least a quarter of a million husbands in the United States are severely beaten by their wives (L. Glick, 1990). Some sociologists see men and women as equal victims of family violence, since the homicides in husband-wife conflicts are fairly equally split between the sexes (L. Glick, 1990).

Child Abuse

A moral obligation to use physical punishment?

With regard to child abuse, parents are legally permitted to use physical punishment on their children. Research indicates that the majority of people in the United States believe it to be a moral obligation to use physical punishment to control their children, if other means fail (Steinmitz, 1974; L. Glick, 1990). It appears that society acknowledges physical punishment as violence only when it reaches extremes of severe child injury or death.

More violence in the past

In previous periods of history, children have experienced more violence than they do today. Historical analysis of child abuse reveals, for example, that for many centuries, the maltreatment of children has been justified by the belief that severe physical punishment was needed to "maintain discipline, to transmit educational ideas, to please certain gods, or to expel evil spirits" (Rabill, 1974; L. Glick, 1990).

Violence and abuse rates against children are not as high today as they have been in the past, but they are high. In America, over 2 million children are abused each year, and many die (L. Glick, 1990). Leavitt reports that more children under 5 years of age die from mistreatment by parents than from tuberculosis, whooping cough, polio, measles, diabetes, rheumatic fever, and appendicitis combined (Leavitt, 1974; Zastrow, 1988).

Motherhood is stressful

Child abuse can include physical abuse and neglect, emotional abuse and neglect, abandonment and inadequate supervision, and exploitation of children. Mothers tend to be more prone to abusing their children than fathers. This has been attributed to the fact that the major burden of child-care responsibilities falls upon women. The birth of a child is restrictive of his or her mother's mobility and freedom, both socially and occupationally. This, combined with the stressful demands of early child rearing, can, for many mothers, produce frustration leading to the greater proneness of mothers to be abusive of their children (L. Glick, 1990).

Three important factors

For Gelles, the most dangerous period for the abused child is from about 3 months to 3 years of age. The abused child is most vulnerable during this period of time, when he or she is the most defenseless and least capable of meaningful social interaction (Gelles, 1974). Sociologists have found three factors to be related to the fact that the frequency of child abuse is highest among 3-month- to three-year-old children: First, the smaller child does not have the ability to withstand violence, unlike the older child who may be able to absorb more physical punishment; second, frustration may be created by the infant's inability to interact with the parent in a more socially meaningful manner; and third, the new child may create, for his or her parents, stress or economic hardship, because of his or her birth (Gelles, 1974; L. Glick, 1990).

Higher demands

Parents who are abusive of their children demand a much higher performance from them than do parents who do not abuse their children. What typically occurs is that the parents "become angry because the child will not stop crying, eats poorly, urinates after being told not to do so . . . " The parents "feel righteous about the punishments they have inflicted on their children. They avoid facing the degree of injury they have caused, but they justify their behavior because they feel their children have been 'bad'" (Gill, 1970; L. Glick, 1990).

Explanations for Violence

Varied explanations for violence

The explanation for violence in the family are varied. Sociologists explain violence in the family in terms of the American culture and the socialization process. They explain that our American culture, in subtle and not so subtle ways, encourages the use of a certain degree of physical force while raising children. Parents are still primarily responsible for the raising, training, and socialization of their children. They have authority over their children, and this authority includes the right to punish them. Corporal punishment is strongly rooted in our culture. This is illustrated by the results of a national opinion survey in which the great majority of respondents were opposed to the punishment of parents who committed violent acts against their children. Also, more than half of the respondents believed that abused children should be removed from the home only as a last resort (L. Glick, 1990).

Punishment and American culture

Abuse and prior socialization

The behavior of abusive parents can also be explained by their prior socialization, when they themselves were deprived of tenderness and motherliness from their parents (Goode, 1974; L. Glick, 1990). This is called intergenerational transmission. When children are socialized in a family where violence and abuse are used to solve problems, they are learning a parental role centered upon violence. When these children are grown and are themselves parents, they reenact, especially in stressful situations, the behavior learned in childhood. Parents who abuse their children have usually had, as a role model, the use of violence as a method of solving family problems.

A psychological problem

The psychopathological explanation of violence in the family stresses that parents who abuse their child are suffering from psychological problems that must be eliminated to prevent further child abuse. The idea of mental illness rather than social learning is inherent in this approach. The case of psychopathy is traced back to the childhood of the abusive parents where they themselves were abused. The cause of the psychopathy in abusive parents is that the parents were reared in the same abusive way, which was recreated in the raising of their children. The cause of the pathology is the parents' early childhood experience (Gelles, 1974).

Economic factors are important

In addition to sociological and psychopathological explanations for violence in the family, there are social and economic explanations as well. There exist a wide variety of stress-producing social situations that tend to occur prior to violent acts of husbands against wives and parents against their children. Studies on unemployment show that economic conditions produce and tend to increase frustration and stress levels, which are vented upon children. In an analysis of "battered children," those who are bruised, drastically injured, and who are physically and psychologically malnourished, Raffali cites the presence of financial as well as marital difficulties among 90 percent of the most abusive families (Raffali, 1975; L. Glick, 1990). Gelles says that the birth of a child who is the product of an unwanted pregnancy is also illustrative of stress-producing situations (Gelles, 1974; L. Glick, 1990).

Responses to Violence

Responses to family violence seem to be related to the theories that have attempted to explain it. These responses have taken the form of individual psychiatric counseling and therapeutic programs, behavior modification, and group and family counseling. These responses reflect an attempt to treat—rather than punish—violent family members in the hope of keeping families intact. One such response is the organization known as Parents Anonymous, founded in 1970. Similar to Alcoholics Anonymous, Parents Anonymous is organized around the support gained from others with similar needs and experiences. Meetings are held by abusive parents to help one another deal with their abusive practices that are directed toward children. Unfortunately, only a small portion of abusive parents is served by this effective community resource. Some of the reasons for this are that in order for a parent to be helped by Parents Anonymous, he or she must admit to being an abusive parent and must be willing to try to change this behavior.

Parents Anonymous

In addition, there have been broader efforts to deal with legal dimensions. Virtually all state laws provide for the effective and immediate protection of children who are endangered by abusive parents or by neglectful home environments. Under many of these laws, caseworkers, or the police, can remove children from dangerous situations immediately without parental consent and without a court order, provided that a complaint is filed the day after the removal (L. Glick, 1990). Unlike the laws that protect children from violence, the laws that protect adults from family violence are much weaker. Adult family members who have been abused—mostly wives and grandparents—must press legal charges against the offender. In the majority of situations, most abused adults discover that the laws, if any, that have been designed to protect them are weak and ineffective against a family member who is abusive.

Laws and violence

NOW, WHAT ABOUT AMERICAN FAMILIES, WHERE ARE THEY GOING?

Paul C. Glick

Given the above, what about the future of marriage and the American family? In the following reading, "Now, What About American Families, Where Are They Going?" Paul C. Glick examines the future of American families.

When asked to comment on the state of American families, knowledgeable people express widely differing opinions (Glenn, 1987). At one extreme are those who believe that the negative aspects of current family life are largely offset by positive gains. At the other extreme are those who are convinced that the family system has undergone fundamental deterioration from which it is unlikely to rebound. In this concluding section, some of the pros and cons about where families are heading will be discussed.

Sociology and Social Research, vol. 74, no. 3, April 1990, pp. 143–145.

On the one hand are those who see the family as undergoing a temporary state of confusion largely because of the suddenness of recent family changes that will be followed by more gradual change. This view holds that we are passing through a period of experimentation with various family forms, after which new family norms will be established (Macklin, 1987; Chilman, 1988). These observers see that marriage is still much more popular than nonmarriage among those in their middle years, even though it may be marriage the second time around (Raschke, 1987). Therefore, being divorced for a while is now regarded as an increasingly acceptable transition period for those who are involved with serious marital problems and who expect to remarry eventually (Spanier and Furstenberg, 1987).

In addition, some of the research on recent trends in family structure has led to the conclusion that the family system has been changing but not necessarily disintegrating. In particular, trends in children's behavior do reflect deterioration in some ways but improvement in other ways (Zill and Rogers, 1988). These trends have been influenced not only by changes in family stability but also by changes in peer culture and the media. Still other research supports the opinion that Americans continue to place a high value on marriage, on family life, and on the role of a spouse (Rodgers and Thornton, 1985). But marriage is not for everyone. Single life has been growing increasingly attractive, and, for those who choose it, the chances are that they will find their later life less problematic than it might have been if recent changes in social conditions had not occurred (Stein, 1981).

These are some of the opinions of observers who detect benefit as well as loss from the recent family changes, thus recognizing that both sides of the situation exist.

On the other hand are those who see more negative than positive consequences from the changes. The recent trend is seen by these observers as a move away from familism and toward individualism, a move that has weakened but not yet killed the ideal of permanence in marriage (Glenn, 1987). This process is regarded as a gain for men and a loss for women and children. Men are accused of more often being the one leaving the marriage, and women are accused of allowing them to do it, while neither accepts the responsibility for keeping the family intact (White, 1987). These critics say that modern lifestyles, including cohabitation, have loosened family ties and placed emphasis on personal values at the expense of family values (Hunt and Hunt, 1987).

In addition, some critical analysts of the current family situation find that young women are becoming increasingly uncertain about their chances of keeping a marriage intact and are therefore acquiring education and work experience that would help them become self-maintaining if their marriage should not last (Sweet and Bumpass, 1988). This situation is seen as a factor also in keeping the birth rate low, for fear that women may be required to have lone custody of their children between divorce and remarriage or until their children grow up. Especially among well-educated women, the task of taking care of one or two children is being considered as much less than a full-time job. So, these mothers return to the labor market soon after their children are born and all too frequently have to leave their children in lower quality child care than they would like.

These are some of the ways that the more critical observers are visualizing family life in America today. From time immemorial, of course, the pessimists have said that the younger generation was going to the dogs, and now these critics say that this time it is for real. But is it?

A balanced position would acknowledge that sound points are made by observers on each side of the issue. The immense changes in society have produced immense changes in family life, and neither set of changes seems likely to be reversed very much. While the gains from marriage and family values may have diminished, there have been gains from enhanced lifestlye options and from greater consumption of material comforts. It is therefore a question as to whether the trade-off has been even or not.

Perhaps too many observers have been emphasizing one side of the situation only. Note that one-half of the mothers are employed outside the home, but one-half remain at home to take care of their children. Single-parenting and living alone have doubled during the present generation, but yet nearly three-fourths of the U.S. population live in the homes of married couples. One-half of marriages end in divorce, but three-fourths of divorced adults remarry. The practice of cohabitation has skyrocketed, but it would probably have been as high a generation or two ago if the young adults at that time thought they could get by with it. And no one knows how many empty marriages of a short while back would have been endured if the choice to end them had been culturally acceptable.

In this context, the family situation may not be as bleak as some people say or as tolerable as other people say. In this writer's opinion, American families are, on the average, somewhere in between the opposing positions and are likely to stay that way for some time to come. This author says this as a research worker attempting to understand what has been happening. But those who want to improve the situation would do well to concentrate on measures designed to help families and individuals of all types to cope intelligently with their serious adjustment problems.

Notes

This is a revised version of a paper presented at the Family Development Conference, University of South Florida, Sarasota, on January 13, 1989.

References

Chilman, C. S., Nunnaly, E. W., & Cox, F. M. 1988. *Variant Family Forms.* Beverly Hills, CA: Sage Publications.

Glenn, N. D. 1987. "A Tentatively Concerned View of American Marriage." *Journal of Family Issues,* 8, 350–354.

Hunt, J. C., & Hunt, L. L. 1987. "Here to Play: From Families to Lifestyles." *Journal of Family Issues,* 8, 440–443.

Macklin, E. 1987. "Nontraditional Family Forms." Pages 317–353 in Sussman, M. S., & Steinmetz, S. K. Eds., *Handbook of Marriage and the Family.* New York: Plenum Press.

Raschke, H. J. 1987. "Divorce." Pages 597–624 in Sussman, M. B., & Steinmetz, S. K. Eds., *Handbook of Marriage and the Family.* New York: Plenum Press.

Rodgers, W. L., & Thornton, A. 1985. "Changing Patterns of First Marriage in the United States." *Demography,* 22, 265–279.

Spanier, G. B., & Furstenberg, F. F., Jr. 1987. "Remarriage and Reconstituted Families." Pages 419–434 in Sussman, M. B., & Steinmetz, S. K. Eds., *Handbook of Marriage and the Family.* New York: Plenum Press.

Stein, P. J. 1981. *Single Life: Unmarried Adults in Social Context.* New York: St. Martin's Press.

Sweet, J. A., & Bumpass, L. L. 1988. *American Families and Households.* New York: Russell Sage Foundation.

White, L. 1987. "Freedom versus Constraint: The New Synthesis." *Journal of Family Issues,* 8, 468–470.

Zill, N., & Rogers, C. C. 1988. "Recent Trends in the Well Being of Children in the United States and Their Implications for Public Health." Pages 31–115 in A. Cherlin Ed., *The Changing American Family and Public Policy.* Washington, D.C.: The Urban Institute Press.

Review Questions

1. Briefly describe P. C. Glick's pros and cons about where American families are heading in the decades to come.
2. Where do you believe members of your family are heading? Why?

Summary

1. A social institution is a pattern of norms centered around a major societal goal, value, or need. Social institutions such as the family and political, educational, religious, and economic institutions are found in every society. They consist of many social groups and have definite procedures for carrying out the activities of the institution.

2. The family is the most fundamental, universal social institution. It is a socially sanctioned, relatively permanent grouping of people who are united by marriage, blood, or adoption and who generally live together and cooperate economically. The functions of the family include reproduction and the regulation of sexual behavior; the care, training, and protection of the young; socialization; ascribing initial status; and providing love and affection.

3. There have been losses and changes in family functions. Other institutions have taken over many family functions. Two major types of family structures are the nuclear family and the extended family. A less common type is the polygamous family. Two major forms of marriage relationships are monogamy and polygamy. Endogamy is marriage within a certain group; exogamy is marriage outside a certain group.

4. The family system in the United States is nuclear and monogamous, as well as endogamous and homogamous. Most marriages are between people of the same social class and religion. Interracial marriages are infrequent. Americans tend to marry within their own ethnic group. The incest taboo is the most widespread norm regarding marriage.

5. Many changes have occurred in the American family. America's average household size has declined. There has also been a decrease in the percentage of married couples among U.S. households, an increase in single-parent families, and an increase in female-headed households.

6. The United States has one of the highest divorce rates in the world. The rate is higher for lower socioeconomic levels, although the difference is decreasing. Divorce rates in the United States vary according to geographic, demographic, and social factors. Desertion and separation are more common forms of dissolving marriages among the lower social classes. Among the many difficulties caused by divorce is a drop in the standard of living.

7. Many social scientists have attributed our high divorce rate to mobility, the various stresses on the nuclear family system, and changes in family functions. It has also been explained in terms of the changing role of women and higher expectations for romantic love in marriage.

8. Violence is very much a part of American family life. Spouse and child abuse exist in all types of families. Violence in families can be accounted for in terms of cultural factors and prior socialization, in addition to psychological and economic variables.

STUDY GUIDE

Chapter Objectives

After studying this chapter, you should be able to:

1. Define "social institution"
2. List and explain the major characteristics and functions of the family as a social institution
3. Briefly describe two recent changes in the functions of the American family
4. List and briefly define the various family structures
5. Define "marriage" and describe its various forms
6. Describe the average American family
7. Describe single-parent families
8. Examine some of the issues in blended families
9. Examine divorce and its explanations
10. Describe spouse and child abuse
11. Briefly examine the explanations for abuse in the American family
12. Briefly examine the future of the American family

Key Terms

Abuse (p. 330)
Bilineal system (p. 308)
Blended families (p. 313)
Child abuse (p. 330)
Desertion (p. 327)
Egalitarian (equalitarian) family (p. 308)
Endogamy (p. 308)
Exogamy (p. 308)
Extended family (p. 305)
Family (p. 303)
Group marriage (p. 307)
Homogamy (p. 309)
Hypergamy (p. 310)
Hypogamy (p. 310)
Incest taboo (p. 310)
Institution (p. 301)
Kin (p. 305)
Marriage (p. 307)
Matriarchy (p. 308)
Matrilineal system (p. 308)
Matrilocal residence (p. 305)
Modified extended family (p. 305)
Monogamy (p. 307)
Neolocal residence (p. 305)
Nuclear family (p. 305)
Patriarchy (p. 308)
Patrilineal system (p. 308)
Patrilocal residence (p. 305)
Polyandry (p. 307)
Polygamous family (p. 305)
Polygamy (p. 307)
Polygyny (p. 307)
Serial monogamy (p. 309)
Single-parent families (p. 311)
Violence (in the family) (p. 330)

Self-Test

Short Answer

(p. 303) 1. Briefly define "family": ______

(p. 303) 2. List three functions of the family:
a. ______
b. ______
c. ______

(p. 304) 3. List two changes in American family functions:
a. ______
b. ______

(p. 305) 4. The nuclear family is ______

(p. 305) 5. The extended family is ______

(p. 308) 6. Briefly describe the average American family: ______

(p. 311) 7. Briefly describe the single-parent family: ______

(p. 330) 8. Briefly describe spouse and child abuse: ______

(p. 327) 9. List three factors that affect the U.S. divorce rate:
a. ______
b. ______
c. ______

(p. 333) 10. Briefly describe the future of the American family: ______

Multiple Choice *(Answers are on page 342.)*

(p. 302) 1. The family can be viewed as:
a. a social institution
b. a group
c. a social system
d. all the above

(p. 308) 2. Exogamy is:
a. marriage within a specific group
b. marriage outside a specific group
c. marriage within and outside a specific group
d. none of the above

(p. 310) 3. The prevailing norm of descent in American family institutions is:

a. patrilineal
b. matrilineal
c. bilineal
d. trilateral

(p. 326) 4. Today in the United States, one out of every _______ marriages end in divorce.
a. two
b. three
c. four
d. five

(p. 307) 5. Marriage is:
a. a socially accepted union of individuals in husband and wife roles, with the key function of legitimation of parenthood
b. a private matter
c. nuclear only
d. none of the above

(p. 308) 6. Descent and inheritance pass through the male side of the family in the:
a. matrilineal system
b. bilineal system
c. trilineal system
d. patrilineal system

(p. 313) 7. Blended families are:
a. one-parent families
b. extended families
c. stepfamilies
d. none of the above

(p. 302) 8. The family is:
a. a dysfunctional system
b. a social institution
c. a dying institution
d. none of the above

(p. 306) 9. Marriage is:
a. a dying social institution
b. basically only an American institution
c. for fools
d. none of the above

(p. 330) 10. Violence in the family:
a. has dramatically increased
b. has dramatically decreased
c. is about the same as it was a century ago
d. none of the above

True/False *(Answers are on page 342.)*

T F 11. The family is found in every known society. (p. 302)
T F 12. The family one establishes through marriage is called the family of kin. (p. 305)
T F 13. Polyandry means many wives or many husbands. (p. 307)
T F 14. The American family is polygamous. (p. 309)
T F 15. In America, descent and inheritance are matrilineal. (p. 310)
T F 16. Exogamy is marriage within a specific group. (p. 308)
T F 17. In the United States, child abuse is on the increase. (p. 331)
T F 18. In the United States, there has been a dramatic increase in single-parent families over the past decade. (p. 311)
T F 19. One out of every two U.S. marriages ends in divorce. (p. 326)
T F 20. The family as a social institution has changed very little in the past decade. (p. 304)

Fill-In *(Answers are on page 342.)*

(p. 305) 21. The ______ consists of a wife, a husband, and their children.

(p. 308) 22. When authority is more equally balanced between husband and wife, an ______, or ______, family exists.

(p. 309) 23. The U.S. family is ______.

(p. 309) 24. ______ is the practice of marrying one person at a time, but marrying more than one time.

(p. 309) 25. When marriage occurs outside one's social class, ______ appears to be more prevalent in our society than ______.

(p. 308) 26. A ______ exists when the authority is vested primarily in the husband.

(p. 308) 27. Descent and inheritance are traced through both sides of the family under the ______ system.

(p. 305) 28. The average American family is ______ in that it establishes a household separate from its family of orientation.

(p. 327) 29. ______ occurs when a wife or husband leaves the family without the approval of the other.

(p. 313) 30. ______ are now called *blended* families.

Matching *(Answers are on page 342.)*

31. ______ The family
32. ______ Basic function of the family
33. ______ Marriage
34. ______ Kin
35. ______ Family of orientation
36. ______ Monogamy
37. ______ Polygamy
38. ______ Incest taboo
39. ______ Divorce rates
40. ______ Homogamy

a. The family into which one is born or adopted
b. Many wives or husbands
c. People who are related by birth or marriage
d. Socialization
e. The prohibition of sexual relationships between members of a family
f. The most basic universal social institution
g. Describes mate selection among people who share similar characteristics
h. Vary with social class
i. Marriage of one male and one female
j. Complex of customs centering upon the relationship between a sexually associating pair of adults within the family

Essay Questions

1. Why are the institutions of marriage and the family important, and how have they been changing?
2. Is there such a thing as a "typical" American family? Explain your answer.
3. What are single-parent and blended families? How do they differ? Will there be more or less of these types of families in the decades to come? Explain your answers.
4. What is meant by "family violence"? How does one explain it?
5. What will the institutions of marriage and the family be like in the future? Explain your answer.

Interactive Exercises

1. As examined in this chapter, the American family is primarily nuclear, monogamous, endogamous, neolocal, bilateral, and increasingly egalitarian.
   a. What are some of your own experiences within the family in terms of the trends examined in the chapter?
   b. In what kind of family did you grow up, that is, "traditional," single-parent, dual-career, and so on, and how do you believe it affected your social and personal development?

2. The institution of marriage has changed significantly during the past couple of decades.
   a. Briefly examine your own plans regarding marriage.
   b. If you do plan marriage (and based upon materials examined in the text), what are your expectations of marriage with respect to children, finances, paid employment, housework, and the like? Are your expectations realistic?
   c. If you do not plan marriage, what are your expectations of a single person's lifestyle? Are they realistic?

3. Are you (or your mother, spouse, daughter, and so on) the primary caregiver of children and parent(s)?
   a. Explain some of the problems you (or they) have encountered.
   b. How have they been dealt with, if at all?

4. Violence exists in many American families.
   a. Briefly examine violence or abuse in your family (or a family that you know well) either in the past or the present.
   b. What caused (or is causing) the abuse or violence?
   c. How is (was) the family coping or dealing with the problem, if at all?

5. Are you an optimist or pessimist regarding the future of the American family? Explain your answer.

Answers

Answers to Self-Test

1. d
2. b
3. c
4. a
5. a
6. d
7. c
8. b
9. d
10. c
11. T
12. F
13. F
14. F
15. F
16. F
17. F
18. T
19. T
20. F
21. nuclear family
22. equalitarian, egalitarian
23. nuclear
24. serial monogamy
25. hypergamy, hypogamy
26. patriarchy
27. bilineal
28. neolocal
29. desertion
30. stepfamilies
31. f
32. d
33. j
34. c
35. a
36. i
37. b
38. e
39. h
40. g

Answers to Pretest

1. F
2. T
3. F
4. F
5. F
6. T
7. F
8. T
9. F
10. F

Chapter 9

Social Institutions: Religion, Education, and Health Care

Chapter Pretest

Let's see how much you already know about topics in this chapter:

1. **Social institutions are simply hospitals or prisons. True/False**
2. **Religion is no longer important to most Americans. True/False**
3. **Church attendance is higher in other countries than it is in the United States. True/False**
4. **The federal government basically controls American school systems. True/False**
5. **The death rate in America has dropped significantly in recent years. True/False**
6. **Japan spends more on health care than does the United States. True/False**
7. **There is a growing incidence of disease conditions in the United States. True/False**
8. **The AIDS problem in America is not as serious as most Americans believe. True/False**
9. **Most Americans are covered by some type of private health insurance. True/False**
10. **Health-care costs are no longer "out of control." True/False**

A social institution is a pattern of social norms centered about a major social goal, value, or need. In the previous chapter, we noted the importance of institutions and how they exist in all societies to meet a variety of goals. We also examined the fundamental social institutions of marriage and the family. In this chapter, we examine the social institutions of religion, education, and health care. In the following chapter, we examine the economic and political institutions.

The Religious Institution

Found in all societies, the **religious institution** meets many basic human needs not met by other social institutions. Religious institutions meet ultimate human concerns with life and death. They meet the basic human need to explain the meaning of existence.

Religion's many functions

The functions of the religious institution are as follows: First, it provides a set of beliefs that explain and interpret occurrences in the social and physical environment that cannot be explained by other means. Second, it serves a basic human need of providing people with ethical principles, morality, and a set of guidelines for appropriate behavior. Third, it provides a set of beliefs for interpreting the causes and consequences of a person's past, present, and future conduct. It provides people with answers to the why's of their existence. Fourth, it provides people with an identity as members of a specific group and a sense of connectedness with the past and future. Fifth, it provides emotional support and consolation in the face of uncertainty, anxiety, defeat, alienation, and disappointment. Other functions of the religious institution are providing unity, cohesiveness, and solidarity in a society; acting as a base from which to criticize existing social organization; and legitimizing existing social arrangements and allocations of scarce and valued rewards. O'Dea (1983) notes that legitimization may be obtained by focusing on a hereafter, by requiring believers to avoid worldly affairs, and by de-emphasizing the importance of worldly accomplishments.

Emile Durkheim

Religion as a human product

Sociologists view religion as a human product. Emile Durkheim, who studied religion among Australian tribes, stressed that religion is entirely a social phenomenon. He believed that the source of religion is group life and that religious ideals and practices symbolize the social group. Religion is also a moral community consisting of people who share common beliefs and practices.

> **A religion is a unified system of beliefs and practices relative to sacred things, that is to say, things set apart and forbidden—beliefs and practices which unite into one single moral community called a church, all those who adhere to them. The second element which thus finds a place in our definition is no less essential than the first; for by showing that the idea of religion is inseparable from that of the church, it makes it clear that religion should be an eminently collective thing (Durkheim, 1915).**

Durkheim believed that the moral community is the foundation of religion. Religion is the collective ideal, with God and heaven as reflections of this ideal. Religion creates, sustains, and celebrates community; they are inseparable. Religion exists when there is a community of believers, a combination or system of beliefs and practices, and some degree or orientation toward the sacred.

Religion itself can be defined as a "system of beliefs and practices relating to sacred things." Sacred beliefs and practices "unify people in a moral community (a church in the most general sense), a collective sharing of beliefs which in turn is essential for the development of religion" (Timasheff, 1977). Durkheim defined the **sacred** as those things set apart by people, including religious beliefs, rites, deities, or anything socially defined as requiring special religious treatment. Transcending everyday existence, the sacred is powerful and ideal, and demands respect and reverence. The *profane* is part of the mundane, ordinary world. An object or symbol becomes sacred only when a community of

Sacred and profane

believers socially define it as sacred. All societies make a distinction between the sacred and the profane. In fact, all aspects of experience can be defined in terms of these two concepts, and the distinction has important implications for social life as a whole, in Durkheim's belief.

Durkheim considered religion universal in human society because it plays a vital role in maintaining the social system as a whole. As an early functional theorist, Durkheim felt that religious ceremonies and rituals perform four significant functions:

1. a cohesive function
2. a revitalizing function
3. a euphoric function
4. a disciplinary and preparatory function

The importance of ceremonies and rituals

Religious ceremonies and rituals perform a *cohesive function* by which the social group periodically reaffirms itself. They also provide a reason for people to assemble, to express common sentiments and common acts.

A society cannot continue unless its traditions are perpetuated and its faith renewed. Many religious rituals and ceremonies therefore perform a *revitalizing function* by which the past is recalled and made present by a dramatic representation. Ceremony functions to "awaken certain ideas and sentiments, to attach the present to the past or the individual to the group" (Durkheim, 1915).

Religious ceremonies and rituals also perform a *euphoric function* by giving people a pleasant feeling of social well-being. Although all groups have crises and losses, through ceremony and ritual, the group attempts to offset these disruptive aspects. For example:

> **The mourning ceremony requires individuals to have and to express certain emotions and sentiments and, more important, to express these sentiments together. This coming together of afflicted persons and sharing of loss renew the collective sentiments and a sensation of comfort is established which compensates for the loss. In these ways, ritual and ceremony serve to remake individuals and groups morally (Vine, 1959).**

Finally, religious rituals perform a *disciplinary and preparatory function* by imposing self-discipline on individuals and preparing them for life.

Karl Marx

A form of false consciousness

Karl Marx's views on religion were quite different from Durkheim's. Durkheim saw religion, with its ceremonies and rituals, as performing a needed function for society. Marx viewed religion as a form of false consciousness and a tool that legitimizes the power of the ruling classes. For Marx, the dominant religion in any society is always the religion of the ruling class. Religion develops as a justification for existing social inequalities and supports the ruling class's economically and politically privileged position.

Marx viewed religion as the "opiate of the people," developing among the oppressed and poor to cope with a life in which they have few advantages. Promised a better situation in the next life, the working classes are blinded to the possibilities of making a better life on earth. All religious institutions inhibit change by supporting and legitimizing the status quo.

Some sociologists believe that Marx's ideas fail to take into account religion's independent status as a social fact apart from its relation to the class structure; moreover, his views do not consider many other functions that religion performs in a society.

Max Weber

Religion influences economic systems

Marx believed that a society's economic system influences the character of its religious belief system, whereas Max Weber (1958) believed that a society's religious beliefs may influence economic systems and cause social change. Interested in the growth of modern capitalism, Weber examined its relationship to early Calvinist Protestantism. He believed that Protestantism, as a set of religious values, resulted in the development of certain western forms of economy and society.

Religion in America

Distinctive features of American religious institutions

Religion in America is different in many ways from religion in many other parts of the world. The following are some of the relatively distinctive features of American religious institutions: First, there is no established church because of the principle of separation of church and state. Second, many different religious groups coexist that embody a society of beliefs. Third, there is an emphasis on religious toleration and a relatively high degree of religious freedom. Fourth, there are pervasive tendencies to emphasize the perfectibility of people and the possibility of human progress.

There also has been a comparatively far-reaching secularization of beliefs in society. **Secularization** is a process by which society's traditional religious beliefs and institutions lose their influence.

Some social scientists believe that religion in the United States is on the decline. It is on a decline because of a general decadence, the expansion of science, and the fact that other social institutions provide value instruction without attention to religious norms. Church attendance has steadily declined during the past 30 years.

Other social scientists believe that religion remains very important and will continue to be important in America. Religion will be important because science and the secular world have failed to provide the explanations that people need. Eighty percent of adult Americans state that religious beliefs are very or fairly important to them. Only 15 percent of American adults claim that religious beliefs are not important to them. The majority of Americans are also formally linked to a church. In the United States, religion is predominantly Christian. Over 90 percent of the population is Protestant or Catholic.

Some studies have indicated that Americans are among the most religious people in the world. In point of fact, a national Associated Press poll reported that 86 percent of the respondents indicated that religion was very or fairly important in their lives. In addition, 62 percent reported that they had attended a religious service in the past month. Also, 64 percent reported that they believed "religion could answer all or most of today's problems" (*The Philadelphia Inquirer*, Jan. 6, 1991).

The most religious people in the world

With respect to American church membership, there have been significant, unprecedented shifts during the past two decades. Mainline Protestantism has experienced a sharp decline in church membership in recent years. Mainline Protestantism generally refers to the old, culturally established white Protestant churches, such as the United Church of Christ, the Presbyterian Church, the Episcopal Church, and others that belong to the National Council of Churches. According to Richard Ostling (*Time*, May 22, 1989), during the past several decades, church membership has dropped 20 percent in the United Church of Christ, 25 percent in the Presbyterian Church, 28 percent in the Episcopal Church, 18 percent in the United Methodist Church, and 43 percent in the Christian Church (Disciples of Christ). On the other hand, during this same period of time, church membership has significantly grown among the black Protestant churches, the Roman Catholic church (16 percent), and the conservative evangelical churches. These changes have been explained in terms of demographic and cultural factors. They have also been explained in terms of the mainline congregations' being preoccupied with social and political issues that have alienated many church members "at the expense of good old-fashioned faith" (*Time*, May 22, 1989).

The mainline decline

In America, the religious institution is related to other social institutions in various ways. For example, with regard to the family, most people marry someone of the same religion, and there are significant differences in marital stability among persons of different religions. An individual's religious beliefs are related to career choices, work habits, and political participation. With respect to education, there is a strong relationship between a person's educational achievement level and how often he or she attends religious services. Catholics and Protestants who have attended college or have a grade school education are more likely to attend church than those who have a high school education. Also there are strong correlations between religious affiliation and educational achievement. Among the major religious denominations in the United States, Jews and Episcopalians are the most likely to have attended college.

The religious institution is related to other social institutions

RELIGION AND THE CONSTITUTION: THE SUPREME COURT SPEAKS AGAIN

D. Grier Stephenson, Jr.

In the following reading, "Religion and the Constitution: The Supreme Court Speaks Again," D. Grier Stephenson, Jr., examines the relationship between religion and government. More specifically, he examines the Supreme Court decision that addresses whether or not the government may observe religious holidays by displaying sectarian symbols on public property.

Among decisions the Supreme Court announced on the closing day of its 1988–89 term (July 3, 1989) was the abortion case, *Webster v. Reproductive Health Services.* It instantly captured the nation's news reporting apparatus and reinvigorated a national debate that shows no sign of abating. Barely noticed was a second and potentially far-reaching decision, *Allegheny County v. American Civil Liberties Union,* that involved an issue of long standing—religion and the Constitution. Specifically, the question was whether government may observe religious holidays by displaying sectarian symbols on public property. The answer the Court gave reflected the contentious nature of church-state relations.

Since the winter holiday season of 1981, officials in Pittsburgh annually had erected a creche on the Grand Staircase in the Allegheny County Courthouse. In 1982, they added a menorah, which was displayed on the steps of the nearby City-County Building. The Pittsburgh chapter of the American Civil Liberties Union filed suit in Federal district court, charging that the displays violated the First Amendment's bans on laws "respecting an establishment of religion."

Controversy over the First Amendment is a reminder that religious freedom in America is a subject even older than the Constitution. The widespread notions today that government should not meddle in religion and that all beliefs should stand equal before the law would have seemed strange to many who settled America before the Revolution. Their tradition was different. The question was not whether government would influence religion and vice versa, but which religion.

In their earliest settlements, for example, some New Englanders bet on the wisdom of a virtual union of *their* church and state. From the beginning, Pennsylvania granted freedom of conscience to all who believed in God, but the Charter of Privileges of 1701 directed would-be officeholders to profess a belief in Christ. Practically on the eve of the Constitutional Convention of 1787, Virginia came close to reinstating a general taxpayer assessment in support of religious congregations. For almost 20 years before the Revolution, the Anglican Church in Georgia was supported by a tax on liquor, giving a new meaning to sin taxes. The state's constitution of 1777 allowed only Protestants to sit in the legislature, but had no religious test for voters. After experimenting with toleration, Maryland denied the vote to Catholics in 1718. Until 1961, the same state required public officeholders to declare belief in the existence of God. From 1796 until at least 1978, the constitutions of several states made members of the clergy ineligible to be legislators.

Such practices and constraints are gone, but new concerns have taken their place. Religious leaders routinely take positions on issues of national importance, including foreign and defense policy, racial justice, income redistribution, and abortion. Two members of the clergy—Pat Robertson and Jesse Jackson—ran for president in 1988. Congregations take in refugees in defiance of the immigration laws. Pres. Ronald Reagan campaigned for the restoration of spoken prayer in the public schools, by constitutional amendment if necessary. Conflict over religious freedom continues to churn, just as it always has.

Understanding how the Supreme Court affects religious freedom today requires a grasp of constitutional context, which has at least three fundamental parts: the existence of the Constitution, with the Bill of Rights; the doctrine of judicial review; and the nationalization of the Bill of Rights.

In the original text of the Constitution, there is only a single, but nonetheless significant, reference to religion. Article VI declares: "no religious Test shall ever be required as a Qualification to any Office or public Trust under the United States." From the beginning, the Constitution precluded a policy for the nation that was followed by most of the American states and virtually every other country at that time. In its leadership, the Federal government could not be sectarian.

The First Amendment, which became part of the Constitution in 1791, declares, "Congress shall make no law respecting an establishment of religion, or prohibiting the free exercise thereof." It should not be surprising that the framers addressed the subject of religion. No government, then or now, stands indifferent on this issue. A nation may protect toleration while permitting establishment—Great Britain, for example; choose establishment and deny toleration—as in Iran; or reject both toleration and establishment—as the Soviet Union has. In America, however, the Constitution says yes to toleration and no to establishment.

The twin provisions of non-establishment and free exercise have complementary objectives—to guard individual liberty and maintain the civil peace. The free exercise clause preserves a sphere of religious practice free of interference by the government. Americans of 200 years ago did not necessarily crave toleration for beliefs other than their own. Given the presence of so many faiths, they simply had no choice. The alternative was unacceptable.

The establishment clause limits government support of religious endeavors and, more importantly, bars it from becoming the tool of one faith against others. That had happened in Europe before and after the Reformation, as well as in the American colonies. Combined with the ban on religious tests for public office in Article VI, the establishment clause commanded that it would not happen again. Even though a few states still maintained some form of established church in 1791, the First Amendment declared that the nation could not have one. Non-establishment was part of the price of union. The first Amendment set the government off limits as a prize in a nation of competing faiths.

With the Bill of Rights as part of the Constitution, it became immensely significant that the Supreme Court shortly assumed the role of guardian of that document. This is the second element in the context of religious freedom. Through the development of judicial review—the authority courts have to invalidate policies and statutes that, in their view, run counter to the Constitution—judges are able to decide what the Constitution means.

Judicial review lies at the heart of the third element in the constitutional context of religious freedom. Initially, the First Amendment and the rest of the Bill of Rights applied only to the national government. Except for a few explicit restrictions in the main body of the Constitution, states were restrained only by their individual state constitutions, not by the Federal Bill of Rights.

It took a long time to close the gap. The first step came with ratification of the Fourteenth Amendment in 1868. With words such as "due process of law" and "liberty," section one contained majestic and undefined checks on state power that begged for interpretation. With revolutionary impact, the justices seized on the ambiguities of the Fourteenth Amendment and gradually read almost every provision of the Bill of Rights, including the religion clauses, into it. This was the second step in closing the gap of 1791. State and local governments became bound by the same restrictions that had applied to the national government all along.

There is some irony in this development. In 1789, some states had favored the establishment clause precisely because it would protect their own forms of state establishment from interference by Congress. Little did they anticipate that a later amendment—the Fourteenth—would aim that same clause at themselves someday.

Thus it was the Fourteenth Amendment that gave the Supreme Court the last word in the Pittsburgh creche/menorah case. Its decision derives from a two-part constitutional tradition. The first includes a line of cases that have challenged public financial support for sectarian schools. The second includes several cases attacking religious observances in public schools. In both parts of this tradition, the Court generally, but not consistently, has taken a "separationist" stance in place of an "accommodationist" one. That is, in most instances, a majority of the justices since World War II have not hesitated to find a transgression of the establishment clause. They have rejected an interpretation which would uphold most government programs challenged under the clause.

At the basis of both halves of this tradition lies *Everson v. Board of Education of Ewing Township* (1947). By five votes to four, this decision upheld the constitutionality of a New Jersey policy allowing reimbursement of bus fares parents paid for transportation of their children to both public and private, sectarian and nonsectarian, schools. Refusing to restrict the meaning of the establishment clause literally to a ban on a state church, the majority set forth the principle that the First Amendment erected a "wall of separation" between church and state. Justice Hugo Black declared: "Neither a state nor the Federal Government can set up a church. Neither can pass laws which aid one religion, aid all religions, or prefer one religion over another. . . . No tax in any amount, large or small, can be levied to support any religious activities or institutions, whatever they may be called, or whatever form they may adopt to teach or practice religion."

That landmark case is noteworthy in at least four respects. For the first time, the Supreme Court applied the establishment clause to the states through the Fourteenth Amendment. Second, Justice Black expressed a 20th-century understanding of religious freedom, not one locked into the 18th-century. He said that government should not take sides between religion and non-religion, not merely that it should avoid favoring one faith over another. A majority of the Constitution's framers would have agreed with the latter view, but it probably would have come as a surprise to most to learn that their Constitution forbade the former.

Third, the analogy of a "wall" separating church and state—the words were Thomas Jefferson's—is not very helpful. Religion and government must interact in numerous ways. To speak of a "wall of separation" thus belies reality. The real difficulty lies in distinguishing permissible from impermissible interactions.

Fourth, even though the Court's language in *Everson* was sweeping, the New Jersey statute providing for reimbursement of bus fares was upheld. The decision was like a foot in the door. Pressures have persisted to see how much additional aid passes muster under the establishment clause.

THE LEMON TEST

In response, the Court developed a three-pronged test, first clearly articulated in *Lemon v. Kurtzman* (1971). This decision also is significant because it was the first case the Supreme Court decided involving substantial public financial assistance for sectarian schools and the first time the Court found a sectarian school aid policy in conflict with the establishment clause. Under the Lemon test, the Court first requires that the statute in question have a secular purpose. Second, the law must have a neutral effect—that is, it must operate primarily neither to hinder nor advance religion. Third, the law must not promote excessive entanglement between church and state—*i.e.,* neither government nor religion should become involved too closely in the affairs of the other. To be snared on any of the three prongs dooms the policy in question. Especially deadly is the combination of prongs two and three. Steps taken to assure a neutral effect have been found to create excessive entanglement. Without entanglement, there can be no assurance of a neutral effect.

The Lemon test has not produced predictable results. The Court has accepted, for example, on-premises diagnostic and off-premises therapeutic services for sectarian school pupils performed by state employees; supplemental grants to schools to pay for testing and scoring required by the state; textbook loans to pupils; bus transportation to and from school; state income tax deductions for educational expenses at private and public schools; and construction funds for church-related colleges.

Judged not acceptable are tuition reimbursement by the state to parents of children in sectarian schools; bus transportation for field trips; state grants for school building maintenance; supplements for teachers' salaries; and loaning instructional materials to pupils or their schools. Also unacceptable are "shared time" programs with supplemental classes in specialized subjects taught by public school teachers to sectarian school pupils on sectarian school premises.

Does this record make sense? Has the Supreme Court been playing darts with the establishment clause and Trivial Pursuit with the Bill of Rights? Nevertheless, the total effect may be clear—direct and substantial support for a healthy sectarian alternative to public education is constitutionally unacceptable.

One should say "may be clear" because of *Bowen v. Kendrick* (1988). The Adolescent Family Life Act of 1981—dubbed the Chastity Act by its opponents—authorizes Federal grants to organizations that provide services related to teenage sexual relations and pregnancy. Some of these subsidies go to religious groups. Five justices, including Anthony Kennedy, the newest member of the court, upheld the law in principle against a challenge that it violated the establishment clause. Only groups which are "pervasively sectarian," as opposed to those that are merely "religion-inspired," might have to be excluded on constitutional grounds. If this program successfully can avoid the prongs of the Lemon test, some direct and substantial school aid conceivably might do so as well.

The second part of the church-state constitutional tradition involves religious observances in public schools. *Engel v. Vitale*

(1962) invalidated the use in New York's public schools of a short prayer, approved by the Board of Regents, which children recited during opening exercises of each school day. The following term, in *Abington Township School Board v. Schempp,* Pennsylvania and Maryland statutes providing for daily Bible reading in public schools met a similar fate. Reaction to the school prayer and Bible reading cases was heated. The House of Representatives unanimously passed a resolution to have the motto "In God We Trust" engraved on the wall above the Speaker's dais in the House chamber. The motto is still there for all to see.

The Supreme Court never has said that students may not pray in school—they have been doing that before exams for years. However, the Court has remained firm in its opposition to *state-sponsored* religious activities in public schools. In *Wallace v. Jaffree* (1985), for instance, an Alabama statute authorizing a period of silence at the start of the school day for "meditation or voluntary prayer" was judged constitutionally defective because the law endorsed religion as a preferred activity. Even Justice Sandra O'Connor, Pres. Reagan's first nominee to the Court, agreed.

However, most justices hinted that it would be all right to have a law setting aside a moment of silence where it is not obvious from the record that the state's purpose is one of restoring prayer to the schools and making an end run around the First Amendment. It was this same strong suspicion of state-sponsored religion that led seven justices, in *Edwards v. Aguillard* (1987), to invalidate a Louisiana law requiring the teaching of creation-science in the public schools if evolution theory was taught.

Yet, could not both the Alabama and Louisiana laws be defended on free exercise grounds? From this perspective, Alabama set aside time in school for students to practice their religious faith. Louisiana assured a balanced education by exposing students to a theory that better fit the biblical account of creation. No, said the Court. The free exercise clause is applicable only where there is a burden on religion imposed by the state, not where government merely seeks to enlarge the religious options of its citizens.

Because of the impressionable nature of school pupils and the unique role schools long have had in the life of the nation, the Court has been quickest to strike down religious influences in the classroom. Elsewhere, the Court sometimes winks. In *Marsh v. Chambers* (1983), for example, six justices approved the Nebraska practice of paying the state legislature's chaplain out of public funds. In *Lynch vs. Donnelly* (1984), five justices (the *Marsh* majority, minus Harry Blackmun) allowed city officials in Pawtucket, R.I., to erect a municipally owned Christmas display, including a creche, in a private park.

MIXED SIGNALS IN PITTSBURGH

Yet, in the Pittsburgh creche/menorah case, the Court limited the degree to which localities may recognize religious holidays through the erection of displays. In the Pawtucket instance, the creche was municipally owned, but placed in a private park. It also was part of a larger holiday display, complete with Santa's house, reindeer, candy-striped poles, carolers, a teddy bear, and a sign reading "Season's Greetings."

In contrast, the creche and menorah in Pittsburgh were privately owned, but displayed on public property. Except for red and white poinsettias and two small evergreen trees, the creche was unadorned by secular holiday trappings. With it was an angel holding a banner that proclaimed *Gloria in Excelsis Deo* ("Glory to God in the Highest") and a sign indicating that the display was the donation of the Holy Name Society. The 18-foot menorah was set next to a 45-foot tree, decorated with holiday ornaments. In front of the tree was a sign bearing the mayor's name and a statement: "During this holiday season, the City of Pittsburgh salutes liberty. Let these festive lights remind us that we are the keepers of the flame of liberty and our legacy of freedom."

In a badly fractured decision, with no one of the five opinions entirely receiving the approval of even a bare majority of the bench, six justices (Blackmun, O'Connor, Kennedy, William Rehnquist, Antonin Scalia, and Byron White) found the exterior menorah and tree display constitutionally acceptable, but five (Blackmun, O'Connor, William Brennan, Thurgood Marshall, and John Stevens) found the interior nativity scene constitutionally offensive. Four justices agreed that both displays were acceptable, while three decided both were unacceptable. Blackmun and O'Connor approved one (the menorah), but not the other (the creche). Of the justices who took part in both the Pawtucket and Pittsburgh cases, only Blackmun and O'Connor deviated—he had voted against the Pawtucket display, while hers had been a reluctant fifth vote upholding it.

The five opinions suggest that the surroundings of the Pittsburgh displays were decisive. The creche with the banner was unacceptable because it "endorsed" religion. The menorah alongside the tree was acceptable since it only "recognized" religion. What does it mean to recognize without endorsing religion? According to the Pittsburgh decision, a display, at most, may suggest religion vaguely. If the religious message is forthright, especially if it appears in a setting undiluted by secular symbols, government crosses the line of constitutionality. So, religous displays on public property are acceptable only if they have become secularized. Religious groups might conclude reasonably that this half-loaf is worse than none.

Meanwhile, separatists should consider the Pittsburgh case a Pyrrhic victory. After all, four justices found no objection to the creche, even though it was unadorned by secular symbols. Moreover, in his opinion for the four, Kennedy, whom the Senate preferred overwhelmingly to Robert Bork, called for modification of the Lemon test. Government violates the establishment clause only when it coerces "anyone to support or participate in any religion or its exercise" or gives "direct benefits to religion" that amount to "proselytizing." If Kennedy acquires a fifth vote for this view, the Court will veer from separation to accommodation. It will move toward outright approval of widespread religious expression in the public life of the nation and, perhaps, toward a more permissive attitude regarding state aid to sectarian schools.

In the coming years, these and other controversies will continue to probe the fuzzy boundaries of the establishment clause. The framers bequeathed certain values by way of a written Constitution and left it to later generations to apply those values to situations they could not foresee. The establishment clause calls for separation, while the free exercise clause leaves Americans free to work for objectives dictated by their faiths. Together, they guarantee that the division mandated by the one forever will be tested because of the freedom assured by the other.

Review Questions

1. Briefly examine what is meant by the "Lemon test."
2. Do you believe government has the right to observe religious holidays by displaying sectarian symbols on public property? Explain your answer.

The Educational Institution

Education has been removed from religious and kinship groupings

A distinguishing mark of modern secular society is that education has been removed from religion and kinship groupings. Even though American religious bodies conduct extensive educational activity and families "do not always turn over their children to the school completely, or without reservations and emotional ambivalence, the degree of separation of formal education from family and church is extraordinarily extensive and sharp" (Williams, 1970). No longer permitted in public schools, religion does not support as much of the educational process as it did in the past.

The continuing goal of socializing the young

The primary goal of the **educational institution** is the socialization of young people. More than 90 years ago, Emile Durkheim (1956) told student teachers at the University of Paris that education "consists of a methodical socialization of the younger generation. . . . [It] is above all the means by which society perpetually recreates the conditions of its very existence."

Education as a conserver of culture

Durkheim stressed the role of formal education as a conserver of culture. The social institution of education reflects rather than transforms the social structure. Lester Ward sees this institution as an instrument of social improvement, where the educated person gains happiness as a valuable by-product. It can also be viewed as the means by which the status quo obtains or keeps power, wealth, and prestige.

Educational institutions are necessary because of two irreducible facts: Human culture is not biologically inherited, but learned; and very young people develop social personalities through adult care and teaching. A society's cultural heritage must be renewed in each generation. For many people in the world today, and throughout most of human history, education has been part of society's ordinary routine and has not been provided by specialized personnel functioning in a separate organization. The young have been instructed in the values, beliefs, customs, knowledge, and skills of their respective cultures by parents, priests, craftspeople, and warriors. Institutionalized education, as we know it in the United States, is not necessary in societies in which the young learn by observing and helping their parents and others. However, even in "simple" cultures, one can find formalized education. As stated by Williams (1970), "Some formalized education is found in even the 'simplest' cultures; if not schools in our sense, there are definitely institutionalized and systematic patterns of indoctrination and instructions—for instance, secret societies or initiation rules."

The Educational Institution in the United States

Large, complex organizational structures meet America's educational needs

In the United States, knowledge and occupational training are too complex to be taught by informal methods. Our society has developed an enormous, complex organizational structure to meet its educational needs. Consisting of administrators, teachers, and students, the public and private schools generally emphasize such cultural values as the practical usefulness of formal education, competitive success, conformity to middle-class group standards, and the creed of patriotic and democratic values.

The educational institution has the continuing goal of socializing the young.

State and local governments control American school systems, although some national controls are visible. Public schools are also funded primarily by property taxes, with some federal and state aid. The almost obvious feature of the school is that it is a formal, highly bureaucratized organization. Authority is centered in the chief administrator at various levels of a firmly established hierarchy whose procedures are standardized to ensure an orderly and predictable functioning. In the interests of efficiency, the American educational process has been rationalized. In many respects, this bureaucratization has resulted in a repressive atmosphere in which students are obliged to sit in a militarylike fashion and remain quiet for hours, to obtain permission to use the toilet, and to walk in straight lines. With an omnipresent grading system, students proceed through a continuous series of stages from the prenursery school to the university.

Functions of the educational institution

The American educational institution performs a number of functions. First, it systematically socializes the young in order that the society may be perpetuated and the status quo preserved. Schools, which are the social organizations of the educational institution, transmit a society's values, attitudes, beliefs, norms, specific skills, and systems of knowledge to young people. Second, it recruits young people for specific occupational and social roles by sorting out those who are "best suited" for the top occupational positions in society. Third, it keeps young people out of the labor market in order to provide older people maximum employment opportunities. Fourth, it promotes technological change in society by providing the basis of knowledge and skills that enable technological innovation to occur.

THINKING GLOBALLY: EDUCATING AMERICANS FOR THE 21st CENTURY

Philip R. Piccigallo

Because there exists a significant link between education, the economy, and our country's ability to compete in a globalized marketplace, there has been an increase in focus on international education. The following reading, "Thinking Globally: Educating Americans for the 21st Century," by Philip R. Piccigallo, emphasizes the point that only an American "workforce sufficiently educated to compete internationally can assure rapid economic growth and the reassertion of American industrial world leadership . . ."

In governors' and state economic development offices, universities and schools, corporate boardrooms, and professional associations across the country, Americans are thinking globally. The focus increasingly is on international education—the formal study of world history and geography, foreign peoples, languages and cultures, and comparative social, political, economic, and education systems. Invariably emphasized in such efforts is the inextricable link between education, the economy, and America's ability to compete in a globalized marketplace. Many ultimately view success in these areas as essential to our national security.

"Yesterday, globalization was a word. Today, it's a reality," trumpeted a recent advertisement by a prominent American bank with worldwide interests. *The Washington Post* observed in September, 1988, that "economic sovereignty is becoming to an important degree an illusion." As historian Paul Gagnon noted, "However banal the phrase 'global consciousness' has become, a number of striking economic realities have fueled a growing interest in an informed citizenry capable of understanding different cultures, languages, business practices, and world affairs." Consider, for example, what the following indicators of economic globalization mean for the U.S.

- Foreign trade accounts for 20% of GNP, up from 10% in 1960.
- One-third of corporate profits, 20% of all jobs, and 80% of new ones are created by world trade.
- One-third of all farm products are sold in foreign markets.
- Virtually all U.S. export products will face stiff foreign competition by 1990, as compared to less than 25% in 1960.
- Exports of goods and services represent more than eight percent of GNP. Meanwhile, the U.S. depends on developing countries for 25% of its exports and well over 50% of vital material resources for its major industries and national defense.

At the same time, many of these developing countries, particularly in Latin America, are beset with serious debt, slow economic development, commodity price collapse, and political difficulties. Failure to solve these problems ultimately means shrinking markets for American exports.

Furthermore, the debt burden of less-developed countries no longer can be treated as merely a private banking problem. "More fundamentally, it is a trade problem, a jobs problem, and a geopolitical problem" of critical significance to U.S. foreign policy and the domestic economy, American Express Company chairman James D. Robinson, 3rd, recently underscored. Studies by the National Academy of Sciences and New York Gov. Mario M. Cuomo's Commission on Trade and Competitiveness emphasized the need to accept American security interests as inseparable from such macroeconomic factors as national economic development, trade, and fiscal policy.

GLOBALIZATION'S DARK SIDE

In short, as one chief executive officer put it, there is a "dark side of globalization." For Americans, it means that our way of life inevitably is intertwined with the economic fortunes of the remaining 95% of the world's population.

State initiatives. Not surprisingly, then, efforts to internationalize school and college curriculums are under way. Consider activity on the state level. "Americans do not realize the effect our international ignorance has on our national security" and ability to conduct business abroad, observed the Southern Governors' Association in 1986. Its report, "International Education: Cornerstone of Competition," outlined a "blueprint for state action to build international perspectives in the school and in the workplace." Also in 1988, the National Governors' Association launched its agenda, "America in Transition: The International Frontier." Foremost, the organization emphasized the need to identify "what skills Americans will need to compete in the global marketplace."

Such efforts are intended to build upon and expand initiatives already under way in various states. These include the establishment of "sister" relationships with schools abroad; student-teacher exchange programs; partnerships between schools, colleges, government, and private businesses; state-sponsored international events (*e.g.,* model United Nations); and programs designed to enrich students' and teachers' international understanding at all levels. Programs focus on five principal areas: geography awareness, international studies, language instruction, teacher training, and programs targeted at businesses and professionals beyond the education field.

The Joint National Committee on Languages reported in 1987 that 25 states either mandate course work in international studies for high school graduation or include a more global perspective in the social studies curriculum from kindergarten through the 12th grade. Thirty states have instituted some form of language requirement. Nearly all states require that secondary schools offer at least two years of a foreign language for accreditation. The National Council for the Accreditation of Teachers, in cooperation with the American Association of Colleges for Teacher Education, has evolved an accreditation standard which recognizes "that global perspectives should permeate all aspects of teacher education programs."

In virtually all states, there are examples of government, state departments of education, public and private schools and colleges, and the professional and business communities working closely together to further international understanding. Joint funding is common. Some state programs operate under grants received from private organizations such as the National Geographic Society and the Rockefeller, Ford, and Danforth Foundations. A number of governors have established broadly representative advisory councils on international education or independent educational units functioning under the auspices of such quasi-public institutions as trade centers or port authorities.

Higher education. Building on a history of support dating to the early 1900's, American colleges and universities warmly have embraced the notion of international studies. A 1988 report sponsored by the American Council on Education (ACE) disclosed that various "centers for international studies" now flourish at hundreds of public and private institutions. They feature a spectrum of international and multilingual course offerings, revitalized international library collections, and opportunities for study and faculty travel abroad. Academics and business people with international backgrounds and former diplomats are recruited vigorously. Campus-wide programs, projects, and special events regularly focus on world issues, business, and politics. While there appeared to be greater involvement in and support for global studies at four-year institutions than two-year colleges, the presidents or chief academic officers at nearly half of the two-year colleges judged international studies "very important."

Support for international studies has come from the highest levels of academia. The ACE, for example, in a 1984 report, "What We Don't Know, Can Hurt Us," noted that "a shrinking, interdependent world has placed an even higher premium on sound levels of international competency." Ernest T. Boyer, president of the Carnegie Foundation for the Advancement of Teaching, similarly identified the educational needs of an increasingly globalized economy in his 1986 study of American undergraduate institutions.

Perhaps most notably, the Commission on National Challenges—comprised of 33 leading citizens, mostly college and university presidents—in its January, 1989, "Memorandum to the 41st President of the United States," placed first among its recommendations the need to "educate Americans for an increasingly interdependent world." It urged strengthening "all fields of international study and research," particularly student and faculty exchange programs, and the teaching and study of foreign languages.

The business community. It is the sobering, bottom-line assessments offered by business leaders that, perhaps more than anything else, are compelling Americans to think broadly about education. David T. Kearns, chairman of the Xerox Corporation, captured national attention in 1987 when he told the Economic Club of Detroit that inadequately prepared workers are costing industry $25,000,000,000 annually in remedial programs. "Public education," he stated, "has put this country at a terrible competitive disadvantage" with other nations. Other business-oriented groups, notably the Committee for Economic Development and the Business Council, have echoed these grim warnings.

At the core of such arguments is the invisible bond between education, the economy, and America's global economic prowess. Only a workforce sufficiently educated to compete internationally can assure rapid economic growth and the reassertion of American industrial world leadership into the next century, said a Hudson Institute study, *Workforce 2000.*

There is another area where business, education, and international concerns directly converge. Since the President's Commission on Industrial Competitiveness allocated top priority to trade in 1985, export promotion initiatives have sprung up and accelerated across the nation. The states have taken the lead in this campaign to compete with aggressive, export-driven global rivals and to redress a trade imbalance currently hovering around $130,000,000,000.

Successful direct exporting, explains the U.S. Department of Commerce's *Guide to Exporting from the United States,* "requires gaining knowledge of foreign buyer needs and tastes, as well as different and more complex channels of distribution." The ability to communicate is paramount, and exporters must cope with different time zones, languages, and customs. Equally important is understanding international business practices, taxes, government regulations, laws, currency, transportation, credit systems, and political conditions. In short, successful exporting demands the multicultural literacy, language skills, and global awareness many Americans, even senior business executives, presently lack.

Education is central to exporting. "The first challenge for state export promotion programs is to stimulate interest in exporting," notes the National Governors' Association. To accomplish this, governors, state economic development offices, and quasi-public world trade centers offer a wide range of seminars, conferences, trade shows, exchange programs, publications, and other initiatives. All are intended to educate the business community and general public on the significance of international trade to the state and national economies. They also are designed to alert prospective exporters of potential opportunities in international markets by providing direct trade leads acquired through developmental offices and overseas representatives.

In addition, a number of working coalitions representing business, educational associations, and universities focus on the international dimensions of education. Such private and quasi-private groups as the Business-Higher Education Forum, the Council on Competitiveness Affiliates, and the American Society for Training and Development promote ways to educate and retrain employees to meet the challenges of emerging technology. All stress the importance of instilling greater global consciousness into every aspect of worker development.

Business schools also have been stirred by globalization. A 1988 report commissioned by the American Assembly of Collegiate Schools of Business, "Management Education and Development: Drift or Thrust Into the 21st Century?," found many schools unresponsive to the new international economic environment. It urged far greater attention to present and future changes in the world arena in which business operates. While noting the relative insularity of business education, Sven Groennings of the New England Board of Higher Education observed the evolution of accreditation standards "which made it very clear that every business student should be exposed to the international dimension through one or more elements of the curriculum."

Furthermore, many business schools participate in state-sponsored activities. In some states, for example, MBA students from leading graduate business schools join with faculty and economic development officers in tailoring international marketing plans for prospective exporters.

THE FEDERAL ROLE

Washington has been relatively frugal in appropriating funds for international studies. Still, one of the three major Federal initiatives, the Fulbright Scholarship exchange program (the National Education Defense Act of 1958 and the International Education Act of 1966 are the other two), has escaped drastic cuts in funding. Moreover, various U.S. departments (Commerce, Agriculture) and agencies (Agency for International Development, Small Business Administration) offer a broad range of informational and financial assistance to businesses, private associations, universities, and schools interested in world affairs. Federal grants help subsidize international studies programs at many schools. There are also a number of smaller, specialty programs, such as the President's International Youth Exchange Initiative and the U.S. Information

Agency (USIA) international visitor's program, administered through the privately run Institute for International Education. In September 1988, USIA officials announced a program that permits the Soviet Union and the U.S. each to exchange up to 1,500 high school students annually by 1991.

Nor did the 100th Congress ignore international education. The trade bill enacted in August, 1988, provided $85,000,000 to improve higher education research facilities and addressed the issue of bottom-up, comprehensive educational improvement to strengthen global competitiveness. Moreover, the Foreign Language Assistance Act of 1988 mandated Federal grants to state educational agencies. The U.S.'s "economic and security interests," it states, "require significant improvement in the quantity and quality of foreign language instruction" in elementary and secondary schools. In 1988, Virginia became the first state to receive Federal funding for half-day "immersion programs" in French, Spanish, and Japanese at the kindergarten and first-grade levels.

Interest in educating Americans to deal effectively and responsibly in the world community is strong and swelling. In December, 1988, President-elect George Bush expressed agreement with 10 university presidents on the "importance of international exchange programs for scholars and students" and global studies in general. Still, there is much to do. The quality and efficacy of many new or revitalized programs await future evaluation.

The present interest reflects to a degree the national mood to improve education generally. It is to be hoped that it also reflects man's nobler instincts, reminiscent of an earlier day. As Peace Corps volunteers spread across the globe in the 1960's, the U.S. enthusiastically endorsed UNESCO's call for "Education for International Understanding, Cooperation and Peace and Education Relating to Human Rights and Fundamental Freedoms." The Foreign Assistance Act of 1975, moreover, encouraged "American agricultural universities to work collaboratively with less-developed countries in solving problems of hunger and inadequate agricultural production." Today, it is 45 university presidents from around the world resolving to develop common curriculums on disarmament and the theory and practice of global conflict management in their institutions.

At the same time, present interest embodies a distinct motivating element of the broader reform movement. There is fear that America is losing its ability to compete internationally, export aggressively, and adapt rapidly to conditions that many feel threaten its national security. It is likely that dynamic international change will heighten these challenges. The U.S. must deal with European unification in 1992, economic maturation of many developing countries, *perestroika* in the Soviet Union, and Green Revolution advances that have eliminated China's, India's, and Bangladesh's need to import food products.

How we respond will determine America's world role in the next century. Rarely have diverse societal forces joined so closely in identifying a national crisis and its intended solution. ". . . Once again it has occurred to policy makers that our success in the marketplace is connected to the way we educate our young people," wrote Evelyn E. Handler, president of Brandeis University, in March, 1987. "So once again education is being asked to solve a national problem." Few would disagree.

No less important, however, must be our departure, once and for all, from a tradition of isolationism deeply rooted in our nation's past. Thinking and learning globally is the first step in the right direction.

Review Questions

1. Briefly comment on the following statement: "Only a workforce sufficiently educated to compete internationally can assure rapid economic growth and the reassertion of American industrial leadership."
2. Do you believe America will have the ability to "think and learn globally" in the 21st century? Explain your answer.

Health and the Health-Care Institution

As with religious and educational needs, the health needs of Americans are important. A society cannot exist unless the health-care needs of its members are adequately met. In the past, the family provided the basic health-care needs of its members. As our society became more complex and technologically advanced, physicians, technicians, hospitals, insurance providers, and the government increasingly have provided much of our health care.

Health care is a complex institution

As we will shortly examine, in America the **health-care institution**—the pattern of norms centered about health-care goals, values, and needs—is quite complex. In fact, in the United States there is a lack of an overall system for providing health care. **Health-care delivery**—the providing of health-care services—is a profusion of ununified systems, some of which are in conflict with one another. Unfortunately, this results in both overlaps and gaps in the comprehensiveness of various health services and in discontinuity of health care. Before exploring this further, we must first examine the meaning of "health" and "health status."

Health and Health Status

Good health is an important goal

No universally accepted index of health status

Good health is one of the most important goals for Americans. The World Health Organization defines "health" as a state of complete mental and physical well-being. Many individuals believe good health to be freedom from disease and pain. Studies have shown that while people can identify or describe healthy people, their conception of health is questioned when an apparently healthy person dies unexpectedly. In many respects, the concepts of **health** and **health status**—health conditions of people—are difficult to define and measure. There is no universally accepted "index of health status," according to the Public Health Services, the Health Resources Administration, and the National Center for Health Statistics and Health Services Research. These health agencies note that no one definition is adequate for the many different types of decisions that must be made about health programs and resources (Census Bureau, U.S. Dept. of H.E.W., 1977, 1990).

There is even more difficulty in categorizing groups of people with respect to their health status because measuring it is an elusive process. In fact, the total death rates, life expectancy rates, and infant mortality rates are commonly used as indicators. According to various federal health agencies, a variety of measures are used because of the absence of a single well-accepted measure of health status. The following measures have been used as indicators: self-perceived health status, the incidence and prevalence of selected diseases, and the measures of disability. A note of caution is needed, however, in that interpretation of these measures is rarely straightforward. An example is given in an analysis of data on the nation's health: "If . . . the number of diseases people report increases over time, it might be concluded that overall health status is deteriorating. However, improvements in the health care system might have resulted in more frequent physician contacts and identification of previously undiagnosed illness. It might also reflect changes in diagnostic procedures used by physicians or changes in levels of awareness or concern. None of these measures would necessarily reflect an actual change in health status, only in how it is measured" (Census Bureau, U.S. Dept. of H.E.W., 1977, 1990).

Indicators of health status

Keeping in mind the above factors, we can now examine the current health status of Americans. We will examine the health-care institution by viewing first, the growing incidence of disease conditions; second, the growing desire by the public for adequate health-care services; and third, the inadequacy of health-care delivery and its costs.

The current health status of Americans

The Growing Incidence of Disease Conditions

The first dimension of the health-care institution to be examined is our nation's health status and the growing incidence of disease conditions. The death rate in America has dropped significantly in recent years. In fact, Americans who are alive today are healthier and will live longer than any other generation in our history. In the 1700s, Americans had an average life span of 35 years. Today it is well over 70 years. Death rates from heart and cerebrovascular disease have declined. In addition, four-fifths of our noninstitutionalized population is in good or excellent health. According to *Barron's*, the United States spends 40 percent more on health care than Canada, 90 percent more than Germany, and over 100 percent more than Japan. However, Americans are not healthier—and they may be less healthy—than the people in the above nations. Professor Karen Davis of Johns Hopkins reports that although per capita health-care outlays in the United States more than doubled during the 1980s, the "measurable improvements in the health status of the nation that were visible in the 1960s and 1970s virtually ground to a halt, and in some cases started to reverse, during the Reagan era. Reason: More stringent eligibility standards for Medicare and Medicaid and the soaring cost of private insurance swelled the ranks of the uninsured" (*Barron's*, June 11, 1990).

Many improvements, yet a growing incidence of disease conditions

Also, evidence exists that shows a growing incidence of disease conditions. For example, statistics reflect an increase in the incidence of cancer, venereal disease, emphysema, AIDS, and a variety of other illnesses. In the current decade of the 1990s, the leading causes of death are heart diseases, cancer, stroke, influenza, and pneumonia. Over 30 million people have some limitation of activity as a result of chronic diseases, which, in many cases, have a long-term impact on these people (Census Bureau, 1990; J. B. McKinlay and S. M. McKinlay, 1987). Chronic illnesses can change their lifestyles to the point where they cannot continue in major activities, such as working at their jobs or at home. They can also be limited in the kind or amount of major activity. Heart problems, arthritis, and orthopedic impairments were among the major causes of limited activity. Many millions of Americans have hypertension, heart disease, and arthritis. Death rates for suicide, cancer, homicide, and alcoholism have increased over the past several decades. More accidents take place than ever before in our history. Infant mortality and tuberculosis rates continue to be high for the poor and for other disadvantaged people (Census Bureau, 1990). In fact, millions of U.S. women give birth without proper prenatal care, and infant mortality rates exceed those of 17 other countries (*USA Today*, March 1990). Even with the availability of immunizations, there are frequent epidemics of communicable diseases. Many American children are not protected against measles, polio, or diphtheria-pertussis-tetanus. Miniepidemics of some diseases have become commonplace in the United States (Census Bureau, 1990).

Many types of health problems

Mini-epidemics

The AIDS Epidemic. The AIDS epidemic has become quite serious in the United States. **AIDS,** or acquired immune deficiency syndrome, is a major health problem and is now affecting all sectors of American society. Over 80,000 Americans have been afflicted with AIDS, and almost 60 percent of those have died from the disease since 1981. No one has recovered completely from the disease. From 365,000 to as many as one-half million Americans will have developed AIDS within the next few years (Centers for Disease Control, 1988; Mantell et al., 1989). Within less than nine years following HIV infection, half of those infected will develop AIDS (Moss et al., 1988). The implications of the above predictions are quite serious considering that scientists indicate that over one and one-half million Americans are infected with the AIDS virus, and 20 percent or more of the American population will become infected (Centers for Disease Control, 1988; Coolfont, 1986; Safyer and Spies-Karotkin, 1988).

Many Americans will get AIDS

Poverty and Health. The effects of poverty are very much evident in the general health and the distribution of disease in the lower classes. In America, there are high degrees of malnutrition and disease among the poor. As noted above, our nation has one of the highest infant mortality rates of the leading industrial nations, and the lower classes have rates of infant mortality higher than that of the rest of the nation. Poor people are hospitalized more frequently than they have been in the past—although many poor are still not admitted to hospitals because they do not have insurance, Medicare, or Medicaid—and when admitted, they remain longer than people in higher income levels. Their longer periods of hospitalization are due, in part, to their having more serious health problems. Their not receiving any prior treatment or only episodic treatment from hospital emergency rooms or outpatient and health department clinics is also a factor.

The poor are in poor health

Poor health is related to our polluted environment

The Environment and Health. America's high incidence of many serious illnesses is strongly related to conditions in our environment. Most forms of cancer have been traced to substances in the environment. Many of our neurological disorders and birth defects are a result of exposure to various drugs, lead, and pesticides. Twenty-first-century noise, stress, overconsumption of food and drugs, and the existence of rural and urban slums will all combine to threaten the health of Americans. The costs that are incurred through our failure to keep our environment clean are prohibitive in terms of declining health, high medical costs, and high death rates.

The Growing Desire for Adequate Health-Care Services

A growing demand for health-care services

The second factor that helps us understand the health-care institution in America is the growing demand by the public for adequate health-care services. Because of the increasing publicity given to health-care issues by the media, government, and others, Americans are becoming more aware of inadequacies in the health-care institution. They are more aware of the facts that millions of people in the lower and middle classes have worse health and receive less and poorer health care than the more affluent classes. People in the middle class and those in poverty very much desire and are demanding health-care services that are available to America's wealthy. In other words, most Americans view health care as a basic right. This attitude has its roots back in the 1950s. As *Barron's* reports, it was "back in 1952 that President Harry Truman's Commission on the Health Care needs of the Nation put an official policy stamp on health care as a basic human right, proclaiming that 'the American people desire and deserve comprehensive health service of the highest quality.' But today the panel's accompanying declaration that 'in our dynamic expanding economy, the means can be found to provide it . . . to all people equally' has the same quality naive ring to it as one of Pat Boone's whitewashed renditions of that era's rhythm and blues classics" (*Barron's*, June 11, 1990).

Health care: a basic right?

The Inadequacy of Health-Care Delivery and Its Costs

The structure of health-care delivery is complex

In addition to the above factors, the health-care institution can be understood by the inadequacies in our health-care delivery system. The present structure of health-care delivery in the United States is quite complex. It is an accumulation of old as well as new social health-care patterns among physicians, other health personnel, and consumers, which has been implanted upon a densely populated, technologically complex society. The evolution of today's health-care delivery system into its entrenchment in the private practice, fee-for-service economic structure is rooted in American history. The roots nourish the remains of earlier styles of health-care delivery. The supporters of this historical pattern of health care have discouraged the planning of more adequate services by their allegiances to present inefficient, costly structures. Also, many dominant health-care professionals have not yet incorporated some of the major changes in social attitudes, such as consumer rights and the acceptance of large organizations as legitimate structures as providers for health and social services.

The High Costs of Health Care. As noted above, a major problem in America's health-care institution is "runaway costs." Each year, health-care spending represents a greater share of our gross national product (GNP). America's health-care bill, which was $42 billion, or almost 6 percent of the GNP in 1965, will be consuming more than 12 percent of the GNP, and be running well over $700 billion each year in the early 1990s (*Barron's,* June 11, 1990). Health-care expenditures are estimated to soar well over $2 billion a day by the mid 1990s (*USA Today,* March 1990). There are many factors or reasons for this sharp rise in health costs. Some of the reasons are charges made by hospitals, physicians' decisions and charges, unnecessary treatment, and high insurance costs.

Health-care expenditures are soaring

One reason for the sharp rise in health costs is charges made by hospitals. A hospital stay that cost $16 per day in 1950 now costs several hundred dollars per day. A large portion of these costs are due to the acquisition of more expensive equipment and an increase in the number of hospital employees and staff in proportion to patient populations. Higher prices for goods and services bought by hospitals and wage increases for hospital employees—especially for nurses and administrators—also account for a high percentage of these spiraling costs. In addition, some of the high costs are due to poor hospital management. Costs increase when hospitals in the same community are competing with one another for the latest, most technologically advanced, and expensive equipment. Duplicated equipment and facilities mean higher health-care prices for the consumer.

High hospital costs

According to the Department of Health, Education, and Welfare (HEW), doctors generate the great bulk of total costs, when one counts bills paid for hospitalization, surgery, drugs, and other medical procedures ordered by physicians. Each doctor, it is estimated by the government, generates several hundred thousand dollars in medical costs every year. This figure excludes the charges for the doctor's own services. A doctor's average yearly income is well over $100,000 a year. Many specialists, and, in particular, surgeons, make several hundred thousand dollars a year (*Burlington County Times,* September 27, 1990). Many doctors, however, believe their incomes are justified by the high costs of medical education, high malpractice insurance premiums, and long work days.

High physician costs

Another factor contributing to the high costs of health care, and one that is directly injurious to the public's health, is the many millions of dollars spent on unnecessary treatments and operations. Unnecessary surgery has been attributed to the large number of surgeons whose livelihoods depend upon performing surgery and to our fee-for-service economic structure, in which doctors are paid each time a patient is treated. Lower rates of surgery occur where there are proportionately fewer surgeons and where patients are not covered by fee-for-service insurance plans. Many millions of dollars are also spent on the unnecessary overprescription of antibiotics and other drugs—several billions of doses consumed yearly.

Unnecessary treatment and drugs

The expense and inadequacy of voluntary health insurance is an additional problem contributing to the high cost of health care in America. It is not uncommon for a family-coverage group health plan to run many hundreds of

Many Americans have no health insurance

dollars each month for those Americans who can afford it. Millions of Americans are not covered by any health insurance. In fact, over 37 million Americans are uninsured for the basic medical and hospital services they need (*USA Today*, March 1990). Those Americans who are covered by some type of health insurance usually find that it is inadequate and unreliable. Many plans do not cover the costs of home care, doctor's office visits, and preventive health examination, but cover only parts of inpatient, medical, and surgical care. What all this means for the average American is that a larger and larger percentage of personal income must go to the increasing health and insurance costs. Even with insurance coverage, the great majority of policies do not protect against serious or long-term illnesses. Many of the Americans who annually file for bankruptcy claim that it is because of medical debts.

An Ununified Health-Care System

A profusion of ununified systems

It is not easy to understand and explain the complexities of health care in the United States. One way of viewing this important institution and some of its problems is by noting the lack of an overall system for providing health care. In the United States, health-care delivery is not a nonsystem, but a profusion of ununified systems, some of which are in conflict with one another. This results in overlaps and gaps in the comprehensiveness of various services and in discontinuity of care. Unlike other industrialized societies, America does not have a comprehensive health-delivery system. Most industrialized nations have a comprehensive national health insurance program. Americans pay for health care through a profusion of private and governmentally sponsored programs designed, in most cases, for particular groups, such as the aged, the poor, union workers, those in group plans, and so on. We also pay directly out of our own pockets for medical care. We operate under the fee-for-service method of remuneration. Physicians still basically set most fees for the specific services delivered, which tends to place more emphasis upon the treatment rather than on preventive aspects of health care. Nations that have comprehensive health-delivery systems have their physicians salaried, and there is, therefore, a greater tendency to stress the preventive aspects of health care.

The above perspective, then, stresses that in the United States, there is a fragmented health-care institution consisting of independent provider units. Lack of effective planning and coordination results in a wide variety of problems, ranging from the maldistribution of resources and the lack of comprehensive care, with continuity, to the duplication of facilities and services and increased costs.

A Medical-Industrial Complex

A second way of viewing the health-care institution is in terms of the "American health industry," or the "medical-industrial complex." This perspective stresses that the "American health industry" consists of doctors, medical schools, hospitals, health insurance companies, and drug companies. Proponents of this perspective report that health care is "no more the top priority of this 'industry' . . . than the production of safe, cheap, efficient, pollution-free transportation is a priority of the American automobile industry." This "health establishment" has been described as "both efficient and systematic in extracting profits in terms of differences between income and expenditures" (Johnson, 1973; Glick and Hebding, 1980). In other words, America's health-care institution is not a chaotic, uncoordinated, unplanned profusion of ununified systems. It is dominated primarily by such entities as hospitals, research laboratories, drug companies, and the like.

Health-care system is dominated by institutions

Complex Forces

A third, and final, perspective views the health-care institution not in terms of an ununified private medical system or a medical-industrial complex, but in terms of complex forces that are outside the control of any medical establishment. These forces—the living patterns and habits of people beyond the control of medicine—affect the birth and death rates and the rates of cancer and heart problems. This point of view admits to some flaws in private medicine, but questions why, with so much dissatisfaction with the way in which our government is run, many reformers want American medicine to be nationalized and bureaucratized.

Living patterns and habits affect health

LOVE AND LET DIE

Nancy Gibbs

In American society, a major issue in health care focuses upon decisions about ending the lives of terminally ill people who are unable to decide for themselves. This is a complex area with many ethical, religious, moral, political, and policy dimensions. The following reading, "Love and Let Die," by Nancy Gibbs, examines this very important agonizing "right to die" dilemma.

> Just as I choose a ship to sail in or a house to live in, so I choose a death for my passage from life.
>
> —Seneca (4 B.C.—A.D. 65)

Nancy Cruzan, now 32, has done nothing for the past seven years. She has not hugged her mother or gazed out the window or played with her nieces. She has neither laughed nor wept, her parents say, nor spoken a word. Since her car crashed on an icy night, she has lain so still for so long that her hands have curled into claws; nurses wedge napkins under her fingers to prevent the nails from piercing her wrists. "She would hate being like this," says her mother Joyce. "It took a long time to accept she wasn't getting better." If they chose, the Cruzans could slip into Nancy's room some night, disconnect her feeding tube, and face the consequences. But instead they have asked the U.S. Supreme

Court for permission to end their daughter's life.

The Cruzan petition not only marks the first time the court has grappled with the agonizing "right to die" dilemma; it may well be the most wrenching medical case ever argued before the high bench. To begin with, Nancy is not dying. She could live 30 years just as she is. And since she is awake but unaware, most doctors agree that she is not suffering. But her parents are suffering, for it is they who live with her living death. They are so convinced Nancy would not want to go on this way that they have asked the courts for authorization to remove her feeding tube and "let her go." A lower-court judge gave that permission, but the Missouri Supreme Court, affirming "the sanctity of life," reversed the ruling. Now the U.S. high court must consider whether the federal Constitution's liberty guarantees, and the privacy rights they imply, include a right to be starved to death for mercy's sake.

Cases that tell people how to live their private lives arouse passionate controversy and are correspondingly difficult to settle, as the court found after its landmark 1973 *Roe v. Wade* decision legalizing abortion. There are 10,000 other patients like Cruzan in the U.S., and their families are waiting and watching. "I'm riding on the Cruzans' coattails," says St. Louis marketing consultant Pete Busalacchi, whose daughter Christine lies in the same Missouri rehabilitation center as Cruzan. "Maybe it would have been best if she had died that night," he says, referring to Christine's 1987 auto accident. "This has been a 34-month funeral." And like many Americans, Pete Busalacchi believes a family's private tragedy should not be a battleground for right-to-life interest groups, politicians or judges. "This is for individuals," he insists. "My suggestion is to take Nancy to the Supreme Court and wheel her in and ask, 'Do you want to live like this?'"

At the moment, most Americans seem to agree with Busalacchi. In a poll conducted last month for TIME/CNN by Yankelovich Clancy Shulman, 80% of those surveyed said decisions about ending the lives of terminally ill patients who cannot decide for themselves should be made by their families and doctors rather than lawmakers. If a patient is terminally ill and unconscious but has left instructions in a living will, 81% believe the doctor should be allowed to withdraw life-sustaining treatment; 57% believe it is all right for doctors in such cases to go even further and administer lethal injections or provide lethal pills.

Right-to-life advocates denounce what they call the "pro-death juggernaut," a shifting of public opinion on death and dying that is affecting not only private decisions but also public policy. Forty states and the District of Columbia have living-will laws that allow people to specify in advance what treatments they would find acceptable in their final days. In January, a New York State Supreme Court justice ruled that a family did not have to pay about two years' worth of $172-a-day fees for tending a comatose patient after they asked to have a feeding tube removed. That same month the Brooklyn district attorney decided not to press any charges against three grown children who had turned off their father's respirator, on the grounds that he was already brain dead.

Though statutes and court rulings may codify what is legal, they cannot ease the acute personal dilemmas of those who must deal directly with right-to-die situations. The issues that patients and families face are not only ethical but also medical, financial, legal and theological. In the last days of a ravaging disease, when the very technology that can save lives is merely prolonging death, how is a family to decide whether to stop the treatment? By adopting the abstract reasoning of jurists and ethicists weighing legal arguments about privacy and moral arguments about mercy? Through some private intuition about how much sorrow they can bear and how much courage they can summon? Or by some blunt utilitarian calculation about whether it is more important to keep Grandmother alive than to send Junior to college? In the end, individuals are left with an intricate puzzle about what is legal—and what is right—in making a decision.

It is not only families that must decide. Doctors are wondering when, in an era of untamed technology, they should stand back and let their patients die—or even help death along. Economists are calculating a sort of social triage: at a time when infant mortality is scandalously high and public health care is a shambles, does it make sense for taxpayers to spend tens of thousands of dollars a year to keep each unconscious patient alive? Lawmakers are struggling with how to draft laws carefully enough to protect life while respecting individual choice. Theologians are debating how sacred life can be if we take it upon ourselves to end it.

It is not surprising that physicians are on the front lines of the euthanasia debate, since they are the only participants for whom life-and-death decisions are as common as they are complex. They are most acutely conscious of the allocation of scarce resources—time, money and their own energy—among patients who might be cured and those who can only be sustained. And it is they who must offer explanations to the anxious families of patients whose lives are lost but not yet gone.

It is a basic premise of medicine that doctors should be healers and care givers; that they must work for their patients' well-being; that if they cannot cure, they should at least do no harm. When they took their Hippocratic oath, they promised, "I will give no deadly medicine to anyone if asked, nor suggest any such counsel . . ." But the plight of the incurably ill has challenged all these premises and left doctors and nurses deeply divided over their duties to the dying.

For many physicians, the actions they take often depend more on circumstance than on moral certainty. How far is the patient from death? How great is the pain? How clear the will? Does the patient just want to be left alone, or is he asking to be killed? The Cruzan case has raised the basic medical issue of whether doctors must continue to treat patients they cannot cure. In its amicus brief to the Supreme Court, the American Academy of Neurology argues that the doctor's duty is to continue treating unconscious patients as long as there is some chance of improvement, which Nancy Cruzan does not have. When hope is gone, the duty ends. But the Association of American Physicians and Surgeons argues precisely the opposite. "The obligation of the physician to the comatose, vegetative, or developmentally disabled patient does not depend upon the prospect for recovery," it wrote in its brief. "The physician must always act on behalf of the patient's well-being."

Taken to the extreme, this principle can mean ignoring or overriding the patient's express wishes. When Dax Cowart was critically burned in a propane-gas explosion near Henderson, Texas, he begged a passing farmer for a gun with which to kill himself. On his way to the hospital, he pleaded with the medic to let him die. For weeks his life hung by a thread. For more than a year, against his will, he endured excruciating treatment: his right eye and several fingers were removed, his left eye was sewn shut. His pain and his protests were unrelenting. One night he crawled out of bed to try to throw himself out a window, but was discovered and prevented.

That was 17 years ago. Cowart is now a law school graduate, married, living in Texas and managing his investments. Yet to this day he argues that doctors violated his right to choose not to be treated. "It doesn't take a genius to know that when you're in that amount of pain, you can either bear it or you can't," he says. "And I couldn't." He still resents the powerlessness of patients who are forced to live when they beg to die. "The physicians say that when a patient is in that much pain, he is not competent to make judgments about himself. It's the pain talking. And then when narcotics are given to subdue the pain, they say it's the narcotics talking. It's a no-win situation."

In Cowart's case, doctors acted paternalistically; they overruled his pleas in the belief that he would one day recover sufficiently to be grateful. But what if there were no chance of recovery: no law school, no wedding, no "life" down the road? Are doctors still obliged to fight on for their patients, even in a losing battle, even against their will? When a patient's time is short and his wishes are clear, many doctors these days would say no to life-at-all-costs heroics. Overtreatment of the terminally ill strikes physicians as both wasteful and inhumane. And patients living within sight of death often find themselves more concerned with the quality of life that remains than with its quantity. Once reconciled to the inevitable, they want to die with dignity, not tethered to a battery of machines in an intensive-care unit like a laboratory specimen under glass.

When her cancer was diagnosed three years ago, Diana Nolan did not need much imagination or prophecy to know what lay ahead. The disease had killed both her parents. Surgeons removed part of her lung, but the cancer spread. Her physician next suggested that she try a potent chemotherapy but warned of the potential side effects—hair loss, nausea and vomiting. "I wanted a full week to think and pray," she recalls. "I am a person who wants to have a part in the treatment. Let me know what my options are." In the end, she told her doctor she wanted only pain-killers. Her two grown sons supported her decision, but some friends urged that she battle on. "They said, 'Go for it at all costs,' but I had seen my father, my mother and several friends go through this." She preferred to stay at home to die, and summoned her Episcopal priest to administer unction. Nolan hopes she will leave a message for those considering decisions like hers. "I wish people wouldn't be frightened about knowing what they're up against. To have a part in my treatment has been so important. I'm part of the team too."

But when doctors cannot consult the patient directly, the issue becomes much harder. Karen Ann Quinlan's was the most celebrated right-to-die case before Cruzan's, and one that seems almost straightforward by comparison. In 1975, after she had been comatose for seven months, Quinlan's father went to the New Jersey Supreme Court to have her respirator turned off. The court agreed, and the U.S. Supreme Court declined to consider the case further. After the ruling, Quinlan lived nine more years breathing on her own. But Nancy Cruzan is not on a life-support system. Her parents are asking doctors to remove a feeding tube. If that petition is granted, Cruzan is sure to die within weeks, if not days.

When it is not high technology but rather basic care that is being withheld, doctors find themselves on shakier ground. Right-to-life proponents, including some physicians, argue that food and water, even supplied artificially, are not "medical treatment." They are the very least that human beings owe one another—and that doctors owe their patients. To keep a heart beating after a brain is dead makes no sense. But Nancy Cruzan is not brain dead; like a baby, she survives on her own if fed.

This distinction can put families and health-care workers at odds, as Robert Hayner found when he went to court in Albany to have his unconscious Aunt Elsie's medication stopped and the feeding tube removed. "How can we be expected to provide care if the tube is pulled?" demanded staff members at her nursing home in a court deposition. "How can we stand by and watch her starve to death? We are her family," they said. "We care about her. We cannot walk down the hall knowing we are killing her."

If doctors and nurses are uncomfortable about withholding food and water, they are profoundly uneasy about actively assisting a suicide. Yet a seemingly inexorable logic enters the picture: once it is acceptable to stand by and allow a patient to die slowly, why is it not more merciful to end life swiftly by lethal injection? What was once taboo is now openly discussed in academic journals: last March the *New England Journal of Medicine* published an article by twelve prominent physicians called "The Physician's Responsibility Toward Hopelessly Ill Patients." "It is difficult to answer such questions," the doctors wrote, "but all but two of us believe that it is not immoral for a physician to assist in the rational suicide of a terminally ill patient."

While such articles challenge doctors to rethink their professional roles, there is no agreement among them on this issue. Some physicians and ethicists warn that active euthanasia, if commonly practiced, could undermine the whole ethos of healing and the doctors' role as care givers. "A patient could never be totally confident that the doctor was coming to help him and not kill him," argues George Annas, director of the Law, Medicine & Ethics Program at Boston University's School of Medicine and Public Health.

Even hospice workers, who are more concerned with controlling pain than delaying death, are firmly opposed to the idea of loading a syringe with an overdose of morphine and handing it over. And doctors who spend all their time treating the incurably ill may still stop short of sanctioning euthanasia. "I don't want that word and my name in the same sentence," says Jeffrey Buckner, medical director for the Jacob Perlow Hospice of Beth Israel Medical Center in New York City. "If you are a physician and that charge is made against you, it sticks."

One of his patients, a 66-year-old writer suffering from a gastrointestinal cancer, came seeking help in committing suicide. He said he had the pills: 60 capsules, 200 mg each, of Seconal. But surgery left him with trouble swallowing, and he wondered if there was a better way to go. In this case it was not so much the physical pain of the cancer that plagued him; it was the mental burden of a lingering illness. "This long farewell performance gets to be a drag on people," the patient said. "It's just not the way you want to see yourself behaving. There's less dignity. Christ, everybody dies. Why does that always have to be the topic of conversation?" Dr. Buckner refused to help with a suicide. "It is reasonable to want to protect yourself from a horrible death," he explains. "But if good medical care is provided, and good pain relief, then those fears can be greatly alleviated."

For active help with a suicide, most patients will have to look elsewhere, well outside the realm of patient care. The spread of AIDS, for instance, has prompted some right-to-die activists to offer support and counseling about pills and occasionally lethal injections to people with the virus. Pierre Ludington, 44, executive director of the American Association of Physicians for Human Rights, has tested HIV-positive: he is stockpiling pills to use when he is ready to go. "I get angry that society wants me to suffer in a hospital," he says. "All I'm doing is feeding its coffers."

Ludington has his own idea of a death with dignity. "I envision having a wonderful meal with friends. After they leave, I'll sit in front of the fire listening to Mozart, mix everything with brandy, sip it, and somebody will find me.'' He is an eloquent if unlikely spokesman for the allocation debate. ''I feel that money belongs to a symphony,'' he says, ''or for an impoverished museum to buy a painting that lasts. I won't last. I won't last. It's an unconscionable act to keep me going.''

Purely economic arguments for euthanasia can sound brutally calculating. But as health-care costs rise annually at double and triple the rate of inflation, and as new technologies promise ever higher bills for ever older patients, the questions grow about how to ration medical care. In 1987 the Oregon legislature voted to deny organ transplants under its Medicaid program and to use that money instead for prenatal care. It is only a matter of time before the issue of continuing care for patients in a vegetative state comes under similar scrutiny.

Jurists and ethicists wrestle with the wider implications of measuring the value of life on a sliding scale. Once a society agrees that at some stage a life is no longer worth sustaining, patients are suddenly vulnerable. ''We would begin with competent people making their own choice,'' warns Daniel Callahan, director of the Hastings Center and an authority on ethical issues in medicine, ''but we would be too easily led into involuntary euthanasia—either manipulating people into asking for suicide or actually doing it to them without their permission because they have become too burdensome or costly.'' The haunting precedent, of course, is the Nazi Holocaust, during which the chronically ill, then the socially unacceptable, and finally all non-Germans were viewed as expendable. In his stark essay ''The Humane Holocaust,'' Christian author Malcolm Muggeridge notes that ''it took no more than three decades to transform a war crime into an act of compassion.''

As the historic taboo about mercy killing gradually erodes, the courts and legislatures are struggling to be sure that the vulnerable are protected—that, in the case of the severely disabled, the right to die not become a duty to die. They fear, for example, that medical care for newborn babies may come to depend on some cost-benefit analysis of their chance of living a ''full healthy and active life.'' In the Baby Doe case in 1982, the Indiana courts allowed a couple to refuse surgery for their baby born with Down's syndrome and an incomplete esophagus; after six days, the baby starved to death. That emotional case raised the concern that some hospitals were not recommending even routine treatment for babies with Down's syndrome, spina bifida, cerebral palsy and other serious but treatable disabilities.

Both the medical and economic arguments for euthanasia are rejected by the powerful right-to-life movement, which commands hundreds of thousands of supporters nationwide. And as on the abortion issue, their stance against mercy killing is based on a theology that places the entire debate in a different context, that of a family of faith that tends most lovingly to its weakest members. The sanctity of a human existence, they argue, does not depend on its quality or its cost. What God gives only he can take away, and to usurp that right is an act of grave hubris. ''Our Lord healed the sick, raised Lazarus from the dead, gave back sanity to the deranged,'' writes Muggeridge, ''but never did He practice or envisage killing as part of the mercy that held possession of His heart.''

But even within the community of faith there is a vast gray area. Though suffering and death underlie Judeo-Christian theology, basic compassion seems to dictate that a patient in terrible pain should be allowed to die. This is a proposition that the Roman Catholic Church appears to endorse. While both suicide and mercy killing are still strictly forbidden, the Vatican in 1980 declared that refusing treatment "is not equivalent to suicide; on the contrary, it should be considered as an acceptance of the human condition . . . or a desire not to impose excessive expenses on the family or community."

Even more active measures have their clerical champions. The late British Methodist clergyman Leslie Weatherhead rejected the idea that death should be left to God. "We do not leave birth to God," he observed. "We space births. We prevent births. We arrange births. Man should learn to become the lord of death as well as the master of birth." At the very least, argue some clerics, the state should stay out of the way. "The *Missouri* decision severs family ties," states a brief by the Evangelical Lutheran Church in America, referring to the ruling against the Cruzans, "by substituting the moral and religious judgment of the state for that of the person."

There is some irony here: the Evangelical Lutherans argue for a family's right to privacy, while the state of Missouri promotes the "sanctity of life." Yet the notion that life is sacred, and worthy of the state's protection, is embedded throughout the American legal tradition, right alongside the protection of individual liberty. When the two rights are at odds, the debates grow fierce. There are specific circumstances in which a society permits the intentional taking of life: in war, in self-defense, as punishment for a heinous crime. The Cruzan case raises the question of whether personal choice and great suffering, by either patients or their families, should join that set of circumstances.

Up until now the legal debate on the right to die has been wildly confused. If a car crashes on the George Washington Bridge and the driver is left comatose, his fate in court may depend on whether the ambulance takes him to New Jersey or New York. In New Jersey his family would probably be able to tell a hospital committee to stop life support. New York State's law is stricter, and without a living will the family would have to prove in court that the driver had left "clear and convincing evidence" that he would not want to be maintained by a machine.

But the laws are so unsettled that even in states where the statutes are strict, they may not necessarily be enforced. Judges and juries across the country have been remarkably lenient on family members who become mercy killers. Rudy Linares, a Chicago landscaper, held off hospital workers with a .357-cal. pistol while he unplugged his baby son's respirator. The 15-month-old boy died in his father's arms. Linares was charged with first-degree murder, but a Cook County grand jury refused to indict him. In fact, out of some 20 U.S. cases of "mercy killings" in the past 50 years, studied by Leonard Glantz of Boston University, only three defendants have been sentenced to jail.

The Cruzan case may finally provide the lower courts with some clear guidance in striking a fundamental balance between the rights of individuals and the duties of the state. If they chose, the Cruzans' lawyers could have suggested that Nancy's "life" is so faint that it does not meet a minimum standard of protection under the law; that, unaware as she is, she has none of those qualities and prospects and experiences that give life its value. But such an argument would require setting some line above which lives are protected, below which they are not. "In the public realm we need general rules that everyone in an institutional setting will follow," says Harvard political philosopher Robert Nozick. "And any line they draw will look arbitrary." Instead the case is being argued on the grounds of liberty and privacy.

The Cruzans' lawyers are asserting that Nancy's constitutional right to liberty has no meaning if it does not protect her from having a feeding tube surgically inserted in her stomach and being force-fed. Though she is unable to refuse the treatment, her parents could act on her behalf. Since the Karen Ann Quinlan case, 50 courts in 17 states have considered the right to have treatment withdrawn. Nearly all have come down on the side of privacy and limited the power of the government to dictate medical care. In a peculiar legal irony, many states make it illegal to assist in suicide; yet again and again, the courts have upheld the rights of conscious but paralyzed patients to have their ventilators and feeding tubes disconnected. In the most recent, highly publicized case, quadriplegic Larry James McAfee, still paralyzed five years after a motorcycle accident, petitioned the Georgia Supreme Court to allow him to disconnect his own ventilator using a special mouth-activated switch. Upholding McAfee's privacy rights, the court granted his petition. But McAfee subsequently decided not to end his life after all.

Unlike Georgia and many other states, however, Missouri has strong pro-life language in its statutes, which the state supreme court invoked in throwing out the lower-court decisions. Though Cruzan had the right to refuse treatment, said the Missouri justices, her parents did not prove to the court that this is what she would have wanted. The "vague and unreliable" recollections by family and friends about Nancy's wishes were not deemed sufficient reason to stop feeding her. "The state's interest," wrote the judges, "is not in quality of life . . . Were quality of life at issue, all manner of handicaps might find the state seeking to terminate their lives. Instead, the state's interest is in life; that interest is unqualified."

Though no one questions the love of Cruzan's parents and their desire to abide by her wishes, what happens when a family's motives are not so clear? The state of Missouri is paying Cruzan's medical bills; but for other families the desire to hasten an inheritance or avoid crushing medical costs could add an ingredient of self-interest to a decision. The Rev. Harry Cole, a Presbyterian minister who faced the dilemma when his wife fell into a coma, admits the complexity of pressures. "If she were to go on that way, our family faced not only the incredible pain of watching her vegetate, but we also faced harsh practical realities." The cost of nursing-home care was likely to top $30,000 a year. "How could I continue to send three kids to college with the additional financial strain?"

The Cole case provides one more reason for courts to be careful about withdrawing life support: medicine is an uncertain science. When Cole's wife Jackie suffered a massive brain hemorrhage four years ago, the blood vessels in her brain ruptured, and she fell into a coma. "The vast majority of patients who have this kind of stroke die within a few hours," Dr. Tad Pula, the head of Maryland General Hospital's division of neurology, told Cole. But Jackie did not die right away; after several crises she stabilized into a vegetative state, which doctors said could last indefinitely. After talking with his children, Cole went to court to remove the respirator. But Baltimore Circuit Court Judge John Carroll Byrnes stayed his decision. Six days later, Jackie Cole woke up.

Today Jackie and Harry still appear on the talk-show circuit. She suffers some short-term memory loss, but otherwise is fully recovered. "When I look back at what the doctors said, I think, 'How wrong they were,'" she says. "What happened to me was truly miraculous." She does not blame Harry for wanting to pull the plug. "I know he loves me. I know he was never trying to do away with me." But the story does highlight the dilemma both judges and family members face. "I thought my decision was well planned, well thought out, responsible," says Cole. "It was what Jackie had asked me to do."

Such situations essentially confront families with a Hobson's choice: either they stand by and allow a loved one to waste away, or else they act to hasten death, with all the guilt and recrimination that entails. A state attorney accused 87-year-old Ruth Hoffmeister of wanting to starve her husband to death. Every evening for the past six years, Ruth has spoon-fed her husband Edward, who has Alzheimer's disease. When he began losing weight, their Pompano Beach, Fla., nursing home would have been obliged by state regulations to force-feed him through a tube. Ruth protested the bureaucratic intrusion. "There is nothing so important to an Alzheimer's patient," she insisted, "as a familiar touch and a familiar voice." She went to court to stop them, and won. "I don't know what the next step will be," she says. "After he had the disease for three years, he said to me, 'I am so tired of dying.' How could I ever justify keeping him alive?"

Although the wishes of patients and their families are often frustrated in court, lawmakers are not insensitive to their plight. Missouri Attorney General William Webster, who has led the legal fight against the Cruzans, may end up their unlikely ally. Webster realizes that few people have living wills, and that the Cruzans' ordeal has been torturous. "Without her case," he says, "I don't think people sitting in their living rooms would have to come face to face with the fact that we have thousands of patients across the country who are never going to recover. They are in this legal, medical nightmare—this limbo."

Webster endorses new legislation that would try to find a careful resolution. He has already met stiff resistance from the Missouri legislature and has a hard fight ahead to change the laws. He proposes that families of patients who have been continuously unconscious for three or more years could petition for withdrawing treatment, including food and water. If they were unanimous that this is what the patient would want, and three independent physicians certified that the coma was irreversible, the patient would be allowed to die.

That would put the decision back in the families' hands and leave them with the ultimate, intimate reckoning—a weighing of needs and fears and risks and possibilities. Long after the decision is made, the resolution may continue to haunt. But, in a sense, the abiding difficulty of these choices has a value of its own. It reflects the deep desire to do the right thing and respect the wishes of a loved one—and also an unshakable sense that life is neither to be taken nor relinquished lightly, even in mercy's name.

Review Questions

1. Briefly examine the pros and cons of euthanasia.
2. If a patient is terminally ill and unconscious, but has left instructions in a living will, do you believe the doctor should be allowed to withdraw life-sustaining treatment? Explain your answer.

Summary

1. A social institution is a pattern of norms centered around a major societal goal, value, or need. Social institutions such as the religious, educational, and health-care institutions are found in every society.
2. The religious institution fills the need of providing explanations for the meaning of human existence.
3. The educational institution is connected with the continuing goal of socializing the young.
4. The health-care institution is concerned with meeting a society's health needs.
5. Social institutions provide stability and consistency in society and regulate human behavior.

STUDY GUIDE

Chapter Objectives

After studying this chapter, you should be able to:

1. Define "institution"
2. List the five major functions of the religious institution
3. Compare and contrast Durkheim's, Marx's, and Weber's views of religion
4. List four distinctive features of American religious institutions
5. List the four major functions of the educational institution
6. Explain the health-care institution in terms of the growing incidence of disease conditions
7. Explain the health-care institution in terms of the growing public desire for adequate health-care coverage
8. Explain the health-care institution in terms of the inadequacy of health-care delivery and its costs

Key Terms

AIDS (p. 365)
Educational institution (p. 356)
Health (p. 363)
Health-care delivery (p. 363)
Health-care institution (p. 363)
Health status (p. 363)
Religion (p. 346)
Religious institution (p. 345)
Sacred (p. 346)
Secularization (p. 348)

Self-Test

Short Answer

(p. 345) 1. "Institution" is defined as ______________________________

(p. 346) 2. "Religion" can be defined as ______________________________

(p. 347) 3. Religion performs the following functions: ______________________________

(p. 346) 4. For Durkheim, religion is ______________________________

(p. 356) 5. For Durkheim, education is ______________________________

(p. 357) 6. Education performs the following functions: ______________________________

(p. 363) 7. The World Health Organization defines "health" as ______________________________

(p. 364) 8. The health-care institution is examined by viewing:
a. ______________________________
b. ______________________________
c. ______________________________

(p. 367) 9. Health-care expenditures in the U.S. are ______________________________

(p. 368) 10. Ununified systems mean ______________________________

Multiple Choice (Answers are on page 383.)

(p. 346) 1. According to Durkheim, religious beliefs and practices relate to:
a. faith
b. mystical moments
c. sacred things
d. secular things

(p. 347) 2. For Durkheim, religious ceremonies and rituals do not perform the following function:
a. a cohesive function
b. a divisive function
c. a euphoric function
d. none of the above

(p. 348) 3. For Marx:
a. religion is the opiate of the people
b. the moral community is the foundation of religion
c. religious ceremonies perform a religious function
d. none of the above

(p. 349) 4. In America, mainline Protestantism has experienced:
a. a sharp increase in church membership
b. a sharp decline in church membership

c. no change in church membership
d. none of the above

(p. 357) 5. In the United States:
a. state and local governments control school systems
b. the most obvious feature of the school is that it is a formal, highly bureaucratized organization
c. knowledge and occupational training are too complex to be taught by informal methods
d. all the above

(p. 357) 6. Education in America:
a. is being replaced by the computer
b. socializes the young
c. has vastly improved
d. none of the above

(p. 364) 7. Some commonly used indicators of health status are:
a. the total death rate and life expectancy rates
b. infant mortality rates
c. self-perceived health status and measures of disability
d. the incidence and prevalence of selected diseases
e. all the above

(p. 364) 8. Dimensions of health-care issues include:
a. the growing incidence of disease conditions and the broad inadequacies in health-care delivery
b. the growing demands by the public for adequate health-care services
c. our health-care delivery system compared with those systems in England and France
d. only *a* and *b* of the above

(p. 365) 9. Which of the following statements is not correct?
a. the poor pay a heavy toll in terms of health for their environment
b. the public is less aware of the fact that the poor have significantly lower levels of health than do the middle and upper classes in America
c. the public is more aware of the fact that the poor receive less and have poorer health care than do the middle and upper classes in America
d. only *a* and *c* of the above

(p. 367) 10. Factors in the high costs of hospital care include:
a. duplicate equipment and facilities
b. poor hospital management
c. more expensive equipment
d. all the above

True/False *(Answers are on page 383.)*

T F 11. For Durkheim, religious ceremonies and rituals perform a cohesive function. (p. 347)

T F 12. Weber viewed religion as the "opiate of the people." (p. 348)

T F 13. The national government controls American school systems. (p. 357)

T F 14. American education has not been influenced by the needs of society. (p. 356)

T F 15. In the past, the family provided the basic health-care needs of its members. (p. 363)

T F 16. The World Health Organization defines "health" as a state of reasonable mental and physical well-being. (p. 363)

T F 17. The concepts of health and health status are no longer difficult to define and measure. (p. 363)

T F 18. Americans who are alive today are healthier and will live longer than any other generation in our history. (p. 364)

T F 19. America spends 100 percent more on health care than does Japan. (p. 364)

T F 20. In the near future, over 50 percent of the American population will be infected with the AIDS virus. (p. 365)

Fill In *(Answers are on page 383.)*

(p. 345) 21. Education, religion, and health care are all social ______.

(p. 346) 22. ______ is a system of beliefs and practices shared by people in a moral community.

(p. 348) 23. ______ is a process by which society's traditional beliefs and institutions lose their influence.

(p. 348) 24. The majority of Americans are formally linked to a ______.

(p. 356) 25. ______ stressed the role of formal education as a conserver of culture.

(p. 356) 26. The primary goal of the ______ and the ______ is the socialization of the young.

(p. 363) 27. ______ delivery is a profusion of ununified systems.

(p. 365) 28. ______ is a major health problem and is now affecting all sectors of American society.

(p. 366) 29. Most Americans view health care as a basic ______.

(p. 368) 30. Millions of Americans are not covered by any health ______.

Matching *(Answers are on page 383.)*

31. ______ Institution
32. ______ Religion
33. ______ Sacred
34. ______ Education
35. ______ Marx
36. ______ Secularization
37. ______ AIDS
38. ______ Health

a. For Durkheim, a conserver of culture

b. Religion is the opiate of the people

c. State of complete physical and mental well-being

d. System of beliefs and practices relating to sacred things

39. ______ Health-care delivery
40. ______ Health-care institution

e. Pattern of norms centered around a major goal, value, or need
f. Many ununified systems
g. Doctors, medical schools, hospitals, health insurance and drug companies
h. That which is set apart by people
i. HIV
j. Traditional beliefs and institutions lose their influence

Essay Questions

1. What is an institution?
2. What is religion?
3. What are the major functions of the religious institution?
4. What are the major functions of the educational institution?
5. What do "health" and "health status" mean?
6. What are the various dimensions of the health-care institution? Explain your answer.

Interactive Exercises

1. Examine the various theoretical views on religion and compare them with the way you view religion's role in society.
2. Examine how the American educational institution has or has not met your career and educational needs.
3. In what ways has the health-care institution had an impact upon your own or your family's personal lives?

Answers

Answers to Self-Test

1. c
2. b
3. a
4. b
5. d
6. b
7. e
8. d
9. b
10. d
11. T
12. F
13. F
14. F
15. T
16. F
17. F
18. T
19. T
20. F
21. institutions
22. religion
23. secularization
24. church
25. Durkheim
26. family, educational institution
27. health-care
28. AIDS
29. right
30. insurance
31. e
32. d
33. h
34. a
35. b
36. j
37. i
38. c
39. f
40. g

Answers to Chapter Pretest

1. F
2. F
3. F
4. F
5. T
6. F
7. T
8. F
9. F
10. F

Chapter 10

Social Institutions: The Political and Economic Institutions

Chapter Pretest

Let's see how much you already know about topics in this chapter:

1. **Power is no longer an important aspect of the political institution. True/False**
2. **No longer is the nation-state the most distinctive and the largest self-sufficient political configuration in the world. True/False**
3. **Politics does not affect my life. True/False**
4. **America is a business civilization. True/False**
5. **Pure capitalism and pure socialism can still be found in a few parts of the world. True/False**
6. **American workers are more independent than in the past. True/False**
7. **America's economic institution is no longer dominated by large corporations the way it was in the past. True/False**
8. **In the near future, the American work force will be growing faster than ever. True/False**
9. **A major shift in the American economy has been one from service to manufacturing. True/False**
10. **In order for U.S. organizations to survive in the future, they must operate in a national rather than an international environment. True/False**

The Political Institution

Inherent in the association of people in any culture is the problem of regulating the power of some people over others. The basic political process is the acquisition and exercise of power by a particular group or particular groups of people over others. The need for maintaining social control and regulating power necessitates the development of political institutions. The **political institution** is the complex of norms that regulates the acquisition and exercise of power by some people in a given territory, through social structures claiming a monopoly of ultimate authority.

Power

Within every society, it is the political institution that determines who should gain power and when and how it should be gained—**power,** according to Max

The political institution determines who should gain power and when and how it should be gained

Weber, being the ability or the potential to influence the thoughts or behavior of others. Legitimate power or authority may be based on the legal norms of society, on tradition, or on charisma. **Charisma** is an uncommon attribute of a person that enables its holder to inspire and lead without formal authority. Max Weber compared charismatic authority with traditional and legal authority. For Weber, an example of traditional and conventional authority is that of a king. Legal authority is that of a president. Charisma is not a rational phenomenon. A charismatic person is perceived by others to have exceptional qualities and powers (Weber, 1958).

Government

The concept of sovereignty

Throughout the world, each **community**—an association of people who share a common identity—is maintained as well as perpetuated by a political order or government. This is why the study of the political institution focuses on processes associated with governance. A government has **sovereignty** when it successfully asserts its claim to make the rules in a given territory. Sovereign states command the obedience of society's members. That is, they exercise authority over their citizens. In addition, sovereign states claim legitimacy to the extent that their claim to rule is willingly accepted.

The Nation-State

The **nation-state** is the major form of political organization in the world. A **nation** is a group of people who share a common background, including all, or at least several of the following characteristics: geographic location, culture, history, religion, race, ethnic characteristics, belief in common political ideas, and language. The concept of **state** refers to a sovereign government exercising power and authority in the name of society. In the modern world, the nation-state is the most distinctive and largest self-sufficient political configuration (Magstadt and Schotten, 1988).

The State, Democracy, and Oligarchy

Democracy and oligarchy

In American society, the most notable political institution is the state. The state is the political and legal institution representing the whole of society, including its people and territory. It has sovereignty and may legally force groups and individuals to obey its laws. The state also has a **government,** the group of people who operate the apparatus of the state, and determine and enforce policies. Control over government may be exercised by all the people—as in a **democracy**—or by only a few people in their own interests—as in an **oligarchy.** In representative democracy, some people are chosen to govern all the people. Democracy may be classified according to mode of participation, method of decision making—majority vote, consensus through discussion, and specialization and division of labor—and according to whether it extends to the political, economic, and social aspects of life.

The political institution institutionalizes and enforces social norms through laws which are established by the government's legislative bodies.

Functions of the Political Institution

Functions of the political institution

In the United States, the political institution has several important functions. First, it institutionalizes and enforces social norms through laws, which are established by the government's legislative bodies. Second, the political institution resolves conflicts among various segments of the society. Third, the political institution provides—through planning, coordinating, and financing—activities believed to be in its citizens' best interests. It provides basic services in such areas as health, education, and welfare. Fourth, the political institution protects its citizens from outside enemies.

POLITICAL INSTITUTIONS AND IDEOLOGIES

Joseph Bensman and Bernard Rosenberg

In the following reading, "Political Institutions and Ideologies," by Joseph Bensman and Bernard Rosenberg, the authors present a sociological perspective on politics and government. The authors examine the effects of governmental policy changes, government in the folk and feudal societies, the centralization of power, and the rise of the state. In addition, they examine such areas as feudal legitimacy, natural law as legitimacy for democracy, and the legitimacy of democratic government.

Sociology does not address itself specifically to the study of government and politics. As with language, economics, religion, and history, whose analysis requires special scholarly skills, so with political institutions. They are hard enough to understand in their own right. Nevertheless, sociology is obliged to consider them in their many and complex relations to other institutions, and thus to go beyond the range of political science *per se*. This is not to be construed as academic imperialism. Sociologists do not wish to misappropriate the data of other sciences, nor to create the Science of Sciences which Auguste Comte hoped to beget. Rather, they flatter sister disciplines by finding it impossible to ignore them; they seek to discover the impact on social life of institutional areas studied by the other sciences, and the limits social life places on these other institutional areas.

What with the tenor and temper of the times, political institutions and ideologies offer the sociologist and the layman alike a particularly interesting field for consideration.

THE EFFECTS OF GOVERNMENTAL POLICY CHANGES

Consider how much our lives are affected by any change in governmental policy. The graduated income tax may serve as an example. Suppose that, as an American citizen, you earned a million or more dollars in any year before 1929. You no doubt made yourself permanently wealthy. With a little foresight, you would have been able to provide not only for yourself but for your heirs and assigns as well. A trust fund you might have set up would enforce frugality and guarantee affluence for many generations to come. However, if you made a million dollars in any year since the Bust . . . most of it would go back to the federal, and possibly the state, government that same year in the form of income taxes. If you did salvage much of your income, a substantial part of it would be confiscated by the state at your death, for inheritance taxes have steadily increased. Try to give it away—and you would be faced with the gift tax. . . .

By its tax policy alone the government can change old classes and create new ones. The least unrealisic proposal of nineteenth-century Utopian schemers was to liquidate an entire élite by stiffening the inheritance tax. This technique has been used, albeit gradually, in Great Britain since World War II. Government subsidies or grants to exploit particular income-producing areas, such as

Mass, Class, and Bureaucracy: The Evolution of Contemporary Society. Englewood Cliffs, N.J.: Prentice-Hall, 1963.

agriculture, education, foreign trade, air, land, and sea transportation, or radio and TV broadcasting, inevitably involve the unequal distribution of opportunity to certain persons belonging to certain classes. As preferment is given to them, other persons in other classes suffer relative deprivation.

There is no end to the immeasurable effect that government has on the rest of society. "Minor" decisions in Washington may cause major upheavals throughout the land and beyond its borders. At the same time, an intricate institutional reciprocity is constantly at work. Thus, almost all modifications in the broader society leave their impact on government in every one of its branches. As new classes emerge they seek political, that is, judicial, legislative, and executive, protection for themselves and their putative rights, while struggling to remove the special protection that has previously been offered to established classes. Urbanism, industrialism, mass production, rapid transportation, electronic communication, and a military economy tend to change the character of politics and of government. We shall now examine some aspects of this change.

GOVERNMENT IN THE FOLK SOCIETY

The folk society may be described as a system in which government does not exist, or alternatively, as a system completely dominated by government. This means only that in the folk society governmental activities cannot be separated from nongovernmental activities. There is no specific sphere of coercion, no independent police force; there is no separate machinery for the application of force or the administration of justice. Such powers are instead predominantly those of the extended family. Anthropologists have known for some time that men's clubs, age-groups and secret organizations, sometimes formed on a territorial basis, may be invested with a political function. However, as Ralph Linton and many others have shown, it is "customary reprobation by kinsmen and co-residents" that almost always proves decisive. This holds even for a civilization undergoing the embryonic stages of statehood. Robert H. Lowie, a distinguished anthropologist, writes of the Icelandic commonwealth that evolved in the Middle Ages, which had a Parliament (called *Althing*) and a "Lawman" chosen by it through a unanimous vote.

> But the Althing had no means of enforcing the laws it passed; and the Lawman was not an executive, though he presided in court and at the legislative assembly. All he was qualified to do was to recite the entire code, and his office expired with the session. He rendered no judgment and he inflicted no penalties.

It is the family head who exercises final authority over all individuals. Their transgressions are more or less spontaneously punished by other members of the society. If a simulacrum of government does exist, it takes shape in tribal councils that are composed of heads of various extended families. However, decisions reached by such councils are carried out within and between the families involved.

GOVERNMENT IN THE FEUDAL SOCIETY

Feudal society resembles folk society politically, since its governmental institutions are also interwoven with dynastic, economic, and religious institutions—and it is an open question whether feudal "government" can be said to exist. In medieval Europe, the many functions of government were so distributed along tortuous chains of command, with exclusive jurisdiction operating at each level, that, whereas there were many feudal governments, there was no feudal *government*. Let us recall that a feudal king was only first lord of the realm. All other chief lords (the barons or the counts) had substantially the same powers as a king. As in the folkish past, politics—loosely defined—consisted of agreements between heads of families or dynasties. And each dynast had his own army and his own police force—big or little.

Government, in any currently intelligible acceptation of the word, means centralized use of force within one administrative body. That body is the state, which has, as its ultimate sanction, a monopoly on the legitimate use of violence. This monopoly is called *sovereignty.* It is therefore a violation of sovereignty, a breach of national or international law, for any other body to commit acts of violence. The state, of course, has other functions, duties and sanctions, but it is most distinctively that institution which alone in the post-feudal world can conduct war abroad and legally incarcerate, fine, or execute persons within its territorial boundaries.

THE CENTRALIZATION OF POWER AND THE RISE OF THE STATE

Students of history are familiar with the general process of centralization that brought the modern state into being. Such a state could not exist until "private" courts, police, and penal systems—all indispensable under feudalism—had been disestablished and superseded by nationally sanctioned systems of law, military service, and the rest. As we have repeatedly indicated, this massive substitution of authority did not take place overnight. However, in Western history, and *mutatis mutandis,* elsewhere as well, it has involved an initial alliance between the bourgeoisie and the king against the feudal lords.

There followed the independent financing and administration of the state. The creation of a national consciousness is an essential part of the process, for without it, acceptance of the state on moral, patriotic, and ideological grounds will be lacking. No state can depend solely on coercion or the threat of violence. Government without some kind of explicit or implicit acceptance of its right to rule by subjects and citizens results either in resistance and revolution or continuous repression, warfare, and tyranny. To all concerned, such government is costly, inefficient, and unstable.

Every government offers a theoretical justification for its existence and for the legality of its actions. This justification, which is conceived to gain general acceptance, has for over a century been formally described as legitimacy. (To be sure, the phenomenon by far predates its label.) The term "legitimacy" originated at the Congress of Vienna in 1815. It was used to describe the conditions of peace negotiated at that conference by the victorious allies in their dealings with France after the final defeat of Napoleon. The delegates understood their objective to be the elimination of certain "lawless" and untraditional changes introduced by Napoleon during his reign, the restoration of monarchies that Napoleon had overthrown, and the reintroduction of "legitimacy" in European government.

FEUDAL LEGITIMACY

Since government was not really an isolable entity even in the feudal order, its legitimacy could only be based upon that of society as a whole. And society or life in *this* world was regarded as profane, from the omnipresent theological worldview which also defined life in the hereafter, in the Heavenly City, as truly sacred. While the best one could do in this world was to remove oneself from it by withdrawing to a monastery, only some men were capable of such discipline. Others did not have the "vocation" and were therefore deemed to be unsuitable for monastic life. Hence, while the really good world might be one huge monastery, not everyone could live in it. Most people had to accept the yoke of temporal existence, trying to lead as pious and proper a life as possible in spite of the human condition—which on this earth was one of irremediable sin. In accepting the temporal yoke, men prepared themselves to lead exalted lives throughout eternity.

Secular society was regarded as an organism each of whose estates had a proper function to perform. The role of the king and of the nobility was essentially to provide protection and order and to rule. The peasant was expected to provide economic goods and the Church to help men achieve salvation. The king and the nobility were anointed: they exercised God-given powers which were, however, subject to Divine Law as interpreted by the Church.

The medieval theory of legitimacy bore heavily upon the Crown and those just below it. In theory they enjoyed great secular power; in fact, they felt continuously restricted by popes and archbishops. The latter were free to use religous authority whenever opportune or necessary. There ensued a great contest in medieval society between the Crown and the Church. It turned, directly or indirectly, around the issue of ecclesiastical limits on secular power, the definition of religious control, and the actual locus of that control. The battle swung back and forth for centuries. Only peasants had no choice but to obey orders—whoever gave them.

In countering the Church's claims, various monarchs advanced theories of their own which, like all theories that conceptualize legitimacy, supported certain claims for the exercise of legal authority by one group at the expense of others. The thesis developed at this time may be called that of *Anointment,* according to which a king, at his coronation, becomes God's steward, God's agent on earth whose authority no terrestrial power can legitimately negate. His authority (only once removed from god's) is absolute. This doctrine is called the Divine Right of Kings. Its appearance signalized a fundamental shift in power which was reinforced by standing armies. European monarchs, especially after the Reformation, wielded such power as they had never before known—and were not to know again when opposition from other sources weakened them.

NATURAL LAW AS LEGITIMACY FOR DEMOCRACY

The Divine Right of Kings came under fire as members of a confident and rising bourgeoisie offered new notions of legitimacy. They were supported by a general trend toward science and skepticism in seventeenth- and eighteenth-century European thought. The idea of Natural Law as a governing principle of the physical universe and of economic relationships was supplemented by the assumption of natural law for government. According to the principal political philosophers of that age, human rights were inherent in nature. It was widely believed that all men were created equal, that they had equal rights to life, liberty, and property or the pursuit of happiness—and that governments existed only to secure these rights. If a state violated the natural rights of man, men had the natural right to revolt and replace an oppressive government with one that would provide for the commonweal. They contended that governments were originally created by voluntary agreement, through a Social Contract which made it possible for men to gratify their needs in effective concert with one another.

There were sharp differences among the proponents of this philosophy, but they tended to share the same first premises. Thus Thomas Hobbes, very much at odds with Locke, Rousseau, and Montesquieu, answered them on their own "naturalistic" grounds. He asserted that men in a state of nature were so selfish and violent that they aboriginally submitted to autocratic control to avoid internecine warfare and total chaos. Hobbes deduced from his interpretation of the prehistoric past that men were naturally suited to autocracy. This was an exceptional variation on the major political theme of his times.

A certain version of the Natural Rights and Social Contract theory of legitimacy is embodied in the Declaration of Independence and the Bill of Rights in the United States; it also animates the French Declaration of the Rights of Man and underlies the English Reforms of 1830 and 1867. In one form or another it has been basic to all democratic reform movements since the eighteenth century.

However, as an ostensibly scientific theory, it is indefensible. Since Darwin's theory of natural selection (modified but intact after a century), it is impossible to speak of "rights" in nature. All that matters in nature is survival. This brute fact Darwin and his successors have made quite clear. For more than a hundred years it has also been apparent (once again!) that man is an historical animal. The rights that we achieve at any time and place are a product of our socially determined evaluation; they are not the expression of abstract Law. At certain times tyranny, autocracy, and plutocracy are as "natural" (that is, as intelligible) as democracy.

THE LEGITIMACY OF DEMOCRATIC GOVERNMENT

The recognition that democracy is an historical phenomenon rather than an absolute imperative in nature produced a crisis among political philosophers of the Western world. Various attempts have been made to repair the damage, chiefly by legitimizing democratic government in the name of science. Nineteenth-century Utilitarians argued in mathematical terms from "the greatest good for the greatest number," postulating that whatever was most good for most people was naturally good. This theory can only be sustained as an article of faith.

Regrettably for most of us, our democratic creed has not so far been empirically validated, and probably never can be. Students of human society should not be dismayed. Belief systems, among them rationalizations of political power, are not of the same order of facts as scientific inferences—though heroic effort to prove otherwise has been made by some latter-day philosophers, who have unavailingly striven to root modern democratic principles in positive law. They argue that scientific knowledge of the probable consequences that will stem from proposed legislation can guarantee laws consistent with the best possible state of affairs. The theory goes: if certain steps now contemplated are actually taken, under specified conditions, then certain results are likely to follow. Such knowledge, if it is systematically applied, can eliminate irrationality in law and government. Science and its handmaidens, logic and research, in such a sphere, would necessarily demand the freedom to propose, experiment, disagree, and decide from the evidence at hand. To the proponents of this position, science means freedom.

In reply we must say that while it is possible, though extremely difficult, to predict the consequences of alternative laws, the judgment that some consequences are "good" and others "less good" or "no good" depends either on one's personal predisposition or on the judges' previously determined agreement. Goodness or badness is not a product of the scientific method; it is a product of individual preference or institutional consensus—and neither of these is a touchstone of objective truth. The scientific study of consequences may be used—or may continue to go unused—within any political context.

For this and other (equally weighty) reasons, Positive Law cannot solve the value problem for democrats. In any case, it has never been accepted by more than a handful of talented political philosophers. The legitimacy of democratic government rests ultimately upon personal belief in human rights, especially in those rights which offer the fullest possible freedom of expression and of growth consistent with the same freedom for others. But this belief is not demonstrably superior to any other, and those of us who subscribe to it must do so without any realistic expectation that it will be validated by science.

Review Questions

1. Briefly examine how change in governmental policy (at the local, state, or federal level) has affected some aspect of your life.
2. Briefly examine one of the following concepts:
   (a) "The Legitimacy of Democratic Government"
   (b) "Natural Law as Legitimacy for Democracy"

The Economic Institution

Definition and Functions of the Economic Institution

The **economic institution** is that social structure or structures related to the production and distribution of goods and services. The economic institution has as its goal the meeting of a society's economic needs, and it performs the following functions to meet these needs: first, the gathering of resources; second, the manufacture of goods and services; third, the distribution of goods and services; and fourth, the consumption of goods and services. In his now-classic analysis of society, Williams (1970) notes that the American economic institution often appears to be the most conspicuous feature of our social structure. America is, above all, a business civilization. Before we examine more closely the American economic institution, an important distinction must be made between capitalism and socialism.

Functions of the economic institution

Capitalism and Socialism

Two types of economic systems primarily regulate the production, distribution, and consumption of goods and services in societies: capitalism and socialism. Capitalism is based on private ownership of the means of production and on competition for profits. This system depends upon the circular relationship of capital investments and workers' labor to produce more goods and services.

Capitalism and socialism

Capitalism, in other words, is an economic system in which the wealth of society is held privately. The wealth is used by its owners to create more wealth.

Socialism is basically aimed to free workers from their dependence on a few wealthy owners of the means of production. It is also aimed to provide a decent living standard for all of society. Profits are reinvested rather than accumulated as wealth. **Socialism,** in other words, is an economic system in which such productive tools as labor, capital, and land are owned and managed by the group as a whole or by its agent—the state. It must be pointed out that one does not find pure capitalism or pure socialism in the world, because economic systems have to adapt to political and other conditions. Economic systems usually combine elements and characteristics of both capitalism and socialism.

THE NEW CAPITALISM: DEMOCRATIC FREE ENTERPRISE

William E. Halal

In the following reading, "The New Capitalism: Democratic Free Enterprise," the author, William E. Halal, reports that the old American capitalism that is based on an industrial paradigm is giving way to a new economic structure that values "smart" growth, market networks, participative leadership, multiple goals, and strategic management.

A historic transformation is taking place as the "Old Capitalism" of the industrial past slowly yields to a "New Capitalism" for the Information Age. More than simply a shift to "knowledge industries," this newly emerging system of business and economics represents a fundamental change in the way we think about goods and services, technology, social structures, and power—even growth and wealth itself.

THE UNLIMITED FRONTIER OF SMART GROWTH

The New Capitalism is opening up a vast new frontier of progress that lies beyond the old unrestrained form of "hard growth," and expanding world population is continuing to industrialize, thereby necessitating a more-balanced type of growth that weighs benefits against costs to improve the quality of life for all—"smart growth."

Sheer material consumption is yielding to an interest in small cars, lean diets, efficient energy use, and other forms of more-intelligent living. Manufacturers like Dow Corning, Armco, and 3M are developing production systems that recycle waste to reduce pollution—while also making bigger profits. High-tech companies are creating a second industrial revolution that improves communications, education, health care, and a vast range of other unmet social needs. Information industries, for instance, are expected to become the biggest economic sector. . . .

From *The Futurist*, January/February 1988, pp. 26–30.

To provide these more-personal services, a client-driven form of marketing is emerging that shifts the focus from selling to genuinely serving customers. Avant-garde companies like Hewlett-Packard, L.L. Bean, and Marriott are measuring customer satisfaction, forming consumer-advisory panels, and generally learning to work with their clients.

Smart growth entails far more complex challenges, but cultivating this *inner* domain of "human economy" offers a wiser, more sustainable form of progress that is almost unlimited.

FREE ENTERPRISE IS MOVING INSIDE CORPORATIONS

To manage this increasing complexity, the New Capitalism is also restructuring institutions. The problems of bureaucracy are becoming prohibitive as corporations grow bigger in a global economy, so hierarchical organizations are being broken up into "market networks" that are flexible and responsive.

Leading-edge firms like IBM, TRW, and GE are developing decentralized forms of control, encouraging small and autonomous business units, helping "intrapreneurs" start new ventures, and allowing people to choose their own jobs. A prominent example is the way IBM took the lead in microcomputers by using a self-contained "independent business unit" free of normal controls. This freedom enabled the unit to develop the personal computer in just a year and a half.

Although market networks are messy, intense competition in a turbulent world is transforming big companies into "confederations of entrepreneurs" that bring the creativity of free markets *inside* organizations themselves.

EXTENDING DEMOCRACY TO DAILY LIFE

A third feature of the New Capitalism is the growth of participative leadership. Demands for higher productivity and the self-confident employees of the "Me" Decade are driving companies to enlist the commitment and talent of their work force.

Firms like Delta Airlines, Motorola, and Ford are working with labor to improve performance, share profits, and safeguard employee rights. For instance, auto makers and airlines signed historic contracts recently in which unions gave up pay increases and work restrictions in return for profit sharing and a say in management decisions.

As a result of unyielding competitive forces, no-nonsense executives who abhor any whiff of lofty ideals are unwittingly moving to democratize the workplace simply because it is efficient. Employees are now seated on the boards of directors of about a dozen major corporations. . . .

A few employee/directors do not make a revolution; however, the extension of democracy to daily life will likely grow because the sharing of rights *and* responsibilities is best for both labor and management.

Other "stakeholders" are being enfranchised to create a broader form of democratic governance that serves all constituencies, which in turn enhances profit. It can be thought of as a better way to make money.

The Europeans, Japanese, and avant-garde American companies like IBM, Dayton Hudson, and Hewlett-Packard work closely with investors, labor, government, customers, and suppliers to foster business success. A good example is the statesmanlike way Lee Iacocca saved Chrysler from bankruptcy by uniting its constituencies to work together for their common good.

This concept is still in an early stage of development, and it involves highly charged, sensitive issues concerning profit versus social welfare. But economic and political pressures will probably continue to urge an "open-system" corporate community that creates not only financial wealth but *social* wealth.

STRATEGIC MANAGEMENT CONVERTS THREATS INTO ADVANTAGES

These moves are leading to a new form of "strategic management," which is needed to cope with today's escalating change. Progressive corporations convert problems of their clients into smart growth, use market networks to foster enterprise at the grass roots, resolve obstacles through participative leadership, and integrate multiple goals into a strategic coalition of interests.

In addition, most large companies and many government agencies now use strategic planning and issue management to gain control over their future. At ARCO, for instance, a committee of representatives from each organizational unit meets to identify issues and then breaks into teams to study the issues and offer recommendations. As many as a hundred issues are tracked until they are resolved or disappear.

The results of these trends should be an "organization–environment symbiosis" that converts external forces for change into strategic advantages—much as the oriental martial arts turn the strength of an aggressor to one's own defense.

TOWARD DEMOCRATIC FREE ENTERPRISE

There are also signs that the old adversarial business–government relationship is being resolved as progressive corporate and civic leaders form partnerships to foster economic progress.

Wang Laboratories worked with the community in Lowell, Massachusetts, to turn this decaying mill town into a model of high-tech prosperity. A coalition of banks, hospitals, and universities made Indianapolis an international center of culture. Michigan, Massachusetts, and Pennsylvania have started labor–management–government alliances to spur economic growth. At the national level, there is interest among many politicians, businesses, and the public in forming tripartite councils to improve macroeconomic policy.

In time, the growth of business–government partnerships may produce a powerful new form of economics that combines *both* democratic collaboration and free-market competition—a system of "Democratic Free Enterprise."

Similar changes are occurring worldwide that may even defuse the tension between the extreme ideologies of the Old Capitalism and the Old Socialism.

Experiments are under way in Europe, the Third World, and even socialist states, which are producing hybrid economies that combine various types of democracy, state control, and free enterprise. China, for instance, seems intent on creating a form of "market socialism," in which managers of state factories have local control, prices are set by a market, and then entrepreneurs can own their own small businesses. And Soviet leader Mikhail Gorbachev is struggling to move the Soviet Union in this same direction.

There are enormous obstacles to be overcome, of course, and a rich diversity of economic systems will flourish among various nations. But such prospects offer the hope of creating a coherent world order that may reconcile the conflict between the superpowers as the New Capitalism becomes not too unlike the New Socialism.

NECESSITY REMAINS THE MOTHER OF INVENTION

If the New Capitalism is so advantageous, why is it that most corporations, government, and other social institutions remain firmly attached to the Old Capitalism that is rapidly becoming outmoded?

Consider General Motors, the giant of industrial America that was once the most successful business in the world. The company has poured $40 billion into an attempt to fend off the Japanese invasion of the auto industry, and it has made some successful moves, such as the famous "downsizing" of its cars and the joint venture with Toyota at the Fremont plant in California. Yet, GM is widely acknowledged to be rapidly losing the battle for world auto markets because it remains mired in bureaucratic habits of the past. A Japanese competitor dismissed GM as "a giant that's sick and in bed."

The problem is not limited to auto making, steel, and other smokestack industries, because many glamorous high-tech firms are also in trouble. Eight out of 10 major high-tech industries are losing out in world markets, according to John Young, president of Hewlett-Packard and chairman of the Reagan Commission on Industrial Competitiveness.

A bright spot in this bleak picture, however, is that crisis is the other side of opportunity. The New Capitalism seems to be moving on inexorably—not out of enlightened ideas, benign intentions, or even good planning, but because of the hard necessities of survival in a turbulent, competitive global economy.

Futurists warned of the need to curb excessive consumption for decades, but it was only the stark necessity of crisis that finally brought about the beginning of a wiser form of growth: Long gas lines drove people to favor small cars, pollution alerts produced demands for environmental controls, and heart attacks created a taste for simpler, healthier diets. Likewise, many experts have long urged flexible, participative forms of organization, but the harsh impetus of Japan's invasion into American markets was required to make these ideas a reality. And the concept of democratic governance remained a lofty ideal until potential bankruptcy forced Chrysler, Eastern, and other firms to share control with their employees.

Thus, the New Capitalism is evolving not out of the promise of a benign world, but because necessity remains the mother of invention. Severe crises are likely to continue threatening us for years, and it is in the crucible of such trials that a hard, enduring new economic system is being forged to withstand the challenge of a difficult future.

THE TWIN IMPERATIVES OF INFORMATION TECHNOLOGY

These crises can be better understood by seeing that deep underlying forces are shifting the technological foundation of economics. The central issue of our time is that an explosion of computer technology is creating a knowledge-based economy. And since knowledge increases when shared, a new economic system is evolving that combines collaborative problem solving and entrepreneurial freedom.

Thus, the New Capitalism that is erratically but inexorably being produced by this "technological imperative" seems—logically enough—to be based on traditional American ideals. That explains why the most striking theme running through all these trends is that the Western principles of democracy and free enterprise are being extended to greater heights and united into an unusual synthesis of cooperation and competition.

Not only are progressive firms developing collaborative relations with their constituencies, as noted above, but they are even working more closely with their competitors. About 55 research consortia have been formed recently to meet foreign competition—such as the Microelectronics and Computer Technology Corporation, a joint venture of 20 firms working together to advance the state of the art in information technology. The advent of cooperative R&D has been called the most significant step forward since the computer chip.

But this is not "socialism," because it is part of the related trend toward greater market competition. Free enterprise is flowering in air travel, telecommunications, banking, and other major economic sectors, while a burgeoning world economy is heightening competition across borders. And, as we've also seen, free enterprise is even moving *into* corporations themselves.

These trends show that a New Capitalism powered by democracy and free enterprise is relentlessly emerging—not because of devotion to principles, but because the Information Age demands it. A massive increase in complexity requires entrepreneurial freedom to handle the needs of a more diverse and more competitive economy, while there is an equally great need for democratic collaboration to bind these volatile differences together.

The compatibility of these twin imperatives is nicely illustrated by the various alliances that American auto makers have formed with their counterparts abroad. While GM, Ford, and Chrysler compete more fiercely against Toyota, Fiat, and Renault, they are also cooperating with these same adversaries by jointly making and selling autos in each other's markets. As noted before, even China, the Soviet Union, and other parts of the socialist bloc seem to be slowly heading toward a modern form of socialism incorporating both democracy and free enterprise, because they know it is essential if they hope to revitalize their economies.

Viewed from a strictly objective, scientific perspective, technological change seems fairly certain to move roughly along the path outlined here, so something resembling the New Capitalism should arrive within a decade or two.

Mendeleev's understanding of the periodic table of elements accurately predicted the discovery of physical elements that occupied feasible niches in atomic structure, and Arthur C. Clarke forecast the development of earth satellites to fill an open niche in spaceflight. Likewise, there exists an empty niche for this more productive, more civilized form of political economy, and the main question is which nation will be the first to develop it.

Review Questions

1. Briefly comment on the following statement: "The Old Capitalism is giving way to a New Capitalism that values smart growth, market networks, participative leadership, multiple goals, and strategic management."
2. Do you see your own career choice as being affected by the New Capitalism? Why or why not?

The American Economic Institution and Industrialism

In less complex, nonindustrialized societies, economic institutions merge with families and tribes. In point of fact, it is difficult to distinguish economic activities from family life, religion, politics, and social relations.

In more complex societies such as the United States, the economic institution is more clearly separated from other social institutions. The primary means of production used by American society is industrialism, not hunting and gathering or agriculture. This type of production influences the character of American social institutions and culture. Industrialism combined with advanced technology influences the size and complexity of our society. Local communities and families no longer function as self-sufficient economic units. Buyer-seller and employer-employee relationships are depersonalized. Few American workers produce complete products themselves. Workers are also more interdependent than in the past. Complex organizations and corporations regulate the activities of many workers and the flow of money.

Industrialism influences the character of our social institutions

Corporations. America's economic institution is very much dominated by large corporations. Fewer than 1 percent of all U.S. corporations—the nation's top 100 corporations—own more than half the manufacturing assets. For the past 25 years, America's 500 largest industrial corporations have accounted for over three-quarters of all industrial sales, profits, and employment. There is also a similar concentration in other business areas, such as banking, finance, transportation, utilities, and communications (Skolnick and Currie, 1985).

U.S. corporate power

The influence and power of corporations have important implications for society. For example, corporations apply political leverage on national policy, gaining favors for themselves and very much influencing the country's tax structure. Economist John Kenneth Galbraith (1971) believes that because corporate capitalism has become so enormous and complex, and because it invests so much time and capital in itself, it cannot chance free competition. The stakes are too high. Government and corporations therefore cooperate in a planned economy, allowing minimal competition among the major enterprises.

Galbraith on corporate capitalism

It is also important to note that the power and growth of U.S. corporations and their impact on social as well as economic life were rarely questioned for almost 25 years after World War II because of the high levels of material wealth. But in the 1970s, throughout the 1980s, and into the 1990s, conditions changed, and America faced the economic crimes of unemployment, inflation, deflation, and the inability of many families to meet basic needs. In addition, more highly visible financial and business corruption, bank failures, industrial pollution, and poor quality consumer goods have made Americans more distrustful of corporations and the government. In any event, corporations are an important component of the American economy. In addition, the American work force is an important component of the economy. It is also changing in many significant ways.

Americans are most distrustful of corporations

The Changing Work Force. The work force is an important component of the American economic institution. Future trends in work-force participation are able to be projected in that people who will enter the labor force in the year 2000 have been born. In point of fact, projections clearly indicate that the work force is significantly changing. Between today and 2030, the Amerian work force will grow more slowly, and newcomers, mainly between the ages of 16 and the mid-20s, will decrease substantially. The work force will include more aged people. Workers between the ages of 45 and 65 will increase 25 percent or more (Fullerton, 1985). The work force will also include more women. Many factors, such as enhanced opportunities, career aspirations, and supportive services

The U.S. work force will grow more slowly

such as flex time and child-care facilities, have contributed to the participation of women in our economy's work force. Even with the greater inclusion of aged and women in the work force, total work-force growth will be lower than in the past. In addition, the percentage of minority workers will substantially increase, and the proportion of white entry-level workers will decline (Cascio and Zammuto, 1987).

More minority workers

Manufacturing to Service. A major shift in the American economy is one from manufacturing to service. There have been and there will continue to be in the decades to come significant shifts from manufacturing to lower-paying service jobs. Well into the future, it is expected that 9 out of 10 jobs will be in the service-producing industries (Personick, 1985). Jobs in service-producing industries are characterized by an increase in the importance of working with clients and customers rather than interacting with material things and co-workers (Klein and Hall, 1988).

There will be more service jobs

Future Work Environments. Future work environments will be technologically sophisticated and complex. Technological systems include such things as "programmable automation, which includes the use of robots that are reprogrammable, multifunctional machines that will manipulate materials, and various forms of computer-assisted design and computer-assisted manufacturing" (Klein and Hall, 1988; Goldstein and Gilliam, 1990). It is projected that this will result in improved product quality and increased production that will permit America to regain a competitive edge in global market competition (Cascio and Zammuto, 1987).

More technologically complex work environments

The International Environment. Future trends also indicate that for U.S. organizations to survive in the future, they need to operate in an international environment. Various corporations and organizations are exploring a wide variety of strategies. For example, researchers have noted that some organizations are "exploring projects in which data entry functions are performed in foreign countries because the advantages of low wages and surplus workers outweigh the disadvantages of long-distance electronic data transmission" (Klein and Hall, 1988; Goldstein and Gilliam, 1990). It is certainly no longer unusual for a manufacturer to produce a product such as a car that is "partially manufactured in the United States and partially manufactured in a foreign country. Sometimes these efforts involve arrangements between liaison teams that direct efforts involving different employees in different organizations in different countries, all contributing to the production of a single final product" (Goldstein and Gilliam, 1990).

A more international environment

NEW WAVE ECONOMICS: TRENDS FOR THE 21st CENTURY

Edward Yardeni and David Moss

In the following reading, "New Wave Economics: Trends for the 21st Century," Edward Yardeni and David Moss stress the point that in the next century, there "won't be one preeminent superpower. Rather, the world will include many highly competitive capitalist economies, all prospering together."

The front cover of the April 7, 1988, issue of *The New York Times Magazine* portrayed an overweight, stooping bald eagle, dressed in red, white, and blue, holding a cane for support and staring anxiously into a small mirror. The cover story was titled "Taking Stock: Is America in Decline?"

Also in 1988, *Newsweek* ran a special front cover report, "The Pacific Century: Is America in Decline?"; *U.S. News and World Report* examined "American Competitiveness: Are We Losing It?"; and, in *The Atlantic,* Peter G. Peterson predicted that "America is about to wake up to a painful new economic reality, following the biggest binge of borrowing in the history of the nation."

Obviously, the decline of America is a very popular subject. In his 1987 book, *Beyond Our Means,* Alfred Malabre, Jr., warned that "we've been living beyond our means—for so long, in fact, that now, sadly, it's beyond our means to put things right, at least in an orderly, reasonably painless manner." Paul Kennedy, a professor of history at Yale University, wrote a recent best-seller, *The Rise and Fall of the Great Powers,* based on the theme that "the United States now runs the risk, so familiar to historians, of the rise and fall of previous Great Powers, of what might roughly be called 'imperial overstretch. . . .' " Benjamin M. Friedman, a Harvard economist and author of *Day of Reckoning: The Consequences of American Economic Policy Under Reagan and After,* told reporters recently that the prosperity of the last eight years was "an illusion." Meanwhile, Ravi Batra still is expecting a Great Depression . . .

We argue that the pessimists are wrong. Americans do face all sorts of challenges as we approach the next decade and the next century. The pessimists do play a very important role in our society by identifying the problems, but they tend to exaggerate. The forces of darkness always seem to be superior to the forces of light.

The pessimistic crowd has inspired us to reexamine the economy. We believe that it is time to change the way we think about it because the economy has changed. The business cycle framework is useful sometimes and downright useless at other times. Keynesian, monetarist, supply-side, rational expectations, and other models of the economy are too dogmatic, rigid, and simplistic.

As an alternative, we offer New Wave Economics, whose roots are in Adam Smith's *The Wealth of Nations,* published in 1776. In Smith's time, pessimism was as prevalent as it is today. Many essayists and pamphleteers

---

were bemoaning the decline of Great Britain and predicting ruin for the country. Smith sought to discredit the pessimists of his day by demonstrating how free markets foster economic growth and increase the wealth of nations. New Wave Economics is an empirically based framework which examines several important new trends in the economy that largely have been ignored by the traditional models and the pessimists. New Wave Economics is not a radically new model of the economy or a theory which explains observed economic behavior. Rather, it is an interdisciplinary approach that extrapolates several important social, political, economic, and demographic trends visible today into the 1990's.

The resulting outlook for the U.S. and other capitalist economies is very upbeat, in stark contrast to the numerous dire predictions. Our optimistic forecast isn't intended to be a down-the-road scenario. Most of the trends we are projecting over the next five years already are under way.

Market capitalism will continue to proliferate and flourish in the global economy. The prosperity created by the capitalist system is especially impressive in comparison to the stagnation of communist economies. The world economy will become more capitalistic as additional countries deregulate their economies. Increasingly, the competitive market will replace state ownership and central planning. In capitalist societies, public policies will become more effective by harnessing, rather than constraining, market forces. Deregulation will spur global competition, which will become even more intense as the capitalist world becomes increasingly multi-polar. The U.S. no longer dominates the capitalist world—Asian and European economies are as large as the North American economy. These markets will grow together, trade will expand, and more prosperity will result. Economic growth disciplined by global competition is not inflationary, so growth should be sustainable.

Capitalism never has been more dynamic. Capitalism produces change, which is occurring more rapidly. Intense global competition is the major cause of the faster pace of capitalism. Managerial and technological innovations are happening more frequently. Competitors are emerging in newly industrializing countries. Many companies are responding successfully to the challenges of dynamic market capitalism; business planners and managers are learning that, to survive and prosper in the New Wave world, they must adapt rapidly to the changes in the global marketplace. They recognize that their companies must produce and distribute goods and services in all the major capitalist markets. In the future, production will be almost as internationally mobile as financial capital. The proliferation of productive capacity around the world will intensify price competition, so inflation should stay low. To remain profitable, companies will continue to cut costs and increase productivity. Prosperity will create labor shortages, but businesses are more likely to boost capital expenditures than inflate their labor costs by bidding up wage rates. Capital spending and technological innovation should accelerate over the next several years in the industrialized economies.

The markets should do a much better job of regulating the capitalist economies than policymakers. Recessions should be less frequent and less severe than in the past. The booms and busts of the business cycle will remain a part of our economic lives, but market forces should dampen the booms. In the global credit markets, bondholders push yields up rapidly when they perceive an inflation threat. Such preemptive strikes reduce the likelihood that inflation will become a serious problem again. Therefore, severe busts no longer will be necessary to unwind the excesses caused by the booms since excesses won't be allowed to build in the first place.

In addition, capitalist economies are becoming more diversified and resilient to shocks such as the global stock market crash of 1987. Major industries can fall into recession without depressing over-all economic growth. Rolling recessions that are limited to certain industries are more likely to occur than economy-wide recessions.

Exchange rate movements can take quite a long time to fix trade imbalances among capitalist economies, but they do work eventually. The U.S. trade deficit should continue to narrow, another achievement of the automatic adjustment mechanism of the marketplace.

In the U.S., powerful demographic forces related to the aging of the baby boom should push the personal savings rate toward 10% and the unemployment rate down to four percent within the next five years. Consumer spending, which in real terms rose close to five percent per year on average from 1983 to 1986, should increase at half this pace over the next five years. Home prices should climb at a much slower pace as the baby boomers settle down. Capital spending should be very strong because the shortage of young new job seekers will force businesses to invest in labor-saving equipment. With the baby boomers now in their 30's and 40's, their work ethic and productivity should improve.

Older baby boomers are likely to borrow less and save more. Some of these savings will go directly (or indirectly through bond funds) into government securities. Savings institutions should enjoy greater deposit inflows just at the point when the mad scramble for housing and mortgage credit of the 1970's and 1980's comes to an end. The traditional lenders to the housing market will have more money to invest at the same time that the demand for mortgage loans cools off. As a result, savings institutions are likely to increase their purchases of other credit market instruments, particularly U.S. Treasury securities.

We wouldn't be surprised if, by the end of the decade, investors complain about a shortage of bonds and nostalgically recall when yields were above nine percent. Such a prospect is even more likely to become reality if the Social Security trust fund surpluses continue to swell as projected by the actuaries. These surpluses combined with sustained economic growth and lower interest rates should balance the Federal budget within the next five years.

THE WEALTH OF NATIONS

Today, the capitalist world is evolving into three enormous, interdependent marketplaces: the North American bloc, which is moving toward a free-trade association between the U.S. and Canada; the newly industralizing countries of Asia, led by Japan; and, the unified economies of Western Europe, which, by 1992, will be the greatest example of economic deregulation in world history.

Economic borders are expanding dramatically and becoming less constrained by political borders. Markets are no longer national, but international. Trade is becoming freer. Competition within and among the capitalist blocs is intensifying. Challengers are cropping up within the newly industrializing nations; countries like Thailand and Malaysia are emerging as new competitors in the global marketplace; and, of course, tremendous potential exists in China and India.

The U.S. is not a loser in this arrangement. Rather, it prospers along with the other capitalist nations because Americans are responding successfully to the global competitive challenges. If the Asian and European blocs are prospering at a more rapid pace, a pessimist could conclude that America is in decline. However, this view is based on a wrong assumption—that the world economy is a zero-sum game. Competition does increase risk, but also raises the rewards enormously by expanding the global marketplace. The three capitalist blocs are huge markets that will continue to grow together.

Some pessimists foresee a grimmer scenario, with tremendous imbalances and tensions in the global economy. However, market forces are working. People are changing in response to the global competitive challenges and sharing a desire to prosper. Increasingly, they believe that capitalism is the means to that end. As trade becomes freer, the differences are likely to diminish. For example:

■ Americans are working harder and productivity is growing at a faster pace, particularly in manufacturing. The threat of deindustrialization forced us to make our businesses more productive to compete in world markets. American companies are implementing Japanese cost-cutting techniques, and workers are settling for smaller wage gains so that their employers will stay in the U.S. Quality and the work ethic are making a comeback. Also, demographic forces should slow consumption and boost savings.

■ As the Japanese have prospered, they've come to recognize that they can afford to improve the quality of their lives. They realize that they won't continue to prosper unless North Americans and Europeans are also. That's why they'll continue to support demands that they should consume and import more. Japanese companies responded to the soaring yen and plummeting exports by designing products that would be more appealing to their domestic customers. As the workweek gradually declines, their consumers will have more time to shop, increasingly at discount stores that sell only imported products. Discounting, a great American tradition, now is becoming popular in Japan.

■ South Korea's era of cheap labor rapidly is coming to an end. Its workers are proud of their country's successes in global markets and, not surprisingly, are demanding much higher wages (1987's average increase was 17%).

■ Even the communists are starting to come around. Under Mikhail Gorbachev's *perestroika,* the Soviet economy will remain planned and, with small exceptions, publicly owned. Still, the Soviet leader wants more local initiative. According to Abel Aganbegyan, a key economic advisor to Gorbachev, "market relations in the U.S.S.R. will be deepened and broadened" and centralized pricing retained only for the most essential products so that "free prices will grow significantly."

Poland and Hungary are permitting more private enterprise. The Vietnamese have a new program of economic renovation which encourages entrepreneurs to start their own small businesses and requires state companies to make a profit. In *The Wall Street Journal,* Boris Konte, vice governor of Yugoslavia's National Bank, explained the forces working to reshape the whole communist landscape: "My country can't compete with [the U.S.] without open borders and a free market. It isn't a matter of politics."

Are the "workers of the world" on the verge of a great transformation? They seem to be, but it probably will take many years before the vast potential of consumers and producers in the communist world is set free from state control and central planning. For example, the Chinese, who are yearning to catch up with their Asian neighbors, have permitted the emergence of free markets, which now determine the prices of about half the country's output. However, in September, 1988, in the face of rampaging inflation, China's leaders moved to strengthen centralized control of the economy.

Today, the European Economic Community (EEC), which was established in 1958 and has grown from six to 12 members, is poised for a great leap forward. At a 1985 summit meeting in Milan, the EEC governments approved the Single European Act, which would create an open market by the end of 1992, promising to eliminate about 300 major economic barriers. Most significantly, these can be removed by "qualified majority voting" among ministers, rather than unanimity.

Why did the Europeans agree to such an unprecedented and extraordinarily ambitious deregulation plan? They feared that they were falling hopelessly behind the U.S. and Japan. For example, the U.S. created 28,000,000 jobs between 1970 and 1986, while the big Western European countries created next to none. Since 1957, a web of red tape and regulations gradually has spread throughout the EEC. A truck driver needs 35 pages of invoices, customs declarations, and import statistical surveys to carry a load of goods from one end of the continent to the other. Fragmented markets force the biggest manufacturer in Europe, Philips NV, to warehouse goods worth 23% of annual sales, while its consumer electronics counterparts in the U.S. and Japan must tie up only 14% of their income on inventory. European leaders hope that freer markets might cure "Eurosclerosis."

If the plan succeeds, the European Economic Community will be the world's greatest market. The potential is impressive: 320,000,000 consumers in the EEC, compared with 240,000,000 in the U.S. and 120,000,000 in Japan. In 1987, the EEC's gross domestic product was $4.2 trillion, almost equal to the U.S.'s and well above the $2.7 trillion combined total of Japan, South Korea, Taiwan, Hong Kong, and Singapore.

Taxes are the greatest obstacle to the formation of a one-market Europe. Value-added tax (VAT) rates vary widely from country to country. High-tax countries fear VAT-dodging by cross-border shoppers. There seems to be a great deal of resistance to proposals that bring tax rates closer together. Nevertheless, the soaring rate of mergers and acquisitions and the quicker pace of corporate restructuring reflect their business community's optimism about the 1992 outcome.

THE PACIFIC CENTURY?

Across the Pacific, changes are just as significant as those under way across the Atlantic. The Europeans responded to the global competitive challenge by adopting the Single European Act, which targets the barriers to free trade that must be removed to create one market. In response to international pressures, the Japanese are making great progress in opening their domestic economy to foreign competitors. The blueprint for the deregulation of the Japanese economy is the 1986 Maekawa Report, which recommended a historic transformation of Japanese society.

Traditionally, most Japanese have believed that theirs was a poor, small, island nation with few natural resources and that everybody had to sacrifice to build it up. This overwhelming consensus helps to explain why the Japanese have worked longer hours and saved more than their Western counterparts. Also, they've favored mercantilist economic policies which encouraged production and exports, and discouraged consumption and imports. This approach was extraordinarily successful, but, in recent years, most of the world started to see Japan as rich, powerful, greedy, and unfair. Resentment was especially strong in the U.S. because of the widening bilateral trade deficit with Japan. Protectionist sentiments in America threatened to disrupt Japan's export-led economy.

The Maekawa Report proposed a revolutionary restructuring of economic priorities including a radical deregulation plan based on two premises: Japan must correct its trade imbalances to relieve international tensions which threaten to devastate its economy; and Japan is no longer poor, so it is time that the people enjoy the fruits of their country's prosperity. The Maekawa Committee recommended that Japan strive for economic growth led by domestic demand instead of exports. Active efforts should be made to encourage imports, particularly of manufactured goods.

The mercantilist approach was swept away. Japan was ready to join the capitalist world—to "strengthen the free trade system and to work for sustained and stable world economic growth." The Maekawa group established the following guiding principle: "In order to make Japan more internationally open, policies based upon market mechanisms should be implemented from the viewpoint of 'freedom in principle, restrictions only as exceptions.' Accordingly, further improvement in market access and thorough promotion of deregulation should be carried out."

Its trading partners and critics were not impressed. Skeptics observed that the Japanese have a long history of broken promises to foreigners who pressured them to open their markets. During April, 1987, the Reagan Administration capitulated to tremendous political pressure at home and slapped a tariff on selected Japanese consumer electronics because the Japanese were violating a 1986 semiconductor trade agreement with the U.S. *Time* noted that "Japanese behavior seemed to U.S. officials to be part of a familiar Japanese attitude toward trade issues: delay followed by nominal agreement followed by intransigence." C. Fred Bergsten, director of the Institute for International Economics, summarized Washington's attitude toward the Japanese: "They give us very clearly the message that they only move when hit over the head by a two-by-four. So we will accommodate and hit them over the head."

Despite these frustrations with the Japanese, the bashing is starting to produce results. Interest rates on loans from Japan's Housing Loan Corporation have been lowered repeatedly. In 1988, its government abolished the tax-exempt status of personal savings accounts in an effort to reduce Japan's high savings rate. The Labor Standards Law was amended to reduce statutory weekly working hours gradually from 48 to 40. The government has called for longer summer vacations and provided incentives to developers of new resorts. Since mid-1985, the Japanese abolished or reduced tariffs on nearly 2,000 imported goods and eased standard requirements and certification procedures. The effects of these efforts have been impressive. Domestic consumption is booming and imported goods are selling particularly well. In 1987, the Japanese built 1,600,000 new homes, the most since 1973.

Now, the Japanese are starting to worry about competition from newly industrializing countries. In 1987, Japan became a net importer of textile products for the first time in recent history. Korean imports account for more than half of the total, causing Japan's knitting industry to complain that the Koreans are dumping sweaters in Japan.

Meanwhile, the Koreans dramatically are expanding their capacity to produce steel, autos, and consumer electronics. Thailand is emerging as a newly industrializing country. The Taiwanese are making significant manufacturing investments in the Philippines. Malaysia is a major supplier of semiconductors.

Will the next century be the Pacific century, as some fear? We doubt it. More likely, it will be the New Wave century. There won't be one preeminent economic superpower. Rather, the world will include many highly competitive capitalist economies, all prospering together.

Review Question

1. Briefly comment on the statement that "there won't be one preeminent superpower in the 21st century . . . the world will include many highly competitive capitalist economies, all prospering together."

Social Institutions: Conclusion

In conclusion, embodying values that are shared by members of society, social institutions provide stability and consistency in society and function as controllers and regulators of behavior. Institutions regulate the ways people meet important recurrent situations such as birth, marriage, family, and death. They also regulate how we believe in God, how we train our young, how we deal with power relations, and how we acquire economic goods. In addition, institutions help ensure that these situations will recur.

In general then, social institutions are not planned entities or deliberate creations of people. In every society, people have basic needs—eating, reproduction, protection, and other needs—that must be met. In their attempts at various ways to meet these needs, they discover that certain patterns of behavior are more effective than others. When groups within a culture believe that a particular set of norms, roles, and values is vital to their survival and that people in society must follow it, the process of institutionalization occurs. Regular and predictable behavior replaces spontaneous and unpredictable behavior.

Summary

1. A social institution is a pattern of norms centered around a major societal goal, value, or need. Social institutions such as the political and economic are found in every society.
2. The political institution exists because of the need for maintaining social control and for regulating the power of some people or groups over others.
3. The economic institution is concerned with meeting a society's economic needs.
4. Social institutions provide stability and consistency in society and regulate human behavior.

STUDY GUIDE

Chapter Objectives

After studying this chapter, you should be able to:

1. Define "political institution," "power" (according to Weber), "state," and "democracy"
2. List the four functions of the political institution
3. Define the concepts of sovereignty and nation
4. Have an understanding of the effects of governmental policy changes
5. Understand what is meant by feudal legitimacy and the legitimacy of democratic government
6. Define "economic institution" and list its four major functions
7. Define and compare "capitalism" and "socialism"
8. Explain how the American economic institution is dominated by large corporations
9. Understand what is meant by the term "New Capitalism"
10. Understand changes in the American work force

Key Terms

Capitalism (p. 394)
Charisma (p. 386)
Community (p. 386)
Corporation (p. 399)
Democracy (p. 386)
Economic institution (p. 393)
Government (p. 386)
Institutions (p. 407)
Nation (p. 386)
Nation-state (p. 386)
Oligarchy (p. 386)
Political institution (p. 385)
Power (p. 385)
Social institution (p. 407)
Socialism (p. 394)
Sovereign state (p. 386)
Sovereignty (p. 386)
State (p. 386)

Self-Test

Short Answer

(p. 407) 1. "Institution" is defined as ______________________________

____

(p. 385) 2. The political institution is ______________________________

____

____

(p. 387) 3. The four functions of the political institution in the United States are:

a. ____________________
b. ____________________
c. ____________________
d. ____________________

(p. 393) 4. The economic institution is ____________________

____

(p. 393) 5. The four functions of the economic institution are:
a. ____________________
b. ____________________
c. ____________________
d. ____________________

Multiple-Choice *(Answers are on page 412.)*

(p. 386) 1. As described by Max Weber, three kinds of authority include all the following except:
a. legal
b. charismatic
c. religious
d. traditional

(p. 386) 2. Legitimated power or authority can be based on:
a. the legal norms of society
b. tradition
c. charisma
d. all the above

(p. 386) 3. According to the text, the state:
a. is the least notable institution
b. has sovereignty whereby it can legally use force to have groups and individuals conform to and obey its laws
c. is the particular group of people who operate the government
d. none of the above

(p. 386) 4. A nation is a group of people who share a common background, including all or at least several of the following:
a. culture, history, language
b. geographic location
c. race, ethnic characteristics
d. all the above

(p. 394) 5. America's economic system is basically:
a. totalitarian
b. socialist
c. traditional
d. capitalist

(p. 393) 6. The economic institution has the following functions:
a. the gathering of resources
b. the manufacturing and consumption of goods and services
c. the consumption of goods and services
d. all the above

(p. 398) 7. The primary means of production used by American society is:

a. hunting
b. industrialism
c. gathering
d. agriculture

(p. 393) 8. The two types of economic systems that regulate the production, distribution, and consumption of goods and services within societies are:
a. capitalism and communism
b. capitalism and socialism
c. socialism and democracy
d. none of the above

(p. 394) 9. A system in which the economy is operated for profit and is in private hands is called:
a. a welfare state
b. socialism
c. a monopoly
d. capitalism

(p. 401) 10. According to Yardeni and Moss:
a. market capitalism will continue to proliferate and flourish in the global economy
b. capitalism has never been more dynamic
c. the markets should do a poorer job of regulating the capitalist economies than policymakers
d. only *a* and *b* of the above

True/False *(Answers are on page 412.)*

T F 11. For Weber, power is the ability or the potential to influence the thoughts or behavior of others. (p. 386)

T F 12. A government has sovereignty when it successfully asserts its claim to make the rules in a given territory. (p. 386)

T F 13. Sovereign states claim illegitimacy to the extent that their claim to rule is willingly accepted. (p. 386)

T F 14. The nation-state is the major form of political organization in the world. (p. 386)

T F 15. The folk society may be described as a system in which government does not exist, or alternatively, as a system completely dominated by government. (p. 389)

T F 16. Capitalism aims to free workers from the wealthy few. (p. 394)

T F 17. Industrialism influences the character of our social institutions. (p. 399)

T F 18. An important feature of the New Capitalism is the growth of participative leadership. (p. 394)

T F 19. Between today and 2030, the American work force will grow more quickly. (p. 399)

T F 20. The future work force will contain fewer women than in the past. (p. 399)

Fill In *(Answers are on page 412.)*

(p. 386) 21. Max Weber defined ______ as the ability not only to control others but also to make people act against their own desires and interests.

(p. 386) 22. ______ is the particular group of people that operates the apparatus of the state.

(p. 386) 23. The concept of ______ refers to a sovereign government exercising power and authority in the name of society.

(p. 386) 24. In the modern world, the ______ is the most distinctive and largest self-sufficient political configuration.

(p. 392) 25. Nineteenth-century ______ argued in mathematical terms from "the greatest good for the greatest number," postulating that whatever was most good for most people was naturally good. This theory can only be sustained as an article of faith.

(p. 400) 26. A major shift in the American economy is one from ______ to ______.

(p. 394) 27. ______ is based on private ownership of the means of production and on competition for profits.

(p. 399) 28. The American economy is dominated by large ______.

(p. 385) 29. ______ is the ability or the potential to influence the thoughts or behavior of others.

(p. 400) 30. Future trends indicate that for U.S. organizations to survive in the future, they need to operate in an ______ environment.

Matching *(Answers are on page 412.)*

31. ______ American work force
32. ______ Community
33. ______ Socialism
34. ______ Capitalism
35. ______ Economic institution
36. ______ Nation-state
37. ______ Sovereign states
38. ______ Max Weber
39. ______ Power
40. ______ Political institution

a. Will grow more slowly
b. Based upon public ownership of wealth
c. The ability to control others
d. A major form of political organization
e. Command the obedience of society's members
f. The free enterprise system
g. Defined and described the major types of political power
h. An association of people who share a common identity
i. Determines who should gain power and when and how it should be gained
j. Its goal is to meet society's economic needs

Essay Questions

1. What is an institution?
2. What is the political institution?
3. What is power?
4. What are the major functions of the political institution?
5. What is the economic institution?
6. What does "capitalism" mean?
7. What does "socialism" mean?
8. What are the major functions of the economic institution?
9. What is the New Capitalism?
10. How is the American work force changing?

Interactive Exercises

1. In what ways has the American economic institution affected your or your family's personal or business lives?
2. In what ways has the American political institution affected your or your family's personal or business lives?

Answers

Answers to Self-Test

1. c
2. d
3. b
4. d
5. d
6. d
7. b
8. b
9. d
10. d
11. T
12. T
13. F
14. T
15. T
16. F
17. T
18. T
19. F
20. F
21. power
22. government
23. state
24. nation-state
25. Utilitarians
26. manufacturing, service
27. capitalism
28. corporations
29. power
30. international
31. a
32. h
33. b
34. f
35. j
36. d
37. e
38. g
39. c
40. i

Answers to Chapter Pretest

1. F
2. F
3. F
4. T
5. F
6. F
7. F
8. F
9. F
10. F

Chapter 11

Population, Urbanization, and the Environment

Chapter Pretest

Let's see how much you already know about topics in this chapter:

1. **In our society, life expectancy for men and women is approximately equal. True/False**
2. **During the period 1990 to 2010, the majority of the growth in the United States population will occur in the west and south regions. True/False**
3. **At present, world population stands at slightly over 6 billion people. True/False**
4. **As of 1987, 62 percent of the United States population lived in metropolitan areas. True/False**
5. **Today 41 percent of the global population is urban. True/False**
6. **In recent decades, urban growth has been occurring at a far more rapid pace in less developed nations than in developed nations. True/False**
7. **The United States relies on oil for approximately 52 percent of its energy. True/False**
8. **During the 1980s, there were substantial declines in levels of lead, carbon monoxide, and sulfur dioxide in our atmosphere. True/False**

In the previous chapters, we have attempted to describe the nature of human society and social behavior. We have described the relationship between culture and human social life, and we have discussed at length the nature and diversity of social relationships, groups, and societies. In order to obtain a fuller understanding of our group and social life, however, we must also consider the topic of population and its influence upon our physical and social world.

Basic Demographic Concepts

Demography is the scientific study of human populations. Demographers are concerned with the measurement, description, and analysis of populations and the ways in which they change. **Formal demography** uses the tools of mathematics to analyze the relationships between the composition of a population and population change. For example, formal demographers would be concerned with studying the effect of declining birthrates (or death rates) on the size of the

Major areas of demography: formal demography and population studies

population itself. **Population studies** concern the examination of the social, economic, and cultural causes and consequences of population change and structure. For example, demographers who specialize in population studies would be interested in studying various social and economic factors associated with a rising birthrate as well as the short- and long-term social and economic effects of continued high fertility on the society at large—such as expansion of the educational system and labor force.

As far as demographers are concerned, population changes in three ways: through fertility, mortality, and migration. Demographers refer to these concepts as demographic processes.

Fertility

Fertility refers to the number of children born to women of reproductive age, usually those between 15 and 45 years old. A basic measure of fertility is the **crude birthrate,** which is the annual number of births per 1000 population. Evidence indicates that there are substantial differences in fertility among different populations and groups within populations. In the United States, for example, fertility differentials exist among social classes and religious and ethnic groups, and between rural and urban dwellers. There are also substantial differences in fertility among nations. In the less developed nations, it is common to find annual birthrates in excess of 35 per 1000 population. In the industrialized nations, however, annual birthrates typically range between 10 and 20 per 1000 population.

Factors related to fertility variations

How do demographers account for fertility differentials? Kingsley Davis and Judith Blake (1956) made up a list of intermediate variables that have a direct influence on fertility. These variables include age of marriage, whether contraception is practiced, and whether abortion is tolerated. Social norms, laws, and values affect fertility by operating through these intermediate variables, for example, by specifying the socially approved age for first marriage, or by indicating social approval or disapproval of contraception and abortion (Heer, 1975).

Mortality

Mortality refers to the incidence of death within a given population. The most frequently employed measure of mortality is the **crude death rate,** which is the annual number of deaths per 1000 population. The mortality rate, like the birthrate, shows considerable variation among different populations. Death rates are highest among the very young (those less than 1 year old) and among the elderly (those age 65 and over). In the United States, women live almost 7 years longer than men; life expectancy is 78.4 years for women born in 1987 compared with 71.5 years for men born in the same year. American whites live longer than blacks and other racial minorities. Even though racial differences in life expectancy have narrowed somewhat during this century, life expectancy for whites born in 1987 stood at 75.6 years compared with a life expectancy of 69.4 years for blacks born in the same year (National Center for Health Statistics,

1990). Mortality rates also vary according to social class and income; the higher socioeconomic groups have lower infant mortality rates and longer life expectancies. People with higher incomes can afford more and better-quality medical treatment, and they receive minimal exposure to health hazards in the form of injury and disease.

Mortality rates vary by social class

Finally, there are also significant differences in mortality among different nations. The crude death rates for the United States, Sweden, and Spain are 9, 11, and 8 per 1000, respectively, compared with 22, 20, and 19 for Afghanistan, Angola, and Mozambique. But the death rates for most of the less developed African, Latin American, and Asian nations have decreased tremendously during this century and particularly since the end of World War II.

Population Growth

Another important demographic measure is called the **rate of natural increase.** This figure is determined by subtracting the crude death rate from the crude birthrate. For example, Colombia has a crude birthrate of 28 per 1000 and a crude death rate of 7 per 1000. Thus Colombia's rate of natural increase (birthrate minus death rate) equals 21 per 1000, or 2.1 percent. As a result of natural increase, the population of Colombia is growing by 2.1 percent each year. As another example, the crude birthrate and death rate for Mexico are 30 and 6, respectively, yielding an annual population increase of 2.4 percent (Population Reference Bureau, 1990).

Exponential growth has many consequences

Growth rates such as these are large because population growth is exponential. **Exponential growth** involves a geometric progression (such as 2, 4, 8, 16, 32, 64 . . .) as opposed to an arithmetic progression, in which the difference between each term and its predecessor is constant (such as 2, 4, 6, 8, 10, 12 . . .). Exponential growth has a number of important consequences. First, exponential growth determines a population's doubling time. A population increasing by 1 percent a year will double in 69 years; one growing at 2 percent will double in 35 years; one growing at 2.5 percent will double in 28 years; and one growing at 3.5 percent will double in only 20 years. Exponential growth also has startling consequences for many of the less developed nations. They already account for approximately three-fourths of the world's total population, and many of them have large population bases and are characterized by high rates of population increase. Finally, of course, exponential growth has major consequences for total world population. At present, world population stands at slightly over 5.3 billion, with a growth rate of 1.8 percent per year. At this rate, world population would double every 39 years, and within the next century, global population would increase to over 25 billion. Although it is doubtful that world population actually will reach this level, population growth already has severe economic, social, and environmental effects in many nations.

Migration

Migration, the movement of people from one place to another, is another of the demographic processes that can affect the size of a population—at least within a certain geographical territory. There are two basic types of migration: international and internal.

International migration

International migration is movement from one nation to another. At one extreme, there are societies that experience no international migration; at the other, whole societies have migrated from one place to another. There are three major types of international migration patterns (Bouvier et al., 1979; Thomlinson, 1965): group, free-individual, and restricted migration. *Group migration* can take various forms:

1. invasion or displacement of entire societies (common until the seventeenth century)
2. forced migration (for example, the involuntary migration of slaves)
3. colonization (for example, the early European settlements in America)

Free-individual migration is the voluntary movement of individuals or families from one well-developed country to another with the intention of remaining there. The European migration to the United States, totaling 30 to 40 million immigrants between colonial days and the present, is an excellent illustration of this. Finally, *restricted migration* refers to the development of barriers and restrictions to limit the types and number of immigrants. Nations such as Australia, Canada, and the United States now have restricted immigration policies.

Internal migration

Internal migration is the movement of people from one area within a nation to another area within the same nation. Historically, Americans have always manifested a high degree of internal migration (or geographic mobility). One of the major internal migration streams has been from east to west; another has been the northward and westward movement of blacks that began in significant numbers during World War I. Regional migration in recent years has revealed distinct patterns. During the mid- to late 1970s, more people moved out of the northeast and north central regions than moved in, while the south and west experienced a net gain in population. During the 1980s, the vast majority of the nation's population growth occurred in the south and west. Between 1980 and 1987, these two regions grew by slightly over 15 million people. Almost half (7.4 million) of the combined increase within these regions resulted from net immigration (with more people entering these areas than leaving). On the other hand, the northeast and midwest faced the situations of net outmigration (totaling 2.5 million) and little overall population increase (*Population Profile of the United States: 1989*, 1989). These regional growth patterns are likely to continue in the future. Projections indicate that during the period 1990 through 2010, the majority of the growth in the United States population will continue to occur in the west and south regions. Given the higher fertility and young population, natural increase will account for most of the west's population growth. However, most of the south's population increase during this period will result from migration—both internal and international. Projections indicate that by the year 2010, 37 percent of the nation's population will reside in the south and 23 percent will reside in the west. In contrast, approximately 19 and 21 percent of the nation's population will be residents of the northeast and midwest, respec-

In the future most of U.S. population growth will occur in the west and south regions

tively (*Projections of the Population of States, by Age, Sex, and Race: 1988 to 2010*, 1988).

Migration (international or internal) affects population size in two major ways. First, an obvious consequence of the movement of people is that some areas will automatically lose population while others gain. Second, because many of those who migrate are young, migrants may have children *after* they relocate. Thus migration can influence fertility levels within various locations.

Population Composition

In addition to the demographic processes—fertility, mortality, and migration—demographers also study **population composition**—the way in which such attributes as age, sex, marital status, ethnic characteristics, and occupational status are distributed throughout a population. Demographers assign prime importance to the study of a population's age and sex composition because these two characteristics have many important effects on society at large and greatly influence a population's potential for future growth and change. The age and sex composition of the United States population is graphically illustrated in Figure 11.1.

A population's age and sex composition influence its potential for future growth and change

An important indicator of sex composition is the **sex ratio,** which is calculated by dividing the number of males in a population by the number of females and multiplying this by 100. In essence, the sex ratio tells us the number of males for every 100 females. In 1989, the sex ratio for the United States was 95.4, indicating that there were 95.4 men for every 100 women (*U.S. Population Estimates, by Age, Sex, Race, and Hispanic Origin: 1989*, 1990). The sex ratio varies over time and geographical area, but whenever or wherever there is a serious imbalance, the probabilities of marriage are lowered.

The age composition of a population has a direct influence on the **dependency ratio,** the ratio of people at dependent ages to people in economically productive ages (Heer, 1975). In essence, the dependency ratio is an expression of the number of people who have to be supported by others. The Bureau of the Census specifies the dependency ratio as the population under age 18 and 65 and over for every 100 people aged 18 to 64. The dependency ratio stood at 62.0 in 1987. The Bureau of the Census projections indicate that the ratio will show an overall decline through the year 2010, reflecting a decrease in the proportion of youthful dependents. Beyond the year 2010, there will be a substantial increase in the dependency ratio, resulting from a growth of the population aged 65 years and older (*Projections of the Population of the United States, by Age, Sex, and Race: 1988 to 2080*, 1989).

In the long run the dependency ratio will increase

The age composition of a population has an extremely broad range of economic and social consequences. It influences a society's consumption requirements, that is, the types of goods and services needed to support a particular population. A society with a large population of young children needs such goods and services as children's food, children's clothing, schools, and day-care centers. A society with a large population of elderly people has different requirements. In addition, age composition also influences many economic and social processes, such as migration, mobility, employment, retirement, and home purchasing.

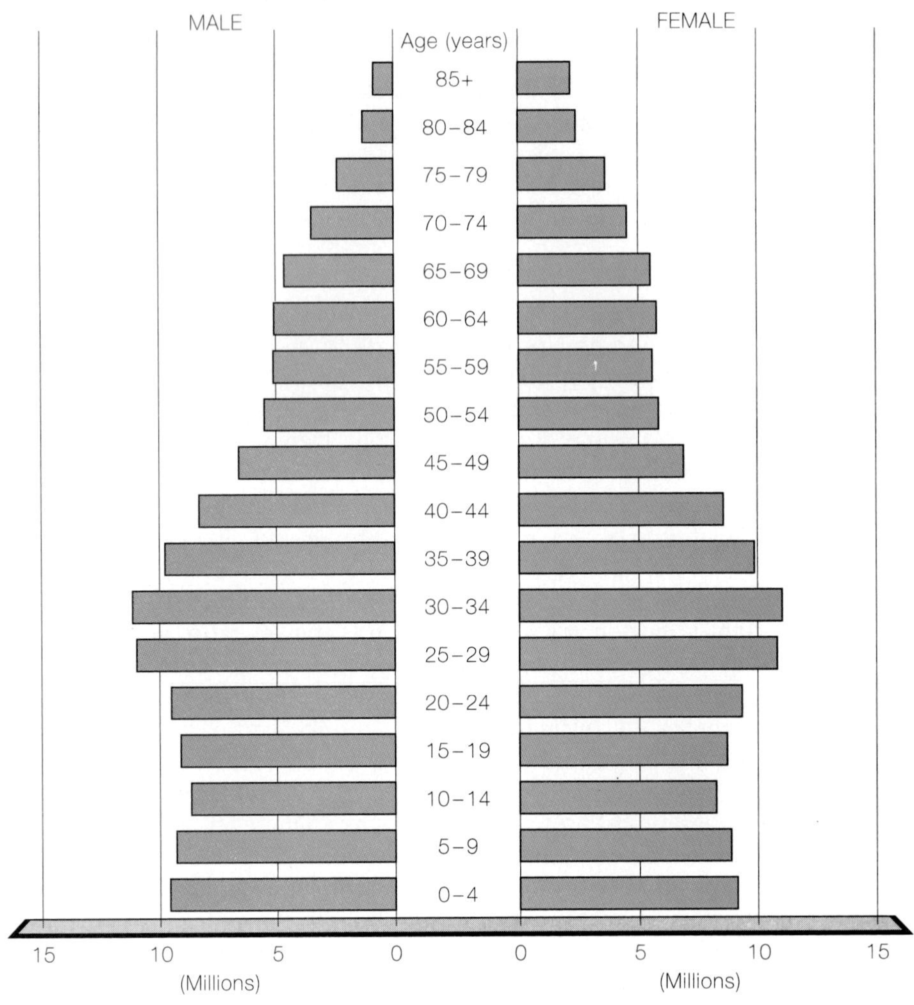

Figure 11.1 United States population by age and sex, 1989.
Source: U.S. Bureau of the Census, Current Population Reports, Series P-25, No. 1057. *U.S. Population Estimates, by Age, Sex, Race, and Hispanic Origin: 1989*. Washington, D.C.: U.S. Government Printing Office, 1990.

World Population: Past and Present

Population growth has strained food and other resources

There has been much public concern about the problems of world population growth. There is, in fact, much cause for alarm today. During the twentieth century, world population has grown faster than ever before. This massive increase in human numbers has already placed severe strains on the supply of food and natural resources within many nations. Each year millions of people in

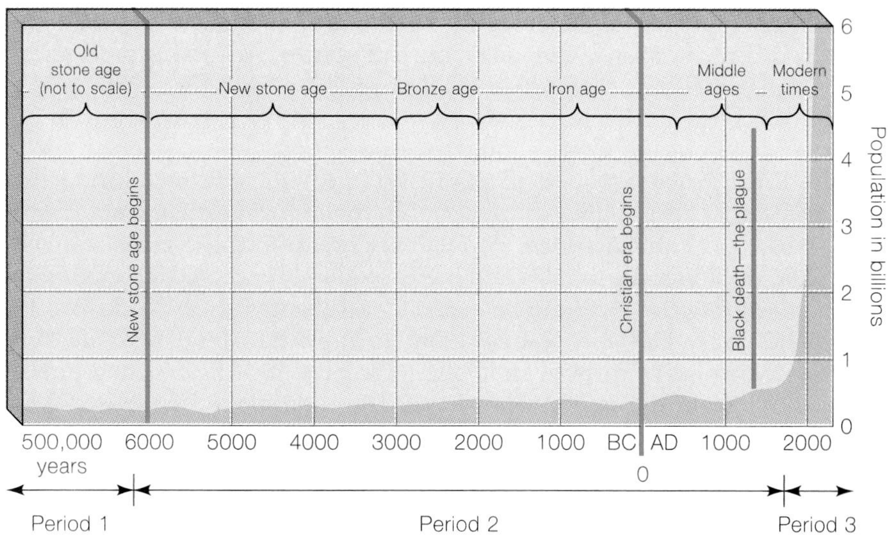

Figure 11.2 **World population growth in history.**
Source: "How Many People Have Ever Lived on Earth?" *The Population Bulletin,* 18 February 1962, p. 5.

the less developed nations suffer malnutrition, starvation, and death, and those who survive often lack basic necessities such as health care and clothing.

We do not have much knowledge about population growth prior to relatively modern times. Demographer Kingsley Davis (1976) estimates that world population around the year 8000 B.C. was only 5 million. By A.D. 1, world population had increased to 300 million; by A.D. 1750, to 791 million; and by 1850, to 1.25 billion people. As we have noted, world population presently stands at slightly over 5.3 billion and is growing at a rate of 1.8 percent per year. This actually represents a slight slowdown in the world's population growth rate, which hit a high of 2 percent around the middle 1960s. However, in terms of absolute quantity, world population continues to grow at a rapid pace. Global population is now increasing by approximately 96 million a year. At current growth levels, it is projected to increase to approximately 6.3 billion by the year 2000 and to 8.2 billion by the year 2020 (Population Reference Bureau, 1990). Moreover, some estimates are that world population may reach 11 billion before stabilization occurs. Projections such as these alert us to the necessity of developing policies and programs to deal with problems of large-scale population growth.

World population is growing at a rapid pace

As indicated in Figure 11.2, throughout most of human existence, world population has actually increased rather slowly. Davis (1976) identifies only three periods manifesting dramatic growth. The first occurred in about 8000 B.C. and was associated with the agricultural revolution. This revolution resulted in a more stable supply of food and more permanent areas of settlement. The second period lasted from around A.D. 1750 to the early 1900s and was associated with the Industrial Revolution in Europe and North America. This revolution brought mechanization to agriculture, advances in science and manufacturing, and improvements in nutrition and general living standards. Advances in medical techniques and sanitation were also made during this period. The result was a decline in death rates and increased life expectancy, with a resulting growth in population throughout the world's industrialized nations.

Finally, a third major period of population growth occurred during the twentieth century. This growth occurred within the less developed countries—in Africa, Asia, and Latin America. Population growth in these areas resulted primarily from declining death rates and increased life expectancy, changes that began to occur during the 1920s but have greatly accelerated since World War II. The sudden decline in mortality resulted from the rapid transfer of scientific and medical technology in the form of antibiotics, vaccines, insecticides, and public health programs from the industrialized to the less developed nations. Davis notes, for example, that the death rate in Sri Lanka (formerly Ceylon) declined 40 percent in only three years (1945–1948), largely due to the control of malaria by DDT. Infectious diseases were steadily conquered, resulting in a massive reduction in death rates within the less developed nations—a faster and greater decline than that experienced by the developed nations during the Industrial Revolution.

Birthrates within most of the world's less developed nations have remained high

At present, the vast majority of the world's population growth is occurring within the less developed African, Asian, and Latin American nations. Estimates are that these nations will account for most of the world's population increase in future decades. As Table 11.1 shows, the rate of natural increase within the world's less developed nations as a whole now averages 2.1 percent a year, which means that these populations will double in approximately 33 years. African nations are now increasing at an annual rate of 2.9 percent, Asian nations at 1.9 percent, and Latin American nations at 2.1 percent. A major factor contributing to population increase within the world's less developed nations is the fact that birthrates within most of these countries have remained high. Birthrates now average 31 per 1000 population, roughly double that in industrialized nations. Social values stressing the importance and desirability of early marriage and large family size are important factors in the perpetuation of these high birthrates. Approximately 36 percent of the population within the less developed nations is now younger than 15 (Population Reference Bureau, 1990). In recent years, there has been a growing consensus among demographers that fertility actually has begun to fall in many less developed nations. This fall was reflected in declining world birth and growth rates during the 1970s (van der Tak et al., 1980; Yaukey, 1985). But even so, birthrates in less developed nations remain high enough to guarantee large world population growth throughout most of the next century.

Industrial nations have low birthrates

In sharp contrast to those within the world's less developed nations, birthrates within the industrialized nations are low, averaging only 15 per 1000. Birthrates for the United States and Canada now stand at 16 and 14 per 1000, respectively, while the birthrates within all northern and western European countries now average 14 and 12 per 1000, respectively. A number of European countries are at or near **zero population growth,** the point at which the ratio of births to deaths is balanced and population ceases to grow. As a whole, the rate

Table 11.1 **Population Growth in Specific Nations: 1990**

NATION	TOTAL POPULATION (MILLIONS)	BIRTHRATE	DEATH RATE	NATURAL INCREASE (ANNUAL %)	NUMBER OF YEARS TO DOUBLE POPULATION
United States	251.4	16	9	0.8	92
United Kingdom	57.4	14	12	0.2	301
West Germany	63.2	11	11	0.0	—
U.S.S.R.	291.0	19	10	0.9	80
China	1,119.9	21	7	1.4	49
Japan	123.6	10	6	0.4	175
India	853.4	32	11	2.1	33
Pakistan	114.6	44	13	3.0	23
Egypt	54.7	38	9	2.9	24
Kenya	24.6	46	7	3.8	18
Brazil	150.4	27	8	1.9	36
Mexico	88.6	30	6	2.4	29
Spain	39.4	11	8	0.3	247
Turkey	56.7	29	8	2.1	32
Less Developed Nations	4,107	31	10	2.1	33
Developed Nations	1,214	15	9	0.5	128

Source: Population Reference Bureau, *1990 World Population Data Sheet* (Washington, D.C., 1990).

of natural increase within the industrialized nations now averages only 0.5 percent each year (Population Reference Bureau, 1990).

As we have pointed out, population increases occurred throughout much of Europe and North America prior to the recent massive population growth within the less developed nations. However, under the long-term effect of industrialization and economic development, birthrates within the industrialized nations have actually shown an overall *decline* since the turn of the century. The only turnabout in this general decline was the baby boom of the late 1940s and 1950s. After this baby boom peaked in the mid-1950s, birthrates within many industrialized nations resumed their decline. Recently, in many cases, this decline has accelerated.

Population Growth in the United States

The United States also has experienced a general decline in birthrates during this century, temporarily interrupted during the baby boom when, in 1957, the fertility rate reached a high of 3.8 children per woman. Since that time, birthrates have shown a fairly steady decline. By the early 1970s, the fertility rate had fallen to 2.1 children per woman—referred to as **replacement level fertility.** At this

Replacement level fertility

point, children are born in numbers sufficient to replace but not to exceed the number of parents. The level is slightly over 2 children per woman, thus allowing for a certain amount of infant mortality and for women who do not bear children. However, replacement level fertility does not mean an automatic halt in population growth. In fact, the U.S. population will continue to grow (probably at a slower rate) for many years to come. As of January 1, 1990, the total population of the United States was 250.1 million, an increase of 23 million over 1980. There were 3,977,000 births in 1989; the birthrate stood at 16.0 per 1000; and the fertility rate was approximately 1.9 children per women. There were more births in 1989 than in any previous year during the decade (*U.S. Population Estimates by Age, Sex, Race, and Hispanic Origin: 1989*, 1990).

Most of the U.S. population lives in metropolitan areas

As of 1987, 76.9 percent of the United States population lived in metropolitan areas. In general, a **metropolitan area** is made up of one or more central cities, their suburbs, and surrounding related areas. As of 1987, almost one-half of the United States population lived in one of the 37 major metropolitan areas having populations of at least 1 million. The five largest metropolitan areas alone, including New York, Los Angeles, Chicago, San Francisco, and Philadelphia, contained nearly 52 million people in 1987. During the 1970s and 1980s, metropolitan areas as a whole showed steady population growth. Nevertheless, in the 1970s, for the first time in many decades, nonmetropolitan areas actually grew at a faster rate (14.3 percent) than metropolitan areas (10.6 percent) (*Patterns of Metropolitan Area and County Population Growth: 1980 to 1987*, 1989; "The 50 Biggest Metro Areas Now," 1984). But during the 1980s, the pattern of the 1970s reversed itself, and metropolitan areas again began to grow faster than nonmetropolitan areas. Between 1980 and 1987, the population of metropolitan areas grew by 8.5 percent—more than double the 4.1 percent growth rate of nonmetropolitan areas. The proximity of a nonmetropolitan area to an urban center also plays a role in population growth. During the period 1970 to 1987, nonmetropolitan growth was highest in counties having easy access, and thus greatest amounts of commuting, to metropolitan areas and lowest in counties remotely located from metropolitan centers (*Population Profile of the United States: 1989*, 1989).

During the 1980s, metropolitan areas grew faster than nonmetropolitan areas

In addition to an increase of some 23 million people during the 1980s, the population of the United States as a whole has grown older. The median age of the population increased from 27.9 years in 1970 to 30.0 years in 1980, to 32.6 years by July 1, 1989. This trend is in large part due to the aging of the baby boomers (the 75 million people born in the 1946 to 1964 period) who entered into their 30s and early 40s during the decade of the 1980s. During the 1980 to 1989 period, while the population of the United States increased as a whole by an average of 1 percent per year, the 25- to 34-year-old population increased by 1.8 percent per year and the population aged 35 to 44 increased by an average of 3.9 percent per year—nearly four times the national rate of growth. The number of elderly has also increased in recent years. The population 65 years of age and over increased from 9.8 percent in 1970 to 11.3 percent in 1980, to 12.5 percent of the total population in 1989. Those aged 65 and over grew by an average annual rate of 2.1 percent during the 1980 to 1989 period. Moreover, in recent decades, the elderly population itself has been aging. Between 1960 and 1989, those aged

In recent decades, the elderly population itself has been aging

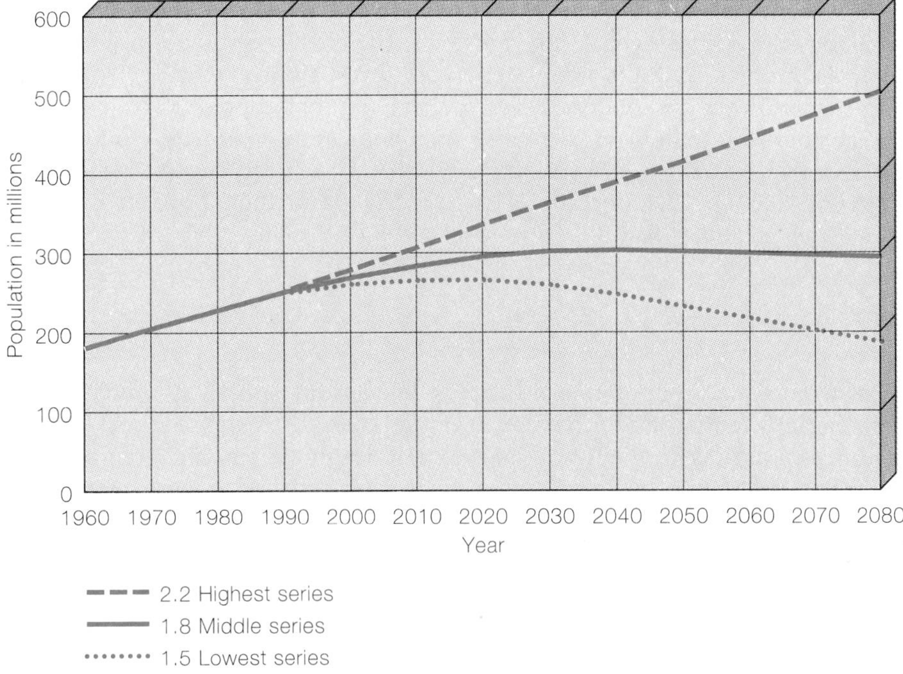

Figure 11.3 **Estimates and projections of total U.S. population: 1960 to 2080.**
Source: U.S. Bureau of the Census, Current Population Reports, Series P-25, No. 1018. *Projections of the Population of the United States, by Age, Sex, and Race: 1988 to 2080,* by Gregory Spencer. Washington, D.C.: U.S. Government Printing Office, 1989.

85 years and over increased from less than 6 percent to almost 10 percent of the population aged 65 years and over. From 1980 to 1989, the population aged 85 years and over grew by an average annual rate of 3.3 percent (*U.S. Population Estimates, by Age, Sex, Race, and Hispanic Origin: 1989,* 1990).

In terms of population growth, what can we expect in the future? As illustrated in Figure 11.3, under the middle series projections, the population of the United States will increase by about 52 million people, to a total of approximately 302 million, between 1990 and the year 2040. This growth will occur slowly—after-1995 growth rates are projected to be less than 0.7 percent per year. Beyond the year 2038, the population of the United States will actually begin to decrease slowly in numbers (*Projections of the Population of the United States, by Age, Sex, and Race: 1988 to 2080,* 1989).

In coming decades, the population of the U.S. will grow older

We also may expect the composition of the U.S. population to change. In general, during the coming decades, the population will grow older as the average age continues to increase. The median age is projected to reach 36.4 years by the year 2000, 40.2 years by 2020, and 41.8 years by 2030. Between 1990 and 2005, the elderly population (aged 65 years and over), will increase by only about 4.7 million. On a percentage basis, this means that the elderly population will grow from 12.6 percent to only 13.2 percent of the entire population during this period. Beyond the year 2010, however, the elderly population will grow quickly as the massive baby boom generation moves into the 65-year-plus age group. According to the middle series projections, those aged 65 and over will increase from 39.4 million in 2010 to 65.6 million (or approximately one out of every five Americans) by the year 2030. By this same year, those aged 85 and over will make up 12.4 percent of the elderly population (*Projections of the Population of the United States, by Age, Sex, and Race: 1988 to 2080*, 1989).

Consequences of Population Growth

The consequences of population growth have been the subject of much recent debate. Social scientists and others have argued that the earth has a vast supply of resources now and for the future. New scientific discoveries and technological innovations will allow humans to get at and use many of these resources. Increasing productivity will help provide adequate living standards for increasing numbers of people worldwide. From this point of view, the earth can comfortably support billions of people in the future. Some social scientists believe that population increase actually benefits economic growth and stimulates technological advances. In Julian Simon's words:

The debate over the consequences of population growth

> **Since ideas come from people, it seems reasonable that the number of improvements depends on the number of people using their heads . . . the bigger the population, the more of everything that is produced. With a greater volume come more chances for people to improve their skills and to devise better methods" (Simon, 1981, pp. 328, 330).**

But other social scientists have been highly critical of this perspective. They point out that population growth already has caused severe economic, social, and environmental problems throughout less developed nations. Moreover, they warn that continued large-scale population growth will likely result in increased environmental deterioration, declines in natural resources, lowered standards of living, famine, and greater political instability for many nations throughout the world.

Population Growth and the Less Developed Nations

There is no question that rapid, large population growth has created severe problems for less developed nations. One of the most severe problems is hunger. It is estimated that half a billion people in the world today are undernourished ("Roots of Africa's Famine Run Deep," 1984). In fact, some estimates have indicated that as many as one-half of the world's population are either starving, chronically hungry, or suffering from malnutrition. Lester Brown,

Estimates of world hunger

president of the World Watch Institute, notes (1984) that between 1950 and the early 1970s, world food production grew at more than 3 percent a year. Since 1973, however, the annual growth has been *under* 2 percent, a rate barely sufficient to keep pace with world population growth (Brown, 1984). Brown cites a number of economic, environmental, and demographic factors underlying this decline, the end result of which is growing hunger for many less developed nations.

Agricultural output and population growth

Africa has experienced an approximate 20 percent decline in per capital grain production since 1970 and, at current population growth rates, will need to feed an additional 223 million people by the year 2000 (Brown and Wolf, 1984; Brown, 1989; Population Reference Bureau, 1990). Brown and Wolf (1984) view the massive drought of the early 1980s as only a trigger for the widespread famine in Africa. Three long-term forces underlie the African food crisis: widespread environmental deterioration, underinvestment in agriculture, and massive population growth. Population growth has brought about changes in land use that, in turn, have altered the water cycle throughout much of the continent ("'Human Element,' not Drought Causes Famine," 1985).

Many factors underlie the problem of hunger in the world today, not the least of which are inadequacies in food distribution and storage systems. But many population experts feel that the problem of hunger results primarily from the fact that in many areas of the world, agriculture cannot keep pace with population growth. By the year 2000, a substantial increase in food production will be required to meet the minimum nutritional levels for an additional 1 billion people. Increases in agricultural productivity also will be expensive, because fertilizers, oil, and farm machinery are expensive. These costs are already too high for many less developed nations. Thus the prospects for feeding many of the world's hungry look bleak.

A substantial increase in food production will be needed in the future

Population growth also has created serious economic problems for many less developed nations. For a country to experience growth in its standard of living, some of the nation's national income must be reinvested into new income-producing investments, such as factories, machinery, and new technology in general. Davis (1976) notes that, given a stable population, a country must invest 3 to 5 percent of its annual national income to create a 1 percent growth in per capita income. However, if a nation's population is growing at 2 to 3 percent per year (which is common for less developed nations), a much higher level of investment is required to raise the standard of living. Recent information ("People, People, People," 1984), indicates that the economies of the less developed nations actually have grown faster in the last two decades than those of western Europe and the United States. But rapid population growth largely diluted the gains. For example, from 1955 to 1980, the per capita income disparity between the United States and India almost doubled in spite of the fact that India's per capita income rose at a slightly higher *rate* than that of the United States. For the individual, lack of economic development means personal poverty and chronic unemployment. As a whole, the per capita gross national product of the less developed nations averaged only $710 in 1988, less than 5 percent of the industrialized nations' per capita average (Population Reference Bureau, 1990). Moreover, estimates indicate that by the year 2000, the number of young workers entering the work force in the less developed nations will

Population growth often retards economic development

increase by approximately 630 million, compared with an increase of only 20 million in industrial nations. The massive growth of the labor force in less developed nations means that low-level wages are likely to continue ("People, People, People," 1984).

Population increase has also brought a host of urban problems to the less developed nations. Birthrates and population increases historically have been greater within the rural areas of these countries. But the number of jobs available in these areas has not kept pace with the number of people. As a result, an increasing percentage of the unemployed and destitute rural population have migrated to the cities in the hope of finding jobs. This pattern of rural-to-urban migration, combined with the city's own natural increase, has been responsible for a vast growth in urban population within the less developed nations. Today many cities—Cairo, Lagos, Mexico City, Manila, plus many cities in Brazil and Kenya—are already overcrowded. Demographic projections indicate continued growth for many cities within the less developed world.

Rural-to-urban migration

Usually, cities offer few solutions to the migrant's problems. The lack of economic development (at least relative to population growth) plus the daily crush of newcomers to the city mean that few jobs are available. Wages are usually low, because the rural migrant tends to be both unskilled and uneducated. Moreover, the vast growth of these cities introduces many other urban problems, such as pollution, overcrowding, poor transportation, and massive housing shortages.

Dealing with Overpopulation

In the present century, world population is growing faster than in any previous period of recorded human history. As we noted earlier, the present global population of 5.3 billion is projected to increase to 6.3 billion by the year 2000, 8.2 billion by the year 2020, and as much as 11 billion before eventually stabilizing. Although most of this population growth will occur within the less developed nations, rapid population growth of this magnitude portends serious global social, economic, and environmental consequences.

Projections such as these raise questions of why populations increase or decrease and what can be done to stem the world population growth. Thomas Malthus (1766–1834), an early demographer, was the first to provide a major theoretical explanation for population growth and its consequences. Malthus emphasized that population growth was a consequence of human beings' powerful urge to reproduce (Weeks, 1981). According to Malthusian theory, populations have a tendency to grow at a geometric rate (2, 4, 8, 16 . . .), whereas food supply and production increase only arithmetically (1, 2, 3, 4, 5 . . .). Given the faster rate of population growth, populations ultimately may exceed their means of support, bringing about famine, disease, and war. Increased mortality then reduces the population to a point compatible with food production and supply. In later writings, Malthus expressed the hope that this

Malthusian theory of population growth

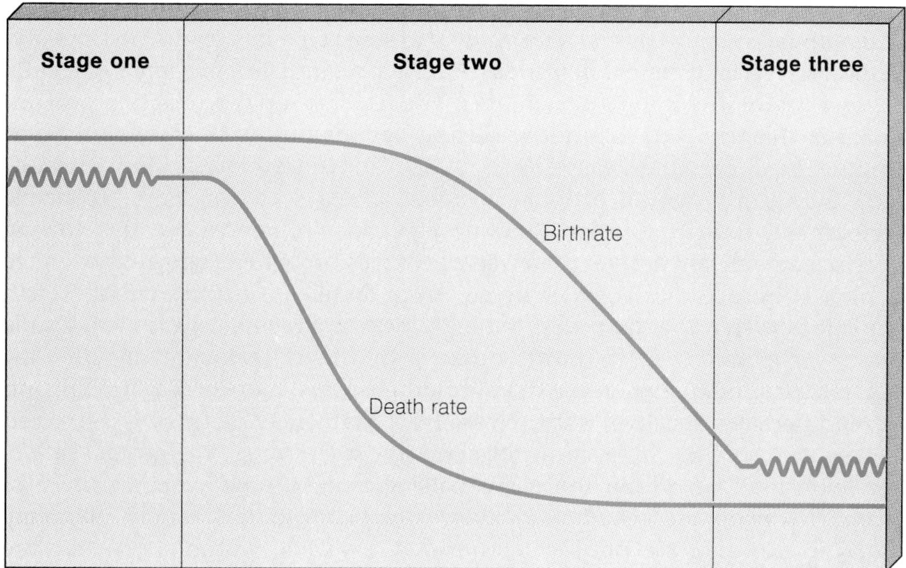

Figure 11.4 The Demographic Transition. *Stage one* is characterized by a high birthrate and a high death rate, resulting in population stability. *Stage two* is marked by a sharp decline in the death rate while the birthrate remains relatively high. The result is rapid population growth. *Stage three* is characterized by low birth- and death rates, once again yielding population stability.

death rate solution to population increase might be avoided if people would employ moral restraint through sexual abstinence, delayed marriage, and continence in marriage (Heer, 1975; Matras, 1973).

Marx: overpopulation was a consequence of capitalism

Over the years, a number of criticisms have been leveled against Malthusian theory. From the Marxist perspective, for example, overpopulation (as well as poverty) is a consequence of the capitalist system, which needs to generate an excess population of workers to keep wages low and profits high. For Marx, the answer to overpopulation and related problems was socialism (Weeks, 1981).

Malthus did not envision the truly massive increases in agricultural productivity that resulted from the growth of industrial technology. Gains in agricultural productivity (the means of subsistence) gave the industrializing nations the capacity to feed and maintain vastly increased numbers of people. Perhaps more important, Malthus did not foresee the eventual effects of industrialization and economic development on fertility.

In recent years, the **demographic transition theory** has been used to describe the pattern of population change found within industrialized societies during the nineteenth and early twentieth centuries. According to the demographic transition theory, a drop in a society's death rate inevitably is followed by a voluntary decline in its birthrate. Factors related to industrial and economic development are responsible for this sequence. In terms of this theory, societies experiencing economic development pass through three basic stages of population growth (see Fig. 11.4).

Stage one is characterized by high fertility and high mortality rates; thus the rate of population growth is virtually nil. This stage characterized American and European societies prior to their industrialization. *Stage two* is characterized by declining death rates but high birthrates. The result is rapid population growth. This stage characterized the industrializing nations during the late eighteenth and nineteenth centuries. *Stage three* is characterized by low fertility and low death rates and is typical of today's industrialized societies. Here, economic development, industrialization, and urbanization influence attitudes toward family size. Small families are preferred as couples come to recognize that, given the high standards and costs of living, large families constitute a substantial economic burden rather than an economic asset. As a result, couples voluntarily have fewer children, the birthrate declines to a level approximating the low death rate, and the rate of population growth declines, more or less holding at a low (and perhaps negative) level (Heer, 1975; Matras, 1973).

The three stages of transition

As a result of declining birthrates and low death rates, the annual rate of population increase within the industrialized nations now averages only 0.5 percent. Many of these nations actively support voluntary family planning. Contraceptives also are popular and widely available within the developed nations. Recent data (Population Reference Bureau, 1990), indicates that within the developed nations, 54 percent of married women of reproductive age use some form of modern contraceptive method such as the pill, sterilization, IUD, or other barrier and chemical methods. Some form of modern contraceptive method was used by 62 percent and by 60 percent of married women of reproductive age in the United States and Japan, respectively. Family planning and contraceptive use have played an important role in bringing about birthrate declines in the industrialized nations. However, as we noted above, birthrates within these nations were in decline well before the existence of family planning programs and modern contraceptive techniques. Ultimately, industrialization and economic development long have played a role in fertility reduction and in shaping attitudes favoring small family size within the developed nations.

In contrast to those in the world's industrialized nations, we have seen that growth rates within less developed nations remain high. Some demographers feel that the less developed nations eventually will experience a demographic transition from high to low rates of fertility similar to that experienced by today's industrialized nations. An important first step in coming to terms with the problem of rapid population growth is to recognize that a problem does exist. Only in recent years, however, have many less developed nations recognized the existence of this problem. The governments of 70 of the less developed nations (which include 93 percent of the people in the developing world) have given official support to family planning programs or have established official policies to reduce the population growth rate. Family planning programs within the less developed nations are often hospital-, clinic-, or health and welfare center-based. A number of governments also have developed mobile teams of personnel to extend family planning information, supplies, and services to those living in remote locations (Nortman and Fisher, 1982; Nortman, 1985).

Many less developed nations have family planning

Family planning programs within less developed countries have had a mixed performance. In nations with recent economic growth, such as South

Korea, Taiwan, Hong Kong, Singapore, and Mauritius, they have been very successful. But in Kenya, India, Bangladesh, and Indonesia, they have had little influence on lowering fertility levels (Weeks, 1981). In some instances, family planning programs have been poorly organized and administered, or inaccessible. In other instances, people have not found family planning consistent with their beliefs and values. Substantial birthrate declines have taken place in China, the world's most populous nation. In China, government has had extensive input into family planning. China has an aggressive population-control policy, currently stressing one child per family and a goal of zero population growth by the year 2000 (Yaukey, 1985). The Chinese program emphasizes family planning, contraceptive use, and an elaborate system of social and economic incentives—payments, housing advantages, increased retirement pensions—for families having only one child, and disincentives for families having two or three children (Nortman and Fisher, 1982; Yaukey, 1985). Whether China will reach its goal of population stability remains to be seen. China's fertility rate is currently above replacement level, and given current growth rates, China's population is projected to increase by 160 million as of the year 2000 (Population Reference Bureau, 1990).

In less developed nations, family planning has had mixed results

China's population policy

In spite of several clearly documented family planning success stories, some demographers are of the opinion that family planning programs alone are not sufficient to reduce population growth in most less developed nations. Although family planning programs may curtail fertility, they nevertheless emphasize that people should have the number of children they desire. In the less developed nations, this number averages around four to five. Thus a number of approaches have been implemented or suggested to hasten fertility declines. These approaches involve family planning services and also a number of "beyond family planning" strategies, which include (van der Tak et al., 1980):

1. expansion and improvement of family planning services
2. more efforts at informing and educating people about contraception
3. improvements in the status of women
4. improvements in nutrition and education
5. efforts in lowering infant mortality
6. systems of incentives and disincentives to encourage small families
7. social sanctions and pressures (such as peer pressure) aimed at encouraging people to limit their fertility

"Beyond family planning" strategies

Today many population experts feel that comprehensive population policies represent an important approach to dealing with the problem of overpopulation. As we have noted, many governments have established official policies to reduce population growth rates and/or have given support to family planning programs. Even where policies and programs do exist, their implementation requires time. When it comes to population growth, however, time is not on our side. Workable population policies and programs must be put into effect quickly if national and possibly global disasters are to be avoided in the future.

Urbanization and Urban Growth

World Urbanization: Past and Present

One of the most important modern demographic processes has been the increasing urbanization of large numbers of the world's population.* **Urbanization** refers to the growth in the percentage or proportion of people living in cities relative to those living in rural areas.

During most of human existence, the vast majority of the human population lived in rural settings. Cities, of course, have existed for thousands of years, but until recent centuries, their presence was rather uncommon. Some of the earliest cities (for example, Babylon, Rome, Athens) date back several thousand years and contained relatively small populations compared with many major cities of today. Although the preindustrial cities of England grew at a somewhat higher rate than the general population, it was not until the Industrial Revolution and the nineteenth century that rapid and substantial urbanization occurred in England and eventually in other European and North American countries as they, too, industrialized.

Urbanization increasing

During the 1800s and 1900s, urbanization and urban growth have increased worldwide. For example, in 1800, only 3 percent of the world's population lived in urban areas. By 1950, nearly 30 percent did. Today 41 percent of the global population is urban (Population Reference Bureau, 1990). Between 1900 and 1975, world population increased two and one-half times. During this same period, the number of cities containing 1 million inhabitants increased 10 times and the number of cities containing over 5 million increased 20 times ("The World's Urban Explosion," 1985). Projections indicate that by the year 2000, about half of the earth's population will be living in urban areas.

Urban growth has been very rapid in less developed nations

In recent decades, urban growth has been occurring at a far more rapid pace in less developed than in developed nations. As of the year 2000, the population of metropolitan areas within less developed nations is estimated to stand at 914 million, over double the number projected for the industrialized nations ("The World's Urban Explosion," 1985). It has been estimated that by the year 2000, 8 out of the world's 10 most populous cities will be located within less developed nations and will range in size from 14.2 million, for Rio de Janeiro, to 27.6 million, for Mexico City ("Ten Top Cities Now and in 2000," 1984). Large-scale urban growth has already created enormous problems in less developed nations. Many large cities within these nations have high unemployment and underemployment rates, people often lack sewage facilities and residential running water, and, in fact, there is often a severe housing shortage. Continued urban growth will make problems such as these all the more difficult to solve.

* Analysis within this and the following section on U.S. urban growth was based, in part, upon information found in Weeks (1981), Weller and Bouvier (1981), Population Reference Bureau (1982), and other specific sources as noted.

Urban Growth in the United States

In the United States over the last 200 years, urbanization has been continuous and rapid. In 1790, the United States population numbered approximately 4 million. Only about 5 percent of this population lived in urban areas. The growth of industrialization in the 1800s was accompanied by a decline in the need for farm labor and a rapid rise in urbanization. In 1850, for example, 15 percent of the United States population lived in urban areas. By 1900, the percentage had increased to 40.

History of U.S. urban growth

During the early 1900s, urban growth continued within the United States. By 1920, slightly over one-half of the United States population lived in urban areas. By 1950, nearly 65 percent of the population could be classified as urban. The post-World War II decades brought various changes in the patterns of United States urban growth. One major change has been the rapid movement of city populations into suburban areas, or rings. The existence of suburbs is not new, of course. Roughly 16 percent of the United States population lived in non-central city "ring" areas in 1900. In recent decades, the growth of suburban areas and populations has been dramatic. Between 1950 and 1986, for example, the suburban population increased from 23 percent to 45 percent of the nation's entire population. During the period 1980 to 1986, the population of central cities throughout the United States increased by 4.7 percent—a growth rate much higher than in the 1970s. Nevertheless, the suburban population grew by 8.9 percent—nearly twice the central city growth rate. By 1986, over 108 million people lived in the suburbs of metropolitan areas (*Patterns of Metropolitan Area and County Population Growth: 1980 to 1987*, 1989).

The megalopolis

Another major change has been the appearance and development of the **megalopolis,** a set of interrelated, adjacent metropolitan areas. Several of these metropolitan forms currently exist in the United States. One is the region stretching from Boston through Washington, D.C. In general, throughout this century, United States metropolitan areas have grown faster than non-metropolitan areas—the only brief reversal period was during the 1970s. As we previously noted, as of 1987, 76.9 percent of the United States population lived in metropolitan areas and almost one-half of the United States population lived in one of the 37 major metropolitan areas having populations of at least 1 million.

Cities and Urban Living: Present and Future

Urbanization will continue

If past and present trends give us any clues as to the future, then we can say with certainty that urbanization will continue to play an increasingly important role within human societies. By the year 2000, approximately one-half of the world will live in urban areas. As we have noted, the metropolitan areas within the less developed nations are faced with the problems of rapid population growth and the need to provide basic goods and services such as food, housing, jobs, sanitation, and transportation for their swelling populations. Meanwhile, urban areas within the industrially developed nations face their own set of challenges. American cities, for example, must often deal with problems of urban blight, shrinking tax revenues, crime, and unemployment. But they also remain as educational and cultural centers and places offering avenues for occupational and social mobility. Some people find the size and heterogeneity of cities alienating. Others thrive on the diversity the city provides and their opportunities for affiliating with social and subcultural networks based on personal interests, neighborhood, and work. The city represents a study in contrasts.

CITIES WITHOUT LIMITS

Rafael M. Salas

As we have seen above, the world is increasingly becoming an urban place. Industrial nations have a higher percentage of urban dwellers than less developed nations. Nevertheless, in recent decades, urban growth has proceeded much faster in less developed nations. The following article, by Rafael M. Salas, discusses the future course of urban growth within the less developed nations, including the appearance of "super-cities"—most of which will be found within these nations. The article focuses particular attention upon a number of problems in the areas of housing, employment, food, health, and education, which are associated with large-scale urban growth within less developed nations.

The world has embarked on a course which will transform it into a predominantly urban planet. By the time population stabilizes at the end of the next century, truly rural populations will have become a very small minority.

More than 40 per cent of the world population currently live in urban areas. This figure will increase to more than 50 per cent shortly after the turn of the century. Developed regions have been more than 50 per cent urban since the mid-20th century. Developing countries are expected to pass the 50 per cent mark in the first quarter of the next century.

Within the less developed regions there are important differences. The developing countries of Africa and Asia are less than 30 per cent urban. Latin America, on the other hand, is nearly 70 per cent urban, reflecting the region's stage of development and the special features of its urban structure and history.

BY THE YEAR 2000: 5 'SUPER-CITIES' OF 15 MILLION

Most of the world's urban population today lives in developing countries. In 1970 the total urban population of the more developed regions was almost 30 million more

The Unesco Courier, January 1987, pp. 10–13, 16–17.

than in the less developed. Five years later the position was reversed and by 1985 the difference had widened to more than 300 million. By the year 2000 the urban population of developing countries will be almost double that of the developed countries. By the year 2025 it will be almost four times as large.

At present the urban population of Africa is smaller than that of North America, but by the beginning of the next century it is expected to be substantially greater, and three times greater by the year 2025.

The proportion of the world population living in the largest cities will almost double between 1970 and 2025, because of the growth of such cities in developing countries. By the year 2025 almost 30 per cent of the urban population in the developing regions will be living in cities of over 4 million, more than double the figure for the more developed regions. Although only a small proportion of the African population today lives in very large cities, by the end of the first quarter of the next century this proportion could be higher than that of any other continent. In developed countries, moreover, there is a trend towards deconcentration.

By the year 2000 there will be five "super-cities" of 15 million or more inhabitants, three of them in the developing regions. Two of them, in Latin America, will have populations of around 25 million. In 1970, nine of the twenty largest cities in the world were in the less developed regions; in 1985 there were ten and by the year 2000 there will be sixteen.

This change signals the end of the close relationship between large cities and economic development. Until recently such cities were because of their size centres of international political and economic networks, a situation which may now begin to change.

The urban population in developing countries is currently increasing three times more quickly than that of developed countries, at a rate of about 3.5 per cent a year, a doubling time of only twenty years.

There are important differences between the developing regions. Latin America has the lowest rates of population growth, followed by Asia. Africa, especially East Africa, has the highest. The current growth rate for Africa is 5 per cent a year, implying a doubling of the urban population every 14 years. The current figure for East Africa is above 6.5 per cent, a doubling time of little more than ten years.

MIGRANTS TO THE CITIES

Such extremely rapid urban growth is without precedent. It confronts the cities, especially in the developing countries, with problems new to human experience, and presents the old problems—urban infrastructure, food, housing, employment, health, education—in new and accentuated forms.

Furthermore, despite migration to the cities, rural population in developing countries will continue to increase, at a rate of around one per cent annually.

Five important points emerge from an analysis of United Nations population figures:

- The world's rural population is now more than 2.5 thousand million;
- Rural population density is already very high in many parts of the less developed regions. Standards of living, while improving, remain low. It is doubtful whether added demographic pressure will benefit agricultural development—on the contrary it may jeopardize the development of many rural areas;
- Increasing rural population in developing countries will make it difficult to reduce the flow of migrants to the cities;
- The natural growth rate (the difference between the number of births and the number of deaths) of the rural population is higher than the one per cent rate—often more than double. The difference is due to the number of migrants to the cities;

■ For most of Africa, unlike the rest of the developing world, rural populations will continue to increase until well into the next century.

Although urban fertility in developing countries tends to be lower than rural fertility, it is still at least twice as high as that in developed countries.

When natural increase in urban areas is high and migrants contribute substantially to it, the migrants' future fertility becomes an important factor. The high fertility typical of rural areas may be carried over into the urban environment; more optimistically, migrants plunging into new endeavours in a different context may adapt rather quickly to urban values, including lower fertility.

Those who consider urbanization to be a blessing hold that migration to the cities is part of a dynamic development process. Those who think that it is a burden believe that rural surplus population becomes an urban surplus, producing "over-urbanization", in which an inefficient and unproductive "informal sector" consisting of street vendors, shoeshine boys, sidewalk repair shops and other so-called marginal occupations becomes more and more important.

Urban life has its positive aspects, but they emphasize employment rather than what workers get for their labour. A city worker may earn more than a rural counterpart, but is it enough to cover the basic needs of food, health, housing and education?

Two important aspects of urban life are income distribution and the number of city-dwellers living below an acceptable and culturally adjusted "poverty line". Reliable data are lacking, but it is probably true that the distribution of incomes is more inequitable in urban than in rural areas, in that there are proportionally more very rich and very poor people in the cities.

This may be as much an indication of economic development in the urban areas as of the privileges enjoyed by urban elites. Rapid demographic growth among the urban masses also contributes to the inequality of income distribution and swells the numbers of the poor.

A MASSIVE HOUSING DEFICIT

The most visible manifestations of the problems of rapid urban population growth are the makeshift settlements on the outskirts of every city in the developing world. They are usually in the worst parts of town as regards health and accessibility, lacking basic services and security of tenure. They are by their nature overcrowded—average occupancy rates of four to five persons per room are common.

The names given to these settlements graphically express their characteristics. In Latin America the word *callampas* (mushrooms) refers to their almost magical overnight growth. The term *bidonvilles* (tin can cities), is often used in Francophone Africa to describe their makeshift nature. There are many other labels, usually given by outsiders; those who live in these settlements might describe them differently, perhaps even considering them as starting points on the path to a higher standard of living.

There is a massive housing deficit in many large cities. The World Bank estimated in 1975 that the poorest quarter of the population in most African and Asian cities cannot afford even minimal housing. Wood and cardboard packing crates, sheets of plastic or corrugated iron, flattened tin cans, leaves, bamboo and beaten earth are the main sources of materials.

Space is also a problem. Landlords may add illegal floors to existing buildings, only to watch their dreams of wealth collapse along with the buildings and the lives of the unfortunate inhabitants. In some cities several workers will use the same "hot bed" in shifts over the twenty-four hours. In Cairo squatters have occupied a large cemetery: the tombs of the wealthy have become homes for the poor.

Colonies of squatters occupy the last areas to be settled, and may be perched on steep hillsides subject to frequent landslides, or installed by rivers or on swampy ground which is flooded regularly. In Mexico City about 1.5 million people live on the drained bed of a salt lake, bedevilled by dust storms in the dry season and floods in rainy months. In Lagos, Nigeria, the proportion of wet land to dry land settled has worsened, while the absolute area of dry land occupied has doubled.

Where squatter settlements have been established near workplaces, the inhabitants may run the risk of pollution and are exposed to dangers such as the leak of poisonous gas in Bhopal, India, or the explosions at oil refineries in Mexico City.

Squatter settlements typically lack water, sewage and waste disposal facilities, electricity and paved streets. In Mexico City, 80 per cent of the population have access to tapwater, but in some squatter settlements the figure is less than 50 per cent. Water consumption in the wealthy quarters of Mexico City is at least five times as high as in the poorer areas. In Lagos, water is strictly rationed and in some parts of the city residents must walk long distances to obtain water from a few pumps which are turned on only in the early morning.

According to a study carried out in Lima, Peru, lower income groups spent three times more per month on water from vendors but consumed less than a sixth as much as those with running water at home.

It is estimated that three million inhabitants of Mexico City do not have access to the sewage system. In São Paulo, Brazil, the absence of sewage systems have turned the two main rivers into moving cesspools.

Because they occupy land owned by the government, private individuals or communal organizations, squatters are frequently subject to harassment, which increases their feeling of insecurity and the precariousness of their existence. Illegal or barely legal occupation does nothing to encourage squatters to improve or even maintain the shaky structures in which they live.

A number of schemes have been devised to give more security to squatters, but there are risks. One is that improving living conditions in the city will encourage people to move there. Another is that improvements to property will increase its value and encourage squatters to sell, while moving it out of the reach of other low-income families.

TWO URGENT PROBLEMS: CHILD HEALTH AND EDUCATION

The health of the poor may be worse in urban than in rural areas. Infant mortality in the Port-au-Prince slums is three times higher than it is in the rural areas of Haiti. In some of the *favelas* of São Paulo, infant mortality is over 100 per thousand live births. The overall infant mortality rate for the slums of Delhi is 221 per thousand, twice that for some castes. In Manila infant mortality is three times higher in the slums than it is in the rest of the city. (Tuberculosis rates are nine times higher; the incidence of diarrhoea is twice as common; twice as many people are anaemic and three times as many are undernourished.) In Panama City, of 1,819 infants with diarrhoeal diseases, 45.5 per cent came from the slums and 22.5 per cent from squatter settlements. Children living in the best housing were not affected.

In most cities in developed countries, young people under 19 constitute less than 30 per cent of the population. In developing countries, the proportion is typically over 40 per cent and may reach 50 per cent in cities such as Manila, Jakarta and Bogotá. If the education system breaks down under this sort of pressure, it will add immeasurably to problems of employment, delinquency and allied problems caused by the existence of "street children".

Education is probably the most pressing of urban problems. A lower rate of population growth would immeasurably help the situation, but such a decrease partly depends on the spread of education. Family planning programmes will certainly be useful, but they must be accompanied by renewed efforts to bring education to the urban masses.

HOW WILL THE CITIES BY FED?

How will agriculture respond to the tremendous pressure of urbanization and the growth of urban population? A recent study by the United Nations Food and Agriculture Organization (FAO) and the United Nations Fund for Population Activities (UNFPA) draws attention to some of the likely effects.

First, urban populations demand cheap food. By weight of numbers they force governments to keep retail prices down. Governments may make up the difference by subsidizing farmers but experience has shown that, once established, such subsidies are difficult to withdraw.

Second, as urban populations grow and indigenous agriculture fails to keep up with demand (for lack of incentive to increase supply), more food is imported. This drains off hard currency intended for capital imports with a view to long-term development.

Third, urban population increase means that rural populations and the agricultural labour force will grow more slowly. But to meet urban needs agricultural productivity should be increasing by 17 per cent for each agricultural worker in developing countries between 1980 and the year 2000. This figure seems high, but recent experience in Asia and Latin America shows that it is possible.

For Africa, however, the increase per worker will have to be almost 25 per cent, an eventuality that seems very doubtful in view of recent events. Research in Africa has shown that lower production gains were made in countries with high rural-urban migration. This contrasts with experience in other regions, where rural-urban migration has been at least partly the consequence of higher agricultural labour productivity.

Fourth, tastes in food change under the influence of urban life-styles, as traditional staples are partly replaced by foods such as bread, meat and vegetables.

Fifth, the growth of urban population intensifies competition for land, water and energy. Cities gobble up agricultural land, often the best land because its fertility was the original attraction which stimulated urban growth. Between 1980 and the year 2000, according to one study, cities will devour four million hectares of land with the potential to feed 84 million people.

Sixth, while malnutrition may be more widespread among rural populations, the urban poor suffer more acutely. People in the lowest income groups normally have to spend more than half of their incomes on food.

BALANCED APPROACHES TO AN URBAN PLANET

The transformation from a rural to an urban planet offers both great blessings and heavy burdens. The transition from agrarian to urban has always been considered a positive step, part of the process of modernization. However, the rapid growth of urban populations in societies rapidly changing in other ways is fraught with enormous tension and tremendously complex problems.

In its search for solutions to problems of urban population dynamics, UNFPA puts continuous emphasis on three fundamental objectives: economic efficiency, social equity and population balance. It recognizes that the solution for many urban problems will only come through economic efficiency and vast growth of the productive forces. Economic growth is essential to any solution of urban problems. At the same time social equity should be pursued, with emphasis on equal opportunity for all.

Neither economic efficiency nor social equity can be attained without demographic balance—balance within and between urban and rural areas, balanced population distribution and balanced population growth.

Review Questions

1. Describe some of the major increases in urban growth within both developed nations and less developed nations that will occur by and beyond the year 2000.
2. Identify the five major points that emerged from analysis of United Nations population figures regarding the rural population.
3. Discuss various problems associated with large-scale urban growth within the less developed nations.
4. List the three fundamental objectives emphasized by the United Nations Fund for Population Activities (UNFPA) in its efforts to find solutions to problems of urban population dynamics.

The Environment

Human beings not only live in a social and cultural world, they also inhabit and are dependent upon a natural environment. Human populations and the environments in which they exist have a reciprocal influence upon one another—each influences the other in rather complex ways.

Ecology is the study of the interrelationships between living organisms and their environment. In studying these relationships, ecologists often speak of **ecosystems,** which "consist of communities of plants, animals, and microorganisms along with the air, water, soil, or other substrate that supports them" (Dasmann, 1976). Ecosystems vary in size and complexity, ranging from small communities of microscopic life to lakes, oceans, forests, and even the entire global ecosystem. Regardless of the complexity of an ecosystem, the organisms that are part of it tend to form a balanced and interdependent "web of relationships" among themselves and with their environment.

Many environmental problems result from human action

Today many environmental problems are the direct result of humans' deliberate attempts to change and exploit the environment. Humans have increasingly interfered with the stability and balance of the earth's ecosystems, disturbing many of nature's life-support cycles. In recent years, world population has grown faster than in any other period of recorded human history. Thus increasing demands are being made on the earth's natural resources. In addition, humans have altered the environment, disturbing or eliminating major ecosystems such as lakes or forests and replacing them with highways, dams, and industrial plants. Likewise, the growth of industrialization and technology has been responsible for vast increases in environmental pollution. Many environmental problems also result from human neglect of and disregard for the environment's delicate ecological balance.

Some consequences of ecological imbalances

This disturbance of ecological balances frequently leads to adverse and unintended consequences for many species of life, including the human species. Increased strains on the earth's resources inevitably result in shortages of basic necessities such as food, fuels, and minerals. Another human-caused problem is pollution of the environment. Water pollution caused by the dumping of chemical wastes into streams and oceans is responsible for the destruction of aquatic life. Air pollution ultimately leads to many health problems. Many environmental problems have to do with declining natural resources, while others are essentially pollution problems. While massive, large-scale population growth, such as we are experiencing in the world today, plays a major causal role in many environmental problems, there are actually a large number of interactive factors at work. G. Tyler Miller, Jr. has identified a number of these factors, some examples of which would include human overpopulation, excessive use of resources on the part of relatively small numbers of people, the distribution of population, the waste of resources, lack of knowledge as to how the earth with its life-support systems works, and "me-first and human-centered" behaviors and view of the world rather than "we-first and earth-centered" behaviors and view of the world (Miller, 1990). In the following sections, we will briefly note a number of our environmental problems and indicate some current responses and suggestions for dealing with them.

Declining Natural Resources

Industrial nations consume much of the world's resources

The depletion of many natural resources (fossil fuels, minerals, and metals) constitutes a severe problem, particularly for industrial societies, which depend on these materials to maintain their high standards of living. Actually, the industrialized nations have been largely responsible for many of the world's natural resource depletion problems because of their disproportionate and often wasteful use of these substances. Although the United States contains only 5 percent of the world's population, it consumes several times this percentage share of the world's nonrenewable resources. On the energy front alone, the United States consumes one-quarter of the world's energy resources. The average American consumes over a dozen times the amount of energy as a citizen of a less developed nation (The Global Tomorrow Coalition, 1990).

Over the years, there have been various estimates as to how long many of the world's natural resources will last. An earlier study by the Massachusetts Institute of Technology projected that the then-known supplies of copper, silver, lead, and zinc would be exhausted within 21 years or less. Chromium and iron would be used up in less than a century; natural gas and petroleum in about 22 years and 20 years, respectively; and nickel in 53 years (Meadows et al., 1974).

While recent estimates with regard to the future supply of many natural resources may differ from some earlier projections, the main issue is one of a growing demand in the midst of finite resource supply (The Global Tomorrow Coalition, 1990). Predicting long-term availability of natural resources is often difficult. Given the current situation of growing world demand and usage rates, it is possible that reserves of a number of minerals and some fossil fuels could suffer depletion in the not too distant future. Recent estimates indicate that reserves of chromite, feldspar, and iron ore may last 100 to 200 years; nickel, phosphate, and bauxite (aluminum ore), 50 to 100 years; mercury, copper, lead, and zinc, less than 50 years. While world reserves of coal are expected to last at least 200 years, reserves of some other fossil fuels could be depleted relatively soon. Based on the 1986 production rate, proven world reserves of oil are estimated to last slightly over 30 years. Natural gas reserves are estimated to last at least 60 years at current usage rates (The Global Tomorrow Coalition, 1990). The United States, the world's largest user of energy, relies on oil for approximately 42 percent of its energy. Coal and natural gas provide an additional 24 percent and 23 percent of U.S. energy needs, respectively (The Global Tomorrow Coalition, 1990).

The U.S. unnecessarily wastes a great deal of the energy it uses

The United States is not only the largest user but also the largest waster of energy. G. Tyler Miller, Jr. has estimated that the United States unnecessarily wastes a minimum of 41 percent of all the energy it uses. A primary source of this problem is energy-wasting factories, vehicles, and buildings. The implementation of an energy policy stressing "least-cost, high-energy-efficiency" beginning in 1973 would, by now, have eliminated the United States's dependency upon imported oil (Miller, 1990). The record is not all bad, of course. In recent years, our cars, houses, and appliances have become more energy-efficient. Still, we could become twice as energy-efficient as we currently are. By becoming as energy-efficient as Sweden or Japan, for example, the United States could reduce its energy bill by about $200 billion annually (Miller, 1990).

Pollution

Sources of air pollution

Nationwide, in recent years, we have annually released in excess of 100 million metric tons of pollutants into the air in the form of carbon monoxide, sulfur oxides, nitrogen oxides, volatile organic compounds, and particulate matter. As we can see from Table 11.2, nearly half of this pollution (particularly carbon monoxide and nitrogen oxides) comes from transportation sources, including automobiles and trucks. Almost one-third (mostly sulfur oxides and nitrogen oxides) comes from fuel combustion sources such as electric utilities. An additional 15 to 20 percent (mostly carbon monoxide, sulfur oxides, and volatile organic compounds) comes from industrial processes. Air pollution has many adverse effects on humans as well as the environment around us. It can impair respiration, cause coughing, and irritate throats and eyes. Sulfur and nitrogen oxides can harm the respiratory tract and lungs; carbon monoxide can harm the pulmonary, nervous, and cardiovascular systems; some volatile organic compounds can cause cancer (The Global Tomorrow Coalition, 1990). Sulfur dioxide and nitrogen oxides, produced by the burning of fossil fuels by power plants, industry, and motor vehicles, are major sources of acid rain, which has caused

Table 11.2 Major Sources of Air Pollution (millions of metric tons annually—1987)

CATEGORY	CARBON MONOXIDE	SULFUR OXIDES	VOLATILE ORGANIC COMPOUNDS	PARTICULATES	NITROGEN OXIDES	TOTAL
Transportation	40.7	0.9	6.0	1.4	8.4	57.4
Fuel combustion	7.2	16.4	2.3	1.8	10.3	38.0
Industrial processes	4.7	3.1	8.3	2.5	0.6	19.2
Solid waste disposal	1.7	—	0.6	0.3	0.1	2.7
						117.3

Source: U.S. Bureau of the Census, *Statistical Abstract of the United States: 1990*, 110th edition (Washington, D.C., 1990), p. 203.

damage to aquatic life, streams, lakes, forests, monuments, and buildings (The Global Tomorrow Coalition, 1990). Carbon dioxide, produced by fossil fuel combustion, chlorofluorocarbons, and methane are the major contributors to global warming and the greenhouse effect. The United States, by the way, is the world's largest contributor of greenhouse gases ("Greenhouse Redesign," 1990). Chlorofluorocarbons, used as spray-can propellants, solvents, and refrigerants, are also a primary source of ozone depletion, which, in turn, can result in greater amounts of ultraviolet radiation reaching the earth. Ultraviolet radiation can adversely affect human health in a number of ways, including aging of the skin and higher incidences of skin cancer and cataracts (The Global Tomorrow Coalition, 1990). In the late 1980s, the Environmental Protection Agency estimated that approximatley 102 million Americans were breathing air that was unsafe. Health-care and lower work productivity costs due to both indoor and outdoor air pollution are estimated to cost our nation a minimum of $110 billion annually (Miller, 1990).

Many Americans are breathing air that is unsafe

Water as well as air is necessary for survival, yet today water is sometimes in scarce supply and too much of it is unclean and unsafe. In recent years, water shortages have become increasingly common throughout the United States—even the northeastern region has experienced occasional droughts. Water shortages have been particularly severe in the west as a result of droughts, development, and inadequate water-management practices ("The U.S.: No Water to Waste," 1990). Agriculture, which uses the vast majority of the available water in the far west region of the country, has been especially hard-hit by rising water prices in recent years. According to the Environmental Protection Agency, almost half of the U.S. rivers, streams, and lakes are either threatened or damaged by pollution ("The U.S.: No Water to Waste," 1990). Typical river and stream contaminants include nitrates, pesticides, phosphates, and additional toxic chemicals. Common lake contaminants are in the form of oil, pesticides, plant nutrients, and various toxic substances (Miller, 1990). Many lakes have been harmed by a process termed "cultural eutrophication"—an excessive buildup of phosphates and nitrates arising from various human actions, including agricultural activities and emissions from sewage treatment facilities and industrial plants (Miller, 1990). Contamination of groundwater is also of growing concern in recent years. Groundwater is an extremely important natural resource—about half of the U.S. population depends on it for drinking water. Groundwater has not been a well-protected resource, however. Instances of

Americans generate millions of tons of solid waste each year.

groundwater contamination from irrigation practices, salt water, and toxic chemicals have been increasing. In 1988, over 50 percent of the states throughout the country identified a number of significant hazards to groundwater quality, including, for example, agricultural activities such as irrigation and crop dusting, underground storage tanks that leaked, and poorly operating septic systems. An added complication is the fact that groundwater pollution is a condition that may not be able to be corrected or remedied (The Global Tomorrow Coalition, 1990; U.S. Environmental Protection Agency, May 1990).

Groundwater has not been a well-protected resource

Another major environmental problem is the growth of solid waste. Although most of our nation's solid waste is generated by industry, mining, and other fossil fuel production-related activities, there has been increased concern regarding the growth of municipal solid waste—the trash, garbage, and numerous other throwaway items disposed of by Americans every day. In 1988, Americans generated 180 million tons of municipal solid waste—that is, about 4 pounds of waste per person each day. During 1988, Americans discarded, for example, 13.2 million tons of food wastes, 12.5 million tons of glass, 14.4 million tons of plastics, 15.3 million tons of metals, and 71.8 million tons of paper and paperboard products. Approximately 13 percent of all 1988 municipal solid waste was recycled, 14 percent was incinerated, and virtually all the remaining 73 percent was sent to landfills. The sheer growth of municipal solid waste in recent years is problematic enough. In 1975, Americans generated 128 million tons of these wastes; by 1988, as we have seen, the figure stood at 180 million tons. Compounding this problem is the fact that in recent years, the number of landfills (the principal method of disposing of such wastes) has been declining

Only a small amount of municipal solid waste is recycled

sharply. Thus we are faced with the situation of increasing waste, yet decreasing capacity to handle it. Moreover, projections indicate that Americans will generate 216 million tons of municipal solid waste in the year 2000 and in excess of 250 million tons by the year 2010 (U.S. Environmental Protection Agency, June 1990). Statistics such as these show the importance, and, in fact, the necessity, of emphasizing different strategies, such as waste reduction and recycling, in order to deal with our nation's waste problems.

There has been some progress in dealing with some of our environmental problems

Despite a number of major environmental problems, the record on the environmental front is not all bad. In terms of air quality, the Environmental Protection Agency reports that between 1979 and 1988, there were substantial declines in levels of particulate matter, lead, carbon monoxide, and sulfur dioxide in our atmosphere (U.S. Environmental Protection Agency, March 1990). Passage of the 1990 Clean Air Act will ensure further reductions in a number of pollutants, such as sulfur dioxide, nitrogen, oxides, and chlorofluorocarbons ("Forecast: Clearer Skies, 1990). Water quality has also shown some improvements. A recent Environmental Protection Agency report indicates, for example, that in 1988, 70 percent of the assessed river and stream miles and 74 percent of the assessed lake acres in the United States were "fully supporting their designated uses," such as water supply and various recreational uses (U.S. Environmental Protection Agency, May 1990). In the area of solid waste, there is a growing awareness of the importance of reducing the amount of waste we generate and more and more communities are placing emphasis upon recycling as a strategy for waste management. In 1989, for example, Seattle recycled 34 percent of its solid waste ("Doing Your Bit to Save the Earth," 1990). The Environmental Protection Agency recently projected that approximately 19 percent of our nation's solid waste generated in 1995 will be recycled (U.S. Environmental Protection Agency, June 1990).

A strong commitment to environmental quality is essential

Solutions to environmental problems require not only an awareness of what the problems are and the reasons for their existence but also a commitment on the part of our society's institutions and people to do something about them. Such a commitment will necessarily require a willingness on our part to reevaluate our relationship to the environment and make certain changes in values, attitudes, and ways of living, which have ultimately caused most of our problems. Some people will have objections to almost any type of remedial change that entails sacrifice on their part. But we are already paying for our attitudes and behaviors that favor exploitation and neglect of our habitat. Fortunately, more and more people are becoming aware of the seriousness of our environmental problems. They are also coming to realize that human life and well-being depend in large measure upon a strong and continuing commitment to environmental quality. Are we willing to pay the price for a sound and healthy environment? Can we afford not to?

PROTECTING THE ENVIRONMENT

Murray Weidenbaum

As we have noted, increasing numbers of people are becoming aware of the seriousness of our environmental problems. A poll by NBC News and *The Wall Street Journal* recently pointed out that nearly three-quarters of Americans feel the environment should rank as one of our government's highest priorities ("Costs and Benefits: Fresh Questions About Clean Air," 1990). Awareness of environmental problems and the importance of dealing with them is one thing, but how do we motivate people to actually clean up the environment and keep it clean? As we shall see in the following article, Professor Murray Weidenbaum feels that this can be accomplished by using a variety of economic incentives.

Every poll of citizen sentiment shows overwhelming support for doing more to clean up the environment. A public opinion survey by *The New York Times* and CBS News reported in 1983 that 58 percent of the sample agreed with the following statement: Protecting the environment is so important that requirements and standards cannot be too high and continuing environmental improvements must be made regardless of cost."

Despite the continuation of such an overwhelming public mandate and a plethora of new laws and directives by the EPA (Environmental Protection Agency) plus hundreds of billions of dollars of compliance costs expended by private industry, the public remains unhappy with the results.

Unfortunately, environmental action is an extremely important example of not wishing to pay the piper. Those same citizens who want environmental improvements "regardless of cost" vociferously and adamantly oppose the location of any hazardous-waste facility in their own neighborhood. Nor are they keen on paying for the cleanup. Of course, they strongly favor cleaning up the environment, but each prefers to have the dump site located in someone else's backyard and to have the other fellow pay for it.

An example of this situation is the reaction of the enlightened citizens of Minnesota to a $3.7 million grant from the EPA to build and operate a state-of-the-art chemical landfill that could handle hazardous wastes with a high assurance of safety. In each of the 16 locations that the state proposed, the local residents raised such a fuss and howl that the state government backed off. Ultimately, the unspent grant was returned to the EPA.

The Minnesota experience is not exceptional. The EPA was also forced to stop a project to test whether the sludge from a municipal waste treatment plant could be used as a low-cost fertilizer. Public opposition was fierce, even though the EPA was going to use federally owned land and the sludge was expected to increase crop yields by 30 percent.

Since 1980, not a single major new disposal facility has been sited anywhere in the United States. According to a state-by-state review, the outlook for the future is "'even

---

Society, vol. 27, no. 1, November/December 1989, pp. 49–56.

more bleak," in large part because of the deteriorating emotional atmosphere surrounding any effort to locate a new dump site. As Peter Sandman of Rutgers University has pointed out, the public perceives environmental matters not only emotionally, but also morally. "Our society," he has written, "has reached near-consensus that pollution is morally wrong—not just harmful or dangerous . . . but wrong." Yet, the individuals who make up that same public are reluctant to personally assume the burdens associated with that strongly held view.

This ambivalent attitude toward the environment is not new. In 1969, the National Wildlife Federation commissioned a national survey to determine how much people were willing to pay for a cleaner environment. At a time of peak enthusiasm for environmental regulation, the public was asked, "To stop pollution destroying our plant life and wildlife, would you be willing to pay an incresae in your monthly electric bill of $1?" The "no" vote won hands down, 62 percent to 28 percent (with 10 percent "not sure"). That study, we should recall, was taken before the big runup in utility bills. Perhaps not too surprisingly, the survey showed strong support for taxing business to finance environmental cleanup.

In other words, most Americans very much want a cleaner environment, but are neither willing to pay for it nor to inconvenience themselves. Americans try to take the easy way out—by imposing the burden on "someone else," preferably a large, impersonal institution.

It is much easier for Congress to express a desire for cleaner air or purer water than for an agency like the EPA to fulfill that desire. Vast sums of money have been spent for these purposes in recent years. From 1970 to 1986, Congress appropriated more than $55 billion for the operation of the EPA. The head-count of EPA employment rose from a few hundred in 1970 to over nine thousand in 1988. These numbers are dwarfed by the costs for the private sector to comply with government's rules on environmental cleanup. The U.S. Council on Environmental Quality estimated the total at more than $100 billion for 1988, and more than $750 billion for the preceding decade (in dollars of 1986 purchasing power). . . .

The EPA can claim important accomplishments. Between 1970 and 1985, air pollution from vehicles fell by 46 percent for hydrocarbons, 34 percent for carbon monoxide, and 75 percent for lead. Rivers that were nearly devoid of life teem with fish once again. Lake Erie, so laden with pollutants in 1969 that a river feeding into it caught fire, has been revived.

Despite these successes, the EPA frequently falls short in meeting congressionally mandated goals for pollution cleanup. The hard fact is that the status quo in environmental policy is not sufficient. Congress continues to pass high-sounding legislation with unrealistic timetables and inflexible deadlines, while the EPA gets ever greater responsibility and private industry spends billions more on environmental compliance. In the words of the EPA's former administrator, William Ruckelshaus, "EPA's statutory framework is less a coherent attack on a complex and integrated societal problem than it is a series of petrified postures."

THE PUBLIC SECTOR DRAGS ITS FEET

Misperceptions of the villains in the pollution story abound. Many people fall into a common trap—that of associating polluters exclusively with business. Many companies do generate lots of pollution. But the same can be said about government agencies, hospitals, schools, and colleges.

The EPA lacks the enforcement power over the public sector that it possesses over the private sector. Reports of plant closings because of the high cost of meeting environmental standards are common. In contrast, there is no record of a single government facility closing down because it was not meeting ecological requirements.

It is not surprising that the GAO (General Accounting Office) says that the performance of federal agencies in the disposal of hazardous waste "has not been exemplary." A GAO report issued in 1986 says that, of 72 federal facilities inspected, 33 were in violation of EPA requirements and 22 had been cited for Class 1 (serious) violations. Sixteen of the thirty-three facilities remained out of compliance for six months or more. Three had been out of compliance for more than three years. A follow-up report by the GAO in 1987 showed little further progress. Only four of eleven federal agencies had completed the identification of hazardous-waste sites and none had finished assessing the environmental problems they had uncovered. Of 511 federal sites failing to meet EPA standards, only 78 had been cleaned up.

A major offender is the DOD (Department of Defense), which now generates more than 500,000 tons of hazardous waste a year. That is more than is produced by the five largest chemical companies combined. The lax situation uncovered by the GAO at Tinker Air Force Base, in Oklahoma, is typical of the way in which many federal agencies respond to the EPA's directives: "Although DOD policy calls for the military services to . . . implement EPA's hazardous waste management regulations, we found that Tinker has been selling . . . waste oil, fuels, and solvents rather than . . . recycling."

The GAO reported that two of the five commercial waste sites receiving the base's wastes had major compliance problems. Also, personnel at Tinker Air Force Base were dumping hazardous wastes in landfills that themselves were in violation of EPA requirements. In one case, the EPA had been urging the Oklahoma Department of Health for several years not to renew a landfill's permit. In another instance, the State Water Resources Board was seeking a court order to close the site. Civilian agencies, including those in state and local governments, continue to be reluctant to follow the same environmental standards that they impose on the private sector.

Federal policy arbitrarily excludes one of the largest single sources of pollution from the EPA's effective jurisdiction: the runoff of pesticides and fertilizers from farms. The EPA reports that in six of the agency's ten regions, pollution from farms and urban streets is the principal cause of water quality problems. But pollution from these sources remains virtually unregulated.

Large quantities of agricultural pollution can be controlled fairly easily at low cost by using limited-till plowing techniques. In striking contrast, industrial pollution control has often been pushed to the limits of economic feasibility. Congress follows a double standard: for urban and industrial pollution it requires the imposition of tough standards to qualify for permits to discharge wastes. For rural and farm pollution, the EPA is merely given money to study the problem.

Congress wants a cleaner environment. But so far it has not mustered the will required to impose the most modest pollution controls on a politically powerful group of constituents. Farm families also want a cleaner environment—but it is always nice to get someone else to pay for your desires. . . .

ECONOMIC INCENTIVES NEEDED

A more clearheaded view of waste disposal problems is needed in the United States. Because definitions vary among levels of government, estimates of the amount of hazardous waste disposed of each year in the United States range from 30 million to 264 million metric tons. Most of this waste is buried in landfills because incineration, the safest and most effective means of disposal, is nearly ten times as costly. Even so, government and industry spend more than $5 billion each year to manage toxic wastes. The annual cost by 1990 is projected to reach $12 billion.

Many experts believe that using landfills is inherently unsafe, if for no other reason than that they are only storage sites. Moreover, there are not enough of them. The EPA estimates that 22,000 waste sites now exist in the United States, and fully ten percent of them are believed to be dangerous and leaking.

The result: not enough reliable environmentally safe places to dump toxic substances. Although the EPA wants to clean up as many landfills as possible, it has very little choice as to where to put the material it removes under the Superfund mandate. Taxpayers may wind up paying for the costly removal of waste from one site, only to find later on that they have to pay again for removing it from yet another dangerous site.

Meanwhile, legal fees mushroom. The litigation costs involving cleanup at the various Superfund sites are estimated to run somewhere between $3.5 billion and $6.4 billion.

Eventually, society will have to face the main reason for the scarcity of hazardous waste sites—the "not in my backyard" syndrome. Sites for the disposal of toxic substances have joined prisons and mental hospitals as things the public wants, but not too close by.

The hazardous-waste disposal problem is not going to disappear unless Americans adopt less polluting methods of production and consumption. Until then, greater understanding is needed on the part of the public, as is a willingness to come to grips with the difficult problems arising from the production and use of hazardous substances. It will cost large amounts of money (probably in the hundreds of billions of private and public expenditures in the next decade) to meet society's environmental expectations. Spending money may be the easiest part of the problem. Getting people to accept dump sites in their neighborhoods is much more difficult.

The answer surely is an appeal not merely to good citizenship, but also to common sense and self-interest. In a totalitarian society, people who do not want to do something the government desires are simply forced to do so, with the threat of physical violence ever present. In a free society with a market economy, we offer to pay people to do something they otherwise would not do. The clearest example in modern times is the successful elimination of the military draft coupled with very substantial increases in pay and fringe benefits for voluntarily serving in the armed forces.

Individual citizens have much to gain by opposing the location of hazardous waste facilities near them, and there is a basic logic to their position. It is not fair for society as a whole to benefit from a new disposal site, while imposing most of the costs (ranging from danger of leakage to depressed property values) on the people in the locality. But local resistance to dealing with hazardous wastes imposes large costs on society as a whole. Those costs are in the form both of inhibiting economic progress and having to ship waste from one temporary site to another.

Individual interests and community concerns can be reconciled by the use of economic incentives. The idea is to look upon environmental pollution not as a sinful act but as an activity costly to society and susceptible to reduction by means of proper incentives. After all, the prospect of jobs and income encourages many communities to offer tax holidays and other enticements to companies considering the location of a new factory—even though it may not exactly improve the physical environment of the region. Under present arrangements, however, there is no incentive for the citizens of an area to accept a site for hazardous wastes in their vicinity, no matter how safe it is.

Some areas might accept such a facility if the state government (financed by all the citizens benefitting from the disposal facility) would pay for something the people in that locality want but cannot afford—such as a new school building, firehouse, or library, or simply lower property taxes. Unlike an industrial factory, a hazardous-waste facility provides few offsetting benefits to the local residents in the form of jobs or tax revenues. Government can do a lot to improve environmental policy in other ways. The EPA could reduce the entire hazardous waste problem by distinguishing between truly lethal wastes—which should be disposed of with great care—and wastes that contain only a trace or minute amounts of undesirable materials. To the extent that this would require changes in legislation, the agency should urge Congress to make them. . . .

A BIRTH CONTROL APPROACH TO POLLUTION

Over 99 percent of environmental spending by government is devoted to controlling pollution after it is generated. Less than one percent is spent to reduce the generation of pollutants. For fiscal 1988, the EPA budgeted only $398,000—or .03 percent of its funds—for "waste minimization." That is an umbrella term that includes recycling and waste reduction.

The most desirable approach is to reduce the generation of pollutants in the first place. Economists have an approach that is useful—providing incentives to manufacturers to change their production processes to reduce the amount of wastes created or to recycle them in a safe and productive manner.

As we noted earlier, the government taxes producers rather than polluters. By doing that, the country misses a real opportunity to curb actual dumping of dangerous waste. The federal Superfund law is financed with taxes levied on producers of chemical "feedstocks" and petroleum plus a surtax on the profits of large manufacturing companies and contributions from the federal Treasury. Thousands of companies outside the oil and chemical industries wind up paying very little, whether they are large polluters or not. Contrary to widely held views, a great deal of pollution occurs in sectors of the economy other than oil and chemicals. The manufacture of a single TV set generates about one hundred pounds of toxic wastes.

Switching to a waste-end fee levied on the amount of hazardous wastes that a company actually generates and disposes of would be far more economically sound than the status quo. This more enlightened approach would require a basic correction in the Comprehensive Environmental Response, Compensation, and Liability Act (or "Superfund"), but it would be a very beneficial form of hazardous waste "birth control."

A GENERAL APPLICATION OF MARKET INCENTIVES

More generally, if the government were to levy a fee on the amount of pollutants discharged, that would provide an incentive to reduce the actual generation of wastes. Some companies would find it cheaper to change their production processes than to pay the tax. Recycling and reuse systems would be encouraged. Moreover, such a tax or fee would cover imports which are now disposed of in our country tax-free. In short, rewriting statutes, such as the Superfund law, so that they are more fair would also help protect the environment—and would probably save money at the same time.

Already, some companies are recycling as they become aware of the economic benefits. One chemical firm burns 165,000 tons of coal a year at one of its textile fibers factories, generating 35,000 tons of waste in the form of fly ash. The company recently found a local cement block company that was testing fly ash as a replacement for limestone in making lightweight cement blocks. The chemical company now sells the fly ash to the cement block manufacturer. What used to be an undesirable waste by-product has been turned into a commercially useful material. The companies are simultaneously conserving the supply of limestone.

A timber company, through its research, developed a new use for tree bark, the last massive waste product of the wood products industry. The firm designed a bark processor that made it the first domestic producer of vegetable wax, an important ingredient in cosmetics and polishes. A factory in Illinois had been creating a veritable sea of calcium fluoride sludge (at a rate of 1,000 cubic yards a month) as a by-product of its manufacture of fluorine-based chemicals. The company found that the sludge could be mixed with another waste product to produce synthetic fluorspar, which it had been buying from other sources. Recycling the two waste products now saves the firm about $1 million a year.

Incentives to do more along these lines could be provided in several ways. The producers could be subsidized to follow the desired approach. In this period of large budget deficits, that would, of course, increase the amount of money that the Treasury must borrow.

A different alternative is to tax the generation and disposal of wastes. The object would not be to punish the polluters, but to get them to change their ways. If something becomes more expensive, business firms have a natural desire to use less of the item. In this case, the production of pollution would become more expensive. Every sensible firm would try to reduce the amount of pollution tax it pays by curbing its wastes. Adjusting to new taxes on pollution would be a matter not of patriotism, but of minimizing cost and maximizing profit. The pollution tax approach appeals to self-interest in order to achieve the public interest.

Charging polluters for the pollution they cause gives companies an incentive to find innovative ways to cut down on their discharges. These fees would raise costs and prices for products whose production generates a lot of pollution. It is wrong to view this as a way of shifting the burden to the public. The relevant factor is that consumer purchasing is not static. Consumer demand would shift to products which pollute less—because they would cost less. To stay competitive, high-polluting producers would have to economize on pollution, just as they do in the case of other costs of production. Since pollution imposes burdens on the environment, it is only fair that the costs of cleaning up that pollution should be reflected in the price of a product whose production generates this burden.

Nine countries in Western Europe have adopted the "polluter pays" principle. In these nations, pollution control is paid for directly by the polluting firm or from the money collected from effluent taxes. The West German effluent-fee system, the oldest in operation, began before World War I. It has succeeded in halting the decline in water quality throughout the Ruhr Valley, the center of West Germany's iron and steel production. It is also serving as a model for a more recent French effort.

Practical problems make changes in pollution policy difficult in the United States. Both the regulators and the regulated have an interest in maintaining the current approach. Pollution taxes have little appeal in the political system, particularly in Congress. Many reject a pollution tax on philosophical grounds, considering pollution charges a "license to pollute." They believe that putting a price on the act of polluting amounts to an attitude of moral indifference towards polluters. The tendency to look at ecological matters as moral issues makes it difficult to adopt a workable approach.

Although economists are often accused of being patsies for the business community, environmental economics makes for strange alliances. So far, business interests have opposed the suggestions of economists for such sweeping changes in the basic structure of government regulation as using taxes on pollution. Despite the shortcomings of the present system of government regulation, many firms have paid the price of complying with existing rules. They have learned to adjust to regulatory requirements and to integrate existing regulatory procedures into their long-term planning.

As any serious student of business-government relations will quickly report, the debate over regulation is miscast when it is described as black-hatted business versus white-hatted public interest groups. Almost every regulatory action creates winners and losers in the business system and often among other interest groups. Clean air legislation, focussing on ensuring that new facilities fully meet standards, is invariably supported by existing firms that are "grandfathered" approval without having to conform to the same high standards as new firms. Regulation thus protects the "ins" from the "outs."

There are many other examples of regulatory bias against change and especially against new products, new processes, and new facilities. Tough emissions standards are set for new automobiles, but not for older ones. Testing and licensing procedures for new chemicals are more rigorous and thoroughly enforced than for existing substances. This ability to profit from the differential impacts of regulation helps to explain why business shows little enthusiasm for the use of economic incentives and prefers current regulatory techniques.

The reform of regulation is truly a consumer issue. The consumer receives the benefits from regulation and bears the burden of the costs of compliance in the form of higher prices and less product variety. The consumer has the key stake in improving the current regulatory morass.

Review Questions

1. List some examples of how the public sector contributes to environmental pollution.
2. Identify and discuss some ways in which economic incentives could be used to help reduce pollution and clean up our environment.
3. What does Weidenbaum mean by a "birth control" approach to pollution?

Summary

1. Demography is the scientific study of human populations. Demographers are primarily interested in studying three demographic processes: fertility, mortality, and migration. Demographers also pay close attention to popu-

lation composition—the way in which such various characteristics as sex, age, and marital status are distributed throughout a population. Characteristics such as these have an important influence on a population's potential for future growth and change.

2. World population during the twentieth century has grown faster than ever before. Given current growth rates, world population is projected to increase from the present 5.3 billion to approximately 6.3 billion by the year 2000 and 8.2 billion by the year 2020. Annual rates of increase within the developed nations now average 0.5 percent per year, with fertility rates close to and frequently below replacement level. Annual rates of increase within the less developed nations now average 2.1 percent a year, yielding a doubling time of only 33 years. Population growth within these nations has already created many serious problems, including hunger, malnutrition, disease, starvation, lack of economic development, and widespread poverty.

3. Industrialization, economic development, family planning, and contraceptive use have contributed to birthrate declines in the industrial nations. Within less developed nations, many governments have given official support to family planning programs or established official policies to reduce population growth. Family planning programs within these nations have had a mixed performance. The clearest successes have been within nations that have experienced economic growth. Recently, a number of approaches have been suggested to lower fertility within less developed nations.

4. Urbanization refers to the growth in the percentage or proportion of people living in cities relative to those living in rural areas. Urbanization has been essentially a nineteenth- and twentieth-century phenomenon. Today 41 percent of the global population is urban. Industrial nations have a higher percentage of urban dwellers than less developed nations. Nevertheless, in recent decades, urban growth has been faster in less developed nations. In general, during this century, United States metropolitan areas have grown faster than nonmetropolitan areas, the only brief reversal having been during the 1970s. As of 1987, 76.9 percent of the United States population lived in metropolitan areas.

5. Humans and other life species depend on the natural environment for survival. Human populations and the environments in which they exist have a reciprocal influence upon one another—each influences the other in rather complex ways. Many environmental problems are essentially pollution problems; others have to do with declining natural resources. While there has been limited progress in dealing with some environmental problems, as in the case of some forms of air and water pollution, much remains to be done. Continuing progress on the environmental front will require an enhanced commitment to environmental quality and a greater willingness on our part to make changes in values, attitudes, and ways of living, which have ultimately caused so many of our environmental problems.

STUDY GUIDE

Chapter Objectives

After studying this chapter, you should be able to:

1. Define "demography" and its two major areas of study
2. Identify and discuss the three major demographic processes
3. Discuss exponential population growth and its consequences
4. Briefly describe the history of world population growth
5. List the factors underlying the current massive population growth in less developed nations
6. Compare statistically contemporary patterns of population growth in developed and less developed nations
7. Describe the present and future patterns of population growth and changing population composition within the United States
8. Discuss both sides of the current debate on the future consequences of world population growth
9. Compare Malthusian and Marxian theories of the causes and consequences of population growth
10. Cite the theory of demographic transition
11. Analyze the effectiveness of family planning in reducing population growth in less developed nations and list effective "beyond family planning" techniques
12. Compare present and future urbanization trends in developed and less developed nations
13. Discuss the history of urban growth in the United States in the last 200 years
14. Define "ecology" and "ecosystems"
15. Cite estimates as to the future availability of various minerals and fossil fuels
16. Identify various types and sources of air, water, and solid waste pollution

Key Terms

Crude birthrate (p. 416)
Crude death rate (p. 416)
Demographic transition theory (p. 429)
Demography (p. 415)
Dependency ratio (p. 419)
Ecology (p. 439)
Ecosystems (p. 439)

Exponential growth (p. 417)
Fertility (p. 416)
Formal demography (p. 415)
Internal migration (p. 418)
International migration (p. 418)
Megalopolis (p. 433)
Metropolitan area (p. 424)
Migration (p. 417)
Mortality (p. 416)
Population composition (p. 419)
Population studies (p. 416)
Rate of natural increase (p. 417)
Replacement level fertility (p. 423)
Sex ratio (p. 419)
Urbanization (p. 432)
Zero population growth (p. 422)

Self-Test

Short Answer

(p. 415) 1. Demography is ________________________________

(p. 415) 2. "Formal demography" (a) and "population" studies (b) can be defined as:
a. ________________________________
b. ________________________________

(p. 416) 3. The three demographic processes are:
a. ________________________________
b. ________________________________
c. ________________________________

(p. 418) 4. The three major types of international migration patterns are:
a. ________________________________
b. ________________________________
c. ________________________________

(p. 419) 5. "Population composition" is defined as ________________________________

(p. 421) 6. According to Kingsley Davis, the three major periods of dramatic world population growth were:
a. ________________________________
b. ________________________________
c. ________________________________

(p. 422) 7. "Zero population growth" (a), "replacement level fertility" (b), and "metropolitan area" (c), can be defined as:
a. ________________________________
b. ________________________________
c. ________________________________

(p. 430) 8. The three stages of the demographic transition are:
a. ________________________________
b. ________________________________
c. ________________________________

(p. 432) 9. "Urbanization" is defined as ______________________
____
____

(p. 442) 10. Three forms of air pollution (a, b, c) and three forms of water pollution (d, e, f) are:
a. ____________________ d. ____________________
b. ____________________ e. ____________________
c. ____________________ f. ____________________

Multiple Choice *(Answers are on page 460.)*

(p. 416) 1. The two major areas of demography are:
a. formal demography and mathematical demography
b. formal demography and population studies
c. migration and demographic transition
d. fertility and population composition

(p. 416) 2. In our society, mortality rates vary by:
a. sex c. race
b. age d. all the above

(p. 418) 3. Thomlinson and Bouvier term the voluntary movement of individuals or families from one well-developed country to another with the intention of remaining there:
a. free-individual migration c. restricted migration
b. group migration d. internal migration

(p. 423) 4. The annual rate of natural increase within the industrialized nations averages:
a. 2.0 percent c. 1.2 percent
b. 0.5 percent d. 2.7 percent

(p. 424) 5. With respect to the population of the United States:
a. most people live within metropolitan areas
b. our population is growing younger
c. we are now at zero population growth
d. our birthrates have shown an uninterrupted decline throughout the twentieth century

(p. 425) 6. Projections indicate that in the future, the United States population will:
a. reach zero population growth by the year 2010
b. increase to about 320 million by the year 2000
c. likely experience another baby boom around the year 2030
d. grow older during the coming decades

(p. 428) 7. The vast growth of urban population in the less developed nations has resulted from:
a. rural-to-urban migration
b. natural increase in the city populations plus rural-to-urban migration
c. increased life expectancy in the city
d. the spread of the city and urban congestion

(p. 429) 8. According to the demographic transition theory, a drop in

a society's death rate inevitably is followed by:
a. an increase in its birthrate
b. a decrease in the society's standard of living
c. a decline in the means of subsistence
d. a voluntary decline in its birthrate

(p. 432) 9. Today the percentage of the global population that can be classified as urban stands at:
a. 75 percent
b. 62 percent
c. 41 percent
d. 24 percent

(p. 440) 10. The United States consumes ______ of the world's energy resources:
a. one-half
b. two-thirds
c. three-quarters
d. one-quarter

True/False *(Answers are on page 460.)*

T F 11. Formal demography analyzes the relationships between the composition of a population and population change. (p. 415)

T F 12. Invasion or displacement of entire societies is a common example of restricted migration. (p. 418)

T F 13. A sex ratio of less than 100 indicates that there are more males than females in a population. (p. 419)

T F 14. According to Kingsley Davis, the second period of dramatic growth of world population was associated with the Industrial Revolution. (p. 421)

T F 15. Massive population growth in the world's less developed nations during the twentieth century is a result of improvements in agriculture and industrialization. (p. 422)

T F 16. In the 1970s, metropolitan areas in the United States grew at a faster rate than nonmetropolitan areas. (p. 424)

T F 17. Along with family planning and contraceptive use, Chinese population policy emphasizes systems of incentives and disincentives to encourage small families. (p. 431)

T F 18. The article "Cities Without Limits" indicates that by the year 2000, the world will have five "super-cities," each with populations of at least 15 million. (p. 435)

T F 19. Sulfur dioxide and nitrogen oxides are major sources of acid rain. (p. 441)

T F 20. According to the article "Protecting the Environment," about 70 percent of environmental spending on the part of government is devoted to reducing the generation of pollutants. (p. 449)

Fill In *(Answers are on page 460.)*

(p. 416) 21. Demographers Davis and Blake have listed a number of ______ that have a direct influence on fertility.

(p. 417) 22. Population growth is ______.

(p. 417) 23. According to the text, world population at present stands at slightly over ______ billion.

(p. 418) 24. There are two basic types of migration: _______ and _______.

(p. 419) 25. _______ refers to the way in which various attributes, such as age, sex, marital status, ethnic characteristics, and occupational status, are distributed throughout a population.

(p. 424) 26. In terms of geographic distribution, most of the United States population lives in _______ areas.

(p. 427) 27. In the less developed nations, population growth often retards _______ development.

(p. 432) 28. Worldwide, between 1900 and 1975, the number of cities containing over 5 million people increased _______ times.

(p. 433) 29. The region stretching from Boston through Washington, D.C., is an example of a _______.

(p. 443) 30. In 1988, Americans generated _______ million tons of municipal solid waste.

Matching *(Answers are on page 460.)*

31. _______ Replacement level fertility
32. _______ Kingsley Davis
33. _______ Demography
34. _______ Megalopolis
35. _______ Exponential growth
36. _______ Karl Marx
37. _______ Ecology
38. _______ Fertility
39. _______ Sex and age composition
40. _______ Zero population growth

a. A set of interrelated, adjacent metropolitan areas
b. Study of the interrelationships between living organisms and their environment
c. Viewed overpopulation as a product of capitalism
d. Point at which ratio of births to deaths is balanced and population ceases to grow
e. Analyzed the history of world population growth
f. Point at which children are born in numbers sufficient to replace but not to exceed the number of parents
g. Greatly influence a population's potential for future growth and change
h. Involves a geometric progression
i. Number of children born to women of reproductive age
j. Scientific study of human populations

Essay Questions

1. What is demography, and what are the three major demographic processes that demographers study?
2. When demographers speak of exponential population growth, what do they mean? What are some of the major consequences of exponential growth?
3. Why has massive population growth occurred within the world's less developed nations during the twentieth century?
4. How will the population of the United States change in the future in terms of size, age composition, and migration patterns?
5. What are the major arguments on both sides of the current debate about the future consequences of world population growth?
6. What are the major problems of population growth in less developed nations?
7. How do Malthusian, Marxist, and demographic transition theories explain population increase and decrease?
8. How effective have family planning programs been in reducing population growth in less developed nations?
9. To what extent has the world's population become urbanized since 1800?
10. What are the positive and negative consequences of urban growth and life?
11. What are some of the various human activities that have brought about and/or contributed to many of our environmental problems?
12. What are the various types and sources of air, water, and solid waste pollution? What are some examples of recent progress in dealing with our environmental problems?

Interactive Exercises

1. At present, the vast majority of the world's population growth is occurring within less developed nations. Natural increase within these nations as a whole now averages 2.1 percent per year, yielding a doubling time of only 33 years. Interview of informally talk with several students from other nations—possibly from one of the countries listed in Table 11.1, page 423. Do they feel that population growth is a problem for their country? If so, in what ways? In general, do people in their country marry early and/or prefer large families? What would these students estimate the average family size to be in their country? Are they aware of any family planning programs or government population policy in their home country? If so, ask them to describe these programs and policies. This exercise should help you gain a deeper and more direct understanding of the influence of social values on family size and the ways in which people in other countries view population growth and its consequences.

2. People in numerous business, governmental, educational, medical, and allied health fields are in constant need of up-to-date information concerning patterns of population growth and changes in population

composition within our society. Regardless of your present occupation or future career plans, it is likely that you will find various forms of demographic information occupationally useful. There are several standard sources of demographic data with which you should familiarize yourself, among them *Statistical Abstracts of the United States,* the *1990 Census of the Population,* and various series of *Current Population Reports,* including series P-23, P-25, and P-60. These are all U.S. Bureau of the Census publications and contain a great deal of information about the social and economic characteristics of our population. Most if not all of these materials can be found in the reference section of your college library, Census Bureau offices, and local libraries. You should make it a point to examine carefully as many of these standard demographic reference sources as possible.

3. Select a particular city, perhaps the one in which you were born, now live, or attend school. How has the population of this city changed over the last 10 or 15 years? Has the city's population increased? What areas within the city have gained or lost population? In general, has the population of the city grown older or younger? How has the city's ethnic composition changed during this period? Information on these topics should be fairly easy to obtain from your school library, regional library, or local Census Bureau office. This exercise should help you become more informed about demographic changes in an urban area that interests you.

4. Energy is an essential resource. As we have seen, however, the United States wastes a considerable amount of the energy it uses. People need to become far more aware and informed about the importance and necessity of energy conservation. Get together with a few other students and develop a list of things people can do in their everyday lives and activities to reduce energy waste. You should also consider steps that business, industry, and transportation could take to lessen their energy waste. What could government do to encourage energy conservation in our society? If possible, share your answers and ideas with other students as well as family and friends.

Answers

Answers to Self-Test

1. b
2. d
3. a
4. b
5. a
6. d
7. b
8. d
9. c
10. d
11. T
12. F
13. F
14. T
15. F
16. F
17. T
18. T
19. T
20. F
21. intermediate variables
22. exponential
23. 5.3
24. international, internal
25. population composition
26. metropolitan
27. economic
28. 20
29. megalopolis
30. 180
31. f
32. e
33. j
34. a
35. h
36. c
37. b
38. i
39. g
40. d

Answers to Chapter Pretest

1. F
2. T
3. F
4. F
5. T
6. T
7. F
8. T

Chapter 12

Collective Behavior, Social Movements, and Social Change

Chapter Pretest

Let's see how much you already know about topics in this chapter:

1. **Collective behavior means the same thing as group behavior. True/False**
2. **People rarely panic in our modern society. True/False**
3. **Contrary to popular belief, mobs and riots are highly predictable, structured, and guided by social norms. True/False**
4. **The federal government makes so many movies that it has become know as "Hollywood on the Potomac." True/False**
5. **The women's movement is essentially dead. True/False**
6. **Society is a social group. True/False**
7. **Urbanization refers to the growth of cities. True/False**
8. **Discovery involves the creation of new things. True/False**
9. **Pajamas, glass, felt, and cigarettes were all invented in America. True/False**
10. **Social change in America has slowed in the late 1980s and early 1990s. True/False**

Collective Behavior

Much human behavior is guided by the cultural patterns of a society. Traditions, customs, and cultural norms guide individuals and groups of people in their interactions with others. Every day, we encounter highly organized situations in which we play well-defined social roles and meet the expectations of others. Our society's structure and norms guide our social behavior, much of which is institutionalized.

However, not all social behavior is so highly predictable, structured, and guided by cultural norms. People, willingly or unwillingly, at times find themselves in situations in which they are unaware of what constitutes proper behavior and in which they are unsure of what is expected of them. The type of social behavior that develops in response to problematic situations has been termed "collective behavior" (G. E. Lang, 1972). **Collective behavior** is not a synonym for group behavior, but refers to social behavior that is relatively

Collective behavior defined

spontaneous, transitory, emotional, and unpredictable. It refers to crowd behavior, riots and panics, social movements, and publics. Collective behavior refers to types of group actions in which the level of institutionalization is low.

Much collective behavior is not stable and predictable, but changeable and episodic. Because rules of behavior are absent, people tend to act spontaneously and in unstructured ways. Behavior tends to change in direction and form more quickly when people become emotional and uninhibited. Collective behavior can be viewed as being at the opposite end of a continuum from formal social organization, which, as we have seen, refers to bureaucracies and other such highly structured entities. Among types of collective behavior, panics (such as when people are fleeing a fire) represent the lowest, if any, degree of institutionalization. Social movements, an additional type of collective behavior, represent a high point of institutionalization. Crowds fall about midway between panics and social movements in institutionalization.

It is important to understand collective behavior because such phenomena as social movements and public opinion are important factors in social change. In many cases, social movements and crowd behavior of the past have formed our present institutional structures. The social movements and protests of the late eighteenth century helped form the basis of contemporary American society. Before examining the major forms of collective behavior, we will examine the social conditions or determinants of collective behavior.

Determinants of Collective Behavior

There are many determinants of collective behavior. A well-known model of the causation of collective behavior has been developed by Neil Smelser (1963). According to Smelser, the first determinant of collective behavior is structural conduciveness. This term refers to social conditions that enable collective behavior to occur. Some of these conditions are heterogeneity, mobility, and large groups of people. In urban societies, these factors encourage and are structurally conducive to collective behavior. Conduciveness does not cause collective behavior. It only enables collective behavior to occur.

The second determinant of collective behavior is structural strain. Social deprivation and frustration from circumstances such as discrimination, persecution, or poverty may create severe strain among people and lead to forms of collective behavior.

There are many determinants of collective behavior

The third determinant is the growth and spread of a generalized belief. This condition occurs when the potential participants in collective behavior interpret the situation of strain, form a belief about the problem's source, and develop an answer as to what might be done about their stressful circumstances.

Conduciveness, strain, and a generalized belief cannot by themselves cause collective behavior. A fourth determinant, some type of event or precipitating factor, must be present if there is to be an episode of collective behavior. The event or factor may be a fight, an arrest, an explosion, or an assassination.

The fifth determinant is the mobilization of participants for action. In other words, the group actively prepares to engage in collective behavior.

The sixth and final determinant of collective behavior is a breakdown in the traditional mechanisms of social control. This is a condition in which the agents of social control—the police, courts, community leaders, and so on—do not adequately perform and therefore break down.

Groups involved in collective behavior are actually social aggregates with the following characteristics: They are composed of a relatively large number of people, relative anonymity prevails, they are usually temporary in nature, and they lack formal organization in terms of an established system of differentiated positions.

As we have mentioned, collective behavior exists in various forms. We will examine in detail three of these forms: crowd behavior, public behavior, and social movements.

Crowd Behavior

A **crowd** is a temporary grouping, collection, or aggregate of people who share a common focus or interest. There are many different types of crowds. There are crowds at rock festivals, at hockey games, and on the beaches. Some crowds are violent and antisocial, such as a rioting mob. Other crowds behave in a socially acceptable manner. Certain occasions provide an opportunity for members of a society to give release to their emotions—the celebration of the new year, for example.

Types of Crowds

Four types of crowds have been identified by social scientists: the casual crowd, the conventionalized crowd, the expressive crowd, and the acting crowd.

Casual crowds form and dissolve rapidly, such as when people visit a park or museum. A group of people watching children play in a fountain is a casual crowd. Emotional involvement is low-keyed, and interest in activities is minimal. Cultural norms guide the actions of individuals in the casual crowd.

In the *conventionalized crowd,* members are aware, to a great extent, of expected ways of acting. It is a deliberately planned, culturally sanctioned crowd situation that is somewhat structured. Theater groups and sports audiences are conventionalized crowds. Definite patterns of action occur in conventionalized crowds because of the participants' common focus.

There are many types of crowds

In an *expressive crowd,* people are able to express themselves freely. They are able to pursue activities that they consider satisfying and release their emotions and tensions through physical activity. This release may take the form of laughing, weeping, shouting, leaping, or dancing. The movement is often rhythmic, and typically, it brings relief and joy to the members. It is sometimes seen at revival meetings, in the "holy dance" of certain religious sects, and at rock concerts (Blumer, 1969).

In the *acting crowd,* such factors as milling, contagion, and suggestibility become important. **Milling** is a spontaneous, elementary collective action in which people move among one another in a somewhat aimless fashion. It makes each individual more sensitive to others. **Contagion** is a process in which crowd members stimulate and respond to one another and consequently increase their responsiveness and emotional intensity. **Suggestibility** is a tendency to respond uncritically to stimuli provided by other members of a crowd.

Herbert Blumer's analysis of collective behavior (1969) illustrates the importance of such factors as milling, contagion, and suggestibility with respect to an acting crowd.

> **The *acting crowd* starts with an exciting event which catches the attention of many. They grow restless because they do not know what to do. Milling will be the first preparation for action: John Doe becomes aware of the excitement shown by others. As the contagion intensifies he begins to respond, without reflecting, to the remarks and actions of others. He will act now, rather than after deliberate thought. In short, he is highly suggestible now.**
>
> **Eventually the impulses, feelings, and imagery of the people will become focused on some object of common attention. It may be the event in which the excitement originated or it may be some common complaint that emerges from the milling and talking. At any rate, the people now share a goal and are in a position to act with unity and purpose.**
>
> **Since the acting crowd is spontaneous, it knows no traditions or rules and has no official leaders. Acting, instead, on the basis of aroused impulses, it tends to be a nonmoral group. Its behavior may be irresponsible, even atrocious, vehement, violent, cruel, and destructive, as in a mob scene. Lynching, beating, stoning, looting, dynamiting, and arson can result from this intense crowd-mindedness in which John Doe's usual critical ability seems to be suppressed (Blumer, 1969).**

In many cases then, the acting crowd is hostile to the social order. It focuses on an objective or external goal. It concerns itself with action, unlike the expressive crowd, which deals with the expression of emotions, feelings, and tension and has no plan of action.

Mobs and Riots

Mobs are also crowds

As noted above, mob behavior is a form of crowd behavior. **Mobs** are crowds that are emotionally charged and oriented toward violence. Emotions are usually focused on a goal or target. Leaders provide direction and affect the intensity of mob behavior. Perhaps one of the best examples of mob behavior in the United States is the lynch mob. Almost 1800 blacks and 200 whites have been lynched in the United States since the turn of the century.

A **riot** occurs when a mob becomes violently aggressive and destructive. The protest riots of the 1960s were oriented toward the looting and destruction of property. The racial riots that occurred in Chicago in 1919 and in Detroit in 1942 involved violence against people. Members of the black and white communities beat and killed one another. Riots also may be religiously oriented, as between the Catholics and the Protestants in Ireland.

Riots have been attributed to a breakdown of society's consensual norms and to social control agencies' inability or unwillingness to restore norms (the social disorganization thesis). These conditions develop from such processes of social change as urbanization, industrialization, and cybernation.* Riots also have been viewed as products of struggle for power among different groups within society (the group conflict thesis) or as legitimate and productive modes of protest (the riot ideology thesis).

Panic and Rumor

When a crowd of people is suddenly overwhelmed by great fright that in many cases leads them to irrational action, **panic** has occurred. It tends to occur when people find themselves trapped in burning buildings or sinking ships. When one thinks of panic, one imagines many frightened people in close physical proximity. Physical proximity, however, is not necessary for the occurrence of this extreme type of crowd behavior. Because the mass media in urban societies can simultaneously reach millions of people living hundreds of miles apart, they may be a critical element in causing panic.

A classic example of large-scale panic occurred in the New York and New Jersey area in the late 1930s when thousands of people believed the country was being invaded by Martians. The realism of a radio dramatization of H. G. Wells's *The War of the Worlds,* combined with the social conditions of the 1930s, caused thousands of Americans to panic. The threat from the Martians was not real, of course; however, it was perceived as real and imminent by those who panicked. Many residents of New Jersey believed that the "invasion" was a physical threat to their very existence. The Wells episode is unusual because of its magnitude. Most panics do not occur on such a large scale.

Historically, many events and disasters have developed into panic. But there have also been many disasters in the world that have not developed into panic. When the bubonic plague swept through Europe in the fourteenth century, panic spread at a devastating rate. Yet it was virtually nonexistent after the northeast blackout of 1965.

Panics, riots, and crowds develop to a great extent because of **rumor,** or the dissemination of information that is distorted, untrue, or unconfirmed and is transmitted during a time of anxiety and stress. Rumors are spread by word of mouth or through the mass media and reflect the feelings of people who find themselves in tenuous, anxiety-producing situations.

Rumor transmission is a social process

In a classic analysis of rumors, Allport and Postman (1965) indicate that rumor transmission is a social process. They examine three progressions that occur in the development of rumors: leveling, sharpening, and assimilation.

1. *Leveling.* As a rumor travels, it tends to grow shorter, more concise, more easily grasped and told. In successive versions, fewer words are used and fewer details are mentioned. The number of details declines most sharply at the beginning of the rumor's dispersion.

---

* Cybernation is the combination of computerization and automation.

2. *Sharpening.* As a rumor travels, the process of selective perception, retention, and the reporting of a limited number of details inevitably takes place. A simple fact or element becomes a dominant one.
3. *Assimilation.* As a rumor travels, it is influenced and shaped by the habits, interests, and sentiments of the individuals who hear and repeat it. The elements of the rumor are forced to fit a general motif.

Sociologists have applied the concept of crowds to a wide range of human behavior. In the following section, these concepts of crowd behavior are explained.

Explanations for Crowd Behavior

Crowd behavior has been explained in various ways. Le Bon (1960), an early French thinker, believed that when people are in crowds, a "collective consciousness" emerges. This collective consciousness supplants individual consciousness. Le Bon perceived this process as the "law of the mental unity of crowds." When immersed in a crowd, personal identity and thus individual mentality is lost. The crowd is an aggregate with a collective mind. People in the crowd are reduced to the lowest common denominator as crowd contagion eliminates its members' educational and cultural differences. By joining an "organized crowd, a man descends several rungs in the ladder of civilization. Isolated, he may be a cultivated individual; in a crowd, he is a barbarian—that is, a creature living by instinct" (Le Bon, 1960). These ideas, to a great extent, have formed the *contagion theory* of crowd behavior. The contagion theory stresses the apparent unanimity of crowds and the "part that rapidly communicated and uncritically accepted feelings, attitudes, and actions play within crowd settings" (Turner, 1964). A high degree of suggestibility results in this situation.

There are many theories of crowd behavior

Other theories, such as the *convergence theory,* stress the idea that participants in crowds are basically revealing their true selves. The crowd functions as a pretext to translate latent impulses into overt action. Convergence theorists stress the convergence of people who share the same disposition and identify a "category of people as 'crowd prone' or focus attention upon latent impulses of hate, frustration, and aggression that purportedly exist among crowd participants" (Vander Zanden, 1990).

Ralph Turner (1964), of the *emergent norm* school, suggests that crowd behavior, like other collective and group processes, should be incorporated within a common theoretical framework of structure and process. He believes that in crowds, situations are defined, norms for sanctioning behavior develop, and action patterns are agreed upon and justified. This theoretical approach challenges those theories stressing contagion and the unanimity of the crowd. The emergent norm theory stresses the absence of unanimity within a crowd and notes the differences in attitudes, beliefs, motives, and actions among crowd members.

These and other interpretations of crowd behavior are complex and contain many contradictions and weaknesses. There is a great need for research in the interpretation of crowd behavior. But these and other theories have provided important insights into the nature of crowd behavior and collective behavior in general.

Public Behavior

The concept of **public** has two different meanings to sociologists. First, a public has been defined as a scattered number of people who share a common interest in a given topic. There are newspaper publics, sports publics, television publics, and so forth. A public is, as noted earlier, an aggregate of people rather than a group of people, because not all members of a public interact.

Second, a public is defined as a collection of people who are concerned over, divided upon, and engaged in discussion about an issue. If no issue exists, there is no public. Each issue has its public. In simple folk societies, few issues cannot be resolved through the folkways of the culture; therefore few publics exist. In complex societies, there are many interests and consequently, many publics. One public favors nuclear power; another favors solar power. Like crowds, then, publics appear in large complex societies. Unlike crowds, members of a public are not gathered together. Members of publics communicate through the mass media and debate a variety of issues. In considering issues, members of publics form opinions, and public opinion develops.

A public requires an issue

Public Opinion

Sociologists are interested in the ways publics define issues and how they implement their goals. Consequently, they are interested in **public opinion**—the opinions and attitudes held by a public about an issue. Public opinion becomes important in complex urban societies where common value systems are diffused because those who are able to greatly influence public opinion can, to some extent, control society.

How does the management of public opinion occur? Without knowing the means of manipulating public opinion, there can be no understanding of how a complex, urban society functions. The formation and control of public opinion is not left to chance. It is influenced and shaped by controlling information, by offering interpretations of what is occurring, or by appealing to a drive or urge created or existing within a public. Public opinion is shaped, to a great extent, by **propaganda**—the deliberate use of communication to influence and persuade individuals to favor one predetermined way of thinking or action over another. Where there is room for the manipulation or interpretation of what is occurring, the propagandist brings into play a repertoire of the classical devices and techniques that have been developed to shape and control public opinion.

In a classic work, A. M. C. Lee and E. B. Lee (1967) have developed the following list of propaganda techniques, which are still very much used today:

Name-calling. Giving an idea a bad label. Used to make people reject and condemn an idea without examining the evidence.

Glittering generality. Associating an idea with a "virtue" word. Used to make people accept and approve an idea without examining the evidence.

Transfer. Associating an idea with a person, image, or symbol that is respected and revered. Makes people accept or reject an idea not on its own merit, but on the basis of the authority and prestige that have been transferred to it.

Testimonial. Having some beloved or hated person approve or condemn a given idea.

Plain folks. Attempting to convince a public that an idea is good because it is held "by the people."

Card-stacking. Using only such highly selected material, whether true or false, as supports one's case.

Bandwagon. Saying "Everybody's doing it," with the implication that people must therefore "jump on the bandwagon."

Public Opinion, Propaganda, and the Government. The formation and control of public opinion are not left to chance by the federal bureaucracy in Washington, D.C. Public opinion is shaped and influenced through the control of information. In fact, the federal government spends about $3 billion annually to influence the way Americans think. The Washington propaganda machine is so vast that no one knows how many civil servants are involved. The following is cited as evidence of the enormous scope of the Washington propaganda machine: "Uncle Sam is one of the nation's top 20 advertisers, with outlays rivaling those of such business giants as Coca-Cola and Procter & Gamble. . . . Washington is coming to be known as 'Hollywood on the Potomac.' Agencies spend as much as $600 million annually making movies. . . . The paper tide of press releases, reports, and documents that flows from government presses each year could fill four Washington Monuments. . . . To finance official activities of federal public relations officials costs more than $400 million annually . . ." (J. S. Lang, 1979).

The government spends billions on what Americans think

A study of federal filmmaking by the White House revealed that the U.S. government owns $2 billion worth of filming facilities and equipment. Taxpayers also have financed such films as "Makeup from the Neck down," "Identification of some Common Sucking Lice," "Sex Life of the Norway Rat," and "Froggy and Friends." Public affairs officers state that their work is vital, because the best-planned programs do little good if the public does not know about them. Critics of the proliferating information systems are concerned about its costs, waste, and potential for thought control (J. S. Lang, 1979).

The Public and the Mass. Herbert Blumer believes that in the modern world, the public is much more likely to be displaced by the mass. For Blumer, a new, wide world of "mass man" has been created by the combined factors of mass education, mass communication, urban migration, and the breakup of small cultures. The mass contains many alienated people facing new conditions of life.

In modern times, Blumer states: "The increasing detachment of people from traditional life, the great number of public issues today, and the expansion of mass communication lead them increasingly to act on the basis of individual selection rather than on the basis of public participation in public discussion. In many ways the public and the mass have become intermingled in modern times" (Blumer, 1969).

Social Movements

The **social movement** is an additional form of collective behavior. A social movement is "a collectivity acting with some continuity to promote or resist a change in the society or group of which it is a part" (Turner and Killian, 1972). Many social movements have originated as crowd phenomena. Social movements also have given rise to crowd activity, both as planned tactics and as spontaneous outbursts.

Defining social movement

Many sociologists distinguish social movements from such processes as social trends and cultural drifts. Social trends are basically unplanned processes that occur over extended periods of time; they are not usually the products of social movements. Examples of such trends are the processes of industrialization, urbanization, and cybernation. Cultural drifts are also social processes. They differ from trends, however, in that they are processes whereby minor changes or alterations in a culture occurring over extended periods of time eventually change a society's entire way of life. Social movements are organized and are more definite than trends. The long-term developments toward equal opportunity for women can be termed a trend or tendency. However, as we shall shortly see, the many groups and organizations involved in the fight for women's rights are part of an authentic social movement.

Social movements that are organized to resist change within society do not require as much attention as those movements organized to bring about some significant degree of change in the basic institutional structures of society.

In a now-classic analysis of collective action and social movements, Stockdale (1970) lists the following five preconditions for collective action: social discontent, structural blockage, contact, efficacy, and ideology.

There are five preconditions for collective action

The first precondition is a high level of *social discontent* and inequality. Social movements, as stated by Blumer (1975), "have their inception in a condition of unrest and derive their motive power on one hand from dissatisfaction with the current form of life, and on the other hand, from wishes and hopes for a new scheme or system of living."

The second precondition, *structural blockage,* occurs when efforts by the people to remove the sources of their discontent to improve their situation are blocked by barriers in the social structure. For example, in many cases, efforts by members of the black community to improve their social and economic situation are blocked by prejudice and discrimination in education, employment, and housing.

Contact or interaction between members of the discontented group is the third precondition for the emergence of collective action. For example, student protests occur only when a critical mass of students are in frequent contact (Hughes, 1972).

The fourth precondition, *efficacy*, is basically the probability that the action proposed by the discontented will relieve the discontent.

The fifth precondition, *ideology*, is a system of values and beliefs that supports and justifies proposed actions. On many college campuses, for example, universities and colleges that invest in South Africa have been viewed by protesting students as greedy organizations that greatly exploit South African blacks.

Collective action and social movements are almost inevitable when all these five structural preconditions are present.

The Life Cycle of Social Movements

In general, social movements go through a life cycle consisting of four basic stages. The *social unrest*, or *preliminary, stage* of a social movement is characterized by a growing dissatisfaction among many people with respect to social or cultural developments. People become alienated, dissatisfied, and restless because of social inequalities, frustrations, and insecurities. This preliminary stage is necessary for the origination of a social movement. It should be noted, however, that not all dissatisfaction results in a social movement.

There exist four basic stages of social movements

The second stage is the *excitement stage*. During this *popular stage*, as it is sometimes called, those people who are dissatisfied with a particular set of conditions become aware that others feel the way they do. In many cases, their attention then focuses on the sources of the conditions and they develop the feeling that something should be done to eliminate them. At this point, a reformist leader emerges. This "prophet" provides slogans, focuses the followers' attention on the problem, and develops plans and solutions for deliverance.

In the third stage, the *formalized organization stage*, members of the movement are formalized. The direction and goals of the movement are clarified, ideologies are developed, and a formal organizational structure emerges. This structure has a hierarchy of leaders or officials and a network of policies and goals.

Institutionalization is the fourth and final stage of social movements. At this point, there is acceptance by the society of the movement's goals. The social movement becomes part of society. When the program and the goals of the movement become institutionalized, the social movement has been successful. The time it takes for social movements to become institutionalized depends on the complexities of the desired changes. If goals sought by the movement are general and complex, such as the goals of the gay liberation movement, it may take an extended period of time for social acceptance. But there may be a more rapid acceptance of goals if they are specific and less complex—such as permitting 18-year-olds to vote.

Resistance movements develop because people are dissatisfied with the fast pace of social change.

Varieties of Social Movements

Sociologists distinguish among several basic types of social movements. The following social movements are some of the most common and provide an understanding of their range.

Reform Movements. One of the most common types of social movements in the United States is the **reform movement.** Reform movements attempt to modify a part of society. Many areas of social life may be affected by reform movements. Our history has been characterized by such movements as Prohibition and the abolition of slavery. Current movements include such varied goals as environmentalism, tax reform, birth control, and equal rights for women. One of the best examples of a reform movement is the women's movement, which will be discussed later in this chapter.

Many types of movements exist in the U.S. today

Revolutionary Movements. Unlike reform movements, which try to modify the existing social system, **revolutionary movements** seek to overthrow the existing social system and replace it with a newer and better social system. The reformer wishes to correct some of society's imperfections. The revolutionist believes that the social system is not worth saving.

The American and French revolutions serve as examples of revolutionary movements. Societies like the United States, which are characterized by many reform movements, tend not to be revolutionary in that the reform movements drain off much of the discontent that is necessary for a revolution. In some cases, it may be difficult to clearly classify a movement as being either revolutionary or reform. The women's movement, for example, has supporters who are revolutionaries and supporters who are moderate reformers.

Resistance Movements. Reform and revolutionary movements arise among those members of a society who are dissatisfied with the slow pace of social change. **Resistance movements** differ from reform and revolutionary movements in that they develop because people are dissatisfied with the fast pace of social change.

Resistance movements arise because of the undesirability of a proposed or impending change or a change that has already occurred. In the south after the Civil War, a resistance movement known as the Ku Klux Klan was organized to keep blacks in their subordinate position. After the 1954 Supreme Court decision on school desegregation, the resistance movement known as the White Citizens' Councils applied economic sanctions to all those people who supported desegregation. The John Birch Society is also known for its capacity to resist many social reforms of the past and present.

Other Types of Social Movements. Other types of social movements include utopian, migratory, and expressive movements. When a social movement has as its goal the "perfect" society, it is termed a *utopian movement.* These movements were particularly popular in the eighteenth and nineteenth centuries, although they are still very much alive today.

Migratory movements involve the large-scale relocation of people who share discontent, hope, and a decision to move from an area of discontent to a new location. The Irish migration to the United States in the nineteenth century, the black migration to the north in the decades following World War I, and the migration of East Germans to West Germany after World War II are examples of migratory social movements.

An *expressive movement* occurs when people come to terms with their external reality not by modifying it, but by modifying their reactions to that reality. It is the result of feelings of powerlessness and an inability to flee from an undesirable situation. The Youth for Christ movement, which attempts to change people rather than society, is an example of an expressive movement. Through emotional expression, rituals, dreams, and so forth, the members of expressive movements find emotional release, allowing them to accept reality more easily.

Some sociologists believe that migratory and expressive movements really represent a different class of phenomenon. They believe, for example, that migratory movements are probably better conceptualized as social trends that may be by-products of reform or revolutionary movements. Expressive movements are more typical of cultural drifts than of social movements.

A social movement, as noted earlier, is an organized effort by a relatively large number of people "either to change a situation that they define as unsatisfactory or to prevent change in a situation that they define as satisfactory" (Vander Zanden, 1990). The idea that a number of people intervene in the process of social change is central to the concept of a social movement. People are not passive but active agents within their culture. Social movements involve many people acting together with a "sense of engaging in a collective enterprise" (Killian, 1964). Social movements such as the American and French revolutions, the Crusades, and the Protestant Reformation greatly affected the societies they touched. Social movements are the means by which people "collectively seek to influence the course of human events" (Vander Zanden, 1990).

People are active agents within their culture

Social movements occur when groups of people, in response to problems and tensions, seek to effect changes in society. Many social changes come about from the organized action of groups like the women's movement, the Nazi movement in Germany, and the civil rights movement. All social movements are not, of course, successful in achieving their goals. They do, however, play an essential role in effecting social change.

AMERICA'S NEW CIVIL WAR

Merrill McLoughlin

In the following reading, "America's New Civil War," Merrill McLoughlin examines the American abortion debate where "both factions invoke the righteous rhetoric of the civil-rights movement."

It is now 15 years since the U.S. Supreme Court ruled that the Constitution protects a woman's right to have an abortion. Fifteen years, and still the war rages. It is a war of words, with one side screaming bloody murder, the other adamantly insisting that abortion is no more than a matter of a woman's right to control her own body. Both factions invoke the righteous rhetoric of the civil-rights movement. Both lay moral claim to the values of liberty, life and happiness. Both clamor for the protection of the law and vow no peace until it is carved in apodictic precedent. The extremes are at an impasse, and the national debate rages relentlessly on.

And with good reason. The abortion issue goes straight to the deepest and most painful questions. Where is the line between an individual's right to privacy and society's duty to protect the powerless? Is it a greater moral evil to end a pregnancy or to bring a child into a world that may be unwelcoming, even openly hostile? At the heart of the matter is a mystery that has been debated for centuries. At what point does a human life, with all the values and perquisites we assign it, really begin?

In *Roe v. Wade*, the 1973 ruling that made abortion legal, the High Court understandably left open that critical question.

"When those trained in . . . medicine, philosophy and theology are unable to arrive at any consensus, the judiciary, at this point in the development of man's knowledge, is not in a position to speculate as to the answer."

Doctors, philosophers and theologians are still arguing the point. And unlike the activists, who on both the left and the right are quite certain that they have the answers, most Americans find themselves unsatisfied by the slogans and are troubled by the issues. Polling indicates that they overwhelmingly support the right to abortion in cases of rape, incest or threat to the mother's health. But those represent a tiny proportion of the 1.6 million abortions that take place each year, ending about one fourth of all pregnancies. About the rest, Americans are not so sure.

In an election year, of course, all the familiar factions are at the barricades. Anti-abortion activists are stalking Michael Dukakis's campaign, waving angry placards and often disrupting the discourse. The reason, put baldly last month by Roman Catholic Archbishop John Whealon of Hartford, Conn., is their shared belief that the Democratic party, whose platform supports the right to choose abortion, "is officially in favor of executing unborn babies whose only crime is that they temporarily occupy their mother's womb." So far, both Dukakis and George Bush, whose GOP platform supports a "human-life amendment to the Constitution," have in the main avoided the divisive issue in their campaigns.

BODIES ON THE LINES

Since last spring, a group called Operation Rescue has been staging large protests in major cities, where participants have been arrested by the hundreds for trying to block the entrances to abortion clinics. Next week in Atlanta, Operation Rescue plans its biggest offensive yet, a six-day "rescue mission" that founder Randall Terry hopes will draw hundreds more—and headlines. The Rev. Jerry Falwell, who has funded Operation Rescue's tactics to the tune of at least $10,000, has suggested that in the future, he and other anti-abortion leaders, perhaps including cardinal archbishops of the Catholic Church, may join the civil disobedience, putting their own bodies on the protest lines and in the jails in an attempt to force the issue to the top of the national agenda. Falwell compares his effort with that of Martin Luther King, Jr., and the protests for civil rights.

Prochoice activists are mobilizing to meet the threat. During Operation Rescue sit-ins, volunteers have showed up to shepherd women past the protesters and into the clinics. And they vehemently object to the co-opting of King. "Civil rights was a movement to *gain* rights," says Molly Yard, president of the National Organization for Women. "They are *denying* women's rights."

But the advocates of choice are clearly worried. For one thing, they point to the legacy of the Reagan years. Despite complaints from the right that the Reagan administration has failed to enact their social agenda, including a constitutional ban on abortions, it has nonetheless chipped steadily away at the margins. The administration has tried to cut off federal funds to prochoice family planners working at home and abroad and to impose regulations that would require minors to get parental permission before having an abortion. This month, with administration support, anti-abortion forces in Congress beat back an attempt to liberalize the Hyde Amendment, which outlaws medicaid funding of abortion except in cases where it would save the mother's life. And against the advice of the National Institutes of Health, which argues strongly that research involving fetal tissue holds enormous promise for people afflicted with ailments like Parkinson's disease and diabetes, the administration is considering an executive order that would ban the use of such tissue, if it is derived from induced abortions in any federally financed scientific experiments or medical treatment.

Then there's the judiciary. Many federal appeals courts are now dominated by conservative Reagan appointees, and decisions in abortion cases are beginning to show their influence. These days, prochoice activists are leery of taking their cases to the highest court in the land. Even though the Supreme Court has regularly struck down attempts by various jurisdictions to restrict abortions, at least four of its members—Chief Justice William Rehnquist, Byron White, Sandra Day O'Connor and Antonin Scalia—have in the past assailed *Roe v. Wade.* If their newest colleague, Reagan-appointee Anthony Kennedy, turns out to be on their side, it could mean a 5-to-4 split against the ruling the next time a major test case reaches the Court. A few weeks ago, Justice Harry Blackmun, author of the 1973 opinion, addressed that issue in a session with University of Arkansas law students: "Will *Roe v. Wade* go down the drain? I think there's a very distinct possibility that it will—this term. You can count the votes."

Most legal experts think it unlikely that the Court will take on *Roe* itself anytime soon. Before that, they predict, the Justices may begin to approve more state regulations that limit abortions. One case that may confront them in the term that begins next week deals with a Missouri statute that declares that life begins at conception, outlaws the use of public funds, facilities and employees in abortions and requires that any abortion performed after the 16th week of pregnancy take place at a hospital, not a clinic.

But all the activity in the public forum tends to obscure the quieter, deeper debate that has been going on for some time in think tanks, in churches, in living rooms. Many Americans got their first real glimpse of it during the 1984 election, when New York Governor Mario Cuomo, responding to suggestions that a Catholic politician cannot in good conscience support a woman's right to choose an abortion, spoke eloquently about the tensions between religious belief and public morality in a pluralistic society.

"As Catholics, my wife and I were enjoined never to use abortion to destroy the life we created, and we never have," said Cuomo. "At the very least, even if the argument is made by some scientists or some theologians that in the early stages of fetal development we can't discern human life, the full potential of human life is indisputably there. That by itself should demand respect, caution, indeed, reverence. But not everyone in our society agrees with me and Matilda. And those who don't—those who endorse legalized abortions—aren't a ruthless, callous alliance of anti-Christians determined to overthrow our moral standards."

CORRUPTED LANGUAGE

Cuomo and many other thoughtful Americans share, deep down, the troubling conviction that we have not yet got public policy quite right. Even the language of the public debate has been corrupted. On the right, for instance, the term *prolife* has too often meant *probirth,* and very little else. All-or-nothing anti-abortionists simply shrug off arguments that there are other life-affirming issues that should weigh on informed judgment, among them, the terror of an impoverished woman who cannot hope to provide proper care for a child.

On the left, similarly, *prochoice* is often an ill-disguised synonym for *proself.* It is surely untrue that 98 percent of all abortions are merely a matter of convenience, as Falwell and others like to claim. And yet some unknown number are precisely that: Routine, easy, safe ways out of a personal problem that might deserve deeper thought. The United States has a far higher annual abortion rate—about 28 for every 1,000 women between the ages of 15 and 44—than other Western nations. In Sweden, by contrast, the rate is 18 per 1,000.

There are those who argue that abortion policy, like some abortions, has become an out-of-sight-out-of-mind "cure" for other, more difficult social ills. It is easier to support the idea of hundreds of thousands of abortions every year, handled privately, individually, than it is to launch a full-scale effort to improve birth-control education, to reform adoption policies, to assault the poverty and despair that push too many women toward the abortion clinics.

It is also easier, in a wildly disparate society, to avoid confronting the core issue head-on. Many liberals say comfortably that they don't *personally* like the idea of abortion, but could not support a law that would restrict others who disagree. Why, they wonder, can't the Falwells of the world be equally tolerant?

The answer is simple. Falwell and others believe abortion is murder, murder of a helpless human being who desperately needs the protection of the law. And if the abortion wars are ever to end, society will have to wrestle with the central question the High Court ducked 15 years ago.

It will not be easy. Most people feel, instinctively, that there is something wrong with the notion that a baby is born truly human only after it has been born. Is the 8-month-old fetus being carried to full term really less human than the one-month-premature infant in the preemie ward? At the same time, they sense that zygotes and blastocysts, the earliest cellular stages of life, should not have quite the same protection under law as newborns—or adult women.

Where is that all-important line between potential human life and the real thing? That is what the debate is about, and no one knows the answer. Old notions relying on when a fetus becomes "viable," able to live outside the womb, are less satisfying now than they were when *Roe* dealt confidently in terms of trimesters. Neonatal technology has steadily improved the chances for infants born far before their time. When *Roe* was written, for instance, a normal 3-pound-5-ounce baby (about average size for the 27th week of development) had only a 50 percent change of survival. By 1985, it had a 90 percent chance. And today, a 2-pound-3-ounce preemie (approximately the 25th gestational week) has a 50-50 chance at a future.

Neonatologists don't think they can push back survival too much more. "Technology will advance," says Dr. David Grimes, a professor of obstetrics and gynecology at the University of Southern California. "The fetal lung will not." Before the 25th week, the fetal lungs are solid. But even there, technology holds out some hope. One day, some researchers think, doctors may be able to help fetal lungs develop outside the womb by stimulating production of surfactant, a substance that causes the lungs to change from a solid mass into meshy air sacs. So when is a fetus "viable"? It depends—on the skill of a particular doctor, on the equipment available to him and on the pace of technology itself.

That is the sort of issue that many find disturbing. Under present law, observes social psychologist Sidney Callahan, it is possible to have babies of the same age "in one part of the hospital being saved and the other part of the hospital being extinguished on the say-so of the mother." It doesn't seem fair for public policy to permit such a state of affairs.

But what is the solution? There are numerous signs that a fuller debate has begun, and that a few on both the right and the left are reconsidering their positions. Among Catholics, there is growing support for a sophisticated position set forth by the American bishops' conference. Called the "consistent life ethic," it argues strongly against single-issue politics and for a moral framework in which all life-and-death issues including abortion, capital punishment and nuclear deterrence must be weighed in the balance in making political decisions. Some evangelicals, too, seem to be paying more attention to the arguments of proponents of choice. Conceding that if they oppose abortions they should offer some alternatives to those who seek them, Falwell's Moral Majority has set a goal of establishing thousands of maternity homes across the country where, at no cost to themselves or the taxpayers, women who choose to forgo abortions can carry their babies to term, assured that adoptive parents will be waiting. So far, there are only about 200 such homes; the independent Edna Gladney Center in Fort Worth is the largest, with room for only 144 women.

"YEARS OF PRAYER"

Meanwhile, some of the mainline Protestant churches, long in the prochoice camp, seem to be having second thoughts. In July, the Episcopal Church repeated its affirmation of years past that abortion is a serious matter that cannot be taken lightly and added the declaration that human life is sacred from conception to birth. The change resulted from "years of prayer and discussion," says the Rev. Richard Henshaw, church spokesman. "We're coming to understand [the issue] more fully than we did 15 or 20 years ago." United Methodists and American Baptists have now challenged the use of abortion as birth control, and the Presbyterian Church (U.S.A.) has established a task force to study the denomination's liberal stance.

Such moves, says Lutheran theologian Richard John Neuhaus, director of the Rockford Institute's Center for Religion and Society, are of "enormous importance." Back in the 1960s, the mainline churches provided "the initial moral legitimation, a kind of blessing, to what was then called the 'liberalization of abortion.'" In fact, says University of Chicago church historian Martin Marty, the mainline churches were always halfhearted in their prochoice positions, which they adopted because they believed in women's right to privacy and feared government intervention in the bedroom and the laboratory. There was always, says Marty, "something in their craw. They also believed there were life issues involved." None of these churches, he points out, has simply declared war on abortion. Their stance is subtler, marked by reservations about both sides in the debate.

SHADES OF RIGHT AND WRONG

No policy, no matter how well reasoned, will satisfy everyone. But at least partisans are starting to concede the awesome complexity of an issue that is at once intimately private and urgently public.

Behind the raucous protests can be heard the ambivalence and pain of individuals who have confronted the complexities themselves, agonizing over shades of right and wrong, sometimes changing their minds. Author Linda Bird Francke, a vocal supporter of the right to choose, several years ago wrote of her own abortion. She already had three children and agreed with her husband that they could not handle another. She went ahead with the operation.

"I have this ghost now," Francke wrote later. "A very little ghost that only appears when I'm seeing something beautiful. . . . And the baby waves at me. And I wave at the baby. 'Of course, we have room,' I cry to the ghost. 'Of course, we do.'"

Francke still "would march myself into blisters for a woman's right to exercise the option of motherhood." But the doubts that haunt her and many other Americans about the act of abortion demand, as Mario Cuomo said, respect and caution, civil discourse instead of civil war.

Review Questions

1. Briefly review each side of the abortion issue.
2. On which side of the abortion issue do you stand? Why?

The Women's Movement

In the 40 years prior to 1960, there was, with little exception, no significant organized women's movement in the United States. During the early 1960s, a variety of events occurred that influenced the development of the women's movement. In 1963, the first official governmental study on the status of women was issued. The President's Commission on the Status of Women report recommended equal opportunity for women in employment and politics, the elimination of property law restrictions, and a greater availability of child-care services. In the same year, after many years of deliberation, Congress passed the Equal Pay Act. For those jobs covered by the act, it required equivalent salaries for men and women doing the same work. *The Feminine Mystique,* by Betty Friedan (1963), was also published in that year. It criticized the traditional social roles of women and examined the psychological costs of the limited homemaker role. The 1964 Civil Rights Act and the establishment of the Equal Employment Opportunity Commission (EEOC) also influenced the movement's development. Title VII of the 1964 Civil Rights Act gives protection against sex discrimination. As amended in 1972, the act prohibits discrimination in employment based on sex, race, religion, color, or national origin. These and other events influenced the development of the women's movement.

Feminism had moved in the direction taken by other social trends in the 1970s. The women's movement had operated from a decentralized, diverse organizational base and had sought those objectives that contended with the basic causes of sexual inequality.

A significant force in the women's movement had been the National Organization for Women (NOW). Founded in 1966, it basically reflected middle-class women's interest in legal, political, and occupational rights. Its early activities focused on women's civil rights, discrimination, and EEOC's enforcement of Title VII. NOW had been to the women's movement what the NAACP had been to the black movement in the United States, in that both had concentrated their efforts on a legal fight against discrimination.

Goals of the women's movement

Three issues for which major goals had been established by most women in the women's movement were equal job opportunities, equal pay for equal work, and the Equal Rights Amendment (ERA) to the United States Constitution. With respect to the first two goals, it was believed that if women were unable to support themselves economically, liberation in other areas of life would be impossible to achieve. The passing of new laws, such as the Equal Pay Act and Title VII of the Civil Rights Act, and women's victories in some sex discrimination court battles had indicated that progress had begun in the critical areas of jobs and equal pay. Problems, however, still existed in the enforcement of these laws.

The third goal of the women's movement had been the passage of the ERA. The major focus of the ERA was the removal of all employment barriers and other types of sex discrimination. The amendment's passage would have meant that sexual equality would have been guaranteed by the constitution and would have discouraged further discrimination against women. In the mid- to late 1970s, however, various ERA opposition groups developed. The conservative groups interpreted the ERA as degrading women in their traditional roles of homemaker and mother. These strong countergroups became sufficiently powerful to prevent the ratification of the ERA in 1982.

The defeat of the ERA proved a serious blow to America's women's movement. Internal dissension over the movement's goals, methods, and procedures impeded its previous strength. The success of the movement also had been blocked by the extent to which people felt that their sociocultural identities had been threatened. As we saw in the chapter on socialization, we are all socialized into sex roles. Our identities, emotions, and reactions are very much defined by our sex roles. Deviations from these culturally set prescriptions and proscriptions cause people stress. Much of the women's movement had stressed the necessity of having people overcome their commitment to the traditional sex roles and institutions of society—and therefore to the values of society as well.

ONWARD, WOMEN!

Claudia Wallis

In the following reading, "Onward, Women!," Claudia Wallis evaluates the current status of the women's movement and stresses that "feminism is not dead."

> Keeping house and caring for the kids fills a woman's day—and more. But what if she had to earn a living too? Your wife will never have to face this double duty if you protect yourself.
>
> —1963 ad for Travelers Insurance

> She had breakfast with the national sales manager, met with the client from 9 to 11, talked at an industry luncheon, raced across town to the plans board meeting and then caught the 8:05 back home.
>
> —1977 ad for Boeing

> I can bring home the bacon, fry it up in a pan. And never, never, never let you forget you're a man.
>
> —1978 ad for Enjoli perfume

My mother was convinced the center of the world was 36 Maplewood Drive. Her idea of a wonderful time was Sunday dinner. She bought UNICEF cards, but what really mattered were the Girl Scouts . . . I'm beginning to think my mother really knew what she was doing.

—Recent ad for *Good Housekeeping* magazine

Now, wait a minute. If Madison Avenue is any indication, American women are going backward. What happened to the superwoman in the tailored suit and floppy bow tie who brought home all that bacon? What happened to breakfast with the national sales manager and racing for the 8:05? What happened to aspiring to the executive suite, to beating men at their own game?

As women head into the 1990s, are they really so burned out from "having it all" (i.e., doing it all), so thoroughly exhausted from putting in a full day at work and then another full evening at home, and they dream nostalgically of the 1950s? Can they really be aching for the dull but dependable days when going to meetings meant the PTA or the Scouts, when business travel meant the car pool, when a budgetary crisis meant the furnace had broken? Is the feminist movement—one of the great social revolutions of contemporary history—truly dead? Or is it merely stalled and in need of a little consciousness raising?

Ask a woman under the age of 30 if she is a feminist, and chances are she will shoot back a decisive, and perhaps even a derisive, no. But in the very next breath, the same young woman will allow that while she does not identify with the angry aspects of the movement in the '60s and '70s or with its clamorous leaders, she certainly plans on a career as well as marriage and three kids. She definitely expects her husband—present or future—to do his share of the dusting, the diapering, the dinner and dishes. She would be outraged were she paid less than a male colleague for doing equal work. Ask about the Supreme Court's *Webster* decision last summer allowing states more leeway to restrict abortions: she'll probably bristle about a woman's right to chose.

Call them the "No, but . . ." generation. No, they are not feminists, or so they say, but they do take certain rights for granted. "I reject the feminist label, but I guess I'd call myself an egalitarian," says Leslie Sandberg, 27, a political-campaign worker in Boston, whose attitude seems typical of her generation. "I'm feminine, not a feminist," insists Linn Thomas, an Auburn University senior, in another variation on the theme. Adds Thomas: "I picture a feminist as someone who is masculine and who doesn't shave her legs and is doing everything she can to deny that she is feminine."

Hairy legs haunt the feminist movement, as do images of being strident and lesbian. Feminine clothing is back; breasts are back; motherhood is in again. To the young, the movement that loudly rejected female stereotypes seems hopelessly dated. The long, ill-fated battle for the Equal Rights Amendment means nothing to young women who already assume they will be treated as equals.

Feminist leaders like Gloria Steinem and Molly Yard, president of the National Organization for Women, are dismissed as out of touch. NOW's call last summer for a third political party that would represent women's concerns seemed laughable to young women who do not want to isolate themselves by gender but prefer to work *with* men. When Sarah Calian, a senior at Brown University, went to hear Yard lecture on campus, she could not connect. Though Calian brims with ambitions for a major career and her first child by 35, she says, "I never felt so not a part of something. I don't know who she was talking to."

Sometimes even the women who participated in the feminist revolution, who shaped their lives according to its ideals, shake their heads and wonder. Call them the "Yes, but . . ." generation. Yes, these women in their 30s and 40s are feminists, but things have not worked out as expected. It is hard for them not to feel resentful: toward society for not coming to the aid of women in their new roles, toward the movement for not anticipating the difficulties. "We were promised that we could do it all and we would be as successful as men," says Carolyn Lo Galbo Goodfriend, 39, a mother of a five-year-old, who manages more than $300 million worth of accounts for Kraft General Foods in Rye Brook, N.Y. "But the trade-offs and sacrifices a woman has to make are far greater than a man's." Lo Galbo once met Steinem at an awards dinner and demanded to know, "Why didn't you tell us that it was going to be like this?" The matriarch of *Ms.* magazine answered with admirable candor: "Well, we didn't know."

Many mid-career women blame the movement for not knowing and for emphasizing the wrong issues. The ERA and lesbian rights, while noble causes, seemed to have garnered more attention than the pressing need for child care and more flexible work schedules. The bitterest complaints come from the growing ranks of women who have reached 40 and find themselves childless, having put their careers first. Is it fair that 90% of male executives 40 and under are fathers but only 35% of their female counterparts have children? "Our generation was the human sacrifice," says Elizabeth Mehren, 42, a feature writer for the Los Angeles *Times.* "We believed the rhetoric. We could control our biological destiny. For a lot of us the clock ran out, and we discovered we couldn't control infertility."

Nonprofessional women, poor women, minority women feel their needs and values have been largely ignored by the organized women's movement, which grew out of white, middle-class women's discontent. Most women of color say their primary concerns—access to education, health care and safe neighborhoods for their children—were not priorities for the women's movement. As for getting out into the workplace, well, poor women have always been there, mopping floors, slinging hash, raising other people's children. "I never saw the feminist movement as liberating me from the home," says L. Clarissa Chandler, a black social worker and feminist who directs the Alcoholism Center for Women in Los Angeles.

On the other hand, stay-at-home mothers, who still make up one-third of all U.S. women with children under 18, feel their status has been depreciated by feminism. Sighs Dabney McKenzie of Montgomery, who describes herself as both a "feminist" and a "typical Southern housewife": "It's almost as if there's a caste system of employment, and motherhood is down there at the bottom."

It might be tempting to conclude from the wide-ranging complaints from so many quarters that the women's movement has failed, that rather than improve the lot of women, it has helped make their lives more complex and difficult. But for all the discontent and frustration expressed by women today, a vast majority revels in the breakthroughs made during the past quarter-century: the explosion of roles for women, their far greater participation in the country's political and intellectual life, the many options that have come to replace their confinement to homemaking. Very few women would like to turn back the clock. A TIME/CNN survey conducted by Yankelovich Clancy Shulman of 1,000 women across the country found that 77% think the women's movement has made life better. Only 8% think it has made things worse. Ninety-four percent said the movement has helped women become more independent; 82% said it was still improving the lives of American women.

Why, then, do so few—33%—identify themselves as "feminists"? Why did 76% of those polled say they pay "not very much" or "no" attention to the women's movement? In many ways, feminism is a victim of its own resounding achievements. Its triumphs—in getting women into the workplace, in elevating their status in society and in shattering the "feminine mystique" that defined female success only in terms of being a wife and a mother—have rendered it obsolete, at least in its original form and rhetoric. "Saying the women's movement is dead is like saying the cold war is dead. No. No. It's over. It's won," insists Carol Gilligan, professor of education at Harvard and author of *In a Different Voice,* which explores the moral values and psychological development of women. "Those changes have been made, and they really are extraordinary."

Consider just a few measures of change. In the 1950s, women made up only 20% of college undergraduates—in contrast to 54% today—and two-thirds did not complete their degrees (conventional wisdom then held that an "M.R.S." was more important). As for aspirations, well, they were limited. When more than 13,000 female college graduates were asked, in the early '60s, how they defined success for themselves, the two most common answers were to be the mother of several accomplished children and to be the wife of a prominent man. In 1960, three years before Betty Friedan's *The Feminine Mystique,* 34.8% of women were in the work force, in contrast to 57.8% today. The number of female lawyers and judges has climbed from 7,500 to 180,000 today, female doctors from 15,672 to 108,200, and female engineers from 7,404 to 174,000. The number of women in elected office has more than tripled since 1975 at the local level, though their presence has barely changed in the U.S. Congress.

Not all the changes were the result of feminist ideology. Female employment in the U.S. has been rising since the 1890s, accompanied, not coincidentally, by a rise in the average age at which women marry, a decline in family size, and a jump in the divorce rate. The sole exceptions to these trends occurred in the 1950s, when, in the prosperous aftermath of World War II, motherhood and babymaking became a kind of national cult: there was a return to earlier marriage, families were bigger and divorce rates stabilized. Though women continued to pour into the workplace during the '50s, this fact was blotted out by the decade's infatuation with blissful domesticity. In the larger historical context, feminism appears to have been a rebellion against the '50s and a course correction. It helped get earlier trends back on track and offered an optimistic, have-it-all ideology to go with them.

It is only now, when 68% of women with children under 18 are in the work force (in contrast to 28% of women with children in 1960), that maternity leave and child care—always issues for the working poor—have become important for the majority of American women. Only today does the women's movement seem remiss in having failed to give greater emphasis to these matters. "The things I fought for are now considered quaint," complains Erica Jong, a best-selling feminist novelist. "We've won the right to be exhausted, to work a 30-hour day. Younger women say, 'Who wants that?' They say, 'We don't need feminism anymore.' They don't understand graduating magna cum laude from Harvard and then being told to go to the typing pool."

Feminism has also been the victim of its own extremist rhetoric and a press that was happy to amplify it. Like any young, energetic social movement, feminism had its share of radicals. Groups like SCUM (Society for Cutting Up Men) made good copy. So did Germaine Greer, who suggested that women be "deliberately promiscuous" and boycott marriage. Bra burning always caught a reader's eye, though none ever took place. (Apparently the closest thing to it occurred at a protest of the 1968 Miss America pageant in Atlantic City, when women tossed their bras into a trash can.) Friedan admits that in the heat of the battle to liberate the suburban housewife the language often became excessive: "It was literally throw the baby out with the bath water, throw out motherhood." Jong recalls a mood among feminists that was "anticosmetics, anti-lacy underwear."

To be sure, NOW always included in its platform demands for maternity leave, day care and respect for stay-at-home mothers. But even within the feminist movement, there was disagreement over strategy. In *Lesser Lives, the Myth of Women's Liberation in America,* author Sylvia Ann Hewlett tells how her late-'70s battle for a maternity policy at Barnard College in New York City was opposed by feminists at the college's own Women's Center. "I was told," she relates, that "if women wanted equality with men they could not ask for special privileges." It was a sentiment often expressed at the peak of the movement, and is still heard in some feminist quarters today.

Such attitudes were more understandable during the early years. If the first women who knocked on the door to the executive suite—or, for that matter, the firehouse or the construction contractor's office—had mentioned maternity-leave benefits, the door would have been slammed in their faces. Similarly, the dress-for-success, male-clone look that now seems so ridiculous was a necessary bit of female camouflage for the first infiltrators of the corporate world.

But if feminism won its war, lifting women's status and self-respect, there are still enormous battles ahead and handicaps for American women to overcome. Among them:

THE WAGE GAP

It is shocking to note that women who work full time still earn only 66¢ to the man's dollar, a difference that has narrowed by less than a dime over the past two decades. One reason: 59% of employed women work in low-paying, "pink-collar" jobs, some because they are trained for nothing else, some because such jobs tend to be more compatible with child rearing. The gap can also be attributed to the relatively recent arrival of women in higher-paying professions and the difficulty they have had in penetrating the so-called glass ceiling, a bias barrier that keeps so many women from moving beyond middle management. Among FORTUNE 500 companies, less than 2% of top executives are female. Harder to explain is the fact that the higher women advance, the larger the wage gap. A May 1987 report by the U.S. Chamber of Commerce found that corporate women at the vice-presidential level and above earn 42% less than their male peers.

DIVORCE AND POVERTY

The wage gap and the segregation of women into low-paying jobs, together with the lack of affordable child care, take their greatest toll on unmarried women, particularly single mothers. Today more than 60% of adults below the federal poverty line are women, and, contrary to popular mythology, the majority are white. More than half the poor families in America are headed by single women. In the early '80s the "feminization of poverty" became an issue for the women's movement, but the situation has barely budged. High divorce rates have added to female destitution. In *The Divorce Revolution* (1985), sociologist Lenore Weitzman showed how no-fault divorce laws—passed in 43 states, largely in response to feminist demand—

have benefited men and impoverished women. Weitzman found that as a result of these laws, which largely eliminated alimony and often forced the sale of the family home, women and their children typically suffer a 73% drop in their standard of living after a divorce while the ex-husband's living standard jumps 42%.

THE SECOND SHIFT

Vernal Brown, 39, does what used to be a man's job: making front bumpers in a Ford auto plant in St. Louis. Though her paycheck was essential for paying the family's bills, she says, her husband "expected the same as if I was a housewife. He told me that if I couldn't take care of the needs at home and have his food ready, I should quit." Instead Brown quit her marriage. Among the upper middle class, male rhetoric may sound enlightened, but the bottom line is much the same. In *The Second Shift*, a study of 50 mostly middle-class, two-career couples published this year, Arlie Hochschild, a sociologist at the University of California, Berkeley, found that wives typically come home from work to another shift: doing 75% of the household tasks. "Men are trying to have it both ways," she charges. "They're trying to have their wives' salaries and still have the traditional roles at home."

Mainstream feminist groups look at the long way to go and wonder how the troops could have grown so complacent. Some see hope of rekindling the flames in the resurgent abortion issue. Membership in NOW, which was down to 160,000 last year (from a peak of 220,000 in 1982), jumped almost 100,000 in the aftermath of *Webster*. Many of the hundreds of thousands who participated in prochoice demonstrations on Nov. 12, organized by NOW and other groups, were marching for the first time in their lives. Among them was Emily Friedan, 33, a Buffalo pediatrician and Betty Friedan's daughter. "For 25 years I have rarely appeared with my mom. This April I marched with her because of the abortion issue," says Friedan, who has organized a local chapter of Physicians for Choice. The abortion issue has helped galvanize college-age women—and men—out of their political inertia. Alexandra Stanton, 20, took a year's leave from Cornell to launch Students Organizing Students, an activist group devoted to protecting reproductive rights. SOS has already launched chapters on 100 college campuses. Says NOW president Molly Yard: "Abortion has strengthened our abilities to campaign on many issues."

Others believe those in the younger generation will catch on to feminism after a little reality therapy. "They don't recognize discrimination as undergraduates because it's so much less overt than in the outside world," says Patricia Ireland, 44, executive vice president of NOW in Washington. Many women do not see sexism as an obstacle until they are well along in their careers and angling for a promotion or until they have their first child and their juggling act begins. Observes Ireland: "Feminism is a movement where women get more radical as they get older."

But reigniting the feminist movement as it used to be is no more possible than a return to the simpler times before feminism. By the early 1980s, more imaginative women in the movement began to speak of a second phase that would be quite different from the first. Friedan, as usual, was out front. In her 1981 book *The Second Stage*, she called on her feminist sisters to go beyond "sexual politics" that cast man as the enemy and denied women's "roots and life connection in the family." The movement must change its focus, she argued, from succeeding in a man's world on a man's terms to achieving a balance between this new role and woman's traditional roles as mother and tender of the hearth. To achieve that balance, urged

Friedan, the structure of the workplace and the home must change. And men must be enlisted to participate.

Friedan was rebuked at first for backtracking, for consorting with the enemy. But slowly her view has prevailed. Asked to select the most important goal for the women's movement today, participants in the TIME/CNN poll rated "helping women balance work and family" as No. 1. Second was "getting government funding for programs such as child care and maternity leave."

The so-called second stage is marked by a discussion about "feminine values" and teaching men and male-dominated institutions to share them. "In the second stage," says Ann Lewis, a founder of the National Women's Political Caucus, "we will not enter the work force as imitators of men. We will not deny the fact that we have children and, yes, think about them during the day. Nor will we deny that we as society's caretakers have responsibility for elderly parents. We bring those values with us."

But what does that mean in practical terms? Some of the needs are obvious. There is no balancing the demands of work and family life—for men or for women—without a national consensus on family policy. Part of this is guaranteeing employed parents the right to take time off after the birth or adoption of a child without risking the loss of their job; more than 100 nations ensure such rights for women workers, according to Sheila Kamerman, a social-policy professor at Columbia University. Equally essential is some sort of financial aid or subsidy to help the working poor and the middle class obtain quality child care; most West European countries have such programs.

Legislation on both parental leave and child care has been inching through Congress. Hopes for passing some version of the Act for Better Child Care (ABC) before year's end were dashed two weeks ago by political wrangling over how to finance it. A family-leave bill is also stalled. Policymakers in some states are not waiting for Washington to act. Seven states, including Minnesota, Oregon and Rhode Island, have already adopted comprehensive parental-leave laws; ten others have passed maternity-leave bills.

Legislation, while vital, will not itself revolutionize the workplace. Parental leave after the birth of an infant quickly comes to an end. The best child care in the world is no substitute for a mother or father being there—at the playground, at the gymnastics competition, at the dinner table. And being there is getting harder for full-time workers. Since 1973, Americans' average workweek has grown six hours, from under 41 hours to nearly 47, according to a Harris survey. Earlier this year Felice Schwartz, president of Catalyst, a research and advisory group that focuses on women in business, proposed a now infamous solution. Writing in the *Harvard Business Review,* she proposed that professional women who prefer not to sacrifice family to ambition be relegated to a slower career path that would top out at middle management. They would get by with shorter hours and schedules flexible enough to permit the occasional trip to the pediatrician or school play.

Schwartz's "Mommy Track" idea unleashed a torrent of condemnation. Critics asked why women, and for that matter men, could not make a temporary switch to a slower track. Why couldn't workers slow down and speed up depending on the changing demands of their personal lives? Author Sylvia Ann Hewlett foresees a "sequencing" pattern in which dual-career couples would alternate the times in which they focus heavily on their work. A mother or father might be intensely involved in a project for a period of time and thereby earn credits for time off to spend with the family during a slower period. To make such a scenario possible, Hewlett points out, the wage gap would have to close. Otherwise the woman's career, being less lucrative, would always seem the more expendable of the two.

Today many major law firms have a slower Mommy Track, but women who choose to switch to such "part-time" positions (as many as 40 hours a week instead of 70) generally do not have the option of picking up speed again; they are out of the race for partnership. Other fields are even less accommodating. "In academic science, the granting situation is so tight that even if you are very creative, if you divert your energy to a child, it will be extremely difficult to compete," says Lola Reid, a research biologist at the Albert Einstein College of Medicine in New York City. Reid, who has a one-year old daughter, advocates a separate pool of grant money for scientists who are in their peak years of child rearing. Otherwise, she says, "we're going to lose a highly trained population; they will simply drop out of the field."

It will take a good deal of pushing and prodding to bring about such developments. But around the U.S., that pushing and prodding is slowly taking place. "There are 600 women's business organizations in America," says Wendy Reid Crisp, director of the National Association for Female Executives, "from women in film to women in construction." Most of the groups were born in the 1980s, says Crisp, and their main focus is changing the workplace, battling the glass ceiling and pushing for child-care benefits. Labor unions are also playing a role in these struggles. In any given month in cities around the country, seminars, workshops and conventions assemble to discuss these same concerns. "This is not the organized women's movement," says Hillary Clinton, a partner in a Little Rock law firm and wife of Arkansas Governor Bill Clinton. "It is not top down. It is bottom up." The emphasis is on practical solutions, not rhetoric. Men are often included, and the tone is less confrontational. "Who wants to walk around with clenched fists all the time?" Clinton asks.

Many feminists believe men will resist these changes. "It means more competition at work and more housework at home," says Patricia Ireland of NOW. Others argue that men will see benefits for themselves. "It's women's demands that are making the workplace more livable," says Warren Farrell, a self-proclaimed "male feminist" and author of *Why Men Are the Way They Are.* "Companies did not have to be flexible in the past because men were their slaves."

Already there are numerous signs that male attitudes and values are becoming "feminized," though most men might reject that description. In a survey conducted last summer for the recruiting firm Robert Half International, 56% of men polled said they would give up as much as a quarter of their salary to have more family or personal time. About 45% said they would probably refuse a promotion that involved sacrificing hours with their family.

That may be a reflection of how things are beginning to change at home. Although married men do only about 30% of the housework today, according to Joseph Pleck, professor of families, change and society at Wheaton College, two decades ago they did just 20%. Pleck sees a "silent revolution" in male attitudes. "I don't predict that we'll be seeing fifty-fifty any time soon," he says, "but a jump of 10% in a national sample is a big change." Other studies have shown a growing role for men in caring for children. For 18% of dual-paycheck couples who work separate shifts, the father is the primary child-care provider during the wife's working hours. The more "women's work" men perform, the more respectable that work becomes and the less men take women for granted. "If men start taking care of children, the job will become more valuable," insists Gloria Steinem.

> My father was convinced the center of the world was 36 Maplewood Drive. His idea of a wonderful time was family dinner . . . I'm beginning to think my father really knew what he was doing.
>
> —Ad campaign circa 2090

Still a little farfetched, perhaps, but it sounds better that way, doesn't it?

Review Questions

1. What do feminists of the 1990s believe? What are their goals?
2. Do you consider yourself a feminist? Explain your answer.

Society

Society defined

A society is the most inclusive group to which human beings belong. It includes all the groups within which they interact. As defined earlier, a **society** is a large number of people who form a relatively organized, self-sufficient, and enduring body. It is a collection of people living in a specific geographic area, sharing a common culture, and thinking of themselves as belonging together. There is great variety among societies in size; complexity; political, economic, educational, and religious systems; and family organization. Some societies are quite large, highly industrialized, and complex, whereas others are small, agrarian, and quite simple in organization.

Many early sociologists distinguished between two major types of societies. Robert MacIver has called these two broad opposite types **communal** and **associational.** Robert Redfield (1947) labels these two types **folk** and **urban.** Ferdinand Tönnies (1957) has made a distinction between the ***Gemeinschaft,*** a community characterized by personal, intimate, stable, overlapping relationships, and ***Gesellschaft,*** a society characterized by impersonal attachments, with an emphasis on such qualities as efficiency, progress, and the pursuit of self-interest.

These broad types—communal-associational, folk-urban, and *Gemeinschaft-Gesellschaft*—are considered **ideal types** in that they are conceptual models that are useful in analyzing various social phenomena. No actual society completely corresponds to the ideal of the communal or associational type of society. No society is entirely folk nor entirely urban. A particular society is more or less folk or more or less urban. The United States approaches the associational, urban type of society. A small, isolated, homogeneous society would approach the communal, or folk, type.

The dichotomous constructs represent similar content and distinguish between two fundamental polar types of social organization so that a range of intermediate or transitional forms of organization may be comprehended (Tönnies, 1957). As Robert Redfield (1947) notes, the folk-urban construct is created only because through it, we may hope to understand reality. Its function is to suggest aspects of real societies that deserve study and especially to suggest hypotheses as to what, under certain defined conditions, may be generally true about society (Redfield, 1947).

Redfield also believes that by examining those societies that are least like our own, that is, folk societies, we will gain a much better understanding of societies in general.

The Communal, or Folk, Society

Most of the world's population lives in societies that approach the communal, or folk, type of society. **Folk societies** are homogeneous, and their members have a strong sense of solidarity. The Native American societies of North America before the twentieth century illustrate the folk type of society. The folk society is typically small and relatively isolated from other societies. People get to know one another well; there are no strangers. A high proportion of social relationships in the folk community are primary, long-lasting, and intimate. They are valued for themselves. There are very few subgroups other than the family in the folk society. Family and the extended kinship network are central to all experience. In fact, the folk society is characterized by "familistic" relationships. These relationships have as their major characteristics devotion, love, and sacrifice. The norms of familistic relationships dictate that participation be all-forgiving, embracing, bestowing, and unlimited, and that the acting members need, seek, sacrifice for, and love one another (Tönnies, 1957).

Folk society: behavior is regulated by custom

There is little need for formal law in a folk society because behavior is largely regulated by custom. Widespread mores are primarily responsible for most social control. Mores as well as informal norms exercise a "strong hold upon behavior; there is little need for formal law. Law we might say is part of the tradition: it is not codified or rationalized; not enacted or dictated; but, emerging from the cumulative experience of the society, it is incorporated in the customs known and accepted by its members" (Chinoy, 1963).

Within folk societies, there is a simple division of labor, and social roles are inclusive and total. They include many aspects of behavior—not merely some limited segment of individual behavior. Sex and age roles are most important because of a division of function between males and females. Sex and age determine much of a person's behavior. In folk communities, if a person's age and sex are known, then much is known about his or her status and function within the society. Besides the division of function between males and females, there is little other division of labor in this technologically simple type of society.

In addition to its simple division of labor, the folk society's limited size and relative isolation tend to make it socially homogeneous, stable, and resistant to change. People in a folk society are not motivated toward innovation, experimentation, or reflection. Consequently, this type of society shows relatively slow change. There are few, if any, specialized associations or impersonal, specialized mechanisms of social control. Behavior is basically traditional and personal. Finally, there is a strong sense of solidarity among members.

The Associational, or Urban, Society

One of the most significant factors affecting human society was the Industrial Revolution, with its systems of technology. This revolution not only gave birth to a new technology, it also brought about newer forms of social organization. The Industrial Revolution and its inevitable corollary, urbanization, caused a multitude of changes in the way people lived. By analyzing the urban type of society, we are able to better understand the types of social transformations and changes in social organization that occurred as a result of the Industrial Revolution.

The ideal type of **urban society** is characterized by the presence of the metropolis, which is highly populated, urbanized, and industrialized. Western social organization, such as the United States, is characteristic of the urban (Gesellschaft or associational) form.

Urban society: more impersonal and contractual

In urban societies, secondary relationships prevail, and social relationships are much more impersonal, instrumental, and transitory than those in the folk community. Contractual relationships predominate. Specified and limited, each covers only a small segment of a participant's life. Examples of contractual relationships are buyer-seller, employee-employer, and teacher-student relationships. Individuals associate for limited purposes. Relationships are instrumental in that they are important for the goals that they bring closer to realization; they are not important for themselves. Each member of the relationship is interested in the other as means to ends and not as ends in themselves. Each member also tries to get from the others as much as he or she can while contributing as little as possible. Means are evaluated according to the norm of efficiency in producing desired ends, which are, in turn, evaluated in terms of "happiness" (Tönnies, 1957). The relationship is usually voluntary, of limited duration, and utilitarian, with each individual's rights and duties specified by contract.

In the urban society, there is a marked division of labor, resulting in a proliferation of occupational roles. The urban individual plays or performs many roles—roles that are segmented in that they are usually limited to specific contexts and involve a narrow range of activities. In the urban community, most people are not directly involved in making their own clothing, growing their own food, or building their own houses. Service occupations tend to predominate in the labor force.

In urban societies, social relationships are not intrinsic, and roles are not inclusive as they are in folk societies. Social relationships in associational societies are instrumental, and social roles are segmental, as shown in Figure 12.1.

In the associational society, there is less consensus among its members, more impersonality, and a diversity of values. Traditional thinking and ritual

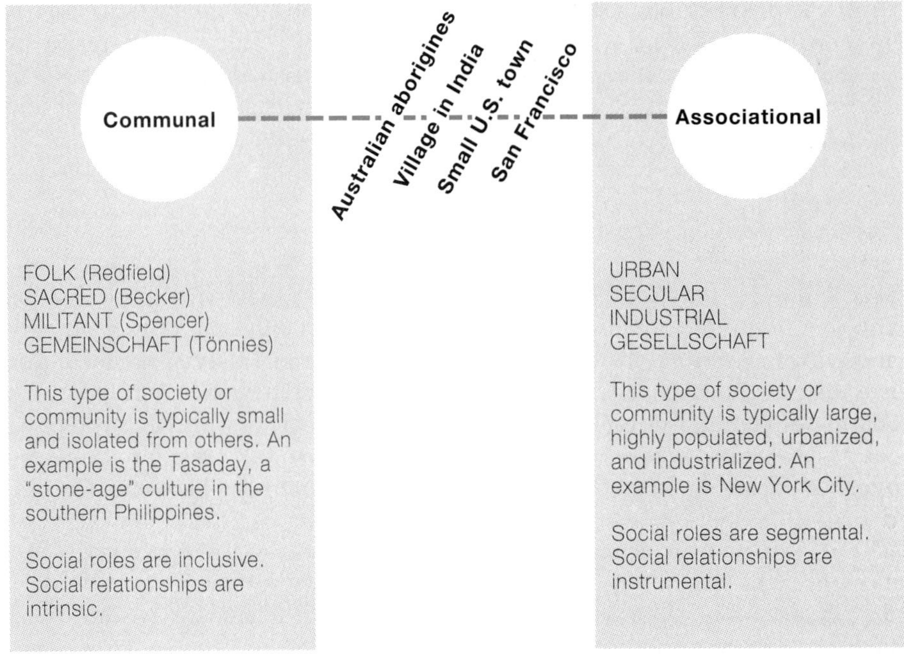

Figure 12.1 **Two broad types of social organization.**

acts are minimal. There is rapid change; in fact, change and innovation become synonymous with progress.

Mores and informal sanctions are weakened; consequently, there is more formal law. Formal law is needed because of the normative and value conflicts that accompany the heterogeneity of the population.

Family life and economics are somewhat separate in the urban society. The family is a consuming rather than a producing unit. Place of work is separated from place of residence. There is a breakdown in the extended kinship network. Many traditional functions of the family, such as education and religious training, are assumed by other organizations. In the urban society, religion tends to be separated from other aspects of life. It no longer permeates a person's entire life, as it does in the communal society.

There are criticisms of the folk-urban dichotomy

Many sociologists have criticized the folk-urban dichotomy. First, the folk-urban perspective assumes that communal, or folk, characteristics do not exist in urban life. There are, however, many urban neighborhoods that reflect the togetherness and interaction patterns attributed to folk societies. Philadelphia, for example, is a city of neighborhoods that can be described as folk communities, with the appropriate qualities of being small, traditional, homogeneous, and isolated. Second, the dichotomy usually identifies the city as the source of social change. However, within relatively isolated societies, social and cultural change also have been known to occur rapidly. Urban communities can be an outgrowth of change rather than the source of change. One must also take into consideration the variable of social change itself. What a person may find today in society may drastically change tomorrow. The folk-urban differences a person observes in a particular place and at a particular time may not hold true for long.

The Growth of Urban Communities

Much of the world has shifted from the folk to the urban type of community. There has been a tremendous growth of urban communities and cities during the past century. Before the Industrial Revolution and its systems of technology changed our social order, the United States was a rural society consisting of farms and small, traditional towns. American societal structure, as well as western society as a whole, is now pluralized into many specialized, complex groups. It is highly segmented and differentiated.

Urbanization: not just "the growth of cities"

Urbanization does not refer simply to the growth of cities but also to the proportion of a society's total population that lives in cities. Cities can develop and grow without appreciable urbanization if the rural population grows as quickly as the urban population. Urbanization increases only if the urban *proportion* of a society increases. Today the urban community is large, densely settled, and complex, with a heterogeneous population that is linked to a highly differentiated institutional social structure.

City Growth and Urbanization. William Dobriner (1969) notes that, in a sense, the term "city" is a recognition of the physical condition of urbanization in terms of size and density. He states: "A city is a large and dense settlement, whereas 'urbanism,' in the sociological sense, constitutes the modal social structure: the groups, distinctive processes, and forms of cities, the heterogeneity, differentiation, specialization and complexity" (Dobriner, 1969).

In general, city growth has been accompanied by urbanization. This occurred in the eighteenth and nineteenth centuries in American and European societies when cities grew by drawing the folk population off the land and into the urban communities that were the focal points of industrialization. People left the farms for jobs in the growing cities.

Dobriner believes that part of the urbanization process is the rise of industrialization accompanied by dramatic improvement in agricultural practices and techniques. As farmers became productively more efficient, excess rural people were drawn to the new factories opening up in the cities: "Hence there was a functional congruence of economic forces in the West (Europe and North America), and urbanization constituted a healthy tension between changing agricultural, technical, industrial forces and a shifting mode of community life" (Dobriner, 1969).

Social Change

Every society is characterized by aspects of social change. Societies may be stable, with little change, or they may be dynamic, with extensive change. No society is completely static. Social change occurs in all societies as a continuous process that is manifested by alterations in social relationships (Rogers and Shoemaker, 1971). Even though social change refers to change in the structure and social relationships of the society, and cultural change specifically refers to change in the culture—such as learned and shared values, beliefs, customs, traditions, and norms—we include them both in the concept of social change.

There are two important ways by which societies change. The first is by invention or discovery of new elements or ideas within the society. The second is by diffusion, or the borrowing of cultural items, traits, or patterns from other societies.

Invention and Discovery

Invention involves the creation of new things. It is a new combination of known elements of a society or new use of existing knowledge. It was, for example, Alexander Graham Bell's combination of elements and the new use of existing knowledge of his era that led to the invention of the telephone.

Invention involves the creation of new things

There are material inventions, such as the automobile and the electronic computer, and nonmaterial inventions, such as a new idea or theory. Unlike a discovery, which involves the perception of something previously unrecognized or an aspect of reality already in existence, an invention requires creation beyond perception. This does not mean that discovery is unimportant. It is important in that discovery contributes to a culture's store of knowledge and is a contributing factor in social change if put to use.

Discovery is basically the perception of previously unrecognized relationships between elements of a culture. Invention is the combination of known devices or elements into new form.

Invention and the Cultural Base. Through invention, societies grow and change. The rate of invention within a given culture or society is affected by a variety of factors.

One variable that affects a society's rate of invention is the intellectual ability of the society. Without being endowed substantially with mental ability, a society cannot be inventive. Demand and existing knowledge are two additional variables functionally related to invention. Ogburn (1946) notes these dimensions and stresses their importance. *Demand* means socially perceived needs that may build to the point where much of a society's energies are diverted to the satisfaction of these needs. Existing knowledge is also an important factor with respect to invention in that an invention is, as noted above, a combination of existing knowledge and inventions (Chinoy, 1963). If a society has a broad, basic foundation in technology, its variety of inventions and rate of invention will be broad and high.

Thus a relation exists between a society's cultural base—its accumulation of knowledge and techniques—and its ability to be inventive. Societies with a large cultural base tend to be much more inventive than those with a smaller base. Inventions are dependent on the state of knowledge, techniques, and skills within a society. Leonardo da Vinci, for example, invented the airplane, air-conditioning units, the machine gun, and many other "modern" inventions. In principle and detail, they were workable; however, the technology of the time lacked the metals, tools, fuels, and skills needed to build his inventions. Leonardo's inventive ideas had to wait until the cultural base of the society provided the necessary knowledge and techniques. It took over 400 years for an adequate cultural foundation to develop.

Invention must be relevant to culture

The survival of an invention depends on its relevance to existing culture. If a particular society is receptive to change, an invention may be accepted and may effect significant social changes. However, if a society is intellectually or emotionally resistant to change, an invention may be discarded before it is tested.

Traditionally oriented cultures or folk societies do not encourage invention. They lack a broad technological base, and there tends to be significant resistance to accepting inventions and change. Invention that challenges stability is not positively sanctioned as it tends to be in highly advanced, urban societies. In advanced societies, inventions, to a great extent, are planned. Much money and facilities are invested in the development of new socially desired material and nonmaterial inventions.

Not only are inventions dependent on a state of knowledge and their relevance to the existing culture, they are also related to need perception. The needs perceived by a society's members affect a society's rate and direction of change. If a society's people do not feel a need for change, there will be no change. The needs of a society, however, do not have to be real for people to perceive a need. Needs are "real" if they are felt or considered to be real by a people. Needs that are recurrent do not necessarily guarantee or induce inventiveness. A needed discovery or invention is not made merely because a need exists. Many needs persist in American society today—a need for energy, a need for a cure for cancer, a need for tax reform, a need for peace in the world. A solution to these needs does not necessarily have to be found, even though the need, in reality, does exist.

Need does not guarantee invention

In American society, as in other modern societies, many inventions are not merely welcomed but are stimulated and encouraged. According to Chinoy (1963), in some fields, invention and innovation represent conformity with significant social values. In general, American society is receptive to the invention of gadgets and implements. Technology and science in America are of great importance to innovation and invention. In the United States, according to Chinoy, technological innovation:

> **is encouraged through the traditional belief that "if a man makes a better mouse trap the world will make a beaten path to his door," through the patent system, and even through suggestion schemes in factories. Efficiency and invention are constantly stimulated by economic pressure. Scientific and technological development has been fostered through the organization of research laboratories and scientific institutes. Few other fields are equal to technology and science in their encouragement of innovation, although in such varied areas of social life as leisure and business procedures there is a wide range of permissiveness and tolerance for new practices, techniques, and ideas (Chinoy, 1963).**

Diffusion

Social change occurs not only through the process of invention and discovery, but also through the process of diffusion. **Diffusion,** as Ralph Linton (1936) notes, is the "transfer of culture elements from one society to another." It involves borrowing and adopting cultural patterns or traits from other groups or societies. Diffusion should be distinguished from *social inheritance,* which is the transmission of culture from one generation to the next through time—not through space and time.

When groups or societies are in contact with one another, diffusion occurs. It can occur indirectly, through the mass media, for example, or it can occur directly when groups of people are in physical contact with one another, as happens in war, migration, or colonization. It is always a two-way process. The contact is essential for the diffusion of traits—a diffusion in both directions. In other words, diffusion occurs not only from western to nonliterate societies or from dominant to minority groups, but in the opposite direction as well. The Native American culture has contributed a multitude of cultural items to American society, ranging from corn and potatoes to tobacco and the game of lacrosse. Whites brought the Native Americans Christianity, the horse, and firearms.

Diffusion involves borrowing and adopting from others

Most of our culture has been borrowed from other societies. That most of our society's content has been diffused from other nations is pointed out by Linton in his classical, much-quoted passage from *The Study of Man:*

> **Our solid American citizen awakens in a bed built on a pattern which originated in the Near East but which was modified in Northern Europe before it was transmitted to America. He throws back covers made from cotton, domesticated in India, or linen, domesticated in the Near East, or silk, the use of which was discovered in China. All of these materials have been spun and woven by processes invented in the Near East. He slips into his moccasins, invented by the Indians of the eastern woodlands, and goes to the bathroom whose fixtures are a mixture of European and American inventions, both of recent date. He takes off his pajamas, a garment invented in India, and washes with soap invented by the ancient Gauls. He then shaves, a masochistic rite which seems to have been derived from either Sumer or ancient Egypt.**
>
> **Returning to the bedroom, he removes his clothes from a chair of southern European type and proceeds to dress. He puts on garments whose form originally derived from the skin clothing of the nomads of the Asiatic steppes, puts on shoes made from skins tanned by a process invented in ancient Egypt and cut to a pattern derived from the classical civilizations of the Mediterranean, and ties around his neck a strip of bright colored cloth which is a vestigial survival of the shoulder shawls worn by seventeenth century Croatians. Before going out for breakfast he glances through the window, made of glass invented in Egypt, and if it is raining puts on overshoes made of rubber discovered by the Central American Indians and takes an umbrella, invented in southeastern Asia. Upon his head he puts a hat made of felt, a material invented in the Asiatic steppes.**
>
> **On his way to breakfast he stops to buy a paper, paying for it with coins, an ancient Lydian invention. At the restaurant a whole new series of borrowed elements confronts him. His plate is made of a form of pottery invented in China. His knife is of steel, an alloy first made in southern India, his fork a medieval Italian invention, and his spoon a derivative of a Roman original. He begins**

breakfast with an orange, from the eastern Mediterranean, a cantaloupe from Persia, or perhaps a piece of African watermelon. With this he has coffee, an Abyssinian plant, with cream and sugar. Both the domestication of cows and the idea of milking them originated in the Near East, while sugar was first made in India. After his fruit and first coffee he goes to waffles, cakes made by a Scandinavian technique from wheat domesticated in Asia Minor. Over these he pours maple syrup invented by the Indians of the eastern woodlands. As a side dish he may have the egg of a species of bird domesticated in Indochina or thin strips of the flesh of an animal domesticated in Eastern Asia which have been salted and smoked by a process developed in northern Europe.

When our friend has finished eating he settles back to smoke, an American Indian habit, consuming a plant domesticated in Brazil in either a pipe, derived from the Indians of Virginia, or a cigarette, derived from Mexico. If he is hardy enough he may even attempt a cigar, transmitted to us from the Antilles by way of Spain. While smoking he reads the news of the day, imprinted in characters invented by the ancient Semites upon a material invented in China by a process invented in Germany. As he absorbs the accounts of foreign troubles he will, if he is a good conservative citizen, thank a Hebrew deity in an Indo European language that he is a 100 percent American (Linton, 1964, pp. 113–119).*

Most Americans, including those with strong nationalistic biases, are unaware of the extent to which our culture is indebted to others. Our society, perhaps more than any other, "represents an amalgamation of contributions from diverse groups—only the most completely isolated societies can be said to have borrowed little or nothing from others" (Chinoy, 1963).

Diffusion involves selection and modification

Diffusion involves both selection and modification. It involves selection in that a culture tends to reject more than it accepts through contact with another culture. China is now adopting many American technological ideas and methods without adopting our institutions, political systems, or philosophies. Diffusion involves modification in that a borrowing culture tends to modify the element borrowed. Americans have accepted Chinese food from the Chinese but have modified it to fit their particular tastes. As cultural traits are diffused, then selection and modification occur.

The **rate of diffusion,** like the rate of invention, is affected by many factors. Societies that are traditionally oriented and revere the past tend to change slowly, so slowly that to our western eyes, they seem not to be changing at all. A cultural taboo or general cultural inertia makes the acceptance of cultural traits from other cultures difficult. In rapidly changing societies, where innovation and sophistication are in many ways positively sanctioned, diffusion, as well as invention and discovery, is likely to occur.

The rate of diffusion is also related to the structure of society. American society, with its many achieved statuses, its stress on individualism, and its open class system is not highly resistant to social change and is very conducive to diffusion. Other societies, because they are highly structured, are strongly resistant to diffusion.

* Ralph Linton, *The Study of Man*, Copyright © 1936, renewed 1964. Reprinted by permission of Prentice-Hall, Inc., Englewood Cliffs, New Jersey.

Population changes and migration also affect the diffusion rate. When a population undergoes a great increase or decrease, social institutions and group relations change. When a migration takes place and large populations shift from one region to another, the diffusion rate is affected by the new social contacts in the environment.

Finally, the diffusion rate is related to need, communication, and transportation. If a society is in need of a particular new element in order to meet a critical situation, the rate of diffusion may increase. With improved communication and transportation, contact between cultures tends to improve and the rate of diffusion usually increases.

Explanations for Social Change

There are many different explanations for social change. The theory of biological determinism explains social change in terms of various characteristics of the human organism. The theory of geographical determinism explains social change as a consequence of features in the natural environment. Cultural determination focuses on elements of the cultural heritage.

The theory of economic determinism accounts for change by means of economic processes and forces. Marx, for example, believed that people have certain needs, such as food, shelter, and clothing, and a means—employment—to obtain these needs. The necessity for these is the primary motive for action. Social classes, according to Marx, are continually in conflict with one another for economic reasons; the conflict between them produces social change (Marx and Engels, 1969). This conflict model views class conflict as the basic cause of all social and political change.

There are many explanations for social change

Unlike Marx, who stressed economics and conflict, Ogburn (1950) stresses the importance of technology with respect to change. Technological changes, Ogburn believes, bring about changes in the culture. Ogburn examines the effect of technological innovation on society and posits the idea that the rate of institutional change is slower than the rate of technological change. He uses the term **cultural lag** to describe this difference. Social systems are strained because technological changes occur more quickly than the society is able to assimilate their implications into the institutional structure. That is, Ogburn believes that, in general, changes occur first in the material segment of culture. Norms, values, systems of beliefs, and knowledge, or the nonmaterial aspects of culture, will later adjust to accommodate the material change, and that adjustment period is called cultural lag. Scientific and medical advances, for example, have prolonged the life expectancy of Americans; however, Medicare benefits have only recently been instituted to meet the needs of the elderly.

Max Weber stressed the importance of a society's ideological commitments, values, and beliefs in explaining social change. His primary focus was on Protestantism and its effect on the social and economic aspects of society. In this sense, Weber was speaking of the role of values (nonmaterial culture) in bringing about changes in the material aspects of life. He felt that Protestantism (as a set of religious values) resulted in the development of capitalistic forms of economy and society. Weber's theory about the roles of values in social change is contained in his book *The Protestant Ethic and the Spirit of Capitalism* (1958).

In any event, sociologists reject the idea that a single factor is able to explain such a complex process as social change. It is not that the theories noted above have not contributed to an understanding of social change. They have made basic contributions. They are inadequate, however, as explanatory models because they tend to be one-sided interpretations.

As we have seen, various forms of collective behavior are important factors in social change. Phenomena from the past, ranging from public opinion to crowd behavior, have formed many of our institutional structures. Americans' discontent with the British in the eighteenth century led to a revolutionary social movement that provided the basis for our American society today. Reform movements through the decades have continued to modify segments of our society and have effected change in many areas of social life. Resistance, migratory, and expressive movements have all functioned as active agents of social change in American history.

Societies grow and change through discovery and the invention of new things and ideas. They also change through the diffusion of cultural items from one society to another. As societies grow and social change occurs, strains, problems, and tensions may be created, which, in turn, lead to further changes. The movement of blacks from the south to the industrial north brought about strain and conflict between black and white workers. This strain then led to attempts to ameliorate racial difficulties and antagonisms. The growth of American unionism was the result of giant corporate growth. Urbanization within the United States has contributed to our declining birth rate and family size.

In periods of rapid social change, social disorganization may develop as new attitudes, values, and norms evolve and take form. Some individuals and institutions are able to adjust to changes in the structure or culture. For others, change means many problems.

Summary

1. Not all social behavior is highly structured, predictable, or guided by cultural norms. Collective behavior refers to social behavior that is relatively spontaneous, transitory, emotional, and somewhat unpredictable.

2. A crowd is a temporary grouping of people who have a common focus or interest. Crowds may be casual, conventionalized, expressive, or acting. Such factors as milling, contagion, and suggestibility are essential to acting crowds.

3. Mobs are crowds that are emotionally charged and oriented toward violence. A riot occurs when a mob becomes violently aggressive and destructive.

4. Panic occurs when a crowd is suddenly overwhelmed by fright that leads to irrational action. Crowds, riots, and panics develop, to a great

extent, because of rumor, which is the dissemination of distorted information. Crowd behavior has been explained in terms of the contagion, convergence, and emergent norm theories.

5. A public is a collection of people who are concerned about, divided upon, and engaged in discussion about an issue. The opinions about an issue held by a public are termed public opinion. Propaganda, to a great extent, shapes public opinion.
6. A social movement is a social aggregate acting with continuity to promote or resist change in the society of which it is a part. Social movements go through a four-stage life cycle, which includes social unrest, excitement, formalized organization, and finally, institutionalization. Many social changes come about from the organized action of various social movements.
7. Society is the most inclusive group to which people belong. Folk societies are small and homogeneous, relationships within them are primary, and behavior is regulated largely by custom. There is a simple division of labor and a strong sense of group solidarity. The characteristics of the urban society are basically opposite to those of the folk society.
8. The Industrial Revolution and urbanization have changed the way people live. With the growth of the urban population in a society, social roles become more segmented, secondary groups and relationships become more important, and the society becomes more heterogeneous. Life in the urban society is now dominated by large, formal organizations.
9. Social change may be explained in terms of discovery, invention, and diffusion. Discovery is the perception of previously unrecognized relations among existing elements of a culture. Invention is the combination of known elements into new form. Diffusion involves the borrowing and adopting of cultural patterns or traits from other groups.
10. As social change occurs, tensions, strains, and problems develop. With periods of rapid change, such as those experienced within the United States, some individuals and social institutions encounter difficulty.

STUDY GUIDE

Chapter Objectives

After studying this chapter, you should be able to:

1. Define "collective behavior"

2. List and briefly explain the six determinants of collective behavior
3. Identify and briefly explain four types of crowds
4. Define "mob," "riot," "panic," and "rumor"
5. Describe crowd behavior
6. Define "public opinion" and explain its importance
7. Define "social movement"
8. List and briefly explain the five preconditions for collective action
9. List and briefly explain the four stages in the life cycle of social movements
10. Identify and briefly explain four types of social movements
11. Describe the women's movement in the United States
12. Define "society"
13. Describe the basic characteristics of a folk society
14. Describe the basic characteristics of an associational society
15. Identify and explain the two important ways by which societies change
16. List 10 items that Americans have borrowed from other societies
17. Compare and contrast three explanations for social change

Key Terms

Associational society (p. 489)
Collective behavior (p. 463)
Communal society (p. 489)
Contagion (p. 466)
Crowd (p. 465)
Cultural lag (p. 498)
Diffusion (p. 496)
Discovery (p. 494)
Folk societies (p. 489)
Gemeinschaft (p. 489)
Gesellschaft (p. 489)
Ideal types (p. 489)
Invention (p. 494)
Milling (p. 465)
Mobs (p. 466)
Panic (p. 467)
Propaganda (p. 469)
Public (p. 469)
Public opinion (p. 469)
Rate of diffusion (p. 497)
Reform movement (p. 473)
Resistance movements (p. 474)
Revolutionary movements (p. 473)
Riot (p. 466)
Rumor (p. 467)
Social movement (p. 471)
Society (p. 489)
Suggestibility (p. 466)
Urban society (p. 489)

Self-Test

Short Answer

(p. 463) 1. Collective behavior is ______________________________
____

(p. 464) 2. Smelser's six determinants of collective behavior are:
a. ______ d. ______
b. ______ e. ______
c. ______ f. ______

(p. 465) 3. A crowd is ______

(p. 465) 4. Four types of crowds are:
a. ______ c. ______
b. ______ d. ______

(p. 467) 5. List Allport and Postman's three progressions that occur in the development of rumors:
a. ______
b. ______
c. ______

(p. 469) 6. A public is:
a. ______
b. ______

(p. 469) 7. List four of Lee and Lee's propaganda techniques:
a. ______ c. ______
b. ______ d. ______

(p. 471) 8. A social movement is ______

(p. 471) 9. Stockdale's five preconditions for collective action are:
a. ______ d. ______
b. ______ e. ______
c. ______

(p. 472) 10. The four basic stages of social movements are:
a. ______ c. ______
b. ______ d. ______

(p. 489) 11. Society is ______

(p. 490) 12. The folk society is characterized by ______
______

(p. 491) 13. The urban society is characterized by ______
______

(p. 494) 14. Invention is ______

(p. 494) 15. Discovery is ______

(p. 496) 16. Diffusion is ______

(p. 496) 17. List three things our American culture has borrowed from other cultures:
a. ______
b. ______
c. ______

Multiple Choice *(Answers are on page 508.)*

(p. 464) 1. Collective behavior is:
a. stable
b. predictable
c. changeable and episodic
d. sharpening

(p. 464) 2. Which of the following is *not* one of Smelser's determinants of collective behavior?
a. structural conduciveness
b. structural strain
c. precipitating factor
d. sharpening

(p. 465) 3. In the acting crowd, which factor(s) becomes important?
a. milling
b. contagion
c. suggestibility
d. all the above

(p. 465) 4. In an expressive crowd:
a. people are able to express themselves freely
b. few people were injured or killed
c. social scientists failed to develop any recommendations
d. none of the above

(p. 467) 5. *The War of the Worlds*
a. was a radio dramatization
b. caused thousands of Americans to panic
c. both of the above
d. neither of the above

(p. 467) 6. Which of the following is *not* one of Allport and Postman's three progressions that occur in the development of rumors?
a. leveling
b. projection
c. sharpening
d. assimilation

(p. 469) 7. Which of the following is *not* one of Lee and Lee's propaganda techniques?
a. name-calling
b. card-stacking
c. mind-constructing
d. testimonial

(p. 471) 8. According to the text, social movements go through a life cycle consisting of the following four basic stages:
a. social unrest, excitement, formalized organization, and institutionalization
b. preliminary, secondary, popular, and resolutional
c. primary, preset, informalized, and resolutional
d. none of the above

(p. 474) 9. Resistance movements:
a. arise because of the undesirability of a proposed or impending change
b. arise because of the undesirability of a change that has already occurred
c. develop because people are dissatisfied with the fast pace of social change
d. all the above

(p. 473) 10. The women's movement is:
a. a migratory movement
b. a resistance movement
c. an expressive movement
d. a reform movement

(p. 489) 11. A society:
- a. is the most inclusive group to which people belong
- b. includes all the groups within which people interact
- c. is a collection of people living in a specific geographic area, sharing a common culture, and thinking of themselves as belonging together
- d. all the above

(p. 490) 12. In the folk society:
- a. social roles are inclusive
- b. social roles are segmental
- c. mores and informal sanctions are weakened
- d. place of work is separated from place of residence

(p. 491) 13. In the urban society:
- a. there is a simple division of labor
- b. there is little need for formal law
- c. change occurs slowly
- d. social relationships are instrumental

(p. 491) 14. In today's world, the urban community is:
- a. large
- b. densely settled
- c. complex
- d. all the above

(p. 493) 15. Dobriner believes that:
- a. part of the urbanization process is the rise of industrialization accompanied by dramatic improvement in agricultural practices and techniques
- b. the urbanization process is a dysfunctional dimension of the ongoing growth in the complexity of our division of labor
- c. urbanization is a dying process
- d. none of the above

(p. 494) 16. Invention involves:
- a. the creation of modified factors
- b. the creation of old things
- c. perception of previously recognized relations
- d. none of the above

(p. 494) 17. Discovery is:
- a. inverted invention
- b. compromised diffusion
- c. perception of previously recognized relations
- d. none of the above

(p. 496) 18. Diffusion is:
- a. the transfer of bilateral elements
- b. the transfer of culture elements from one society to another
- c. the discovery of elements and their inventive process
- d. none of the above

(p. 497) 19. The rate of diffusion, like the rate of invention, is:
- a. affected by many factors
- b. not affected by many factors

c. bimodal
d. trilateral

(p. 498) 20. Cultural lag is:
a. the same as a cultural leg
b. a conflict model
c. a diffusionary model
d. none of the above

True/False *(Answers are on page 508.)*

T F 21. The type of behavior that develops in response to problematic situations is termed collective behavior. (p. 463)

T F 22. A crowd is a temporary grouping, collection, or aggregate of people who share a common focus or interest. (p. 465)

T F 23. Riots have been viewed as a product of a struggle for power among different groups within society. (p. 466)

T F 24. The Chicago riot of 1919 was oriented toward looting and destruction of property. (p. 466)

T F 25. For panic to occur, physical proximity is always necessary. (p. 467)

T F 26. Public opinion is the deliberate use of communication to influence and persuade individuals to favor one predetermined way of thinking or action over another. (p. 469)

T F 27. On the whole, social movements are organized to bring about some significant degree of change in the basic institutional structures of society. (p. 471)

T F 28. Institutionalization is the fourth and final stage of social movements. (p. 472)

T F 29. There has been a significant organized women's movement in the United States since 1910. (p. 480)

T F 30. The defeat of the ERA proved to be a serious blow to America's women's movement. (p. 481)

T F 31. A society is the most inclusive group to which humans belong. (p. 489)

T F 32. Contractual relationships predominate in an associational society. (p. 489)

T F 33. In the associational society, mores and informal sanctions are weakened. (p. 489)

T F 34. Much of the world has shifted from the urban to the folk type of community. (p. 490)

T F 35. Urbanization refers to the growth of cities. (p. 493)

T F 36. Invention involves the creation of new things. (p. 494)

T F 37. Discovery is the perception of previously unrecognized relationships between elements of a culture. (p. 494)

T F 38. Diffusion is basically the same as social inheritance. (p. 496)

T F 39. Very little of American culture has been borrowed from other societies. (p. 495)

T F 40. Cultural lag occurs when the migration rate affects the diffusion rate. (p. 498)

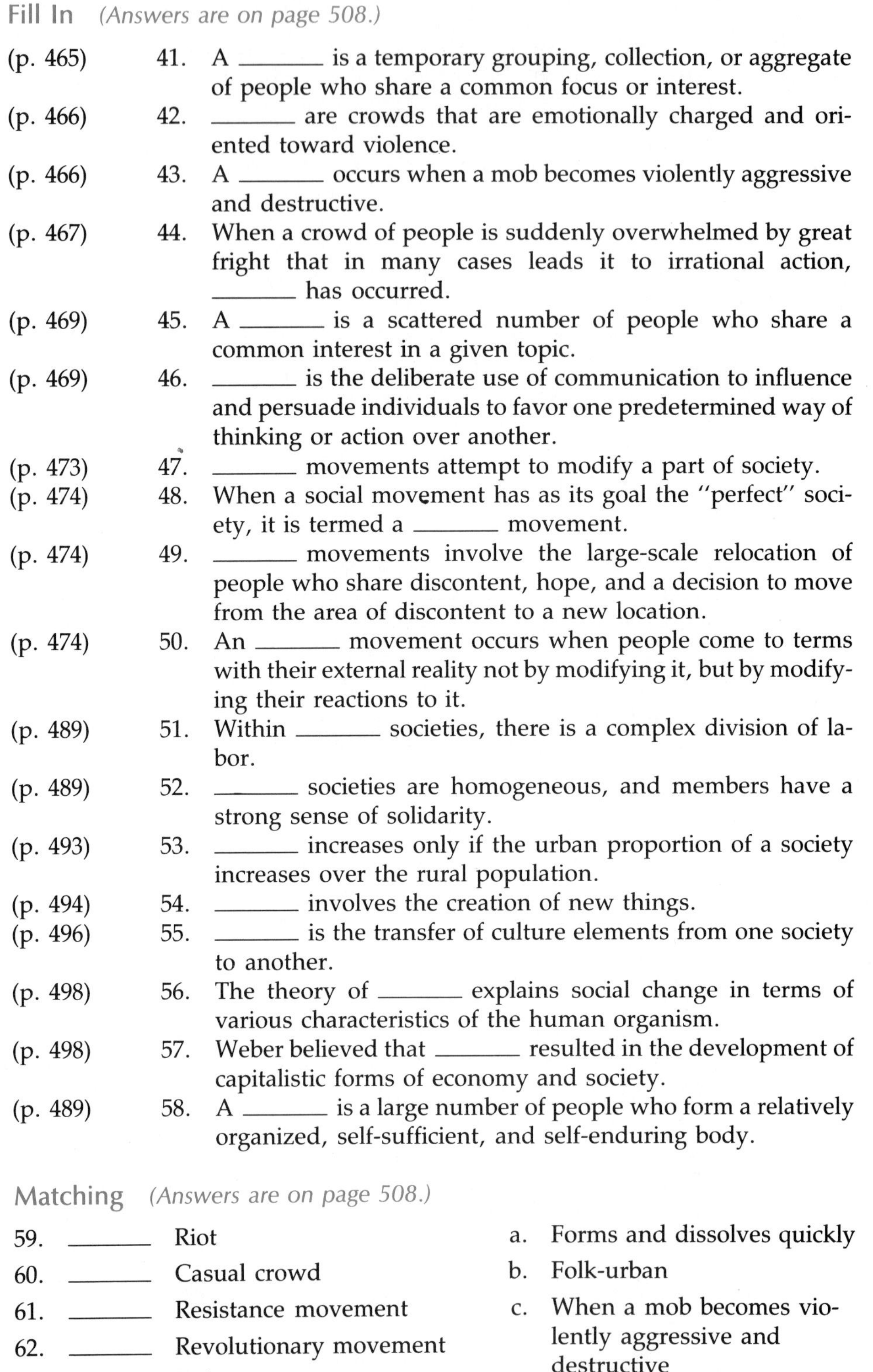

Fill In *(Answers are on page 508.)*

(p. 465) 41. A _______ is a temporary grouping, collection, or aggregate of people who share a common focus or interest.

(p. 466) 42. _______ are crowds that are emotionally charged and oriented toward violence.

(p. 466) 43. A _______ occurs when a mob becomes violently aggressive and destructive.

(p. 467) 44. When a crowd of people is suddenly overwhelmed by great fright that in many cases leads it to irrational action, _______ has occurred.

(p. 469) 45. A _______ is a scattered number of people who share a common interest in a given topic.

(p. 469) 46. _______ is the deliberate use of communication to influence and persuade individuals to favor one predetermined way of thinking or action over another.

(p. 473) 47. _______ movements attempt to modify a part of society.

(p. 474) 48. When a social movement has as its goal the "perfect" society, it is termed a _______ movement.

(p. 474) 49. _______ movements involve the large-scale relocation of people who share discontent, hope, and a decision to move from the area of discontent to a new location.

(p. 474) 50. An _______ movement occurs when people come to terms with their external reality not by modifying it, but by modifying their reactions to it.

(p. 489) 51. Within _______ societies, there is a complex division of labor.

(p. 489) 52. _______ societies are homogeneous, and members have a strong sense of solidarity.

(p. 493) 53. _______ increases only if the urban proportion of a society increases over the rural population.

(p. 494) 54. _______ involves the creation of new things.

(p. 496) 55. _______ is the transfer of culture elements from one society to another.

(p. 498) 56. The theory of _______ explains social change in terms of various characteristics of the human organism.

(p. 498) 57. Weber believed that _______ resulted in the development of capitalistic forms of economy and society.

(p. 489) 58. A _______ is a large number of people who form a relatively organized, self-sufficient, and self-enduring body.

Matching *(Answers are on page 508.)*

59. _______ Riot
60. _______ Casual crowd
61. _______ Resistance movement
62. _______ Revolutionary movement
63. _______ Reform movement

a. Forms and dissolves quickly
b. Folk-urban
c. When a mob becomes violently aggressive and destructive

64.	______	Society	d.	Creation of new things
65.	______	Invention	e.	Ku Klux Klan
66.	______	Linton	f.	*The Study of Man*
67.	______	Redfield	g.	Women's movement
68.	______	Diffusion	h.	Transfer of cultural elements
			i.	The most inclusive group
			j.	American Revolution

Essay Questions

1. What is collective behavior?
2. What are the determinants of collective behavior?
3. What are crowds?
4. What are publics?
5. What is a social movement?
6. What are the preconditions for a social movement?
7. What are the stages in the life cycle of a social movement?
8. What are the basic types of social movements?
9. What is a society?
10. What are the differences between a communal and an associational society?
11. How do societies change?
12. What is invention?
13. What is discovery?
14. What is diffusion?

Interactive Exercises

1. At one time or another in the past, you have been a part of a crowd. Identify a type of crowd in which you have participated. Which theory best explains the behavior that occurred in that crowd?
2. Given today's technological advances in communication, do you believe that there could be a reoccurrence of a "War of the Worlds" type of panic? Why or why not?
3. Briefly define "cultural lag," and give two examples of how it has had an effect on your current or future occupational or professional field.

Answers

Answers to Self-Test

1. c
2. d
3. d
4. a
5. c
6. b
7. c
8. a
9. d
10. d
11. d
12. a
13. d
14. d
15. a
16. c
17. d
18. b
19. a
20. d
21. T
22. T
23. T
24. F
25. F
26. F
27. T
28. T
29. F
30. T
31. T
32. T
33. T
34. F
35. F
36. T
37. T
38. F
39. F
40. F
41. crowd
42. mobs
43. riot
44. panic
45. public
46. propaganda
47. reform
48. utopian
49. migratory
50. expressive
51. urban
52. folk
53. urbanization
54. invention
55. diffusion
56. biological determinism
57. Protestantism
58. society
59. c
60. a
61. e
62. j
63. g
64. i
65. d
66. f
67. b
68. h

Answers to Chapter Pretest

1. F
2. F
3. F
4. T
5. F
6. T
7. F
8. F
9. F
10. F

References

Chapter 1

Baker, T. L. *Doing Social Research.* New York: McGraw-Hill, 1988, pp. 15–16.

Cohen, A. K. *Delinquent Boys.* New York: Free Press, 1955.

Comte, A. *The Positive Philosophy.* Harriet Martineau, trans. and ed. London: Bell, 1915.

Durkheim, E. *Suicide.* Translated by J. A. Spaulding and G. Simpson. New York: Free Press, 1951.

Hunt, M. *Profiles of Social Research: The Scientific Study of Human Interactions.* New York: Russell Sage Foundation, 1985, pp. 10–11.

Larsen, O. N. "Need for Continuing Support for Social Sciences," *ASA Footnotes,* vol. 9, no. 3, March 1981.

Liebow, E. *Tally's Corner: A Study of Negro Streetcorner Men.* Boston: Little, Brown, 1967.

Mills, C. W. *The Sociological Imagination.* New York: Oxford University Press, 1959.

Roethlisberger, F. J., and Dickson, W. J. *Management and the Worker.* Cambridge, Mass.: Harvard University Press, 1939.

Chapter 2

Benet, S. "Why They Live to Be 100 or Even Older, in Abkhasia." *New York Times Magazine,* December 26, 1971.

Chinoy, E. *Sociological Perspective.* New York: Random House, 1963.

Hall, E. T. "The Silent Language." *Américas,* vol. 14, 1962.

Homans, G. C. *The Human Group.* San Diego, Calif.: Harcourt, Brace, Jovanovich, 1950.

Kluckhohn, C. *Mirror for Man.* New York: McGraw-Hill, 1949.

Mead, M. *Sex and Temperament in Three Primitive Societies.* New York: Morrow, 1935.

Mechanic, D. "Promoting Health." *Society,* vol. 27, no. 2, January/February 1990, pp. 16–22.

Mills, T. M. *The Sociology of Small Groups.* Englewood Cliffs, N.J.: Prentice-Hall, 1967.

Miner, H. "Body Ritual Among the Nacirema." *American Anthropologist,* vol. 58, no. 3, 1956.

Murdock, G. P. "The Common Denominator of Cultures," In R. Linton (ed.), *The Science of Man in the World Crisis.* New York: Columbia University Press, 1945.

Sumner, W. G. *Folkways.* Boston: Ginn, 1940.

Tylor, E. *Primitive Culture.* London: J. Murray, 1871.

Yinger, J. M. "Contraculture and Subculture." *American Sociological Review,* vol. 25, 1960.

———. "Countercultures and Social Change." *American Sociological Review,* vol. 42, no. 6, December 1977.

Chapter 3

Cooley, C. H. *Human Nature and the Social Order.* New York: Scribner, 1922.

———. *Social Organization.* New York: Free Press of Glenco, 1956.

Davis, K. "Extreme Social Isolation of a Child." *American Journal of Sociology,* vol. 45, 1940.

———. "Final Note on a Case of Extreme Isolation." *American Journal of Sociology,* vol. 50, 1947.

Elkin, F., and Handel, G. *The Child and Society: The Process of Socialization.* New York: Random House, 1972.

Erikson, E. *Childhood and Society*, 2nd ed. New York: Norton, 1963.

Feldman, S. *The Rights of Women.* Rochelle Park, New Jersey: Hayden, 1974.

Freud, S. *An Outline of Psychoanalysis.* New York: Norton, 1963.

Goffman, E. *The Presentation of Self in Everyday Life.* Garden City, New York: Anchor Books, 1959.

Linton, R. *The Study of Man.* New York: Appleton Century Crofts, 1936.

McLoughlin, M., with T. L. Shryer, E. E. Goode, and K. McAuliffe. "Men Vs. Women." *U.S. News & World Report*, August 8, 1988.

Mead, G. H. *Mind, Self and Society.* Chicago: University of Chicago Press, 1934.

Mead, M. *Sex and Temperament in Three Primitive Societies.* New York: Morrow, 1935.

Montague, A. *The Natural Superiority of Women*, revised edition. New York: Macmillan, 1968.

Munson, H. "Teenage Violence and the Telly." *Psychology Today*, March 1978.

Neugarten, B. L. and Neugarten, D. A. "The Changing Meanings of Age." *Psychology Today*, May 1987.

Piaget, J. "Piaget's Theory." In P. H. Munson (ed.), *Carmichael's Manual of Child Psychology.* 3rd ed., vol. 1. New York: Wiley, 1970.

Shapiro, L. "Guns and Dolls." *Newsweek*, May 28, 1990.

Chapter 4

Blau, P. M. *Bureaucracy in Modern Society.* New York: Random House, 1956.

Cartwright, D., and Zander, A. *Group Dynamics: Research and Theory.* 3rd ed. New York: Harper & Row, 1968.

Cooley, C. H. *Human Nature and the Social Order.* New York: Scribner, 1922.

———. *Social Organization.* New York: Free Press of Glenco, 1956.

Darnton, N. "Mommy vs. Mommy." *Newsweek*, June 14, 1990.

Davis, K. *Human Society.* New York: Macmillan, 1949.

Dobriner, W. M. *Social Structures and Systems.* Pacific Palisades, Calif.: Goodyear, 1969.

Ehrenreich, B. "Strategies of Corporate Women." *The New Republic*, January 27, 1986.

Etzioni, A. *Modern Organizations.* Englewood Cliffs, N.J.: Prentice-Hall, 1964.

Hochschild, A. *The Second Shift: Inside the Two-Job Marriage.* New York: Viking, 1989.

Maslow, A. *Motivation and Personality.* New York: Harper & Row, 1964.

Merton, R. K. *Social Theory and Social Structure.* New York: Free Press, 1957.

National Opinion Research Center, General Social Surveys, 1978–1984. New York: New York Times, 1985.

Parsons, T. *Structure and Process in Modern Societies.* New York: Free Press, 1960.

Peter, K. and Hall, R. *The Peter Principle.* New York: Morrow, 1969.

Roethlisberger, F. J., and Dickson, W. J. *Management and the Worker.* Cambridge, Mass.: Harvard University Press, 1939.

Special Task Force to the Secretary of Health, Education, and Welfare. *Work in America.* Cambridge, Mass.: M.I.T. Press, 1980.

Weber, M. In *Max Weber: Essays in Sociology.* Edited and translated by H. H. Gerth and C. W. Mills. New York: Oxford University Press, 1964.

Chapter 5

Barlow, H. D. *Introduction to Criminology*, 5th ed. Glenview, Ill.: Scott Foresman/Little, Brown, 1990, p. 295.

Becker, H. S. *Outsiders: Studies in the Sociology of Deviance.* New York: Free Press, 1963.

Clinard, M. B. *The Sociology of Deviant Behavior*, 3rd ed. New York: Holt, Rinehart & Winston, 1968.

Clinard, M. B., and Meier, R. F. *The Sociology of Deviant Behavior*, 5th ed. New York: Holt, Rinehart, & Winston, 1979.

Cloward, R. A., and Ohlin, L. E. *Delinquency and Opportunity.* New York: Free Press, 1960.

Cohen, A. K. *Delinquent Boys.* New York: Free Press, 1955.

Diagnostic and Statistical Manual of Mental Disorders, 3rd ed., revised. American Psychiatric Association, 1987.

Durkheim, E. *Suicide.* Translated by J. A. Spaulding and G. Simpson. New York: Free Press, 1951.

Facts About Mental Illness. National Mental Health Association, 1979.

Facts on Alcoholism and Alcohol-Related Problems. National Council on Alcoholism, 1987.

Goode, E. *Deviant Behavior,* 2nd ed. Englewood Cliffs, N.J.: Prentice-Hall, 1984.

———. *Deviant Behavior,* 3rd ed. Englewood Cliffs, N.J.: Prentice-Hall, 1990, p. 107.

Gottfredson, M., and Hirschi, T. "Why We're Losing the War on Crime." *The Washington Post Magazine,* September 10, 1989.

"Ground Rules for Telling Lies." *Time,* April 3, 1978.

"Heroin Curb." *U.S. News & World Report,* January 14, 1985, p. 66.

Hurley, D. "Cycles of Craving." *Psychology Today,* July/August 1989, pp. 54–58.

Lindesmith, A. R., and Gagnon, J. H. "Anomie and Drug Addiction." In M. B. Clinard (ed.), *Anomie and Deviant Behavior: A Critique and Discussion.* New York: Free Press, 1964.

Mannle, H. W., and Hirschel, J. D. *Fundamentals of Criminology,* 2nd ed. Englewood Cliffs, N.J.: Prentice-Hall, 1988.

Merton, R. K. *Social Theory and Social Structure.* New York: Free Press, 1957.

National Institute on Drug Abuse. *Cocaine/Crack: The Big Lie.* DHHS Publication No. (ADM) 89-1427, 1989.

National Institute on Drug Abuse. *National Household Survey On Drug Abuse: Population Estimates 1988.* DHHS Publication No. (ADM) 89-1636, 1989.

Quinney, R. *Critique of the Legal Order.* Boston: Little, Brown, 1974.

———. "Crime Control in Capitalist Society." In *Critical Criminology,* Taylor, Walton, and Young (eds.). London: Routledge and Kegan Paul, 1975.

Regier, D. A., et al. "One-Month Prevalence of Mental Disorders in the United States." *Archives of General Psychiatry,* vol. 45, November 1988.

Scheff, T. J. "The Role of the Mentally Ill and the Dynamics of Mental Disorder." *Sociometry,* vol. 26, 1963.

———. *Being Mentally Ill.* Chicago: Aldine, 1966.

Siegel, L. J. *Criminology,* 3rd ed. St. Paul, Minn.: West, 1989.

Sutherland, E. H. *White Collar Crime.* New York: Holt, Rinehart & Winston, 1949.

Swanson, C. R., and Territo, L. "Computer Crime: Dimensions, Types, Causes, and Investigation." *Journal of Police Science and Administration,* vol. 8, no. 3, 1980, pp. 306–307.

Sykes, G. M., and Matza, D. "Techniques of Neutralization: A Theory of Delinquency." *American Sociological Review,* vol. 22, December 1957.

Uniform Crime Reports, 1989. Federal Bureau of Investigation, United States Department of Justice, August 1990.

United Nations Demographic Yearbook, 1987. United Nations, 1989.

Velocci, T. "Can Business Collar White-Collar Crime?" *Nation's Business,* November 1978.

Williams, G. D., et al. "Demographic Trends, Alcohol Abuse and Alcoholism, 1985–1995." *Alcohol Health and Research World,* vol. 11, no. 3, 1987, p. 80.

Yablonsky, L. "The Delinquent Gang as a Near Group." *Social Problems,* vol. 9, 1961.

Chapter 6

Beeghley, L. *Social Stratification in America: A Critical Analysis of Theory and Research.* Santa Monica, Calif.: Goodyear, 1978, pp. 1–91, 141–144.

Bendix, R., and Lipset, S. (eds.). *Class, Status, and Power.* New York: Free Press, 1957.

Coleman, R. P., and Neugarten, B. L. *Social Status in the City.* San Francisco: Jossey-Bass, 1971.

Coward, B., Feagin, J., and Williams, J. A., Jr. "The Culture of Poverty Debate: Some Additional Data." *Social Problems*, vol. 21, no. 5, June 1974, pp. 621–634.

Davis, K., and Moore, W. "Some Principles of Stratification." *American Sociological Review*, vol. 10, April 1945, pp. 242–249.

Fave, R. D., "The Culture of Poverty Revisited: A Strategy for Research." *Social Problems*, vol. 21, no. 5, June 1974.

Galbraith, J. K. *American Capitalism: The Concept of Countervailing Power.* Boston: Houghton Mifflin, 1956.

Gans, H. J. "The Uses of Poverty: the Poor Pay All." *Social Policy*, July–August 1971.

Gerth, H. H., and Mills, C. W. (eds.). *From Max Weber: Essays in Sociology.* New York: Oxford University Press, 1946, pp. 181–182.

Glazer, N. From "Why Isn't There More Equality?" *This World*, no. 6, Fall 1983. Copyright © 1983 This World.

Hodges, H. M., Jr. "Peninsula People: Social Stratification in a Metropolitan Complex." In W. C. Lane (ed.), *Permanence and Change in Social Class.* Cambridge, Mass.: Schenkman, 1961.

———. *Social Stratification.* Cambridge, Mass.: Schenkman, 1968.

Lenski, G. E. *Power and Privilege: A Theory of Social Stratification.* New York: McGraw-Hill, 1966.

Lewis, O. "The Culture of Poverty." In J. J. Tepaske and S. N. Fisher (eds.), *Explosive Forces in Latin America.* Columbus, Ohio: Ohio State University Press, 1964.

Lynd, R., and Lynd, H. *Middletown.* New York: Harcourt, Brace, 1929.

———. *Middletown in Transition.* New York: Harcourt, Brace, 1937.

Miller, S. M. "Comparative Social Mobility." In C. Heller (ed.), *Structural Social Inequality.* New York: Macmillan, 1969.

Mills, C. W. *The Power Elite.* New York: Oxford University Press, 1956.

Riesman, D., Glazer, N., and Denney, R. *The Lonely Crowd.* New Haven, Conn.: Yale University Press, 1950.

Rossides, D. W. *Social Stratification: The American Class System in Comparative Perspective.* Englewood Cliffs, N.J.: Prentice-Hall, 1990, pp. 405–416.

Tausky, C. *Work and Society: An Introduction to Industrial Sociology.* Itasca, Ill.: F. E. Peacock Publishers, 1984, pp. 115–117.

U.S. Bureau of the Census, Current Population Reports, Series P-60, No. 162. *Money Income of Households, Families, and Persons in the United States: 1987.* Washington, D.C.: U.S. Government Printing Office, 1989, pp. 10, 11, 42, 107–108.

U.S. Bureau of the Census, Current Population Reports, Series P-60, No. 166. *Money Income and Poverty Status in the United States: 1988 (Advance Data from the March 1989 Current Population Survey).* Washington, D.C.: U.S. Government Printing Office, 1989, pp. 5–9, 12, 57, 58, 60, 61, 68.

U.S. Bureau of the Census. *Statistical Abstract of the United States: 1990.* (110th ed.) Washington, D.C.: U.S. Government Printing Office, 1990, pp. 392, 451.

U.S. Department of Commerce, Bureau of the Census. *Social Indicators: 1976.* Washington, D.C.: U.S. Government Printing Office, 1977.

Valentine, C. *Culture and Poverty.* Chicago: University of Chicago Press, 1968, pp. 114–120.

Vanfossen, Beth E. *The Structure of Social Inequality.* Boston: Little, Brown, 1979, pp. 21–51, 355–372.

Warner, W. L., and Lunt, P. S. *The Social Life of a Modern Community.* New Haven, Conn.: Yale University Press, 1941.

Williams, R., "Some Further Comments on Chronic Controversies." *American Journal of Sociology*, vol. 71, 1966, pp. 717–721.

———. *American Society: a Sociological Interpretation*, 3rd ed. New York: Knopf, 1970.

Wright, J. D. "Address Unknown: Homelessness in Contemporary America." *Society*, vol. 26, no. 6, September/October 1989, pp. 45–53.

Chapter 7

Allport, G. *ABC's of Scapegoating.* New York: Anti-Defamation League of B'nai B'rith, 1948.

———. *The Nature of Prejudice.* Reading, Mass.: Addison-Wesley, 1954.

Blumer, H. "Race Prejudice as a Sense of Group Position." In J. Masuaka and P. Valien (eds.), *Race Relations.* Chapel Hill, N.C.: University of North Carolina Press, 1961.

Burlington County Times, Willingboro, N.J., April 5, 1990.

Cox, O. C. *Caste, Class and Race.* Garden City, N.Y.: Doubleday, 1948.

Daniels, R., and Kitano, H. H. L. *American Racism: Exploration of the Nature of Prejudice.* Englewood Cliffs, N.J.: Prentice-Hall, 1970.

Henry, W. A., III. "Beyond the Melting Pot." *Time,* April 9, 1990.

Kasschau, P. L. "Age and Race Discrimination Reported by Middle-Aged and Older Persons." *Social Forces,* vol. 3, March 1977, 728–742.

Killian, L. M. *White Southerners.* New York: Random House, 1970.

Layng, A. "What Keeps Women 'In Their Place'?" *USA Today,* May 1989.

Office of Technology Assessment (OTA), Washington, D.C. in *Philadelphia Inquirer,* December 25, 1985.

Payne, B., and Whittington, F. "Older Women: An Examination of Popular Stereotypes and Research Evidence." *Social Problems,* vol. 23, no. 4, April 1976, pp. 400–504.

Rose, P. I., *They and We.* New York: Random House, 1974.

The United Nations Decade for Women, 1976–1985: Employment in the United States. Report for the World Conference on the United Nations Decade for Women 1976–1985, Office of the Secretary, Women's Bureau, U.S. Department of Labor, Washington, D.C., July 1985.

U.S. Bureau of the Census. *Statistical Abstract of the United States: 1990.* (110th ed.) Washington, D.C.: U.S. Government Printing Office, 1990.

Vander Zanden, J. W. *American Minority Relations.* New York: Random House, 1982.

———. *Sociology: The Core.* New York: McGraw-Hill, 1990.

Writh, L. "The Problem of Minority Groups." In R. Linton (ed.), *The Science of Man in the World Crisis.* New York: Columbia University Press, 1945.

Wright, R. *Black Boy.* New York: Signet, 1945.

Chapter 8

Beals, R. L., and Hoijer, H. *An Introduction to Anthropology,* 4th ed. New York: Macmillan, 1971.

Beck, M., et al. "Trading Places." *Newsweek,* July 16, 1990.

Bumpass, L. L., Sweet, J. A., and Castro, T. "Why Separated Wives Are Slow to Remarry." Paper presented at the annual meeting of the American Sociological Society, Atlanta, August 28, 1988.

Burgess, E. W., Locke, H. J., and Thomas, M. M. *The Family,* 3rd ed. New York: American Book, 1963.

Clingempeel, G. In V. Jarmulowski, "The Blended Family: Who Are They?" *Ms. Magazine,* February 1985.

Eshleman, J. R. *The Family: an Introduction.* Boston: Allyn and Bacon, 1981, 1985.

Gallup, G., Jr. "What Americans Think about Their Lives and Families." In *Families,* vol. 2, no. 6, June 1982. Also "Good Family Life Tops Priority List." Gallup Poll, *San Francisco Chronicle,* February 27, 1989, p. B-6.

Gelles, R. J. "Child Abuse as Psychopathology: A Sociological Critique and Reformulation." In S. Steinmetz and M. A. Straus (eds.), *Violence in the Family.* New York: Dodd, Mead and Co., 1974.

Gill, D. G. *Violence Against Children.* Boston: Harvard University Press, 1970.

Glenn, N. D., and Weaver, C. N. "The Changing Relationship of Marital Status to Reported Happiness." *Journal of Marriage and the Family,* vol. 50, 1988, pp. 317–324.

Glick, L. *Focus on Sociology.* Riverton, N.J.: C-R Press, 1990.

Glick, P. C. "The Role of Divorce in the Changing Family Structure." In S. Wolchik and P.

Karoly (eds.), *Children of Divorce: Empirical Perspectives on Adjustment*. New York: Gilford Press, 1988.

———. "Remarried Families, Stepfamilies, and Stepchildren." *Family Relations*, vol. 38, 1989, pp. 24–27.

———. "American Families: As They Are and Were." *Sociology and Social Research*, vol. 74, no. 3, April 1990.

Glick, P. C., and Lin, S. L. "Recent Changes in Divorce and Remarriage." *Journal of Marriage and the Family*, vol. 48, 1987, pp. 737–747.

Goode, W. J. "Force and Violence in the Family." *Journal of Marriage and the Family*, vol. 33, November, 1971, pp. 624–636.

———. "Family Disorganization." In R. K. Merton and R. Nisbet (eds.), *Contemporary Social Problems*. San Diego, Calif.: Harcourt, Brace, Jovanovich, 1976.

Jarmulowski, V. "The Blended Family: Who Are They?" *Ms. Magazine*, February 1985.

Leavitt, J. E. *The Battered Child*. Morristown, N.J.: General Learning Press, 1974.

LeMasters, E. E. *Parents in Modern America: a Sociological Analysis*. Homewood, Ill.: Dorsey Press, 1970.

Morgan, S. P., Lye, D. N., and Condran, G. A. "Sons and Daughters and the Risk of Marital Disruption." *American Journal of Sociology*, vol. 94, 1988, pp. 110–129.

Murdock, G. P. *Social Structure*. New York: Macmillan, 1949.

———. "The Nuclear Family." In D. W. McCurdy and J. P. Spradley (eds.), *Issues in Cultural Anthropology*. Boston: Little, Brown, 1974.

Parsons, T. *Essays in Sociological Theory: Pure and Applied*. Cambridge, Mass.: Harvard University Press, 1958.

Pasley, K., and Tallman, M. In V. Jarmulowski, "The Blended Family: Who Are They?" *Ms. Magazine*, February 1985.

Rabbill, S. X. "A History of Child Abuse and Infanticide." In S. Steinmetz and M. A. Strauss, *Violence in the Family*. New York: Dodd, Mead, 1974.

Skolnick, A. *The Intimate Environment*, 2nd ed. Boston: Little, Brown, 1978.

Skolnick, A., and Skolnick, J. *Family in Transition*. Glenview, Ill.: Scott Foresman/Little, Brown, 1989.

Spanier, G. B., and Glick, P. C. "Marital Instability in the United States: Some Correlates and Recent Changes." *Family Relations*, vol. 31, 1981.

Steinmetz, S. and Strauss, M. A. *Violence in the Family*. New York: Dodd, Mead, 1974.

Thorton, A. "Cohabitation and Marriage in the 1980s." *Demography*, vol. 25, 1988, pp. 497–508.

Visher, E. In V. Jarmulowski, "The Blended Family: Who Are They?" *Ms. Magazine*, February 1985.

Wallerstein, J. In V. Jarmulowski, "The Blended Family: Who Are They?" *Ms. Magazine*, February 1985.

Zastrow, C. *Social Problems*. Chicago, Ill.: Nelson-Hall, 1988.

Chapter 9

Barron's. June 11, 1990.

Burlington County Times, Willingboro, N.J., September 27, 1990.

Centers for Disease Control. "Update: Acquired Immunodeficiency Syndrome (AIDS)—Worldwide." *Morbidity and Mortality Weekly*, vol. 37, 1988.

"Coolfont Report: A PHS Plan for Prevention and Control of AIDS and the AIDS Virus." *Public Health Reports*, vol. 101, 1986, pp. 341–348.

Durkheim, E. *The Elementary Forms of Religion*. Translated by J. W. Swain. London: George Allen and Unwin, 1915.

———. *Sociology and Education*. New York: Free Press, 1956.

Encyclopedia of Society. Guilford, Conn.: Dushkin Publishing Group, 1974.

Gallup Poll, *New York Times*, March 11, 1984.

Gibbs, N. "Love and Let Die." *Time*, March 19, 1990, pp. 62–71.

Glick, L., and Hebding, D. *Introduction to Social Problems*. Reading, Mass.: Addison-Wesley, 1980.

Johnson, E. *Social Problems of Urban Man*. Homewood, Ill.: Dorsey, 1973, pp. 450–460.

Mantell, J. E., Schulman, L. C., Belmont, M. F., and Spivak, H. B. "Social Workers Respond to the AIDS Epidemic at an Acute Care Hospital." *Health and Social Work*, February 1989, pp. 41–51.

McKinlay, J. B., and McKinlay, S. M. "Medical Measures and the Decline of Mortality." In Howard D. Schwartz (ed.), *Dominant Issues in Medical Sociology*, 2nd ed. New York: Random House, 1987, pp. 691–702.

Moss, A. R., Bacchetti, P., Osmond, D., Krampf, N., Chaisson, R. E., Stites, D., Wilber, J., Allain, J. P., and Carlson, J. "Seropositivity for HIV and the Development of AIDS or AIDS-Related Condition: Three-year Follow-up of the San Francisco General Hospital Cohort." *British Medical Journal*, vol. 296, 1988, pp. 745–750.

National Center for Educational Statistics. Washington, D.C.: U.S. Government Printing Office, 1984, 1990.

O'Dea, T. *The Sociology of Religion*. Englewood Cliffs, N.J.: Prentice-Hall, 1960.

Philadelphia Inquirer, Philadelphia, Penn., January 6, 1991.

Piccigallo, P. R. "Thinking Globally: Educating Americans for the 21st Century." *USA Today*, November 1989, pp. 29–31.

Safyer, A. W., and Spies-Karotkin, G. "The Biology of AIDS." *Health and Social Work*, Fall 1988, pp. 251–258.

Skolnick, J. H., and Currie, E. *Crisis in American Institutions*. Boston: Little, Brown, 1985.

Stephenson, D. G., Jr. "Religion and the Constitution." *USA Today*, March 1990, pp. 21–23.

Timascheff, N. S. *Sociological Theory*. Random House, 1977.

Time, May 22, 1989.

U.S. Bureau of the Census. *Statistical Abstract of the United States: 1990*. (110th ed.) Washington, D.C.: U.S. Government Printing Office, 1990.

USA Today, March 1990.

Vine, M. W. *An Introduction to Sociological Theory*. New York: David McKay, 1959.

Weber, M. *The Protestant Ethic and the Spirit of Capitalism*. Translated by T. Parsons. New York: Free Press, 1958.

Williams, R. M., Jr. *American Society: A Sociological Interpretation*. New York: Knopf, 1970.

Chapter 10

Bensman, J., and Rosenberg, B. *Mass, Class, and Bureaucracy: The Evolution of Contemporary Society*. Englewood Cliffs, N.J.: Prentice-Hall, 1963.

Cascio, W. F., and Zammuto, R. F. *Societal Trends and Staffing Policies*. Denver: University of Colorado Press, 1987.

Fullerton, H. N., Jr. "The 1995 Labor Force: BLS' Latest Projections." *Monthly Labor Review*, vol. 117, 1985, pp. 17–25.

Galbraith, J. K. *American Capitalism: The Concept of Countervailing Power*. Boston: Houghton Mifflin, 1971.

Goldstein, I. L., and Gilliam, P. "Training System Issues in the Year 2000." *The American Psychologist*, February 1990, pp. 134–143.

Halal, W. E. "The New Capitalism." From *The Futurist*, January/February 1988, pp. 26–30.

Klein, K. J., and Hall, R. J. "Innovations in Human Resource Management: Strategies for the Future." In J. Hage (ed.), *Future of Organizations*. Lexington, Mass.: Lexington, 1988.

Magstadt, T. M., and Schotten, P. M. *Understanding Politics, Ideas, Institutions, and Issues*, 2nd ed. New York: St. Martins Press, 1988.

Personick, V. A. "A Second Look at Industry Output and Employment Trends Through 1995." *Monthly Labor Review*, Nov. 1985, pp. 26–41.

Skolnick, J. H., and Currie, E. *Crisis in American Institutions*. Boston: Little, Brown, 1985.

Weber, M. *The Protestant Ethic and the Spirit of Capitalism*. Translated by T. Parsons. New York: Free Press, 1958.

Williams, R. M., Jr. *American Society: A Sociological Interpretation*. New York: Knopf, 1970.

Yardeni, E., and Moss, D. "New Wave Economics: Trends for the 21st Century." *USA Today*, January 1990, pp. 68–70.

Chapter 11

Bouvier, L. F., Shryock, H. S., and Henderson, H. W. "International Migration: Yesterday, Today, and Tomorrow." Population Reference Bureau, *Population Bulletin*, vol. 32, no. 4, August 1, 1979.

Brown, L. R. (1989). "Feeding Six Billion." In Robert M. Jackson (ed.), *Global Issues 90/91 Annual Editions Series*. Guilford, Conn.: The Dushkin Publishing Group, Inc., 1990, p. 84.

———. (1984). "Putting Food on the World's Table." In LeRoy Barnes (ed.), *Social Problems 85/86 Annual Editions Series*. Guilford, Conn.: The Dushkin Publishing Group, Inc., 1985, p. 219.

Brown, L. R. and Wolf, E. (1984). "Food Crisis in Africa." In Robert M. Jackson (ed.), *Global Issues 85/86 Annual Editions Series*. Guilford, Conn.: The Dushkin Publishing Group, Inc., 1985, p. 103.

"Costs and Benefits: Fresh Questions About Clean Air." *U.S. News & World Report*, July 30, 1990, p. 40.

Dasmann, R. F. *Environmental Conservation*, 4th ed. New York: Wiley, 1976, p. 6.

Davis, K. "The World's Population Crisis." In R. K. Merton and R. Nisbet (eds.), *Contemporary Social Problems*, 4th ed. New York: Harcourt Brace Jovanovich, 1976.

Davis, K., and Blake, J. "Social Structure and Fertility: An Analytic Framework." *Economic Development and Cultural Change*, vol. 4, 1956, pp. 211–235.

"Doing Your Bit to Save the Earth." *U.S. News & World Report*, April 2, 1990, p. 63.

"Forecast: Clearer Skies." *Time*, November 5, 1990, p. 33.

The Global Tomorrow Coalition. *The Global Ecology Handbook: What You Can Do about the Environmental Crisis*. Walter H. Corson (ed.). Boston: Beacon Press, 1990, pp. 31, 164, 165, 176, 180, 192, 194, 195, 220, 223, 224, 226, 230.

"Greenhouse Redesign." *U.S. News & World Report*, June 18, 1990, p. 47.

Heer, D. *Society and Population*, 2nd ed. Englewood Cliffs, N.J.: Prentice-Hall, 1975, pp. 13, 19, 68–69, 107.

"'Human Element,' not Drought Causes Famine." *U.S. News & World Report*, February 25, 1985, p. 71.

Matras, J. *Populations and Societies*. Englewood Cliffs, N.J.: Prentice-Hall, 1973.

Meadows, D. H., et al. *The Limits to Growth*, 2nd ed. New York: Universe Books, 1974.

Miller, G. T., Jr. *Living in the Environment: An Introduction to Environmental Science*, 6th ed. Belmont, Calif.: Wadsworth Publishing Company, 1990, pp. 20, 21, 414, 415, 498, 522–526, 547, A39.

National Center for Health Statistics. *Vital Statistics of the United States, 1987*, vol. II, sec. 6, life tables. Washington, D.C.: Public Health Service, 1990, pp. 6, 7, 9.

Nortman, D. L. *Population and Family Planning Programs: A Compendium of Data Through 1983*, 12th ed. New York: The Population Council, 1985.

Nortman, D. L., and Fisher, J. *Population and Family Planning Programs: A Compendium of Data Through 1981*, 11th ed. New York: The Population Council, 1982.

"People, People, People." *Time*, August 6, 1984, pp. 24, 25.

Population Reference Bureau. "U.S. Population: Where We Are; Where We're Going." *Population Bulletin*, vol. 37, no. 2. Washington, D.C.: 1982, pp. 28–29.

———. *1990 World Population Data Sheet*. Washington, D.C.: April 1990.

"Roots of Africa's Famine Run Deep." *U.S. News & World Report*, December 3, 1984, p. 32.

Salas, R. M. "Cities Without Limits," *The Unesco Courier*, January 1987, pp. 10–13, 16–17.

Simon, J. L. (1981). "People Are the Ultimate Resource." In Kurt Finsterbusch and George McKenna (eds.), *Taking Sides*, 3rd ed. Guilford, Conn.: The Dushkin Publishing Group, 1984.

"Ten Top Cities Now and in 2000." *U.S. News & World Report*, January 9, 1984.

"The U.S.: No Water to Waste." *Time*, August 20, 1990, p. 61.

"The World's Urban Explosion." *The Unesco Courier*, March 1985.

"The 50 Biggest Metro Areas Now." *U.S. News & World Report*, May 14, 1984, p. 16.

Thomlinson, R. *Population Dynamics*. New York: Random House, 1965.

U.S. Bureau of the Census, Current Population Reports, Series P-23, No. 159. *Population Profile of the United States: 1989.* Washington, D.C.: U.S. Government Printing Office, 1989, pp. 1, 2, 8, 12, 13.

U.S. Bureau of the Census, Current Population Reports, Series P-25, No. 1017. *Projections of the Population of States, by Age, Sex, and Race: 1988 to 2010.* Washington, D.C.: U.S. Government Printing Office, 1988, pp. 2, 3.

U.S. Bureau of the Census, Current Population Reports, Series P-25, No. 1018. *Projections of the Population of the United States, by Age, Sex, and Race: 1988 to 2080.* Gregory Spencer. Washington, D.C.: U.S. Government Printing Office, 1989, pp. 3, 4, 6, 7, 8.

U.S. Bureau of the Census, Current Population Reports, Series P-25, No. 1039. *Patterns of the Metropolitan Area and County Population Growth: 1980 to 1987.* Washington, D.C.: U.S. Government Printing Office, 1989, pp. 2, 18, 19.

U.S. Bureau of the Census, Current Population Reports, Series P-25, No. 1057. *U.S. Population Estimates, by Age, Sex, Race, and Hispanic Origin: 1989.* Washington, D.C.: U.S. Government Printing Office, 1990, pp. 1, 2, 3, 4.

U.S. Bureau of the Census. *Statistical Abstract of the United States: 1990.* (110th ed.) Washington, D.C.: U.S. Government Printing Office, 1990, p. 203.

U.S. Environmental Protection Agency. *Characterization of Municipal Solid Waste in the United States: 1990 Update.* June 1990, pp. ES-1–ES-15, 55, 74.

U.S. Environmental Protection Agency. *National Air Quality and Emissions Trends Report, 1988.* March 1990, pp. 2–7, 12, 13.

U.S. Environmental Protection Agency. *The Quality of Our Nation's Water.* May 1990, pp. 9, 11, 18.

van der Tak, J., Haub, C. H., and Murphy, E. "A New Look At the Population Problem." In Kurt Finsterbusch (ed.), *Sociology 85/86 Annual Editions Series.* Guilford, Conn.: The Dushkin Publishing Group, Inc., 1985, pp. 191–192, 195.

Weeks, John R. *Population: An Introduction to Concepts and Issues*, 2nd ed. Belmont, Calif.: Wadsworth, 1981.

Weidenbaum, Murray. "Protecting the Environment." *Society*, vol. 27, no. 1, November/December 1989, pp. 49–56.

Weller, R., and Bouvier, L. F., *Population Demography and Policy*. New York: St. Martin's Press, 1981.

Yaukey, D. *Demography: The Study of Human Population.* New York: St. Martin's Press, 1985.

Chapter 12

Allport, G., and Postman, L. *The Psychology of Rumor*. New York: Russell and Russell, 1965.

Blumer, H. "Collective Behavior." In A. M. Lee (ed.), *Principles of Sociology*. New York: Barnes and Noble, 1969.

———. "Outline of Collective Behavior." In R. E. Evans (ed.), *Readings in Collective Behavior*, 2nd ed. Chicago: Rand McNally, 1975.

Chicago Commission on Race Relations. *The Negro in Chicago: A Study of Race Relations and a Race Riot*. Chicago, 1922.

Chinoy, E. *Sociological Perspective*. New York: Random House, 1963.

Dobriner, W. M. *Social Structures and Systems.* Pacific Palisades, Calif.: Goodyear, 1969.

Friedan, B. *The Feminine Mystique.* New York: Dell, 1963.

Hughes, H. M. *Crowds and Mass Behavior.* Boston: Holbrook Press, 1972.

Killian, L. M. "Social Movements." In R. Faris (ed.), *Handbook of Modern Sociology.* Chicago: Rand McNally, 1964.

Lang, G. E. "Sociologists Look at Crowds and Mass Behavior." In H. M. Hughes (ed.), *Crowds and Mass Behavior.* Boston: Holbrook Press, 1972.

Lang, J. S. "The Great American Bureaucratic Propaganda Machine." *U.S. News & World Report,* August 27, 1979.

Le Bon, G. *The Crowd: A Study of the Popular Mind.* New York: Viking, 1960.

Lee, A. M. C., and Lee, E. B. *The Fine Art of Propaganda.* New York: Octagon Books, 1967.

Linton, R. *The Study of Man.* New York: Appleton Century Crofts, 1936 (renewed 1964).

Marx, K. *Selected Writings in Sociology and Social Philosophy.* T. B. Bottomore and M. Rubel (eds.). Baltimore: Penguin Books, 1964. Originally published in 1848.

Marx, K., and Engels, F. *The Communist Manifesto.* Baltimore: Penguin Books, 1969. Originally published in 1848.

McLoughlin, M. "America's New Civil War." *U.S. News & World Report,* October 3, 1988, pp. 23–25, 27–30.

Naisbitt, J. "The Bottom-Up Society: America Between Eras," *Public Opinion,* April/May, 1981.

Ogburn, W. F. *The Social Effects of Aviation.* Boston: Houghton Mifflin, 1946. *Social Change with Respect to Culture and Original Nature.* (Rev. ed.) New York: Viking Press, 1950.

Rogers, E. M., and Shoemaker, E. F. *Communication of Innovations: A Cross-Cultural Approach.* 2nd ed. New York: Free Press, 1971.

Redfield, R. "The Folk Society." *American Journal of Sociology,* vol. 52, 1947.

Smelser, N. J. *The Theory of Collective Behavior.* New York: Free Press, 1963.

Stockdale, J. D. "Structured Preconditions for Collective Action." Paper presented at the Society for the Study of Social Problems, Washington, D.C., 1970.

Tönnies, F. *Community and Society.* Translated and edited by C. P. Loomis. East Lansing, Mich.: Michigan State University Press, 1957.

Turner, R. H. "Collective Behavior." In R. Faris (ed.), *Handbook of Modern Sociology.* Chicago: Rand McNally, 1964.

Turner, R. H., and Killian, L. M. *Collective Behavior.* Englewood Cliffs, N.J.: Prentice-Hall, 1972.

Vander Zanden, J. W. "Resistance and Social Movements," *Social Forces,* vol. 37, 1959.

———. *Sociology: A Systematic Approach.* New York: Ronald Press, 1990.

Wallis, Claudia. "Onward, Women!" *Time,* December 4, 1989, pp. 80–89.

Weber, M. *The Protestant Ethic and the Spirit of Capitalism.* Translated by T. Parsons. New York: Free Press, 1958.

Glossary

Acceptance (Vander Zanden) Minority group members may come to acquiesce to their disadvantaged and subordinate status.

Achieved status or role A status or role attained through individual efforts, action, or accomplishment.

Aggregate A set of individuals who happen to be in the same place at the same time.

Aggression When minority group members respond to dominance by striking out against a status that is subordinate and disadvantaged.

Agism The system of social, economic, political, and psychological pressures that suppress groups because they exhibit the biologically determined characteristics of old age.

AIDS Acquired immune deficiency syndrome.

Altruistic suicide That which results from excessive integration into a group or society to the point at which the person would willingly give his or her life if group values and norms so required.

Anomic suicide That which results from a breakdown or weakening of the values and norms of the group or of society itself.

Anomie (Merton) A state of disjunction or lack of integration between cultural goals and the availability of legitimate means for attaining these goals.

Applied science An orientation that incorporates the use of scientific knowledge to solve some sort of practical question or problem.

Ascribed status or role A status or role assigned to an individual at birth. It is based on factors beyond the individual's control.

Assimilation (Vander Zanden) Minority group members may attempt to become socially and culturally fused with the dominant group.

Assimilationist minority A minority that desires to be absorbed into the dominant group.

Association A social group characterized by its own administrative structure and organized to pursue the common interest of its members.

Associational society A heterogeneous society in which secondary relationships constitute a high proportion of relations and where there is a complex division of labor and a proliferation of social roles.

Avoidance (Vander Zanden) Minority group members may attempt to shun situations in which they are likely to experience prejudice and discrimination.

Beliefs Ideas that people hold about the universe or any part of the total reality surrounding them.

Bilineal system A system of descent and inheritance whereby property passes through both the male and female sides of the family.

Blended family Stepfamilies have been renamed blended families.

Bourgeoisie The capitalist class that owned productive property such as land, factories, and machinery.

Bureaucracy A hierarchical pyramid of officials who rationally conduct the work of a large organization.

Capitalism An economic system that is based on private ownership of the means of production and on competition for profits.

Career (Weber) A promotion system based on merit, seniority, or both, so that officials typically anticipate a lifelong career in the organization.

Caste A particular level found within the caste system of stratification.

Caste system A form of stratification based exclusively on factors of birth.

Category A collection of people with similar characteristics but with *no* common identity, understanding of membership, and *no* involvement in patterned social interaction.

Child abuse The intentional use of violence toward, or the intentional neglect of, children on the part of parents or other caretakers.

Children of divorce The children living in one parent families that have been broken by divorce.

Chronic alcoholic The most serious type of excessive drinker. The term applies to those who have lost total control over their drinking to the point where they cannot function and/or maintain stable relationships with others.

Class (Marx) Those holding similar productive positions.

Class (Weber) Those who possess similar economic standing in the society based on ownership or nonownership of property and similar wealth and incomes.

Cognition (Piaget) The use of thinking and language that develops in stages.

Collective behavior Social behavior that is relatively spontaneous, transitory, emotional, and somewhat unpredictable.

Commune An alternative to the nuclear family, in which a group of people live together and share family functions.

Communal society (see *Folk society*)

Competition The basic form of social interaction, according to conflict theorists.

Conflict A product of social interaction and an effort that is directed toward resolving a decision-making impasse.

Conflict subculture (Cloward and Ohlin) A subculture composed of delinquents who achieve status through acts of violence or force.

Conflict theory The theoretical perspective that sees competition and social conflict as forming the basis of group and social life.

Conflict theory (of deviance) A theory that stresses the importance of power and political processes in both defining and controlling deviant behavior.

Contagion A process whereby crowd members stimulate and respond to one another and constantly increase their responsiveness and emotional intensity.

Continued subjugation When a dominant group wants neither to incorporate the minority nor to drive it out, but wants to keep it around in a servile, exploitable state.

Control group The group that receives no stimulus in an experiment.

Controlled experiment A method of data collection involving an experimental group and a control group. The experimental group receives the stimulus and the control group does not.

Cooperation The interaction among individuals or groups to achieve shared goals or promote common interests.

Counterculture A subculture having values and norms that sharply contradict the dominant values and norms of the larger society.

Crime The violation of specific types of norms called laws.

Criminal subculture (Cloward and Ohlin) A subculture composed of delinquent youth who typically engage in robbery, fraud, and theft.

Crowd A temporary grouping or collection of people who have a common focus or interest. There are four types of crowds: casual, conventionalized, expressive, and acting.

Crude birthrate The annual number of births per thousand members of the population.

Crude death rate The annual number of deaths per thousand members of the population.

Cultural lag The time lag between the adoption of an innovation and the accomplishment of cultural adjustments made necessary by the innovation.

Cultural relativism The idea that each culture should be evaluated from the standpoint of its own setting.

Cultural universals Similar or common elements that are found within every culture.

Cultural variation The wide differences and diversity of "ways of living" both within and between cultures.

Culture (explicit) Those aspects of culture that people are aware of and consciously recognize.

Culture (implicit) Those aspects of culture that are unrecognized by people but that give direction to behavior.

Culture (Tylor) That complex whole which includes knowledge, beliefs, art, morals, law, custom, and any other capabilities and habits acquired by humans as members of society.

Culture of poverty A perspective of poverty stressing the idea that the different social strata manifest cultures distinctive of those various strata and that the values of the poor are substantially different from the values of those in the mainstream of society.

Delinquency The violation of laws on the part of people eighteen years of age and younger.

Delinquent subculture (Cohen) The subculture of working class boys who manifest a "delinquent response." Cohen sees the delinquent subculture as malicious, nonutilitarian, and negativistic.

Demographic transition theory A theory that examines the impact of industrial and economic development on population growth. According to this theory, a drop in a society's death rate inevitably is followed by a voluntary decline in its birthrate.

Demography The scientific study of human populations.

Dependency ratio The ratio of people of dependent ages to people of economically productive ages.

Desertion The permanent departure from the family of either husband or wife, against the other's will.

Deviant behavior Behavior that does not conform to norms or that does not meet with the expectations of a group or society. More specifically, it refers only to those deviations in which behavior is in a disapproved direction and of sufficient degree to exceed the tolerance limit of the community.

Diffusion The transfer of cultural elements from one society to another.

Discovery The perception of previously unrecognized relationships between elements of a culture.

Discrimination An act or actual response whereby members of a particular group are accorded negative treatment on the basis of a certain characteristic or combination of traits, such as sex or race.

Divorce Dissolution of a marriage by law.

Ecology The study of the interrelationships between living organisms and their environment.

Economic institution That social structure or structures related to the production and distribution of goods and services.

Ecosystems Communities of plants, animals, and microorganisms along with the air, water, soil, or other substrate that supports them.

Ectomorph (Sheldon) A person with a tall, lean, and flat-chested body type.

Ego (Freud) That segment of the personality that is conscious and rational. It acts as a mediator between the demands of the *id* (biological needs) and the *superego* (demands of society).

Egoistic suicide That which results from a lack of full participation in group life together with the emotional attachments and supports that participation entails.

Endogamy A method for selecting marriage partners from within one's own specific group.

Endomorph (Sheldon) A person with a predominantly soft, round, and heavy-set body type.

Equal Rights Amendment (ERA) A defeated amendment to the U.S. Constitution. Its major focus was the removal of all employment inequities based on sex.

Equalitarian or egalitarian family A family authority pattern whereby authority is equally balanced between husband and wife.

Estates system A stratification system characteristic of feudal Europe.

Ethnic group A group whose members share a unique social and cultural heritage passed on from one generation to the next. Members are identified by distinctive patterns of family life, language, religion, and other customs that cause them to be differentiated from others.

Ethnocentrism The tendency to feel that one's own culture is superior, right, and natural, and that all other cultures are inferior and often wrong and unnatural.

Exogamy A method for selecting a marriage partner from outside of one's own specific group.

Experimental group The group receiving the stimulus in an experiment.

Exponential growth A geometric progression in population growth (2, 4, 8, 16, 32, 64, . . .).

Extended family A family consisting of several generations of blood relatives.

Extermination (Allport) Lynchings, pogroms, and massacres marking the ultimate expression of prejudice to eradicate a racial or ethnic group.

Family A socially sanctioned, relatively permanent grouping of people united by blood, marriage, or adoption ties who generally live together and cooperate economically.

Felony A serious crime such as criminal homicide, rape, or robbery.

Fertility The number of children born to women of childbearing age, usually between the ages of fifteen to forty-five years.

Field experiments Experiments conducted away from the laboratory in more natural social settings.

Folk society A small, homogeneous, often nonliterate society characterized by a high degree of group solidarity, a simple division of labor, informal social control, and traditionalism.

Folkways Rules of conduct that are felt to be "appropriate" but that are not seen as vital to the welfare or survival of the group.

Formal demography The area of demography that analyzes the relationships between the composition or structure of a population and population change.

Formal organizations Organizations that have been formally established for the explicit purpose of achieving certain goals.

Functionalism The theoretical perspective that considers society to be a system of interrelated parts, each fulfilling a particular purpose in helping to maintain the total social system.

Gemeinschaft A society or community based on traditional relationships.

Generalized other (G. H. Mead) The attitude of the entire community or organized social group whose judgments people apply to their own behavior in forming their concept of self.

Gesellschaft A society or community based on contractual rather than traditional relationships.

Group Two or more people who come into contact for a purpose and who consider the contact meaningful.

Group marriage A marriage pattern in which sets of women and men enjoy more or less equal conjugal rights with each other.

Hawthorne effect The effect of the experimental situation itself on the subjects.

Health (World Health Organization) A state of complete mental and physical well-being.

Health-care delivery The providing of health-care services.

Health-care institution The pattern of norms centered about health-care goals, values, and needs.

Health status Health conditions of people.

Heterogeneous society A society containing many different types of groups and categories of people.

Hierarchy A hierarchical authority structure, with the scope of each individual's responsibility clearly defined.

Homogamy A term used to describe mate selection among people who share similar characteristics. It means that people marry others like themselves.

Horizontal mobility A change in one's social or economic position so small as to not significantly affect one's general position in the stratification system.

Hypergamy Marriage of a female into a higher social class.

Hypogamy Marriage of a female into a lower social class.

Hypothesis A tentative statement capable of being tested by the scientific method.

I (G. H. Mead) The unsocialized, impulsive, and creative part of the self.

Id (Freud) The segment of the personality consisting only of primitive impulses and unconscious drives.

Ideal types Conceptual models that are useful in analyzing various social phenomena.

Impersonality (Weber) An impersonal orientation by the officials toward their clients, who are treated as "cases."

Incest taboo The prohibition of sexual relations between members of a family.

Informal group A group within which the members' social as well as personal relations are not prescribed or defined by the formal organization.

Innovation (Merton) Rejection of legitimate means and the use of illegitimate means to get to legitimate goals or ends.

Instinct A complex, genetically inherited pattern of behavior that is universal for all members of a species.

Institution A pattern of norms centered around a major goal, value, or need for society.

Integration (Rose) The minority rejects the idea that it is inferior.

Intergenerational mobility Mobility between parents and children usually based on occupational differences between generations.

Internal migration The movement of people from one area within a nation to another area within the same nation.

International migration The movement of people from one nation to another.

Invention The combination of known devices or elements into new form.

Kin Persons related by birth or marriage.

Labeling theory Theory that analyzes the social definitions of deviance and the social reactions and consequences of such for those persons identified as deviant.

Language A highly intricate set of symbols that is made by humans.

Laws "Formal" norms; written or codified standards.

Learning theory A theory that sees deviant behavior as learned or acquired through one's interactions with others.

Legal protection Protecting minority groups by legal, constitutional, or diplomatic means.

Life chances The chances of a person to fulfill or not fulfill his or her potential and abilities as a member of society.

Looking glass self (Cooley) Perception of the self that an individual forms by interpreting the reactions of others to him or her.

Macrosociology Level of sociological analysis that studies the broad structure, organization, and features of society.

Marriage (Murdock) A complex set of customs centering upon the relationship between a sexually associating pair of adults within the family.

Material culture The material objects that people produce and use.

Matriarchy A family authority pattern whereby the authority is vested primarily in the wife.

Matrilineal system A system of descent and inheritance whereby property passes through the female side of the family.

Matrilocal residence When a newly married couple move in with the wife's parents.

Me (G. H. Mead) The socialized or conventional part of the self.

Megalopolis A set of interrelated, adjacent metropolitan areas.

Mental disorder From a psychiatric point of view, a disorder labeled *neurosis* or *psychosis*.

Mesomorph (Sheldon) A person with a predominantly heavy-chested, muscular, and athletic body type. Sheldon felt that mesomorphic persons were the most prone to crime and delinquency.

Metropolitan area An area made up of one or more central cities, their suburbs, and surrounding related areas.

Microsociology Level of sociological analysis that studies how people behave and interact in everyday social settings.

Migration The movement of people from one place to another.

Militant minority A minority that desires and demands domination over others.

Milling A spontaneous, elementary, collective mechanism whereby people move among one another in a somewhat aimless fashion.

Minority group Any culturally or physically distinctive, self-conscious social aggregate that is subject to political, economic, or social discrimination by a dominant segment of a surrounding political society.

Misdemeanors Relatively minor types of crime, such as petty theft, disorderly conduct, and vagrancy.

Mob A crowd that is emotionally charged and oriented toward violence.

Modified extended family When a relative other than a parent, such as an aunt, uncle, or grandparent, moves into the household of a nuclear family.

Monogamy The marriage of one male and one female.

Mores Norms that are highly respected and valued by the group. Their fulfillment is felt to be necessary and vital to group welfare.

Mortality The incidence of death within a human population.

Neolocal residence When a newly married couple live in their own residence.

Nonmaterial culture That part of culture consisting of various elements such as norms, values, beliefs, and language.

Norm (ideal) A standard of expected behavior.

Norm (statistical) A mathematical average; what is most frequently or typically done.

Nuclear family A family consisting of a wife and husband plus their children.

Objectivity The ability and willingness to make observations and draw conclusions without personal bias, preconceptions, or personal feelings.

Observation (detached) Form of observation in which the researcher remains "outside" the group under study and records his or her observations in a precise, systematic, and controlled way.

Observation (participant) Form of observation in which the researcher joins and participates in the group being studied.

Office (Weber) A clear-cut division of labor among the individual officials.

One parent family A family that was originally intact, with parents married to each other, but has been broken by divorce, desertion, separation, or death.

Open class system A stratification system of high upward and downward mobility that is based on individual effort and achievement rather than factors relating to birth.

Organizations Human groupings or social units that are deliberately constructed and reconstructed to meet specific goals.

Panic The sudden overwhelming of a crowd of people by great fear which leads them to irrational action.

Patriarchy A family authority pattern in which the authority is vested primarily in the husband.

Patrilineal system A system of descent and inheritance whereby property passes through the male side of the family.

Patrilocal residence When a newly married couple move in with the husband's parents.

Peer group (child's) All the groups of children of similar age in which the child participates.

Personality The organization of attitudes, beliefs, habits, and behavior, in addition to other characteristics that are developed through interaction with others.

Pluralistic minority A minority that desires a peaceful side-by-side existence with the dominant group.

Political institution The social institution that determines when, how, and who should gain power.

Polyandry The marriage of one woman to two or more men.

Polygamous family A type of family organization that is formed by the marriage of one woman to two or more men or the marriage of one man to two or more women.

Polygamy Marriage between one person of one sex and a minimum of two persons of the other sex.

Polygyny The marriage of one man to two or more women.

Population (survey research) A large category of people from which a sample is selected.

Population composition The way in which various characteristics, such as age, sex, marital status, ethnic characteristics, and occupational status, are distributed throughout a population.

Population studies The area of demography that examines the social, economic, and cultural causes and consequences of population change and structure.

Positivism A method of study advocated by Auguste Comte that emphasizes the techniques of observation, comparison, and experimentation in developing knowledge.

Power (Weber) The chance for people to realize their own will even against the resistance of others.

Power elite (Mills) Those individuals who hold a monopoly of corporate, military, and political power within a society.

Prejudice An emotional, rigid attitude, belief, or predisposition to respond in a certain way to a group of people.

Primary group A small group characterized by intimate, intrinsically valued relationships that involve many aspects of an individual's life experiences.

Primary relationship A relationship that is emotional, informal, and unspecialized and that involves the whole personality of the individual participants.

Probability The likelihood that certain things will be found to exist or occur given the presence of other things.

Proletariat The workers who constitute the exploited laboring class.

Propaganda The deliberate use of communication to influence and persuade individuals to favor one predetermined way of thinking or acting over another.

Public A scattered number of people who have a common interest in a given topic. Also, a collection of people who are concerned about, divided upon, and engaged in discussion about an issue.

Public opinion The opinions and attitudes about an issue held by a public.

Pure science An orientation that incorporates the idea of acquiring knowledge for the purpose of understanding more adequately the subject matter within its field of inquiry.

Race (biological definition) Populations differing in the incidence of certain genes.

Race (social definition) A group of people who identify themselves or are identified by others as being different from other groups on the basis of physical characteristics.

Racism A system of social, economic, political, and psychological activities and pressures that suppresses groups because they exhibit biologically determined racial characteristics.

Random sample One in which people are selected at random from the entire population, with each individual having an equal chance of being picked.

Rate of diffusion Rate of transfer of cultural elements from one society to another.

Rate of natural increase A demographic measure determined by subtracting the crude death rate of a population from the crude birthrate.

Rebellion (Merton) Rejection of either goals or means coupled with the attempt to substitute new ones for the society.

Reference group Any group that an individual takes into account when evaluating his or her own behavior and self-concept.

Reform movement A social movement that attempts to modify parts of the society and effect change in many areas of social life.

Religion (Durkheim) A system of beliefs and practices relating to sacred things.

Replacement level fertility The point where children are born in numbers sufficient to replace but not to exceed the number of parents.

Residual rule breaking Varieties of deviance for which the group has no specific labels and thus become packaged under the broad category of mental disorder.

Resistance movement A social movement that develops because people are dissatisfied with the fast pace of social change.

Retreatism (Merton) The total withdrawal from goals as well as means to goals.

Retreatist subculture (Cloward and Ohlin) A subculture composed of delinquents who for the most part are involved in the consumption of drugs.

Revolutionary movement A social movement that seeks to overthrow the existing social system.

Riot Mob behavior that is violently aggressive and destructive.

Ritualism (Merton) The inward abandonment of goal attainment coupled with the external appearance of goal striving. Means to goals become ends in themselves.

Role A pattern of behavior that is expected of an individual who occupies a particular position or status in society.

Role conflict When two or more roles are in conflict.

Role expectancy The way in which an individual of a particular status is expected to act.

Role performance An individual's actual response to the way he or she is expected to act.

Role strain A condition wherein an individual has too many role obligations and experiences difficulty in fulfilling them all.

Rules (Weber) A formal system of rules and regulations governing decisions and actions.

Rumor The dissemination of information that is distorted, untrue, or unconfirmed. It is usually transmitted during a time of anxiety and stress.

Sacred (Durkheim) Those things set apart by people, including religious beliefs, rites, deities, or anything socially defined as requiring special religious treatment.

Scapegoat A group, or someone or something, that is forced to bear the blame or misfortune for others.

Science A method of study whereby a body of organized and verified knowledge is obtained.

Secessionist minority A minority that desires full political self-determination and independence.

Secondary group A group that is usually large and that is created for a clearly defined, limited purpose.

Secondary relationship A relationship that is nonemotional, formal, and specialized, and that does not involve the whole personality of the individual participants.

Secularization A process by which society's traditional religious beliefs and institutions lose their influence.

Segregation An institutionalized form of discrimination, enforced by custom or by law.

Self (see *Social self*)

Separation (Rose) The minority group does not accept the dominant group's negative image and avoids contact with the dominant group.

Serial monogamy An alternative to the nuclear family pattern in which a person continues on a cycle of marriage and divorce.

Sex ratio The number of males for every one hundred females.

Sexism A system of social, economic, political, and psychological activities and pressures that suppresses groups because they exhibit certain biologically determined sexual characteristics.

Single parent family An unmarried, divorced, or widowed mother or father with at least one child.

Social action (Weber) "Meaningful" social behavior.

Social change Change in the structure and social relationships of a society.

Social class A number of people who have relatively equal status (position or rank) within a hierarchy of class statuses or positions.

Social determinism The idea that social interactions cause or at least greatly influence people's behavior.

Social facts (Durkheim) Ways of acting, thinking, and feeling that are characteristic of a group or society.

Social group A unit "composed of two or more persons who come into contact for a purpose and who consider the contact meaningful" (T. M. Mills, 1967).

Social movement A collectivity acting with some continuity to promote or resist change in the society or group of which it is a part (Turner and Killian, 1957).

Social organization The actual regularity of human interaction.

Social self An individual's awareness of his or her social or personal identity.

Social structure Patterns of interactions and networks of relationships found within a society.

Socialization The process by which a person acquires the attitudes, beliefs, and values of his or her culture.

Society A large number of people who form a relatively organized, self-sufficient, enduring body and who learn and share a particular culture.

Sociological imagination A quality of mind that lets people understand the relation between biography and history. It involves an awareness of how events in personal life often are shaped by social forces.

Sociology The scientific study of human interaction and the products of such interaction.

Specialization (Weber) A specialized administrative staff that maintains the organization and its internal communication system.

State The political and legal institution representing the whole of a society, including its people and territory.

Status A position relative to other positions.

Status (Weber) The amount of prestige held by individuals and groups within society.

Stratification A system whereby people rank and evaluate each other as superior or inferior and, on the basis of such evaluations, unequally reward one another in terms of factors such as wealth, authority, power, and prestige.

Subculture Somewhat distinctive patterns of thinking, acting, and feeling shared by subgroups within society.

Submission (Rose) The acceptance of a subordinate status.

Suggestibility A tendency to respond uncritically to stimuli provided by other members of a crowd.

Suicide Intentional self-destruction or taking one's life.

Superego The social values and ideas that a person internalizes and that form the conscience.

Survey A method of data collection carried out by means of questionnaires or interviews given to a representative sample of the population under study.

Symbol Something that stands for something else, such as words or language.

Symbolic interactionism The theoretical perspective that seeks to understand social life and human behavior from the standpoint of the interacting individuals themselves.

Theory A set of general statements or principles that attempts to explain observations, experiences, or research findings.

Tolerance limit The degree to which norm violations are tolerated or suppressed by a group.

Trial marriage Living together without a marriage license.

Urban society A large, heterogeneous society characterized by a complex division of labor, formal social control, and a low degree of group solidarity.

Urbanization Growth in the percentage or proportion of people living in cities relative to those living in rural areas.

Values Estimates of "worth" or "desirability."

Verstehen (Weber) A method whereby the sociologist can make interpretations of the actions and intentions of others. Means "understanding."

Vertical mobility A change of position with a significant movement up or down in the stratification system.

White collar crime (Sutherland) A crime committed by a person of respectability and high social status in the course of his or her occupation.

Withdrawal (Rose) When minority individuals deny their identity and accept the image that the majority has of their group.

Work An activity that produces something of value for others.

Zero population growth The point at which the ratio of births to deaths is balanced and population ceases to grow.

Answer Key: Kezins' Sociological I.Q. Test

Answer		Statement
(True)	False	1. Psychological disorders are more common among people in the lower class.
(True)	False	2. Heart disease is far more likely to kill poor people than the affluent.
True	(False)	3. Most suicides are committed by people in their 30s and 40s.
True	(False)	4. Per-pupil expenditures by American school systems significantly affect student scores on achievement tests.
(True)	False	5. More women are graduating from professional schools today than ever before.
True	(False)	6. The vast majority of women today support sexual equality in the home.
True	(False)	7. Most elderly persons ($\geq$ 65 years) depend on their children for at least some amount of financial assistance.
(True)	False	8. Less than 1 percent of all welfare recipients are able-bodied employable males.
(True)	False	9. Most welfare recipients are white.
True	(False)	10. Approximately half the families on welfare have been on the rolls for five years or more.
True	(False)	11. Whites have higher self-esteem than blacks.
True	(False)	12. The suicide rate is higher among women than men.
True	(False)	13. Suicide rates in the United States are higher among upper class people than among lower class people.
True	(False)	14. Largely as a result of women's liberation, the frequency of marital coitus has declined noticeably over the last decade.
(True)	False	15. Most married women work.
(True)	False	16. Three out of four divorced women remarry within three years.
True	(False)	17. It is more difficult for men to remarry than it is for women.
True	(False)	18. In dating and mating, "absence makes the heart grow fonder."
True	(False)	19. States with the death penalty have a lower murder rate than those without the death penalty.
(True)	False	20. Crimes of violence and theft are far more likely to occur among teen-agers than among any other age group in our society.

True (False) **21.** The United States has one of the lowest rates of infant mortality in the world.

True (False) **22.** The soaring birth rates in developing countries make it difficult, if not impossible, for those countries to feed their rapidly growing populations.

(True) False **23.** Almost half the people currently in jail in this country have not been convicted of a crime.

True (False) **24.** Northern schools are more integrated than schools in the South.

(True) False **25.** Suicide is more prevalent in the South than in any other region of the United States.

True (False) **26.** Rape is usually an impulsive uncontrollable act of sexual gratification.

True (False) **27.** In dating and mate selection, "opposites attract."

(True) False **28.** Women are more likely than men to abuse children.

True (False) **29.** In most instances, marital happiness is likely to increase following the birth of children.

(True) False **30.** By age 45, more than one-third of all males in this country have engaged in at least one homosexual act.

RESPONDENT BACKGROUND INFORMATION

SEX (Female = 1, Male = 2)

TERM STANDING (Freshman = 1, Sophomore = 2, Junior = 3, Senior = 4)

MAJOR (Liberal Arts = 1; Business = 2; Engineering = 3; Education = 4; Physical Sciences = 5; Other = 6)

AGE (18 or less = 1; 19 = 2; 20 = 3; 21 or more = 4)

Index